The Time Traveller's Guide
to Restoration Britain

BY THE SAME AUTHOR

The Greatest Traitor:
The Life of Roger Mortimer,
1st Earl of March,
Ruler of England, 1327–1330

The Perfect King:
The Life of Edward III,
Father of the English Nation

The Fears of Henry IV:
The Life of England's Self-made King

1415: Henry V's Year of Glory

The Time Traveller's Guide to
Medieval England:
A Handbook for Visitors to the
Fourteenth Century

The Time Traveller's Guide to
Elizabethan England

Human Race:
Ten Centuries of Change on Earth

The Time Traveller's Guide to Restoration Britain

A Handbook for Visitors to the Years 1660–1700

IAN MORTIMER

THE BODLEY HEAD
LONDON

1 3 5 7 9 10 8 6 4 2

The Bodley Head, an imprint of Vintage,
20 Vauxhall Bridge Road,
London SW1V 2SA

The Bodley Head is part of the Penguin Random House group of companies
whose addresses can be found at global.penguinrandomhouse.com.

Penguin
Random House
UK

First published by The Bodley Head in 2017

www.penguin.co.uk/vintage

A CIP catalogue record for this book is available from the British Library

ISBN 9781847923042

Printed and bound by Clays Ltd, St Ives plc

Penguin Random House is committed to a sustainable future for our
business, our readers and our planet. This book is made from
Forest Stewardship Council® certified paper.

Contents

This book is dedicated to my son, Oliver Mortimer,
who ran a weekly parkrun with me during
the writing of this book.

Running teaches us many truths, not least that
happiness and satisfaction are not the same thing.
I hope that you'll be happy as long as you live
but I hope even more that you'll be satisfied.

Acknowledgements

I am grateful to several people for their assistance with this book. First, the team of Jörg Hensgen and Stuart Williams and all their colleagues at The Bodley Head and Vintage. Authors depend on publishers for many things – and most people think in terms of printing books and persuading shops to sell them – but we also rely heavily on our publisher's encouragement, confidence and patience. *Especially* the patience. You have been very supportive. I am enormously grateful.

A big Thank You is similarly due to my agent, Georgina Capel, for her advice and her diplomacy. I would like also to record my gratitude to my previous agent, Jim Gill of United Agents, who negotiated the original UK contract for this book and helped me place it and the earlier volumes in the right hands. Thanks are due too to Mandy Greenfield for copy-editing and to Alison Rae for proofreading this book.

As always, I am hugely indebted to my wife, Sophie. Without her love and companionship, I simply could not have spent the required number of hours at my desk to complete this project, nor would I have been contented enough in the twenty-first century to want to enter the late seventeenth century so completely. I owe her yet another century of gratitude.

Ian Mortimer
Moretonhampstead, Devon
12 November 2016

Introduction

> The mind is its own place, and in itself
> Can make a Heaven of Hell, a Hell of Heaven.
>
> John Milton, *Paradise Lost*, book one, lines 254–5

As you lie down on your feather bed on your first night in Restoration Britain, you will notice the quiet. If you're visiting during the 1690s, maybe you can hear a longcase clock chiming downstairs, in the parlour. If you're here in the 1660s, probably the only sound will be the creak of the staircase as the maid gently makes her way up to sleep in the attic, or that of a dog outside barking at the night watchmen. The bell in the church tower will ring the hour throughout the night, sounding in the starlit darkness beyond your shuttered window. Otherwise there is silence. Like many people, you may let the nightlight burn down, so there is a glow beyond the bed hangings. If you've left them open, you'll see the candle flame shining on the wooden panelling of your chamber. On a linen-covered table are the looking glass you'll gaze into in the morning, and the combs your maidservant will use to dress your hair in preparation for the day ahead. But therein lies a question: what does the day ahead hold?

The chances are that, even though you come from the modern world and can look back on the period from 1660 to 1700 with the benefit of hindsight, you don't know what destiny awaits you here. These four decades are tumultuous. People experience everything from rapturous enthusiasm for one king to the violent expulsion of his successor. There are wars abroad and riots at home; persecutions of some religious minorities and greater toleration of others; expanding trade in the Far East and the disappearance of the plague from British shores. Most significantly, there is a marked rise of rational, scientific thinking. Professionalism enters many walks of life, the city of London grows into an international capital, and the middle sorts suddenly spring up, with their refined ways of living and fashion-conscious tastes. It is the age of many geniuses. It produces the greatest British architect of all time in Christopher Wren, the greatest British scientist in Isaac Newton and the greatest diarist in Samuel Pepys. It also heralds the greatest composer in Henry Purcell, the greatest woodcarver in Grinling Gibbons and the greatest clockmaker in Thomas Tompion. It sees the heyday of Peter Lely and Godfrey Kneller in the world of painting, the apogee of John Milton and John Dryden in poetry, and it applauds a mass of brilliant actors, actresses and drama-tists, including Thomas Otway, Aphra Behn and William Congreve. And don't forget those three other geniuses in science, Robert Boyle, Robert Hooke and Edmond Halley, whose achievements would place them in the front rank, if it were not for Newton. It is the age of innovations, of the arrival of tea, coffee and chocolate, exotic fruit, fine wines and new medicines. Great houses are built in the baroque style, their interiors filled with new fashions in Indian fabric and Chinese furniture and porcelain. Last but not least, this is the great age of the English constitution, during which the ideas of John Locke, the most influential philosopher in the English language, come to be espoused in the Bill of Rights, limiting the power of the king. As a result, whichever year in the late seventeenth century you visit Britain, the day ahead is likely to be full of surprises.

All these changes in society are confusing enough for the indigenous inhabitants. You, the modern visitor, will have the additional difficulty of not being familiar with even the basics of life in the seventeenth-century home. What are you going to eat for breakfast? How do you control the itching of nits and the lice in your clothes? What should you use to brush your teeth? As you wake, the noises of the carts and carriages in the cobbled thoroughfare outside sound strange; so too do the calls and greetings of the street vendors and the pedestrians on their way to market or to church. Open the curtains of your chamber and you will look down through the small panes of uneven, slightly distorting glass to see women's bonnets and gentlemen's periwigs as people greet each other in their various stilted or informal fashions. How are you going to get on in this society, which is so unfamiliar to you?

This book will tell you how to live, day by day, in the late seven-teenth century. You will learn what to wear and what to eat and drink, which places are the best to stay in, what money can buy, and how to get around. You will learn about lice control and dental hygiene, even if the seventeenth-century practices cause you to squirm. As you will see, the general approach of a *Time Traveller's Guide* is that the past is best viewed close up and personally – in contrast to traditional history, which emphasises the value of objectivity and distance. Hence you are very much at the centre of this story. The past might have been 'solitary, poor, nasty, brutish and short' for some, and grandiose and luxurious for others, but simply to be told these things does not compare with seeing life at close hand, albeit in your mind's eye.

Before we travel to the Britain of 1660–1700, however, there are a few key facts you need to have at your disposal. First, you need to understand why we use the term 'Restoration' to describe the period. It refers to the return of the monarchy in 1660, after what the diarist John Evelyn describes as 'a most bloody rebellion of nearly twenty years'. This 'rebellion' breaks out in 1642, when forces loyal to King Charles I gather to oppose those who support Parliament, led by Oliver Cromwell. At stake is the matter of who has absolute authority in England. Are the people bound to obey the monarch because he rules by divine right, as a conduit of the will of God? Or do they have a right to self-government, through Parliament? It is one of the most profound questions of political life, and the answer can hardly be decided by a debate. Four years of intermittent warfare ensue. Judgement comes down first on the side of the people, led by Cromwell and Parliament. In April 1646, after a string of military setbacks, the king seeks refuge among his Scottish subjects. A few months later, the Scots give him up and send him as a prisoner to the English Parliament. After a brief second civil war in 1648, which ends in defeat for the royalists, Charles is tried for high treason: he is found guilty and beheaded at Whitehall on 30 January 1649. A few days later the monarchy and the House of Lords are abolished. England, Wales, Scotland and Ireland are collectively declared a republic – a 'Commonwealth and Free State' – and Parliament formally confirms itself as the source of all just power in the British Isles.

Parliament in these years is dominated by a Puritan outlook, characterised by a set of stringent religious and moral concerns that take precedence over the old traditions and customs of the country. The bishops are abolished, as are the church courts. A measure of how extreme things become in these years is the Adultery Act of 1650.

Under this law, anyone found guilty of adultery is to be hanged. In 1654, Susan Bounty, the wife of Richard Bounty of Bideford, Devon, falls pregnant with another man's child. She is tried at the Exeter assizes for the crime of adultery and sentenced to death. She pleads her pregnancy and is allowed to remain in gaol until her child is born. Then she is hanged.[1]

The truly frightening thing is that very few people criticise such 'justice'. Indeed, many magistrates up and down the country want *more* people hanged for moral lapses, not fewer. The 1650s are probably the most religious decade Britain has seen since the Middle Ages – 'most religious' in the sense that society is completely dominated by Christian beliefs and more willing to punish people for ungodly behaviour than at any other time. If you have a choice as to which part of the seventeenth century you would like to visit and are *not* of a Puritanical disposition, I would strongly recommend avoiding the Commonwealth.

Times change, influential men grow old and die, and extreme forms of government sooner or later become unacceptable. The collapse of the Commonwealth is thus perhaps an inevitability. Its demise is helped by economic turbulence, which makes people question whether Puritanism is truly the right and godly path. When Cromwell dies in September 1658, the government is heavily in debt and both royalists and republicans realise they have a common enemy in religious extremism. A period of chaos follows. On 11 October 1659, John Evelyn writes in his diary: 'The army now turned out Parliament. We had now no government in the nation; all in confusion; no magistrate either owned or pretended but the soldiers, and they not agreed. God almighty have mercy on us and settle us!' Others record similar fears. In Essex, Ralph Josselin, the Puritan vicar of Earls Colne, writes on 14 October: 'Heard ... that the army ... interrupted the Parliament. Our sins threaten our ruin.' On 20 November he adds: 'men's minds exceedingly discontent; the soldiers at present give law unto us, God give a law to us all'. The following month, the London barber Thomas Rugg writes of his fellow citizens that 'their minds were very unquiet, and all grieved ... now to be ruled by the sword and the committee of swordmen, which was called the Committee of Safety'.

Into the midst of this crisis steps George Monck, the army's commander in Scotland. He is widely respected, having proved himself in campaigns in Ireland and Scotland as well as at sea in the First

Dutch War (1652–4). He communicates secretly with Charles I's son and heir, Prince Charles, who is in exile in France, and then arranges for the surviving members of the last elected Parliament to gather at Westminster. On 1 May 1660 the MPs unanimously agree to invite the prince to take the throne. Charles II is duly proclaimed on 8 May, and lands at Dover on the 25th. On 29 May 1660, his thirtieth birthday, he rides in procession through the city of London. It is a brave move on both men's parts: General Monck risks being branded a traitor to republicanism, and Prince Charles can hardly feel relaxed about returning to a country whose Parliament cut off his father's head. But there is a general recognition that the Commonwealth has no other possible successor, and that only a man whose acknowledged authority transcends religious and secular factionalism has a chance of reuniting the nation.

To understand the outpouring of joy that greets Charles II's accession you have to bear in mind the fear of another civil war erupting and of law and order breaking down again. You also have to remember the victims of Puritanism like Susan Bounty. The king not only represents stability and unity; he also stands for freedom from oppression (initially, at least) and the end of religious extremism. On the same day that Parliament agrees to ask Prince Charles to return, General Monck reveals that the prince has signed a declaration, later known as the Declaration of Breda. This document promises a pardon to all those who committed crimes against the prince and his father during the Civil Wars and the Commonwealth (except those who signed Charles I's death warrant). The prince also undertakes to honour all sales and purchases of land in that time; to tolerate people of all religious faiths; to pay the army its back-pay and to recommission the troops in the service of the Crown. For the first time in over a decade, there is optimism in Britain.

The return of the king allows people to recover their cherished traditions and pleasures. People can look forward to dancing round the Maypole on Mayday again, going to the theatre, holding horse races and attending other forms of entertainment prohibited by the Puritans. They can expect the swift resurrection of the bishops and the House of Lords. As the proposed king has already acknowledged an illegitimate son of his own, it goes without saying that he will abolish the Adultery Act. Thus the 'Restoration' not only refers to the reintroduction of the royal family; it also denotes the restoration of principles of legislation, age-old institutions and ancient customs. Unlike most key dates that mark the beginning of a new historical period in British history, which often have little real significance except to denote the death of one monarch and the succession of another, 1660 has an enormous impact on daily life. In English history, probably the only year that stands comparison as a turning point is 1066.

So much for the start of the Restoration; when does it end?

Some historians apply the term 'Restoration' only to the 1660s, the period immediately after Charles II returned. The great diarist Samuel Pepys has unwittingly had a part to play in this, for he describes the years 1660–69 so vividly that the decade attracts almost all the attention, distracting people from the later years of the seventeenth century. At the other extreme, literary critics refer to English plays written as late as the 1690s and early 1700s as 'Restoration Comedies': stylistically, they are notable for their sexual innuendo, satirical wit and sense of immoral fun, all of which characterise English society after 1660. Thus the Restoration has no commonly accepted termination. I have chosen the end of the century for several reasons. First, there is a unifying spirit of licentiousness that is noticeable throughout the period, even if it starts to decline in the 1690s. Second, another 'restoration' of sorts takes place when James II's daughter Mary and her husband William become monarchs in 1689. And third, very little has been written about ordinary people in the last three decades of the seventeenth century. Pepys dominates our understanding of the daily life of the period to such an extent that, apart from academic tomes, you won't find many books on late-seventeenth-century England except those dealing with the Glorious Revolution of 1688 and the biographies of great men. But life after Pepys is fascinating too and deserves greater attention than it has hitherto received.

Geographically, the authority of the king of England expands considerably over this period. In 1660 Charles II reigns over the British Isles, the port of Dunkirk in France and 'the Plantations', which are the British territories in the New World. In that year these include the small colonies of Massachusetts Bay, New Plymouth, Connecticut, Rhode Island, Virginia, Maryland, Nova Scotia and Newfoundland on the eastern seaboard of North America; and Jamaica, the Leeward Islands and Barbados in the West Indies. By 1700 the Plantations have grown to include thirteen greatly enlarged colonies in North America as well as most of the West Indies. In addition, the king now rules stretches of the coast of India (including Bombay and Calcutta) and parts of the coast of West Africa. It is no exaggeration to say that the British Empire dates from this period, even if it does not yet go by that name. This book, however, is intended for those interested in visiting Great Britain, the largest island in the British Isles. It does not touch on Dunkirk, which is sold to the French in 1662; or Tangiers in North Africa, which is ruled by the English from 1660 to 1684. Nor is it intended as a guide for visitors to seventeenth-century Ireland. The emphasis remains on England, by far the most populous country in Great Britain, but elements of late-seventeenth-century Scottish and Welsh culture are also included. In this respect it is important to remember that the United Kingdom has yet to become a political reality: Wales has been administered as part of the kingdom of England since 1536, but England and Scotland will not become one state until 1707, even though both kingdoms are ruled by the same king. For the period covered in this book, Scotland remains a separate political entity, with its own legal system, Parliament, currency, language and culture.

A last general point you need to bear in mind before stepping into Restoration Britain concerns the weather. Do wrap up warm. Britain is still experiencing the Little Ice Age of the seventeenth century, which leads to some bitterly cold winters, harvest failures and food shortages. 1675 is known as a 'year without a summer', for obvious reasons.[2] The Long Frost of December 1683 to February 1684 remains the coldest three-month period ever recorded. The River Thames remains frozen from 2 January to 20 February; the ground is frozen to the depth of three feet in Kent, and at the Downs 'the sea is frozen above a mile about the shore', as *The London Gazette* reports.[3] Gentlemen with thermometers busily measure the temperatures in the staircases and libraries of their country houses and find that even indoor temperatures are well below freezing. Water freezes in ewers in the corners of bedchambers, as does the milk in dairies and the ink in shopkeepers' inkwells. Across the country, snow lies in glistening stillness. Water wheels stand still. Ships remain motionless in their harbours, their rigging sparkling uselessly in the cold sunlight.

As you snuggle down in your feather bed in Restoration Britain and stare at the light of a guttering candle, trying to keep warm, you will probably start to wonder what you have let yourself in for. I want to add something else for you to think about. A well-respected historian once declared that 'the changes in English society that affected England between the reign of Elizabeth and the reign of Anne were not revolutionary'.[4] I suspect that reading this book and perhaps comparing it with *The Time Traveller's Guide to Elizabethan England* will make you think otherwise. Elizabeth died in 1603, Anne ascends the throne in 1702, and the years in between those two dates see many dramatic changes. We may think of the 'bloody rebellion of nearly twenty years' as the 'English Revolution', but in truth the decades that follow are just as revolutionary. In terms of the decline of super-stition, enhanced individualism, greater professionalism and clearer scientific understanding, this is truly an age of radical development. In fact, some of the most profound changes the British people have ever experienced take place between 1660 and 1700. It is a time when the last dying notes of the medieval world are drowned out by the rising trumpet fanfare of modernity, and the rationalism that you take for granted comes to be the dominant way of thinking.

But don't take my word for it. Read on. See for yourself.

I

London

It is Sunday, 2 June 1661 – and it is raining hard. Water trickles into puddles in the muddy alleys and swells in the drains that flow down the middle of the cobbled streets. Most people have returned from church to eat their dinner, peering out through windows spattered with raindrops as the church clocks of the city chime a dull midday. The few who are still braving the weather stride along beneath the overhanging jetties of the houses, hunched in their bedraggled hats and cloaks. They glance up at you as they approach: those gentlemen who are worried about their expensive clothes turn their shoulders to the wall to keep to the driest path, forcing you to step away from it. A horse-drawn coach speeds past, its wheels clattering over the uneven stones and sending water flying from the puddles. A stray dog hurries out of its path. But although you may find the weather inclement, there is a reason why you are out and about. This is when you get the clearest view of the city. Normally there are just too many carriages and people in your way. And that's not to mention the pollution. Some days a pall of smoke hangs over the roofs: it gets in your eyes, and the stonework of every church in the city is blackened with it. Today the houses might be dripping from the eaves but at least you can see them.

When you walk through the heart of London you realise that the city is practically a living museum. It is not that the citizens are careful to preserve old structures, but rather that they are reluctant to pull them down. Almost every building you see is old. On the east side you have the Tower of London, the stern castle of the Norman and Plantagenet kings of England, which is now a storehouse for gunpowder and armaments and a prison for high-ranking figures. To the north of the Tower is the city wall, first built by the Romans and subsequently heavily patched, but still standing in most places to its battlement height of 18 feet. The wall encloses a mass of medieval streets, lanes and alleys, twisting and weaving intricately around old houses and churches. Some of the streets are too narrow to allow two coaches to pass, and some of the alleys so tight that even a single vehicle cannot enter. Thames Street, one of the busiest thoroughfares of the whole city, has pinch points just 11ft wide, where traffic frequently comes to a stop.

Many of the houses are several hundred years old, their blackened oak timbers deeply scarred with the fissures of so many seasons. The rat holes in their walls are similarly ancient and, like the houses themselves, are teeming with life. The older properties have been modernised with glass windows but they preserve their essential character, the first floor projecting out about 18 inches over the ground floor, and the second jettied out about a foot over the first, with a gabled roof facing the street. On narrow alleys, the occupants of second-floor chambers can reach out and touch hands with their opposite numbers on the other side. Such jetties block out much of the light, so they make the alleys dark at the best of times; on grey days such as today they are particularly dim. Grand old stone mansions are still to be found on the principal streets, their halls now heated by fireplaces and tall brick chimneys. But even the terraces of four-, five- and six-storey town houses date from between sixty and a hundred years ago. What's more, if you take just a few steps down one of these dark alleys, you'll see that tucked in behind these tottering edifices are older structures divided up into tenements without any regular plan. Here's a chamber above a kitchen, there's a chamber above a hall. Many of these were once the buildings of medieval monasteries and friaries. Even old barns have been turned into houses. As you can see, London has developed not by being demolished and rebuilt but by constantly adapting, little by little, to people's changing demands.

Even if you are familiar with the twenty-first-century city, you will not recognise much here. The Tower may look more or less the same, but the other structures are all very different from their modern successors. The tall limestone obelisk bound with iron on the south side of Cannon Street is an ancient landmark called London Stone. Some people will tell you it was erected by King Lud, the mythical founder of London; others that it was the stone from which all milestones in Roman Britain measured their distances from the capital. Moving north to Cornhill, you will find the Standard, the great conduit that provides the citizens hereabouts with water. On the north side of the street you will see a fine old building of four arcades around a quadrangle: this is the Royal Exchange, built by Sir Thomas Gresham and named by Queen Elizabeth in 1571. You can see statues of all the kings and queens since the Norman Conquest in the niches above the arcades. Sometimes you'll hear the Royal Exchange described as the most valuable three-quarters of an acre in the world, due to the trade carried on here, but on a wet Sunday afternoon it feels more like a sepulchral monument, dripping with raindrops and absence. Nearby is one of the city's pillories, where trading offenders are publicly humiliated with their heads and hands trapped between wooden boards; today that too is as damp and silent as the puddles welling up across the courtyard of the Exchange.

Everything appears ancient – from the seven medieval gates of the city to the livery halls of the powerful guilds and the Guildhall itself, built in 1411. Some of the finest merchants' and goldsmiths' houses are to be seen on Cheapside, the main trading street, but these too are almost a century old. The buildings on the southern edge of the city, where the waters of the River Thames lap at the quays, are similarly venerable. If you can turn your attention away from the vast number of ships on the river you'll see the waterline marked by a whole gamut of antiquated and decrepit walls and roofs. Here is London's second royal fortress, the gaunt Baynard's Castle, rebuilt in the fifteenth century and remodelled at the start of the sixteenth. Further along the bank are the weather-boarded and pitch-covered warehouses of merchants whose ships have been returning for the last forty years with cargoes of Virginia tobacco or spices from the East Indies. On a weekday the rain would not have stopped the three wooden cranes on the wharf at Queenhithe from loading and unloading the tuns of wine but, today being Sunday, they too are motionless. Further along the river still is the Steelyard, where the merchants of the Hanseatic League have had their trading centre for the last seven centuries. They are no longer the powerful economic force they once were, and the old buildings are now sinking into decay.

The most striking structure along the river is London's only bridge, built in the twelfth century. It stands 910ft long and connects London proper with its southern suburb of Southwark and the roads leading into Kent, Surrey and Sussex. Each of its nineteen arches has a name, such as 'Queen's Lock', 'Narrow Entry', 'Rock Lock' and the charmingly named 'Gut Lock'. These arches are built on boat-shaped starlings or piers in the water, forcing the fast-changing tides to gush through the channels between them. The roadway of the bridge is lined with houses that peer over the turbulent flow. At the southern end is the medieval gatehouse, where about two dozen decayed heads and skulls are to be seen – these being the remnants of traitors, placed there as examples to the citizens.[1] At the northern end there is a gap between the houses, following a major fire in 1633. It is ironic that the most significant modern change to the bridge is an empty space.[2]

Gradually you will realise that there is almost nothing visible that dates from the seventeenth century. Here and there you'll see a recent house, built where a fire has destroyed a dwelling, but two-thirds of the buildings within the city walls are medieval and almost all the rest are Elizabethan. Leathersellers' Hall has an impressive portico dating from the 1620s. Denmark House, the queen's royal palace designed by the royal surveyor, Inigo Jones, has some fine additions: a suite of royal apartments, new stables and coach houses. Otherwise, very little in the heart of the city post-dates 1600. The most significant piece of seventeenth-century architecture within the city walls is a 120ft-wide portico with Corinthian columns, which has been added to the west end of St Paul's Cathedral. This too is the work of Inigo Jones. But just look how incongruous it appears, forced on to the massive church, whose high lead roofs look black and gloweringly gothic in the rain. Note too the contrast between Jones's work and the worn sculpture of the masonry of the nave. One hundred years ago, lightning struck the tower and, in the ensuing fire, the spire collapsed; it has not yet been replaced. Shops and stalls have been constructed at the foot of the cathedral's soot-blackened stone walls, between the mighty buttresses. When you step inside, you'll see the pillars on either side are all out of alignment, sometimes leaning by more than six inches, even though they are a solid-looking 11 feet in diameter. Hundreds of monuments of London dignitaries and noblemen fill the spaces between the columns and cover the walls; among them King Ethelred the Unready, John of Gaunt, Sir Nicholas Bacon, Sir Francis Walsingham, Sir Philip Sidney, Sir Christopher Hatton, John Donne and Anthony van Dyck. Many have been defaced by vandalism or accidents. Much of the damage is a result of the Civil Wars, when the cathedral served as a stable for more than 800 horses – a sign of the contempt that Cromwell's forces had for the old religion. At the same time the choir stalls, bishop's throne and organ were destroyed, and saw-pits were dug in the floor. When a committee visits the cathedral in 1666 with a view to improving and updating it – and Christopher Wren first suggests topping the whole edifice with an enormous baroque dome – its members sadly conclude that the old building just won't take the strain.

This then is the heart of London: a decaying mass of antiquity, adaptation and dilapidation, collapsing beneath the weight of its age. However, step beyond the city walls and into the suburbs and you will be amazed by the difference. First, pinch your nose and walk past the old warehouses and collapsing timber buildings that surround Fleet Ditch. As you cross the bridge over the River Fleet you will see all sorts of refuse floating in the swollen river below: 'sweepings from butchers' stalls, dung, guts, and blood, drowned puppies, stinking sprats, all drenched in mud, dead cats and turnip tops'.[3] Keep going westwards up Fleet Street; as you approach the bottom of Drury Lane and enter the area that will one day be called the West End, you will find yourself surrounded by tall flat-fronted houses that are made of fine red-brown bricks, with tall glass windows facing the streets. Between the windows are elaborate classical columns. The doorways are recessed and covered with elegant canopies and have glass panels above the doors to let light into the hallways within. Whole streets stand to a uniform height, so that ten or twelve town houses look more like a great palace than a series of private dwellings belonging to individual gentlemen and 'men of ability' (as contemporaries refer to the upwardly mobile). The eaves of these do not drip on a rainy day such as this, because they have gutters and downpipes that conduct the roof water into the streets. And, just as significantly, the streets themselves are not cobbled or dressed with gravel, but paved. They even have a camber, so that the rainwater does not run into a channel in the middle but into gullies on the sides, adjacent to a raised pavement.

Here, on the edge of the old city, the elegant town house has arrived.

What has brought on this transition? One of the reasons is simply the massive growth of London's population. In 1550, there were about 50,000 Londoners. That number quadrupled to about 200,000 in 1600. It almost doubled again over the next fifty years, reaching about 375,000. Since 1650 it has increased by another 10 per cent, and now in 1661 stands at about 410,000. But the population increase only accounts for the need to provide more housing; it does not explain the change in the standard of architecture. For this you need to consider the attitude of the English monarchs, who reside at Whitehall Palace, at the end of the Strand. Queen Elizabeth I forbade the expansion of the city to the west of Drury Lane, just over half a mile from the palace. Her successors have similarly attempted to restrict all house building to previously developed sites. They have failed – partly because they have allowed the lords who own the land west of Drury Lane to buy licences to build on virgin soil, and partly because such fine new houses are now considered to contribute to 'the honour of the nation' and thus fall outside the scope of restrictive legislation.[4] In other words, new houses in this area are not illegal as long as they are for the wealthy. But as these new buildings creep closer and closer to Whitehall, the royal family becomes more and more anxious about their architecture. Proclamations are issued stipulating how high and wide each house should be, how thick its walls, and how each one must fit in with its neighbour and thus form an elegant unity. This is why the lines of new housing look more like palaces than narrow town houses: the kings and their courtiers prefer to be surrounded by elegant buildings rather than the unplanned slums of the riff-raff.

The major showpiece is the Covent Garden piazza. The houses here are so different from the timber-framed buildings of the old city that you may be forgiven for thinking you are entering a different country. A wide, paved square greets you, with handsome three-storey mansions around the perimeter. On the south side are the gardens of Bedford House, the London home of William Russell, fifth earl of Bedford, whose father commissioned Inigo Jones to design the piazza in 1631. On the western side you find the parish church, also designed by Inigo Jones, and two brick-fronted town houses built by the fourth earl. To the north and east elegant residences have been developed by a string of private developers, all fronted with a 20ft-high arcade. Given that the fourth earl paid £2,000 to the king for the licence to build the piazza, and spent more than £4,000 on the church and £4,700 on his three town houses, you can see why Covent Garden in 1661 is a byword for high living.[5] Anyone resident in the old heart of the city must feel like the poor relation of those rich enough to live here.

Covent Garden marks the beginning of modern town planning in Britain. It inspires many elegant developments to the west and north of the city. No one builds jettied wooden houses any more; everyone wants flat-fronted brick ones, with wide streets, drains, neat gutters and lots of light. Gabled roofs are out – people want pilasters with Corinthian or Ionic capitals and balustrades along the roof. Most of all, those with money want to live in a well-proportioned square. Near Holborn, Lord Hatton has laid out Hatton Garden as a handsome street with a square of fine town houses at one end. Even more impressive are the recent developments in Lincoln's Inn Fields and in Great Queen Street, both built by William Newton. The Dutch artist Willem Schellinks, who visits London in 1661, describes Lincoln's Inn Fields as 'a large square lying behind Lincoln College, where law students are taught. Round this square are many fine palace-like houses, all with forecourts behind high walls; one can count there seventy entrances with stone pillars and double doors, and many of the nobility live there.'[6] A few years later, Lorenzo Magalotti, a Florentine nobleman travelling in the train of the Grand Duke of Tuscany, Cosimo III, adds his words of praise, calling Lincoln's Inn Fields 'one of the largest and handsomest squares in London, in respect to both the uniformity and size of its buildings'.[7] If your architect manages to impress both the Dutch and the Florentines – two of the most urbane and sophisticated nations in Christendom – then you are creating quite an impression.

As a result of this, there are really two Londons: the old and the new. The old is largely confined within the ancient city walls and in the areas immediately outside the gates, as well as the suburb of Southwark, on the south side of the river. The new London envelops the old, running from Spitalfields in the north-east across to Hatton Garden – including the new developments to the south of Theobalds Road – and as far as Piccadilly. But the new city is not stopping there: if you walk all the way around the perimeter, you will see a great deal of building work under way. Southampton Square (better known to you as Bloomsbury Square), laid out by the earl of Southampton in 1660, is currently being developed as a piazza of high-quality houses. Although it is still possible to see 'the Lines of Communication' – the half-moon defences constructed to defend London during the Civil Wars – these will soon disappear under the new streets. At the south-west extreme of the conurbation, the palaces of Whitehall and Westminster still sprawl in all their medieval angularity, but you cannot help but feel it is only a matter of time before these too are engulfed in the great tide of construction that is lapping at the city walls.

The heavy rain does not abate all day. In his house in Seething Lane, to the north of the Tower, Samuel Pepys looks out at the downpour.

He is the Clerk of the Acts, one of the most important positions in the administration of the navy, and a prosperous man with interests in a great many subjects, including scientific innovations. However, having already spent a couple of hours drinking wine and eating anchovies with Ralph Greatorex, a maker of mathematical instruments, he has had enough of discussing the mathematical properties of levers. He is now wishing the rain would stop, so the man could go. But if you come back to call on him the following Thursday, when the weather is fine and warm, you'll find him in a much better frame of mind, sitting on his roof terrace with his neighbour, Sir William Penn, playing his lute and drinking wine (again). And on that sunny day the old city will give you quite a different experience from the wet Sunday you have just seen.

Although the heat means that there are few domestic fires burning, the many industrial ones around the city make the air acrid with the smell of coal smoke. But it is not just burning coal that will affect your nostrils. You will gag on the noxious fumes coming from the riverside and those parts of the city where tanning and fulling take place. In the main streets, the piles of dung left by the horses also emit an aroma. So do the splashes of urine where men have pissed in alleyways. As the heat of the day intensifies, these smells tend to be overpowered by the stench of the cesspits in the cellars. Pigeons fly out from under the eaves of the old houses, their droppings leaving a white streak on the timberwork. Rats scavenge behind barrels and under and over crates. Kitchen rubbish collectors lead their horse-drawn carts from door to door, collecting rotting matter. Rakers, whose business it is to empty private cesspits, lead their horse-drawn carts filled with dung-pots through the streets. Flocks of sheep and herds of cattle are driven on the hoof to the abattoirs and meat markets, where their dung and their blood add to the stink of the street.

You could say that walking through old London is still the same multi-sensory experience it was in the Middle Ages. In fact, it is even more overwhelming, due to the larger population. Ten times as many people live here these days as did in the late fourteenth century, and that means ten times as many sheep and cattle, and ten times as much human waste. And it is not just the permanent residents who contribute to the sense of overcrowding: hundreds of thousands of people come into town daily for business or pleasure – to go to market, attend a fair, do business in the city or see a play at one of the theatres. As a result, there are crowds of people and animals everywhere you go.

Just listen to the sounds of a London street. More than 3,000 oxen are led into the city and slaughtered here every day, besides a huge number of other animals. The noise they make as they pass by or wait in pens is considerable; their squeals, bleats and bellows as they are being slaughtered are raucous and disturbing. Then there is the sound of the iron-shod wheels of more than 2,000 coaches, and many more thousands of carts and wagons, grinding over the cobbles of the old streets, and the metallic hammering of blacksmiths and candlestick makers. When the traffic grinds to a halt because too many coaches are simultaneously trying to pass the same point, you will hear loud altercations between the drivers. You will hardly be able to avoid the bells and loud clappers of the rakers driving their dung-carts, with which they announce their presence. Nor will you be able to ignore the yelling of those gathering around a cockfight or wrestling match, especially if many bets have been placed. If you then add the hourly chimes of more than a hundred churches, the cries of street vendors pushing their way through the crowds – 'Mackerel, two a groat and four for sixpence', 'Flounders, buy my flounders', 'Frying pans mended' – and the calls of householders leaning out of their upstairs windows, trying to attract the attention of the sellers in the street, you can see that old London is not just so crowded and smelly: it is also so loud that you can barely hear yourself think.

If you are looking to escape the hubbub, there are gardens and parks laid out for recreation. This is a new cultural aspect of the city: a hundred years ago the urban centre was the main and only attraction, and if you needed to renew your connection to nature, you could go for a stroll into the fields. The idea of a horticultural experience was something that only occurred to gentlemen who installed pleasure gardens in their country houses. But these days Londoners increasingly feel the need to leave the congested streets, if only temporarily. Those who can afford it might take a coach to Hyde Park, to wander in the grounds or follow the parade of other fashionable coaches around its perimeter. If you're on foot, you might saunter over to St James's Park where you can enjoy a long, straight walk between the lines of mature elms, along the path known as the Mall, and, at the same time, watch the aquatic birds on the nearby ornamental canal. On the north side, beyond St James's Palace in what will one day become Green Park, you will find a woodland where people come to see deer; and on the southern side of the park is the royal aviary, Birdcage Walk. Another

fashionable option is to take a boat to Vauxhall to see the New Spring
Gardens. These are a series of covered walks among flowerbeds, where
people stroll up and down or stop at huts where they can buy an
overpriced glass of wine or beer, for which there are long queues. At
this time of year it is very pleasant to wander there gathering roses
or pinks and then return to the city by a wherry, trailing your fingers
in the water as the waterman guides you to the nearest 'stairs' or
small dock, from which you can walk home.

At the end of the evening, London undergoes yet another transformation. The commotion dies down, the colour fades from the
streets and the traffic dwindles. In the public gardens the decent and
self-respecting people withdraw and less-respectable characters make
their shadowy appearances. If you go for a walk among the tall elms
in St James's Park by night, you are entering a different world. In the
words of the poet John Wilmot, earl of Rochester:[8]

> And nightly now beneath their shade
> are buggeries, rapes, and incests made.
> Unto this all-sin-sheltering grove
> whores of the bulk and the alcove,
> great ladies, chambermaids, and drudges,
> the ragpicker, and heiress trudges.
> Carmen, divines, great lords, and tailors,
> 'prentices, poets, pimps, and jailers,
> footmen, fine fops do here arrive,
> and here promiscuously they swive.

Similar things go on in Hyde Park. At the end of the century
William III is so anxious about what is going on in the darkness outside
his carriage that he has 300 oil lamps installed along what is now Rotten
Row, to light his way back to Kensington Palace.[9] In the city itself, lanterns
are lit and fixed above the doors. Some trading places, like Leadenhall
Market, open late, displaying the meat on sale by candlelight. Elsewhere
lanterns are carried up and down the streets as the official watchmen
perform their night patrols, past the closed shops and shuttered houses.
Only at midnight are the street lights allowed to burn down. After that,
you are unlikely to see any lights except those attached to coaches or
'links' – flaming torches carried by boys to illuminate the way of
gentlemen who have been carousing late. Apart from at Smithfield, where

the market traders gather by torchlight to conduct business from about midnight until daybreak, the city returns to a few hours of silence, darkness and stillness.

All this should give you some idea as to why people's opinions of London are so wildly divided. For those who were born here, London is not just a city, it's everything that life promises. It's a religion, a mythology, a law and a tradition. It's a great experiment in how to live and, as such, it contains all that is good and bad about life. Ask any Londoner what he thinks of the place and he will tell you that it is the flower of all cities. Richard Newcourt declares in his new map of London (published in 1658) that London is 'the most magnificent and renowned city in Europe, both for the antiquity of her foundation as also for honour, wealth and beauty'. John Brydall in his *Camera Regis* (1676) states that London 'is styled the epitome or breviary of all England, the seat of the British Empire, the king of England's chamber'.[10] Foreigners readily agree with such pronouncements, largely because of the sheer size of the place. The number of ships moored in the Thames always grabs their attention, with estimates ranging from 1,400 to 2,000 vessels at various times. But visitors also pass negative comments. Most agree that sprawling Whitehall is not only the largest palace in Europe but also the ugliest. Lorenzo Magalotti admits that no city in the world has so many fine shops, but is unimpressed by most of London's public buildings – except for the Tower of London, the Banqueting Hall in Whitehall Palace (designed by Inigo Jones), Westminster Hall and St Paul's Cathedral. He also cannot reconcile being held up by the heavy traffic on London Bridge with the idea of a Renaissance city. Monsieur Misson, a French gentleman who spends some time in England, declares the houses of old London to be 'the scurviest things in the world ... nothing but wood and plaster and nasty little windows'.[11] And, dare it be said, some English writers also voice their complaints about the state of the metropolis. Daniel Defoe describes the Fleet as 'a nauseous and abominable sink of public nastiness'.[12] John Lanyon gives a fuller account of the city's unsavoury features, declaring:

It is too apparent that notwithstanding many persons and considerable sums of money are employed for cleansing the streets yet they grow daily more offensive with dust and unwholesome stenches in summer and in wet weather with dirt, which occasions a swarm of coaches, to the disturbance of the city and the increase of noisome soil that whereof being by rain washed into the common sewers and passages and thence into the Thames, the sewers are much obstructed, the common passages (particularly Holborn Ditch, formerly of great convenience) now rendered useless and the greatest annoyance in the city, and the river itself, especially above [the] bridge, made daily less navigable. Besides the avenues to the city are almost all day pestered with those carts which only carry away some small part of the soil [i.e. dung] out of the streets and are made exceeding noisome and almost impassable with dirt carelessly spilt by the way to the common laystalls [dung-heaps], which being many and so near the city yield a great and contagious stench, offensive to passengers but especially to the skirts of the town, which else would be the most delightful places, and what wind so ever blows brings those noisome vapours into the city itself, sometimes to increase the beginning of infection.[13]

You cannot help but feel that what London really needs is a major surgical operation to cut out its old, irregular and decaying heart and replace it with a new, well-designed one.

The Great Fire

In the early hours of Sunday, 2 September 1666, the king's baker Thomas Farynor wakes up in his house in Pudding Lane to find himself choked by smoke. He sees flames rising rapidly up his staircase. Rousing his son, daughter and maidservant, he tells them to climb through an upstairs window. The maidservant refuses, too scared of heights, and remains in the house. He therefore leads just his children along the edge of the roof to the safety of their neighbour's house. The maidservant becomes the first victim of the Great Fire of London.

Three hours later, in Seething Lane on the other side of the city, Samuel Pepys and his wife are woken by their maidservant, Jane Birch, who tells them of a large fire she has seen from her chamber window. Pepys puts on his nightgown and goes to her room to look for himself, but thinks the fire of little consequence and goes back to bed. When he gets up again at 7 a.m., Jane tells him that more than 300 houses have been destroyed overnight. That gets his attention. Pepys leaves the house and walks to the river, from which he looks out towards the bridge from an elevated spot. He sees 'an infinite great fire' in the streets around the northern side of the bridge.[14] As he watches, flames race along the riverbank as far as the Steelyard. People are struggling to remove their goods from their houses, dragging them to the river and hurling them down into boats. As Pepys walks back through the streets he sees other men and women hurriedly carrying their valuables to the nearest parish church, confident that such stone buildings will not burn. The poor, he notices, endeavour to remain in their homes for as long as possible, until the fire reaches them; then they run for the nearest waterside stairs and try to clamber into boats. Pepys notes that the pigeons are similarly loath to leave the houses, but hover about the windows and balconies until their wings are burnt and they drop to the ground.

Londoners are used to fires – Pepys mentions another fifteen incidents in his diary – but they have never seen anything like this. The combination of the dry weather, the strong easterly wind, the firewood stored in cellars and back yards against the forthcoming winter, and the fact that the fire takes hold in the dead of night (and so has progressed considerably before people wake up) all contribute to the difficulty of containing it. The complacency of the authorities does not help. The lord mayor of London, Sir Thomas Bludworth, is too slow to order the destruction of houses with gunpowder. But the fundamental problem is the fabric of the buildings themselves. There are too many old, wooden houses packed closely together, leaning towards one another across streets and alleyways. Moreover, when wooden houses burn, they fall outwards, spilling fire in all directions. By the riverside there are wooden warehouses full of oil, pitch, tar, resin, hemp, cordage, brandy and similarly combustible materials, all in close proximity to one another. The result is a rapidly expanding sheet of flame that engulfs many streets at once. The Reverend Thomas Vincent recalls:

> Rattle, rattle, rattle was the noise which the fire struck upon the ear round about, as if there had been a thousand iron chariots beating upon the stones; and if you opened your eyes to the opening of the streets, where the fire was come, you might see in some places whole streets at once in flames, that issued forth as if they had been so many great forges from the opposite windows, which folding together, were united together in one great flame throughout the whole street, and then you might see

the houses tumble, tumble, tumble from one end of the street to the other with a great crash, leaving the foundations open to the view of the heavens.[15]

At dusk on the evening of 2 September, Pepys boards a small boat to observe the fire from the river, but is driven back by the heat and the burning material floating in the hot air. He ties up on the safe side of the river and heads to an alehouse, from where he stares across at the burning city. As he later puts it:

> As it grew darker, [the fire] appeared more and more, and in corners and upon steeples and between churches and houses, as far as we could see up the hill of the city, in a most horrid malicious bloody flame, not like the fine flame of an ordinary fire ... We stayed till, it being darkish, we saw the fire as only one entire arch of fire from this to the other side of the bridge, and in a bow up the hill, for an arch of about a mile long. It made me weep to see it. The churches, houses, and all on fire and flaming at once, and a horrid noise the flames made, and the cracking of houses at their ruin.[16]

The following day, Monday, 3 September, John Evelyn too looks out from the south bank of the river to observe the city's destruction. In his words:

> All the sky was of a fiery aspect, like the top of a burning oven ... God grant mine eyes may never behold the like, who now saw above ten thousand houses all in one flame! The noise and cracking and thunder of the impetuous flames, the shrieking of women and children, the hurry of people, the fall of towers, houses and churches, was like a hideous storm.[17]

If you join Pepys or Evelyn on the riverbank you too will see the river strewn with prized possessions, flung into the water to save them, and boats filled with people, clinging on to their furniture, musical instruments, rugs, chests of money and silverware. All over the city, the towers and steeples of dozens of parish churches are silhouetted by a colossal flame, which fills the sky with burning debris and consumes everything in its path. In places, the temperature is approaching 1,700°C.[18] And in the middle of it all stands the greatest building in the city, St Paul's Cathedral, which has withstood every calamity to befall London for nearly 600 years. Now the lead is melting from its roof and flowing down the walls and spilling over the tombs of the great men. The stones of its immense pillars are cracking in the intense heat. The monuments of London's ancient glory are crumbling to dust.

Some people will tell you it takes four days for the fire to burn itself out; others insist it lasts five or six. However, for months afterwards, pockets of material continue to smoulder in basements, flaring up suddenly when the air enters them. Pepys notices smoke coming from cellars all through the winter; the last such occasion being 16 March 1667, more than six months after the start of the fire.[19]

As soon as the blaze has started to die down, the ruins attract attention. William Taswell, a fifteen-year-old schoolboy, describes making his way to the cathedral on the morning of 6 September, while the fire is still burning:

On Thursday, soon after sunrise, I endeavoured to reach St Paul's. The ground was so hot as almost to scorch my shoes, and the air so intensely warm that unless I had stopped some time upon Fleet Bridge to rest myself, I must have fainted under the extreme languor of my spirits. After giving myself time to breathe, I made the best of my way to St Paul's. And now let any person judge of the violent emotion I was in when I perceived the metal belonging to the bells melting; the ruinous condition of its walls; whole heaps of stone of a large circumference tumbling down with a great noise just upon my feet, ready to crush me to death ... I forgot to mention that near the east wall of St Paul's a human body presented itself to me, parched up as it were with the flames: whole as to skin, meagre as to flesh, yellow as to colour. This was an old decrepit woman who had fled here for safety, imagining the flames would not have reached her there. Her clothes were burnt and every limb reduced to coal.[20]

John Evelyn walks through the city the day after Taswell:

I went this morning on foot from Whitehall as far as London Bridge through the late Fleet Street, Ludgate Hill by St Paul's, Cheapside, Exchange, Bishopsgate, Aldersgate and out to Moorfields, thence through Cornhill etcetera with extraordinary difficulty, clambering over heaps of yet smoking rubbish, and frequently mistaking where I was: the ground under my feet so hot that it even burnt the soles of my shoes ... At my return I was infinitely concerned to find that goodly church St Paul's now a sad ruin ... The lead, iron-work, bells, plate etcetera melted; the exquisitely wrought Mercers' Chapel, the sumptuous Exchange, the august fabric of Christ Church, all the rest of the Companies' halls, splendid buildings, arches, entries all in dust; the fountains dried up and ruined while the very waters remained boiling; the voragos [chasms] of subterranean cellars, wells and dungeons, formerly warehouses, still burning in stench and dark clouds of smoke, so that in five or six miles of traversing about I did not see one load of timber unconsumed nor many stones but what were calcined white as snow.

The people who now walked about the ruins appeared like men in some dismal desert, or, rather, in some great city laid waste by a cruel enemy; to which was added the stench that came from some poor creatures' bodies, beds and other combustible goods ... Nor was I yet able to pass through any of the narrow streets but kept [to] the widest: the ground and air, smoke and fiery vapour continued so intense that my hair was almost singed and my feet insufferably surbated [made sore]. The bye-lanes and narrow streets were quite filled up with rubbish; nor could one have possibly known where he was but by the ruins of some church or hall that had some remarkable tower or pinnacle remaining.[21]

When the fire has died down enough for people to be able to see the full extent of the damage, they find that all the city from the Tower to the Temple Church has been destroyed, from the river all the way up to the northern city wall. Apart from the cathedral, eighty-seven churches and six chapels are in ruins or have fallen completely. The halls of fifty-two livery companies have gone, as has the Royal Exchange, the Customs House and four prisons (many of the inmates escaping during the fire). London Stone lies shattered in fragments, the largest surviving piece being barely two feet long. The devastated area amounts to 436 acres; no fewer than 13,200 houses lie in ashes. Although that amounts to only one-fifth of the city, it is nevertheless the most important part in terms of civic pride and heritage, urban administration and trade. The fire leaves 80,000 people homeless. Yet, surprisingly, almost everyone has found shelter within four days.

Whereas on Thursday the 6th and Friday the 7th you will see people who have lost everything camping on the sides of the roads leading to Islington and Highgate, by the Wednesday of the following week they have all vacated the area. Temporary churches and places of business are set up promptly. Property prices and rents rocket, naturally, but people share rooms and houses. Some resort to building small brick shacks on the sites of their former premises, although the onset of winter and the lack of protection soon persuade many to move. Be warned that the old parish watch system no longer operates in the desolation: if you are attacked at night, no constables with torches will come to your aid. When Pepys takes a coach through the ruins after dark, he travels with a drawn sword.[22]

The Great Rebuilding

The Great Fire is an astonishing spectacle, but the rebuilding of London is even more remarkable. It is much easier to burn down an old wooden city in five days than it is to build a fine new one in five years. Nevertheless, that is what happens. Within two weeks of the fire, John Evelyn and Christopher Wren have each independently drawn up a new layout for the city. Wren's plan, informed by Inigo Jones's work at Covent Garden, envisages piazzas adjacent to the principal public buildings, such as the cathedral and the Royal Exchange, and long, wide streets connecting them. Evelyn's plan similarly incorporates many piazzas but it is more regular, arranged around square and rectangular blocks. However, both plans are set to one side, due to issues arising from ownership of the land. The law of property has proved one of the most enduring and stabilising factors down the centuries: people trust that no one can simply take away their land from them. The last thing they want now is to be forced to give up the site of their home; many of them don't have any other assets left. Besides, the government cannot afford to buy all the ruins at the market price. There are many other legal questions that complicate the matter. What happens to the people whose income depends on rent paid by their tenants? Many landlords continue to demand payment, even though the Fire has destroyed their houses. What should happen in the interim to the people who urgently need a new place of business, or who are sharing rooms with their kin? They can't afford to wait until the government has raised enough money to buy their land. For all these reasons, it is highly desirable that the city is rebuilt as quickly as possible, and this means simply going ahead without lengthy legal battles over land acquisition. Thus the original street layout is retained. In the end, only two new roads are created: King Street and Queen Street, crossing the city from the Guildhall to the Thames.

The ruins soon become a hive of activity, as workmen pull down the remains of walls, remove the old burnt timber and cart away stone to be reused elsewhere. Demolition is already complete by the end of November. The livery companies are swift to re-establish themselves; three halls are finished by the end of 1668. The Royal Exchange is rebuilt the following year. As for St Paul's Cathedral, the king initially vows that it will be restored, despite Wren's advice that it should be demolished. But in the spring of 1668, while reconstruction is in progress, part of the nave wall collapses, revealing hitherto unsuspected weaknesses in the surviving fabric. At this news, the king reconsiders the building's future, and in July he asks Wren to draw up a plan for a new cathedral. Funnily enough, Wren already has some ideas up his sleeve. Demolition of the remains of Old St Paul's starts the following month. The medieval stones are taken down the hill to the Fleet Ditch and used to canalise the river and raise the level of the ground there.

It is at this point that the tradition of controlling the quality of building in London bears new fruit. An Act is passed establishing four different categories of house, all of which must be built in brick or stone, with roofs of tile or slate. The smallest category, two storeys with an attic and a cellar, is intended for alleys and lanes; each storey is required to be 9ft high. The next size up, of three storeys plus an attic, is for streets and principal lanes, and roads facing the river; the ground floor and first floor are to be 10ft high, the second floor 9ft. The third type comprises four-storey houses 'fronting all high streets and lanes of note', the storeys from the ground up being 10ft, 10½ft, 9ft and 8½ft high.[23] All the houses along one street are meant to have the same height of roofline and be contiguous. The fourth category is 'mansion houses for citizens and other persons of extraordinary quality'. These too are limited to four storeys. Not all the high-quality features of William Newton's developments in Lincoln's Inn Fields are adopted; most houses cannot have forecourts behind high walls, and the high construction costs mean that most buildings do not have pilasters and balustrades on the roof. But the Act is effective in permitting the design and construction of affordable high-quality residences. By the end of 1667, 650 have been completed by private developers. The next year sees another 1,450 finished. Eventually, 8,000 are erected on the sites of the original 13,200: there are fewer dwellings because all the back-yard tenements have been eradicated. In addition, streets have been widened and drainage channels built. Wren starts rebuilding the parish churches in 1670: he designs seventeen of them in that year alone, and eventually completes fifty-one. He also designs the new baroque cathedral, which is sufficiently complete for a service to be held there in 1696, although it won't be finished until 1710. The Monument to the Fire, located near Pudding Lane and designed by Christopher Wren and Robert Hooke, is completed in 1676.

While the old city is being rebuilt, the suburbs keep growing. To the east of the Tower, the construction of small houses for workers continues apace: in Shadwell as many as fifty houses are built per acre of ground.[24] To the west and north of the city, new houses are built for the wealthy. Henry Jermyn, earl of St Albans, starts building St James's Square in 1665 and sees his aristocratic town houses take pride of place as the most luxurious in London in the 1670s. Just to the north, on Piccadilly, three massive mansions are built in the 1660s. In 1667 Richard Boyle, earl of Burlington, acquires and completes Burlington House (better known to you as the Royal Academy), designed by the royal surveyor, Sir John Denham. Further west along the same street, Edward Hyde, earl of Clarendon, is building Clarendon House, designed by Roger Pratt and widely considered the finest residence in London. And further west still, there is the huge Berkeley House, built by Hugh May for Lord Berkeley and completed in 1666. Leicester Square, Soho Square and Golden Square are laid out in the 1670s, as are the streets between them. Devonshire Square dates from 1678. Red Lion Square and Marine Square (later known as Wellclose Square) are two of the many building projects of the 1680s undertaken by the strangely named Nicholas If-Jesus-Christ-Had-Not-Died-For-Thee-Thou-Hadst-Been-Damned Barbon (a name thrust upon him by his Puritan father, Praise-God Barebones). Ironically, Barbon's damnation is something heartily desired by many of his contemporaries, on account of his initial building projects in Mincing Lane, whose houses have such weak foundations that they collapse, and his willingness to demolish properties without the owner's consent, which leads to litigation. He is not the only unscrupulous developer. In 1682 Sir George Downing builds Downing Street – a development of houses which are structurally so weak that only four of them survive, and those four will require frequent rebuilding over the subsequent centuries. Pity the poor people who have to live there.

To be fair to Barbon, he does build many solidly constructed houses in London as well, such as those along the Strand, in Chancery Lane and Red Lion Square. Even more positively, he pioneers the practice of insuring buildings against fire in the 1670s. In 1680 he relaunches the service as a joint-stock company, 'The Insurance Office for Houses'. Soon it has a number of competitors, including the Friendly Society for Securing Houses from Loss by Fire (founded in 1683) and the even-more snappily titled 'Contributors for Insuring Houses, Chambers or Rooms from Loss by Fire, by Amicable Contribution' (founded in 1696).[25] Having paid your deposit and a subscription, you will have a metal plaque attached to the wall of your house to verify that you are insured and that the insurance company's firemen may attempt to put out any fire that affects your property. Of course, if you haven't paid your subscription, or don't display a proper plaque, they will just stand by and watch your house burn.

Fire insurance is something Londoners badly need, for they continue to be somewhat cavalier with the candles. If you miss the Great Fire of London in 1666, you might choose to watch the Theatre Royal burn down in January 1672. The Navy Office buildings in Seething Lane, including Pepys's own house, catch light in January 1673, taking another thirty houses with them. A fire in Shadwell consumes about a hundred old houses the same year. Then, on Friday, 26 May 1676, the Little Fire of London breaks out in Southwark, on the south bank of the Thames. Like its 'Great' predecessor, it starts at night in an old, overcrowded area of narrow alleys and timber-framed houses. By the time it is brought under control – at ten o'clock the following night – it has consumed 624 properties. Private mansions regularly burn down too. Hungerford House (on the site of the modern Charing Cross Station) goes up in smoke in 1669. Goring House does likewise in 1674; this is replaced by Arlington House (which will become the south wing of the modern Buckingham Palace). The grand Montagu House, the Bloomsbury home of the duke of Montagu, designed by Robert Hooke, is sadly reduced to ashes in 1686. Tragically, Bridgewater

House is engulfed in flames the following year, with the deaths of two of the earl of Bridgewater's sons and their tutor.

The two most shocking of all these noble conflagrations are those that engulf the royal palace of Whitehall. In April 1691, a maidservant who cannot be bothered to find a knife to cut a candle from a bundle of them decides to burn one off, and then tosses the first candle aside without thinking. As Evelyn notes in his diary, 'this night a sudden and terrible fire burnt down all the buildings over the Stone Gallery at Whitehall, to the waterside, beginning at the apartment of the late duchess of Portsmouth, which had been pulled down and rebuilt no less than three times to please her!' Worse is to come. In January 1698, the remainder of 'the largest and ugliest palace in Europe' is destroyed when a Dutch laundress leaves some clothes to dry in front of a charcoal fire and then forgets about them. Only Inigo Jones's great Banqueting Hall and the gatehouses are saved. Sculptures by Michelangelo and Bernini perish in the flames, as does Holbein's great portrait of Henry VIII and many other priceless treasures. So too does the laundress responsible.[26] The completeness of the destruction enables developers to build more houses and offices on the extensive site of the old palace, with its courtyards, bowling green and gardens.

As a result of all this building and rebuilding, the city can accommodate more and more people and the population continues to grow at an extraordinary rate. Between 1660 and 1700 the number living in the poorer parishes to the east of the city increases by over half, from about 59,000 to 92,000.[27] To the west, the fashionable parish of St Martin-in-the-Fields sees even more dramatic growth, from 19,000 in 1660 to 69,000 by 1685.[28] Across London as a whole, the population of 410,000 in 1660 rises to about 475,000 by 1670 and to 575,000 by 1700. That is more than Paris (488,000 inhabitants), more than four times the size of Rome (125,000) and nearly ten times the size of Dublin (60,000).[29] What's more, London now accommodates about 11.4 per cent of the population of England (compared to just 5 per cent in 1600). If you add the many commuters and visitors – the farmers from nearby villages bringing their livestock into the city, the tourists coming to view the sights, and people from all over the kingdom coming to town to attend the law courts or transact financial business – the importance of the capital increases still further. At least one-sixth of all English people spend some portion of their lives in the capital.

All this makes London dominant in English affairs, although the full extent of its dominance is not often appreciated. In the years 1670–1700, its population is around 420 per cent of the size of the ten next largest places in England put together. Never before has it been so strikingly out in front. Nor will it ever be so again (in the modern world it is about 163 per cent).[30] And this primacy is more than just a question of numbers. For most of this period, only three places in England are permitted to print books – Oxford, Cambridge and London – and of those, London produces by far the majority. It is also where all the newspapers are printed, where Parliament sits, where the stock market is established and where the banks are based. If you want to see the king, you'll need to come to court, which is based in London. If a wealthy man dies with goods worth £5 in more than one diocese, the chances are that his executor will have to come to London to prove the will. For all these reasons, London attracts people from all over the country. By 1700, London is vital to a significant proportion of the people of Britain.

This dominance and intensity of activity mean that London increasingly acts as a magnifying glass on people's lives, bringing out their key characteristics. It makes the wealthy wealthier, the poor poorer and the avaricious more greedy. It allows the poetic to dream. It drives the lonely to despair. It encourages the curious to experiment, the gluttonous to eat, inebriates to drink, gamblers to take risks, extroverts to show off and shy people to retreat into themselves. In short, it is a great amplifier of the English spirit, and therefore an excellent place to begin your journey into Restoration Britain. However, although tiredness with London may well equate to tiredness with life (as Dr Johnson will famously say in the next century), it is only a small part of the island of Great Britain.

Traveller, your carriage awaits.

2

Beyond London

One of the most interesting things about the British countryside in the late seventeenth century is how differently people see it, compared to the modern world. While out riding, they don't pull on their reins at the top of a hill and exclaim, 'Oh, isn't that a lovely view!' They just don't associate nature with beauty in the same way that we do. When the antiquary Ralph Thoresby travels throughout northern England in the 1690s he never once expresses any admiration of the scenery. Coming to Lake Windermere, in what we know as the Lake District, he simply remarks that it is 'the most spacious lake in England'. Ascending the mountain to Hardknott Pass, he talks of the mountains being 'terrible' and 'dangerous' and of the rivers in the valleys as 'hideous in places'.[1] Celia Fiennes, an intrepid gentlewoman who travels the length and breadth of England in her thirties, similarly talks about 'those high inaccessible rocky barren hills which hang over one's head in some places and appear very terrible'.[2] When she visits Lake Windermere in 1698 she notes all she has learnt about the manorial rights and customs, how the locals make bread and so on, but there is no indication that she is moved by the view. She pays close attention to rivers and other watercourses – but only because they yield fish and drinking water and drive the mills. She never says that a lake looks beautiful or a high peak wonderful. At Blackstone Edge in Lancashire, she comments that it is 'known all over England for a dismal high precipice and steep in the ascent and descent at either end; it is a very moorish ground all about ... which is very troublesome'.[3] When she descends again to Rochdale, she declares it to be both 'pretty' and 'neat'. And that just about sums up how most people in seventeenth-century Britain view the environment. If it looks well maintained and is productive, then it may be deemed fine and admirable; but if it is natural, there is something primitive about it and, more often than not, it is 'troublesome'.

This attitude is also reflected in how people regard the landscape in its painted form. You will have to search very hard indeed to find a landscape painting by a British artist except as a backdrop to a portrait. There are a few (Robert Aggas, Robert Robinson and Robert Streater each produce a handful), but the man celebrated as the founding father of British landscape painting, Richard Wilson, won't even be born until 1713. On the rare occasion that you do come across a representation of natural scenery in the gallery of a stately home, it will be by a Dutch or French artist. The fact is that British people don't take an objective view of the countryside because their lives are still entwined with fields, woods, hedgerows and country lanes. They do not feel the need to praise or replicate nature because it is all around them. They find pictures of cattle and mountains crude and not at all charming. Who wants to look at a painting of cows standing in a muddy field?

What is remarkable about Thoresby and Fiennes is not so much their blindness to natural beauty as the fact that they venture out to these places at all. This in itself hints that attitudes towards the countryside are beginning to change. Another such sign is a growing fashion for great landowners to commission artists from the Low Countries to paint their estates. Jan Siberechts, who comes to England in 1674, is just one of many Dutch and Flemish landscape painters who make a living out of 'portraits' of English country houses and their grounds. Such artists naturally set their subjects against the backdrop of the local scenery. Another such artist is Willem Schellinks, mentioned in the previous chapter. Now *he* appreciates a good view. Having climbed to the top of a hill in Essex, he describes seeing 'a beautiful view over the finest landscape we have so far seen in England, towards the county of Kent just across the River Thames'.[4] Later he stays at the house of Sir Arnold Braems, which he declares lies 'in a valley of outstanding beauty'.[5]

The thing is, in order to appreciate a view so fine, you need something to compare it to – a view that is not so pleasant. Up to now, though, when English people have looked around them, they have simply seen miles of fields and trees. A field of corn might look beautiful next to a craggy mountain but, other than that, it is all just as God intended. However, little by little, people in the densely populated towns are beginning to appreciate that country views offer the mind an escape. Every so often, visiting a town house, such as the elegantly furnished home of Elizabeth Manby in Lincoln, your eye will alight on a 'landskip'.[6] At the same time, the difficulty of escaping a city's noxious fumes makes people much more appreciative of country air. John Evelyn not only rants against the smoke of London in his *Fumifugium* (1661), but also remarks that regular visits to the country are necessary to maintain good health. The religious writer John Bunyan is of a like mind. 'Who would not exchange the stench and fogs of a city for the open balmy air?' he writes. It seems as if people are opening their eyes to the beauty around them for the first time – or, at least, some of them are.

So much for what seventeenth-century people *think* of the countryside. But what will you *see*?

Let us begin with the kingdom of England, which at this time officially incorporates the principality of Wales (we will consider Scotland separately). As you are no doubt aware, the landscape is extremely varied. It ranges from the fells of the north to the fens of the east, from the sparsely populated Welsh mountains to the drained marshes of Kent and Somerset. Generally speaking, the south is richer than the north, and the east richer than the west. Wales is considered particularly poor: one-third of its populace does not earn enough to be eligible to pay the hearth tax. Nor is there any easy collective description for the agriculture of these places. In Kent, travelling in the footsteps of Thomas Baskerville, you will pass vast orchards of cherries, pears and apples and great hop gardens. If you journey through Dorset, you might find yourself overwhelmed by flocks of sheep: it is said there are 300,000 of them within six miles of Dorchester alone; nationally the sheep population in 1660 is more than twelve million and rising fast.[7] Some industries also show regional variation. On many rivers in Devon and Cornwall you will hear the heavy stamping sound of blowing houses, where tin ore is crushed by massive hammers, powered by water wheels and smelted. Coal mining is carried on in counties such as Berkshire and Shropshire as well as Nottinghamshire and County Durham. Other industries are less localised: the processing of woollen cloth, for example, takes place all over England. Likewise in all regions you will see active woodland management: coppices are maintained for fuel, fencing and coach-building. Foresters pollard oaks and beeches: the timber goes for building houses and ships, the foliage serves as animal fodder and the sticks are used for fuel. In most counties, stacks of willow and alder are covered with turf and burnt slowly for charcoal, which is used in such rural industries as blacksmithing, brewing and gunpowder manu-facture. Although you might not instinctively place making explosives alongside thatching and basket weaving as a rural craft, when you consider that, for safety's sake, gunpowder needs to be produced in damp conditions in isolated buildings with very thick walls and weak roofs, you can see why the mills are located in remote areas.

To give you an idea of the agricultural character of England and Wales at this time, the seventeenth-century statistician Gregory King has helpfully put together a schedule of his estimates for the year 1695. By his reckoning, $7/13$ of the total area of the kingdom is used for agriculture. Given that England and Wales have areas of 50,350 and 8,015 square miles respectively, this amounts to 31,427 square miles of farmland, which is more than 20 million acres.[8] Roughly half of this is arable and half pasture or meadow. Another $1/13$ of the total area (roughly 2.9 million acres) is occupied by managed woods and coppices; another $1/13$ is forests, parks and commons; and a further $3/13$ are heaths, moors, mountains and barren land. A quarter of the last $1/13$ is roadways, another quarter is waterways and the remaining half is developed land: houses and other buildings, plus their associated gardens, orchards and churchyards. By anybody's reckoning, the country is still very green. But this does not mean that the land is underused. King estimates that 75 per cent of the population lives and works in the countryside and villages, and about 80 per cent of these people work in agriculture.[9] Overall, the population of England in 1695 is about 5.06 million, which implies a rural density of seventy-five people per square mile.[10] Wales is much less populous, with around 400,000 individuals and a total density of about fifty people per square mile, including its towns. As you are more used to modern densities of 1,112 per square mile in England and 390 per square mile in Wales, you will feel that there is hardly anyone at home.

As you walk through the English countryside you will notice that many fields are 'open' – that is to say, unenclosed by a hedgerow or fence. But that number is rapidly dwindling. For hundreds of years villagers in England have managed the land in common, dividing it up into two, three or more great fields of several hundred acres, which are then subdivided into furlongs, so that every yeoman or tenant farmer has a few strips of land in each of the great fields. In addition, he has certain grazing rights on the commons and regularly attends a court that oversees the administration of the whole manor. Land managed in this way is called 'champion' or 'champaign' country. But now more and more of these great fields are being divided up and physically separated by hedges, walls and fences. The process started in the Middle Ages, when lords of manors started to replace underused arable land with pasture for their wool-bearing flocks of sheep, but it has gathered great momentum since 1600. In fact, more enclosure takes place in the seventeenth century than in any other: about a quarter of the entire area of England is enclosed, with the greatest level of hedge-planting and wall-building taking place in the years from 1630 to 1680.[11] Only nineteen of the 139 parishes in Berkshire have been entirely enclosed by 1634, but two-thirds of the county has been appropriated for the sole use of its owners by 1700.[12] Wiltshire experiences a similar fate, being mostly open in the early seventeenth century but mostly enclosed by the end of it. Some counties never had open fields in the first place: Kent, parts of Sussex, Cornwall and Cheshire. In these regions the only unenclosed areas are the commons where farmers might retain the right to graze their sheep and cattle. In 1700 just eleven of England's forty counties still consist predominantly of unenclosed arable land.[13] In all, over the course of the seventeenth century, the proportion of England that remains champion country shrinks from about 55 per cent to 23 per cent.[14]

'So what?' you might ask. Big fields, small fields: does it really make any difference? Yes, it does. Think how often you hear someone in the modern world ask, 'Why do so few people today own so much of the countryside?' Part of the answer lies wrapped up in the systematic process of enclosure, and in the meaning of that word 'own'. At the start of the seventeenth century, most of rural England and Wales is owned by the nobility and landed gentry, but while it is unenclosed, it is not theirs to do with as they wish. Their tenants have rights over it. Almost every householder in an open-field manor will have a few strips of arable land. Even if he only has the use of an acre or two, he will still have the right to graze a proportionate number of animals on the common. In some places he will be entitled to use the collectively owned oxen, which are grazed on the fallow field, to pull a plough across his strips of land. Every man, woman and child in the community joins forces to help with the harvest. They may also have the right to take wood and fruit from hedgerows and woodlands, or to trap birds in the great fields and in a few places to fish in the rivers. What's more, a manorial lord cannot simply evict his tenants and do what he wants with the land, because their tenures are guaranteed, normally by a copyhold agreement or a lease, and each agreement may cover two or three generations. In other words, an unenclosed manor is not so much a parcel of land as a self-sufficient community, and the lord's 'ownership' does not imply much more than an income from that community and the right to sit in judgement on its disputes; it does not mean he can do what he wants with the land. Hence this change from big fields to small fields represents a massive shift in English society. It means the shift of control from local communities to landowners.

Why, then, does it happen?

Landowners will often tell you that the principal reason is efficiency, and that not just the great fields but also the commons and meadows can be made more productive by enclosure. In unenclosed manors, tenants with larger flocks and herds tend to overstock the pasture, so that there is insufficient grass for those who own fewer sheep and cattle. People are reluctant to plant new trees when all the land is managed in common. They are happy to cut wood down and fell timber, but are not so keen to replace it when they know it will be someone else who reaps the benefit; enclosures that incorporate bushes and trees in their hedgerows are therefore a good thing. As for the arable land, leaving a whole great field fallow every other year is no longer necessary as methods of fertilisation improve; yet it is very difficult to change working practices when so many tenant farmers are working in each field and they all tend to adhere to traditional ways of doing things. Finally, there is the basic inefficiency of having to till strips of land that are in different places; it's much easier to farm your acres if they are all in one block.

Those in favour of open fields and the communal culture of the countryside have much to say in defence of the old way of life. Tilling the land supports large numbers of people who have no other form of livelihood. As customary tenants of the manor, their rents are cheap and they often cannot legally be increased. Farming collectively allows the less well off to benefit from communal assets, such as teams of oxen. Thus, in many small ways, the wealthier tenants support the poorer ones. As for the opinion that open-field farming prevents inno-vation, villagers point out that they *can* adapt: they can select specific furlongs to leave fallow rather than whole fields; they can introduce different spring crops or turn areas over to grass for more animal husbandry.[15] And the scattered ownership of strips of land is not without its benefits: in years of heavy rainfall, your low-lying strips might be waterlogged but the higher ones will drain well; and when there is little rainfall, the lower ones make up for the withered crops on the high ground. What's more, although it might seem that leaving a great field fallow every other year is inefficient, it serves a purpose if it is feeding the cattle. Lastly, what will the rural farmer be, if he does not have a part in the management of the land? He will simply be an individual renter. All the ties of loyalty, community support and mutual respect will be commuted to a single money payment.

This is the battle for the heart of England. However, as you will be aware, the outcome is a foregone conclusion. The plain fact is that enclosures are indeed more efficient than open fields. Old-style collective farming might be able to innovate to a degree, but not to the same extent that an outright owner can. The new forms of fertilising the land – such as the sowing of turnips and clover to replenish the soil's nutrients (introduced from Flanders by Sir Richard Weston in the 1640s) or 'denshiring' it (burning the vegetation and digging in the ashes, as they do in Devonshire) – are more easily adopted over an enclosed field than over individual strips in a great field. At the end of the day, these economies all add up; they make farming more profitable, and serious farmers who want to improve their land are prepared to pay higher rents to do so. Last but not least, if landlords can enclose the land (either by agreement or by Act of Parliament), they can extinguish all those customary tenancies and cheap rents, and instead lease out the land at market rates.

This suggests that avaricious landlords are to blame for the transformation of the English countryside and its outright ownership. However, chatting to a few of them will show you that this is only partly true. When there is a dire harvest or a particularly bad winter on an unenclosed manor, the small husbandmen with only a couple of acres cannot make ends meet. Some give up farming their own land, choosing instead to earn their living by manual labour; others leave the manor. In such cases, the steward has to reallocate the redundant strips of land to other tenant farmers. Gradually, as the bad weather continues, the land is concentrated in fewer hands. Before long the farmers who are left in business want all their lands to be in one place, for ease of sowing, fertilising and harvesting. Thus pressure to enclose the land grows from the major tenants too, and not just from the landlords. When enclosure finally takes place, the smallest farmers are forced off the land altogether. Two or three small enclosures by themselves are not enough to enable a poor husbandman to sustain a family – especially when he has lost his use of the communal oxen, meadows, commons, firewood and the rights to trap game, birds or fish. By separating the working practices of big and small farmers, the big ones no longer help the small, and the small ones are forced to sell up. Your typical manor of sixty or seventy tenant farmers, working collectively, is suddenly reduced to two dozen farmers working independently, employing twenty or thirty labourers between them. The unemployed remainder have little choice but to head off to the nearest town and look for a job.

The drive to improve the land is gradually reshaping the countryside in other ways too. The boundaries of the newly enclosed fields are designed to run in dead-straight lines; hence you can easily tell them apart from the ancient hedgerows of the medieval period, which are never straight. Similarly, when the open fields were laid out in the Middle Ages, the villages where the people lived were all built as groups of cottages, often around a village green. In those days it was unusual for farmers in these regions to live in isolated farmhouses. Now, with communal farming coming to an end and farmers having all their fields in one block, it is sensible for them to live in the middle of their land, where they can keep an eye on their animals. Therefore many new farmhouses are being built in the open countryside. Naturally, the roads leading to these new dwellings are straight, leading from the highway to the farmyard – quite unlike the lanes twisting between ancient hedgerows such as you find in Devon, Cornwall, Kent and Sussex. As for the old farmhouses in the villages, they are frequently converted into rows of cottages for rural labourers.

As farmers stop using communal oxen they start to employ their own teams of plough horses. These are less costly to keep, faster and more versatile, so although you will still see oxen here and there, their numbers are rapidly declining. At the same time, the horse population of England almost doubles over the period 1660–1700.[16] The massive growth of London's population leads to an ever-increasing demand for meat and dairy products. As meat has to be transported on the hoof, and dairy products have to be moved quickly in order to be sold fresh, large enclosed farms are established in the counties surrounding the capital. The growing demand for meat, coupled with the mass of new enclosures, means that the national sheep population increases to over seventeen million by the end of the century – more than three sheep for every person in the kingdom.[17] In the north of England, farmers start planting fields of potatoes for the first time. Elsewhere, from about 1670, you will start to see large areas planted with turnips, to be mashed up for cattle feed.[18]

There are other dramatic changes in the countryside too. If you venture into the Fenlands of Norfolk, Cambridgeshire and Lincolnshire, you will find an area of wetland extending to about 300,000 acres gradually being drained. Pepys's mathematical friend Ralph Greatorex designs an engine for pumping water into deep, straight channels built for the purpose.[19] John Evelyn goes to see a set of windmills and water pumps in the Fens in 1670. He remarks that the reclaimed land is exceptionally fertile, and that the draining of the marshes has removed the swarms of mosquitoes that hitherto infested the area. You would have thought that such work would be widely welcomed but, as with enclosure, what is progress for some is the very opposite for others. In this case, the Slodgers take a dim view of proceedings. These are the people who live amidst the waterways and marshes and who wish to preserve their independent, semi-aquatic way of life: cutting reeds, fishing and snaring. Accordingly they sabotage the pumps, mills and dams in the hope of flooding the land again. Even in the seventeenth century you can't please everybody all of the time.

Not every part of England and Wales is seeing agricultural change. In the south-west peninsula, the fields have all been enclosed for centuries. Large numbers of Red Devon cattle are driven annually in a 'red tide' along the deep lanes on their way up to the summer pastures on Dartmoor. Hereabouts you will come across many people living in houses and cottages built of cob – a mixture of earth or clay, straw and sometimes animal hair – with thatched roofs. Thatch tends to last only about thirty years, after which it needs replacing, but in Devon only the top level is removed, so that more and more layers of thatch are built up on top of the straw base. As a result, many houses in this county look ungainly and humped, with thatch six feet deep and wide, overhanging eaves. Around Dartmoor, you will still find many longhouses – medieval granite buildings in which cattle live at one end and the farmer and his family live at the other, all under the same roof, and all entering and leaving by the same door.

The landscape is also largely unchanged in remote parts of northern England. In Cumberland, for example, each countryman continues to live on his own tenement with a handful of pigs and half a dozen chickens. He keeps his other livestock – perhaps ten cows and about fifty sheep – in small fields or 'closes' near his farmhouse. In the autumn you'll see a black tide of Scottish cattle coming south for sale in Carlisle and wintering on the lowlands, to be resold to graziers further south the following year, or to be slaughtered and salted down for use in ships' stores. Oats and bigg (a coarse form of barley) are the principal crops grown here, chosen for their hardiness. As for the houses, many are single-storey 'clay dabbins' built of cob around a cruck frame and thatched. Sometimes the whole community comes together to build such a house in a single day for a newly married couple.[20] Other dwellings are single-storey stone buildings with slate roofs around which the wind whips cruelly in winter. Older versions of these are called 'bastles' – farmhouses that have been fortified against the intrusions of Scots reivers, who until relatively recently came south to raid cattle. On high ground you come across stone shielings, where farmers stay temporarily when driving their cattle long distances, or where cowherds live when looking after their grazing animals. When Celia Fiennes is making her way to Carlisle in 1698, she passes through Cumberland and describes the houses there as

> sad little huts made up of dry walls, only stones piled together and the roofs of the same slate. There seemed to be little or no tunnels for their chimneys and [they] have no plaster within or without. For the most part I took them at first sight for a sort of houses or barns to fodder cattle in, not thinking them to be dwelling houses, they being scattered, here one, there another ... it must needs be a very cold dwelling but it shows something of the laziness of the people.[21]

I suspect that the inhabitants will have their own views on that last comment.

Towns, Boroughs and Cities

As mentioned above, Gregory King estimates that 75 per cent of the people of England and Wales live in the villages and countryside. That figure is worth dwelling on for a moment, because as you walk through some of the settlements that he describes as *towns*, you might think they are more like villages. Some of them have just 400 inhabitants living in about eighty houses. The reason for this is that a settlement is not called a town on account of its size, but by virtue of it having a market. Likewise, a city is not necessarily a bustling place: it is called a city if it has a cathedral, regardless of whether it has 30,000 inhabitants, like Norwich, or 3,000 like Ely, or just a few hundred, like the Welsh city of St David's. In total, the number of market towns in England in 1693 is 614 (including 22 cities); and in Wales there are 66 (including 4 cities).[22] As for 'boroughs', these might be one of several things: a market town that is governed by a mayor and corporation of aldermen; or a place that sends an MP (or two) to Westminster; or a settlement that is simply called a 'borough' by tradition. In all, there are 202 Parliamentary boroughs in England and 13 in Wales.[23] Not all Parliamentary boroughs are towns, it should be noted. A few are leftovers of a different medieval settlement pattern and have very few residents. Old Sarum has none at all – 'not as much as the ruins of a house', as one contemporary puts it – but it still sends two MPs to Parliament.[24] Dunwich, once a prosperous port, also sends two MPs even though there are waves lapping at its marketplace in 1677.

With regard to the larger towns, in 1670 about 680,000 people in England (13.6 per cent of the population) live in a town of at least 5,000 inhabitants. That means more than 86 per cent of the population lives in what you (as opposed to Gregory King) might regard as a rural area. By 1700 that figure has declined only slightly, to 83 per cent. By this reckoning, Wales is 100 per cent 'rural' throughout the period: there are no towns of 5,000 people in the principality. The largest settlement, Wrexham, has about 3,500 inhabitants in 1700.[25]

English towns with more than 5,000 inhabitants (cities are in capitals)[26]

c. 1670	Population	c. 1700	Population
LONDON	475,000	LONDON	575,000
NORWICH	20,000	NORWICH	30,000
BRISTOL	20,000	BRISTOL	21,000
YORK	12,000	Newcastle	16,000
Newcastle	12,000	EXETER	14,000
Colchester	9,000	YORK	12,000
EXETER	9,000	Great Yarmouth	10,000
CHESTER	8,000	Birmingham	8–9,000
Ipswich	8,000	CHESTER	8–9,000

c. 1670	Population	c. 1700	Population
Great Yarmouth	8,000	Colchester	8–9,000
Plymouth	8,000	Ipswich	8–9,000
WORCESTER	8,000	Manchester	8–9,000
Coventry	7,000	Plymouth	8–9,000
King's Lynn	7,000	WORCESTER	8–9,000
Manchester	6,000	Bury St Edmunds	5–7,000
CANTERBURY	6,000	Cambridge	5–7,000
Leeds	6,000	CANTERBURY	5–7,000
Birmingham	6,000	Chatham	5–7,000
Cambridge	6,000	Coventry	5–7,000
Kingston upon Hull	6,000	GLOUCESTER	5–7,000
SALISBURY	6,000	Kingston upon Hull	5–7,000
Bury St Edmunds	5,000	King's Lynn	5–7,000
Leicester	5,000	Leeds	5–7,000
OXFORD	5,000	Leicester	5–7,000
Shrewsbury	5,000	Liverpool	5–7,000
GLOUCESTER	5,000	Nottingham	5–7,000
		OXFORD	5–7,000
		Portsmouth	5–7,000
		SALISBURY	5–7,000
		Shrewsbury	5–7,000
		Sunderland	5–7,000
		Tiverton	5–7,000
Total urban population	c. 678,000	*Total urban population*	c. 850,000
Population of England	4,980,000	*Population of England*	5,060,000
London as % of pop.	9.5%	London as % of pop.	11.4%
Other urban as % of pop.	4.1%	Other urban as % of pop.	5.4%
Total urban as % of pop.	13.6%	Total urban as % of pop.	16.8%

As you wander through the streets of a provincial city, quite a few things will remind you of your visit to the capital. Take Exeter, for example. Like London, it is a river port and growing rapidly, but due to the failure of any local bakers to burn it down, it resembles the old heart of London rather more than the new aristocratic piazzas of the capital. It has a medieval bridge and a medieval castle, and the two towers of its ancient cathedral stand high above every other building, including the city's medieval Guildhall. The city streets and lanes are narrow, and as you climb the hill up into the city centre, you will see that most of them still have central drains and are cobbled, not paved. Thick stone walls stand to the height of about 13 feet around much of the city, and the five substantial stone gates still give a guarded access. The alleys are muddy, narrow and dark where the old houses are jettied out over them. Some are even narrower and darker here than those in London, for when they were built in the Middle Ages, local transport in Devon was more frequently undertaken by packhorse than cart, so people had scant regard for wheeled traffic when they laid out the smaller rights of way. As in many other towns and cities, the private houses of Exeter are predominantly old and timber-framed: as you walk around, note how many jetties and beams are decorated with carved figures – here the head of a Moor, there a griffin, there a unicorn, and so on.[27] The city has an Exchange, where you find high-quality shops. There is also a second Exchange for merchants, in the remains of the cathedral cloisters, where cloth dealers and manufacturers meet twice a day, as they do in London.[28] The markets are still held in the middle of town and so you will smell the blood of slaughtered animals in the streets and the effluent seeping through cellars. You will hear the cries of street vendors and see people queuing for water from the conduit at the top of South Street, just as they do at the Standard on Cornhill, in London.

Exeter still has its old inns, of course: dozens of them, from the renowned Bear Inn in South Street, to nondescript taverns with a spare bed or two in the suburbs. When Grand Duke Cosimo III arrives in Exeter in 1669, the whole of his entourage stays at the finest hostelry in town, the forty-room New Inn in the High Street, which has been known as the 'New Inn' ever since it was built in about 1445. There he graciously receives the gentry of the county, and Lorenzo Magalotti writes down his impressions of Exeter. He describes it as 'a small city' (even though it is the seventh largest in the kingdom). He carefully notes that ships of 300 tons burden can navigate as far as Topsham, a small town nearby, from where the merchants send their goods by barge up the canal to Exeter Quay. He is impressed by the reach of the trade in woollen cloth such as bays and serge, which are sent all over the world – to the West Indies, Spain, France, Holland, Italy and the Middle East. As for the public buildings, he admires the cathedral, the Bishop's Palace, the ancient walls and the old castle.[29] However, he does not remark on any other structure. There is no doubt as to what he thinks is the chief attraction of the place: 'the city is intersected almost in the middle by a very large and straight street, full of very rich shops, which is its best and most considerable part'.[30] In Exeter, as in London, Magalotti's real interest lies in shopping.

All this will remind you of the old heart of London before the Fire. But as you look around you will also see signs of change. The old cathedral yard has been given a new, fashionable function, akin to the walks in London's St James's Park. 'In the square of the cathedral is a most beautiful summer walk, under the shade of trees, which are divided into several rows, as they often are in Holland,' writes Magalotti.[31] If you leave the city by the South Gate and look east, you will see streets of fine new houses under construction. The three buildings directly to your right have recently been built by prosperous tradesmen. They are two storeys high, with a third attic storey; the gable ends face the street in the style of older buildings, and the timber frames are square and infilled with lath and plaster. However, they are wider than Tudor houses, with tall brick chimneys, and they are flat-fronted, not jettied out over the roadway. They are typical of the new structures being built to house the growing population of the city. Here and there among them you will find a fine brick building, proudly declaiming its newness and high level of comfort. There's a handsome example on Magdalen Road: a substantial mansion of three storeys, built for Thomas Mathew in 1659.[32] Initially the bricks for such buildings are imported as ballast in Dutch merchants' ships. By the 1690s, new brickfields in the parish of St Sidwell, just to the east of the city, lead to the building of many more brick houses. It all creates a favourable impression on Celia Fiennes when she visits in 1698: 'Exeter is a town very well built: the streets are well-pitched noble streets and a vast trade is carried on.'[33]

Exeter is just 2 per cent of the size of London. Although it has many of the same features that the capital enjoys, there are also many it lacks. It has no royal palace and few members of the aristocracy spend any time here. Thus its prosperity depends far more heavily on its economic dynamism than on its position as a social nexus – even if the Grand Duke of Tuscany stays at the New Inn. Celia Fiennes goes into considerable detail about the serges traded in the city, describing how the carriers who bring the wool into town on their loaded horses are 'thick along the highways', and how the fleeces are taken to the fulling mills. She notes approvingly that the canal by which the merchandise arrives in barges is being upgraded, so that seagoing ships can sail right up to the city. She describes how the quay has recently been extended to allow for the extra business, and a handsome new customs house has been constructed in red brick, on the ground floor of which the merchandise is unloaded. 'Serge is the chief manufacture,' she declares. 'As Norwich is for copes, calico and damask, so Exeter is for serges – there is an incredible quantity of them made and sold in the town.'[34] Seventeenth-century people see towns differently from us too, just as they do the countryside.

Not all of the old towns are experiencing the same levels of fortune. Although a few (such as Norwich) have growth rates even greater than that of London, many towns are not growing at all. Their expansion is often restricted by their customs and restrictive trading practices, such as keeping out all 'foreign' traders. Indeed, some places seem stuck in a rut. When Thomas Baskerville visits Leicester he remarks:

> It is now an old stinking town, situated upon a dull river, inhabited for the most part by tradesmen, viz: worsted combers and clothiers, for the streets being then swept and cleansed against the judges coming in the next morning, the stinking puddles of —— and water being then stirred made me go spewing through all the streets.[35]

Manchester, on the other hand, is growing rapidly on the strength of its textiles. Birmingham has strong growth, on account of its metal-working. Among the other large towns undergoing rapid development are Chatham, because of its dockyard; Liverpool and Portsmouth, because of the shift towards the Atlantic trade; Sunderland, on account of its port and its salt processing, dye manufacture and glassmaking; Tiverton, because of the burgeoning wool trade; and Nottingham, as a result of the wool trade and hosiery manufacture. In Plymouth, another port benefiting from the booming Atlantic trade, Magalotti notes that so many men are employed in the export of lead and tin that 'only women and boys are to be seen – for the men are all at sea'.[36] These towns exemplify the industrial bubbling that you will see across the country, as it experiences the challenges and opportunities of economic improvement.

Alongside these large towns of 5,000 people or more, there are approximately fifty further towns in England with 2,000 inhabitants; in Wales, only Wrexham, Brecon, Carmarthen, Haverfordwest and Swansea fall into this category.[37] These too are experiencing a range of fortunes. Many of them are simply carrying on in the way that old market towns do. The population of the city of Lincoln steadily increases from about 3,500 to 4,500, its inhabitants growing more prosperous from its many trades.[38] Carlisle, a small city of about 3,000 people on the border with Scotland, is benefiting hugely from the fact that the two kingdoms are no longer at war, so the succession of sieges it has had to endure down the centuries is apparently at an end (there is still the siege of 1745 to come, but don't tell them that). In Abbey Street there are some handsome new structures of stone and brick, including Tullie House, built in 1689 for the future dean of Carlisle. When Celia Fiennes visits nine years later, she mentions some 'graceful' houses, such as the chancellor's residence, which is 'built of stone [and] very lofty with five good sash windows in the front'.[39] Faring less well in these peaceful times is a town like Ludlow, in Shropshire. It is only slowly recovering from a long siege in 1646. Before the conflict, its population stood at 2,600; by 1660 it has fallen to 1,600. Among the crumbling remnants of the town walls and old timber-framed houses, you will find a profitable market but few signs of urban expansion. In 1700 the town still has only 2,200 inhabitants.[40]

If you want to see the most impressive examples of economic dynamism at this time, you need to visit the new ports on the west coast. Smithwick in Cornwall is a striking example. At the start of the century there is nothing here except the manor house belonging to the Killigrew family, and Pendennis Castle, a coastal fortification built by Henry VIII. The Killigrews then construct a port, which they call Falmouth. In 1660 Sir Peter Killigrew obtains a grant of a market for Falmouth; he also builds a prison and two inns. Four years later the place has more than 200 houses. The Killigrews build the custom-house quay in the 1670s. Thereafter the economic growth is rapid, on account of the depth of the harbour and Britain's growing overseas interests. From 1688 Falmouth is recognised as the official despatch point for the packet ships sailing to British overseas territories in India, the West Indies and America. By 1700 it has 350 houses and the population is approaching 1,500 people.[41]

Even more impressive is a little fishing village called Whitehaven in Cumberland, not many miles from Celia Fiennes's 'sad little huts'. This has only nine thatched cottages when the Lowther family acquires it in 1631. From that moment on, however, the Lowthers are to Whitehaven what the Killigrews are to Falmouth. Sir Christopher Lowther builds the harbour to export his locally mined coal to Ireland, and his son Sir John obtains the right to hold a market there in 1660. Sir John lays out the settlement with straight roads in a grid; he builds a church and other public buildings, and in many ways provides the prototype for the northern industrial factory town. In 1685 the population passes 1,000 people; in 1700 it is about 3,000 – a massive rate of expansion in just fifteen years.[42]

If you have a head for sums, you will have worked out from the above figures that the vast majority of towns in England and Wales – about 650 of them – have fewer than 2,000 inhabitants. In fact, if you exclude all those towns with a population of 5,000 or more, the average size of all the other towns in 1700 is just 810 people, or about 200 families – barely a village, by modern reckoning.[43] Yet these towns all have their own public buildings, services and hinterlands. The focal point in each place is the market. Willem Schellinks neatly illustrates this in his description of Brentford. 'As it was Tuesday, which is the usual market day there, there was a great deal of merchandise brought to market, and lots of people come from the neighbouring villages to hawk their goods or lay in supplies.'[44] Thus, although Magalotti might declare that Axminster has 'nothing considerable apart from the church', and Celia Fiennes might ride through Richmond (a town of about 1,400 people) and say it looks like a 'sad, shattered town and fallen much to decay and like a disregarded place', such settlements are important elements of the nation's infrastructure.[45]

Take Moretonhampstead, for example, where I am writing this book. Sitting on the edge of Dartmoor in Devon, the town has a population in the 1660s of about 700 people, with a further 1,000 living in the hill farms dotted around the parish. There are no proper roads across the moor yet, just a track; nevertheless in this town you will find a marketplace and a market cross, a parish church and, from 1672, a Presbyterian chapel. The main market is held on Saturdays, with subsidiary markets held at various places around the town, including a shambles for selling meat, a butter market, an apple market and a corn market. There are two annual fairs for selling cattle – one held in July, the other in November – and another great market for cattle on the Saturday before Whitsun week. In the Church House across the road from where I am writing, a schoolmaster teaches local boys to read and write. Nearby is the town blacksmith (I can hear the clanging of his hammer and anvil from here). Not far from the church is an almshouse, built in 1637, which provides accommodation for sixteen poor people. From 1662 the town has a resident licensed physician; by 1700 there are two resident medical men, both licensed surgeons. There are several alehouses serving food and drink, and a newly established inn provides accommodation for visitors. Wheeled vehicles never come here because of the steepness and roughness of the terrain – commodities are brought in on packhorses – but the town is thus more important to people in the wider area as it provides a local centre for them to sell produce and obtain supplies. Thus the country folk come in on market days from up to seven miles away, which in this region means that the town serves a hinterland of about seven thousand people, in addition to its own population.[46]

Finally, there is one thing all towns have in common, and it concerns the F-word. *Fire* does not just affect London. On 25 April 1659, almost the whole of Southwold burns down, with the loss of no fewer than 238 dwelling houses in addition to its town hall, market house, prison, granaries and warehouses. When Bungay goes up in smoke on 1 March 1688, 200 houses are destroyed: only the Guildhall and the Fleece Inn are left intact. Half the town of Newmarket burns down on 22 March 1683. Add to these Rolvenden (Kent) in 1665; Prestonfield near Edinburgh in 1681; the Walks in Tunbridge Wells (subsequently known as the Pantiles) in 1687; St Ives (Huntingdonshire) in 1689; thirty houses in Morpeth in 1689; and much of Builth in 1690, and you can see that fire poses a risk wherever you are. People just don't learn. The month of September is particularly dangerous. On 20 September 1675 the Great Fire of Northampton destroys 700 houses – more than three-quarters of the town. On 12 September 1681, seventy-two houses in the Welsh town of Presteigne are lost. And on 5 September 1694, 150 houses in Warwick are reduced to cinders. You might want to bear these dates in mind if you go travelling in September. Some tips about how to save your accommodation, should it go up in flames, may therefore come in handy. When Thomas Baskerville visits Northampton a few weeks after the fire there, he records:

> I found about the middle of the town an indifferent house standing, and all the other houses for a good distance round about it burnt down, and yet the upper storeys of it were only studded with lathe and plaster work. It was a small inn and had for the sign a shoemaker's last with this motto: 'I have sought after good ale over the town and here I have found it at last'. The strangeness of the preservation made me alight to discover of the innkeeper how it could possibly be effected. [He] told me, by the help of some friends hoisting some hogsheads of beer out of the cellar and, being very diligent to cool those parts of the house which were very hot, they did preserve it.[47]

Surely this is one of the greatest events in the annals of British fire-fighting. Not only do these tipplers refuse to abandon their local, even though the rest of the town is on fire (including, presumably, some of their own homes), but they gallantly fight the fire with *beer* – and win.

Scotland

The geography of Scotland is unlike that of either England or Wales. Quite apart from the fact that the Scottish Highlands are considerably more mountainous than anything to be found south of the border, the population is much smaller – about 1.2 million people – and consequently more spread out.[48] Covering an area, including the islands, of 30,420 square miles, Scotland has a population density of just forty-one people per square mile. This is only slightly less than that of Wales. However, unlike Wales, Scotland has several large towns of more than 5,000 people. The majority of the population live in the central waist of the country (Glasgow, Edinburgh and the area between them) or in the ports on the east coast. With these large settlements and a dominant capital, Edinburgh, Scotland is more like England than Wales.

It is the wildness of the Scottish landscape that sticks in most people's minds. The Highlands in particular are made up of many miles of uninhabited moor, heath and mountain. Even in the Lowlands there is relatively little enclosed ground, due to the scarcity of timber for building fences. The natural state of the landscape is matched by the survival of much of the indigenous fauna. The wildcat is still to be found in places. If you are lucky, you may catch a sight of one of the few remaining British wolves, the very last of which is shot in 1690.[49] However, it will not surprise you to learn that not everyone will think it a blessing to encounter a wild animal. In fact, most people will only find it fortuitous in so far as it will give them a chance to kill it.

'Barren' and 'barbarous' are the two adjectives most commonly used to describe Scotland. No kings visit their northern kingdom in these years. Few Englishmen of any sort go there. Pepys sails to Edinburgh in the company of the duke of York in 1682 and travels on to Stirling, Linlithgow and Glasgow, and although he admires the last of these places as 'an extraordinary town for beauty and trade, much superior to anything [else] to be seen in Scotland', he adds, 'so universal a rooted nastiness hangs about the person of every Scot (man and woman) that [it] renders the finest show they can make nauseous, even among those of the first quality'.[50] Another English gentleman traveller describes the houses of the common Scottish people as 'very mean, mud-wall and thatch the best; but the poorer sort live in such miserable huts as never eye beheld'.[51] Celia Fiennes, bless her, crosses the border in 1698 but, having travelled only a couple of miles into the country, is so shocked by the unappetising food, the clothing of the native women (or the lack of it) and the primitive state of the houses that she turns around and heads back to England as fast as she can.[52]

In many respects, Scotland has not yet changed from its medieval state. It shows few signs of cultivation to the contemporary eye, and contains a great deal that people associate with natural squalor. The Highlands are still dotted with lairds' castles, or peel towers, since the Scottish kings of the sixteenth century were less successful than their English counterparts in suppressing the private armies of the nobility. The sixty-six towns or royal burghs are still dominated by their churches and tollbooths – the latter being the local centres for administration and justice, where tolls are collected and councils and courts are held. Prior to the abolition of the rule of bishops in 1689, Scotland still has its fourteen medieval cathedrals. Most of these are relatively small buildings, located in burghs with fewer than a thousand inhabitants, just as they were in the Middle Ages; only three (Glasgow,

Edinburgh and Aberdeen) are situated in large settlements.[53] The majority of country folk live in 'touns': small communities of four to ten families working the land together.[54] The inhabitants of these touns operate an agricultural system called runrig – the allocation of strips of land in an arable infield to the tenants on a periodic basis, and the collective use of an outfield, further away from the toun, for grazing cattle or growing hardy crops, such as oats. These touns also have their common grazing lands and their shielings up on summer pastures. Near the coasts and the salt-water lochs, people supplement their farming with fishing.

There are some signs of economic innovation. In the south and south-west of the country, some touns are specialising in rearing sheep.[55] The surpluses derived from such specialisation allow farmers to move from subsistence farming to commerce, which in turn leads to economic growth in the market towns or 'burghs'. Partly because of this, you will increasingly notice large numbers of people on the move, travelling with their cattle from high ground to sell them in the Lowlands, or transporting grain in the other direction. Young men and women walk from rural areas into the burghs looking for work as apprentices and servants.

It is the large settlements, and above all the ports, that are showing the strongest signs of economic vitality. Glasgow has been growing steadily for the last 400 years, so that by 1700 its population has reached 15,000, making it the second-largest city north of the border.[56] In 1668 the town council purchases land at Newark in order to build a deep-water harbour, called Port Glasgow, to encourage trade. Although this is slow to yield profit, it coincides with the rise of Atlantic commerce and sows the seeds for Glasgow's phenomenal growth in the next two centuries. On the east coast, the largest ports – Perth, Dundee, Aberdeen and Leith (an adjunct to Edinburgh) – have long been recognised on the Continent for their exports of salmon, coal, linen, salt, beef, wool, coarse cloth and hides.[57] Now they are importing luxury items too, such as fine cloth from England and wine from Bordeaux. As a result of their country's prosperity, at least 6.6 per cent of the Scottish population lives in a town of 5,000 people or more in 1691 – compared to 5.4 per cent in England (excluding London).[58] Although Scotland might appear to be predominantly an impoverished barren wilderness, overall it is just as urbanised as provincial England.

Pride of place in the ranks of Scottish towns goes to Edinburgh. With a population (including Leith) of 40,000 or more in 1700, it is easily the second-largest city in Great Britain. Its growth is partly to do with the fact that it is a national capital, not just a regional one, even though royal rule has been sporadic for the last century or so. In fact, the absence of an active king on Scottish soil for most of the period since 1542 accentuates Edinburgh's importance, as the Scottish government no longer has to follow the king on his peregrinations around his kingdom, as it did in the Middle Ages. Regents, councils, ministers and their households are based firmly in Edinburgh. As a result, Scottish noblemen build substantial stone houses for themselves in the city. Merchants too start to demonstrate their increasing wealth in new, more impressive houses. For example, Gladstone's Land is rebuilt by a merchant as a flat-fronted six-storey town house with an arcade on the ground floor incorporating a shop, twenty years before Inigo Jones executes his arcade design for Covent Garden. The merchants' trade corporations also build striking new halls for themselves, such as the Tailors' Hall on Cowgate. The highlight of all this civic rebuilding is undoubtedly Parliament Hall, built in the 1630s, where the Scottish Parliament meets.

After the Scots rapturously welcome back the monarchy in 1660, Edinburgh becomes even more a centre of national attention. But it is not just the nobility and the merchants who are making the running, it is also the new professionals or 'men of ability'. The Royal College of Physicians of Edinburgh is founded in 1681 and the same year sees the establishment of the Advocates Library. By 1690, there are more than 200 lawyers, 33 physicians and 24 surgeons resident in the city.[59] Heriot's Hospital finally opens its doors in 1659, in a splendid turreted building that differs strikingly from the mountains of irregular masonry that form most of the noble houses in the city. Under the superintendence of Robert Mylne, Master Mason to the kings of Scotland, more elegant structures appear, not least of which is Mylne's Square, in the heart of the city, and Mylne's Court, on the Royal Mile. Holyroodhouse, the palace of the kings of Scotland, is remodelled along Palladian lines by Mylne and Sir William Bruce in 1671. A water supply is piped to the city from Comiston Springs in 1675, with well-heads and cisterns designed by Mylne and Bruce. The Bank of Scotland is established in 1695 to lend money to Scottish businesses. In 1685, the old College of King James comes to be known as the University of Edinburgh.[60] Gradually Edinburgh is turning itself into that most unusual thing: a capital city without a resident head of state.

As you wander through the streets of the city, two things are likely to strike you above all others: the stench of the place and the height of the buildings. With regard to the first, the town regulations stipulate that no refuse and excrement is to be put out for collection on a Sunday. That's all well and good – except that you will still find rakers leading their carts through the streets on the other six days. Thus you will find buckets of rotting fish heads and bones, scraps of skin and offal, bloody linen, urine and excrement waiting in the street to be collected. In summer months the problem is particularly acute, as the heat hastens the rotting of the buckets' contents and the streams around the city dry up, preventing the washing away of such waste. A visitor from Cheshire describes the olfactory condition of Edinburgh in these words: 'the sluttishness and nastiness of this people is such ... their houses and halls and kitchens have such a noisome taste, a savour, and that so strong, as it doth offend you so soon as you come within their wall'.[61] Another visitor recalls that 'the scent was so offensive that we were forced to hold our noses as we passed the streets'. In contrast, Glasgow smells as sweet as a rose. 'For pleasantness of sight, sweetness of air, and delightfulness of its gardens and orchards, it surpasseth all other places,' writes a visitor in 1669, foreshadowing Samuel Pepys's similar comments a few years later.

With regard to the buildings, a great number of the houses in the town are six or seven storeys high. Some are eleven, twelve or thirteen storeys. Others resemble a huge cliff face of tenements, with a central stair turret protruding into the street. You will find the very highest buildings around Parliament Square. If you are more familiar with the new four-storey houses in London, these will seem like skyscrapers in comparison. In fact, you might feel a little nervous climbing a dozen flights of stairs to visit someone at the top of one of these structures. After all, there are no fire escapes. What if the worst should happen?

On Saturday, 3 February 1700, at about ten o'clock at night, the worst *does* happen. Fire breaks out in a group of buildings around a small courtyard chiefly occupied by lawyers, immediately behind Parliament Close. The buildings in question are fifteen storeys high;

people regularly point them out as the highest in Edinburgh. Duncan Forbes discusses the consequent Great Fire in a letter to his brother:

> It continued till eleven o'clock of the day with the greatest fervour and vehemence that ever I saw fire do, notwithstanding that I saw London burn. There are burnt by the easiest computation between three and four hundred families' [homes]; all the pride of Edinburgh is sunk; from the Cowgate to the High Street all is burnt and hardly is one stone left upon another. The [houses of the] Commissioner, the President of Parliament, the President of the Court of Session, the Bank, most of the Lords, lawyers and clerks, were all burnt, besides many poor and great families ... Few people are lost, if any at all, but there was neither heart nor hand left among them for saving [the buildings] from the fire, nor a drop of water in the cisterns. Twenty thousand hands [removing] their trash they knew not where, and hardly twenty at work. These Babels, of ten and fourteen storeys high, are down to the ground, and their fall is very terrible ... The Exchange, vaults and coal cellars under Parliament Close still burning. This epitome of Dissolution I send to you without saying any more but that the Lord is angry with us, and I see no intercessor.[62]

Forbes is wrong in one respect. The pride of Edinburgh is not 'sunk'. In fact, like London, its great days are just beginning. The city goes on to provide much of the impetus for the Scottish Enlightenment in the next century. Furthermore, one particular triumph arises from the ashes. In 1703 the good people of Edinburgh set up a 'Company for quenching of fire' – and thereby establish the first municipal fire brigade in Britain.[63]

3

The People

In 1695 Gregory King attempts to calculate the size of the future population of the kingdom. This is a truly radical idea: in the past, people would not have believed such things could be predicted; they assumed they were wholly subordinate to the will of God. Nevertheless, King carefully analyses the past data and concludes that the population of England and Wales will increase from the 5.5 million people of his own time to 6.42 million in 1800, 7.35 million in 1900, and 8.28 million in the year 2000.[1] He further predicts that, by the year 2300, the population will have hit a ceiling of 11 million; it will not grow beyond this, for the simple reason that there is not enough land in the kingdom to feed more people. It is a brilliant piece of analysis: perceptive, well evidenced and well argued. The only snag is that it is completely wrong. The population will reach 11 million by 1820, not 2300. At the time of writing (2016), it is almost five times King's absolute maximum.

How can the best statistician of the age make such a mistake?

It goes without saying that King cannot take into consideration the consequences of the improvements in agriculture over the next 200 years. Nor can he possibly foresee the impact of mechanisation. He thus cannot consider how mankind will eventually overcome the constraints on its growth. However, he can – and does – consider the constraints themselves. He knows that the birth rate is roughly 1 in 28 while the natural death rate is 1 in 32, so there should be an extra 20,000 people born in England every year. At the same time he calculates that illness and famine carry away an average of 4,000 people per annum. A further 3,500 are killed in Britain's wars, and 2,500 mariners are lost every year due to the dangers of their work. As for the Plantations in America and the West Indies, 1,000 Englishmen die there annually, not including the slave casualties.

As a result of all these adversities, average population growth is much smaller than 20,000 people every year.

As you can see, King's mistake is not just a result of his failure to foresee the innovations of the future; it also lies in his assumption that all these constraints will continue. With the benefit of hindsight, we know they won't, but in 1695 there is simply no justification for such optimism. The population of England has been declining for the last forty-five years. In 1650 it stands at 5.23 million. By 1660 it has decreased to 5.14 million; a decade later it drops to 4.98 million. Thereafter the rate of decrease slows, reaching a low of 4.93 million in 1680 and staying at that level until 1690.[2] Only in the last decade of the century does it perk up, recovering to 5.06 million. But England in the 1690s is not typical of the whole of Europe – or even the whole of Britain. In 1696–9 much of northern Europe is hit by a famine that decimates the population. Scotland, which has about 1.2 million people in 1695, sees one-tenth of them die or emigrate over the last four years of the century (many of the men go to Poland).[3] France likewise loses one-tenth of its population – about 2 million people. Although England and Wales do not suffer to the same extent, it is a bold step by Gregory King to estimate that there will be *any* rise in the population at all.

When you walk down a street in 1680, you will see that there are many more young people compared to our own time. Children under the age of fifteen make up 30 per cent of the population (compared to 17.6 per cent in the modern world). As for older people, less than 10 per cent of the population is aged sixty or more (in the modern world it is 23 per cent). It is a sad irony that a society in which child mortality is very high is heavily populated by children. They simply never get the chance to grow up. Infant mortality is above 21 per cent; in the modern world only 0.4 per cent of children die in the first year of life. If you add those dying between the ages of one and fourteen, you are left cowering in the shadow of a daunting statistic: 37 per cent of all the children born in England do not make it to the age of fifteen.[4]

As a result of this, a married woman in Restoration Britain has to give birth more than four times in order to maintain the population at a static level.[5] This is quite something to ask, especially if she does not marry until relatively late in life. Although girls can legally marry at twelve and boys at fourteen, such matches are rare. Charles II marries

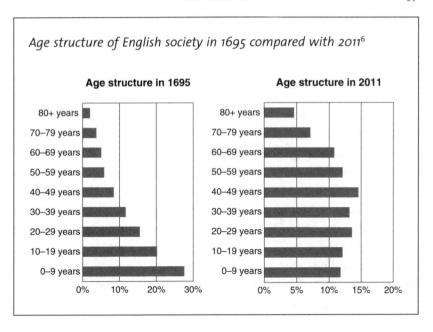

Age structure of English society in 1695 compared with 2011[6]

off two of his illegitimate sons at the age of fourteen to twelve-year-old girls, but they are hardly representative of ordinary folk.[7] John Evelyn's wife, Mary, is twelve on her wedding day, fourteen years younger than her husband; and Samuel Pepys's wife, Elizabeth, is not quite fifteen when she marries the twenty-two-year-old future diarist in 1655; but again these cases are unusual. The vast majority of women do not marry until they are well into their twenties: the average age for women is twenty-four, and for men it is twenty-eight. Despite this late age, however, many women rise to the challenge of enlarging the population, some having ten or more children. Alice George, a servant in Oxford, does not marry until she is thirty, but then has fifteen children as well as three miscarriages.[8] Giving birth to so many babies is, of course, dangerous in itself; every single pregnancy – and not just the first – is a matter of life and death. Barbara, Lady Fleming, dies giving birth to her fifteenth child in April 1675.[9] But don't be complacent even if you are an adult man. The average life expectancy at birth for both sexes is about thirty-three years – considerably less than half what you might hope for in the modern world, and about five years *less* than it was a century earlier.

Having said all this, you will come across some old people in society, and the age of sixty is clearly the point at which they start to consider themselves *properly* old. Ralph Josselin, the rector of Earls Colne in Essex, writes in his diary on 26 January 1675, 'Sensible [that] this [day I] entered my sixtieth year: I grow an old man.'[10] John Evelyn is similarly aware of the great turning point when he records on 30 October 1680, 'I now arrived at my sixtieth year, on which I began a more solemn survey of my whole life, in order to the making and confirming my peace with God.'[11] Three years later, he starts commenting on those very old people who are still fit and able, such as his godmother Mrs Keightley, who is now 'eighty-six years of age, sprightly, and in perfect health, her eyes serving her as well as ever, and of a comely countenance, that one would not suppose her above fifty'.[12] You can see what he is thinking: if *she* can still be active at eighty-six, so might I be. As it happens, he dies at the age of eighty-five.

Ralph Josselin is another diarist who starts to look for consolation in the healthiness of very old people. In his case, he goes to see Lady Vere, who is eighty-eight years old. He remarks with some amazement that 'her senses continue'.[13] Lady Vere lasts until ninety. Sadly, Josselin only lives to sixty-six. But that is still twelve years longer than King Charles II. Celia Fiennes pauses for thought when she comes across the tomb of Elizabeth Heyrick in a church in Leicester: this lady lived to ninety-seven, and saw 140 of her progeny. Celia herself dies a few weeks short of her eightieth birthday.[14] Lady Anne Clifford continues to write her diary until the day before she greets eternity with an indignant frown at the age of eighty-six. Thomas Hobbes, the philosopher, lives to ninety-one; Thomas Mace, the lutenist, to ninety-three; and Sir Hans Sloane, the collector, also to ninety-three. However, all these people are mere whippersnappers compared to some. In 1681 Alice George – the woman who marries at thirty and has eighteen pregnancies – tells the philosopher John Locke that she is 108 years of age, and that her father lived to eighty-three, her mother to ninety-six and her maternal grandmother to 111.[15] She herself lives for another eleven years. Over that time she is visited by many people at her home in Oxford, where she repeatedly shows off her party trick of threading a needle without any need of spectacles, confounding those who associate extreme old age with poor vision and unsteady hands. Her portrait is painted in 1691, when she attains the reputed age of 120. She rather casts into shadow the old man who shows Willem Schellinks around his garden in 1661: he claims to be a mere 114.[16]

The Social Order

It is often said that the wealth of society can be represented by a pyramid. This is certainly true of Restoration England. At the bottom of the pyramid there are many families who have to make do with less than £20 per year. Above them, somewhat less than half the population has £30 per year or more. Next up, about 8 per cent have £60 or more; above them, about 3 per cent have an income of £150 or more; and right at the top, 0.1 per cent have at least £600.

Gregory King provides us with a contemporary estimate of how this breaks down according to the various 'sorts' of people.

Gregory King's scheme of income, 1688[17]

No. of households	Rank, degrees, titles and qualifications	People per household, incl. servants	Average annual house- hold income
160	Peers of the realm	40	£2,800
26	Prelates	20	£1,300
800	Baronets	16	£880
600	Knights	13	£650
3,000	Esquires	10	£450
2,000	Greater merchants and traders by sea	8	£400
12,000	Gentlemen	8	£280
5,000	Men in greater administrative offices	8	£240
8,000	Lesser merchants and traders by sea	6	£200
10,000	Lawyers	7	£140
5,000	Men in lesser administrative offices	6	£120
40,000	Greater freeholders	7	£84
2,000	Greater clergy	6	£60

No. of households	Rank, degrees, titles and qualifications	People per household, incl. servants	Average annual house-hold income
16,000	Men in the sciences and liberal arts	5	£60
5,000	Naval officers	4	£80
4,000	Military officers	4	£60
140,000	Lesser freeholders	5	£50
8,000	Lesser clergy	5	£45
40,000	Shopkeepers and tradesmen	4½	£45
60,000	Artisans and handicraft workers	4	£40
150,000	Farmers	5	£44
50,000	Common seamen	3	£20
35,000	Common soldiers	2	£14
364,000	Labouring people and outservants	3½	£15
400,000	Cottagers and paupers	3¼	£6½
30,000	Vagrants, gypsies, thieves and beggars	1	£2

King is particularly keen to differentiate between those who add to the wealth of the nation – those whose income is in excess of £30 per year – and those who, being poor, decrease it. No fewer than 849,000 households (62 per cent) fall into the latter category, along with 30,000 vagrants, gypsies, thieves and beggars. Thus this chart goes some way to demonstrate the inequalities of wealth in society. However, King's figures only relate to *incomes*; if you were to look at *capital* ownership, you'd find a much greater proportion of it in the hands of the richest 1 per cent, the nobility and gentry. But even that does not begin to reflect the true disparities in society. For it is your status, more than your wealth, which determines how people will treat you. Financial fortunes wax and wane, but your position in society is fixed according to your family background and upbringing, and that is what other people really want to know about you. Well-educated and well-connected gentlemen who have lost all their money through reckless gambling or unwise investments may still be entertained in houses where a prosperous farmer would not be permitted to cross the threshold. Similarly, a widow from an old gentry family who lives in a rented room in a tradesman's house in a county town, but who can still proudly boast a coat of arms and a nephew with a commission in the navy, will be welcome in places where the tradesman's wife will merely be tolerated. The fact is that, when confronting the inequalities of society, we are not just dealing with how much money you have but with social hierarchies that reflect political influence, ancestry and connections, clothing, manners, education and region of origin. Lack of money is just one of many factors separating the poor from the rich and influential.

All this raises the question of class – and it is here, in this period, that the English start to become obsessed by the 'class system'. Of course there is no official 'system' as such: it is largely a matter of perception, and people's perceptions are beginning to shift. There is an awareness that a new class is emerging: wealthy, fashionable townsmen. They have large amounts of disposable income, considerable periods of leisure time, an obsession with their own status and a delight in novelties. In Paris they are already being described as *bourgeois*, following the production of Molière's play, *Le bourgeois gentilhomme*, in 1670. In fact, Samuel Pepys is a prime example of the type, with his attention to everything that is fashionable, his obsession with money and his constant concern with being seen in good company. As a naval official, Pepys is unlike many other Londoners – but that is beside the point. Although the ranks of the *bourgeoisie* are filled with people from a wide range of professions and backgrounds, they all have much in common, not least their social climbing and exquisite self-consciousness. A new category is therefore needed to describe them according to their lifestyle, not their occupation. Hence the word 'class' enters the English language. Thomas Blount helpfully includes it in the second edition of his dictionary, *Glossographia*, in 1661.[18] He particularly uses it to describe groups of people of a similar 'degree'. However, the term really catches on because 'class' is not just a way of describing people who have something in common; it is also the perfect way for men and women to set themselves apart from those with whom they have *nothing* in common.

Terms such as 'bourgeoisie' and 'class' have yet to achieve widespread circulation in this period. Therefore you should stick to those terms that Restoration people understand, such as 'citizen', 'degree' and 'sort'. Daniel Defoe identifies seven different 'sorts' of people:[19]

> The great, who live profusely;
> The rich, who live very plentifully;
> The middle sort, who live very well;
> The working trades, who labour hard but feel no want;
> The country people, farmers etcetera, who fare indifferently;
> The poor, who fare hard; and
> The miserable, who really pinch and suffer want.

These seven 'sorts' – which are more succinct than Gregory King's twenty-six income groups – will form the basis in this book for looking at people according to their status.

THE GREAT

'The great' are not merely rich, they are the people with the highest status in the two realms. Their ranks include the nobility – all the lords who are entitled to attend the English and Scottish Parliaments by hereditary succession, plus the English, Welsh and Scottish bishops – together with those gentlemen who enjoy the dignity of a baronetcy or a personal knighthood. These titles are highly regarded and convey a precise legal status. For example, along with the right to attend Parliament, a nobleman is entitled to be tried by his peers for a crime, and cannot be imprisoned for debt. In 1676 there are eleven English dukes (the highest rank), three marquesses, sixty-six earls, eleven viscounts and sixty-five barons – a total of 156 secular lords – in addition to the twenty-six English and Welsh bishops.[20] Scotland has a similar hierarchy of nobles, although there are fewer of them: there are just four non-royal Scottish dukes in 1676. 'The great' is therefore a tiny group, relatively speaking. In England, according to Gregory King, all the lords, bishops, baronets and knights together number just 1,586: about 0.03 per cent of the population. Yet this group has an average income per head in excess of £1,000 per year and holds the title deeds to considerably more than half of Great Britain. Some lords are far wealthier. The duke of Newcastle, Henry Cavendish, has an annual income of £11,344; and George Villiers, second duke of Buckingham, is worth about £19,000 per year in the late 1660s. That doesn't stop them squandering the lot. The duke of Newcastle manages to accumulate debts amounting to £72,580 by the time of his death in 1691. The duke of Buckingham too loses most of his fortune, so in 1671 he places what remains in a trust, in return for a fixed allowance of £5,000 per year. The fifth earl of Bedford, who is created the first duke of Bedford in 1694, is far more careful with his income, which fluctuates between £10,000 and £14,000 in his youth; as a result of his prudence, it has risen to about £20,000 per year by the time he dies in 1700.[21]

Another thing you may have noticed from Gregory King's schedule of incomes is the importance of the *household* in understanding the social order. Often you will hear lords and ladies use the word 'family' to describe their household, meaning all the servants as well as the children, which gives you an idea of how tightly knit large households are. Unsurprisingly, the nobility have the most servants, and of course the greatest of 'the great' have the most of all. For them, even leaving the house or going to the loo requires staff. The average of forty people per household given by Gregory King masks the fact that some dukes and earls have eighty or ninety men and women on the payroll. In the households of some dukes and earls, the principal servants have their own servants. Most knights and baronets with £1,000 per year employ between twenty and thirty staff, incurring a wage bill of about £200. At Woburn Abbey, the earl of Bedford pays between £600 and £700 in salaries to a staff of forty people.[22] This includes a team of a dozen footmen all dressed in his livery of 'broadcloth lined with orange baize' – a sign of conspicuous consumption that truly reflects what Defoe means when he says the great 'live profusely'.

As you would expect, 'the great' have the best of everything, especially those things that are tangible and long-lasting – the best art collections, the best libraries, the best suites of furniture and the best collections of houses. Yes, *collections* of houses. Many among 'the great' have inherited a string of country seats. The duke of Beaufort has twelve in 1680; the duke of Norfolk ten. Although many of these are unoccupied and some are in ruins – being damp castles no longer fit to house a nobleman's family – they nevertheless attest to the greatness of their owner's authority. The indefatigable Lady Anne

Clifford, eventual heiress to the earldom of Westmorland, has five castles in her domain: she repairs them all and resides in them, proudly reminding everyone of her ancestors' personal rule over the region. Most of the men in this category will have at least two houses: a London residence as well as a country seat. When they move from one to the other, their whole household (or the major part thereof) packs everything up and accompanies them. Call in at Bedford House on the south side of Covent Garden in the 1660s when the earl of Bedford is not at home and you will find no one there, except for a housekeeper, a watchman and a gardener. It is quite an eerie feeling, walking through room after room in a grand house when the family is away, hearing the echo of your footsteps on the floorboards.

THE RICH

When we talk of 'the rich' as a group, we are talking about two sorts of people. First, those who make money exploiting their own talents; and second, those who inherit a large estate and receive hundreds of pounds in rent, regardless of whether or not they have any talents. It might surprise you that, in Restoration Britain, those without talent are accorded the higher status of the two.

Let's begin with this second group, the untitled landed gentry. Here we have a large number of gentlemen and esquires (an esquire being a gentleman entitled to bear a coat of arms) with average incomes of £280 and £450 respectively, according to Gregory King. In reality, those who may be classed among 'the rich' have a vast range of fortunes. At the top end of the scale are a few dozen esquires who can afford to buy out two or three baronets. At the bottom there are country yeomen who rent out their lands to others to farm and thus are called 'gentle' by their neighbours, on account of the fact that they do no manual work; their incomes may be as little as £100 per year. Approximately 10 per cent of Gregory King's 15,000 gentlemen and esquires enjoy £1,000 per year or more. Such men are more like the heads of landowning corporations than individuals: when they die, their heirs simply take over the running of the estate. But whether their incomes are £100 or £10,000, they are all officially recognised in that, as substantial freeholders, they are entitled to vote for a county Member of Parliament.

Among the self-made members of 'the rich' it is the businessmen who build the largest fortunes. Perhaps the most astonishing example is that of Hugh Audley, who begins with £200 in 1605 and dies worth £400,000 in 1662. The story of how he builds such a massive fortune makes for a compelling book; Samuel Pepys, ever conscious of his personal wealth, buys a copy and reads it in January 1663.[23] But he finds little therein to inspire him. Audley is essentially a moneylender – and thus remains merely one of 'the rich' and never becomes one of 'the great'.

It *is* possible to pass from a lower sort to a higher one. A hugely rich man can do this either by marrying the heiress of a great family that has fallen on hard times, or by lending money to the king. Those who choose the latter course are rewarded with a knighthood and sometimes even a baronetcy. Sir Robert Vyner, baronet, starts off life as the third son of a man of no great wealth from Warwick, but by 1672 the king owes him the colossal sum of £400,000. Sir John Banks, baronet, comes from Maidstone but now lives in a house on the grandest side of Lincoln's Inn Fields; he is worth an estimated £100,000 when John Evelyn visits him in 1676. When he dies in 1699, his assets amount to £180,000.[24] Evelyn thinks Sir Stephen Fox and Sir Josiah Child are even richer; Sir Stephen leaves an estate worth £172,024 and Sir Josiah's wealth is probably greater still.[25] This is impressive when you consider that Sir Stephen is the seventh son of a Wiltshire squire of modest means, and Sir Josiah started off as a brewer supplying the navy. All these stories show that opportunities do exist for men of talent to enter the hallowed halls of 'the great'. Having said that, even sociable and generous financiers can never quite shrug off the stigma of having made their money in trade. Sir George Downing charmingly refers to them as 'cheats, blood-suckers and extortionists'.[26] People have a higher regard for those whose ancestors achieved their wealth by hacking other people to death in the service of a medieval king than for those who win their own fortunes through the barbaric practice of lending money.

Wealth is, of course, a relative matter. However, it is fair to say that, as only one in thirty people has £100 or more per year at his disposal, the great majority will regard anyone with an income of twice this as belonging to 'the rich'. Some of those who clearly fall into this category have worked their way up from the rank of tradesman. Samuel Pepys is a good example. He does not have a

country estate or a private income – he is the fifth child of a London
tailor and a laundress – but, due to Mrs Mary Robinson's legacy of
£500 to benefit poor London boys with a good education, he is able
to go to Cambridge University. In addition, he has a useful family
connection in Edward Mountagu, his first cousin once removed.
Mountagu has a country estate and an additional income of £2,000
per year from his offices as Councillor of State and General-at-Sea.
More importantly, he also has the ear of Charles II, who showers him
with rewards on his return to England in 1660: the king creates
him earl of Sandwich and appoints him Master of the Great Wardrobe,
Clerk of the Privy Seal and Vice-Admiral of the Kingdom. Soon after
leaving university, Pepys gets a job as a clerk in Mountagu's household
and, about five years later, his employer uses his influence at court to
obtain for Pepys the position of Clerk of the Acts, with an annual
income of £350 and the possibility of making further profits through
perks and bribes. Hence this tailor's son enters the echelons of 'the
rich'. Eventually he rises to become the chief officer of the navy staff
under James II. And, as anyone who has read Pepys's diary will know,
he certainly has the wherewithal 'to live plentifully'. If the extent to
which a young man can fill his life with wine, women and song is
indicative of his true wealth, then there are few richer men in England
than Samuel Pepys.

THE MIDDLE SORT

In turning to 'the middle sort' in England, we encounter about 238,000
households in which around 1.3 million people live, either as family
members or live-in servants. Most of this sort are yeomen who own
and work their own land, and prosperous citizens who have bought
multiple houses as investments. The remainder are salaried military
and naval officers or what contemporaries call 'professionals' – people
who profess to follow a calling – clergymen, physicians, surgeons and
school teachers. Such a range of activities means that this is the most
varied group of all. What they have in common is their disposable
income, their reliance on their own abilities to make ends meet, and
the fact that they do not have the social connections or the financial
safety net of 'the great' or 'the rich'. As Gregory King's schedule
indicates, most have an income between £50 and £100.

This category is changing faster than all the others, due to increased professionalisation. Physicians have been treating the rich for centuries but it is only in this period that there are enough of them for the majority of ordinary people to become used to paying for a medical consultation and receiving a prescription for a medicine, which they can have made up at an apothecary's shop. Likewise, there have been grammar schools teaching Latin in most towns since the thirteenth century but it is only now that they also require specialists to teach Hebrew, Greek and mathematics. Thus more and more professional teachers are required. In Scotland, too, every community is now supposed to have a school, as laid down in an Act of 1646. In addition, the innovations of the age create a number of new professions – banking, insurance, statistics, clockmaking, engineering, newspaper journalism, surveying, and so forth. The Restoration period as a whole is marked by the rise of professional men and the commensurate ascendancy of 'the middle sort'.

THE WORKING TRADES

Gregory King's schedule of incomes includes 100,000 households dependent on tradesmen who run shops or manufacturing businesses. The vast majority of them are town dwellers, performing services that generally date back to the Middle Ages. In most small towns, men carry on their trade in an informal way, normally operating from their homes. In larger places, however, there is a degree of formality, which permits certain people to cater to the townsfolk and prevents strangers from competing with them.

A city like Exeter controls its working tradesmen through the guild merchant system, in this case administered by the mayor's court. On completion of an apprenticeship, on payment of a fee or on proving his right of succession to his father's position, a tradesman becomes a member of a trade guild and a freeman of the city. He swears an oath of loyalty to the Crown and to the mayor and bailiffs of the city. In addition, he promises to pay his taxes and not to sue a fellow citizen anywhere but in the mayor's court, and to follow all the bye-laws. He is then free to carry on his trade within the city's boundaries and to take part in the selection of the city's mayor and its two Members of

Parliament. In reality, the civic authorities no longer go out of their way to impede traders who are not freemen. Innkeepers, alehouse keepers and victuallers rarely obtain the freedom of the city, having a separate licensing system. Nevertheless, if you are a tradesman yourself, you will want to become a member of the relevant guild. And if you want to have an overview of the vast range of trades carried out in the city, looking through the rolls of freemen can be most enlightening.

Admissions to the Freedom of Exeter, 1659–99

#	Trade	No. of freemen	#	Trade	No. of freemen
1	Fuller	289	23=	Brewer	29
2	Grocer	144	23=	Haberdasher	29
3	Tailor	129	25	Mason	23
[4	Gentleman	127]	26	Cutler	22
5	Mercer/ Merchant	117	27	Saddler	22
			28	Fellmonger	21
6	Cordwainer	104	29	Glover	20
7	Butcher	76	30	Blacksmith	18
8	Joiner	75	31	Pewterer	16
9	Weaver	66	32	Woollen draper	15
10	Carpenter	61			
11	Baker	60	33=	Feltmaker	13
12=	Silk weaver	57	33=	Painter	13
12=	Woolcomber	57	35=	Currier	10
14	Hellier	55	35=	Tobacco pipe-maker	10
15	Goldsmith	53			
16	Clothier	52	35=	Upholsterer	10
17	Cooper	45	35=	Worsted-comber	10
18	Apothecary	39			
19	Chandler	38	39=	Bookseller	8
20	Barber	36	39=	Capper	8
21=	Ironmonger	31	39=	Glazier	8
21=	Locksmith	31	39=	Linen draper	8

#	Trade	No. of freemen	#	Trade	No. of freemen
39=	Needle-maker	8	64=	Milliner	2
39=	Sleigh-maker	8	64=	Petty chapman	2
45=	Druggist	7			
45=	Stationer	7	64=	Retailer	2
45=	Vintner	7	64=	Scrivener	2
48=	Cook	6	64=	Surgeon	2
48=	Hosier	6	64=	Surveyor of Port of Exeter	2
48=	Plumber	6			
48=	Trunk-maker	6			
52=	Horner	5	64=	Watchmaker	2
52=	Musician	5	64=	Woolman	2
52=	Point-maker	5	82=	Bellfounder	1
52=	Tinplate-maker	5	82=	Bricklayer	1
56=	Pressman	4	82=	Carver	1
56=	Distiller	4	82=	Comber	1
58=	Comb-maker	3	82=	Confectioner	1
58=	Paviour	3	82=	Coroner	1
58=	Pin-maker	3	82=	Doctor	1
58=	Serge weaver	3	82=	Girdler	1
58=	Tobacconist	3	82=	Innkeeper	1
58=	Tobacco cutter	3	82=	Lantern-maker	1
64=	Barber-surgeon	2			
			82=	Leather-dresser	1
64=	Basket-maker	2			
64=	Bookbinder	2	82=	Maltmaker	1
64=	Brazier	2	82=	Mariner	1
64=	Cotton-weaver	2	82=	Plasterer	1
64=	Counsel-at-law	2	82=	Shoemaker	1
64=	Dyer	2	82=	Silk dyer	1
64=	Fletcher	2	82=	Soapmaker	1
64=	Gunsmith	2	82=	Turner	1
64=	Instrument-maker	2	82=	Wool stapler	1
				Total	2,089

If you compare this list with a similar one drawn up for Exeter in the Elizabethan period (see *The Time Traveller's Guide to Elizabethan England*), you will see just how much has changed in three generations. These days the fulling of serges is the predominant trade. A hundred years earlier, the group now called 'fullers' were described as 'tuckers', and there were fifty-seven of them admitted to the freedom of the city, making them only the third-largest trade in Exeter. There were no 'pressmen' (printers) back then, either, or any distillers. There were no bricklayers, soapmakers, confectioners, watchmakers, tobacconists or grocers. There were very few silk-weavers. The largest contingent by a long way was formed by the merchants, whose ranks included the tradesmen now known as 'grocers'.

This system of officially recognising the city's tradesmen sounds very official, but in truth its formality masks a welter of problems. First and foremost is the fact that tradesmen simply are not paid enough. Even if a man works six days a week for fifty weeks in the year (allowing time off for holy days and Christmas) and earns 20d per day, or £25 per year, and has six children, he will be hard-pressed to feed, clothe and educate them. The crushing fact is that wages have been declining for generations and now, in real terms, they are *less than half* of what they were in the mid-fifteenth century.[27] Back then was the golden age for tradesmen, when skilled workers could earn enough to keep their families without having to worry all the time. Now, rather than minimum wages for their work, *maximum* wages are set by magistrates, limiting what men and women can earn. For instance, in Bedfordshire in 1684 it is laid down that a master carpenter should be paid 1s 4d per day (8s per week or about £20 per year) and if he receives food and drink from his employer his wages should be reduced to just 10d (5s per week, £12 10s per year). But these rates are only for the daylight-filled summer months; from mid-September to mid-March those rates should be reduced to 1s and 8d respectively, giving a carpenter an income of just £17 10s per year. And these are the wages for a *master* carpenter: while he is still a journeyman, they are limited to 1s per day without food in summer and 10d in winter (£13 15s per year). If you refuse to work, in an attempt to raise these wages, you are likely to lose your job and end up in prison. In 1677 a group of workers in the Wiltshire cloth town of Trowbridge parade through the streets following a fiddle player, demanding that their weekly wages rise from 6s to 6s 6d for a twelve-hour day, and calling on all the folk of the town to join them in the procession. The ring-leader, Aaron Atkins, is arrested, thrown in gaol and tried at the following quarter sessions.[28]

Another problem tradesmen face is that of property prices. You may think the modern world is facing a particularly acute problem, in that its skilled tradesmen are priced out of living in the towns and cities where they are employed. The same is true in the late seventeenth century. Look at their account books and you will soon see that Defoe's declaration that the working trades 'feel no want' is open to question. As mentioned above, I am writing this book in a small town thirteen miles to the west of Exeter, called Moretonhampstead. My host is a weaver, called Thomas Mardon, and his house is well situated in the middle of town, within a stone's throw of the church-yard. He is not doing badly for a weaver in 1692: he has an annual income of about £25, on which he keeps his wife, Anne, two children (they have already buried three others) and one servant. That just about covers all the bills. The problem is that he doesn't own this house; he has a lease on it, granted more than fifty years ago to his now-deceased father-in-law. That lease expires after the death of the third person named in its conditions. As it happens, all three of those named people are dead already. The only reason that Thomas and his family have not been evicted is because, before he died, his father-in-law paid to have the name of his last surviving daughter, Thomas's wife, added to the lease. As she is fifty-one years old in 1692, the family has to face the fact that she may not live much longer. What is to happen when she dies? Thomas will lose his workplace and the family their home. Thomas has therefore spoken to his landlord's steward and has arranged a new lease. It is going to cost him the huge sum of £102.[29] But what choice does he have? Suitable houses don't come up very often. This is why tradesmen like him are correctly described as 'labouring hard'. Men like Thomas can only look after their families by constantly planning for the lean times that undoubtedly lie ahead.

THE COUNTRY PEOPLE

The problems that beset a tradesman like Thomas Mardon also affect his rural counterparts. But not everyone in the country suffers in the same way. The great dividing line is whether you are working for yourself or whether you are merely labouring for a husbandman. If the latter, then life is tough at the best of times, and the chances are that you will be one of the next sort down, the habitually poor. Agricultural wages, like those of tradesmen, are less than half of what they were in the fifteenth century, although not quite as low as the nadir of the early seventeenth century. The wages for a male haymaker in 1684 are set at 10d per day, or 6d if he is given food and drink. Women are paid 6d or 3d for the same work. However, haymaking is a seasonal activity, so there is no payment for such work in winter. Likewise reaping: men can earn 1s 6d per day (without food) reaping in summer and women can earn 10d but, again, there is no winter work. Families must seek out what work they can, and take in extra jobs such as sewing and washing, as well as growing their own herbs and vegetables. Such people can rarely afford to eat meat with the regularity that their ancestors did. But even better-off husbandmen with 20–50 acres live precariously. The land they farm is rented or leased, and when some of it has to be left fallow, the challenge of making enough on the remainder to pay the rent or save for a new lease pushes many farmers into penury.

Let's get hard-nosed about this and look at the economic effects of the freezing winters that Britain experiences during this period. If you are a husbandman with a relatively large farm of 40 enclosed acres, and that land is fertile and yields 18 bushels of wheat per acre in a good year, then, having set aside 4 bushels of seed per acre for replanting, you will potentially have a crop of 560 bushels or 70 quarters. What is that worth? In a year of great plenty, such as 1688, you might receive as little as 20s per quarter, so you'll earn £70. After you have paid your three farmhands their summer wages of £18, you will still have £52 in hand. But you will probably want to use some of that grain yourself, for your own family, rather than selling it. There may well be some rent to pay too, on top of the lease. Then there's the cost of maintaining the animals to pull the plough and produce the manure to enrich the soil. In addition there are parish rates and taxes to pay. And we have not factored in the necessity of leaving some land fallow, to recover its fertility. If you were to farm only half your 40 acres each year, your gross income would be about £26, before rates and taxes. But remember that we are talking here about a good harvest – what happens if the year is a bad one? Imagine you are leaving half your land fallow, and heavy rain in August wipes out half your crop: you will only take 9 bushels per acre off your land, four of which you'll need to set aside as seed for next year. Even at the very high price of £2 10s per quarter, your gross turnover will be just £31 5s. After you've paid your farmhands reduced wages of £12, paid your rent and set aside enough to maintain your plough animals, you will be lucky to have £15 left for the whole year.

Of course, losing half your crop is not the worst-case scenario. You might lose it all.

Country folk, you will soon find, are shrewd, thrifty and cautious. They have to be. They spend their entire lives being heaved to and fro on the great pitchfork of the British weather. But they do have one great advantage over townsmen and tradesmen: they can at least eat the fruit of their own labour. Even if disaster strikes and half the season's grain is lost to frost or flood, then what remains can at least sustain the desperate family. Farm labourers, on the other hand, might not be so lucky.

For this reason, you will find sacks of grain and piles of cheese stored in the barns and in the farmhouse itself. Have a look at Skiggs Farm in Writtle, Essex, in the early 1680s.[30] The farmhouse is basically three rooms upstairs and three down, with a few extensions and outbuildings. The contents are worth £259 – including such luxuries as silver spoons, a silver bowl, a silver porringer, a Bible, a couple of carpets and a gun. The owner, Edmund Sterne, is clearly a prosperous man. But every item he possesses – every piece of furniture, the silver, all the farm implements and tools, everything in his kitchen and his stores – only adds up to about £40. The vast majority of his wealth is in the form of food. Some is stored in sacks – £34 of wheat, £24 of rye, £16 of oats, £18 of barley – and cheese worth £3 10s is in the cheese chamber; the rest of his wealth is out grazing in the fields and rooting around in a pig sty. This is how husbandmen cope with the unpredictable weather. Defoe is quite correct to describe the country folk as 'living indifferently'. The very precariousness of their way of life precludes them from ever living well.

THE POOR

This is where we sink below the breadline. As Gregory King's schedule of incomes makes clear, 60 per cent of the population lives at or below this level. Just as the modern term 'upper class' is insufficient to preserve the subtle distinctions that separate 'the great' from 'the rich', so the modern term 'working class' is inadequate to explain the gradations between workers who make ends meet, hard-pressed labourers, poor servants, paupers, the destitute and the truly pitiful.

Let's start with the best-off members of this sort: ordinary mariners. Abroad for most of the year, they have few children at home requiring support, if any at all. Many never marry. If a mariner doesn't have a house and keeps all his possessions in his trunk aboard his ship, he won't have to pay any rent, rates or taxes. On board ship, all his food may well be paid for – especially if he is serving in the navy. There are irregular but not insubstantial rewards too, such as prize money when an enemy vessel is captured, or when he buys goods in one port and sells them in another for a profit. So a single seaman earning £20 per year might be better off than many tradesmen and farmers – as long as he avoids being captured by Barbary pirates, and doesn't mind having to fight a skirmish every so often, and is happy climbing the rigging of a ship when caught in 50ft waves in the middle of the wholly inaccurately named Pacific Ocean at night. There is also the small matter of the 1 in 16 risk of being lost overboard ... So you've got to be fairly desperate to want to spend your whole life aboard ship. When you meet some of those who do sail from port to port and hear them say how much they love being at sea, you will understand why when they tell you how they started: almost all of them come from a background of grinding poverty.

Take Edward Barlow, for example. You may not have heard about him, but he is the Samuel Pepys of the high seas. He is raised at Prestwich, near Manchester, along with his two brothers and three sisters. Their father is a husbandman with an income of just £8–9 per year. No man can feed and clothe his wife and six children on so little – and the children know it. Their family does not go to church because their parents cannot afford to clothe them; it is not thought seemly for people to enter the house of God in rags. So when Edward reaches the age of twelve, he gets a job. He works for a while in the coal delivery business, earning 2–3d a day. When he has conscientiously saved up enough, he buys himself a set of clothes so that he can fulfil his ambition and go to church on Sundays. Next he tries to become an apprentice 'whitester' (whitening yarn); he spends his spare time looking after cattle, and hedging and ditching. Underfed, underpaid and beaten, he abandons his apprenticeship and, aged thirteen, walks to London to seek his fortune, with two shillings in his pocket. He goes to find one of his older sisters, who works as a servant in the city; although she cannot help him, she suggests that he become a servant in their uncle's alehouse in Southwark. It proves hard work. His aunt constantly accuses him of defrauding her when serving guests with beer or tobacco. Edward is forced to become a stable boy, to avoid such accusations. His uncle regularly beats him – on one occasion simply because he went to see a whale stranded in the Thames without permission. So his spirits are low when a 'spirit' approaches him with an offer of a rewarding job at sea. In reality, such men 'spirit away' their victims and do not let them see land again until they have landed in Jamaica, where they sell them as indentured servants (unfree, unpaid labourers). His uncle, to his credit, saves him from such a fate and eventually arranges that Barlow be made apprentice to the Chief Master's Mate of the *Naseby*, the flag-ship of Edward Mountagu, Samuel Pepys's kinsman and patron. After fifteen years at sea, his wages are 25s per month (£15 per year).[31] He remains at sea for most of the rest of his life, teaching himself to read and write and drawing up his journal in a large, leather-bound book, which he manages to save from all the shipwrecks and other disasters that befall him.

If you are one of 'the poor' and not a mariner or soldier, you are probably serving as a farm labourer or a servant in someone else's house. As we have just seen, farm labourers depend entirely on the quality of the harvest. A bad year might result in you not being paid – exactly when food prices are double their usual level. You and your family will have to live on beans or mashed turnips, and make your bread from oats or ground acorns. For this reason, particularly if you are unmarried, you may well be better off if you are employed as a live-in servant in a gentleman's household. But be warned: 'employment' is a relative term here: sometimes servants are not paid for years. And they are often subjected to beatings. Samuel Pepys is not a cruel man by the standards of the time but he thrashes his servants. In 1660 he beats a maidservant with a broom for laying out things incorrectly about the house. The following year, he whips a servant for stupidity after the man puts gunpowder and match in the same pocket. He boxes the ears of one servant boy simply for wearing his cloak slung over his shoulder.[32] His female servants can expect a degree of sexual attention, whether they invite it or not. In some houses the master's sons and male visitors will take advantage of low-status women, safe in the knowledge that, if they are reported for their licentiousness, it will generally be to the servant's discredit and the loss of her position. If you want to know what life in service is like for many women, think in terms of Cinderella's daily grind of scouring, scrubbing, washing and polishing from before dawn to late at night – and having to comb the lice out of the hair of a man who regularly beats you and forces you to have sex with him.

The financial rewards for this semi-ritualised mass exploitation of the poor are, as you might expect, minimal. Gregory King's detailed notes show that he thinks about 150,000–200,000 live-in servants have wages of £3 or more per year, but 350,000–400,000 earn less than this.[33] Normally £2 per year plus board and lodging will pay for a chambermaid, a dairy maid or a laundry maid. A housekeeper normally earns £6 or more; a male cook £4; a female cook about £2 5s. Butlers and coachmen earn £3 or more.[34] Young boys and girls earn less – often nothing at all – on account of their serving an apprenticeship. The famously miserly Robert Hooke pays his housekeeper Nell Young £4 per annum in 1672, which includes having sex with her; her successors as housekeepers receive just £3.[35] Ralph Josselin pays his maidservant £2 10s per year.[36] Pepys pays his maidservant Jane Birch £3 per year in 1662 and thinks it a lot of money to pay a woman. The following year he engages a cook's maid for £4 per year and exclaims that it is 'the first time that ever I paid so much'.[37] While it is possible that tips might increase a servant's earnings, very few people tip their own servants. Pepys and his guests each give his cook 12d for clearing up after a feast in 1663, but that is largely because they make such a colossal mess.[38]

All this illustrates why there is no such thing as a 'servant class' in Restoration Britain. There is a world of difference between the earl of Bedford's steward – educated, respected and paid £40 per annum, plus board and lodging – and a menial drudge who is regularly abused and paid just £2. Both are servants, yet the steward is squarely in the third of Defoe's status groups – the middle sort, along with professional men – while the drudge is in the sixth, 'the poor'. If it weren't for the fact that her board and lodging are provided by her master, she'd sink right to the bottom. You can hardly doubt that Defoe is right when he declares that people like her 'fare hard'.

THE MISERABLE

People do not ignore the miserable. They can't – because they are everywhere. When John Evelyn visits Ipswich in 1677 and is not pestered by a single beggar, he is astounded and remarks on the fact in his journal as 'a thing very extraordinary'.[39] However, he adds that this is not because there are no beggars in the town: it is because begging is prohibited 'by the prudence of the magistrates'. The distressing fact is that 'the miserable' are not a small minority. In Devon in the 1690s, approximately one-fifth of the population falls into this category, being dependent on poor relief.

As a result of this ubiquity, high-status people discuss the question of poverty on a regular basis. Why do the poor exist? they ask. What should be done about them, for the benefit of society? What should be done for them for their own benefit, if anything?

Daniel Defoe has an answer to the first of these questions. Extreme poverty exists, he believes, for two reasons: casualty and crime. The first means that people end up as penniless beggars and thieves because of a sickness in the family or an accident resulting in the loss of a limb or eyesight. The second reason is that some people are too given over to luxury, sloth or pride to work for a living. As he puts it:

> There is a general taint of slothfulness upon our poor; there's nothing more frequent than for an Englishman to work till he has got his pocket full of money, and then go and be idle, or perhaps drunk, till it is all gone, and perhaps himself in debt; and ask him in his cups what he intends, he'll tell you honestly, he'll drink as long as it lasts, and then go to work for more.[40]

As you can see, Defoe does not believe that a shortage of work leads to poverty. He would rather blame the poor themselves for their plight. As a workaholic himself, he is not alone in finding the accusation of laziness a convenient way to remove any vestige of responsibility from his own shoulders. But 'responsibility' is a moot point. Who should take responsibility for the poor?

The starting point is the Poor Law Act of 1601, which directs parish overseers to levy a rate on solvent householders to pay for the maintenance of the impoverished people of the parish. (The Scots receive a similar piece of legislation in 1649.) The able-bodied are set to work; children are placed as apprentices with those who will feed them in return for their service; and the infirm are sheltered and given food. By the end of the century, more than £400,000 is raised in England every year to assist the poor.[41] Most of this is distributed as cash payments of between 6d and 12d per week per person, with widows receiving the most. Money is also paid by overseers to medical professionals for the treatment of sick paupers. The system is regulated by a settlement policy: if a destitute stranger enters a parish and seeks help, he is to be interviewed and sent home to his place of birth, where the overseers have a duty to look after him. Despite these measures, groups of vagrant thieves and beggars still threaten the occupants of isolated rural houses. Measures are accordingly passed in some places to pursue all strangers, interrogate them and commit them to the local magistrates if they cannot give a good reason for being where they are.[42] Very few people are as philanthropic as Hannibal Baskerville (father of the aforementioned traveller Thomas Baskerville). At his Berkshire home he builds a large dormitory for vagrants, and puts up a little bell at his back door so that any beggar who requires anything may summon a servant and ask for it. Hannibal spends three-quarters of his income on helping the poor.[43]

Apart from the parish poor-relief system, there are two new strategies employed by the authorities to deal with those who cannot support themselves. The first is the system of 'indentured servants', briefly mentioned above. This entails you agreeing to the terms set out in a legal document (an 'indenture') that you will be bound as an unfree servant in 'the Plantations' (the West Indies or America) for four years. You are completely under the orders of your new employer and will obey him in everything. The costs of your emigration, your food and accommodation will be paid for, and when you come to the end of your term, you will be allowed to settle freely in your adopted country. It is only one step up from slavery. On the plus side, some men sentenced to death are offered indentured labour as an alternative to execution. The problem for the law-abiding poor is that unscrupulous people take advantage of the system. Some children are kidnapped, sold off as indentured servants and sent to the Plantations – and never find their way home.

The other new measure for dealing with extreme poverty is the workhouse. That very word might make you shudder but the idea of resolving poverty and its attendant hunger by providing work is not to be dismissed out of hand. Also, as many people will tell you, the work is therapeutic, in keeping you safe from 'idleness and debauchery'.[44] The first workhouse is set up by the London Corporation of the Poor during Cromwell's administration. The 1662 Settlement Act allows for official workhouses to be established in and around the capital, and in 1665 a businessmen, Thomas Firmin, sets up a private workhouse in London to teach children from the age of three to read and to spin. This, mind you, is only for children: Firmin's view of adult paupers is even more extreme than Defoe's – in his opinion, they come 'from the suburbs of Hell itself'.[45] Although other work-houses follow, it is only at the end of the century that they become properly established as a means of providing for the poor. The first of the type that will become common in the eighteenth century is set up at Bristol in 1696. By 1712, there will be fourteen towns in England with fully functioning workhouses. Grim though they may be, for many people they mark a step up from the days when, to quote Defoe, the miserable 'pinch and really suffer want'.

THE PROBLEMS OF PRECEDENCE

There is every reason why you should take one look at the foregoing hierarchy and feel fury and rebellion bubbling in your veins. But that is a sign of your modernity. Most people in Restoration Britain simply accept it. They realise that the people shouting at them do not have anything against them personally, it is simply due to their low birth. At the same time, everyone is aware of how they are viewed by those of higher and lower status. A tradesman and a farmer of similar rank might meet as equals in a town, but if the tradesman is significantly wealthier than the farmer, and dresses accordingly, there will be no pretence at equality. In this period, fawning and forelock-tugging are as natural as coughing and scratching. An apprentice will rarely look his master in the eye. In church, even if you think you are equal in the eyes of God to everyone else who has come to worship, don't presume that you can just sit anywhere: pews are private and are allocated according to social rank. Even within the family there is a hierarchy at work, so an older daughter gets a better place in the family pew than a younger one, *unless* her younger sibling is married and she is not, in which case the order of precedence is reversed. Samuel Pepys relates the story of how, when the young heir to the earldom of Kent is waiting on the earl of Bedford as a gentleman servant, a letter arrives informing them that the old earl of Kent has died. As the earldom of Kent is older than that of Bedford, it takes precedence, so the earl of Bedford dutifully gets up out of his seat, bows to the new earl of Kent, invites him to sit in the place of honour that he has occupied and waits on the new earl as *his* servant for the rest of the meal.[46]

In no area of life is status as important as it is in marriage. It does not matter whether the apple of your eye is a suitable age (sometimes people marry partners thirty or forty years older); nor does it matter whether he or she is similarly attractive. What matters is whether your intended partner is of a suitable social status. On the whole, 'the great' marry among themselves. A duke might marry a commoner, in the shape of a knight's or baronet's daughter, but it is rare for a lord to marry outside the ranks of 'the great' unless he himself was originally of humble stock, like General Monck, duke of Albemarle (who, when he was a prisoner in the Tower in the 1640s, seduced his servant and later married her). Huge dowries might be arranged between a gentleman's daughter and a lord's son, but money only becomes a factor when the match is appropriate in terms of rank. The earl of Sandwich is absolutely furious when his wife suggests that their daughter should marry a rich merchant: he declares 'he would rather see her with a pedlar's pack on her back but that she should not marry a gentleman'.[47] Rarely does love get a say in the matter. In 1675, a young gentleman, James Graham, falls in love with the beautiful Dorothy Howard, the daughter of Lord Dundas and the widow of an earl's son. Mr Graham asks John Evelyn to speak on his behalf. Evelyn agrees to do so 'more out of pity than that she deserved no better match, for although he was a gentleman of good family, yet there was great inequality'.[48] Thanks to Evelyn's silver tongue, Mr Graham does win the honourable lady's hand. When it comes to his own family, however, Evelyn is less amenable to overlooking differences of rank. When Sir Gilbert Gerrard comes to see him about wedlock between his son and Evelyn's daughter, Evelyn is horrified to learn that Sir Gilbert's fortune is based on coal pits near Newcastle, and forbids the marriage.[49] Such concerns affect the 'middle sort' too; for them, the wealth conveyed by marriage is even more of a sticking point. In 1662 Samuel Pepys's brother, Tom, who has no great income, falls in love with a woman whose parents initially offer a meagre dowry of £200. Pepys persuades his brother to refuse. The parents scrape together £400, but Pepys demands £500. After lengthy negotiations between them and Pepys, nothing can be done. The relationship is terminated, leaving Tom broken-hearted.[50]

THE KING

Now that you have been introduced to the multi-tiered society of Restoration Britain, it is time to look at the figure on top of the whole wedding cake. Three men rule the kingdoms of England and Scotland in our period: Charles II (1660–85), James II (1685–8) and William III (1689–1702). William *reigns* jointly with his wife, Mary II (daughter of James II), until her death in 1694, but she does not *rule* equally with him: power is vested in him alone. Thus three men serve as the royal lynchpin that holds the whole of the social structure together.

It is important to recognise at the outset that the king is not 'first among equals': he possesses a unique pre-eminence in both spiritual and temporal matters. He is the Head of the Church of England and, because of that semi-divine status, he affects the lives of everyone in the country. For example, he appoints the bishops and archbishops who govern the religious and moral life of the people. No one is permitted to curse the king – whether in private or in public. Even to *imagine* his death is treason. He can pardon anyone for any transgression of the law. His predecessors were the feudal lords of England – outright owners of the whole country, from whom the lords and prelates merely held their land – and although the feudal system is formally abolished in 1660, the monarchy is reimbursed with a permanent grant, funded by the taxpayer. A committee of the House of Commons decides this should amount to £1.2 million per year, for the maintenance of the royal household and the government of the country. Consider this massive sum in relation to the incomes we've just discussed, from the earl of Bedford's £20,000 down to a chambermaid's £2, and you can see how far the king stands outside the normal parameters of society. Moreover, he has powers of patronage: the ability to confer titles on people and thus ennoble them, and to appoint men as magistrates to govern locally. He can summon and dissolve Parliament. He is commander-in-chief of the armed forces. He can sue anyone in any court. And yet he himself stands above the law. He cannot personally commit a crime – with the sole exception of treason, as Charles I clearly demonstrated.

But no one mentions that.

In theory, Charles II rules on the same basis as his father. In practice, he rules with far less authority. No one can escape the fact that a revolution has taken place (in the form of the Civil Wars) and that Charles I was powerless to stop his trial. It is therefore tacitly acknowledged that the king is not at liberty to enact policies against the will of the people. This is demonstrated in 1662 and 1672, when Charles II tries to deliver religious toleration for all and is forced to back down. It is shown again in 1688, when James II's religious policy proves so unpopular that he has to flee for his life. As for William III, he is forced to accept the Bill of Rights in 1689, which further limits what a king can practically do. All three kings thus have less *authority* than Charles I. However, in administrative terms, they are more powerful than he was. This is not because they can defy Parliament but because they increasingly work *with* Parliament. From early in Charles II's reign, the king rules with the advice of a 'cabinet' of ministers – so named after the 'cabinet' or private chamber where they meet – and the king himself normally attends their meetings. He also occasionally attends debates in the House of Lords. In short, as Parliament grows more powerful, so does the king.

THE THREE RESTORATION KINGS

Charles II is often described as 'the merry monarch' on account of his taste for gambling, mistresses, horse racing and general high living. The Frenchman Monsieur Misson describes him as 'fonder of women, ease and pleasure than of Dunkirk, England and all the crowns in the universe'.[51] But this playful image conceals a cautious, calculating, pragmatic survivor, whose only unshakable principle is never to risk being ousted from his throne. Faced with a disaster, he will readily sacrifice one of his ministers as a scapegoat. As Lord Halifax says of him: he 'lives with his ministers as he does with his mistresses; he uses them but he is not in love with them'.[52] His mistresses would no doubt agree, although Charles remains close to two of them – Lady Castlemaine (by whom he has four children) and Nell Gwyn (by whom he has two). Sadly, he has no children by his Portuguese wife, Catherine of Braganza, whose repeated miscarriages merely add to the humiliation of her husband's public philandering.

Charles is a cultivated man – devoted to music, art, the theatre, science and technology, and highly knowledgeable of naval affairs. Anatomy in particular fascinates him, and he attends dissections of human corpses. In 1663, after learning that a horse has passed four kidney stones of enormous size, he orders the horse's dung to be searched every day for more examples.[53] In politics, he is duplicitous. He secretly promises the French king in 1670 that he will convert to Catholicism but, knowing it will cause another revolution in England if he does so publicly, fulfils his vow only when he is on his deathbed, fifteen years later. It is not surprising that he acquires a reputation for untrustworthiness. The earl of Rochester writes a mock epitaph on him:

> Here lies our Sovereign Lord, the King
> Whose word no man relies on
> Who never said a foolish thing
> Nor ever did a wise one.

To which the king replies, 'My words are my own but my actions those of my ministers' – a witty reply, but one that, yet again, shows his readiness to blame someone else.

Perhaps Charles's biggest political gamble as king is to support his brother James as his heir apparent, after it becomes widely known that James has converted to Catholicism. The result is a protracted political battle. The so-called Exclusion Crisis of 1679–81 gives rise to the forerunners of Britain's modern political parties. Those who want James excluded from the throne and the king's authority curbed are called Whigs – 'whigs' being slang for rabidly anti-Catholic Scottish cattlemen. They are met head-on by those who intend to uphold the king's prerogative, who are called Tories – slang for Irish Catholic thieves. The Whigs raise the spectre of the pope and burn his effigy; the Tories respond by reminding people of the extremism of Cromwell's government. Eventually, the king and the Tories are victorious. When Charles dies on 6 February 1685, the crown passes to James without opposition. By the time of his death, Charles has succeeded in creating a form of kingship that is rich, dynamic, colourful and responsible, and yet is still imbued with mystique and majesty. He is one of the great innovators in the development of the monarchy.

★

James II does not have his brother's political judgement, or his wit. Worst of all, he lacks his pragmatism and flexibility. His outlook on the monarchy is that it 'must be either more absolute or quite abolished'. And absolutism presents a significant problem for a Catholic who rules over an Anglican country – and is officially head of its Church.

Over the course of his lifetime, James gradually becomes obsessed with the idea that it is his duty to restore the Catholic faith in England. His long period of exile in France before 1660 convinces him that Catholicism is the one true religion. His much-loved first wife, Anne Hyde, daughter of the earl of Clarendon, converts to Catholicism in 1669; James himself secretly does likewise not long afterwards. After Anne's death in 1671, he decides to go public with his faith: at Christmas 1672 he refuses to take communion alongside his brother, the king. The following year he openly acknowledges his conversion to Catholicism, and in September he marries the Catholic princess Mary of Modena, by proxy, in a Catholic ceremony. The success of the king and the Tories in the Exclusion Crisis that follows only reinforces James's conviction that God's providence is directing him to bring about the restoration of English Catholicism. This in turn strengthens his resolve that he must stand firm in all his unpopular dealings with the British people.

At the outset of James II's reign, the people are on his side. An uprising in Scotland, led by the earl of Argyll, is crushed by the Scots. In England, a rebellion led by the duke of Monmouth (Charles II's eldest illegitimate son) is defeated at the Battle of Sedgemoor on 6 July 1685. But this is the high-water mark of James's popularity. The Bloody Assizes that follow the battle, in which James refuses to pardon any of those who are sentenced to death, become notorious. Thereafter he loses the confidence of the people. High-handed actions in bullying Parliament into suspending anti-Catholic legislation, refusing to accept the outcomes of elections by the Fellows of Magdalen College, Oxford, and locking up seven bishops in the Tower of London only underline the dangers to Protestants. To be fair to James, his vision of tolerating all religions is heartfelt. But what he does not appreciate is that such toleration is widely perceived as a pretext for encouraging Catholicism and, in Protestants' eyes, Catholic practices that have no foundation in the Bible are heretical. His arrogant determination to pursue a policy of toleration is thus the cause of his downfall – which, you have to admit, is something of an irony.

James II reigns for less than four years. Unable to believe that his own daughter, Mary, and her husband, Prince William of Orange (who is also his nephew), will invade England in defence of Protestantism, he leaves it too late to take appropriate military measures. William lands in Torbay on 5 November 1688 and marches to Exeter, where he sets up his headquarters. The local gentry flock to him. James II sets out to rally his troops at Salisbury, but all the providential signs are against him. Memorably, he has a series of terrible nosebleeds, which rather prevent him from striking a dramatic warrior-hero pose. His advisors tell him to retreat to London. On 11 December he attempts to flee the country, but he is recognised in Faversham and brought back to the city. When Prince William requests James to leave the capital, he sheepishly goes to Rochester and from there finally sails for France.

If you visit Britain in the early days of 1689 you will find that neither England nor Scotland has a head of state. William of Orange, however, is recognised as the sole guarantor of peace throughout both realms, and that is important. The memory of the breakdown of law and order in 1658–60 makes everyone fear what will happen if William returns to Holland. Parliament is summoned and charged with debating the question of the succession. The MPs decide to offer William the throne, on four conditions. First, he has to agree to share the throne with his wife in a joint monarchy, so that there is no break in the succession (although actual power is vested in William alone). Second, he has to accept new oaths of loyalty. Third, he has to listen to a Bill of Rights that outlines limitations on the powers of the monarch. And fourth, he has to acknowledge that the children of his sister-in-law, Anne, will take precedence in the succession over any children of his by a later marriage, in the event of Mary's death.

William III, as a result, rules on a very different basis from his grand-father, Charles I. He has to listen to a declaration by both Houses of Parliament that the king may not suspend any statute legislation, tax people without the consent of Parliament, maintain an army in peace-time without Parliament's approval or inflict excessive fines or 'cruel and unusual punishments' on his subjects. In addition, the king must henceforth allow Protestants to bear arms to defend themselves, permit his subjects to petition him without fear of persecution, guarantee the freedom of elections, allow free speech in Parliament without the speaker being liable in any court, and summon Parliament to meet regularly. Parliament sits every year from 1689, and from 1694 is freshly elected every three years.

Historians refer to the events of 1688–9 as 'The Glorious Revolution'. Sometimes you hear modern commentators cast doubt on this, arguing that, as no blood is spilled, it is insufficiently radical to be a true revolution. However, when you look at the transition of government from near absolutism to constitutional monarchy over the whole period of the Restoration, it is difficult to think of a better word to describe it other than 'revolutionary'.

Women

Just as there is enormous inequality between the various sorts of people, so too there is great inequality between the sexes. It amounts to sexism on a scale that you will barely be able to countenance. And there is nothing hidden or underhand about it. As the marquess of Halifax puts it, in his advice to his own daughter:

> You must first lay it down for a foundation in general that there is inequality in the sexes, and that for the better economy of the world the men, who were to be the lawgivers, had the larger share of reason bestowed upon them ... We are made of different tempers that our defects might be mutually supplied. Your sex wanteth our reason for your conduct, and our strength for your protection; ours wanteth your gentleness to soften and entertain us.[54]

This attitude should not be confused with misogyny, a hatred of women. There are plenty of men who deeply love their wives (and are loved by them in return) and yet such men still chastise their partners and beat them, often genuinely thinking it is for their own good. Also, you need to be aware that not all women think that greater equality between the sexes is desirable, let alone possible; a great many believe that women should be subordinate to men because that is the natural order of things. Even some well-educated women hold this view. Mrs Lucy Hutchinson, for example, is a translator of Latin prose and poetry, a poetess in her own right and the author of a biography of her husband, as well as an autobiography. She is exactly the sort of person whom you would expect to make a stand for women. Instead she maintains that they are intellectually inferior to men.[55] This is the amazing thing about sexism in Restoration Britain: the prejudices against females are so deep-seated that many women share them.

The legal position of women in England is much the same as it has been for centuries. In short, a husband is lord and master of his wife and of his unmarried daughters, and of all their possessions. As Edward Chamberlayne neatly puts it in his *Anglia Notitia, or The Present State of England* (1669), 'if any goods or chattels be given to a married woman, they all immediately become her husband's. She cannot let, set, sell or give away anything without her husband's consent.'[56] Even her clothes do not belong to her. Wives cannot borrow money without their husband's permission, nor can they make a will. They may not admit a person into the matrimonial home against their husband's command. If a wife runs away from her husband, he has the right to enter someone else's property to drag her home. A husband can beat his wife with impunity as long as he does not actually kill her. If she refuses to make love with him, he is within his rights to force her. She cannot give evidence against him in any court, no matter what the charge. Therefore, if she catches him in flagrante making love to another woman, she cannot give evidence in court of his adultery. And so on. There are few things you can be sure of in seventeenth-century Britain, but one of them is this: if there is a disagreement between husband and wife, the woman is legally in the wrong, even if she is actually in the right.

It is not so much the laws themselves that affect married life as the framework they provide for everyday relations. A 'good woman' is not one who behaves in a natural way but one who represses her instincts. As one writer puts it, a woman 'may do nothing against God's will but many things must she do against her own will, if her husband require her'.[57] You get repeated glimpses of this in the relationship between Samuel and Elizabeth Pepys. On 9 January 1663, Elizabeth reads aloud to her husband a copy of a letter outlining her grievances (she has already given him a copy but he burnt it without reading it). The letter is full of sadness for her lonely life without a companion when he is away at the office. Pepys is horrified that she has committed such criticisms of their home life to paper, which could be read by other people. He not only rips up the copy of the letter she has just read, but a whole bundle of other letters she has been keeping, including his early love letters to her, forcing them from her hands and tearing them up in front of her as she cries floods of tears.[58] It does not matter that he is totally within his rights to do this. It does not matter that later that same day, when writing his diary, he regrets his actions. What matters is that the law justifies a husband's actions against his wife so completely that it makes him arrogant and uncompromising. Mere disagreements escalate into personal humiliations. You cannot help but feel for Elizabeth: it is simply oppressive to live with someone who believes he is wholly in the right and justified in his anger towards you, even if he later regrets causing you harm.

The general prejudices against women (as opposed to wives) are no less depressing. A girl has great difficulty obtaining a Latin education and therefore most women are not properly schooled, by the standards of the time. Even if they *are* taught by private tutors, they cannot go to university or obtain a professional post, such as that of a lawyer or a schoolmaster. If a woman does practise medicine, she is not allowed to charge a fee for her services. Women cannot be MPs or magistrates; nor can they be freemen of a town – so they cannot become aldermen or mayors, either. Nor can they vote for an MP. Even if a woman is a duchess in her own right, she cannot sit in the House of Lords. Amongst the high-born, a lord's daughter must stand by and watch each and every one of her younger brothers inherit, before she has a chance of seeing anything of her father's estate, and sometimes this includes males in collateral branches too. Lady Anne Clifford, the only surviving daughter of the third earl of Cumberland, has to wait for her uncle and cousin (the fourth and fifth earls) to die before she can take possession of her father's estate and ancestral castles. In the meantime she has to put up with two unhappy marriages. Scolding women are punished by being strapped into a cucking stool on the end of two long beams and then dunked into a pond or stream: a humiliation amplified by the jeering delight of all the community who come to watch. Argumentative men, it should be noted, face no such reprimand.

Despite all this, you will hear people say things like 'if there were a bridge over into England, it is thought that all the women in Europe would run thither'; or 'in some things, the laws of England are, above other nations, so favourable to that sex, as if the women had voted at the making of them'.[59] Given what you've just learnt, this begs an explanation: Elizabeth Pepys, for example, might consider running in exactly the opposite direction if there were a bridge over the Channel.

Part of the answer can be found in what Lorenzo Magalotti writes about London women in his journal:

> The women of London are not inferior to the men either in stature or in beauty, for they are all of them handsome, and for the most part tall, with black eyes, abundance of light-coloured hair, and a neatness which is extreme, their own personal defect being their teeth, which are not, generally speaking, very white. They live with all the liberty that the custom of the country authorises. This custom dispenses with that rigorous constraint and reservedness which are practised by the women of other countries, and they go whithersoever they please, either alone or in company; and those of the lower order frequently go so far as to play at ball publicly in the streets ... They do not easily fall in love, nor throw themselves into the arms of men, but if they are smitten by the amorous passion they become infatuated and sacrifice all their substance for the sake of the beloved object, and if he deserts them, they are sunk into great despair and affliction. Their style of dressing is very elegant, entirely after the French fashion, and they take more pride in rich clothes (which are worn of value even by women of the lowest rank) than in precious jewels, all their expense in the latter article being confined to pearls; consequently pearls are of great esteem and request in England ... Such and so great is the respect which the English entertain for their women that in their houses, the latter govern everything despotically, making themselves feared by the men.[60]

Here Magalotti is looking beyond the letter of the law and observing women's actual lives. Englishwomen, in his eyes, have both greater liberty than their Italian cousins and more control over their husbands because their menfolk respect and, indeed, *fear* them. And that pattern of greater liberty and male fear is also true of the relationship between Samuel and Elizabeth Pepys. Samuel allows his wife to stay out at entertainments by herself, even though he can be insanely jealous of the thought that she might fancy another man. As for his fear of her, when he considers one day in 1662 whether or not he dare try to seduce a maidservant, he decides against the idea 'for fear she should prove honest and refuse and then tell my wife' – and there is no saying to what that might lead.[61] On 25 October 1668 he finds out, when his wife walks in on him with his hand up a maidservant's skirts and, as he admits in his diary, 'with my hand in her cunny'.[62] This does not go down well with Mrs Pepys. Her quiet wrath reduces her proud and arrogant husband to a shivering, apologetic wreck. For several weeks afterwards she gives him grief, or, as he puts it, 'the greatest sorrow to me that ever I knew in this world'.

In some respects, both the law and customs protect women. For example, if a man travels abroad for a long time and returns to find his wife pregnant, he has to bring the child up as his own, even if he has been away for more than a year.[63] Likewise, if a woman is pregnant when she marries, the child is deemed to have been fathered by the husband and, if male, will become his heir, whether or not he is the biological father. The law is so adamant that a man should control his wife that it necessarily follows that married women guilty of treason can only have been obeying their husbands' commands, and thus be not guilty. A woman automatically acquires the rank of her husband by marrying – so, if he is a lord, she becomes a lady – but a woman of higher rank than her husband does not sink down the pecking order; a duke's daughter retains her status as a 'lady' even if she marries a mere tradesman. As for the customs of the country, these make even more of a difference. A wife is her husband's right hand in all domestic arrangements. Defoe declares that 'a man with good husbandry, and thought in his head, brings home his earnings honestly to his family [and] commits it to the management of his wife.'[64] Although divorce is nigh on impossible, and does not always permit you to remarry, a couple can choose formally to separate, and in such cases a court may determine that a husband should pay his estranged wife alimony. In 1677 the Court of Arches orders Sir Francis Throckmorton to pay his wife £300 per year while they live apart.[65] On top of these formal arrangements are those old customs that empower women in ways that make the modern mind boggle. Monsieur Misson tells us that

> I have sometimes met in the streets of London a woman carrying a figure of straw representing a man crowned with very ample horns, preceded by a drum, and followed by a mob, making a most grating noise with tongs, grid-irons, frying pans and saucepans. I asked what was the meaning of all this; they told me that a woman had given her husband a sound beating for accusing her of making him a cuckold, and that upon such occasions some kind neighbour of the poor inno-cent injured creature generally performed this ceremony.[66]

Between the alimony and the cuckold's horns, you can see why many men live in fear of their wives.

You might well ask whether things are getting better or worse for women. One of the few clear legal improvements is that, from 1691, women are allowed to claim Benefit of the Clergy in the same way that men are. This allows them to escape being hanged for a number of felonies if it is their first offence (for further details, see chapter 11). Beyond this, the answer depends heavily on your status. If you are a poor farmer's wife, you will probably conclude that life is getting worse. For a start, everybody in this group is finding times tough, with high food prices and low wages. But on top of these problems, the enclosure movement has a particularly negative effect on the social position of country women. In the last century, many more wives worked alongside their husbands in the great fields. Now, however, as they lose their strips of land and their rights of firewood-gathering and pasturage, and their husbands are forced to find paid employment elsewhere, the wives are left at home doing all the functions that their husbands would otherwise do, in addition to their own duties. The result is that the husbands earn all the hard cash (and thus have a greater say in what it is spent on) and the wives' role becomes increasingly that of unpaid drudge. Rather than being co-workers and joint contributors to the family coffers, the wives become the prime servants.

Women who fall into the 'middle sort' face a different problem: the educational barrier. In this age of professionalisation, people increasingly expect their physicians and surgeons to be qualified in some way, and ideally to hold a medical degree. Self-taught women are perceived more and more often as second-rate practitioners, suitable only for consultation over children's diseases and minor ailments. Experience becomes less important; education and formal qualifications more so. A bishop's licence is required to be a surgeon or a schoolmaster, and women without a formal education cannot obtain one. The demand for qualifications means that men even start to impinge on that most female-dominated of all occupations, midwifery.

It is the gradual collapse of Puritan ethics that most clearly benefits well-off women. The greater licentiousness of the court permits rich ladies to take a string of lovers in a way that would have been unthinkable before 1660. Creative women start to find a freedom that has hitherto been denied them. From 1661, women are no longer barred from appearing on the London stage, and many actresses become prosperous. Those who excel at painting can now make a living from it, whereas in the days of Puritan England it would have been frowned upon for them even to set up a studio. Women find it easier to publish their plays, poems and novels. And other wealthy women take on great building projects: Elizabeth Wilbraham personally oversees the building of Weston Park, her husband's family's stately home in Staffordshire. Other wives take on their husband's accounts and business interests.[67] Another freedom that gentlewomen discover in this period is travelling, as shown by Celia Fiennes. Prior to the Civil Wars it was rare for women to journey alone far from home. The conflict sees many royalist families go abroad, and as a result of this enforced wandering, many women discover the delights of travelling for the sake of self-education, and the taboos against them following such practices start to break down.

Overall, most women have a tough time of it, but it is not as starkly one-sided as the law suggests. Indeed, some people think that working women are among the most contented people you could meet. One May evening Dorothy Osborne walks out across a common near where she lives:

> where a great many wenches keep sheep and cows and sit in the shade singing of ballads ... I talk to them, and find they want nothing to make them the happiest people in the world but the knowledge that they are so. Most commonly, when we are in the midst of our discourse, one looks about her, and spies her cows going into the corn, and then away they all run as if they had wings at their heels.[68]

Despite all the sexism and the prejudices against the poor, the childbirth mortality and the hardships of poverty, you have to wonder whether these women aren't just as happy as their descendants in the modern world.

4

Character

Do you believe in witchcraft? Do you believe in God? You don't have to say 'yes' to either of those questions, but it might help. Superstition and religion both underpin a great deal of seventeenth-century thought and behaviour. However, if you answer 'no', you might find it easier to understand the scientific outlook emerging in some parts of society. For it is really quite a remarkable change. The last death sentence for witchcraft in England is passed down in 1685; in 1687 the Royal Society publishes Isaac Newton's *Philosophiae Naturalis Principia Mathematica* ('The Mathematical Principles of Natural Philosophy'). Just two years separate a belief in witches strong enough to warrant the death penalty from the publication of the fundamental work underlying modern science. Now, this does not imply that one moment everybody is anxiously watching out for flying broomsticks, and the next they are all calculating the gravitational pull of the Sun on the Earth. In reality, if people are superstitious they tend to remain so for life; it is the younger generation who doubt their parents' old-fashioned beliefs and let them die out. Similarly you should not think that hard-headed, evidence-based thinking is wholly new in 1687. Newton's ideas about gravity may well fall out of a tree but he is not the first natural philosopher (or scientist, to use the modern term) to be a blue-skies thinker. But what makes the period you are visiting unique is that it is the tipping point for society – when the majority cease to uphold old superstitions and start to prioritise scientific ways of deducing the truth.

The second half of the seventeenth century is a tipping point in several other respects too. We have already touched upon the shift from amateur to professional practice in education and medicine. Dramatic changes in military organisation started before the Restoration but it is after 1660 that the new professionalism becomes the norm.

It is in this period that the nation first acquires a standing army, and that naval officers are selected and promoted on merit, not social status. As for architecture, it is in the Restoration period that traditional building styles give way to houses, churches, streets and squares designed by architects and professional developers working in the wake of Inigo Jones. Portraiture, drama and sports all have their watersheds, as we will see in chapter 12. A tipping point is also reached in political thinking. Society starts to care less about *who* is the rightful ruler and recognises that two things are far more important: what the ruler does, and whether he is accountable to his subjects. And in religion, people increasingly realise they can no longer expect to understand Creation simply by way of what is written in the Bible; they must go out into the world and investigate for themselves. Thus religion loses some of its authority but gives impetus to scientific enquiry, resulting in a huge number of discoveries – in physics, chemistry, botany, astronomy, mathematics, statistics, microscopy and economics.

In all these things people are driven by an intense curiosity – a child-like sense of wonder – and this is the real spirit of the age. People look around themselves as if they have just emerged from a dark cave. And they look *at* themselves with a similar sense of amazement. Restoration men and women can open a Bible and read God's words for themselves and explore what God's will is for each of them. They are increasingly interested in themselves as individuals. Indeed, they think of themselves as private people more than they ever did in the past. In the old days of communal living and farming there was little personal life, and people considered themselves to be primarily members of a larger group – their parish, tithing, manor, hundred or town guild – but now an individual's sense of himself is much more like our modern one. It is not surprising that this is the great age of diary-keeping. The individual person is now the centre of his or her own world, whereas before, for most people, that position was occupied by God.

The fact that so many aspects of society alter fundamentally in these years means that you need to be careful about the assumptions you make as you travel the length and breadth of the country. For example, blithely predicting the return of Halley's Comet in rural parts of the country in 1682 is likely to shock the natives. Conversely, declaring someone guilty of being a witch at a ball in a smart London mansion in 1699 is likely to see people swiftly look for alternative dance partners. Just as there are two Londons before the Great Fire, so there are two sides to British society – the old and the new – but there is no clear geographical divide between them. England, Wales and Scotland are a patchwork of ideas, attitudes and prejudices, and you generalise at your peril.

Superstition and Magic

You'd have thought that after sixteen years at sea Edward Barlow would have given short shrift to anyone claiming to work magical incantations. This is, after all, a man who has sailed to Japan, Indonesia, China, Africa and Brazil and has seen the strangest animals that the world has to offer, including lions, porcupines, elephants, rhinoceroses, ostriches, toucans and monkeys. He is as careful a witness as they come. Yet he does not doubt that, after his shipmates have left a number of debts unpaid in the Norwegian port of Bergen, the women whom they defrauded are responsible for the storm that drives their ship on to the Goodwin Sands.[1] His superstition is a reminder of how everyone has their own belief system and, through it, makes sense of the world – especially when facing the unknown.

Superstitions, large and small, are everywhere. Monsieur Misson notes that some Englishmen are intent on preserving the hairs that grow out of their warts, as tokens of good luck. Most tradespeople in London have a particular regard for the first coin that they receive in the morning: they kiss it, spit on it and then put it in a pocket by itself, in the expectation of good fortune.[2] Magistrates and judges alike listen in sober consternation to stories of the Devil assuming the form of a cat or a magpie to visit a witch. Even though Ralph Josselin is a clergyman, he is quite capable of believing that the Devil takes the form of a bull to force one of his parishioners into a river.[3] In some places it is still held that if a murdered person's corpse is touched by the murderer, it will bleed. In Orkney in 1666 four men who have died in suspicious circumstances are exhumed so that all the suspects can be made to touch their putrefying corpses and the authorities can check for bleeding (strangely, no blood is to be seen).[4] When it comes to ghosts, even sober, educated men are affected. John Aubrey, a Fellow of the Royal Society, publishes a book in 1696 in which he attests to the authenticity of portents, omens, dreams, apparitions, disembodied voices, knockings, invisible blows, prophecies, magic, transportation by invisible powers, visions in crystal balls, conversations with angels, oracles and instances of second sight.[5] John Mompesson, a magistrate living in Tidworth, Wiltshire, has to put up with the haunting sound of a drum beating in his house night after night, from March 1662 to April 1663. It terrifies the life out of his children when its disembodied rhythm moves to their room.[6]

One of the most common superstitions is that the future can be foretold from interpreting certain events. A violent storm might be taken as a portent of some dire calamity shortly to befall a community. So might the beaching of a whale or the birth of a calf with two heads. The news that earthquakes have destroyed ancient Smyrna and several other places in the Mediterranean causes the scientifically minded Evelyn to think they must be the forerunners of greater calamities: 'God Almighty preserve His Church and all who put themselves under the shadow of His wings, till these things be overpast!' he writes.[7] Every autumn you can buy cheap almanacs that tell you what the following year might hold. All sorts of people believe that an accurately cast horoscope will reveal what is to befall them. Others anxious to know the future will seek out practitioners of palmistry or fortune-telling gypsies. In August 1663 a gypsy woman tells Pepys that he should watch out for two men called John and Tom, who will be with him within a week hoping to borrow money. Shortly afterwards he receives a letter by the hand of his brother, John Pepys, from their brother Tom, seeking £20. Pepys – a future president of the Royal Society – is impressed that this prognostication turns out 'to be so true'.[8]

When it comes to health, the highest people in the land are not above accepting the efficacy of superstitions. The queen falls desperately ill of a fever in October 1663 and is expected to die. In desperation, her physicians turn to the last resort of medicine: applying live pigeons to her feet.[9] She recovers. How much the pigeons have to do with it, no one knows. The royal family's own claim to have healing powers can't be ignored either. Since medieval times, the king of England has been associated with the ability to cure scrofula, a form of tuberculosis (otherwise known as 'the King's Evil'). Charles II is rather keen to maintain this tradition – largely because the ceremony underlines the divine status of his kingship. Observers are invited to witness him touching for the disease. The sufferers pass in a line between two rails in front of the enthroned sovereign. One by one they go on their knees;

the king touches both their cheeks as a clergyman exclaims, 'The king touches thee, God heal thee.' Then they are each given a gold medal on a ribbon. Whether all this does any good is a moot point. Mr Hollier, a surgeon of St Thomas's Hospital, tells people that the king's touch does no good whatsoever.[10] On the other hand, large numbers of people want to be touched each year. In 1684 so many apply for tickets to be cured that half a dozen of them are crushed to death.[11] You might well suspect the reason is the value of the gold medal, not the king's magic properties – and you would probably be right. As Monsieur Misson notes, after the ceremony, 'those that are really ill are put in the hands of physicians and those that have come only for the medal have no need of other remedies'.

The king is not the only thaumaturgist in town. In fact, the Restoration period is when you can visit one of the most remarkable British faith healers of all time: Mr Valentine Greatrakes, also known as 'The Stroker'. He comes from an English landowning family in Ireland, so he is not at all like your usual travelling confidence trickster. To begin with, he modestly tries to stop people talking about his strange power. But after he starts healing people through rubbing or stroking them, his fame spreads. People travel from England as well as Ireland to see him, including the scientist and future Astronomer Royal John Flamsteed. Clergymen try to stop him, partly on account of the miraculous character of his abilities and partly because he also can heal scrofula, which is supposed to be something only the king can do. But desperate people do not listen to doubters. The king, hearing of Greatrakes's ability, invites him to perform a cure in front of the court. The invitation is, of course, a ruse, and on this occasion his stroking the proffered patient is unsuccessful. But in the eyes of his followers, one failure does not undermine his many other successes, and Greatrakes himself is the first to admit that his laying on of hands does not always work. Those attesting to his genuine skill in effecting miraculous cures include Thomas Sydenham, the leading physician of the age, and Robert Boyle, one of the greatest scientists, who attends more than sixty healing sessions.[12] Greatrakes goes back to Ireland in 1666 but returns to England every few years, performing many more cures before his death in 1683. If you are looking for a simple explanation as to why superstition remains so strong in the British Isles, you need look no further than the widespread belief in the efficacy of Greatrakes's touch.

Witchcraft

At the other end of the spectrum of supernatural benevolence lies witchcraft, the sin of the century. You've missed the real fireworks of occultism: most of the indictments and executions for witchcraft fall between 1590 and 1660.[13] Nevertheless, you need to remember that witchcraft remains a criminal act recognised in statute law throughout the Restoration period: it is not just a curious set of quaint and curious folk beliefs. In England and Wales the legal punishment is to be hanged. In Scotland, witches are strangled and burnt. And although in 1685 Alice Molland becomes the last witch to be sentenced to death in England, you are not safe even after this date: the Witchcraft Act will not be formally repealed until 1736. In Scotland, you'll have to wait until 1727 for the sad sight of the last woman being covered in pitch and set alight on account of her fellow countrymen's belief in sorcery.

The key Acts defining witchcraft are those of 1604 in England and 1563 and 1649 in Scotland. The English Act, replacing an earlier piece of legislation, makes it a felony to conjure up evil spirits, to dig up a dead body for magical purposes or to practise any sort of witchcraft that results in the death of, or injury to, another person. People found guilty receive the death penalty. The same Act also prohibits relatively harmless supernatural services, such as using a witch to discover the whereabouts of lost items and to provoke someone to commit acts of 'unlawful love'. These practices, and those leading to the death of cattle, result in the supposed witch being imprisoned for one year. If found guilty a second time, for even one of these minor crimes, the witch is hanged. The law in Scotland is slightly different. As they put it there: 'Thou shalt not suffer a witch to live'. Everyone found guilty of witchcraft is burnt at the stake, including necromancers, whose crime is nothing more sinister than trying to make contact with the spirits of the dead.[14]

As you will soon discover, the application of the law is extremely uneven, both geographically and over time. Generally speaking, the more remote an area, the greater the likelihood that the local people believe in witches, so witch hunts and trials in such regions are more common. The exception is Wales: over the whole period from 1563 to 1735, only thirty-four cases of witchcraft are reported there.[15] In those parts of Britain that are prone to belief in witchcraft, accusations don't proceed at a steady rate but in sudden bursts of paranoia. Take great care if you visit Scotland in the years 1661–2 and 1677–8, as major witch hunts are then under way. In total, just over a thousand men and women – about one-third of all those ever charged with witchcraft north of the border – are accused between 1660 and 1700.[16] The English are less inclined to charge witches during this period. Between 1563 and 1735 they hold a similar number of trials as the Scots, but the vast majority of them pre-date 1660.

So what does a trial for witchcraft look like? Isobel Gowdie is perhaps the best-known self-confessed witch of all. She is a farmer's wife from Auldearn in the north of Scotland. In 1662, the minister of her kirk, Henry Forbes, accuses her of attempting to harm him with witchcraft. She responds by making four voluntary confessions in front of him and the Scottish justices. She explains that she was out walking with a neighbour one day fifteen years earlier when she met the Devil. He gave her his mark on her shoulder and, while her neighbour held her firm, the Devil sucked blood from the mark, then spouted it into his hands and poured it over her head, baptising her 'Janet' in his own name. At their next meeting, she allowed the Devil to copulate with her. She found him a 'very black, hairy man, very cold', with cloven feet, and he lay very heavily upon her. His member was enormous – far larger than any normal man's – and his semen was 'as cold within her as spring well-water'. Later, when she joined a coven, he would copulate with each of the women within sight of all the others, without any shame. Her coven dug up the corpse of an unbaptised child in the graveyard at Nairn, hacked it up and mixed the pieces with their fingernails and toenails, grain and kale leaves, and then spread the potion on a dung-heap belonging to one of their enemies, to kill his crops. With the aid of her familiar spirit, 'Janet' ruined men's harvests and soured their milk. She admitted turning herself into a hare, a jackdaw and a crow. She and her coven broke into the houses of the rich to eat their food and drink their wine, and when they emptied a barrel, they filled it with their piss. While flying on straws or broomsticks, she and other members of her coven shot people dead with special elf-arrows, given to them by the Devil himself. Because she hated Forbes but had failed to kill him, she asked the Devil if she could take another shot at him. She and her coven then made an incantation against him with the flesh and guts of toads. They made a clay image with which to kill a local laird's male children, roasting the figure in a fire. They raised the wind and storms to do their bidding. And so on.[17]

Gowdie seems willing to confess to everything she can possibly think of that was associated with witchcraft. Taken together, it all reads as if she is laughing at the minister and justices for believing such a load of rubbish. However, her accomplices are arrested and they back up her story – from her diabolical baptism to her orgies with the Devil and her shooting of elf-arrows. I am not sure if she burns or not – no one I have spoken to is clear on the matter – but I would not be surprised: many women are burnt for much less. In 1661 Isobel Fergussone is arrested for committing adultery with the Devil in the form of her landlord's half-brother, who flees to Ireland just afterwards. She is found to have the Devil's mark on her. Her confession results in her being ordered to be executed by burning – although, in line with Scottish law, she is mercifully strangled on the pyre before the flames reach her body.[18]

In England, the cosmopolitan south-east sees relatively few accusations of witchcraft in this period. The attitude there is one of cautious disbelief. Monsieur Misson notes that people nail up horseshoes to keep witches at bay, adding: 'it is true they laugh when they say this but they do not laugh at it altogether'.[19] In the remote south-west, however, belief in witchcraft is still strong. As at Auldearn, 500 miles away, fairy lore is still firmly rooted in this part of the world, as well as the idea that old women can transmogrify themselves into cats and birds.[20] As Willem Schellinks ventures into Cornwall in 1661, he nervously reports that he has heard that the region is alive with witches and sorcerers.[21] And plenty of people are on hand to tell you from personal experience that he is not wrong.

In 1682, three old women from Bideford are accused of witchcraft – their names being Susanna Edwards, Temperance Lloyd and Mary Trembles. A witness giving evidence against them, Dorcas Coleman, reports that she went to see a physician, Dr Beare, to discuss some pricking sensations she felt in her body. Dr Beare airily dismissed her, saying he could do nothing for her as she was bewitched. Dorcas says that she then sought out the cause of her bewitchment and found it was Susanna Edwards, for when she met Edwards, she found herself compelled to crawl towards her to draw blood with her nails – this apparently being the only way to break a witch's spell. Another woman, Grace Thomas, also testifies that she felt pricking sensations, and blames Temperance for causing them. Temperance, who is eighty years of age and finding it difficult to deal with the onslaught of questioning in court, confirms that she did indeed cause the pricking by repeatedly piercing a piece of leather. Further questioning and more rumours of their evil doings bring the women's defences down. Temperance confirms that she was led by the Devil in the form of a small black man, with whom she had had sex, to pinch Grace Thomas. On examination, she is found to have two teats, each about an inch long, near her pudenda. These are definitely the Devil's marks, the court decides. Susanna Edwards is led to confess that she too has met the Devil in the form of a small boy and that, in that guise, he has sucked blood from her breast and had sex with her. Mary Trembles, who stands accused of hurting another woman by witchcraft, is also duped into confessing that she met the Devil in the shape of a lion and that he sucked her so hard that she screamed with pain. Thereafter the accusations flow: these women can travel invisibly, have killed a woman, made cows barren of milk and caused shipwrecks. In their confusion – and, frankly, who would not be confused by this welter of bitterness and bizarre accusation – the women do not deny all these things. They are found guilty by the mayor and taken to Exeter to face a judge, who confirms the verdict. All three are hanged on 25 August 1682.

From all this you may infer several things. Witchcraft is not as ubiquitous as some people claim. However, in those rural areas where it does persist, it is dangerous and frightening. Even a circuit judge from London, sitting in Exeter – one of the biggest and most prosperous cities in the kingdom – will uphold the law against witchcraft. It is not a matter of what *you* do and believe; it is more a case of what other people think of you, and what *they* believe. The implications of this are quite disconcerting. In the modern world, we assume that the truth is something we share with all those around us. If something is a fact – that people cannot change into cats or jackdaws – then it is as true for you as it is for me. In the seventeenth century, things are not like that. Many people believe that the laws of nature affect us in different ways: that witches can do things we cannot. Thus the truth of how the world operates is something that divides people as much as it unites them. And, when it comes to witchcraft, there is no saying that your version of reality will prevail.

Religion

You could be forgiven for thinking that Restoration society is less religious than it has ever been before. Many years have passed since the last heretic was burnt in England – Edward Wightman, way back in 1612 – and the law enforcing such burning is repealed in 1677. Compulsory church attendance is on the wane. Pepys sometimes goes to church alone, leaving his wife behind. In some places the poor are expected not to attend services at all. Increasingly the wealthy want to be seen in their finery in church, and don't want to be reminded of those less fortunate than themselves. By this token, those who do attend are not necessarily there purely for the good of their souls. Pepys is not the only one to spend church services eyeing up the ladies. When Thomas Baskerville visits the Dutch church in Yarmouth, he notes that 'thither the people go every afternoon to hear prayers and where their fine women may be seen'.[22]

Despite all these things, there are plenty of indicators that religious conviction is as strong as ever. You need only reflect on the fact that James II loses his throne on account of his promotion of his fellow Catholics to realise that faith continues to be of prime importance to many people. And this is by no means an unprecedented reaction. In 1661 Parliament introduces the Corporation Act, requiring everyone serving in a local administrative office in England to obtain a certificate confirming that he has attended an Anglican service within the last twelve months, and to swear oaths of allegiance to the king, recognising his supremacy in spiritual matters. When Charles II tries to introduce religious toleration for all in 1672, he is thwarted by the strength of Protestant feeling: the most he can achieve is to issue a Declaration of Indulgence, by which nonconformists are permitted to worship in licensed buildings, and Catholics in their own homes. Even this modest step in the direction of toleration is withdrawn the following year, when the king is forced to accept the Test Act. This requires every office-holder to swear three oaths: those of allegiance to the Crown and of the king's supremacy in spiritual matters, and a third one asserting that the Catholic doctrine of transubstantiation is untrue. This bars the king's own brother from holding office. If kings and dukes cannot stand against the tide of popular religious feeling, how can ordinary individuals hope to do so? In 1697 a Scottish student called Thomas Aikenhead is reported to have ridiculed the Old Testament as 'Ezra's Fables' and to have declared that Christ learnt magic in Egypt so that he could perform miracles. On a cold night, after a few drinks, he jokes with some friends, 'I wish I were in that place Ezra calls Hell so I could warm myself.' His companions turn out not to be his friends. Thomas is arrested, tried and sentenced to death. He begs for mercy on the grounds that he is only eighteen years old and this is his first offence. But when the question is put to the Church of Scotland ministers, they urge that he be executed, as an example to others. He is hanged outside the walls of Edinburgh, watched by the ministers who condemned him.

Perhaps the clearest sign of the vitality of faith amongst the people generally is the number of dissenting churches and sects that exist after 1660. Edward Chamberlayne, writing in 1676, lists all those that he has heard of – Presbyterians, Independents, Anabaptists (or Baptists), Quakers, Fifth-Monarchy Men, Ranters, Adamites, Antinomians, Sabbatarians, Perfectionists and the Family of Love – and expresses the hope that all these 'mushrooms of Christianity', which sprang up under Cromwell, will soon vanish.[23] Signor Magalotti and Monsieur Misson are similarly intrigued by the number of nonconformists in England and add yet more sects to Chamberlayne's list. Among them are Muggletonians, followers of Lodowicke Muggleton, who teaches that God and Christ are one and the same thing; and Photinians, who believe that God and Christ are wholly independent of one other. In addition, Magalotti and Misson mention Arians, Brownists, Antiscripturists, Hederingtonians, Theaurian-Joanites, Seekers, Waiters, Reevists, Baronists, Wilkinsonians, Millenarians, Arminians, Socinians, Origenists, Levellers, Quintinists, Mennonites and Libertines.[24] Had they looked further, they could have named even more.

In theory, almost all these sects should vanish in 1662, when the Act of Uniformity requires everyone to accept the new Book of Common Prayer, published that year. They don't. More than two thousand dissenting clergymen are ejected from the Church of England, largely because they are opposed to the restoration of the rule of bishops. In Scotland, 270 ministers are similarly forced out of office. The ousted Scots clergy promptly hold a series of 'conventicles' – illegal religious meetings – and this ushers in a period of bloody persecution that is only resolved in 1689 when the Scottish Parliament abolishes the bishops in favour of a Presbyterian Church of Scotland. If society really were becoming more secular, clergymen on both sides of the border would simply accept the Act of Uniformity with a shrug of the shoulders. Their congregations too would accept the new Book of Common Prayer. But dissenting ministers and their followers are of one mind: their religion is more important than obeying the letter of the law. In the 1690s, in England alone, nonconformist ministers preach to more than 200,000 followers – more than 10 per cent of the adult population.[25] If Restoration society seems less religious than it has ever been before, it is only because it immediately follows the Commonwealth, the most religious period we have seen for centuries.

All this prompts me to suggest that you should keep four fundamental things in mind about religion in Restoration Britain:

1. Society is not growing less religious, but the channels of divine intervention are becoming more secular. People no longer expect their prayers to be answered directly by God; they increasingly believe that God will act through other individuals. Thus, if people are ill, they don't expect a miracle, but they might pray that God will cure them through the auspices of a physician. Of course, this makes it all the more important that the physician from whom they seek help is of impeccable spiritual correctness. And that normally means he needs to be of the same religious disposition as them. Most God-fearing people will not believe that an atheist will be able to do them any good, whatever his medical qualifications.

2. Never forget that your fellow Christians are not necessarily your friends. And if you are not a Christian, you probably don't have any friends.

3. It is a good idea to attend at least one service every Sunday. If you don't, people will talk. If you fail to go for a whole month, you may be arrested on suspicion of being a Catholic.[26] If that happens, you will need swiftly to obtain a certificate from a minister, confirming that you have taken communion in an Anglican church recently. It is safest just to go. Pepys isn't very religious, yet he usually goes twice: once in the morning, to his parish church, and once after his Sunday dinner, to a church of his choice.

4. Choose your religious denomination very carefully. If you want to play it safe, stick to Anglicanism. Clasp the 1662 Book of Common Prayer to your chest, tell everyone that you despise Catholics, Quakers

and atheists, curse the pope, praise the king, and commemorate the anniversary of Charles I's execution each year on 30 January as the death of a martyr. Thus you may avoid the pitfalls of sectarian religion. However, if you are of an anti-establishment disposition and truly cannot abide the thought of attending a Protestant service, then read the following brief guide to radical Restoration sects carefully – to identify which beliefs are merely awkward and which are positively dangerous.

A BRIEF GUIDE TO RADICAL RESTORATION SECTS

Fanatics. We have all come across people in the modern world who are convinced that the end of the world is nigh, and who urge the rest of us to repent of our sins. They have their precursors in this period, and ordinary citizens call them 'fanatics'. Pepys notes on Tuesday, 25 November 1663 that there is 'great talk among people how some of the fanatics do say that the end of the world is at hand and that next Tuesday is to be the day – against which, whenever it shall be, God fit us all'.[27]

Fifth Monarchists. This sect believes that Christ's return to Earth is imminent, and that they must prepare the way for the Fifth Monarchy of the prophecy of Daniel – when the Jews will be converted, the Turks destroyed, and Christ will again rule the Earth in glory. These people don't approve of the return of Charles II and are even unhappier to see the restoration of the Church of England. On 6 January 1661, they take up arms under the leadership of a wine merchant called James Venner and stage a rebellion in the streets of London. When the Trained Bands of the militia confront them and demand to know whom they serve, they answer 'King Jesus!' and open fire. A two-day skirmish follows; about twenty men are killed on each side.

Quakers. In the 1660s, Quakers are the most hated and persecuted nonconformist sect of all. They are variously called 'the most incorrigible sinners', 'heretics', 'a dangerous sort of people', 'a vessel of fanaticism', 'the fag-end of the Reformation with a sullen, meagre look' and 'clownish hypocrites'.[28] They manage to enrage both the clergy and the wealthy by refusing to pay tithes and swear oaths of allegiance, and by declining to offer the usual marks of respect to their social superiors. Most shocking of all, they allow women to speak in their meetings. They are more threatening than Fifth Monarchists, on account of their numbers. Their founder, George Fox, only starts preaching in 1647 and spends several lengthy spells in prison, yet by 1660 there are more than 30,000 Quakers in England. In 1662 the Quaker Act is passed, making it illegal to refuse to take an oath of loyalty and prohibiting meetings of five or more members of the sect. Visit any prison and you will see Quakers solemnly sitting there in the cells. One hundred of them are rounded up in Southwark on a single day in August 1663. In 1668 a group of Quakers build a meeting house in London: if you join the stout of heart in going there, you will be arrested and fined £10 for each service you attend. It is not until the passing of the Toleration Act of 1689 that you can attend such meetings in peace.[29]

Atheists. Atheism is not a sect as such, as it lacks organisation and leadership. Otherwise it would displace Quakerism as the most hated religious group. To quote Magalotti, it is

> the very abyss of blindness and the uttermost limit of the pestilential heresy of Calvin. The professors of it say there is no God; they do not believe in a Resurrection to come; they deny the immortality of the soul; and teach that everything happens by chance; and as a natural consequence, they follow their own perverse inclinations, without having any regard to futurity but thinking only of the present time.[30]

And that is about as polite an appreciation as you will hear. Most people regard atheism as repugnant and any discussion of it as taboo. In 1698 Parliament passes a law making it illegal to deny the divinity of Christ, which effectively criminalises both atheism and deism (which is the belief that God exists as a Creator, but that he does not intervene in the workings of the world). Obviously, if you fall into either of these camps, you won't be able to swear the Oath of Supremacy required by the Test Act of 1673. However, if you swear an oath in bad faith in order to acquire public office, you will be guilty of perjury. You can't win. Even being a genius won't help you. The scientist Edmond Halley is rejected for the post of Savilian Professor of Astronomy at Oxford in 1691 due to a rumour that he does not believe in God. The only way to be an atheist and flourish is to be very wealthy and/or enormously charismatic. It is permissible for the flamboyant earl of Rochester to profess his atheism openly, but not for a humble tradesman or a farmer, who will simply be shunned by his neighbours.

Presbyterians, Congregationalists, Independents, Unitarians and Baptists. Things are somewhat easier if you are a follower of one of these groups – but not that much easier. There remains a basic assumption that all nonconformists are republicans at heart. Many moderate Presbyterian clergy who are ejected from their churches in 1662 keep a low profile for the next ten years; they then are among the 1,500 nonconformists who obtain licences to preach in 1672. Those who are more radical face further intolerance and persecution. The father of the Unitarians, John Biddle, spends much of his life in chains and is still incarcerated when he dies in 1662. The entire Seventh Day Baptist congregation of Bulstake Alley, Whitechapel, is imprisoned in Newgate Gaol in 1661; their preacher, John James, is found guilty of high treason and hanged, disembowelled and quartered at Tyburn. As an Independent Congregationalist strongly influenced by the Fifth Monarchists, John Bunyan spends the first twelve years of the Restoration period in prison. He could obtain his freedom if he wanted – by undertaking not to preach – but he refuses. Such is the fire within him that he writes a total of forty-two religious books and holds illegal conventicles – for which he is locked up again in 1676.

Suffice to say, unless you really know what you are doing, it is best not to try to join any nonconformist groups before the Toleration Act of 1689. They are all dangerous. However, if you do find yourself moved to join them, or see your children falling in with them, you can take solace from this fact.

At least they are not Roman Catholics.

ROMAN CATHOLICISM

If you are a Roman Catholic in Restoration Britain, you'd better have your wits about you. You are in a distinct minority – less than 0.5 per cent of the country is Catholic – and there is a long history of popular intimidation as well as official persecution. You are not allowed to travel more than five miles from your home. You may not go to school. You cannot attend a university. You pay taxes at double the rate. There is a fine of £100 for marrying in a Catholic ceremony. Catholic physicians and surgeons cannot obtain licences to practise. Catholic lawyers likewise cannot represent their clients in court, and the aforementioned Corporation Act (1661) and Test Act (1673) prohibit Catholics from holding official posts. And if you think things cannot get worse, think again.

In 1678 an anti-Catholic panic attack called the 'Popish Plot' breaks out. A ne'er-do-well Catholic convert called Titus Oates reveals to the authorities that the English Catholics are conspiring to kill Charles II so that his convert brother, James, can take the throne. The king himself interrogates Oates and finds he is a duplicitous, self-interested schemer and has him arrested, but Parliament is scared enough to overrule the king. Oates is given his own band of armed constables and is ordered to discover all the supposed Catholic conspirators. When Sir Edmund Godfrey, the magistrate to whom Oates has revealed the names of dozens of plotters, is found strangled and run through with his own sword, popular feeling against the Catholics runs even higher. The Trained Bands are put in readiness. Hundreds of 'Godfrey daggers' are sold so that Anglicans can protect themselves against the murderous Catholics. The gates of London are guarded around the clock. Houses of leading Catholics are searched. Anyone found to have been in contact with the Jesuits is arrested and sent to the Tower. An MP is hounded out of town simply for denying that there is any plot. Oates then implicates five Catholic lords, who are arrested, tried and found guilty. One of them, Lord Stafford, is executed. A second Test Act banning Catholic noblemen from sitting in the House of Lords is immediately passed. Then Oates and his accomplices implicate the Catholic queen in the plot, stating that she is trying to poison her Protestant husband. Rumours spread that the Great Fire of London was started by the Catholics and that they plan to burn down the city again. By the time the extent of Oates's fantasies becomes clear, in 1681, thirty-five men have been executed as a result of his false evidence.

Hardly has the fear died down when two new crises hit English Catholics. The first is the death of Charles II on 6 February 1685, which brings his politically inflexible Catholic brother to the throne. The second is the French king's revocation of the Edict of Nantes, which has hitherto guaranteed Huguenots (French Protestants) the freedom to live and practise their religion in France. Suddenly they are faced with a choice: convert to Catholicism, die or escape. Thousands are executed and murdered. All their churches are demolished and the schools closed. Hundreds of thousands of Huguenots flee, and many of them come to England, telling stories of terrible suffering at the hands of Catholics. With such stories circulating, it is extremely unwise of James II to choose this moment to promote tolerance of Catholicism, and to allow Catholics to join his government. He appoints a Catholic to be a privy councillor, and encourages members of the court to attend Mass: John Dryden the poet and Nell Gwyn both do so. He allows Catholic books and pictures to be sold openly. Friars are seen walking along the streets, laughing. It is only a matter of time before the mob takes things into their own hands. When the news breaks that the Protestant William of Orange is coming to rescue England from the Catholic king, every Catholic chapel in London is demolished or burnt. The embassies of the Catholic states of Venice, Spain, Tuscany and the Palatinate of the Rhine are also attacked and looted.[31]

Wise Catholics keep their heads down through all of this. In fact, if you are Catholic, it is best to keep your head down until the next century. Catholics are still excluded from William III's Toleration Act of 1689, which only allows freedom of worship to *Protestant* noncon-formists. But even more importantly, the ousted James II repeatedly threatens to return to England with the help of the French in order to seize back the throne. In 1690 he invades Ireland. William III defeats him at the Battle of the Boyne, but James does not give up. There are further Jacobite plots in 1692, 1694 and 1696. The last of these sees a failed attempt to assassinate the new king, William III. After this, Catholics are not allowed to come within ten miles of London.

JEWS

Before we leave the subject of religion, you might like to know that one previously persecuted minority group does see a slight upturn in its fortunes. The Jews were expelled from England in the thirteenth century and subsequently could not live openly in the kingdom. A few Jewish families settled in London in the 1580s and

1590s, but to all intents and purposes it was not possible to be a Jew in England before 1656. In that year Oliver Cromwell relaxed this prohibition and invited Jews to settle here. In 1660, there are about thirty-five Jewish families in London and by the end of the century that number has doubled. They are mostly Sephardic Jews and Ashkenazim from Poland and Germany, living around Whitechapel and Petticoat Lane. Don't imagine, though, that this is a sign of general rapprochement. Soon after the Restoration, the lord mayor and the Corporation of London petition Charles II to expel the Jews once more.[32] However, on this occasion the king refuses the petition and permits the Jews to stay.

Immorality

I mentioned in the introduction to this book that there is widespread relief when, in 1660, the Adultery Act is repealed by the English Parliament. Most people are indeed happy to wave goodbye to the bulk of such legislation. However, a significant minority do not see things this way, preferring the moral austerity of Cromwell's time. The overthrow of James II in 1688 and the accession of the much more strait-laced William and Mary give Puritans a new lease of life, which in turn leads to calls for a stronger moral law. In 1690 a group of bishops and judges draft a bill to put the Adultery Act back on the statute books. In order to make convictions easier, they propose that there should be an assumption of guilt if two people are found in bed together or naked in the same room. Fortunately the Bill fails. A further attempt to punish adultery with hanging – or at least branding and transportation – is narrowly defeated in 1698.[33] Frustrated by these setbacks, the morally upstanding people of London take matters into their own hands and establish societies for the reformation of morals, in order to prosecute individuals for any offence they can pin on them. The return of the king in 1660 might herald a restoration of libertinism for some but don't presume the result is a free-for-all thereafter.

In Scotland, moral austerity remains the norm. Although the Scottish Parliament in 1649 refrained from passing an Act punishing adultery with death, there is a tottering pile of other moral legislation in force, including an 'Act against the horrible crime of blasphemy', an 'Act against swearing, drunkenness, scolding and other profanities', an 'Act against fornication' and an 'Act for punishing the horrible crime of incest with death'. This last one makes it a capital offence not just to lie with your own relations, but with any of your in-laws – be it your stepfather or stepmother, your spouse's nephews, nieces, aunts or uncles, or anybody who is married to one of your relations. It is not unknown for a man in Scotland to be burnt at the stake for having sex with his sister-in-law.[34] These laws continue to be enforced throughout the period. And as the case of Thomas Aikenhead shows, when it comes to blasphemy, the Scottish authorities see no reason to show clemency on the grounds of youth.

Such attitudes might make you wonder what you can and can't get away with. Just how naughty can you be?

Immorality lies in the mind of the perpetrator as well as in the eye of the legislator, so let's begin with your conscience. Some people feel guilty about the slightest things. Edward Barlow thinks his greatest vice is that, every time he falls in love with a girl, he promises to return to her after his next voyage – but then he meets another girl on the said voyage and says the same to her.[35] Pepys is racked with guilt just for playing music on a Sunday. He is not alone. Monsieur Misson observes that 'those to be hanged for murdering their parents will first confess that they broke the Sabbath', and when Ralph Thoresby visits Rotterdam he is appalled to see people 'singing, playing, walking and *sewing*' on the Lord's day.[36] Apart from clergymen, the only people allowed to work on Sundays are miners – because the mines will flood if they don't. But while Sabbath-breaking is reprehensible in some people's minds, there are worse crimes. It hardly matters that it is upon a Sunday in 1660 that Mr Pepys meets up with Mistress Lane of Westminster Hall and takes her to Lord Sandwich's house, where he shares a bottle of wine with her in the garden, before having sex with her in his old house in Axe Yard. The following month he puts his empty house to the same use with another woman.[37] Over the ten years of his diary he has affairs with about ten women and sexual frolics with about forty others, most of which involve him fondling their private parts and them his. He knows it is wrong – worse even than playing his lute on a Sunday – but he just can't stop himself. In June 1663, after spending an afternoon groping Mistress Lane in a wine tavern, and having a stone thrown at him by someone who sees him at it through a window, he reflects, 'I have used of late, since my wife went [away from London], to make a bad use of my fancy with whatever woman I have a mind to – which I am ashamed of and shall endeavour to do so no more.'

When an immoral act becomes publicly known, it assumes a whole new dimension, and certain deeds can still prove fatal. If Pepys were homosexual, for example, he would suffer more than stone-flinging. Male–male desire is viewed not as a matter of natural affection, but only in terms of its physical manifestation – sodomy – and, as such, it is deemed entirely unnatural. Like bestiality, it is a capital offence under the terms of the Buggery Act of 1533. Several notable executions have taken place over the years, including those of the earl of Castlehaven in 1631 and of John Atherton, bishop of Waterford, in 1640. Few cases come to light for the obvious reason that it is not normally something done in the presence of witnesses. Moreover, those giving evidence who have been party to the act will also be hanged: a servant who testifies that his master sodomised him is signing his own death warrant. For this reason, homosexual men are not normally accused of sodomy itself, but of 'assault with intent to commit sodomy', so that the witness does not suffer too.

All this gives you some idea of the moral tempest through which you will have to navigate. The legal framework within which people live does not correspond with their natural urges, whether those be sexual or more to do with a spot of embroidery on a Sunday afternoon. Ultimately everyone has to find their own way of dealing with the problem. Robert Hooke's method is to sleep with his housekeeper, Nell Young, and after she leaves his employment, to have a passionate affair with his niece, Grace. Their love being against the law, she also lives with him as his 'housekeeper'. Pepys's way of coping with the mismatch of desire and morality is, broadly speaking, subterfuge – until he gets caught. Others resort to prostitution. For the wealthy, this often takes the form of maintaining a mistress. Lord Sandwich has a house in Chelsea where he keeps his girlfriend – or his 'slut' as Pepys refers to her (look who's talking!). Men who are unwilling or unable to maintain a mistress may find temporary relief in London's Fleet Alley, and you will find similar streets in most major towns. Unsurprisingly, as London grows in size, so does the sex industry; by the 1690s prostitutes are to be found all over the city, not just in one street. In 1691 a correspondent to a journal suggests that an area be set aside where all the London street walkers can ply their trade legally every evening, as they do in Amsterdam.[38]

Above all else, however, it is the immorality of the court that is the talk of the town. People fear that the king's outrageous behaviour will bring harm upon them all. The royal chaplain is bold enough to preach in a sermon before the king in July 1667 that, on account of King David's sin of adultery, 'the whole nation was undone'.[39] Before 1660 the punishment of libertines had the royal seal of approval – but Charles II encourages them to be *more* immoral. You can see the clergy's problem: how can they possibly hope to maintain strict discipline among their flocks if the fount of all power in the land, and the head of their Church, is so openly leading them astray?

It is well over a hundred years since there was last a royal mistress in England – people don't know quite what to expect. Charles doesn't worry about that: in fact, he seems determined to make up for the whole century's worth of missed opportunities. In all, he has about fourteen illegitimate children by seven women, and numerous other affairs. But it is the sheer ostentation of his liaisons that leaves people dumbfounded. In January 1663 he spends four or five nights a week at Lady Castlemaine's apartments, and each morning he is seen walking back to the palace by all those who live close by. Their servants talk about it. The palace sentries do too. Everyone does. Pepys opines that 'there is nothing but bawdry at court'. A few days later he himself sees the king leave his mistress's rooms and declares that it is 'a poor thing for a prince to do'.[40] The following week he hears from Captain Fenner that Lady Castlemaine recently invited the beautiful Frances Stuart to an entertainment and the two women performed a marriage ceremony together for the king's amusement. They exchanged rings and even went so far as to perform the flinging of the stocking – whereby the naked bride throws her stocking to the womenfolk who are there to witness her nuptials. Captain Fenner adds that Lady Castlemaine then made room in the bed for the king, who took her place in acting the part of the bridegroom. Such are the stories circulating about the king and, whether they are true or not, the king's public behaviour encourages people to believe them.

Charles's use of the peerage system to reward his libido is just as outrageous. He creates Lady Castlemaine, who is his first mistress after becoming king, duchess of Cleveland. A duchess! You might just accept that giving a mistress a title helps her get around at court, as it allows her to join the ranks of 'the great' so that people have to look up to her, but still, does he have to elevate her above upstanding earls' wives? Not only that, he ennobles her illegitimate sons: the dukes of Southampton, Grafton and Northumberland are all his offspring by her. He also creates James Scott, his son by an earlier mistress, duke of Monmouth. In 1670 Louise de Kéroualle, a famous French beauty, comes to England: she is meant to tempt Charles into making a treaty between England and France. She succeeds magnificently. In 1673 she is created duchess of Portsmouth and, in due course, the king's son by her becomes duke of Richmond. Although Nell Gwyn remains a commoner, she does not do badly by her royal bedfellow, either. She is given a freehold house in Pall Mall, and her royal bastard is eventually created duke of St Albans. That's six illegitimate dukes. Add the earl of Plymouth (the king's son by Catherine Pegg) and you can see that a large proportion of the front rank of the English aristocracy is privileged purely on the grounds that it is the result of Charles's unashamed lust.

The king is not the only immoralist in town. In 1663 Sir Charles Sedley, baronet and rake, strips off and parades naked on the balcony of the Cock, a cookshop in Bow Street. He plays out 'all the postures of lust and buggery that can be imagined' and preaches a highly blasphemous sermon. In the course of this he declares to the crowd of about a thousand people gathered below that he has a powder such as will make all the women of the town run after him – except that he does not use the word 'women' but calls them by their sexual organs. Next he takes a glass of wine, washes his private parts in it and then drinks it. After that he drinks the king's health. In all this he is supported by his friend Charles Sackville, Lord Buckhurst, an aristocrat and suspected highwayman. In 1668 these two men run through the streets of London by night 'with their arses bare', staging a fight until they are arrested by the city watch.[41] It is Buckhurst who lures Nell Gwyn away from the stage and beds her before he hands her over to be the king's mistress.

A more famous and shocking libertine than either Sedley or Buckhurst is the arch-rake John Wilmot, earl of Rochester. Talk about immorality! Wine, women and syphilis are just the starter. The main course of his life includes the abduction of his chosen bride, serial adultery, self-confessed claims of sodomy, blasphemy, insults directed at anyone and everyone (even the king), extreme lewdness, rudeness, atheism, reckless courage in warfare, fighting duels, punching royal servants in the king's presence, selling fake medicines, writing poetry,

unlawful appearances on the London stage, imprisonment in
the Tower and banishment from court. He is also suspected of being the
author of *Sodom*, almost certainly the rudest play ever written, about
a debauched king who encourages his sex-crazed subjects to indulge
themselves in as much sodomy as they like. Just to give you a flavour
of its lewdness, the *dramatis personae* includes: King Bolloximian and
Queen Cuntigratia; Prince Prickett, Princess Swivia and General
Buggeranthus; Pockenello (a pimp, catamite and the king's favourite),
Borastus (the buggermaster-general), Pene, Tooly and Lady Officina
(pimps and she-pimp of honour); Fuckadilla, Cunticula and Clitoris
(maids of honour); Flux (physician-in-ordinary to the king) and
Virtuoso (dildo-maker to the court).

Enough. There have always been transgressors of social norms – so
what makes this different? Is this just not sordid? Many people think
so. But there is more going on here than will ever meet a moralist's eye.

You can call Samuel Pepys a hypocrite for his immorality. *His* outrageousness lies in that very hypocrisy: saying one thing and doing
another. But the king, Rochester, Buckhurst and Sedley are not hypocrites; *their* outrageousness is that they do not pretend to subscribe
to normal standards of morality. They are asking a wider question:
how should men fight against a system of Puritanical repression that
is so sanctimonious that it borders on inhumanity? It hangs women
for adultery and witchcraft, and men for homosexuality and blasphemy; it prohibits free speech, restricts free thinking and imposes a
religious structure on almost everything that is said and done. Ordinary
people can do next to nothing to kick against the control of the
Church, but these rich and privileged young men *can* do something –
even if it is only a matter of breaking all the rules. There is a reason
why they strip off and simulate acts of buggery on a balcony, and it
is not because they are buffoons or idiots. They are all educated men
of the stage and they know exactly what they are doing in invoking
such taboos. What's more, they can write too. They can add a literary
flourish to Charles II's two-fingered gesture towards the Puritanism
that killed his father and forced him into exile. At its best, their contribution amounts to brilliant poetry. Yes, it incorporates language so
vulgar that even in the modern world it is shocking, but men who
can write as well as Rochester do not choose such words gratuitously.
They choose them because the Puritans banned them. Thus their
immorality is more than just profane: it is revolutionary, deliberately

offensive, public and proud – and a world apart from Pepys's furtive fumbling with maidservants' petticoats in attic rooms.

Attitudes to Foreigners

None of the people of Britain are famed for their welcoming smiles to strangers. Ask almost any foreigner who visits and you will hear the same old story: the English are unfriendly, proud and treacherous, and the Scots and Welsh are cruel and barbarous. Their redeeming features are a sense of fair play (in the case of the English) and an indomitable courage (in both the Scots and the Welsh). If you come across a variation on these themes, it will be to differentiate between the attitudes of the wealthy and the common rabble. In describing the Scots, Monsieur Misson distinguishes between 'those who have civilised themselves by their travels and by their commerce with France and England' and the common folk who are 'half-barbarous'. He goes on to explain that the well travelled are 'courteous, good-natured ... men of wit, more subtle and cunning than their neighbours and very capable in the sciences'. The poorer sort, however, 'are mere savages'.[42] In describing Londoners, Magalotti makes a similar distinction, only he puts it more elegantly:

> The common people of London, giving way to their natural inclination, are proud, arrogant and uncivil to foreigners, especially the French, against whom, they entertain a great prejudice and cherish a profound hatred, treating such as come among them with contempt and insult. The nobility, though also proud, have not so usually the defects of the lower orders, displaying a certain degree of politeness and courtesy towards strangers; and this is still more the case with those gentlemen who have been out of the kingdom, and travelled, they having taken a lesson in politeness from the manners of other nations.[43]

These views are not surprising. A Continental traveller in Britain has, by definition, broader horizons than the majority of those he meets here, as few ordinary Englishmen have journeyed abroad. Moreover, in order to have come here in the first place, the said traveller must be reasonably well off. And if he writes down his views, he also needs to have been educated. Therefore a great many contemporary comments on the people of Britain are blunt opinions held by educated gentlemen about the illiterate lower orders. British travellers say similar things about the unfriendliness of the common people when they go abroad. Nevertheless, such opinions are a good indicator as to how a stranger like you will be received in Restoration Britain. The educated and wealthy will do their best to welcome those of a similar rank; the middle sort will be suspicious of you, and the poor will not go out of their way for you at all – unless you pay them enough to make it worth their while.

This, by and large, is true whichever country you are from and however exotic your appearance. When the Russian ambassador arrives in London in November 1662 and makes his procession through the streets of the city in his native garb, the ordinary citizens' reaction is not exactly respectful. 'But Lord, to see the absurd nature of Englishmen, who cannot forbear laughing and jeering at everything that looks strange,' writes Pepys.[44] At the end of our period, when Tsar Peter I visits England to view the shipyards, he stays at Sayes Court, which is owned by John Evelyn. One of Evelyn's servants writes to his master and describes the Russian people staying in the house as 'right nasty'.[45] Yet both embassies are most cordially received at a higher social level, as indeed are most diplomatic missions to England. Evelyn makes a special point of going to see that Russian procession in 1662 and describes the visitors 'on horseback clad in their vests after the Eastern manner, rich furs and caps, and carrying the presents, some carrying hawks, furs, teeth [ivory], bows etcetera'. He concludes, 'it was a very magnificent show'.[46]

So much for Continental travellers; what about strangers from other parts of Britain?

It perhaps goes without saying that relations between the English, Welsh and Scots have always been awkward. An English traveller describes the Scots as 'proud, arrogant, vainglorious boasters, bloody, barbarous and inhuman butchers'.[47] As for the Welsh, if you are in London on 1 March 1662, which is St David's Day, you will see all the Welshmen in town wearing a leek in their hats. This is widely believed to commemorate an ancient battle in which the Welsh beat the English. The English custom is to mock the Welsh by putting up dolls and scarecrows with leeks in *their* hats. Both sides drink heavily and soon get rowdy. On this occasion an English cook puts a leek in his own hat and drunkenly addresses a Welsh lord as 'fellow countryman'. The Welsh lord is not amused and replies sharply in Welsh, prompting the cook to sneer back at him in English. The lord draws his rapier and goes for him. The cook runs into his shop and grabs a hot spit from the fire to defend himself. The lord's retainers draw their swords to defend their master, but the crowd now joins in, throwing mud and stones and whatever else is to hand, eventually driving the Welshmen to the river to flee by boat.[48]

These infelicitous moments are not just confined to rivalries between the separate countries within Britain. Similar tensions can erupt into violence between groups of Yorkshiremen and Londoners, or even between people from separate villages within the same county. Indeed, the word 'foreigner' is used in rural parishes to denote anyone not normally resident in the community, and that can even include the lord of the manor.[49] This universal 'foreignness' presents impecunious travellers with the danger of being seen as a vagrant. You may be a gambler, a beggar or a servant looking for work; perhaps you are a seaman sleeping rough as you return to your ship, or a decommissioned soldier on his way home; or a pedlar, a released prisoner, a labourer, a musician or an actor travelling from town to town – strangers who are poorly dressed and who have no money are seen as a threat and if the local constable decides you are indeed a vagrant, he will be after you. The punishment is simple: you will be stripped from the waist up and 'whipped till your back be bloody'.[50] Then you will be driven out of the parish. And remember this is not a punishment for any particular crime, only for being an unwelcome visitor – a 'foreigner' without any money.

That sounds a pretty grim prospect, so consider something much more positive. When the French king starts murdering his own people on account of their Protestantism, the English set aside their prejudices and provide a safe haven. Scottish towns too play their part in welcoming French refugees in the 1680s. Perhaps more than 70,000 Huguenots settle in Britain. In 1697 there are twenty-two French churches in London (nine of them in Spitalfields) and a hundred Huguenot clergymen administering to them.[51] Other nations have established colonies in London too. There are Dutch, Italian and Danish churches and, by 1700, a second synagogue.[52] There are also French and Dutch churches in other towns. Given all this, it is misleading to say that the people of Britain are unfriendly towards foreigners. There is just a greater antipathy to strangers in general – which, in an age of plague, religious war and daily violence, is unsurprising.

BLACK PEOPLE

There are relatively few black people in Britain during this period – probably 2,000–3,000 in 1660 and about 5,000 in 1700.[53] The great majority of them are the servants of the rich. Almost everyone with pretensions to fashionable living wants to have a black pageboy in his or her household, dressed in the finest livery. Wealthy ladies keep their black boys practically as pets. Charles II's mistress, the new duchess of Portsmouth, has herself painted by Sir Godfrey Kneller with her black pageboy in a fine coat. Plantation owners want to be waited on by black servants in their English homes in the same way as they are in the West Indies. Slavers whose ships take blacks from Africa to the West Indies like to be followed by teenage black servants as they stroll around Bristol or Liverpool. So if you find the name of a 'negro' or a 'blackamoor' in a country parish register, it is invariably because the local lord of the manor or his wife likes to have exotic servants about the house.

How are black people treated? It is difficult to generalise on this point. The concept of racism, as it exists in the modern world, has yet to develop, but there is certainly a sense of 'otherness' about those with a dark skin colour. That implies a number of preconceptions, some of which are deeply unpleasant. People associate blacks with godlessness, on account of their pagan origins in sub-Saharan Africa. On the whole the slave trade is approved of by society, for otherwise how else would the plantation owners obtain the labour necessary to produce the sugar that everyone craves these days? If people hear the word 'slave', they don't necessarily think of the transatlantic slave trade, let alone the working conditions in far-flung parts of the world; they think of the plight of enslaved white Christians in North Africa. Many maritime families have lost kinsmen to Barbary pirates, who raid villages and take ships at sea and sell those they capture in the slave markets of Tunis, Tripoli and Algiers. Some individuals do point out the inhumanity of the slave trade – the writer Aphra Behn is one, in her novel *Oroonoko* (1688) – but most people either don't think about the black slave trade or regard it as a necessary evil.

The association of blacks with godlessness and slavery leads to some searching questions about the nature of liberty. If a plantation owner brings a slave to England, is he still a slave on these shores? English law does not recognise a state of slavery, so the answer is a

clear-cut 'no' in many people's eyes. Edward Chamberlayne, writing
in 1676, declares that 'a foreign slave brought into England is, *ipso
facto*, free from slavery but not from ordinary service'.[54] This view is
upheld by the Lord Chief Justice, Sir John Holt, whose opinion is that
'as soon as a Negro comes into England he becomes free; one may
be a villein in England but not a slave'.[55] On top of this, many people
hold that, since it would be wrong to enslave another Christian, the
act of baptism liberates a slave. In 1667 a baptised black woman, Dinah
Black, who has been a servant to a rich woman in Bristol for the last
five years, is sold by her employer to a slave trader. The purchaser
intends to take her back to the West Indies, but Dinah refuses to go.
The aldermen of Bristol decide she cannot be compelled and order
her to be taken off the boat. Since her former employer does not wish
to take her back, she is free to work for someone else. Not all courts
see things this way, though. So strong is the law of property that many
decide that, if individuals have been bought in the past, then their
purchasers have the right to sell them again. In two legal cases in 1677
royal judges declare that, as non-Christians, blacks are not entitled to
the rights of ordinary men and thus, being merely property, their legal
owners have a right to compensation for losing them if they come to
Britain. The bishop of London worsens their plight still further in
1680 when he states categorically that baptism does not mean the
emancipation of a slave.[56]

Regardless of the legal position, the plain fact is that black people
are bought and sold in Britain as if they were slaves. When William
Hoyle is baptised in Bishopsteignton in Devon, he is described in the
parish register as 'a Negro belonging to the above Mr Cove, aged
about 17 or 18, his grandfathers were his Master and Mr William
Cumes'.[57] Note the language used here: William 'belongs' to his
'master', even though that man is his grandfather. Note also that he
is described as a 'negro' even though he is half white. The treatment
of black servants in England can be harsh too, reminiscent of slavery
conditions in the Plantations. Katherine Auker, a black woman, is
brought to London in 1684 by Robert Rich, a planter in Barbados.
She is tortured by her master and mistress and turned out, without
a discharge, so that no one else can employ her. Instead Mr Rich
arranges that she be arrested and locked up. He and his wife then
return to Barbados, leaving her in prison. Katherine applies to a court
in 1690 to be discharged from her employer's service so that she can

work for her living; the court releases her and allows her to work for whosoever will employ her – but only 'until such time as the said Rich shall return from Barbados'.[58] Clearly she will never be entirely free of this man. He owns her.

Although black servants in Britain are not called slaves, that is effectively what they are. Charles II buys a black pageboy from the marquess of Antrim for £50: that is not a contract with the servant, but with his vendor. Lord Sandwich similarly obtains 'a little Turk and a negro', as 'presents' for his daughters in 1662.[59] Blacks are generally made to wear collars of silver, copper or brass engraved with the name and coat of arms of their master or mistress. Even William III's favourite black servant wears one. If they run away, the advertisements in the press refer to their ages, the scars they bear, how well they speak English and the inscriptions on their collars. A few black men and women do manage to live independently, working as paid employees in other people's houses, but returning at night to their own homes. However, the vast majority are live-in servants. Pepys is pleased with his black kitchen maid's culinary skills in 1669, and his neighbour Sir William Batten has great respect for his own black manservant, Mingo, who accompanies his master to the tavern and turns out to be a surprisingly good dancer. However, you only have to go to the house of Sir Robert Vyner to see how some people view someone with black skin. After Sir Robert's black pageboy dies of consumption, he does not give him a Christian burial. Instead he has his body dried in an oven and keeps it as a curio in his house, on display in a box.[60]

Violence

You won't be surprised to hear that the society you are visiting is far more violent than the modern world. Britain has emerged from a prolonged period of civil war and bitter animosity. But still, with regard to England in particular, it is not as dangerous as you might think. The annual homicide rate is only about four deaths per 100,000: half the rate it was earlier in the century.[61] Three times as many people are killed in Scandinavia and six times as many in Italy. In fact, you're twice as likely to be murdered in late-seventeenth-century Belgium as you are in England.[62]

Nevertheless, you don't want to take any chances. After all, that homicide rate of four per 100,000 is four times higher than that of modern Britain. What's more, it does not reflect the greater level of non-fatal violence in society. As Monsieur Misson tells us:

> Anything that looks like fighting is delicious to an Englishman. If two little boys quarrel in the street, the passengers stop, make a ring around them in a moment, and set them against one another, that they may come to fisticuffs. When 'tis come to a fight, each pulls off his neckcloth and his waistcoat and gives them to hold to some of the standers-by; then they begin to brandish their fists in the air. The blows are all aimed at the face, they kick one another's shins, they tug one another by the hair, etcetera. He that has got the other down may give him one blow or two before he rises but no more; and let the boy get up ever so often, the other is obliged to box him again as often as he requires it. During the fight the ring of bystanders encourage the combatants with great delight of heart and never part them while they fight according to the rules. And these bystanders are not only other boys, porters and rabble but all sorts of men of fashion, some thrusting by the mob that they may see plain, others getting up on stalls, and all would hire places if scaffolds could be built.[63]

Given this propensity to violence, you need to be careful. Remember how easily that Welsh lord and the London cook come to blows. Don't presume that the crowd is more given over to fighting than gentlemen: 'the great' and 'the rich' are just as eager to punch, thump and stab people. In fact, gentlemen are among the worst offenders of the lot. The well off tend to be rather taller and stronger than ordinary working men, on account of their better diet in youth; they thus grow up believing that they can bully their way to getting what they want. In 1665 Lord Morley takes exception to something said to him in a tavern by one Henry Hastings, so he beats him to death. In 1685 the earl of Morton has an argument about a dog with one of his footmen and runs him through with his sword. In 1666 the marquess of Dorchester and the duke of Buckingham end up shoving each other and pulling hair and wigs in an argument over who is going to sit where in the House of Lords. The same year the duke of Buckingham proposes in the House of Lords to ban the importation of Irish beef and is challenged to a duel by the earl of Ossory for insulting his countrymen.

The duke accepts! Sadly, on this occasion, the king intervenes and sends both men to the Tower of London to calm down. Two days later the duke of Buckingham argues with the marquess of Dorchester about a patent and challenges him to a duel – and back to the Tower he goes.[64]

As you can tell, this is the golden age of the duel.[65] Whereas most aspects of fisticuffs, fighting, brawling, wrestling, scrapping, skirmishing and rioting are self-explanatory and don't differ that much down the ages, duelling is another story. Duels are private fights in which gentlemen may settle their personal differences with honour. The emphasis is heavily on the *gentlemen*: ordinary people do not fight duels. Tradesmen and labourers simply go outside to beat the living daylights out of each other – and sometimes don't even bother leaving the room. For gentlemen, everything is governed by etiquette. And whereas most of the time tradesmen and labourers give each other sore heads and bloody noses, gentlemen frequently kill each other.

So why do men fight duels? The general answer seems to be: why not? Lord Chesterfield fights a duel over the price of a mare. The earl of Tankerville calls the duke of Albemarle's new gun a 'coxcomb's fancy', whereupon the latter challenges him to a duel – with swords (guns won't be used for duels until 1711). Sherrington Talbot is killed in a duel that follows an argument about which side fought best during the rebellion of the duke of Monmouth. The duke of Buckingham is challenged to a duel by the earl of Sandwich about the duke's refusal to pay his losses on a game of cards. Conyers Seymour is killed in a duel after being challenged by someone who doesn't like the way he dresses. Robert Wolseley fights the Honourable William Wharton in 1689 on the grounds that he doesn't like the man's poetry: he kills him with a wound to the buttocks. (How very honourable.) But perhaps the prize for the most pointless duel ever goes to Henry Bellasis and his great friend and drinking partner Tom Porter, the playwright. While they are drinking in a coffee house and speaking a little too loudly, someone asks Bellasis if he and Porter are arguing. Bellasis says no, he is only giving Porter some advice, adding that 'I never quarrel, I strike'. Porter carelessly quips that he doubts any man in England would dare strike him, whereupon Bellasis does exactly that: he punches Porter playfully on the ear. Porter is a bit put out by this and asks Bellasis to step outside with him. They do so, but Bellasis is so drunk he simply gets into his coach to go home. Porter stops the driver and invites

Bellasis down to fight him. Having allowed Bellasis to descend in peace, Porter draws his sword. In the fight that ensues both men are injured – Bellasis fatally so. As he gushes blood, he urges Porter to flee quickly: he will endeavour to stand on his feet as long as he can so that Porter can get away. Bellasis is as good as his word. The coroner later returns a verdict of death 'from unknown causes'.[66]

Traditionally a duel only involves the offended person and the offender; however, during this period the opponents appoint seconds to support them, and frequently the seconds fight too. Henry Jermyn (nephew of the man who built so much of the West End of London) entices a succession of well-to-do ladies into bed with him, including the countess of Shrewsbury. As a result, he is challenged to a duel by Colonel Thomas Howard. Each man chooses a second: Jermyn chooses Giles Rawlings and Howard selects Colonel Cary Dillon. They all meet in St James's Park on 19 August 1662. In the ensuing fight, Jermyn is run through three times by Colonel Howard and left for dead; Rawlings is killed outright by Colonel Dillon. The victors flee on horseback. What is remarkable about this duel is that Jermyn and Rawlings don't actually know what the duel is about; only later, after he has recovered, does Jermyn find out that Howard has also been sleeping with the countess of Shrewsbury. Another example of an extended duel is also the result of the countess of Shrewsbury's intimate favours. Her husband challenges her new lover, the duke of Buckingham, to a duel. It takes place on 16 January 1668 in a field at Barn Elms. The duke chooses two seconds to fight alongside him, Sir Robert Holmes, a naval hero, and Captain William Jenkins, an officer in the Horse Guards. The earl of Shrewsbury is assisted by Sir John Talbot (father of the aforementioned Sherrington Talbot) and Bernard Howard. The earl is mortally wounded by the duke, who runs his sword through Shrewsbury's right breast. Sir Robert wounds Sir John in the arm. On the duke's side, Mr Howard kills Captain Jenkins. If you take my advice, I would steer clear of the countess of Shrewsbury's many lovers, just in case you are asked to be a second. And certainly don't get entangled with the lady herself.

Why does the government not stop duelling? Easier said than done. Ever since the practice was introduced in the sixteenth century (from its spiritual home, Italy) monarchs have been trying to ban it. However, men who are angry enough to fight to the death are not put off by the prospect of a heavy fine. Charles II issues proclamations against duelling in 1660 and 1680; otherwise he does nothing to stop it.[67] He doesn't want to alienate those aristocrats and gentlemen for whom honour is so important. Nor do Members of Parliament, who debate several Bills that would entail duellists forfeiting half, or all, of their estate to the Crown. The basic fact is that duelling with swords is dangerous – far more so than fighting with pistols – and it requires enormous courage.[68] That in turn commands respect. If men stare death in the face, overcome their fear and prove victorious – demonstrating many of the virtues that society admires – it seems churlish and ignoble to punish them.

Cruelty

Monsieur Misson thinks there is something soft about the English. He observes that they do not hurt criminals in the extreme ways they employ in France – that is, they do not break people on the wheel, they do not rip them apart by having their limbs tied to four horses, which are then driven in opposite directions, and they do not tear their flesh from their bones with red-hot pincers.[69] And it is true that, if you have been watching the English for a *very* long time – say, the last 150 years – you will notice that society is not as brutal as it once was. As we have seen, the hanging of witches is in decline, they don't burn heretics any more and they don't boil poisoners to death (as they did in the reign of Henry VIII). In Halifax, the famous 'gibbet' or guillotine used to behead malefactors since the Middle Ages is employed for the last time in 1650. In 1661 the king offers fifty people condemned to death the option of being transported to Jamaica as indentured servants; they all accept.[70] The Bill of Rights read to William III in 1689 specifically forbids the king from using 'cruel and unusual punishments' on his subjects, thereby practically outlawing torture. Some would say that no longer hanging women for many first felonies, from 1691, is a sign that Misson is right: the English really have gone soft.

You, however, will no doubt find this new, 'softer' England still incredibly barbaric. Even some of the clemency is not what it seems. The reason why the king offers transportation as an alternative to being hanged is the labour shortage in the Plantations. In England, you will see traitors cut down from the gallows and eviscerated alive. Heretics are no longer burnt at the stake, but women still are – for killing a husband or an employer, or for counterfeiting the coin of the realm. Every county town has its gallows and its droves of vagrants and thieves being flogged until their backs are bloody. Indeed, the liberal use of the whip is seen by many as merciful, for it inflicts a punishment from which the culprit will soon recover, whereas cutting off a man's ears and branding him tends to be permanent.

Cruelty extends far beyond the methods of punishing people. You see it reflected in those who 'spirit away' men and women to become indentured servants in the West Indies – the fate that so nearly befalls Edward Barlow. These days Londoners have to worry that, when they walk down an alley, someone will bundle them down to the riverbank and put them in a boat bound for the West Indies. In 1670 a young apprentice called Roger Pym is seized by a mariner and forced on to a ship, sold to the captain and taken off to the Plantations, never to be seen again.[71] Samuel Embry goes to court to prosecute Simon Harris 'for spiriting away one Mary Embry his sister and selling her for 48s., to be transported beyond the seas to Barbados'. Some cases are utterly tragic. A man called Walter Scot loses his wife when she is kidnapped and put on board a ship bound for Barbados. Margaret Caser loses her only son Thomas and a two-month-old baby in her charge when Richard Specke, a waterman of Shadwell, abducts them and sells them to the boatswain of the *John and Katherine* to take to Barbados. Women can be just as cruel as men in this regard. Sarah Sharp is

> a common taker up of children, and a setter to betray young men and maidens to be conveyed into ships ... She confessed to one Mr Guy that she hath at this time four persons aboard a ship whereof one is a child about eleven years of age, all to be transported to foreign parts as Barbados and Virginia.[72]

In the home, behaviour that seems cruel to us is considered normal, even a moral duty. When Pepys discovers that one of his servant boys has stolen and drunk some whey from the kitchen, he

> with my whip did whip him until I was not able to stir, and yet I could not make him confess ... And last, not willing to let him go away a conqueror, I took him in task again and pulled off his frock to his shirt, and whipped him till he did confess that he did drink the whey, which he hath denied ... So to bed with my arm very weary.[73]

The servant boy, Wayneman Birch, suffers considerably from Pepys's repeated attempts to thrash him into an acceptable moral shape. And this is a boy whom Pepys claims to love, if only for the sake of his sister (for whom Pepys has a great fondness). Eventually, in the summer of 1663, Wayneman is dismissed. The following November, he is sent to Barbados.[74]

When men fight publicly to the death and privately beat their women, children and servants, you can imagine how they treat animals. As you will see in the final chapter of this book, cockfighting, bull baiting and bear baiting are all still extremely popular. The Commonwealth banned these games not because they are cruel sports, but because people enjoyed them too much – they were too much of an indulgence, in Puritan eyes. In 1656 all the bears at the Bear Garden in London were shot by a firing squad, with the sole exception of one cub. It is fair to say that most people are delighted to see blood sports back. Besides being popular entertainments, they form an important part of the ritual year. Schellinks records that on Shrove Tuesday 1662:

> In London one sees in every street, wherever one goes, many apprentice boys running with, under their arms, a cock with a string on its foot, on which is a spike, which they push firmly into the ground between the stones. They always look for an open space and, for a penny, let the people throw their cudgel from a good distance at the cock, and he who kills the cock gets it. In the country or with country folk they bury a cock with only its head above the ground and blindfold a person and turn him two or three times round himself, and he then tries to hit the cock with a flail, and the one who hits it or comes closest to it gets the prize.[75]

It gets worse. Often on some of the steeper streets of the city, such as Fish Street, you'll see carters and carriage drivers whipping their horses, and all the street boys and passers-by joining in, thrashing the poor beasts.[76] Cats are rounded up and burnt alive on 5 November – the gruesome details follow in the next chapter. Across the country, hedgehogs, badgers, foxes and stoats are all killed on sight. So too are whales, especially when they swim up a river like the Thames, as they do in 1658 and 1699. In the modern world, we would try to guide a whale back to open sea. In the seventeenth century, people's instinct is to kill it first, then consider what they are going to do with it. All that flesh and oil – it has to be good for something.

There are some signs that attitudes are changing. Cultivated men such as John Evelyn are disgusted by the restoration of baiting games:

> I was forced to accompany some friends to the Bear Garden etcetera, where there was cock fighting, dog-fighting, bear & bull baiting, it being a famous day for all these butcherly sports, or rather barbarous cruelties ... There were two poor dogs killed & so all ended with the ape on horseback, & I most heartily weary of the rude & dirty pastime.[77]

The 'ape on horseback' refers to what is traditionally the final act at a bear-baiting show. A monkey is tied fast to an old horse and then the young dogs are released to bring it down; the monkey screams in panic as the dogs bite the horse and kill it. Most of the crowd loves the spectacle, but clearly not John Evelyn.

He is not alone. Chamberlayne declares in 1676 that 'cock-fighting seems to all foreigners too childish and unsuitable for the gentry, and for the common people, bull-baiting and bear-baiting seem too cruel; and for the citizens football and throwing at cocks very uncivil, rude and barbarous'.[78] I wonder if townsmen and -women are becoming more considerate towards animals through having pets, and thus thinking of creatures in terms of sentiment rather than as either food or vermin. King Charles keeps spaniels and allows them to roam wherever they want, even during state occasions. Elizabeth Pepys buys a pet dog to accompany her in her loneliness in 1660 (although her husband shuts it in the cellar as it is very poorly house-trained). At the end of 1660 the Pepys household also acquires a cat to control a mouse problem at home, and in January 1661 two canaries enter the small menagerie. A whistling blackbird later comes to join them. Pepys also has a monkey but, when it escapes, he grows angry 'and so I did strike her till she was almost dead'.[79]

So much for my theory about sentiment. Clearly, the shift away from cruelty to animals is a long, slow, complicated process.

The Spirit of Adventure

All the negative things you've heard about the character of the people in this chapter – the superstitions, witchcraft, religious hatred, xeno-phobia, violence and cruelty – might leave you with the impression that the British are a miserable, prickly, narrow-minded, selfish bunch. Only the rakes sound like any fun. But these people have a light side as well as a dark one. As we saw at the start of this chapter, they are driven by an intense curiosity. One of the ways in which this is manifested is through the travels of those who desire to see the world. The fruit of their exploits and enquiries inform and affect the whole population.

To appreciate their drive, you need to have an idea of how far people normally travel. Although 'the poor' and 'the miserable' at the very bottom of society might be permanently on the move – whether as beggars or as conscripts in the armed forces – generally speaking, crossing long distances is governed by wealth and necessity. Country folk regularly attend their local market, but in England that will always be within 6 or 7 miles of their home. On occasion, they may have to visit a church court in another town or cathedral city, forcing them to travel 10–20 miles. Some tradesmen, such as masons and ship's carpenters, cover considerable distances on account of their work. A schoolmaster may travel to a different part of the country to serve as a tutor or take up a teaching position in a grammar school. Over the course of a year, a sought-after physician may be called to attend patients up to 30 or 40 miles away, depending on his reputation. The wealthier sorts undertake long journeys for education, to vote, to prove a will or to attend a law court. The families of the great and the rich tend to be spread across the nation, living in different counties. They and their servants frequently have to make long journeys for social visits and estate administration. They also have to travel to London for business affairs or to attend Parliament and the court. In the country, they have to move around their locality a great deal in order to fulfil their responsibilities as magistrates, lords lieutenant and military officers.

All these reasons to travel have been established for centuries. What is novel is the desire to travel for the sake of travelling – to see new sights, learn new things and maintain or improve one's health. Celia Fiennes expresses the reasons why ladies and gentlemen should travel around Britain:

> If all persons, both ladies [and] much more gentlemen, would spend some of their time in journeys to visit their native land, and be curious to inform themselves and make observations of the pleasant prospects, good buildings, different produces and manufactures of each place ... [it] would be a sovereign remedy to cure or preserve [them] from these

epidemic diseases of vapours, [to which] should I add laziness? It would also form such an idea of England, add much to its glory and esteem in our minds and cure the evil itch of over-valuing foreign parts, [and] at least furnish them with an equivalent to entertain strangers when among us, or inform them when abroad of their native country, which has often been a reproach to the English: ignorance, and being strangers to themselves. Nay the ladies might have matter not unworthy their observation, so subject for conversation ... which would spare them the uneasy thoughts [of] how to pass away tedious days, and time would not be a burden when not at a card or dice table ... But [it is] much more requisite for gentlemen in the general service of their country at home or abroad, in town or country, especially those that serve in Parliament, to know and inform themselves [of] the nature of [the] land, the genius of the inhabitants, so as to promote and improve manufacture and trade.[80]

Many of the virtues that Celia Fiennes associates with domestic travel can be applied to foreign trips too. The term 'Grand Tour' is first coined in 1670 by Richard Lassels in his book *An Italian Voyage* to describe the Continental journeys undertaken by hundreds of young English gentlemen each year. They make their way to Dover, cross the Channel to Calais and aim straight for Paris. From there they journey down to Italy. Rome is always the most popular destination, followed closely by Venice. Other must-see places for Englishmen are Parma, Piacenza, Bologna, Genoa, Lucca, Florence, Siena, Viterbo, Arezzo, Perugia, Terni and Naples. The southernmost destination for most gentlemen is Paestum, at which point they will turn back and visit all the places they missed on the way south, delaying their return to England for as long as possible. Most young men spend between eighteen months and two years on such a journey. Some Grand Tours last even longer. Thomas Herbert, the brother of the earl of Pembroke, spends three years travelling around France and Italy in 1676–9. Robert Spencer, earl of Sunderland, spends four years in France, Spain, Switzerland and Italy in 1661–5. Parents hope that their sons will learn something along the way, so they send them in the company of tutors, whose duty it is to keep their charges' attention focused on the artworks and architecture of the Italian Renaissance, and to steer them away from all the pretty Italian women. This is quite a tall order – especially when the tutor is effectively a servant and not in a position to tell his young lord what not to do. Many Grand Tours descend into debauchery and whoring as soon as the newly liberated young buck reaches Paris. To be fair, however, many are genuinely educational. The naturalist John Ray sails to Calais in 1663 specifically to record all the birds, beasts, fish and insects that are not to be found in England: over the next three years he travels through Flanders, the Low Countries, southern Germany, Austria, Italy, Sicily, Switzerland and France. Robert Boyle's five years abroad are spent studying subjects as diverse as ethics, history, natural philosophy and fortification. Edmond Halley's Grand Tour in 1680–82 sees him monitoring the progress of comets with Giovanni Cassini at the Paris Observatory.

English gentlemen and ladies are also able to learn from those foreign travellers who come to these shores. We have already encountered some of them – Willem Schellinks from Holland, Lorenzo Magalotti from Italy and Monsieur Misson from France. Thousands of others arrive from almost every corner of the world. Ambassadors from the king of Siam (Thailand) come to London in 1682. John Evelyn entertains the Frenchman Jean-Baptiste Chardin in 1680, hearing of his travels to the East Indies, Persia, the Black Sea, the Caspian Sea, Baghdad, Nineveh and Persepolis. One of the most remarkable of all visitors is the Latin-speaking Chinese intellectual Shen Fuzong. When he comes to England with the Flemish Jesuit Philippe Couplet, in 1687, James II orders Godfrey Kneller to paint a portrait of him in his Chinese robes. Shen spends some time at Oxford helping to catalogue the Chinese books in the Bodleian Library and providing information on everything from Chinese maps and calendars to mathematics and games. The same year, Couplet produces *Confucius Sinarum philosophus*, which introduces three of the four canonical works of Confucianism to Western scholars. Items brought to these shores by traders hint at some of the cultural differences to be encountered on the other side of the world – Chinese porcelain and furniture, for example, or Indian cotton, chintzes, rugs and tea. In these respects, the English are the very opposite of 'unfriendly' to foreigners: exotic goods from the Middle East and Far East are welcomed as never before.

On top of all these different ways of learning about the rest of the world, you must bear in mind the growing diplomatic reach of the king of England. There are English ambassadors resident at the courts of Denmark, Flanders, France, the Holy Roman Empire, the Imperial Diet, the Hanseatic League, Tuscany, Venice, Poland, Portugal, Prussia,

Russia, Savoy, Spain, Sweden and Turkey.[81] Additionally in 1676 there are consuls stationed in Aleppo, Smyrna, Zante, Algiers, Tunis, Tripoli, Messina, Naples, Leghorn, Genoa, Marseilles, Alicante, Malaga, Cadiz, Seville and the Canary Islands. Not only do diplomats in these places despatch information about their host countries back to Britain, but they also dine out themselves on their experiences when they return. Then there are the overseas possessions of the English Crown. Governors or deputy governors exercise British rule over New England, Virginia, Carolina, New York, Newfoundland, Jamaica, Barbados, Bermuda, the Leeward Islands, St Christopher Island (St Kitts), Nevis, Jersey, Guernsey, Bombay (India), Fort St George (India), Bantam (Indonesia), Tangiers (North Africa) and Guinea (West Africa), as well as other territories that are dependent on these states.[82] Further settlements, such as Willoughbyland (now Suriname) and British Honduras (Belize), have only recently been settled. The East India Company, the Royal Africa Company, the Levant Company and the Hudson's Bay Company all trade with their respective parts of the world, bringing back information and local products. Although the British do not have a settlement in Australasia, the land is known about: Australia was discovered in 1607 and New Zealand in 1642. Thus atlases and globes produced in this period will look familiar to you: they just lack a few details here and there.[83]

The enormous reach of Britain means that it is not just gentlemen who bring back knowledge of the rest of the world. Most of the 50,000 seamen employed by the Royal Navy and English merchant ships travel far from home and see things they could never have anticipated in their home parishes. Edward Barlow's long career endows him with anecdotes that would make any barnacled midshipman proud – except that he does not simply tell tall stories: he really has seen the world. William Dampier, who also goes to sea as a boy, becomes the third Englishman to circumnavigate the Earth in the years 1679–91 (after Sir Francis Drake in 1577–80 and Thomas Cavendish in 1586–8). He first leaves for the Mosquito Coast, but soon finds himself in the company of buccaneers in the West Indies and Virginia; he then sails around Cape Horn and across the Pacific in search of the Manila treasure galleon and lands on the coast of New Holland (Australia), which he explores for two months in early 1688. Returning home via Vietnam, Sumatra and India, he finally comes ashore in England on 16 September 1691. His memoir of the trip, *A*

New Voyage Round the World (1697), is an instant bestseller, full of information about the flora and fauna of the places he has visited, as well as the people, the islands and the buccaneers. Everyone wants to meet him. Pepys and Evelyn both invite him to dinner. He goes on to sail around the world twice more, becoming the first man ever to circumnavigate the world three times.

Joseph Pitts is another accidental explorer: a seaman remarkable for being the first Englishman to travel to Mecca and write an appraisal of the holy place, which is forbidden to non-Muslims. He is born in Exeter and in 1678, at the age of fourteen, joins a fishing boat bound for Newfoundland. On the ship's return, off the coast of Spain, the crew is captured by Algerian slavers; Pitts and his shipmates are all cast into the hold in chains. In Algiers he is sold in the slave market and is beaten by his master for being Christian. Having been sold a second time, his new owner decides he must convert Pitts to Islam. So he has him strung up by his feet and beaten on his soles until the blood runs down his legs. After several days of this, having his bloody feet thrust into salt water and being beaten on the belly while still suspended, Pitts agrees to convert. One positive result of his conversion is that, after he is sold a third time to a kindly old man, he is able to accompany his master on the pilgrimage to Mecca. He travels throughout North Africa, visiting the ruins of Alexandria on the way. At the port there he notices an English ship from Lympstone in Devon and meets a sailor whom he knows from home (now that's a 'small-world story' if ever there was one). After returning from the pilgrimage he is set free and sails to Smyrna, where a Cornishman pays for his voyage to Leghorn in Italy. From there he walks home, arriving back in England after being away for sixteen years. Pitts writes and publishes a book called *A faithful account of the Religion and the Manners of Mahometans* in which he explains, in an extraordinarily fair and level-headed way, what Islam is like and how people in Algiers really live. As an objective and dispassionate account of a foreign people and their religion and customs, it is worthy of the pen of a Fellow of the Royal Society.

The result of all these much-publicised travels is that, wherever you go, people talk about the world. The poor are amazed by the stories brought back by sailors. The rich discuss the further-flung reaches of the globe with the sure knowledge relayed to them by their peers and what they have read in books by men such as Dampier and Pitts. The wider world becomes a great topic of debate to which everyone can add their own opinion. Pepys sits down one afternoon in the Fleece Tavern and argues with two escaped white slaves that Algiers is more lenient to Christian slaves than the Plantations are to black ones: they soon put him right on the subject, telling him about the constant beatings on the feet and the belly. Evelyn has dinner-table conversations about events in China and Japan. Merchants from Königsberg tell their hosts in London how people in their country live in winter, fishing with nets half a mile long through holes in the ice and taking the fish to market in sledges, packed with snow.[84] One day you may be discussing the Turkish military advance into Germany and how the German emperor drinks too much, and another day you might be talking about the unscrupulousness of Moroccan warlords, or chatting about the Hottentots' practice of semi-castration, or gazing in astonishment at a book in Chinese or Russian.[85] The newspapers help circulate the knowledge of foreign events, so that you may find yourself in a London coffee shop reading about the defeat of Don John of Austria at Ameixial at the end of June 1663, or the destruction of Lima in a major earthquake at the end of May 1688.[86] In fact, literate Londoners are just as much aware of recent events elsewhere in the known world as most modern people – with the principal difference that there is a time delay proportionate to the distance that the news has to travel. The Battle of Ameixial in Portugal, for example, takes place on 8 June 1663, three weeks before it appears in a London newspaper. The earthquake that destroys Lima actually happens on 20 October 1687, seven months before the London newspapers report it.

Scientific Knowledge

On 28 November 1660, a committee of learned gentlemen meets in London to discuss the formation of a new college or philosophical society for the exploration of scientific matters. Two years later their organisation receives a royal charter and becomes the Royal Society. Three years after that it starts publishing its *Philosophical Transactions*. As you are no doubt aware, this is a supremely important development in the history of science. It provides the institutional focus for inter-national excellence in natural philosophy (as science is called at this time), which is just emerging as the prime discipline for understanding the depth and breadth of Creation.

This emphasis on Creation, with its religious connotations, is important. In the modern world we are prone to see religion and science as operating antagonistically, but in the seventeenth century they are one and the same thing. Previously unknown plants and animals discovered in the New World are immediately understood to have been created by God. People want to know their properties, to see whether they were put on Earth to be useful to mankind in some way – as medicines or dyes, for instance. Scientists are thus driven on by both their thirst for knowledge and by their quest for spiritual enlightenment. Robert Boyle is particularly interested in the nature and extent of Creation: not only does this intensify his interest in the natural world but it leads him to pay for the translation of the Bible into foreign languages and to send out missionaries to convert indigenous peoples of other continents. Isaac Newton knows the Bible better than anyone, and writes several theological treatises alongside his scientific works. The astronomer John Flamsteed is an ordained clergyman. Robert Hooke's depictions of the minutiae of life are part of his attempt to show the machinery of Creation in greater detail. It is hardly surprising that so many scientific breakthroughs are made in this period. As history has shown repeatedly over the centuries, if you really want to make something happen, make it a spiritual quest.

The religious aspect of scientific discovery is, however, only half the story. The other half is collaboration – and that is where the Royal Society proves to be so important. All these men could have pursued their research independently, treading their separate paths as pilgrims of truth. But the Royal Society brings them together in a great scientific crusade, and the publication of the *Philosophical Transactions* embodies and invigorates this collective enterprise. Ideas don't just filter down into society, they positively cascade. Robert Hooke is engaged by the Royal Society to undertake new experiments every week – thereby becoming the world's first paid professional research scientist. He demonstrates that he can keep a dog alive by blowing air into its motionless lungs, facilitates a blood transfusion and gives a report of skin grafting on a dog. Hundreds of discoveries are reported, not only in the pages of the *Philosophical Transactions* but also in the scientists' own books. The leading figures become internationally famous. John Evelyn remarks that a traveller in England who has not visited Robert Boyle at work in his laboratory is 'missing one of the most valuable objects of our nation'.[87] Hooke is no less renowned after his *Micrographia* is published in 1665, largely on account of its incredibly detailed illustrations of familiar objects observed through a microscope. You are probably familiar with the massive, 18-inch image of a flea, as well as his fine engravings of a gnat, a fly's eye and a louse. Astronomers like John Flamsteed and Edmond Halley reveal that there are thousands of stars that the naked eye cannot perceive. Isaac Newton's fame spreads abroad with his papers on optics and, later, his *Principia Mathematica*. All these men become household names – to the extent that playwrights lampoon them on the London stage. Even if you are not a natural philosopher, you can hardly be unaware of what is happening around you.

The Scientific Revolution (as it will become known to future historians) is heavily centred on London. Of course other countries contribute ideas and discoveries – some of the most important thinkers of the age are based on the Continent, including Gottfried Leibniz, Christiaan Huygens and Jakob Bernoulli – but London is the epicentre. The Royal Society is one reason. Another is the number of instrument makers based in the capital. If you want to buy a microscope, telescope, thermometer, barometer or clock, London is the place to visit. If you are a maker of such objects, again London is the place to be, for this is where people will pay for precision devices.

There is no better example of a craftsman who takes advantage of the demand for scientific instruments than Thomas Tompion, the father of English watchmaking. A blacksmith's son from Bedfordshire, he moves to London in about 1660 to learn the trade of a clockmaker. It is perfect timing, if you will pardon the pun. In 1657 the Dutch mathematician Christiaan Huygens builds the first pendulum clock and, almost immediately, it is copied everywhere. Soon Tompion is making better pendulum clocks than everyone else. When Huygens writes to the Royal Society in 1675 announcing his invention of a watch with a balance-spring, Robert Hooke complains to Charles II that he had the same idea fifteen years earlier; so the king asks Tompion to make just such a watch to Hooke's design. The following year Tompion becomes the obvious choice to make a pair of highly accurate clocks for the newly built Royal Observatory. The resulting machines, with 13ft-long pendulums, are so sophisticated that they run for a whole year on a single wind and have mechanisms to facilitate their continued action even while being wound. Their accuracy (within two seconds a day) is a phenomenal achievement, coming less than twenty years after the invention of the pendulum. Tompion's business grows rapidly after that. He employs dozens of apprentices and skilled workers on his production line of precision timepieces. In his highly regulated factory, six sequences of manufacturer's reference numbers are developed, for watches (from 1681), spring-driven clocks (from 1682), weight-driven clocks (from 1682), repeating watches (from 1688), alarm watches (from 1692) and watches with a special virgule escapement (from 1695). He also continues to make highly specialised instruments for astronomers, and barometers and clocks of exceptional craftsmanship for the royal families of Europe.[88]

Science is more noticeable than ever in the form of domestic technology and machines. It enters Samuel Pepys's house in the form of a watch, a thermometer, a microscope, a telescope, a monetary calculator and a pantograph (a device for copying images at the same scale). Even those who cannot afford such expensive instruments can see technology in public places. If you stroll through St James's Park in October 1660 you'll see a whole display of water-lifting machines, including an Archimedes screw designed by Ralph Greatorex.[89] Sir Samuel Morland sends a jet of water 60ft high over the top of Windsor Castle in 1681; smaller and more practical machines for use in mines, houses, ships, wells, draining schemes, garden water fountains and public drinking-water pumps are available from his London shop in Great Russell Street. Morland also develops a speaking trumpet or loudhailer that can make the human voice heard over the distance of a mile.[90] Right at the end of our period, Thomas Savery, a gentleman from Devon, devises a steam engine for pumping water out of mines. He obtains a patent for it in 1698 and demonstrates it in front of the Royal Society the following year.

The zeal of all these scientists and engineers allows them to break boundaries that have restrained mankind for centuries. Nothing seems to daunt them. When experiments with blood transfusions in dogs prove promising, the question arises as to whether humans can benefit too. Accordingly a gentleman called Arthur Coga is recruited to have sheep's blood pumped into his veins: a procedure that he survives more than once. Charles II is in stitches when he is told that the Royal Society is trying to establish the weight of air. Hooke proceeds nonetheless and manages to weigh 119 pints of air at $2\frac{1}{8}$ ounces, which is not that far off (the correct weight is just over 3 ounces).[91] When a treasure ship laden with gold and ivory goes down off the south coast of England in April 1691, Edmond Halley proposes a new form of diving suit to allow the recovery of the valuable cargo. Flying is another subject to which the scientists return time and time again. Hooke experiments with gunpowder-fired flight, and with gears to give men mechanical wings; he is likely to bore you for hours with his discussions on the subject. One of the few barriers they do not tackle is that of distant time. Everyone still believes the world was created just before dusk on 23 October 4004 BC, in line with Bishop Ussher's calculations. As a result, when John Conyers discovers a flint hand-axe near some elephant bones in London in 1679, people conclude that it must have been used by an Ancient Briton to kill one of the elephants brought to Britain by the Emperor Claudius in AD 43 – for how else could the elephant have arrived on these shores?[92] No one imagines that the axe is 350,000 years old and that elephants were then indigenous to Britain.

Perhaps the most significant shift of thinking connected with all this scientific work is the belief that everything can be subject to quantification. Newton can mathematically determine the depth of a film of air between a lens and flat sheet of glass to the accuracy of $\frac{1}{100,000}$ of an inch; Robert Boyle can calculate the relationship between the volume and pressure of a gas; Flamsteed the progress of comets; Halley the life expectancy of the population; and so on. Quantification allows certainty and, in a highly uncertain world, that appeals to many people in many walks of life. Bishop Ussher's calculation of the date of Creation might seem silly to us but it needs to be seen in the context of this desire to resolve everything into exact quantities, for the sake of certainty. For this reason, quantification quickly becomes fundamental to practical as well as theoretical initiatives, and mathematics acquires a new status. It underpins the novel business of fire insurance in London. It is important for the building of larger ships and the more accurate surveying of land for new streets and squares. People start to quantify society and its problems too. In 1662 John Graunt attempts to calculate for the first time the true population of the city of London, the age bands of its inhabitants and other factors. His influential friend William Petty takes up the quantitative baton in his *Political Arthithmetick* (1676) and declares: 'instead of using only comparative and superlative words and intellectual arguments, I have taken the course (as a specimen of the political arithmetic I have long aimed at) to express myself in terms of number, weight or measure'.[93] You don't need to be a scientist to see how much the modern world owes to the rise of statistical thinking in the Restoration period: it underpins all the technological and social progress on which we depend.

Education

This burning desire to find out about the Earth and to measure every-thing in it might give you the impression that educational standards are riding the crest of a wave. This is, sadly, not the case. Schools have failed to move with the times. They tend to be bound by their charters and the restrictive statutes of their well-meaning founders, who could never have foreseen the different demands on young minds. Thus many old grammar schools teach Greek, Latin and Hebrew, but not mathematics, chemistry or physics. When you come across someone celebrating a child prodigy, it is never because he has achieved a breakthrough in natural philosophy: it is normally because he has mastered a biblical language at a very young age. William Wotton, for example, is praised by Evelyn for his ability to read Latin, Greek and Hebrew at five years old, and Arabic and Aramaic at thirteen.[94] The fire that excites members of the Royal Society tends not to burn in the hearts of those whose sole ambition is to spend their careers bedecked with laurel wreaths in ivy-clad educational establishments.

Not everyone goes to school. Most boys whose fathers are husbandmen or labourers receive no more education than regular admonishments on a Sunday from their resident clergyman. However, if you are lucky enough to be launched on the path of learning, you will begin by being taught to read at a petty school for a couple of years, from the age of five or six, principally using a hornbook. This is a single page on which the letters of the alphabet, the numerals and the Lord's Prayer are written or printed, set in a wooden frame and covered with a thin sheet of translucent horn. The idea is that you will learn to recognise and copy these symbols. By the age of seven or eight you should have learnt to read and be ready for the next stage of your education. However, this is where you might start to doubt that going to school in Restoration Britain marks you out as 'lucky'.

A great deal of teaching comes down to discipline. Rows of boys sit on long hard benches or 'forms' in unheated schoolrooms from 6 a.m. to 6 p.m. in summer (7 a.m. to 5 p.m. in winter), forced by their masters to repeat old texts parrot-fashion, and they are beaten if they fail. Schools are not places that encourage enquiry but, rather, subservience to tradition. In fact, the Royal Society's motto *Nullius in Verba* ('Take nobody's word for it') is directly aimed at this intellectual obsequiousness. Various educational reformers try to introduce more practical syllabuses but, even in their academic utopias, the teaching is invariably conducted in Latin and is backward-looking.

You might wonder why anyone should want their son to go to a school where he will freeze, have to speak in Latin and be beaten regularly. The answer is, of course, that it will elevate him in the social hierarchy. A public school like Westminster, whose pupils learn to make speeches and compose verses in Latin, Greek and Hebrew – and even in Arabic – costs the princely sum of £40 per boy per year.[95] On top of this there are extra fees for penmanship, provision of Bibles and other texts, paper and school uniforms. It all adds up to far more than most people earn. You might wonder whether it is worth it, when your ability to write verses in Ancient Greek is unlikely to be in demand at court (or anywhere else, for that matter). But it is not *what* you learn that matters so much as *where* you learn it. An expensive education leaves the have-nots in no doubt that they will never achieve parity with you – the cream of society – no matter how clever they are. The few exceptions to this are those boys who are able to take advantage of educational endowments to get a free place at a grammar school and then secure themselves a place at a university by going up as a *servitor* (a quasi-servant to richer students). If they don't go to university, most grammar-school boys will leave school at about fifteen and follow their father's trade or commence a seven-year apprenticeship. If you do not follow the path from petty school to grammar school, you might be given a place at a charity school (if you are an orphan) or be sent to a private boarding school, but most probably you will not benefit from any further formal education. The sailor Edward Barlow is quite remarkable in that he teaches himself to read and write – but he does so while a prisoner of war in Batavia (modern Jakarta), in Indonesia. Conditions there are almost as bad as those in an English public school.

As you can see, literacy is very closely related to status. Almost all of 'the great', 'the rich' and 'the middle sort' are literate and many of them trilingual – in English, Latin and French. If you serve an apprenticeship and become one of 'the working trades', your master will probably encourage you to practise your reading and writing: two out of three English craftsmen and tradesmen can write in the 1680s and 1690s. Literacy is less common among country people: about half of all yeomen can write their names, but only a quarter of husbandmen. As for the poor, only about one in five servants in England can sign their names, and even fewer labourers. Overall, 55 per cent of Englishmen are signature-literate by 1700. This is good in comparison to most of Europe but not as impressive as Scotland, where, thanks to the Calvinist educational tradition and a national network of parish schools, 67 per cent of people can sign their names. To be precise: literacy among Scottish tradesmen increases from about 50 per cent in 1660 to 80 per cent by 1700. Almost three-quarters of Scottish farmers can sign their names by 1700, and the number of servants and labourers who can do so increases from one in ten in 1660 to one in three by the end of the century.[96]

The education of women is a very different matter. As Hannah Woolley puts it in her *Guide to the Female Sex*, 'I cannot but complain of, and must condemn, the great negligence of parents, in letting the fertile ground of their daughters lie fallow, yet send[ing] the barren noddles of their sons to the University.'[97] She is of course talking about the great and the rich, but it is fair to say that parents across the social spectrum consider it more important for their daughters to acquire *accomplishments* than formal academic training. Thus, in the 1680s, only 13 per cent of Englishwomen and 12 per cent of Scotswomen can sign their name.[98] Having said this, for every woman who can write, two or three more can read – reading is one of those 'accomplishments' that well-to-do people feel their daughters should acquire, as well as needlecraft, singing, dancing and speaking French. Mary Evelyn, the diarist's much-loved daughter, is literate in French and Italian, well read in history and the classics, sings well and plays the harpsichord. Her sister Susanna has a particular talent for design and painting in oils, and displays great dexterity in needlecraft. She also speaks French and is familiar with most of the works of the Greek and Latin authors of antiquity. And it has to be said that educational opportunities for girls are improving. There are now schools for gentlemen's daughters in places such as London, Shrewsbury, Leeds and Manchester. But as with male education, schooling reinforces the social hierarchy. If you are not sent to school, you might still learn from a personal tutor. Or, if your father owns a copy of the Bible in English, then you might have the opportunity to teach yourself how to read. If neither of these applies, then the delights of reading will probably never be known to you. Some charity schools that look after orphans take in girls as well as boys: Christ's Hospital is one, although the girls are taught separately and are only instructed in 'such work as becomes their sex and may fit them for good wives'.[99] How many girls can read and write when they leave is a moot point. There are many men who clearly do not want to educate the poor, especially the *female* poor, above their station.

The same problems that prevent schools moving with the times beset all six of the universities in Britain – Oxford and Cambridge in England and St Andrews, Glasgow, Aberdeen and Edinburgh in Scotland. Generations of benefactors have left them well endowed, but have prescribed too closely how those endowments will be spent. Tradition, privilege and tenure have done the rest. In 1676, fourteen of the sixteen colleges at Cambridge are headed by men holding the degree of Doctor of Divinity. The university has eight professors: two of divinity and one each of civil law, medicine, mathematics, Hebrew, Greek and Arabic. At Oxford, the five Regius Professors lecture in theology, medicine, civil law, Hebrew and Greek; there are also professors of anatomy, history, natural philosophy, astronomy, geometry, moral philosophy and botany.[100] It is noticeable that only two of all these distinguished academics are Fellows of the Royal Society. If it were not for Isaac Newton, FRS, professor of mathematics at Cambridge, and John Wallis, FRS, Savilian Professor of Geometry at Oxford, you could be forgiven for thinking that the two English universities have nothing to do with the revolution in knowledge that is under way in London. Nevertheless, approximately a thousand boys aged between fourteen and seventeen go up to Oxford each year, and another thousand to Cambridge, to study what amounts to a year of rhetoric (based on a selection of Greek and Latin authors, plus a lot of theology), followed by two years of Aristotelian logic. A hundred or so young men go up to each of the Scottish establishments. In a welcome move, Charles II establishes a chair of mathematics at St Andrews in 1668, and the first professor, James Graham, sets up an observatory there in 1673. But only gradually do the Scottish universities start to reach for the new learning. George Sinclair, who ends his career as professor of mathematics and experimental philosophy at Glasgow, breaks new ground in measuring depths using barometers, astronomical observations, developing diving bells and surveying and draining mines. However, his best-known work is his *Satan's Invisible World Discovered* (1685), in which he describes many supposed cases of witchcraft, poltergeists and other demoniac phenomena, in an attempt to prove that they really exist.

Nonconformists are not allowed to attend the English universities but they are not barred from the Scottish ones. From 1670, if you are an English Presbyterian or a Quaker in need of a degree, you can attend a Dissenting Academy. These are small higher-education establishments, often run by a single polymath, who will teach a few boys at a time so that they are fully prepared to take their degree at a Scottish university or one in the Low Countries, such as Leiden or Utrecht. Although Daniel Defoe does not go on to university, this is how he obtains his education, first going to a private boarding school, before being sent to Mr Charles Morton, the minister of the best-known Dissenting Academy at Newington Green, just north of London. Samuel Wesley, father of John and Charles Wesley (the future founders of Methodism), is also taught by Morton at Newington Green. Teaching is in English and includes instruction in theology, classical studies, history, geography, modern languages, politics, mathematics and natural philosophy. There is a laboratory equipped with air pumps, thermometers and mathematical instruments. Whereas most Dissenting Academies have just half a dozen or so students, Morton's attracts fifty a year. It is too good to last. Alas, the disgruntled bishop of London closes the school down in 1685, after just ten years. Morton himself emigrates to America in 1686, where he ends his days as vice-principal of Harvard College.[101] But Dissenting Academies continue elsewhere for many years afterwards.

Grief

Men and women have always had the capacity for happiness, sadness and all the emotions with which you and I are familiar. But as we have seen, life expectancy in the Restoration period is not great. This raises an important question: how do people cope with grief? This is especially the case with regard to the loss of children, for parents will on average see half their children die before they are fully grown. Are seventeenth-century fathers and mothers inured to death? Are their lives merely tinged with sadness? Or do they feel such losses as sharply and deeply as we do?

If you sit with a father or mother at the bedside of one of their dying children, you will soon see that the emotional impact depends very much on the child's age. When Ralph Josselin loses a ten-day-old son, he records that the child's extreme youth has not allowed him to form a strong bond with the boy. The death of a thirteen-month-old child causes him and his wife only slightly more grief. However, when it comes to the death of their eight-year-old daughter Mary, a huge wave of sorrow engulfs them:

> [she] was a precious child, a bundle of myrrh, a bundle of sweetness; she was a child of ten thousand, full of wisdom, womanlike gravity, knowledge, sweet expressions of God, apt in her learning ... Lord I rejoice I had such a present for thee ... [she] lived desired and died lamented, thy memory is and will be sweet unto me.[102]

This pattern of being utterly distraught by losing children over the age of two or three, yet simply noting with resignation the deaths of younger infants, is also to be seen in John Evelyn. When he loses his youngest son, aged seven months, he writes a short paragraph in his diary, saying, 'The afflicting hand of God being still upon us, it pleased Him also to take away from us this morning my youngest son George, now seven weeks languishing at nurse, breeding teeth and ending in a dropsy. God's holy will be done!' His distress when his five-year-old son dies from a fever is much more marked. He recalls that the boy, as he lay dying, asked if it was permissible to pray to God without putting his hands together, because the doctors had instructed him firmly to keep them under the bedclothes. At the end of the long entry Evelyn writes: 'here ends the joy of my life'. But when he suddenly loses his eighteen-year-old daughter, Mary, whose accomplishments we noted above, his anguish is extreme. Pages and pages of the most bitter lamentation fill the diary:

> She died the 14th [March 1685] to our unspeakable sorrow and affliction, and not to our's only but that of all who knew her ... What shall I say, or rather not say, of the cheerfulness and agreeableness of her humour? Condescending to the meanest servant in the family, or others,

she still kept up respect, without the least pride ... Oh dear, sweet and desirable child, how shall I part with all this goodness and virtue without the bitterness of sorrow and the reluctancy of a tender parent! Thy affection, duty and love to me was that of a friend as well as a child. Nor less dear to thy mother, whose example and tender care of thee was unparalleled ... Oh how she mourns thy loss! How desolate thou hast left us! To the grave shall we both carry thy memory.[103]

When it comes to young adults dying, especially young women in childbirth, the heartbreak is every bit as deep and soul-destroying as in modern times. And that makes you think. When you recall how cruel Restoration society is, how violent and disease-ridden, you almost *want* people to be inured to the loss of family members. But the fact is that they are just as vulnerable and as easily hurt as we are.

Humour

Let's face it, you're going to need a good sense of humour to get by in Restoration Britain. You're also going to want to share a joke or two, just to lighten things up a bit. I don't suggest that you hang out with many nonconformist churchmen, if it's a laugh you are after. Nor would I suggest the company of Samuel Pepys. It is not that he does not do humour but rather that his jokes are either very poor or in very poor taste. For example, he finds it enormously funny that a man manages to convince a virtuous woman that he is a physician so that he can feel her sexual organs. An uproarious joke for Pepys is that a man might helpfully offer to gut another man's oysters to stop them stinking. He is most amused by a chair that, when you sit on it, suddenly claps your body with mechanical arms and imprisons you. In April 1661 he is in a particularly 'strange mood for mirth'. He asks some women if he can buy their children, and takes the ale that two little schoolboys are carrying to their schoolmaster and drinks it. Pepys also agrees with Captain Pett to put it about that he himself is actually the father of Pett's expected child.[104] As you can see, practical jokes and any sort of jape that exploits someone's foolishness or ignorance are considered a merriment by our Sam. Bless him, he has many virtues and vices – but you are likely to place his sense of humour among the latter, not the former.

The same ill-shaped humour is to be found in almost every inn, tavern, alehouse and drinking establishment in the country. Ned Ward is in a London coffee house one day listening to someone playing the violin badly when two sailors, spying a stout hook driven into the wall above the fireplace, seize the fiddler and hook him up by the slit in the back of his breeches. Everybody laughs. When the poor man manages to free himself by much wriggling and falls to the floor, they laugh so much that 'had we seen a fellow break his neck at football, it could not have been a greater jest'.[105] There you have it. The popular sense of humour of this period, like that of most past societies, fits modern sensibilities about as well as a three-fingered glove.

For real wit, you need to pay heed to the poets of the court. They all have great fun with the king and his womanising. One anonymous courtier, referring to the attack by the Dutch on the English fleet in the Medway in June 1667, writes:

> As Nero once with harp in hand surveyed
> His flaming Rome, and as that burnt he played,
> So our great prince, when the Dutch fleet arrived,
> Saw his ships burn and, as they burnt, he swived.
> So kind was he in our extremest need,
> He would those flames extinguish with his seed.[106]

Even more cutting is the earl of Rochester's 'Satire upon Charles II':

> Peace is his aim, his gentleness is such,
> And love he loves, for he loves fucking much.
> Nor are his high desires above his strength;
> His sceptre and his prick are of a length;
> And she may sway the one who plays with th'other,
> And make him little wiser than his brother.
> Poor Prince! Thy prick, like thy buffoons at Court,
> Will govern thee because it makes thee sport.
> 'Tis sure the sauciest prick that e'er did swive,
> The proudest, peremptoriest prick alive.
> Though safety, law, religion, life lay on't,
> 'Twould break through all to make its way to cunt.
> Restless he rolls about from whore to whore,
> A merry monarch, scandalous and poor.[107]

Of course, to appreciate the humour in the above doggerel, you have to be there when Rochester accidentally hands a copy of it to the king himself.

In an age of wits, it is difficult to decide to whom should be given the last word and, with it, the last laugh. But let me finish with five quips from a range of people – a scientist, a peer, a lady, a rake and an MP – that between them neatly illustrate the sense of humour of the age:

• When Fellows of the Royal Society witness the experiment of draining the blood of one dog into another, whose own blood is removed, it is observed that it stands to be of great benefit to a man's health if bad blood can be replaced with good. At which one Fellow asks what would happen if the blood of a Quaker were let into the body of an archbishop.[108]

• In 1660, the marquess of Dorchester, who is an amateur physician, challenges his son-in-law, Lord Ros, to a duel, telling him he will ram his sword down his throat. To which Lord Ros replies, 'If by your threatening words you do not mean your pills, the worst is past. I am safe enough.'[109]

• Catherine Sedley is most surprised that James, duke of York – the future James II – takes her as his mistress. She wonders what he sees in her, saying, 'It cannot be my beauty for he must see I have none. And it cannot be my wit, for he has not enough to know that I have any.'[110]

• Catherine Sedley's father is Sir Charles Sedley, and she is his only legitimate daughter. Therefore he is none too happy that James takes her to bed. He is not placated when, as king, James creates her countess of Dorchester. Therefore, when in 1689 it comes to a vote in Parliament as to who should be king, he votes in favour of William III and Mary. Asked why, he explains: 'James II made my daughter a countess, and I have been helping to make his daughter a queen.'[111]

• When Sir William Petty, the author of Political Arthithmetick, is challenged to a duel by Sir Aleyn Broderick, who doesn't like something Petty has written about Ireland, he accepts the challenge. But Petty's sight is not good. In fact, he is practically blind. He accordingly accepts Sir Aleyn's challenge on one condition: that they fight in a dark cellar, with axes.[112]

5

Basic Essentials

'When in Rome, do as the Romans do,' runs the old saying, and it is advice that you would be well advised to follow in any place or time. But hang on: there are things you don't know about this place and this time. When is Britain at war? The British fight three wars during this period: the Second Dutch War, from March 1665 to July 1667; the Third Dutch War, from April 1672 to February 1674; and the Nine Years' War, which has already been going for a year by the time the British join in May 1689 and which does not come to an end until May 1697. I strongly recommend not joining the navy during these years unless you are particularly prone to extreme violence, in which case you have found your spiritual home. But for the rest of us, what about matters of ordinary life? There are things you don't know that you don't know. What coins do you use? Where do you go shopping? How do you tell the time? All these daily functions are different from the ways we do things in the modern world. Therefore in this chapter we will deal with those basic aspects of life that are easily taken for granted, but which you need to understand in order to get by.

The Weather

On Thursday night, about two or three o'clock, there was a most terrible storm of rain, hail and violent winds, accompanied with such dreadful thunder and lightning that some started up half distracted, thinking it to be the day of judgement; it was indeed the most formidable, unparalleled tempest that ever I knew; the wind blustering and beating great hailstones with such force against the windows and walls as did awaken very hard sleepers with fear.[1]

So Ralph Thoresby describes the night of 19 January 1678, when he is nineteen. Most people say that 'the Great Wind' of 18 February 1662 is the most destructive storm in living memory. Several Londoners are killed by falling tiles. The streets are left full of 'brick bats, tile-shards, sheets of lead … hats and feathers and perriwigs'. Lady Saltonstall is killed in her bed when her house collapses on top of her. On the other side of England, in the Forest of Dean, 3,000 trees are blown down.[2]

The other contender for the worst storm of the period is the hurricane of 11 January 1690. As Evelyn describes it:

> This day there was a most extraordinary storm of wind, accompanied with snow and sharp weather; it did great harm in many places, blowing down houses, trees, etc, killing many people. It began about two in the morning, and lasted till five, being a kind of hurricane, which mariners observe have begun of late years to come northward.[3]

Despite the severity of these storms, it is probably the incessant cold that will bother you most. The modern average annual temperature for England is 9.7°C – in the 1660s it is 9.0°C; in the 1670s, 8.6°C; in the 1680s, 8.7°C; and in the 1690s a decidedly chilly 8.1°C. As for extremes, brace yourself. Four of the twelve months of the year are at their coldest ever in these forty years: the coldest March recorded is that of 1674; the coldest May that of 1698; the coldest July that of 1695; and the coldest September that of 1694.[4] On top of these records, I am sure that you have not forgotten 1675, a 'year without a summer', and the Long Frost of 1683–4, when the three-month average drops to –1.2°C, the coldest three-month period ever recorded in England. (For comparison, the modern average for December–February is 3.7°C.) It is at times like these that you notice how badly the window shutters fit, and how the wind whips under the front door.

The Calendar

There are two calendars in use in Europe in the late seventeenth century. The official one for the kingdom of England is the Julian Calendar, which we have been using since the Middle Ages. This starts each new year on Lady Day (25 March) and celebrates a leap year every fourth year, so there are 100 leap years in four centuries. The other is the Gregorian Calendar, which has been in use across most of the Continent since 1582 and is the one with which you are familiar. New Year's Day in this system is 1 January, and there are 97 leap years every four centuries. The result is a slight time discrepancy between England and the rest of Europe. The Scots use the Julian Calendar, like the English, but with the important exception that they start a new year on 1 January, as they do on the Continent. Astronomers thus have to keep their wits about them when comparing notes. If a cosmic event is seen by an astronomer at the observatory in St Andrews on 5 January 1691, then the same event might be witnessed on 5 January 1690 by John Flamsteed at the Royal Observatory in Greenwich and on 15 January 1691 by Giovanni Cassini at the Paris Observatory. The difference is particularly confusing for travellers. For example, if you spend Christmas Day 1668 in Paris and set out the following morning on a nine-day journey to London, you will arrive on Christmas Day 1668. If you set out the following day and travel north for the next sixteen days, as you cross the border into Scotland you will move from 12 January 1669 to 12 January 1670.

One further complication is that people don't stick to one or the other system. Some English people (like Pepys) celebrate New Year's Day on 1 January even though the year does not officially change until 25 March. Others use both the old and the new years to describe the period from 1 January to 24 March, thus they write Valentine's Day 1676 as 14 February 1675/6. There are a couple more things that might catch you out. For example, which is the shortest day of the year in Britain? The answer is 10 or 11 December. And when do you think Easter Day is in 1667? On 7 April *and* 22 March. The reason is that the year lasts from 25 March 1667 to the following 24 March, and two Easter Days fall in this period. The year 1694 also has two Easters, with the added oddity that Easter Day 1694 is followed by Easter Monday 1695.

People note their birthdays, even if they do not celebrate them as we do in the modern world, and contrary to what you might have heard, they *do* know how old they are. This was not always the case: in past centuries, remembering your age was a tricky business, especially if all you had to go on was a vague memory of your mother telling you that you were born on the Wednesday after Whitsun in the thirteenth year of the reign of the previous king. By 1660, everyone

(*Above*) Charles II, painted by John Michael Wright. It is easy to underestimate Charles as a monarch, especially with regard to his scandalous private life. But his political flexibility is what makes the Restoration of the monarchy a success, and his patronage of the arts and sports transform social life in Britain.

(*Right*) James II, portrayed by Sir Peter Lely. A great patron and a noble prince but a failure as a king. His determination to pursue a policy of tolerance towards Catholics turns a loyal nation against him within four years of his accession.

Queen Catherine of Braganza. You have to feel sorry for her, married to the openly adulterous Charles II. She also fails in her one constitutionally vital role of providing an heir. After a serious illness, in which she is delirious, she recovers and asks 'How are the children?' only to be told she does not actually have any.

William III, prince of Orange and nephew of Charles II. The country flocks to support him as the Protestant defender against his cousin James II in 1688.

Queen Mary II, daughter of James II, painted by William Wissing. She reigns jointly with her husband, William III, until her death in 1694.

Barbara Villiers, Lady Castlemaine and duchess of Cleveland. Charles II's first mistress after his return to England – and later the mistress to several other gentlemen mentioned in this book.

Louise de Kéroualle, duchess of Portsmouth, arrives from France in the train of the duchess of Orléans and soon is made a duchess herself – for services rendered to the king.

Nell Gwynn. Not considered the most attractive of the king's mistresses but probably the woman who inspires the most affection in him and among her fellow Londoners. It's her personality that makes the difference. Honestly.

In the Restoration period, London dominates England more than at any other time in history. Here it is viewed from the south bank of the Thames, before the Great Fire.

According to Pepys, who watches the Great Fire from the south bank, it consumes the heart of the city in a single 'malicious bloody flame'.

Covent Garden, designed by Inigo Jones for the earl of Bedford, sets the pattern for town planning in Britain. An elegant arcade and some of the finest houses in the city surround the central piazza, which becomes home to an extensive market around 1670. Note the yellow hackney carriages carrying fare-paying passengers.

Golden Square, laid out in the 1670s, is just one of many well-proportioned squares constructed as London expands westwards.

Michael Dahl's portrait of Sir George Rooke shows the classic coat and waistcoat design of the 1690s that sets the standard for English gentlemen for the next century.

Lord Mungo Murray, painted by John Michael Wright, is shown dressed in the full Scottish plaid as worn in the 1690s.

Bridget Holmes, depicted by John Riley, is a royal 'necessary woman' who lives to 100 years of age. Here she is shown in her working clothes in 1686, at the age of 95.

Lady Anne de Vere Capel here models a fine dress for her portrait by Michael Dahl, showing the fashionable gown of the 1690s.

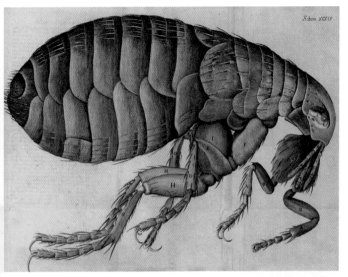

Robert Hooke's book *Micrographia* causes a sensation when it appears in 1665. The image of a flea, engraved by Hooke himself, is 18 inches across. It introduces people for the first time to a new microscopic world they have not even imagined.

(*Right*) The agony of toothache is easy to imagine in an age without anaesthetics. But the pain is not half the problem. Abscesses in rotten teeth kill about 6 per cent of the urban population in these years.

(*Below*) The earliest surviving cheque, drawn on the bank of Clayton and Morris in the year 1659/60. The Restoration sees a series of revolutions in the financial world – from the development of the Stock Exchange to recoinage, fire insurance and the establishment of the Bank of England.

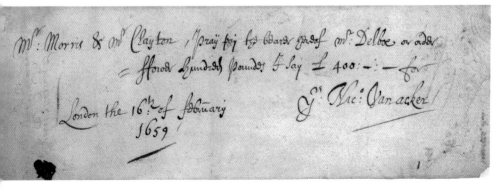

The Thames freezes during the Long Frost of 1683–4 – so much so that a fair is held on its surface. It remains the coldest winter on record.

The King's Bath at Bath. All social ranks take the waters regularly – drinking them, bathing in them and having them sprayed over them. However, as Pepys notes, the communal bathing probably spreads as many diseases as the mineral waters cure.

is familiar with *Anno Domini*, even if they start the *annus* on different dates. Those who place great store in astrological prognostication are particularly keen to recall their birthdate. It is no coincidence that Charles II rides into London in 1660 on his thirtieth birthday. As for Pepys, not only does he celebrate his birthdays and wedding anniversaries but he also holds dinners to commemorate his operation to remove a bladder stone, a particularly nasty bit of surgery that proves fatal to many people. In 1663 he invites eight friends to join him in celebrating his survival with a slap-up meal.

'Let's dance and sing and make good cheer, since Christmas comes but once a year,' writes the royalist poet John Taylor. No doubt his words and sentiments are familiar to you. Although there are no Christmas trees, cards, crackers or tinsel, the Nativity is festooned with traditions and merriment. People love to hang holly and ivy about their halls and to burn the Yule log. They wish each other happiness, and they drink and bid each other 'good cheer', 'welcome' and 'God be with you'. In some towns, such as Cirencester, you can hear carol singers in the streets. In London the carol singers go from house to house carrying a wassail bowl (a bowl of spiced ale).[5] Some old-fashioned manorial lords still provide huge dinners in their halls for all their servants and tenants.[6] Employers might give their servants 'treats' in boxes (hence 'Boxing Day') and fathers might similarly give small gifts to their children. The 'twelve days' of Christmas are fully observed: with an emphasis on driving away melancholy for the whole duration, so games, music, dancing and fine food and drink are the order of the season. Mince pies, turkey and plum porridge have all become established as Christmas foods. Note, however, that the mince pies might not be quite what you are expecting: their ingredients include chicken, eggs, sugar, raisins, lemon peel, orange peel, spices and cow's tongue.[7]

All this goodwill, carol singing, turkey eating and mince-pie scoffing is especially welcome in the Restoration period for a very sound reason: Christmas was banned by the Puritans. Of all the things to abolish! It does not appear in the Bible, the Puritans argued; therefore it is nothing more than an element of popery. You would have thought they would have insisted on religious observance on such a day but no, they wanted nothing to do with it. Theological writers argued that the date of Christ's Nativity is not in the Bible, therefore it must be an invention of the Catholic Church.[8] Ministers were forbidden from preaching on Christmas Day. Shops were required to be open. Amazing though it may seem, in the 1650s it was considered superstitious to eat mince pies, plum porridge or brawn in December. People did not like this, as you can imagine, and they started to personify the banished feast as 'Old Father Christmas': an old man with a white beard on trial for his life, who is innocent of any wrongdoing. But now Old Father Christmas is back, and you may freely eat mince pies during the twelve days' feast. You can also deck churches and houses with boughs of holly and ivy, and spear pieces of roast beef with rosemary, play cards and bowls, go hawking or hunting, give money or boxes of presents to your children, servants and apprentices, and send the traditional present of a couple of capons to a friend – all of which were banned under the Commonwealth.[9]

St Valentine's Day is traditionally when birds choose their mate, and so the day has all the frisson of a betrothal about it. Even married people choose valentines – and they don't have to be their spouse. There are several ways of selecting someone. One is simply to choose a partner: a dangerous strategy, unless you do choose your spouse. Alternatively, you and your friends can all put each other's names in a hat, on different-coloured paper for the sexes, and draw them out. A third option is to take as your valentine the first member of the opposite sex you see on the morning of 14 February (other than your own family and servants). In 1662 Elizabeth Pepys has to keep her eyes shut and hide from the workmen to avoid seeing one of them first. As the man must buy presents for his valentine, women will hope that the first person they clap eyes on is a handsome prince. Frances Stuart strikes lucky in 1668 and receives a jewel worth £800 from the duke of York.[10]

Gunpowder Plot Day (5 November) is much more significant in Restoration Britain than it is in the modern world. All the shops remain closed and a special church service is held, at which people hear sermons about the deliverance of the kingdom from Guy Fawkes and the Catholic plotters in 1605. You won't be surprised to hear that the celebrations include processions and bonfires. However, as the 1670s wear on, and people grow more and more anxious about the succession of the Catholic duke of York, the day becomes an excuse for popular demonstration. By the end of the decade, at the height of the fear during the Popish Plot, the guy is dressed as the pope and stuffed with live cats, which are burnt to death on the bonfires.[11] When he becomes king, James II tries in vain to forbid such gruesome ceremonies. But then the Protestant champion William III lands on the coast of Devon on 5 November 1688. Now there are two reasons for Protestants to celebrate the date – England has been saved by God from Catholicism twice on the same day; this calls for twice the celebrations! November the 5th is thus a great day to be visiting England. Unless you are a Catholic. Or a cat.

Telling the Time

You might think that the act of telling the time is itself a 'timeless' activity. Two hands on a dial, twelve figures around it – it couldn't be simpler. Well, that would be true if there were *two* hands on the dial; most longcase clocks built in this period have only the one, an hour hand. Some old church clocks and country-house clocks – turret clocks – do not have a face at all but simply ring the hour. Many people are still using sundials, including pocket ones that can be corrected for the time of year. Longcase clocks built by the best London makers do have two hands, and truly fine table clocks like those built by Tompion even have a dial that shows the days of the week. Watches too mostly have two hands, but note that they do not fit around your wrist but rest in your pocket, often attached to a chain or a cord.

Clocks are not cheap items. A standard clock in the 1670s has a second-hand value of £2, which is more or less the going rate for a tradesman's timepiece.[12] Monsieur Misson remarks after his journey of 1697 that clocks are still comparatively rare in England, but that almost everyone of any substance has a watch: Tompion's workshop turns out more than 5,000 watches but only about 650 clocks.[13] Everyone else has to rely on the ringing of church clocks and 'the bell man' – a chap who walks around the neighbourhood at night, slow-ringing a hand-bell and calling the hour. On 16 January 1660 Pepys notes that he stays up 'till the bell-man came by with his bell just under my window as I was writing of this very line, and cried, "Past one of the clock, and a cold, frosty, windy morning."'[14] Church clocks also ring through the night, so that if you start work at 4 a.m., you may well hear the hurry-on from your local parish tower.

Start work at 4 a.m.? Yes, you may have to, especially in summer. And this does not just apply to bakers and market traders. The ability to work depends on there being enough light. Thus Pepys will often be at his office at 4 a.m. in June, July and August, and at 5 a.m. in May and September. In winter, in contrast, he sometimes won't get out of bed until 8 a.m.[15] Those intending to travel long distances get up early to take advantage of the light. King Charles sets out from Newmarket at 4 a.m. to travel back to London in summer; if Pepys has to go on a long journey, he will get up even earlier, at 3 a.m. or thereabouts.[16] Ralph Thoresby is a glutton for punishment – rising early even in winter. In November 1680 he resolves on 'getting an alarm put to the clock, and that set at my bed's head, to arise every morning by five', in order to have more time to pray and read about the saints.[17] An alternative – if you can afford it – is one of Thomas Tompion's clocks with a built-in alarm.

As for bedtimes, most people have their heads on the pillow by 11 p.m. In summer it is quite usual for people to go to bed at 9 p.m. or even earlier if they are planning to be up at 4 a.m. John Milton, the poet, goes to bed at 9 p.m., rises at 4 a.m. and has a man read the Hebrew Bible to him from 4.30 a.m.[18] You do get night owls of course, as well as carousers. Pepys often stays up till the early hours. After dining with the king in June 1660, Lord Sandwich does not get home to go to bed until 5 a.m., and sleeps in afterwards until 11 a.m.[19] By then, most travellers and workers will have been up for seven hours already.

Language

The language you will hear spoken in England is broadly familiar, as the diarists you have encountered in this book demonstrate. Whereas you would find it difficult to follow the speech of 1500, that of 1660 is much easier to understand, largely due to the unifying and harmonising effect of William Tyndale's great Bible translations of the 1520s and early 1530s. More than three-quarters of the Bible used in Anglican church services – known as the King James Version – is his work, and so Tyndale's syntax and phraseology have permeated the language everywhere it is spoken.[20] However, the speech you will hear in the street is not quite the same as modern English. Some past participles are different: people often say 'he ris' (rather than 'he rose'); 'he durst' ('he dared'); 'he ketched' ('he caught'); and 'he drownded' ('he drowned'). The use of 'thee', 'thou' and 'ye' is still common. As for spellings, some have yet to be modernised, so you will see 'ambassadors' spelled 'imbassadors' and 'embassadors', 'pensions' written as 'pentions', and 'stationers' described as 'stacioners'. Foreign words are prone to phonetic spellings, so Londoners may well write about the 'piatzza' in Covent Garden. 'Hath' and 'doth' are still used by old-fashioned types instead of 'has' and 'does', but the '-th' forms of other words are fast dropping out of usage.

Much more confusing for the average time traveller is the fact that words shift in meaning. The result is that you will sometimes believe you understand a man perfectly, when in reality you have misunderstood him completely. For example, in the seventeenth century the word 'to discover' means 'to uncover' or 'to reveal'. So if I were to say, 'The bishop discovered me in bed with his sister', I do not mean that he pulled back the curtains and got the shock of his life, but that he told someone about the two of us cavorting together. Here is an illustrative selection of ways in which the shifts of language can trip you up:

Restoration phrase	Meaning in modern English
'she hath a fine carriage'	You might presume the speaker is referring to a lady's mode of transport. Think again. It means 'she dances [or walks] well'.
'his third sermon was his most painful'	I know what you are thinking. Three hours on a wooden pew listening to a preacher can be hard on the buttocks. Actually the meaning is 'he took the most care over his third sermon'.
'he read my book with great affection'	Dismiss images from your mind of someone stroking this volume lovingly. It means 'he read my book carefully'.
'the beer there is rarely good'	If someone said this to me about a modern hostelry, I would avoid it. However, it is a recommendation – for it indicates that 'the beer there is of an unusually high quality'.
'I lost my wig in my toilet'	It doesn't mean the article has been flushed away but that 'my wig came off while getting dressed'.

'Mr Pepys is a most effeminate man'	Well, he most certainly is. In this period 'effeminate' means 'fond of women'.
'she is licensed to be a badger'	She is permitted to buy essential commodities at market and sell them elsewhere for profit.
'she is the meanest woman I ever met'	Nothing to do with how nasty she is: it indicates that 'she is the poorest woman I ever met'.
'the dancing was interrupted by divers who had not been invited'	Not men in flippers. Rather, it means that 'the dancing temporarily came to a halt when various uninvited people turned up'.
'His schoolmaster tells me that my grandson is the most pregnant boy he has ever met'	John Evelyn writes something like this in his diary. He is not referring to a medical miracle but that his grandson 'is full of potential'.

As you can see, there are many possibilities for making a fool of yourself. When Pepys describes Commissioner Pett's daughter as 'a very comely black woman', he means that she is very pretty and has dark hair, not that she has black skin. If he meant the latter, he would have called her a 'negress' or a 'blackamoor'. However, in other contexts people do use the word 'black' to refer to race. As with all languages, only half the meaning lies in the words themselves: the rest is context and cultural understanding.

When it comes to more difficult words, the late seventeenth century has a great advantage over previous ages in that there are good English dictionaries to help you. The earliest such works are lists of hard words, with very basic definitions. Then Thomas Blount's *Glossographia* (first edition 1656; second edition 1661) hits the booksellers' stalls. As with the earlier writers, Blount defines all the technical terms he has come across in such specialist subjects as law, science, music, architecture and mathematics, but he also includes many new words that are being used by people in the street, such as 'coffee', 'chocolate', 'drapery', 'omelette' and 'balcony'. In total, he carefully defines more than 11,000 words, producing etymologies for very many of them and thus opening the door to lexicography. *Glossographia* also paves the way for an increasingly sophisticated array of English dictionaries. Most impressive of these is Edward Phillips's five-volume *New World of English Words* (1662), which includes names of places, peoples and personages from European and classical history, as well as definitions of words. It informs you as to the original language from which every word was derived, whether Hebrew, Arabic, Aramaic, Greek, Latin, Italian, French, Spanish, Gaelic, Dutch or Saxon. It also explains certain antiquated words: readers learn that 'myriad' is from Greek and means 'ten thousand', that a 'molar' or grinding tooth is from the Latin word for a mill, that a 'muricide' ('mouse-killer' in Latin) is a cowardly fellow and that 'mixen' is an archaic term for dung or a dung-hill.

If you travel around Britain you will soon realise that people do not all speak the same way. Dialect words will skitter off your understanding like hailstones bouncing on cobbles. In Devon, for example, the country folk still use many words that Phillips and Blount refer to as archaic: 'muxy' for example, which relates to the archaic 'mixen', is the way you will hear Devonians talking about a muddy lane. In the far west of Cornwall, beyond the Fal estuary, you might well still hear Cornish spoken: this is a completely different language – a form of Brythonic Gaelic, like Welsh. However, the last sermon in Cornish is preached at Landewednack in 1678; after that date you will not find many Cornish speakers who do not also understand English.[21] That is not the case in Wales and Scotland, where Welsh and Scottish Gaelic are still strong. Celia Fiennes notes that there are so many people speaking Welsh on market day in Shrewsbury that you can easily believe you are in Wales.[22] About a hundred books have been published in Welsh by 1660 and thereafter they continue to appear at the rate of about seven or eight a year – a marked contrast to Cornish, which has no books at all. Gaelic sees only a handful of publications, but the large number of speakers in the Highlands – about 200,000 – means that very little English is used there. Even where English is spoken, it is either in the vernacular Scots dialect or pronounced with such a broad Scottish accent that anyone other than a local will have difficulty understanding it.[23]

Most well-educated Englishmen can speak some French, albeit haltingly, but very few foreigners coming to England can speak any English – rather the reverse of the situation in the modern world. The next most widely spoken languages are Italian and Spanish, which are both popular with gentlemen who go on a Grand Tour. As the knowledge of languages separates the educated from the uneducated, gentlemen sometimes use French to discuss things of a private nature so that the servants cannot spy on them. When Lord Sandwich tells Samuel Pepys about the duke of York's affair with Anne Hyde, for example, he does so in French.[24] Latin is widely read and used as a superior language for scientific books and anything scholarly that is aimed at an international readership, and a few people can converse fluently in Latin. However, it is not quite the universal language that some people suppose: it is pronounced differently in England from the rest of Europe. Magalotti relates how the professors and heads of colleges at the university of Cambridge all gather to welcome Cosimo III in 1669. The Grand Duke is led into the Senate House, where he is seated at a place of honour at a large table, with all the dignitaries at a respectful distance around him; then he is addressed in Latin by a worthy professor. As he speaks, the Italians look at each other in bewilderment, for the Latin is delivered with such a thick accent that they find it as unintelligible as English.[25]

Communications and Writing

Writing a letter, like telling the time, is likely to catch you out. What should you write with? What should you write on? What script should you use? And where can you post your letter once you have written it? You'll notice that people write differently according to their reasons for writing. If they are writing a note, a letter, an account or a private memorandum, they will write on paper. Of course, the quality of the paper will be selected to suit the nature of the work: many types are manufactured, from fine white writing paper costing 6s 8d per ream to coarse white paper at 2s.[26] If, however, they are writing a legal document or something that needs to stand the test of time, like an indenture or a parish register, they will choose to write on vellum, which is a specially processed sheep's skin. If kept dry and away from rats, it will last for thousands of years. As for what you might write with, you have a choice of a quill, a metal pen, a pencil or even a fountain pen. The best quills are cut from the flight feathers of geese and swans. A thin cut in the nib draws up the ink from the inkwell and allows it to flow back down as the pen is moved across the page. The same principle enables you to employ a metal pen, which can be used for finer drawing work.

However, as you will see, it is easy to have too much ink on the nib, which then soaks the paper and not only blots it but causes it to tear. Pencils avoid this, being made of graphite strips encased in wood, very similar to their modern equivalents (except that they are oval in cross-section). As for fountain pens, these are a new innovation and not yet wholly practical. Nevertheless, Pepys – always eager to try out anything new – receives a silver pen that carries its own ink in August 1663.[27]

Script-wise, you have a choice. Most printed lettering is described as 'italic'. This needs no introduction: it is the script you are reading now (whether slanted or not). The only differences are that in the seventeenth century 'u' and 'v' are the same letter (but 'v' is normally used at the start of the word and 'u' in the middle); 'i' and 'j' are similarly interchangeable; and the letter 's' is frequently written in a long form, like an uncrossed 'f'. What you might find a little harder to follow is the form of writing called 'secretary hand'. This is never printed but is rather a cursive script: the letters are joined together so that the pen does not leave the page in the middle of a word (in theory), allowing you to write quickly. Several of the letter shapes are different, in upper-case forms as well as lower-case, so that at first sight it will prove difficult to read. But you will soon get used to it. Far harder are the forms of shorthand or tachygraphy (literally 'quick writing') that people employ for speed. In a system like that of Thomas Shelton, many words are represented by a single symbol; it does not look like normal writing at all. Most people cannot read it. This is precisely why Pepys chooses to write his diary this way. Only by concealing his confessions from his wife and servants can he risk setting down the naked truth in its full technicoloured detail.

Let's say you've written a letter. What next? First, there is no point looking for an envelope: they have yet to be invented. Instead you will write the name and address of the intended recipient on the outside of the folded letter itself. Then you need to seal it, using sealing wax and, if you have one, an engraved signet ring. Finally, you need to post it. If you're in London, you might take it straight to the General Letter Office. This is on Threadneedle Street, more or less where the modern Bank of England is situated. After the Fire, it moves first to a couple of temporary locations and, in 1678, to Lombard Street. You can hand your letter in there to one of the 'window men' and pay him the postage: a single-sheet letter can be sent up to 80 miles within England for 2d, and more than 80 miles for 3d. If you send two sheets, it will cost you double, three sheets treble, and so on. Your letter will then be postmarked with the date (from 1661) and placed in a sack for despatch. Letters and packets for Kent are sent out every day except Sunday. Other parts of the British Isles are served by collections on Tuesdays, Thursdays and Saturdays.[28]

The London postal service

Destination or postal route	Cost of posting a letter, per page	Cost of sending a parcel	Items despatched
England and Wales	2d if less than 80 miles 3d if over 80 miles	8d per oz if less than 80 miles 1s per oz if more than 80 miles	Tuesday, Thursday, Saturday
Scotland	4d	1s 6d per oz	*as above*
Ireland	6d	2s per oz	Tuesday, Saturday
Low Countries and Germany (via Hamburg, Frankfurt, Cologne)	8d	2s per oz	Monday, Tuesday, Friday
France and Spain (via Bordeaux, Rochelle, Nantes, Bayonne, Cadiz, Madrid)	9d	2s per oz	Monday, Thursday
France, Italy and the Eastern Mediterranean (via Leghorn, Genoa, Florence, Lyons, Marseilles, Smyrna, Aleppo, Constantinople)	1s	3s 9d per oz	Monday, Thursday

Eastern Europe	1s	4s per oz	Monday,
and Scandinavia			Friday
(via Danzig, Leipzig,			
Lübeck, Stockholm,			
Copenhagen,			
Elsinore,			
Königsberg)			

The sophistication of the English postal system is impressive. Fifty sorters work at the General Letter Office, besides the 'window men'. The post-boys ride at rapid speeds along six main routes, night and day, so that in twenty-four hours your letter might travel up to 120 miles.[29] Local carriers then take the mail to the addressee. You can write to someone on the far side of the country on a Monday and expect to hear back from them by the end of the week. In addition, the above postal rates are fixed for the whole nation, so you can post your letter wherever there is a deputy postmaster. There are 182 in Great Britain in 1676, so most substantial towns are covered. In London there are more than 500 receiving houses or shops where you can drop off or collect your letter or parcel and messengers will convey it to the General Letter Office. Lists of these places are published in the newspapers.

From 1683 there is an additional London postal service: the Penny Post, devised by William Dockwra. You can post any London-bound letter or parcel weighing 1lb or less at one of six sorting offices in the capital: it costs you nothing to send it, but the recipient pays a penny to receive it. There are collections and deliveries every two hours, every day of the week except Sunday. You can send letters in the same way twice a day into the suburbs. If you need to send something into the country, up to 10 miles from London (to 148 towns and villages), you will pay 1d per item and the recipient will pay the same again. Monsieur Misson exclaims that it is a wonder that not every city has set up such a system. Other writers agree that England has the best, cheapest and fastest postal service in the world; they add that, in the past, few people sent letters, but these days almost everyone does. Sir William Petty, writing in 1676, reckons that the number of letters posted has increased twenty times over the last forty years.[30] Organised transport systems and high levels of male literacy have transformed things. Back in 1603 it took three days for news of Elizabeth I's death at Richmond to reach Edinburgh, 397 miles away, carried by a special messenger changing horses regularly along the way. That is an average of 132 miles per day. Now only slightly lower speeds of communication are available to everyone, and not just the government acting on matters of national importance. Moreover, it costs only a few pence.

Not every message is conveyed around the country at breakneck speed. Generally you can assume that reports of important events are circulated at roughly 30 miles per day. The duke of Gloucester, the brother of Charles II, dies of smallpox on 13 September 1660; at Earls Colne, about 60 miles away, Ralph Josselin notes the fact in his diary two days later.[31] Although the French attack Teignmouth at 4 a.m. on 26 July 1690, the news does not come to the attention of John Evelyn in London (200 miles away) until a week later.[32] International news may take a long time to arrive, due to the great distances involved, but sometimes it may be travelling just as fast as domestic information. An attack on the British port of Tangiers on 14 June 1663 is known about in London forty-two days later (thus travelling at about 40 miles per day, by sea).[33]

We in the modern world believe we are living through a communications revolution – and no one in his or her right mind would doubt it. But people in Restoration Britain are experiencing a similar transformation. Faster, affordable communications are a major part of that story. Even more noticeable, however, are the newspapers sold at stationers and read in coffee houses. By 1663 the bibliophile George Thomason has managed to collect more than 7,200 editions of English newspapers and news-sheets published since 1640 (as well as a further 15,000 pamphlets). There were no newspapers before the Civil Wars, largely due to the legal restrictions on printing, but now that the publishing cat is out of the bag, it is very difficult for the government to return things to the way they were. Although Charles II reintroduces control of the press by way of the Licensing Act of 1662, a stream of newspapers pour out of the capital with names such as *Mercurius Politicus*, *The Public Intelligencer* and *The True Protestant Mercury*, each appearing once a week. Samuel Pepys's newspaper of choice in the early 1660s is *The Kingdom's Intelligencer*.[34] From 1665, *The Oxford Gazette* is published: this is the government's official newspaper, which is renamed *The London Gazette* in 1666.

A Scottish equivalent, *The Edinburgh Gazette*, first appears in 1699. Similar official publications from foreign countries, such as the *Gazette de France*, the *Gazeta ordinaria de Madrid* and the *Lisbon Gazeta*, and unofficial English newsletters such as *The Weekly Pacquet of Advice from Rome*, are sent to London; the news they contain is quickly recycled, so that important events are made known to everyone who cares to be informed. In their old age, Evelyn and his wife set aside Wednesday and Saturday nights as 'lecture nights', when they read out the newspapers to each other. During the Long Frost, the ports are all frozen and Britain is cut off from the rest of Europe; the thaw thus brings a flood of news, as all the European newspapers for the last two months arrive at once.[35] Mr and Mrs Evelyn have difficulty keeping up.

The real communications revolution – as far as the media are concerned – comes at the end of the Restoration period. Before then, the terms of the Licensing Act of 1662 restrict printing presses in England to London and the universities of Oxford and Cambridge – and what is to be printed requires the permission of a 'surveyor' or censor. In 1663 this role is filled by Sir Roger l'Estrange, an editor of three newspapers who, ironically, opposes the general public reading them, 'because I think it makes the multitude too familiar with the actions and the counsels of their superiors'.[36] (You can't help but feel he is in the wrong job.) That year a pamphlet justifying the execution of Charles I is discovered in the press of John Twyn, who is tried for the crime of printing it. Despite his protestations of innocence, he is found guilty and hanged and quartered, his head being set on Ludgate and the four quarters of his body displayed above the other gates of the city. People are appalled and, indeed, the rigidity of press control contributes to calls for a change in the law. In 1695 Parliament refuses to renew the Licensing Act, thereby making way for the first time for a free press. New journals are swiftly published, with titles such as *The Post Man*, *The Post Boy* and *The Flying Post* emphasising their speed and thus their up-to-dateness. These are printed two or three times a week and in editions of 3,000–4,000, not far short of *The London Gazette*'s print run of 6,000 copies.[37] Sitting down in a coffee house in 1695, with the sun streaming through the windows on the printed newspaper on the table before you, and the steam of your coffee rising in the sunlight, you may well think that you're not so far from home.

Politeness

Monsieur Misson remarks that 'the people of England when they meet, never salute one another otherwise than by giving one another their hands and shaking them heartily; they no more dream of pulling off their hats than women do of pulling off their head cloths.'[38] This is not quite true: men do take off their hats to one another, especially to social superiors; however, you need to note the importance of the handshake. Other forms of greeting will similarly be familiar to you. If you meet Pepys, he may well say 'How do you do?' as a form of welcome. If you meet the king, he will hold out his hand for you to bow to and kiss. Ladies should hold up their heads to a gentleman to kiss them on greeting, but they should bow to kiss the king's hand. For people who are significantly higher in status than you but not royal, removing the hat and bowing is the norm. As for saying goodbye, that word 'good-bye' itself is appropriate. Restoration people understand it to mean either 'God b[less] ye' or 'God be [with] ye'.[39]

When it comes to addressing important people, modern practice is useful in so far as forms have not greatly changed. You should address the king as 'Your majesty' and a duke or an archbishop as 'Your grace'. Speaking to lesser lords and bishops or their wives, you can simply say 'Your lordship' or 'Your ladyship', and to clergymen 'Your reverence'. If a man is a knight or a baronet, then call him 'Sir John' or whatever his first name is. His wife is 'Your ladyship', 'Dame Alice' or 'Lady Smith'. Gentlemen are referred to as 'Mister' or 'Master' (both written 'Mr'). The term 'Esquire' is used after a gentleman's name to indicate that he has a coat of arms – note that it is not used for non-armigerous gentlemen. Nor do you call a tradesman or ordinary farmer 'Mr' – at this time he does not have a pre-title, only his name. Wives, sisters and daughters of gentlemen are addressed as 'Mistress' (written 'Mrs' or 'Mtress'), whether they are married or not, and letters should be directed to them as 'Mrs Smith', even if they are under the age of ten. I would strongly recommend that you do not address an unmarried woman in the 1660s as 'Miss': this is the way people refer to noblemen's concubines.[40]

Most other aspects of politeness are much as they are in the modern world. All the social norms about spitting and blowing your nose in public were laid down in the Middle Ages (see *The Time Traveller's Guide to Medieval England* for details). Certain things do change, however: the wearing of hats is one. Men should take off their hats indoors unless they are working, so a tradesman might wear one in his shop but not in another man's house, especially if it is the house of a social superior. It is not acceptable for men to wear hats in church but some nonconformist ministers do, on the basis that preaching is their job.[41] Until about 1680 hats are put on to eat dinner (to avoid catching cold), but are removed when drinking someone's health. By that date most gentlemen habitually wear a wig so there is no need for a hat; the rest of society follows their example, giving up wearing hats indoors altogether, even at mealtimes.[42]

The etiquette of the nobility is extraordinary: it will amuse you greatly to watch the excruciating politeness of those who have practised the art for years, and I mean both the fawning servants and the noblemen themselves. Best of all is when two high-ranking aristocrats from foreign countries meet. Each of them is of course unfamiliar with the protocol in the other's country. Therefore, intensely aware that the honour of their homeland is at stake, they both feel obliged to express even more politeness than might normally be expected of them. How far Grand Duke Cosimo must stand beyond the front door of his house in London to welcome the king's brother is crucial: he must go so far out of his mansion to make the greeting look generous – but not too far, as he is a head of state and James is merely a royal duke. Cosimo must allow James to enter the house first but then, when going up the stairs, it is necessary for Cosimo's gentlemen to precede him and his guests, as they are receiving the Englishman, not vice versa. At the top, Cosimo must turn to the duke to invite him into the drawing room, where all the assembled Italian gentlemen there should bow to him as he makes his way through to the room where he and Cosimo will finally be able to talk to one another.[43]

At the other extreme, the art of the insult is a highly polished one. Ned Ward is with a friend in a coffee house one day, listening to the banter between some women from Billingsgate Market. His friend remarks in a low voice, 'Come away. Let's seek another apartment or these saucy-tongued old whores will tease us to death.' Unfortunately his words are overheard by one of the women, who stands up and 'gives her lungs a breathing':

You white-livered son of a Fleet Street bumsitter begot upon a chair at noonday between Ludgate and Temple Bar! You puppily offspring of a mangy nightwalker who was forced to play the whore an hour before she cried out to pay the bawd, her midwife, for bringing you, you bastard, into the world. Who is it you call whore?[44]

One other little piece of advice that you're unlikely to find in traditional history books: where do you go to the loo, if you are caught short away from home? Most towns are still small enough that you can take yourself off discreetly to find a bush on the roadside. In London, however, this is not possible. You will therefore find 'houses of office' at certain points, such as over the Fleet (before the Great Fire) or on London Bridge. You will also find them by the stairs leading down to the Thames. Most men can, of course, relieve themselves in the river itself, but those with more pressing needs and females will want to resort to one of these public conveniences. If you are nowhere near the river or a public house of office, then the thing to do is to visit a public house and pay for something that entitles you to use the facilities. In 1660, faced with a sudden looseness in the bowels, Pepys does exactly that: 'I went into a little alehouse at the end of Ratliffe and did give a groat for a pot of ale and there I did shit.'[45]

Thank you, Samuel, for recording it for posterity.

Units of Measurement

The measurement of distance, area, volume and weight is slowly becoming standardised across England. Most people recognise a standardised *inch*, and a *foot* of twelve inches, a *yard* of three feet, a *chain* of twenty-two yards, a *furlong* of ten chains and a statute *mile* of eight furlongs. For some specific distances you have specific measures. In measuring the height of a horse, for instance, you use the *hand* of four inches. In measuring depth, you use the *fathom* of six feet. In measuring cloth you use the *ell* of 45 inches. With regard to area, the standard form is based on the *pole* (or *rod*) of five and a half yards; a *rood* is a pole wide and a furlong long, and four roods make an *acre*. However, 'most people' does not mean everyone. There are parts of the country where locals will recognise few of the above measurements apart from the inch, and in Scotland even the inch is different.

As Celia Fiennes travels through northern England, she reflects on a hard day's travelling and remarks, 'the miles here are very long so that at least it may be esteemed the last 20 mile as long as the 30 mile gone in the morning'. It is not just that the miles *seem* very long, they really *are* longer than usual.[46] Although the statute mile of 1,760 yards referred to above was standardised back in 1593, many northerners still use the old English mile of 1,500 paces, each pace being five feet, so a mile is 2,500 yards. Just to confuse you, there is another 'old English mile' of eleven furlongs, or 2,420 yards, and an 'old British mile' of 2,428 yards.[47] In Oxfordshire three different sorts of 'mile' are in use, according to Robert Plot's *Natural History of Oxfordshire* (1677), including one of nine and a quarter furlongs (2,035 yards). Hampshire miles are similarly a little longer than a statute mile, varying from place to place, but mostly at this time being about ten furlongs (2,200 yards). The only thing of which you can be certain, wherever you are in the country, is that the person telling you the mileage from here to there is surer of the actual distance than you are.

Miles are easy by comparison with other measures. Area is especially complicated – for the simple reason that standardisation tends to take place when people trade their goods, and acres of land can't be taken to market. Purchasers have to accept the local customary ways when they buy land. Although in most places an acre is an area 40 poles by 4, the eventual size of your acre depends on how big your pole is. The standard size is 16.5 feet, but in Cumbria you will come across poles or rods of 18, 20 or 21 feet.[48] And that's just in Cumbria. Go to Cornwall and everything is madly different. There a fathom is 5 feet, not the usual 6. A mile is much longer than a statute mile (although no one seems to know exactly how long), and an acre is a similarly ill-defined area, often the equivalent of an ancient hide or 120 statute acres.

Weight is even more complicated, as it depends on what you are weighing. If it is bread, grain, gold, pearls, silver or apothecaries' drugs, then you weigh according to *troy* pounds. In this system there are only 12 ounces per pound – but note that the ounces in question are a little heavier than the ounces you know. Almost all household items except bread are weighed according to the *avoirdupois* pound: this has 16 ounces to the pound, but using an ounce that is only $^{73}/_{80}$ of a troy ounce. Hence the old quip: 'a pound of iron weighs more than a pound of gold but an ounce of gold weighs more than an ounce of iron'. Confused yet? Wait until you get to the West Country: in Cornwall and Devon there are 18 ounces to the pound, not 12 or 16.

Complications increase further with volume. You probably know that four *gills* make a *pint*, and eight pints make a *gallon*. You may also be aware that 54 gallons make a *hogshead*, two hogsheads make a *butt* and two butts make a *tun*. That is true of beer – but only in London, and then only when measuring *beer*; if it is *ale* (brewed without hops) then there are 48 gallons to the hogshead. Outside London a hogshead of beer or ale is 51 gallons. But note that these are *ale and beer* gallons of 282 cubic inches, which are larger than wine gallons (231 cubic inches); you need 63 of the latter to make a hogshead of wine.[49] Some imported wines come in hogsheads of yet different volumes: a hogshead of claret is 46 wine gallons. A hogshead of brandy is 57 wine gallons. It's enough to drive you to drink.

Now is probably not the moment to tell you that Scottish weights and measures are all different from the English ones. But just in case: four Scottish *gills* make a *mutchkin*, and two mutchkins make a *chopin*, two chopins make a Scottish *pint*, and eight pints make a Scottish *gallon*. Therefore although a Scottish gill is only three-quarters the size of an English gill, a Scottish gallon is more than three times its English namesake. A Scottish ell is 37 inches and a Scottish *fall* is 6 ells, and a Scottish chain is 4 falls, a Scottish furlong 10 chains and a Scottish mile 8 furlongs. This would make a Scottish mile longer than an English one by 640 feet, *except* that a Scottish inch as standardised in 1661 is fractionally longer than an English inch, making a Scottish mile longer than an English one by just under 650 feet.[50] Frankly, the complexities of weights and measures are such that you cannot possibly hope to understand them all. You simply have to do what everyone else does, and that is become familiar with local measurements and learn by experience not to pay over the odds. This is why local customs have lasted such a long time. And if you are travelling away from London, you just have to accept that some miles really are longer than others.

Money

Look at the coins in your purse. Pick one out. Think of all the hands it has passed through, whether being spat on for luck by a London market trader first thing in the morning or daintily pushed across a counter at the Royal Exchange. It may have travelled the length and breadth of the kingdom several times over, passing through thousands – if not tens of thousands – of hands. It may have travelled around a city many times, and through the centre over and over again, sewing itself into the social fabric as it goes in and out of pockets and purses, money boxes and palms. It has been everywhere and has bought almost everything: rent, debts, bread, wine, houses, sex, clocks, jewels, books, guns, loyalty and betrayal. To a thief, a half-crown may mean death; to a beggar, life. It is like a memory-less ghost passing between us, part of the indefinable essence of humanity that makes society more than the sum of its parts.

Despite all this strange mystery that coins represent, they are also subject to change. And the second half of the seventeenth century is probably the most revolutionary period in the entire history of money.

Let's begin with the coins themselves. At the start of the period, the currency is a bit of a mess. The denominations are much the same as in previous and later centuries – the pound sterling in England and Wales is composed of 20 shillings, each shilling being of 12 pence (written '12d'), and each penny (1d) being four farthings (¼d) – but apart from a few machine-made or 'milled' examples from the reigns of Elizabeth I and Charles I, the coins in your purse are all hammered. That is to say, they have been minted by being placed between two die and struck hard with a heavy hammer, by hand. They are generally of a low quality; they wear easily and are liable to be clipped around the edges by people hoping to take a little of the precious metal and sell it on. This practice is technically treason and is punishable by hanging, drawing and quartering or burning alive, but it still continues. There is also an acute shortage of small change; many tradesmen (especially in London) have taken to minting their own ½d and ¼d tokens in copper, tin and lead. These are accepted and collected by the proprietors of shops who, when they have a sufficiency, exchange them with the issuer for silver. For a few years in the 1660s, Irish shillings of the reign of James I are used as 9d pieces.[51] Obviously a money supply that includes thousands of unofficial and outdated coins is unsatisfactory. And Charles II has no wish for people to see Cromwell's head on a coin. For all these reasons and many more, coinage reform is desperately needed.

The new coins start to appear in 1662 with a handsome silver crown of 5 shillings. They are milled on heavy machines that leave a far clearer imprint, and have a raised edge to reduce the level of clipping. The crown is followed in 1663 by a silver half-crown, a silver shilling and a golden guinea – a new denomination so called because it is made from gold that comes from Guinea in Africa. Its value is initially set at 20s but fluctuates thereafter with the price of bullion, rising as high as 30s in the 1690s, before settling down to 21s 6d for the last few years of the century. Over the next decade, high-quality five-guinea, two-guinea and half-guinea pieces are also minted in gold, and sixpences, groats (4d), threepences, tuppences (2d) and pennies are produced in silver. From 1672 the government starts to mint good copper halfpennies and farthings (although tin is used from 1684, to help the Cornish tin industry). Charles II orders this new copper coinage to bear the image of Britannia ruling the waves, thereby giving us a national icon at the same time. The unofficial tokens quickly fall out of use.

If you cross the border into Scotland, you are in for a shock. All the prices will sound outrageously expensive to you. This is because the Scottish pound is valued at one-twelfth of an English one. So when a Scotsman asks 60 shillings for a pair of woollen stockings – and there you are thinking he wants £3 sterling – he is actually demanding the equivalent of an English crown, 5s. The easiest way to bear in mind the difference is to remember that a Scottish shilling has the same value as an English penny. Old coins continue in circulation, but in Charles II's reign you have the following Scottish denominations freshly milled in silver: a merk (worth 13s 4d in Scottish shillings, or 13$\frac{1}{3}$d in English money), and four-merk, half-merk and quarter-merk pieces. The Scottish moneyers also turn out copper sixpences and tuppences (equating to $\frac{1}{2}$d and $\frac{1}{6}$d in English currency). In James II's reign, only 10s coins are minted (English 10d). In the reign of William and Mary, more silver coins appear – 60s, 40s, 20s, 10s and 5s – but no gold coins are produced in Scotland. Foreign gold coins are accepted for their bullion value, particularly the Venetian ducat, the French louis d'or and, dare it be said, the English guinea.

Despite all the hard work improving the coinage in the 1660s and 1670s, by the mid-1690s England is once more undergoing a crisis. Coin clippers have practically devoured the currency, damaging not only the coins themselves but also trust in their value. Some have been trimmed to little more than half their original size: when you now go into a shop and pay with silver, it is likely that the shop attendant will weigh your money.[52] Part of the problem is that the silver is worth more than the face value of the currency: goldsmiths and bankers take in coins and melt them down, and make more in selling the metal than the coins were worth. Evelyn records on 11 May 1696 that there is 'want of current money to carry on the smallest concerns, even for daily provisions in the markets ... causing such a scarcity that every day tumults are feared'.[53] The same month a riot almost breaks out in Derbyshire when, to their horror, a group of miners see their heavily clipped wages refused by the local tradesmen.[54] The difficulties of financing the war with France add to the problem: if the army cannot be paid, who knows what might happen. So the government calls in its team of advisors, which includes a certain professor of mathematics called Isaac Newton. He suggests a complete recoinage – and thereby lands himself a job. Over the next two and a half years, under Newton's watchful eye, the Royal Mint produces new coins to the value of £6.8 million: more than twice the value it has minted in the previous three decades.[55] If you put your hand in your pocket in 1700 and look at your change, you will see a fine array of milled coins that, in respect of the silver and copper, will closely resemble their successors in the early twentieth century. And if you meet Isaac Newton in person, you will observe that he is now a very rich man.

Impressive though the changes in the coinage undoubtedly are, the real revolutions in money are to be found elsewhere – in the flexibility of finance and in attitudes to borrowing. Cast your mind back to all those exceptionally rich men mentioned in chapter 3, with fortunes of £100,000 or more. Their wealth is principally built on lending money. Merchants are becoming businessmen, and goldsmiths are becoming bankers. The cities of London, Edinburgh and Glasgow in particular are seeing the professionalisation of providing finance. Partnerships and companies are being established to fund entrepreneurs, pay interest on deposits and deal in government bonds. Edward Backwell, Francis Child, John Freame, Thomas Gould and Richard Hoare all serve apprenticeships as members of the Goldsmiths' Company in London but none of them goes on to become a craftsman. They all become bankers, with ledgers full of clients' details concerning loans and agreements. Edward Backwell has a thousand customers with a total of £500,000 on deposit with him in September 1664.[56] Francis Child establishes Child's Bank. Richard Hoare starts the bank bearing his name that his descendants will own for centuries to come. The partnership of Freame & Gould will later become better known as Barclays Bank. Coutts Bank is also founded in this period, by John Campbell in 1692. If you want to look for any other bankers, forty-four partnerships and companies are listed in *A Collection of the Names of the Merchants Living in and about the City of London* (1677), the world's first trade directory, where they appear as 'goldsmiths who keep running cashes'. Two scriveners, Robert Clayton and John Morris, start up an innovative bank that caters to landowners: in the 1660s they have deposits of about £1.5 million on their books. Over the course of the Restoration period the world of finance shifts from personal borrowing to multimillion-pound banking.

Alongside the establishment of banks, a whole new approach to financial services develops. People start writing cheques. The earliest known example dates from February 1660: it has all the major features of a modern cheque, namely a request to a bank (Clayton & Morris) to pay the named bearer a specified sum, this sum being written in words as well as in figures, together with the date and the account holder's signature.[57] Bills of Exchange continue to be used for overseas transfers. When gentlemen send their sons abroad on the Grand Tour, they are not so foolish as to stuff their pockets with gold; instead they periodically send them Bills of Exchange for £100 or £200, which they can cash at bankers in major cities.[58] The new service of buildings insurance takes off, as mentioned in chapter 1. In the 1680s, Edward Lloyd opens a coffee house in London where the underwriters of shipping insurance meet; by January 1692 he is publishing a weekly professional news-sheet entitled *Ships Arrived at, and Departed from several Ports of England* – the forerunner of Lloyd's List. In 1698, at another coffee house near the Royal Exchange, John Castaing starts to publish a twice-weekly newsletter called *The Course of the Exchange*, which gives prices for traded stocks – the forerunner of the modern stock market. With the number of joint-stock companies in London increasing from 15 to 140 in just five years (1690–95), you can see why such a list is needed.[59]

On top of all these changes, the government's attitude to trade and finance undergoes a series of important developments. From 1660 it is advised by a Committee on the Plantations and a Committee on Trade. Over the next three decades these committees collect data regarding Britain's overseas financial interests until they are reconstituted as the Board of Trade in 1696. In 1696, too, the Chancellor of the Exchequer presents the first Budget to Parliament.[60] These important reforms follow shortly after the establishment of the Bank of England in 1694. As the war with France costs the government more than £5 million per year, it becomes imperative to get the nation's finances on a sound footing. The Bank of England successfully attracts investors. The idea is for the government to charge extra duties for four years on certain imports in order to pay 8 per cent interest on an advance of £1.2 million by the bank's subscribers. This it does but, having advanced all its capital, the bank has no means to pay those who wish to withdraw their cash. As a result, it starts issuing promissory notes, which can be drawn on the bank or transferred to other people. Herein lie the origins of England's banknotes. You will see them with the familiar 'I promise to pay ...' but in strange denominations, such as 'I promise to pay [name of original depositor] or Bearer on demand the Sum of Five Hundred and Fifty-Five pounds'. The reason is that early notes relate to the actual sum originally deposited or withdrawn. In 1695 the Bank of Scotland is established, and it too starts issuing banknotes.

Private banks, milled coins, cheques, banknotes, insurance, bonds, the Bank of England, Lloyd's of London and the stock market – it all seems a world away from the hammered coins of 1660. And, as if to cap it all, there's one further icon of modern finance that develops at this time. Charles's government never properly recovers from its over-expenditure in the 1660s. The debt remains on the books for evermore – and thus it is from this period that we date our National Debt.

Taxes and Lotteries

As the old saying goes, nothing is certain but death and taxes – although the rich in all ages like to think that at least one of the two is open to negotiation.[61] The good news for you is that no Restoration Parliament would dream of taxing you as heavily as you are taxed in the modern world. There is no Value Added Tax on purchasable items. There is no income tax on what you earn. There is no inheritance tax. Instead there is a range of minor taxes which, more or less, are means-tested. Some may seem a little bizarre to you, or even silly – until, that is, you have to pay them.

A substantial revenue stream for the king is the customs paid on goods that are imported and exported and duties on other specific items. The list of these, as agreed by Parliament in 1660, is extraordinarily extensive and detailed. Take pans, for instance: if they are frying pans or dripping pans, the importer has to pay a duty of £3 per hundredweight (112lbs *avoirdupois*); if they are warming pans, they are charged at £4 per dozen. There are forty-four rates for different sorts of linen cloth, twenty-three rates for silk and nine for the various types of lace. There are ten rates for different patterns of knife, some charged by the dicker (10 knives), some by the dozen and some by the gross (a dozen dozen, 144). The high levels of duty on many items mean that imported goods are luxury items, beyond the reach of most ordinary people. But with regard to alcohol, everyone is liable to pay a rate of duty. For every barrel of ale or beer sold at 6s or more, the brewer has to pay 15d. There is a 1d duty on every gallon of spirits, and the duties on imported beer and wine are heavy: for example, £4 10s on every tun of wine (252 gallons) imported to London from Bordeaux.[62]

The traditional form of extra taxation is the subsidy: a levy on income from land at 4s per pound, or on the value of goods at 2s 8d per pound. The thresholds for this are quite high, so it really only affects the rich. But more than a few manage to avoid it. The king is astonished that individuals with an income of £3,000 a year can get away with paying just £16 tax. The reason – you will be shocked to hear – is that they lie about their incomes. Some people in Bristol assess themselves at 1 per cent of their real wealth, so after 1663 this tax is rarely levied.[63] By then Charles II's government has introduced the poll tax, a charge levied on everyone according to his or her status. Ordinary people over the age of sixteen pay 6d per head if they are married and 12d if they are single. Lords pay according to their rank: for example, dukes pay £100, earls £60, barons £40 and knights £20. Gentlemen pay £5 if they do not have a coat of arms, £10 if they do. Poll taxes are levied seven times between 1660 and 1697, before being abandoned as inefficient. In the intervening years other taxes are deployed. The most unusual is the 'Free and Voluntary Present' to the king – a voluntary tax in which you can give the government whatever you want, up to a maximum of £200 (or £400 if you are a lord). You might think that the whole idea is madness – I mean, who would? – but it yields more than £229,000.[64]

The hearth tax is levied in England from 1662 to 1689. Every householder is liable to pay 1s, twice a year, for every fireplace in his or her house. The idea is that the rich pay more, because their houses have more fireplaces. That is all very well in theory, but a problem arises in that a surveyor has to enter every house to count the number of hearths. If there is a chimney, does it serve just the one hearth on the ground floor or is there a hearth on the upper floor as well? It is easier to count the windows of a property, because you can see them from outside. Consequently the government institutes a window tax in 1696: owners of houses with ten windows or fewer pay a tax of 2s, but owners with more than ten windows pay 10s. More bizarre even than taxing windows is the marriage tax, levied from 1695. Ordinary people have to pay 2s to register a baptism, 2s 6d for a marriage and 4s for a burial. Noblemen and the rich pay more: a duke or an archbishop must pay £50 4s to be buried; a gentleman must pay £1 4s to bury his wife or one of his children. The new land tax that is introduced in 1692 is much more sensible: landowners pay £2 for every £100 of income from land. Simple and proportionate.

Taxes are not the only way by which the government extracts money from your purse. The other is the lottery. The first successful enterprise is the Royal Oak, a monopoly that proves so popular that by 1688 its commissioners are willing to pay the Crown £4,200 per year to run it. The monopoly is challenged in 1693 by a government official, Thomas Neale, who sets up the Million Adventure the following year. The idea is to raise £1 million for public funds by selling 100,000 tickets at £10 each. The first prize is £1,000 per year for sixteen years; there are nine prizes of £500 per year; the lowest of the 2,500 prizes is £10 per year. The clever part is that even tickets that do not win earn £1 per year interest for sixteen years, so everyone who subscribes wins. It opens the flood-gates. Dozens of lotteries start up in the mid-1690s, with names such as Good Luck to the Fortunate, the Unparallel'd Adventure, the Ladies Invention and the Honest Proposal. The popularity increases as they become more affordable. In the years 1694–6 most of them require a stake of £1; in 1696–7 the amount required tumbles to mere pennies. The lowest is just one penny – for the Wheel of Fortune in 1698 – which promises to pay £1,000 to one of its 1.65 million ticket-holders. These private lotteries undercut the government's second venture into the business, the Malt Lottery in 1697, which raises just £17,000. Accordingly Parliament puts a stop to all lotteries in 1699; only the Royal Oak Lottery and the Charitable Adventure for the Benefit of Greenwich Hospital are allowed to continue.[65]

There is one other 'lottery' that continues after 1699: the tontine, a scheme whereby greater benefits accrue to those who live longest.

In 1693 the Chancellor of the Exchequer starts to sell annuities on this basis, in order to raise £1 million. If you buy a £100 share, you'll receive 10 per cent interest until 1700 and thereafter a 14 per cent annuity. However, if other investors predecease you, then their benefits come to you too. You could call it the ultimate lottery – the lottery of life. The last beneficiary will not die until 1783, by which time he has an annual income of more than £1,000.[66]

Shopping

In the modern world you go shopping; in Restoration Britain, frequently the shopping comes to you. In Doncaster, where they make high-quality woollen stockings of various colours, the women 'go with bundles of the stockings on their arms from inn to inn where travellers are, that you can hardly evade laying out money with them, for they will follow you up into your chamber and will not be denied without a great deal of trouble'.[67] In most towns you have much the same attention from pedlars, hawkers and petty chapmen. Small hardware items such as mops, mats, baskets, brooms, penknives, quills, combs, inkhorns, bootlaces, playing cards, newspapers and printed broadsides are hawked from door to door, as are services such as sweeping chimneys, repairing chairs, mending pots and pans and sharpening knives and scissors. Water carriers will bring water to your house for a penny. Women parade the streets with enormous baskets balanced on their heads, selling fish, vegetables, herbs and fruit.

If the hawkers can't persuade you to buy, then it is to the shops or the market that you must go, depending on what you require. Broadly speaking, you go to a market for food; for anything high in value, you go to a shop. The most important exception to this rule is bread: loaves are occasionally sold in markets but it is more usual to buy direct from the bakery.

The marketplaces themselves are open areas in the middle of towns, where temporary wooden stalls are set up for the day. Trading begins very early: the stall keepers tend to set up before daylight, around 3 a.m. in summer or 5 a.m. in winter. In most towns there is just the one marketplace but in a large settlement there may be several. York has two main markets: Thursday Market, for poultry, meat, dairy produce, oatmeal, salt, herbs, vegetables, wildfowl and rabbits, as well as candles, hemp and coarse cloth; and Pavement Market, for poultry, vegetables, wildfowl, rabbits, roasting pigs, eggs, corn, sieves, baskets, woodenware, shoes and leather goods. In addition there are specialist markets for malt, butter, hay, wool, leather, fish and cattle.[68] Norwich is unusual in being a large city with just the one marketplace where everything is sold. Prices tend to be steady or slightly in decline in the 1670s and 1680s – they don't start to rise until the 1690s – but in times of dearth the cost of basic foodstuffs can double.[69] Be prepared to haggle. Although traders will be reluctant to compromise on price early in the morning, as the day wears on they may well do so, especially for perishables. Take a basket with you, as no one will give you any packaging with your goods. Most housewives drape a cloth over the top of their basket to protect the contents from flies, dust and all the other infelicities of a crowded space. Others take napkins or similar cloths to wrap around their cheese and fish, so that they do not taint the other purchases. An earthenware pot is a good idea if you plan to buy butter on a warm day; the vendors will bring it to market in a small wooden barrel and will scoop it out to weigh it in front of you, but after you've paid for it, it's your responsibility.

Shops are very different from their modern equivalent. Large expanses of plate glass have yet to be invented, and indeed very few shops have any glass in their windows at all. Most have shutters that open in the middle, with hinges at the top and bottom: the top part swings upwards to provide shelter from the rain, and the lower shutter hinges down to form a table for displaying goods. Shops selling high-value merchandise, such as clocks, musical and scientific instruments and jewellery, do not have such open fronts but windows like a normal house: it is the sign hanging outside that denotes the premises as a shop. If you enter, you'll be served at a counter in the front parlour. Note that shops open later than the market, about 6 a.m. in summer and 8 a.m. in winter. For some commodities you will need to visit a workshop. Furniture, for example, is made to order. Large items of metalwork also need to be specifically commissioned from a blacksmith, although small objects like candlesticks and knives may be available from a mercer's shop or in the market.

The other place you might go shopping is a fair. In the seventeenth century these are nearing the end of their long history, but some are still vibrant. They used to supply all the things that you couldn't get in a market; effectively they were moveable towns that came to a locality for two or three days every year. Now they broadly fall into one of two sorts: those in which one or two major commodities are traded in bulk, such as wool, horses, cattle, sheep or cheese; and those that have become recreational fairs, where the principal commodities are drinking, dancing, sex and merriment. There are about ten or twelve of both sort in each county, all of which are held between Easter and early November.

Without doubt, the greatest fair in the country at this time is 'Stir-Bitch' or Stourbridge Fair, which takes place in early September on the banks of the River Cam, near Cambridge. It is a must-see: Daniel Defoe regards it as 'not only the greatest [fair] in the whole nation but in the world'.[70] The London publican and satirist Ned Ward puts it in terms that are both more poetic and earthier. According to him, it is

> where vice, merchandise and diversion draw the Cambridge youth, London traders, Lynn whores and abundance of ubiquitarian strollers into a promiscuous assembly, all contributing something to either the pleasure or profit of one another; some coming to spend money, others to get it ... I beheld such a number of wooden edifices, and such a multitude of gentry, scholars, tradesmen, whores, hawkers, pedlars, and pick-pockets, that it seemed to me like an abstract of all sorts of mankind, drawn into a lesser body, to show the world in epitome.[71]

Thomas Baskerville is equally astonished by the place:

> It was, methought, a goodly sight to see the vast quantities of earthenware there spread upon the turf ... here you shall see large streets and shops full of all the variety of wares that are to be sold in London, and great quantities of iron brought from several parts of the nation and elsewhere. The wool fair there to which they come from all parts of England at that time to be furnished is no less. Here you shall see carts laden with oysters; here you shall see great heaps of salt fish; and here you shall see on the bankside great heaps of coal to be sold; and the river thick set with boats for a mile or more in length with all sorts of provisions ...[72]

You'll also see traffic jams of coaches and hackney cabs on the road between Cambridge and the fair, carrying people each way for the price of 3d a head. Wandering through the fair itself, you'll see the timber stalls and tents placed in rows like streets: Oyster Row, Garlic Row, Mercers' Row and Cheddars' Lane. The street called Cheapside is where the London retailers gather: the goldsmiths, toy makers, brass workers, turners, milliners, haberdashers, hatters, mercers, drapers, pewterers and china-goods importers. Interspersed amongst them are coffee houses, taverns, brandy shops and eating houses. Nearby there is a large square called the Duddery, where the wholesalers unload their packs and there is a pulpit for the clergy to preach on the Sunday during the fair. Near the Duddery you can buy woollen goods, brought by dealers from as far away as Yorkshire, Lancashire, Somerset and Devon; over the course of the week more than £100,000 of cloth will be sold here. You can buy Yorkshire kerseys, Manchester fustians, Kidderminster blankets, Norwich stuffs and Devon serges. In addition, immense sacks of wool called 'pockets', which weigh 25 hundredweight each (2,800lbs), are sold to mill owners. The trade in raw wool alone exceeds £50,000 at each fair. The hop business is no less impressive, with a significant proportion of all the hops in the country changing hands here. Other important markets within the fair are for wrought iron and brassware from Birmingham, edged tools and knives from Sheffield, and glassware and stockings from Nottingham and Leicester. Isaac Newton even manages to buy here the glass prisms he needs to prove that light splits into a spectrum of colours.[73]

For a keen observer like Ned Ward, the real delight lies not in the shopping but in the people. As he walks along Cheapside he comes across 'linen drapers, silk men, ironmongers, leather-sellers, tobacconists, etc., who, swelled in their shops, looked as big above the rest of the petty dealers as the bluff well-fed senior fellows of a college do above the lean, thin-gutted poor sizers'. At the end of the street, he turns left and walks along by the river, where:

> my nostrils were saluted with such a saline savoury whiff, as if I had been walking in a dry fishmongers shop in Thames Street; at last I came into a Dutch market of red and pickled herrings, salt-fish, oysters, pitch, tar, soap, &c. Next [to] these a parcel of wooden trumpery, ranged in as much order as a cupboard of plate, where bacchanalian students may furnish themselves with punch-bowls agreeable to their own bibacity, sots supply themselves with cans sizable to their own humours, and beggars accommodate themselves with spoons and porridge-dishes of any dimension, suitable to their own appetites. Adjoining to this place stand about a dozen suttlers' [provisioners']

boozing-kens, distinguished by the name of the Lynn-booths; the good people that keep 'em being inhabitants of that town, and have so fair a reputation for the foul practice of venery that their sinful hovels have always maintained the character of being notorious bawdy-houses; the scholars, to encourage the old trade of basket-making, have great resort to these up-tail academies, where they are often presented with a Lynn fairing [a present from a fair], which brings 'em to thin jaws, and a month or two's spare diet, as a penance for a minute's titillation; giving many of 'em reason to say with a scholar under the same affliction, who being at chapel whispered to his chamber-fellow, 'Chum, chum, though I have the Word of God in my mouth, to tell thee the truth on it, I have a Lynn devil in my breeches.'[74]

It takes all sorts to make a world, they say, and as Ward rightly remarks, you will find the world in epitome at Stourbridge Fair.

If you love shopping, London is the place for you. Whatever it is you seek, you will find it in abundance: whole lines of emporia selling not just every commodity but every *variety* of every commodity. Thames Street is known for its candlemakers' shops, Canon Street is famous for its linen shops, Cheapside for its goldsmiths and drapers. Little Britain is where you go for second-hand books, St Paul's Churchyard for new ones. At the junction of Fleet Street and Water Lane you will find Thomas Tompion's shop selling clocks, watches and barometers; next door is the cabinet-maker and marquetry-layer Jasper Braem. Step into an apothecary's shop and see the wall-mounted shelves with rows of coloured bottles, the spoons hanging on the wall, an apprentice grinding away at the mortar, and the hatted apothecary waiting to serve you behind his shop counter, beside a cabinet of drawers marked with Latin names. Or enter a cobbler's shop and see all the fine leather boots and shoes hanging in their pairs from the ceiling, while the cobblers themselves work hunched over their lasts, with trimmings of shoe leather scattered across the tables. The baker stands behind his counter with shelves of loaves behind him and a few on the counter, the sweet smell of freshly baked bread tempting you to buy.

The most luxurious shops of all are in the four exchanges. The Royal Exchange in the heart of the city, rebuilt after the Fire, is still the great gathering place for merchants and news circulation. Advertisements are plastered all over the pillars of the four colonnades around the central square, and such is the noise of so many conversations that you have to shout to make yourself heard to your companion. As Ned Ward observes, the flat-hatted and richly dressed merchants do a fair bit of talking with their heads and hands, commonly sneezing with the snuff they take; and if they sit on one of the benches, they do so as if taking their place on a great saddle. For shoppers, the main attractions are not down here, but upstairs in the galleries of high-quality small booths, where you can buy draperies and high-value items, such as Chinese porcelain, musical instruments, tobacco pipes, clocks and watches, guns, lacquered cabinets from Japan, mathematical instruments, haberdashery and gold and silverware. The New Exchange, just to the south of the Strand, is a similar two-storey building containing galleries of small shops, largely attended by women selling hosiery and similar luxury goods to the Royal Exchange. The Middle Exchange, also on the Strand, which does business from 1671 to 1696, sells hosiery, jewellery and books. The fourth exchange is the Exeter Exchange, which opens in 1676; this also sells hosiery and luxury household items such as drapery and books, but it has an auction house on its upper floor. Note that even in these luxurious shops you will need to haggle. Pepys goes shopping for an instrument with which to measure timber in March 1663 and finds one, but cannot agree on the price. As for auctions, these are sometimes held 'by the candle'. A candle an inch long is lit and the winning buyer is the one who shouts out his price last before the flame goes out.[75]

As you will see, many shops are staffed by women. In fact, the higher quality the goods, the prettier the woman who will serve you. Walking past the rich premises on Cheapside, you will see the merchants' wives at their doors, beckoning you with a sweet smile. Enticement, flirtation and feminine pulchritude are tricks of the salesman's trade: sex sells, even in the seventeenth century. In fact, *especially* in the seventeenth century. The galleries of the Royal Exchange are attended by the most attractive young females, so much so that people call it 'the merchants' seraglio'. When he pays a visit to the Exchange, Ned Ward comments that

> We went up where women sat in their pinfolds [pens], begging of custom, with such amorous looks, and affable tones, that I could not but fancy they had as much mind to dispose of themselves as the commodities they deal in. My ears on both sides were so baited with 'Fine linens, Sir,' and 'Gloves and ribbons, Sir,' that I had a milliner's and a seamstress's shop in my head for a week after.[76]

The real glory of London shopping for the modern observer lies in its markets. There is a plethora of these in the capital, and you will have to elbow your way through the crowds that throng them early in the morning just to see what they have on offer. Before the Great Fire there are two general markets in the city, Cheapside and Gracechurch Street. In addition there are many specialist markets, namely: Aldersgate Street (fruit and vegetables), Billingsgate (fish and coal), Bishopsgate (meal), Blackwell Hall (cloth), Eastcheap (meat), Fish Street Hill (fish), Leadenhall (skins, hides and meat), Newgate Street (meal), Old Fish Street (fish), Queenhithe (meal and flour), St Nicholas Shambles (meat), St Paul's Churchyard (fruit and vegetables), Smithfield (cattle, horses, sheep and hay) and Stocks (meat and fish). After 1666, six of those are no longer held,[77] but you can add instead Bear Key Market (for corn), and three more markets for general food supplies: Honey Lane, Holborn Bars and Butcher Row. In addition, to cater for the citizens in the rapidly expanding suburbs, you have many markets outside the city walls, several of which have recently been established in or near the great squares.[78] Note that not all markets operate all days of the week: some do – such as Newgate, Covent Garden, Honey Lane and Stocks – but others are held on only one or two days.[79] Leadenhall sells meat on Mondays, Wednesdays and Saturdays, leather on Tuesdays, and hides on Thursdays and Fridays. Hours vary from market to market, but most start selling around 3 a.m. in summer and 5 a.m. in winter, so that the majority of the trade is done before the retail shops open. Late-night opening, from 1674, is on Saturdays, when the markets can stay open to 10 p.m.[80]

Of all the London markets, Smithfield is the most dramatic. You might not think of a market in terms of drama but just you go and see it when they start doing business, sometimes as early as midnight. It is a huge space: five muddy acres are set aside for the trade in live animals. They all give voice loudly to their discomfort in the darkness, the cows lowing repeatedly in their pens in the centre of the area, the sheep bleating back at them. Braziers around the edge light the animals' heads as they are lifted suddenly above the tide of the cattle. Here a black eye gleams in the light of your lantern; there a man with a flaming torch corrals yet more sheep into a pen, shouting at them all the while, and with his dog barking at the creatures as they veer this way and that. Other dogs join in with the canine cacophony. Pigs grunt angrily. Sheep accompany the din. Market traders call out, prodding the animals to show prospective dealers the quality of the beasts. And all this has the backdrop of music playing in the nearby alehouses around the perimeter, and people standing and laughing in their groups as they drink their beer.

Finally, we return to Covent Garden. Whereas in 1660 it is still an elegant residential square, with aristocrats' carriages setting down or picking up their noble cargoes, over the rest of the decade flower traders start to set up stalls around its perimeter. Then the vegetable sellers join them. The wealthy residents try at first to clear them off but in 1670 the earl of Bedford decides that the potential revenue from the area is just too great, positioned as it is between the old city and the fashionable West End, and he obtains a charter for the burgeoning market. Within a very short time it grows to become the pre-eminent place in London to buy fruit and vegetables. Booths are set up along the south side: wooden arcades where men and women call out their wares from behind the most colourful food displays you'll see anywhere. Walking beneath Inigo Jones's covered walkway at the end of the century, you will look out on a pullulating mass of people drawn in by the arrangements and by exotic new plants and vegetables. Women especially cherish this hour or so of freedom from the household to exchange the day's gossip and buy amid a profusion of produce, or to meet a secret admirer, while buying a few herbs or some gingerbread to explain where they have been. Men stroll through the centre discussing business on their way to and fro between the workplace and the coffee house, or on the lookout for flirtatious young women. It is as if all the pleasure gardens, herb gardens, vegetable patches, fields and orchards of the kingdom – and many from abroad – have come to this magnificent square to offer the greatest delight to the housewife, the cook, the epicure and the botanist. No one can hope to visit the Garden of Eden but, on a fine day, the Garden of London is a most satisfying substitute.

6

What to Wear

It seems that people in all times have an irresistible urge to develop a particularly ridiculous garment that marks out the fashion of their generation to those who come after them. Shoes with toes so long you cannot climb stairs, cuffs that hang so low you could trip over them, horned headdresses, codpieces, skirts so wide that you have to turn sideways to walk through doorways, and ruffs – all these garments make you scratch your head and wonder how on earth they came to be so popular. Surely, you think to yourself, people in the Restoration period – the age of Christopher Wren, Isaac Newton and the Scientific Revolution – have grown up and are above all that nonsense? But as soon as you think it, you just *know* that some friend of the king's is going to come up with something else even more bizarre. And you would not be wrong. This is the period when the male elite decided it was a good idea to cut off their hair and start wearing cascading wigs.

Restoration fashionistas come up with quite a few odd garments, actually. Gentlemen might have difficulty dealing with petticoat breeches covered in ribbons, and little matching skirts just below their knees. Ladies might be reluctant to start wearing patches on the face – and just wait until you hear about the 'fontage'. But before delving into such specific matters there are some general points about Restoration appearances that you need to bear in mind, if you want to fit in.

The first thing is that unless you are small, 'fitting in' is going to be tricky: Restoration men on average are just 5ft 7 inches (1.70m) and women 5ft 1 inch (1.55m); it will not be until the nineteenth century that people start to reach their modern average heights.[1] Most Restoration people who are on the tall side are likely to come from the well-nourished sectors of society – the great, the rich and the middle sort – so if you are tall and you dress in the clothes of the working trades, the country people and the poor, you are likely to stand out all the more. The second point is that, when it comes to fashion, the whole 'Island Story' of British history is fundamentally misleading. English fashion closely follows French and Dutch fashions in the seventeenth century, just as it followed French and Spanish styles in the sixteenth. The fascination with the wig starts in France. The surge in the silk-weaving industry in England is partly triggered by Louis XIV's expulsion of the Huguenots in 1685. One word from the king and suddenly the whole court can be sent scurrying to find tailors to produce fashionable new clothes – and the inspiration for such alternative directions nearly always comes from abroad.

A third point you need to bear in mind is that changes in fashion do not affect just the great and the rich; they have a knock-on effect throughout most of society, including the poor. Clothes that are out of date are generally handed down by the wealthy to their servants. Men and women of the 'middle sort' – who tend to copy the fashionable dress of the gentry – realise that they too must constantly change style. Not only do they want to be seen dressed in the latest fashions, but they really don't want to be mistaken for a servant. This can happen quite easily, even to a prosperous gentleman like Samuel Pepys: in March 1667 he accompanies his wife to church and is mistaken by the verger for Mrs Pepys's servant. The passing down of clothing explains why the clothes regarded as suitable for a maidservant in the 1690s are based on the court fashions of about 1680. The materials are not the same, of course, but if you come to grips with the fashions of the wealthy, you will also understand the developing dress sense of the rest of society.

When it comes to colour, you need to remember that your visual palette has been conditioned by the invention of aniline dyes in the nineteenth century. In Restoration Britain, only natural dyes are available, and they are not all equally affordable. If you look at the folk travelling the highways, the colours of their clothes will be red, blue, black, white (in the form of natural linen) and a whole range of shades of brown and russet. The traditional sources for these are madder root (red), woad (blue), oak galls (black), walnut (brown), weld (yellow) and orchil lichens (violet). People don't often wear green, even though it can be made by dyeing a garment with weld and overdyeing with woad. Other dyes found naturally in Europe, such as the crushed *kermes* insect (scarlet) and secretions of the *murex* sea-snail (imperial purple), are very expensive and scarce. Brazilwood (red) and indigo (blue) have been imported for centuries from Asia but they too have traditionally been expensive and are rarely used. Change has been in the air for a number of years, though, as the opening up of the world's trade routes is bringing new dyes to Britain. Fustic (yellow), logwood (grey-purple) and cochineal (red) are being imported from South America. Lac (red) and cutch (yellow), as well as increasing amounts of indigo, are arriving from India. At home, the production of copperas – iron sulphate, a black dye – expands in southern England.[2] Alum and other metal-based mordants necessary to fix these dyes are also more easily available. A dyer's workshop in Lincoln in 1664 contains large amounts of woad, fustic, brazilwood, logwood, madder, orchil, indigo, copperas and alum.[3] In short, although the colours will appear relatively unexciting to your jaded modern eye, seventeenth-century clothing is becoming more colourful, especially among the profligate courtiers.

Men's Clothing

UNDERWEAR

The closest garment to a man's heart – physically, if not metaphorically – is his shirt. Invariably this is made of 3 ells of undyed linen. Holland and cambric are the best quality, although the much coarser lockram, Osenbridge and even linsey-woolsey might be employed for a worker's garment. The full shirt consists of long sleeves and a trunk that reaches down below the buttocks, without buttons or opening at the front, but with open seams between the front and back of the garment, which sometimes ascend as high as the waist. The sleeves of gentlemen's shirts are gathered at the wrist with ribbons; expensive examples may be cut more voluminously in the sleeve, with pleats and tucks at the shoulder and wrist. An even more expensive version might have a panel of finely sewn picots at the neckline and patterns embroidered in the linen.[4] Push the boat out further and you might have a very fine shirt embroidered with silk and bordered with lace. Obviously these refinements will cost you. Three ells of fine holland at 6s per ell is going to be 18s, just for the material. After you have added in the cost of making it, and embellishing it with pleats and picots, you can expect to pay 20–30s. Lace trimmings can increase that significantly – by several pounds. Note also that, although some holland costs as little as 3s an ell, the very finest holland can cost 12s or more. And that won't include a collar: 'bands' to go around the neck are separate. In summer you might choose to wear a shorter half-shirt of linen. Half-shirts are also useful in cold weather as they are worn as a second shirt. Given how cold it is throughout this period, you may well decide to wear the half-shirt as an undergarment beneath your main shirt as a matter of course.[5]

The point above, about the cost of linen, applies equally to other undergarments. A linen nightshirt may well reach down below the knee, and thus costs a small packet if made in cambric or fine holland. Note that you should have a nightcap to match your nightshirt. Gentlemen in mourning should wear black nightclothes and black nightcaps – an extra expense that you could probably do without at a time of loss. As for a man's drawers, these tend to be of plain cut, especially if they are of the short variety, fastened with a ribbon at the front. Expect to pay 2s 6d for an ordinary pair, or 1s 6d for second-hand.[6] There is a longer sort for use in winter, with loops or stirrups beneath the foot to keep them from riding up your leg. On a very hot summer's day you probably will want short holland drawers cut at an angle, with a wide gusset, to permit maximum air circulation. Pepys once recalls lounging around in his 'cool holland drawers' until 5 p.m.

OUTER CLOTHES

The year 1668 marks a watershed in the design of men's suits. Before then, the style might be loosely described as 'doublet and skirts'. Some come with proper skirts, some with skirt-like trousers called 'petticoat breeches', and others covered all over with ribbons and tassels so that you can't tell whether it is a skirt, breeches or what. Most have a jacket-like doublet of wool or fustian (heavy cotton cloth), which is worn unbuttoned at the waist, showing off the shirt beneath. To the modern eye, all of these look more like female dress than male, and the most excessive specimens look like a cascading waterfall of tasselled cloth. They are also likely to make you the object of ridicule: some petticoat breeches are so wide about the knee – more than a yard in circumference – that you can easily put both legs through one hole and not notice, and thus go about all day with a loose trouser leg, to the great amusement of all those you meet.

This style of 'doublet and skirts' starts to come under threat in about 1664. The waistcoat or vest is the key. Previously this was an undergarment worn by men and women for warmth; now it acquires a new prominence as a comfortable collarless, short-sleeved men's item, fitted to the waist, with a skirt reaching down to the knee. Over this is worn a tunic or surcoat, shorter than the waistcoat by six inches, and worn unbuttoned and loose, to show off the waistcoat beneath.[7] Finally in 1668 the suit acquires the full long coat and knee-length waistcoat that will remain standard for the next hundred years or more. On Sunday, 17 May of that year Pepys proudly struts off to church in his 'new stuff-suit, with a shoulder-belt, according to the new fashion'. The shoulder belt is like a wide sash on which a gentleman wears his sword, so Pepys looks very swish. Over the rest of the period, the coat and waistcoat see various refinements. The coat sometimes acquires pockets low down at the front, or has its cuffs turned back to an ostentatiously large degree; the waistcoat might be given a belt or buttonholes all the way down. But whatever form it takes, you will recognise this ensemble.

Take, for example, the suit worn by James, duke of York, when he is married for the second time, in 1673. This comes in three parts: coat, waistcoat and breeches. All three are made of a grey wool broadcloth, heavily embroidered with floral patterns of gilt-silver and silver threads. The long coat reaches down to the thigh; it has buttons all the way down, but is worn open. Two horizontal pockets are low down at the front, one on either side, fastened shut by buttons to stop them sagging open. At the back you can see the wide pleats that enable the skirts of the coat to fan out. The lining is an orange-red ribbed silk. The loose breeches are fastened just below the knee. The coat sleeves are three-quarter-length and folded back in large cuffs known as 'hounds-ears', as they look like the floppy ears of hunting dogs. The matching waistcoat has long fitted sleeves over the shirt, which protrude beyond the hounds-ear cuffs, buttoned around the wrist.[8]

Suits tailored later in the century hardly vary from this design. Some gentlemen's coats have lapels; some have vertical pockets and full-length sleeves; some have embroidered cuffs; some have their cuffs trimmed with fur; and some have side-pleats and a single vent at the back – but overall the long coat and waistcoat with breeches are the norm from 1680. And the breeches are 'closed' – that is, fastened below the knee, and not left open as they are in the days of petticoat breeches in the 1660s. Often they are made of black velvet and fastened with ribbons. After 1680 they tend to be less flouncy and cut closer to the leg. By 1700 braces or 'gallowses' have been invented to hold them up, but these remain rare. Most breeches are supported by being hooked to the doublet (in the earlier days), tied with a cord, or cut tight enough to the hip that they need no other support.

Neckwear also undergoes something of a revolution in this period. To begin with, in the 1660s, the falling band is the thing: a piece of fine cloth suspended from a high neckband that goes all the way around the neck and is sometimes left open at the front and sometimes tied with band-strings. From about 1665 the man of style starts to wear a cravat instead: a scarf of fine linen or muslin that is tied at the front and covers the throat. The most ostentatious cravats are trimmed with lace and hang down over the whole chest. At the end of the century, this develops into the steinkirk: a very long cravat that is tied by being twisted into a loose rope and tucked into the waistcoat, or pinned to one side of the coat with a brooch. Matching the lace of the cravat are the ruffles tied around the wrists: linen, muslin or lace flounces that demonstrate the high status of the wearer. All these garments are pricey: a fine muslin cravat suitable for an earl will cost in the region of 7s, and a pair of muslin cuffs to match, 2s 2d. Lace can cost much more. James II pays £36 10s for a cravat of Venetian lace to wear at his coronation.[9]

And then we come to the stockings. Gentlemen, you will get used to wearing them, I assure you. If you have previously made forays into medieval and Elizabethan times, you will find Restoration stockings no humiliation at all; you are not expected to reveal your thigh, let alone your buttocks, as was the case in previous ages. You don't even have to reveal your knees, after the demise of petticoat breeches in the 1660s. What will be on show is your bestockinged lower leg. The garments themselves may be made of knitted silk – the most attractive and most fashionable material – but these are expensive. Pepys pays 15s for a pair of silk stockings in 1663.[10] Alternatives include woollens such as kersey, worsted, jersey and serge, and various forms of linen. An ordinary pair of woollen stockings will set you back 1s 2d.[11] For the socks, which are worn outside the stockings, linen is the usual material. These too can be costly, even though they are hardly seen. The earl of Bedford pays 1s 3d for each pair of socks made for him in 1689 – the equivalent of a day's wages for many working men. Note that if you visit in the 1660s, when petticoat breeches are in vogue, you may find yourself wearing 'canons' or 'port canons'. These are little skirts that go around the knee, decorating each stocking, often made to match the skirts of the suits and petticoat breeches. They are frivolous and highly impractical, so you won't be sad to see them fall out of fashion in 1668.

Foolish though port canons and petticoat breeches might appear to you and me – and, indeed, to many people at the time – they will not actually cause you physical pain. The same cannot be said for the shoes and boots. In September 1662, Pepys buys a new pair of jack boots of hard leather and, putting them on two weeks later when he sets out for Cambridge, gets as far as Ware before he is in such agony that he has to buy an old pair of shoes for 4s from the landlord of his inn in order to be able to continue on his way. And the offending items weren't cheap; in fact, they cost him £1 10s – more than three weeks' wages for many ordinary tradesmen, and considerably more than the 9s that a run-of-the-mill pair would have cost.[12] Gradually hard jack boots are reserved for military pursuits and riding. From the mid-1670s a lighter version is introduced: this is made of soft leather and is buttoned, laced or buckled up the side of the calf, thereby allowing a closer, more comfortable fit. All these boots are made of black leather, as are almost all men's shoes (although for 'dress' wear, men might still have red heels and soles).[13] Buckles are introduced around 1660; at first these are small and oval, but after 1680 they are large and square. Shoe tongues grow in length, rising up in front of the ankle for several inches after 1680, and after 1690 they are turned down or allowed to flop over the buckle to reveal the red lining of the shoe.[14]

Given the cold, you will undoubtedly want to have an overcoat for outdoors. The term used in the 1660s is 'cassock', which at this time is a long, loose coat buttoned down the front, with a turned-down collar, which normally hangs down to the thighs. After about 1670 the word is used exclusively for ecclesiastical garments. The alternative to the cassock is a cloak, which is worn over both shoulders as protection against the weather. After 1670 these also fall from favour and are only used for riding. From that year the fashionable item of outer dress is the Brandenburg (named after the Prussian state). This is a large, long woollen overcoat reaching down as far as the calf. Alternatively, you could wear a 'jump', which is a loose short coat with long sleeves and buttons down the front.

In this period a hat is a necessity. The upturned-flowerpot hats of
the 1650s, which are also known as 'sugar-loaf hats', with their high
flat crowns and wide flat brims, do last into the 1660s but they are
quite impractical, blowing off in the slightest gust of wind. Their
replacements, made from velvet stiffened with buckram, felt and beaver,
have a much lower crown but retain the broad brim; they are best
worn cocked at an angle, to appear as rakish as possible. Pepys notes
seeing 'a brisk young fellow with his hat cocked like a fool behind, as
the present fashion among the blades is', in June 1667.[15] Feathers of
course abound in a gentleman's hat – frequently several plumes will
be worn at once. As the 1690s draw near, the felt hat starts to take on
a three-cornered shape, with its edges turned up, foreshadowing the
tricorn hat of the eighteenth century. If you see this as your style,
remember that the point of the hat – not the flat side – goes in front.

The clothes of Montague Drake, Esq., 1698[16]

Woollen wearing clothes, viz: seven suits, two odd waistcoats, a scarlet cloak, ten pairs of stockings, a muff and a hat	£18
Four pairs of boots, being two pairs of jack boots and two pairs of lammer boots; one pair of splatterlashes [leggings to wear when riding], nine pairs of near-sides [?] and a parcel of old ones	£3
Wearing linen: thirty-four holland shirts, eleven coarser holland shirts; two large trimming cloths of holland	£20 10s
Nine periwigs, four quilted night caps, two waist-coats of dimity [stout cotton, woven with raised stripes], two flannel ones, four pairs of thread stock-ings, six pairs of cotton ones, three lace cravats, three large muslin neck cloths, nine pair of lace sleeves, four handkerchiefs, four turnover neck cloths, seven-teen long muslin neck cloths	£10
Nine pairs of stockings and ten pairs of gloves; a shoe-ing iron, a knife and a small hammer; a small pair of gold scales; a small parcel of seven books	£1 12s
Six swords, a pair of files and a belt	£4

HAIR

The vast majority of gentlemen do not wear any facial hair. There is an important exception in Charles II, who sports a small moustache from the time of his return as king until the late 1670s. This is not a fashion you should feel obliged to follow; his brother, James, for example, never wears one. Nor do most courtiers. Pepys has a moustache until January 1664, when he dispenses with it for good. Most gentlemen by this time shave at home: the expectation is that men will be properly clean-shaven, and that means eradicating any stubble every other day. You might attend a barber's shop to have your beard trimmed, if you are having your hair cut at the same time. Alternatively, if you can afford the extra cost, you may prefer to have your barber come to you. Pepys has a barber shave him at his house on Sundays prior to going to church. Otherwise, he uses a pumice stone to shave himself until January 1664. After that he takes up using a razor (of the 'cut-throat' variety).[17]

When Charles II returns to England in 1660 his hair is his own. Although the French started wearing *perruques* or wigs as fashion accessories way back in the 1630s when Louis XIII went bald, the English have yet to do so. In fact it is not until 1663, when Charles himself starts going grey, that he and his brother adopt the practice of wearing a 'peruke' or 'periwig' – or 'wig' as it is called from the 1670s. Almost overnight, the fashion switches from long, luscious, natural locks to artificial hairpieces. Predictably, Samuel Pepys wants one. In October 1663 he visits a couple of periwig shops, although he is almost put off by the sight of a greasy old-woman's hair on sale in one of them. He orders two wigs: one costing £3, made of someone else's hair, and another worth £2 but actually costing 21s 6d, as it will be made of his own hair.[18] It is true that there are practical arguments in favour of cutting off all your hair and making a wig out of the results: a wig is much easier to clean, and thus you'll find it simpler to rid yourself of nits. But on the whole it seems slightly ludicrous, especially when the fashion for wigs inclines men to wear larger and larger perukes, more lavishly perfumed and powdered than before. Maintaining a couple of wigs can cost up to 20s per year.[19] Moreover, as Pepys's perruquier says, the wig will only last him two years, yet in that time he will regularly have to have his hair cut short. Thus the man of fashion ends

up paying twice for his hair: once to the barber and once more to the
perruquier. And Pepys's wigs are at the cheap end of the spectrum.
The earl of Bedford's four new wigs in 1672 cost £20, £18, £10 and £6;
normally he spends £14 or £15 a year on new wigs and wig maintenance – and that does not include having his hair cut so that they fit.[20]

ACCESSORIES

The well-dressed gentleman knows that presenting himself well is
not just about wearing the right clothes but also about having all
the right accessories. In the Restoration period these might include
anything from a muff to an umbrella. A muff, you ask? Surprisingly,
yes: in the 1680s and 1690s it becomes fashionable for gentlemen
to carry a muff, normally made of fur, satin or velvet, suspended
from a ribbon attached to the waistband. Scarves, combs, snuff-boxes
and handkerchiefs are also frequently carried about town. Another
new fashion is for gentlemen to carry silver-headed polished
Japanese canes. These are very elegant and you may well choose
to sport one instead of a sword. Men of wealth continue to wear
a sword at their side throughout the period but increasingly it is
for show.

Gloves you might find perfectly straightforward – until you realise
that there is a huge range, from sheepskin gloves at 8d a pair and
dog-skin ones at 1s, to the most expensive sort, costing several pounds,
which are not actually meant to be used. They are covered in furls of
silver and silk ribbon and are intended only for show, being carried,
not worn.[21] Similarly, some gloves are valued for the scents imbued
in the leather. The earl of Bedford has gloves into which 'jessemy
butter' has been rubbed to give them a jasmine aroma. He has other
pairs scented with frangipane or musk mallow.[22] As for his umbrellas
or 'umbrelloes' – the very latest in fashion accessories in 1687 – he
pays 16s 6d for one that year. This is the ultimate in conspicuous
consumption. Two years later, he pays £4 2s 2d for two more
umbrellas.[23] That's the equivalent of two months' wages for many
tradesmen. For just two umbrellas! It is even more incredible when
you reflect that they are designed to keep off the driving heat of the
oriental sun, not the rain, which is rather more common in
Buckinghamshire.

THE WORKING TRADES, COUNTRY PEOPLE
AND THE POOR

It goes without saying that not everyone can afford to dress in the aforementioned manner. However, as stated at the outset, this style sets the pattern for others to follow – albeit with some constraints of practicality and affordability. Both are important issues. A working man needs to look prosperous in order to convey the impression that he is good at his trade; however, there is no point dressing a blacksmith in lace. The basic clothes of a working man in the 1660s include his doublet or jerkin, breeches, shirt, stockings, shoes and hat or cap. Just one such set of new garments is likely to set you back in the region of 12–15s: working men's shirts are rarely cheaper than 2s 8d, shoes the same, stockings 12d, hat 2s, breeches 2s and doublet 3s. That is a considerable amount of money for someone earning just £10 or £15 per year. It is hardly surprising, therefore, that there is a considerable trade in second-hand clothes. When a man dies, his clothes are not simply thrown away, but are handed out to those who will use them. If you do have to buy new, remember that, even at this social level, the practice is to buy the cloth you require and then have it made up for you by your wife or a tailor. Occasionally you do find a business that sells ready-made clothes. Thomas Feris, a glover from Lincoln, has made-up leather breeches for sale in his shop, alongside his gloves.[24] A widow in the same city uses her dressmaking skills to sell made-up clothes in her haber-dashery, including mantles (long cloaks) and loose gowns for men and women, shirts, petticoats and coats, as well as the usual array of gloves and hosiery.[25]

SCOTTISH CLOTHING

You may have some notion that, as soon as you head north of the border, all the men you meet will be wearing a kilt and a sporran. That is, after all, the traditional Scottish dress, is it not? Well, not exactly. Tartan woollen cloth is traditional but the idea that all the clans have their own design of tartan will not catch on until about 1745. What's more, the kilt as you know it is unknown before the 1730s – and then,

dare it be said, it will be an Englishman who invents it.[26] But traditional
Scottish dress does exist and is widely worn, in the form of the belted
plaid. This is an enormous tartan garment, between 12 and 18ft long
and about 5ft wide, wrapped around the body to form both a skirt and
a trunk, thrown over the shoulder, wrapped around the chest
and pinned. The skirts are kept in pleats by the belt and the top half
is turned over in such a way that items can be carried in its front fold.
The whole ensemble is that of a man wearing a huge tartan blanket.

Walking around the streets in Glasgow or Edinburgh, you will
notice that not everyone wears the plaid. Follow a tradesman down
a city street on a summer's day in the 1690s and the chances are that
he'll be wearing a long coat over a long waistcoat and a pair of
breeches that end just below the knee, with stockings below and
shoes with square silver buckles.[27] He'll also have a hat or a wig –
very similar to the men in an English town. But then you see a group
of countrymen, some of them riding perhaps, or driving their cattle
to market on foot. All of them are wearing plaids. And in the cold
of winter, the tradesman you followed earlier will be wearing a great
overcoat, which might well be made of tartan. The patterns of
woollen cloth all around you will leave you in no doubt that you're
north of the border.

Contemporaries draw a distinction between the use of the plaid in
the Lowlands and its more frequent use in the Highlands. One visitor
states that:

The low-land gentry go well enough habited but the poorer sort go
(almost) naked, only an old cloak, or a part of their bedclothes
thrown over them. The highlanders wear slashed doublets, commonly
without breeches, only a plaid tied around their waists, etcetera
[and] thrown over one shoulder, with short stockings to the gartering
place, their knees and part of their thighs being naked: others have
breeches and stockings all of a piece of plaid wear, close to their
thighs.[28]

That last point, about 'breeches and stockings all of a piece', is a
reference to 'trews' or long breeches of tartan, which are worn by
those wealthy enough to ride a horse. Such gentlemen wear a tartan
jacket or a plaid over the top, and a flat hat or bonnet, which is often
coloured blue. Common men go bare-headed. The reference to some

Lowlanders wearing their bedclothes is a reminder that many poor men sleep in the same plaid they wear during the day. It does not often get washed. You may start to associate plaids with a certain aroma.

The best description of the Highlanders' dress is in William Cleland's poem of 1678. In this he reveals that Highlanders might wear the plaid over a jacket, or clothing dipped in tar to protect them from the weather:

> But those who were their chief commanders,
> as such who bore the pirnie [*striped cloth*] standards;
> who led the van, and drove the rear
> were right well mounted of their gear:
> with brogues, trews, and pirnie plaids,
> with good blew bonnets on their heads,
> which on the one side had a flipe,
> adorned with a tobacco pipe.
> with dirk, and snap-work, and snuff-mill,
> a bag which they with onions fill,
> and as their strict observers say,
> a tame horn filled with usquebay [*whisky*].
> A slashed-out coat beneath their plaids,
> a targe [*shield*] of timber, nails, and hides;
> with a long two-handed sword,
> as good as the country can afford –
> had they not need of bulk and bones,
> who fight with all these arms at once?
> It's marvellous how in such weather
> O'er hill and moss they came together;
> how in such storms they came so far;
> the reason is, they're smeared with tar
> which doth defend them heel and neck,
> just as it doth their sheep protect ...[29]

If you do visit the Highlands and see a large group of fellows dressed in the manner described above, carrying two-handed swords and wearing dirks between their legs, just remember there is a reason. In these parts they still continue the custom of the blood feud.

These are their work clothes.

Women's Clothing

UNDERWEAR

It is a bit of a leap from tar-streaked hairy Highlanders to women's underwear but, nevertheless, this is where our story now takes us. A woman's principal undergarment is her smock or shift. In some ways this has much in common with a man's shirt. It is made of undyed linen on account of the coolness of the fabric in hot weather, its absorbent properties (which allow it to soak up sweat and thus clean the body) and its softness, which means it can be worn under much heavier, coarser garments and protect the sensitive areas from chafing. As you don't have the option of wearing a brassiere at this time, a good linen smock is a necessity. Again, the best-quality cloth is holland, followed by cambric and coarser forms of linen. Also like men's shirts, the addition of picots, lace trimmings and specially embroidered sections bump up the price. Unlike men's shirts, however, women's smocks are tailored with gores in the side seams, rather than being left open. They are thigh-length, with bunched sleeves that are closed around the upper arm, and cut low over the breast. Often they are perfumed.[30] A cord draws the linen together in folds over the neck opening at the front, creating the effect of a series of pleats where the fabric lands over the breasts. Some women fold the linen over this cord so that it bunches up and creates an attractive ruffled effect.

Most of the time you will not be showing your smock. Even if it happens to be laden with lace, only you and your maidservants will appreciate it. Showing your bare arms above the elbow is risqué. Showing your bare legs is considered even more erotic. But in certain circumstances you might end up revealing all. There is a tradition of holding smock races around the country, in which women run against each other, dressed only in their smocks, in order to win a prize. Crowds turn up, hoping that the drawstring comes undone, and more than one competitor has had to decide between losing a race and running naked.[31] Another reason for revealing your smock is debt. It is widely believed that if a girl gets married in nothing but her smock, she will be cleared of all her debts. The thinking is that if a husband takes her with nothing in the world, then if she has debts, he won't have to take them on with her and, because she is now his wife, she won't have to

pay them. What's more, if *he* has debts, then nothing of hers by inheritance can be taken by his creditors. Thus the smock wedding is, in
theory, to the bride's advantage, whether or not she has debts. The
actual legalities do not accord with this belief but that does not stop
a few women standing at the altar, shivering in next to nothing, feeling
the eyes of all the congregation on their bare arms and legs.[32]

Women's undergarments tend not to be the most straightforward
subject for a man to describe at any time in history, and the Restoration
is no exception. Corsets (otherwise known as 'stays'), petticoats, under-
petticoats, waistcoats and bustles all have their place in a lady's clothes
chest. Be glad you don't have to wear them all at once. In fact, with regard
to the stays, be wary about wearing them at all. They are not designed
for your comfort but to appeal to your vanity and the appreciative male
gaze. They are a development of the bodice, which is an outer garment
in the 1660s but by the 1680s has sunk beneath the folds of the gown.
Several pieces of whalebone reinforcement running up and down through
the stays give shape to them; thus, when tightened appropriately, they
make the wearer appear to have a narrow waist and a fuller upper body,
pushing up the breasts for the cleavage to be displayed to maximum effect.
They can be uncomfortable to wear, even painful, if over-tightened. With
regard to the other items of underwear in the above list, a woman's
waistcoat is a form of vest, made of linen and put on over the head, and
is worn for warmth over the smock. Petticoats are similarly meant to
keep you warm. Sometimes they are designed to be visible, under the
open section of an overskirt or gown, in which case they will be made
of a showy material like sarcenet (a fine silk), taffeta (woven silk) or
tuftafetta (a form of taffeta, also known as 'tuff'). Striped patterns are
generally considered fashionable, perhaps with a slight train and trimmed
with lace, if you can afford it. Under-petticoats are shorter and meant
never to be visible to the public; these are often made of linen for comfort,
but the most expensive are of silk. The bustle is an innovation of the 1680s:
a fashionable bolster to make the skirt protrude more over the bottom.
Strange though it may seem to our generation, for whom 'Does my bum
look big in this?' is a catchphrase, some Restoration women looking in
the mirror wonder 'Does my bum look *big enough* in this?'

It is possible you will hear people speak of women wearing drawers.
This is very unusual.[33] Short drawers are a man's undergarment, and the
impression given when a woman wears a man's undergarments is – how
should I put this? – that she's on the pull. When Samuel Pepys suspects

his wife of having an affair with her dancing master, he hides 'to see whether my wife did wear drawers today as she used to do'.[34] If someone shows you a pair of ladies' drawers, you'll realise from the shape and the embroidery that they are garments designed to be seen, and no one can show off that much leg in the seventeenth century without giving out powerful messages of enticement. Some smock races are actually run in men's drawers. Don't be fooled into thinking this is an early indication of women wearing appropriate athletic costume. The purpose is to allow spectators more than a glimpse of the young women's legs. A ballad you might hear, called 'The Virgins' Race', tells the story of some Yorkshire women who run in half-shirts and drawers for the prize of a silver spoon. Similarly, you'll come across advertisements for races between local beauties for the prize of a new holland smock: these often have the purpose of drawing in a larger crowd to another event, such as a cricket match. Sometimes these announce that the competitors will run *only* in drawers. Rest assured, if someone refers to a woman wearing drawers, it is not her warmth or her athletic performance that he has in mind.[35]

OUTER CLOTHES

Many of the most famous images of Restoration ladies, especially those painted by Sir Peter Lely, show them wearing voluminous gowns of dazzling colours over a loose chemise. The ensemble creates a romantic image of wantonness, not least because such huge garments are nightgowns and are not worn out of doors. It is all a bit misleading as to what women actually wear on those rare occasions when they are *not* sitting for their portrait in front of a Delphic temple in an Arcadian grove. In reality, women's clothing is more restrained than this – and more restraining too. Thomas Mace writes in 1676 that until recently women have been

> so pent-up by the straightness and stiffness of the gown-shoulder sleeves that they could not so much as scratch their heads for the necessary removal of a biting louse; nor elevate their arms scarcely to feed themselves handsomely; nor carve a dish of meat at a table, but their whole body must needs bend towards the dish.[36]

Changes in women's fashion occur just as frequently as those in men's styles. In 1662 Pepys and his wife go for a walk to Gray's Inn

specifically to observe women of fashion because Mrs Pepys is planning to make some clothes for herself. If you follow her example, I
would recommend that you do not cut your cloth before Easter, for
only then are you likely to see the new fashions that will be in vogue
in summer.[37] As with men's clothing, most of the changes from year
to year are in the little refinements. Thomas Rugg notes in his diary
for July 1660 that 'this month came up a fashion that women did wear
satin and taffeta gloves'.[38] It is this sort of detail that catches the eye –
the attention to minutiae that shows you are both aware and up to
date. Over the whole period, however, women's clothing goes through
a transformation as significant as that of men's clothing.

In the 1660s and 1670s, the usual style is for women to wear a
bodice and skirt. The bodice or 'pair of bodies' is the predecessor to
a pair of stays and very similar, in that it is a whalebone-lined garment
designed to shape a woman's upper body into a desirable form. The
main difference is that, as it is worn as an outer garment, it is much
more lavishly decorated. It is no more comfortable, however: one
male contemporary describes it as 'pernicious beyond imagination'.
He adds that 'by straight-lacing themselves, to attain a wand-like
smallness of waist ... [young women] shut up their waists in a whalebone prison' and make themselves ill.[39] On the positive side, not only
do women like the shapely results but the garments can be spectacular
in their own right. A fine bodice may have very thin ribbings encased in
silk, with a tapering of the waist and a tailpiece of ribbon. It may also
have a matching busk or stomacher at the front – a piece of tailored
fabric that fills the gap where the bodice is drawn together. Necklines
are usually low and edged with lace. Sleeves (which may be detach-
able) are worn full to the elbow and then turned back in cuffs or
decorated with frothy bunches of lace just above the wrist.

A major new trend sweeps across London around 1680 as women
take to wearing a gown instead of a bodice and skirt. Often the skirt
of the gown is left open at the front to reveal the petticoat beneath.
The gown may be loose all over, as in the French *sac* or nightgown,
or it may be tight to the upper part of the body. In the latter instance
it is drawn into a V shape at the front, where it may reveal a stomacher
or an embroidered pair of stays. You will be glad to know that the
bodice of a gown is not constrained by whalebone. Often the skirts are
worn hitched up to reveal the petticoat, and from the 1680s they
are worn over a bustle. A popular form of gown from the early 1680s,

the mantua, is made of silk and has a long train sweeping elegantly along behind the wearer. Another is the sultane, which is trimmed with buttons or loops.

Women's cleavage tends to be revealed most deeply in the 1660s, when the rakes are striking their blows for free love, but throughout the period bodices and gowns are cut low. This does not mean everything is always on show, however; a judicious use of neckwear can be employed, as the occasion demands. The bosom might be draped in diaphanous silk scarves or, until the 1680s, covered by a gorget. This is a sort of shoulder-cape, normally of lace. From the 1690s you might wear a steinkirk muslin scarf like the men, or a 'pinner' – a piece of muslin, lawn or lace pinned to cover your modesty. Don't worry too much about its arrangement. As Robert Herrick puts it so perfectly in *Hesperides* (first published in 1648):

> A sweet disorder in the dress
> kindles in clothes a wantonness:
> a lawn about the shoulders thrown
> into a fine distractión,
> an erring lace, which here and there
> enthralls the crimson stomacher,
> a cuff neglectful, and thereby
> ribbands to flow confusedly,
> a winning wave, deserving note,
> in the tempestuous petticoat,
> a careless shoe-string, in whose tie
> I see a wild civility,
> do more bewitch me, than when art
> is too precise in every part.

Thus the only people who are likely to complain about your casualness are those women whose smartness cannot match it.

When it comes to stockings, bright colours are all the rage, with knitted wool or silk being the preferred materials. Women's shoes are most frequently made of leather and pointed, with a high heel; other materials include velvet and embroidered cloth for some slippers and 'mules' (slippers with heels), and silk and satin for the linings. Gold or coloured braid is used for decorating fine leather and suede shoes, which may also be perfumed. If you really want to dazzle, try a pair of slip-on red velvet pantofles with an inch-wide square toe, a low heel and a mass of exquisite patterns in silver-gilt thread embroidery on the upper part.[40]

Red velvet shoes aren't that well suited for walking through the mud and muck of a city's streets. In such cases you may well choose to use a patten, an iron frame that raises your feet to keep them from the trampled dung.[41] Alternatively you might take off your shoes altogether and wear something more practical. Ladies don't wear jack boots (for which be grateful); instead, soft-leather boots called buskins are made for outdoor wear or riding long-distance. Women's outdoor coats are similar to men's; alternatively you might choose to wear a tippet (a waist-length cape) from the 1680s. Note, however, that some tippets are just for show: a velvet or fur-trimmed one is no good in a storm. Nor is a palatine: a tippet made of sable that simply covers the shoulders and has two flaps hanging down over the breast. More practical by far is the mantle – a voluminous cloak that reaches to the feet, tied in front of the throat. Celia Fiennes goes for a walk one day on a windswept moor and gets caught in a hailstorm but does not mind particularly because she is wearing her 'dust coat'.[42]

Until the 1670s women regularly wear hats – wide-brimmed sugar-loaf hats, not dissimilar to men's, or straw hats. Curiously, hats then quickly fall out of fashion. Women still use a variety of types of

---

The clothes of Sarah Kitchen, single woman, of Christchurch parish, Bristol, 1672[43]

One cotton mantle, one worsted mantle, one white serge petticoat, one Indian fustian petticoat, one red cloth petticoat with gold and silver lace, one plain tabby petticoat, one sad [dull-coloured] serge petticoat and gown of the same, one wrought fustian waistcoat, one black silk Mantua gown, one black sarcenet petticoat, one serge cloak, one silk cloak, one morning coat, one riding suit, one holland tuff petticoat	£10
Eleven pairs of sleeves, eight skull caps, five calico hoods, eight stock neckcloths, sixteen dressings, eleven forehead cloths, six bibs, six handkerchiefs, six pocket handkerchiefs, nine aprons, eleven coifs, one tuff waistcoat, four other waistcoats, five shifts, ten laced stock neckcloths	£3 3s 3d

headwear, and the coif remains especially common. This is a close-fitting plain linen head covering that comes down the sides, to be fastened beneath the chin. Often it is worn with a crosscloth or forehead cloth: a triangular piece of material with one point to the back of the head beneath the coif, and the sides tied under the chin. Alternatives include a plain linen skullcap or a linen scarf tied around the head.

HAIR

Specialist hairdressers are just starting to establish themselves in London in this period – and well they might, for women start to experiment with their hair as never before.[44] In 1660 Pepys sees the new queen, Catherine of Braganza, with hers all frizzed up, and he is not sure he likes it.[45] Later in this decade women have their hair drawn back from the face and arranged in an oval 'bun' at the back of the head, decorating it with ribbons or artificial flowers. It also becomes fashionable to insert locks into the hair, which are plaited and curled and secured by pins. Further change sweeps across fashionable London when the glamorous Madame Kéroualle arrives to seduce the king in 1670. Ladies ask for their hairdressers to give them a *hurluberlu* – a mass of close curls all over the head, with stray ringlets at the back. In 1674 the 'bullhead coiffure' comes in from France: a forehead fringe of thick curls. In 1680 curls with a centre parting are all the rage. And then in 1690 the 'fontage' arrives.

Women are far too sensible to embrace the male fashion of cutting off their hair to replace it with a wig. Why should they? The only time they wear a periwig is when out riding, and then they put it over their *own* hair. However, the fontage is proof that Restoration ladies are just as vain and fashion-addicted as their menfolk. To build a fontage on your head, first you need a 'commode' or wire frame, which is attached to a close-fitting linen cap at the back of the head. The commode is covered with lace and linen and a shape built up that leans slightly forward, resembling a half-closed fan. Then the woman's hair is built up at the front to form a 'palisade', so that the hair rises directly in curls up the commode and is crowned with a mass of lace at the top, about 10 inches or a foot above the head, framed by ribbons on all sides. It looks dazzling, but I imagine women can't do anything under such a construction except ... well, look dazzling.[46]

MAKE-UP AND BEAUTY

Rouge, white powder and perfumes should be on any self-respecting lady's make-up table in this period. When so many other women are staring at you, fluttering their fans just below their eyes, you have little choice. But you might think twice about the full extent of beauty products employed at this time. Would you wash your face in puppy water? It's not what you're thinking it is. I also thought it was puppy's urine when I heard that Samuel Pepys's wife bought some at the suggestion of his aunt, who uses it for her ugly visage.[47] It is worse than that. Basically it is oil of distilled dog. There are various recipes; this one is from Nicholas Culpeper's *Pharmacopoeia Londinensis*:

> Takes four pounds of sallet oil [olive oil], two puppy-dogs newly whelped, a pound of earthworms washed in white wine; boil the whelps till they fall in pieces then put in the worms; strain it after a while, then with three ounces of cypress, turpentine, and one ounce of spirits of wine, perfect the oil according to art.[48]

Alternatively you could try the recipe published in 1690 by John Evelyn's daughter, Mary. This prefers the puppies to be roasted at nine days old and their skulls broken open after roasting, and snail shells to be used instead of earthworms. Who would have thought this, coming from such a sweet girl! She is most insistent on the addition of *canary* wine and a lemon, with the whole lot being distilled and dripped over a lump of sugar and a little gold leaf. But whichever recipe you use, you've then got to rub the oil all over your face.

Strangely, puppy water is not controversial, even if Samuel Pepys does not approve. Painting your face, however, is. For many people this is what prostitutes do, and actresses (who are normally presumed to be gentlemen's mistresses). Certain women do it to enhance their beauty. Others feel shape is more important than colour and carry cork 'plumpers'. Mary Evelyn describes these as 'very thin round and light balls to plump out and fill up the cavities of the cheeks, much used by old court countesses'.[49] If you hang around court long enough, sooner or later you will see some of them fall out. Another affectation that spreads far and wide is the practice of wearing little black patches on the face. This begins back in the 1650s, when women start to mark themselves with artificial moles or beauty spots. Pepys is unimpressed when his wife applies her first patches in 1660; his opinion is not changed in October 1662 when he sees a pretty girl in the Exchange with 'her face full of black patches'.[50] Young women are still wearing them when Monsieur Misson visits England in 1697. 'The young, old, handsome, ugly, all are bepatched till they are bid-ridden,' he declares. 'I have often counted fifteen patches or more upon the swarthy wrinkled phiz of an old hag threescore and ten and upwards.'[51]

Finally, it is important that fashionable ladies are seen to have soft, white hands. Willem Schellinks notes one method of making sure of this. One day in August 1660 he is out hunting in Kent with his host and a large party of men and women. Someone shoots a deer with a crossbow: immediately, all the ladies dismount and rush forward to wash their hands in its blood, which is supposed to keep them tender and white. Yuk, you might think. And yes, it's not to everyone's taste. So here's an alternative recommended by Mary Evelyn: last thing before you go to bed at night, put on gloves made out of chicken skin.[52]

ACCESSORIES

Just as gentlemen carry their swords and their muffs when leaving the house, so women also pick up a few accessories. Ladies might carry a muff, as the gentlemen do. What's more, they might actually use it to keep their hands warm, as opposed to simply hanging it on a ribbon for show. If they are very wealthy, ladies might also employ an umbrella to shield them from the heat, and wear kid gloves perfumed with jessemy butter. They might use short, wrist-length gloves fringed with lace or, from about 1670, close-fitting elbow-length ones of fine leather or silk. Mittens too are popular: long lace or silk ones, or shorter ones with a separate thumb. Obviously handkerchiefs go without saying but remember that when you read about *pocket* handkerchiefs, the pocket itself is not necessarily part of a garment. Linen pockets are themselves accessories: pouches sewn separately and held inside the clothes on linen ties. Aprons are self-explanatory, as are fans (often elaborately painted) and jewellery, especially pearls. Diamond pendant earrings are popular, as are gold rings carrying turquoises, sapphires, rubies and emeralds. Perhaps the most unexpected item you will have to deal with is a mask. For the last hundred years or so, women have been finding occasion to cover their faces when out in public. This might be when travelling from town to town – to keep their complexion free from dust – or it might be in the theatre or in a London park – to keep their reputation free from gossip. There are two sorts: the full mask or vizard, which is an oval shape that covers the whole face; and the half-mask or 'loo-mask', which only covers the eyes. Either will conceal your identity if you wear it with a hooded cloak. Bear in mind, though, that at the end of the period masks are seen as symbols of prostitution.

THE WORKING TRADES, COUNTRY PEOPLE
AND THE POOR

The vast majority of women can only imitate the fashions of the day. The very idea that a butcher's wife might have a silk petticoat or carry a sable muff is ludicrous. Whereas an elegant London woman might wear a fine mantle and buskins as she rides along the street, her poor West Country cousins will be soldiering through the weather on foot in a 'rocket' (cloak) and wooden clogs. You get a picture of what clothes most tradesmen's wives have in the chest when you consider the possessions they leave behind. In Essex, in 1672, Widow Poole dies leaving £40 of cash; her possessions besides amount to a further £8 8s. Of this sum, four petticoats and one waistcoat amount to £1; a hat is another 3s; a black scarf and a green apron add another 5s; and some old petticoats and bodices, and another hat and a waist-coat, add 5s to that total. It looks as if her best skirts have already been given away, but the clothes remaining add up to just 33s – a fraction of her modest wealth.[53] Although you might presume that women are very conscious of their appearance and keen to invest in beautiful clothes, the reality is that expensive garments are beyond the reach of those whose husbands work at a trade or farm a few acres. Then, when they grow old and are widowed, appearance takes a marked second place to the simple struggle to stay alive. Sarah Kitchen, the prosperous single woman whose clothing is listed above, has an estate of £462 – a substantial sum indeed – but £423 of this is in the form of leases, money and plate. It is security. Many widows follow the same model of life: it is better to be financially secure than dressed in fine clothes.

SCOTTISH CLOTHING

Like their menfolk, Scotswomen wear the plaid (or the 'arisaid', as
the female version is also called). As soon as Celia Fiennes crosses the
border in 1698 she comes across women thus attired. She describes
them: 'though with naked legs are yet wrapped up in plaids, a piece
of woollen like a blanket or else riding hoods, and this when they
are in their houses'.[54] Another English commentator notes of
Scotswomen that

> the meaner [i.e. less well off] go barefoot and bareheaded, with two
> black elflocks on either side of their faces; some of them have scarce
> any clothes at all, save part of their bedclothes pinned about their
> shoulders, and their children have nothing else on them but a little
> blanket. Those women that can purchase plaids need not bestow much
> upon other clothes, these coversluts being sufficient. Those of the best
> sort are very well habited in their modish silks yet must wear a plaid
> over all for the credit of their country.[55]

Generally at this time every woman except the very poor will have
a plaid to her name. Sophia Petticrew, the widow of an Edinburgh
vintner at the end of the period, has two, both described as Glasgow
plaids. Her other clothes are as follows:

> A twilted [quilted] black killimankie petticoat
> A striped and flowered killimankie petticoat
> A fine black cloth petticoat
> A blue and red serge petticoat
> A black moskered [decayed] petticoat
> A light-coloured silk and worsted gown with lemon-coloured
>   Persian lining
> A moskered gown lined with black serge
> A black serge apron
> A black killimankie apron
> A blue and white apron
> A black short ruffled silk apron
> A pair of stays and a stomacher
> An old dark-coloured rocolar [cloak?]

A pair of shoes

A night cap

21 coarse clothes, laced and plain

2 muslin pinners with lace

4 laced mutches

Two plain muslin hoods

A striped muslin hood

A suite of damask head cloths

Half a muslin napkin with lace

A cambric napkin[56]

As you can see, some of the wording is unusual. 'Killimankie' is calamanco, a glossy woollen cloth woven with a satin twill; 'mutches' are close-fitting day-caps made of linen or muslin; and 'damask' is a twilled linen fabric with patterns that show up from reflected light. Despite this, the actual garments would be recognisable to an Englishwoman of similar rank. Indeed, she might well admire them. Needless to say, Sophia Petticrew is not one of those poor women who sleeps in her plaid. In fact I expect she takes a dim view of those women who do.

Cleaning Clothes

If you don't wash your fine clothes, they will not have the desired effect, regardless of the quality of the material. As for your linen, there is a reason why everyone wears undergarments of this fabric: it is to soak up the sweat and dirt from the body, so that smelly excretions can be removed when the linen is washed. From this you will see that cleanliness is as essential to fashion as expensive fabric and tailoring.

Not everything can be cleaned easily, however. Silk, lace, lawn, tiffanies (pieces of very fine gauze) and sarsenet are singled out as fabrics that you simply do not hand over to your laundry maid or a washerwoman, because she will ruin them. If you can afford such things, you will either wash and starch them yourself (if you are a woman) or hand them to your wife or her chambermaid to clean.[57] Coats and items that are best cleaned by brushing go to the house-maid. Only wool and regular linen items go to laundry maids or, if you prefer, the town washerwomen. If the laundry is being done by your own staff, they will save everything up for the household's 'great wash'. The regularity of this varies from family to family, but John Houghton writes in 1695 that 'I find upon enquiry that in good citizens' houses they wash once a month, and they use, if they wash all the clothes at home, about as many pounds of soap as there be heads in the family'.[58]

So, what does the great wash involve? First there may be some preparation. If you have managed to spill drops of ink on your shirt, you will need to soak the affected area overnight in urine – so says Hannah Woolley in her book, The Compleat Servant-Maid (1677). When the ammonia has started to break down the stain, then the garment is ready for the great wash. Traditionally this happens very early in the morning – a 2 a.m. start in winter is not unusual.[59] When a great household, such as that of a lord, undertakes a great wash, extra women are hired to help – at the rate of 1s 6d per day per woman, in the case of Lord Bedford's household, reflecting just how hard the work is.[60] In those areas where they burn wood to make potash, the clothes are layered into washing vats with the resulting lye and then beaten or trampled. In Scotland the women who do this hitch up their skirts to the tops of their thighs, exposing themselves far more than they would normally; therefore one of their number is usually stationed nearby to chase off any peeping Toms in the neighbourhood. Elsewhere people use soap – either black soap (½d per lb), grey soap (1d per lb) or castile (3d per lb), the most expensive. Black soap smells, being made out of train oil; it also stains linen, so don't use it on cambric or holland cloth, but only on wool. When everything is clean it is laid out flat in the sun or hung on a clothes line to dry.

What about the dolly stick, you might ask? What about the washboard? The mangle? The clothes horse? All of these things lie in the future – although bats for beating the dirt out of recalcitrant woollens are in use. The one striking innovation that comes in at this time is ironing. In the past, if you wanted to flatten your clothes, you either had to use smoothing stones or, if you could afford one, a screw press. But from about 1670 you come across people talking about irons and 'smoothing irons' – for flattening lace bands, for example. They aren't cheap: about a shilling, if you buy them second-hand.[61] When in the 1680s the well-to-do start to talk about having their 'ironing' done, the iron as we know it has definitely arrived.[62]

Pity the ironing board won't be along for another thirty years.

7

Travelling

Long-distance travel is one of the most important aspects of our whole cultural journey from the medieval world to the modern. It underpins our well-being in almost every way – from feeding ourselves in times of want, and warning each other in times of danger, to sharing the benefits of international trade and the spread of scientific and technological ideas. In addition, travel is essential for the justice system and holding political elections. Thus the whole question of getting around is of the utmost importance. Yet you will undoubtedly find travel very frustrating in the late seventeenth century. The state of the roads, suspicion of strangers and the cost of accommodation all present problems. So too do ancient traditions. As Willem Schellinks notes with some exasperation, 'in the whole of England it is not permitted to travel on the Sabbath by water or on land in any vehicle, or to hire horses, carriages or coaches'.[1] There is a 10s fine for travelling on a Sunday unless you have first obtained consent from a magistrate, and, although the law is increasingly flouted, people *will* ask you to show your permit.

Road Transport

The roads in all parts of Britain leave a lot to be desired. Many of them date back to Roman times, and their surfaces are now so uneven that travellers are forced to take a detour through the surrounding soil, which quickly becomes rutted and muddy. Another problem is the damage caused by the increased number of travellers. For centuries, only pedestrians, cattle, horseriders, packhorses and carts have used the roads and, of those, only pedestrians care if occasionally they have to make their way through a bit of mud. In these days of international trade, however, not only are there more people and animals on the move but there are large numbers of carriages too, as well as many more carts and wagons. These cause a much greater problem: their iron-rimmed tyres create deep ruts in earthen roads, scatter gravel and lever apart the old flagstones where these still form part of the surface.

The roads are in such a state all over Britain. Celia Fiennes is a good guide to their condition: in the south she observes that respectable ladies sometimes have to be taken to church in ox-drawn wagons and that 'Sussex men and animals have grown long-legged from pulling their feet out of the clay'.[2] 'The roads to Bridport are stony and narrow,' she declares as she labours through Dorset. Travelling on into Devon, she finds that the large number of ancient enclosed fields 'makes the ways very narrow, so as in some places a coach and wagons cannot pass'. She observes that Devon people 'are forced to carry their corn and carriages on horseback with frames of wood like panniers on either side of the horse, so load it high and tie it with cords'.[3] Cornwall is similar. There the narrow lanes make for a death trap after heavy rain. One day when Celia is out riding, her horse steps straight into a very deep puddle and she knows she is lucky they both survive the experience.[4]

Drowning is perhaps something you don't immediately associate with road transport; nevertheless, it is a real possibility. Ralph Thoresby is caught in a downpour in May 1695 and bides his time at Ware, noting that the rain 'raised the washes along the road to that height that passengers from London that were upon the road swam, and a poor higgler [pedlar] was drowned, which prevented our travelling for many hours'.[5] In 1698 our redoubtable Celia finds the floodwaters in Devon rising and rising until they are up around the windows of her coach; outside she can see cattle swimming in the fields.[6] In such conditions the dangers are exacerbated by rickety bridges. Thomas Baskerville's travels take him across several old wooden bridges in Cambridgeshire, and more than once he crosses in fear of the rotten timbers giving way beneath him.[7] In terrible storms, even stone bridges might collapse. In May 1663 two men crossing a river in Northamptonshire are lucky to survive after both the arch in front of them and the one behind are suddenly swept away, leaving them stranded.[8]

People tend to exaggerate such awkward experiences, and it is worth remembering that, just like the streets of London, there are good examples as well as bad. Good roads generally have stone underpinnings, are raised above the floodplain and are surfaced with gravel. Charles II remarks that there are so many excellent highways in Norfolk that the county should be cut up to provide a few for the rest of the kingdom.[9] Generally speaking, however, the roads of England are not fit for purpose. Those in Scotland are even worse. The rough state of the trackways north of the border and the scarcity of the bridges is of no concern to the drovers who guide their cattle and flocks across moors and through fords. In both kingdoms, the only systematic form of maintenance is the requirement that local people fix their own roads. In England and Wales this amounts to parishioners having to provide six days' labour per year on road maintenance or pay a fine to the Surveyor of Highways. A similar system exists in Scotland, whereby parishioners have to provide three days' work in summer and three in the autumn.[10] But what do you do if, like the twenty or so families who live in Radwell, Hertfordshire, you have two miles of the Great North Road running through your tiny parish? They can't possibly afford to maintain such a long stretch. If a rich traveller's coach occasionally breaks an axle or has to be lifted out of a rut in the road, then so be it. There's probably a sixpence tip in it for them.

Parliament recognises the problem but attends to it with a spectacular lack of urgency. In 1662 an Act is passed requiring every parish to levy a Highway Rate for three years to repair the roads. Not much happens. The following year an Act is passed to allow three turnpikes – barriers lifted on payment of a toll – to be set up to fund the repair of the Great North Road: at Wadesmill in Hertfordshire, Stilton in Huntingdonshire and Caxton in Cambridgeshire. But such is the backlash in Stilton that the barrier is never erected. And as Caxton's turnpike is easily evaded, only the toll at Wadesmill provides funds for the scheme. Thus Parliament falls back on the old strategy of local coercion. In 1670 it passes a temporary Act putting the obligation on Justices of the Peace to raise a rate to repair routes where parishioners cannot meet the expense themselves. In 1691, another Act gives the Surveyors of Highways the power to call upon JPs to raise rates to buy materials for mending roads.[11] These measures are woefully inadequate. Finally, in 1695, with even more coaches on the roads than before, Parliament once again picks up the idea of using tolls to fund maintenance. The second and third Turnpike Acts are passed

to fund the Shenfield-to-Harwich road in Essex and the highway
between Wymondham and Attleborough in Norfolk. A fourth Act is
passed in 1697 for the way between Reigate and Crawley, and a fifth
in 1698 for the route from Birdlip to Gloucester.[12] The principle that
the user pays underlies road-maintenance strategy from now on.

FINDING YOUR WAY

Signposts are one of the most useful contributions to civilisation
but they are few and far between prior to the 1690s.[13] One erected
in 1669 at Chipping Campden shows the ways to the neighbouring
county towns of Gloucester, Oxford, Worcester and Warwick, with
the miles to each place marked in Roman numerals on each hand.
But you will have to walk a long way in any of those directions to
find the *next* sign. The great step forward comes in 1697, when an
Act of Parliament orders Surveyors of the Highways throughout
England and Wales to erect a 'direction stone or post' at every
crossroads in their parish.[14] The following year, as Celia Fiennes
makes her way through Lancashire, she remarks approvingly that
'at all crossways there are posts with hands pointing to each road
with the names of the great town or market towns that it leads to'.[15]
Not every county is so quick to erect them. Many parishes in rural
Devon won't get round to setting up direction stones for at least
another fifteen years.[16]

So, how do you find your way around if there is no signpost? You
could try asking for directions. However, in some rural places, locals
won't be able to direct you to places more than three miles away.[17] In
more remote areas it is advisable to hire a guide: he will not only lead
you to your destination, but will also warn you of areas where you
might be particularly vulnerable to flooding or highwaymen. The
other option is to buy a road atlas. Fortunately the first such publication, John Ogilby's *Britannia*, appears in 1675. This depicts 2,519 miles
of roads in 100 strip maps: a pioneering form of cartography that will
become very popular over the next century or so. His method of
compilation is remarkably thorough. He uses his 'waywiser' or measuring wheel to record the actual lengths of the roads, and he
standardises his measurements not on the various local miles in use
but on the statute mile of 1,760 yards. He claims to have surveyed

23,000 miles of roads in all, making his survey the most significant advance on domestic cartography for more than a hundred years.

The whole question of navigation becomes much more complicated after the sun has gone down. In champaign country, even if you have the benefit of moonlight or a lantern, you may well find yourself walking across a road one minute and through an open field the next. In East Anglia, where the fens are being drained by the building of deep ditches on either side of the road, there is a serious risk of accidentally ending up in the dark water on a moonless night. Wide expanses of waste ground and commons are also a cause for concern. In December 1682 Thomas Baskerville and six companions go off the beaten track in Gloucestershire. They ride into fog, miss a turning and carry on for four or five miles. 'We found ourselves shut up in darkness upon these comfortless downs where I knew we might ride ten miles forwards and perhaps not find a house,' writes Baskerville. Eventually the company meet a man who directs them to the nearest inn, where they find good fires, excellent ale and food and beds for the night.[18]

Travelling across London after dark is somewhat easier, especially after 1662. In that year an Act of Parliament requires the main streets to be lit until 9 p.m. by lanterns fixed above the doors of houses at regular intervals. In 1683 Anthony Vernatty obtains a patent to light the streets and installs new lamps with thick convex glass coverings, which magnify the light for the benefit of pedestrians.[19] Note, however, that although these burn until midnight, they are only lit from Michaelmas to Lady Day (29 September to 25 March), and then only from the third day after the Full Moon to the sixth day after the New Moon. They are also expensive to maintain, so many streets and alleys are left in the dark.[20] Most other towns do not follow London's example, on account of the expense. In those places you will need to use your own lantern. The best sort has special glass, like the aforementioned lamps, which magnifies the light and carries it further. If you don't have a lantern and there is no moon and the street lamps are out, then you'll have to hire one of the 'links' – the torches carried by boys who, for a penny or two, will offer to guide you home. Be careful, though, for unless you know the city well, you cannot be sure exactly where the boy will lead you – perhaps into some dark alley where he will extinguish his lantern suddenly and leave you to the mercy of his friends.

COACHES

A hundred years ago it was not seemly for men to take a coach. It was a form of transport for ladies; gentlemen rode alongside or behind on horseback. Nowadays men take coaches and carriages without a second thought. When Pepys says he is 'almost ashamed to be seen in a hackney' it is not because it reflects badly on his manliness but because it is such a common thing to do: he would prefer a coach of his own.[21] But with many Londoners thinking likewise – there are about 9,000 coaches on the streets of the capital in the 1660s – you can just imagine the effect on the traffic.[22] Travellers are constantly cursing about being caught in a 'stop', as too many coaches and carts block a narrow street. When a coach driver carelessly knocks an item off a market stall and has to pause to make amends, or a drayman and a coachman exchange angry words due to some reckless driving, and one descends from his vehicle and grabs the reins of the other and starts threatening him, the traffic yet again grinds to a halt.[23]

There are many varieties of passenger vehicle on the roads. The slowest and most uncomfortable are the stage wagons or caravans, which carry people and merchandise from town to town. With four large wheels and a cloth awning, and drawn by a long line of horses in a row, they can accommodate up to twenty people.[24] The driver normally walks along beside the horses, cracking his whip, which gives you an idea as to how slow they are. Travelling this way will make you think you are about to head out for the American West. But they have their place, moving the less well off and their possessions from town to town. They are also a very safe way to travel, as highwaymen tend not to bother holding up large numbers of poor people. There are about 300 carriers operating between provincial towns and London in 1681.[25]

Private coaches are a much faster mode of transport. At the start of the period, these are mainly square cabs with large wheels at the rear and smaller ones at the front. The cab itself is normally a leather-covered wooden frame suspended from the chassis; this leads to a fair bit of swinging about, and you may feel a little seasick. From the 1660s new designs proliferate. The cab of the average coach is given a more distinct taper, so that it is wider at the top than it is at the bottom. The best examples are given spring suspension. Windows, which were previously covered with leather blinds to keep out the weather, are increasingly glazed.[26] Vehicles with seating for six passengers, pulled by four or six horses (hence 'a coach and four' or 'a coach and six'), are built to carry gentlemen from their country seats into town. Some of these are gilt but, after Charles II expresses his dissatisfaction with ostentatious coaches, most are simply painted black and decorated only with the owner's coat of arms on the door.

In London you'll see a large number of small four-wheeled carriages with a yellow cab and red wheels drawn by two horses. These are hackney carriages, so called because *hacquenee* is an old French word for horse. You'll also see quite a few open-top chariots, driven by the occupants themselves. Some of these have bodies of wickerwork, for extra speed. The general trend is to design faster, lighter coaches for the city. In 1665 Robert Hooke produces a prototype for a speedy two-wheeled, two-passenger chariot drawn by a single horse. Then there are calashes – small chariot-coaches with collapsible tops – a sort of early convertible. Right at the end of our period the chaise makes its appearance: a light, open-top fast vehicle drawn by one or two horses.[27] You can see where all this is heading ... Samuel Pepys has a lot of fun in Sir William Pen's chariot, which is drawn by two horses, competing against Sir William Batten's coach and four. The chariot wins – although the occupants' clothes, including Pepys's velvet coat, are covered in dust and grime as a result.[28]

Okay, practicalities. If you are in London and you need a cab, you can hail a hackney carriage. They are not meant to loiter in the street, as the result of a 1660 Act to stop them blocking thoroughfares, but you will still find them waiting wherever there is a convenient spot. Lorenzo Magalotti notices them on almost every street in 1669. Alternatively, there is a cab rank at the Maypole in the Strand. Each vehicle for hire can carry up to four passengers anywhere in the city or the suburbs. The number of cabs is limited to 400, so you will find it hard to obtain one at times of great demand, such as in bad weather or after the theatre. Before 1670, most do not have glass windows, so you will travel in the dark. From 1662 drivers are all supposed to be licensed (at a one-off fee of £5) and the cab should display the driver's licence number on the outside. The standard charge is 12d per hour. According to Monsieur Misson, the normal way of settling a dispute about a fare is by fighting your coachman. Even the duke of Grafton – the king's illegitimate son – has been known to fight a hackney-carriage driver over the cost of a journey.[29]

If you plan on heading further afield, you will need to obtain a coach of your own. At the bottom end of the market, professional men tend to buy vehicles in the £15–25 range. If you are prepared to buy second-hand, you can obtain them even more cheaply. One belonging to the Lincoln physician Dr Henry Corbet is valued at £13 10s with all its harness in 1680.[30] Alternatively, you can get yourself a little open-top chariot for running around town: the historian Sir William Dugdale buys a new one in 1681 for £23 13s, plus £4 for the harness and £1 for a cover for it when not in use.[31] Sir William Penn's speedy chariot costs £32. A good-quality covered glass coach will set you back considerably more. Samuel Pepys agrees to pay £53 for one in 1668. At the top end of the spectrum, the earl of Bedford's new coach in May 1682 comes to £127 4s.[32] Add a team of suitable horses (at £25 each) and suitable livery for the ducal coachman and a couple of footmen – and the earl won't have any change from £300.[33] Then there are the running costs. Dr Henry Corbet has four horses, worth an average of £7 each, and needs to rent at least four acres to keep them all in grass, at approximately 10s per acre, plus hay in winter.[34] Don't forget the veterinary bills, farriers' bills and the maintenance of the coach itself. At the expensive end of the scale, just feeding the earl of Bedford's six horses when he is staying in London costs about £1 10s *per week*. And, really, an earl should not have to make do with just the one coach; he ought to have several. The earl of Bedford never spends less than £1,000 per year on his stables and coaches, and in some years more than £1,500.[35]

The principal advantage of the coach and six over the coach and four is not that the extra two horses make you go that much faster – horses can only canter so quickly – but that you can travel at high speed for longer. In 1667 Pepys travels 18 miles to Epsom in a coach and four, which, at 6mph, is not bad going, but the same horses take an extra hour to make the return journey.[36] John Evelyn, travelling to Althorpe in 1688, covers the first 32 miles in a coach and four at a similar 5–6mph but then, after lunch, is given the use of a coach and six for the remaining 40 miles and does an impressive 8mph all the way.[37] The other factor to bear in mind about a coach and six is the prestige value. Wherever these vehicles go, they turn heads. You definitely want to be seen in one, even if you don't need to travel fast. Pepys is delighted when he receives a letter from Lord Howe telling him that his lordship is sending his coach and six to collect him the following morning.[38] Many ladies and gentlemen who cannot attend a funeral send their coaches to represent them, with their coat of arms displayed on the sides of the cab. Evelyn proudly notes in his diary that no fewer than six coach and sixes attend the funeral of his daughter Mary in 1685.[39]

Presuming you don't have enough money to buy your own coach, what other options do you have? You can hire one: standard London rates are 18d for the first hour and 12d per hour after that.[40] Alternatively you can catch a stagecoach. This is truly radical: an efficient *public* transport system, open to anyone who can pay and much faster than those lumbering old carriers mentioned earlier. Nor is the excitement lost on contemporaries. Edward Chamberlayne has this to say on the subject in 1676:

> There is of late such an admirable commodiousness, both for men and
> women of better rank, to travel from London to almost any great
> town of England, and to almost all the villages near this great city,
> that the like hath not been known in the world, and that is by stage-
> coaches, wherein one may be transported to any place; sheltered from
> foul weather and foul ways, free from damaging one's health or body
> by hard jogging or over violent motion, and this not only at a low
> price, about a shilling for every five miles, but with such velocity and
> speed as that the posts in some foreign countries make not more miles
> in a day; for the stage coaches, called Flying Coaches, make forty or
> fifty miles in a day, as from London to Oxford or Cambridge, and that
> in the space of twelve hours, not counting the time for dining, setting
> forth not too early, nor coming in too late.[41]

It all sounds rather wonderful. So what is the reality?

A fledgling stagecoach network already exists in 1660. You can buy a journey from London to any of a few dozen major towns on major routes: Dover in the south-east; Exeter in the south-west; Bristol in the west; Chester in the north-west; and Edinburgh in the far north. They depart regularly – coaches bound for Exeter, Chester and York leave every Monday, Wednesday and Friday – but their slowness and expense are significant drawbacks.[42] They rarely exceed 30 miles per day, even in summer. The 70-mile journey from London to Dover via Canterbury takes two days, which is only a little faster. And sometimes there are delays: in November 1661 it takes a stagecoach four hours to cover just the 17 miles between Canterbury and Sittingbourne.[43] Thus the network in 1660 does not yet have the 'velocity' that Chamberlayne's 1676 account suggests. Nor is it as cheap as he claims. Fares to Exeter, Chester and York are indeed about a shilling for every five miles – £2 in summer or £2 5s in winter – but on top of this you will have to tip the coachman or, rather, coachmen, because on long distances there will be three or four drivers.[44] The passengers also have to pay for the drivers' beer at each inn. And you will need to pay for your own meals during your journey. Slowness thus means greater expense.

For this reason, the Flying Coaches, which start with the London–Oxford route in 1669, are significant advances in transport efficiency. In truth, they only 'fly' between March and September; in winter they revert to the usual two-day journeys. Even in the summer their speeds are only about 5mph. But they introduce a new sense of urgency to public transport. The widespread advertising of a 59-mile daily service to Oxford does wonders for the trade as a whole. It pushes many other carriers towards greater efficiency: the London–Chester connection is reduced to five days' travelling (46 miles per day), and the 65-mile route from London to Northampton is occasionally covered in a single day.[45] The reduction in time leads to lower costs to passengers and much greater demand. This in turn attracts others to the business and creates more competition. In 1681 you can catch a stagecoach from London to any one of 88 towns in Britain, and that number is rapidly increasing: it will be 180 towns in 1705.[46]

It is when you get into a stagecoach that you might start to have your doubts about this form of transport. Just try travelling in a cheap six-seater that has been made to take eight passengers. Ned Ward journeys from London to Stourbridge Fair with five women, an infant and an old man, in a 'dirty, lumbering, wooden hovel', and describes his experience as the vehicle sets off over a cobbled street:

> The rest of the company, being most of 'em pretty burly, had made a shift to leave me a nook in the back part of the coach, not much wider than a chair for a jointed baby. I nestled and I squeezed and drew in my sides like a fat man going through a narrow stile, till with much ado, I had wedged in my buttocks between the side of the coach and the hip of a bouncing blowsabella, who sat next to me ...
>
> We, at every swog, kneaded our elbows in one another's sides, till I had the ill fortune to so raise the old gentleman's spleen that he

grinned and snarled like a towzer at a bone when a strange dog is near him, being ready to bite my nose off ... In a little time we got off the stones [cobbles] and had done cursing of the pavier, and then began to swim as easily along the road as a Gravesend barge in fair weather, though wedged as close in one by another as a barrel of red herrings.[47]

Another point against coaches is that they can be dangerous. While anyone travelling on a highway is vulnerable to attack by brigands, those travelling by coach are especially susceptible, even on the streets of a city. An old trick is for one man to stop a coachman to ask him for directions and for his accomplice to snatch whatever he can, from the occupants of the coach, through the open window. The thieves then make their getaway through the warren of narrow lanes.[48] Out on the open road, travellers are even more at risk. You are miles from anywhere, your robber is mounted and armed, while you sit helplessly in a slow-moving coach. Both John Evelyn and Celia Fiennes run into highwaymen in the course of their travels. And while you have probably only heard of a few famous brigands, there are hundreds of them up and down the country. A report compiled in the reign of Charles II names nineteen highwaymen known to be active in East Anglia alone. One of them, William Dowsing, is a gentleman who rents Shotley Hall in Suffolk from Sir Henry Felton, MP. Another is a butcher by trade; another a physician.[49] But the real danger is the first-timer, the nervous desperado who, with a starving family and a couple of accomplices, has hit upon the idea of robbing a coach in order to clear his debts. Lack of experience in such matters means that many men panic and shoot, when they should simply flee.

Then there is the danger of a road-traffic accident. Although your coach itself might be going no more than 8mph, you can imagine the danger posed to pedestrians in a narrow street by the hooves and the swinging weight of the cab. The coachman and his passengers are at risk too, especially from overturning on corners. John Evelyn's coach overturns in October 1666, and the smashed glass injures his son.[50] Even the royal family has to put up with the odd upset. In the early hours of 8 March 1669 the royal coach tips over in Holborn on the way to Newmarket. The torches fixed to the coach do not light the street well enough, it hits a rut and over it goes, with the king, the duke of York, the duke of Monmouth and Prince Rupert (the king's nephew) tossed about inside.[51] On this occasion, no one is injured – although I would not like to have been that coachman afterwards. Other dangers presented by coaches include putting your head through the window of a coach to greet a friend, only to find there is glass in it; falling out of the coach because the door is not shut properly and being run over by the rear wheels; and going to a stately home in a coach where the coachman is plied with alcohol by the servants and is consequently unable to drive – a misfortune that befalls John Evelyn and Lord Howard.[52]

HORSES

If you are intending to travel off the beaten track, you will need a horse. The same thing applies if you want to travel fast, or simply travel with dignity – high-status people don't walk through the dust and mud of the highways. Buying a steed, though, can be tricky. There are hundreds of horse fairs and markets up and down the country, but there is no guarantee that you will get your money's worth. When Willem Schellinks goes to Smithfield to buy horses he finds 'clear enough proof of the dishonesty of this horse market, as our horses were really nothing special and therefore [we] overpaid by half ... They were miserable beasts.'[53] Ned Ward describes horse dealers as

> A sort of Smithfield fox ... who swear every morning by the bridle that they will never suffer from any man a knavish trick or ever do an honest one. They ... have a rare faculty of swearing a man out of his senses, lying him out of his reason and cozening him out of his money. If they have a horse to sell that is stone blind, they'll call a hundred gods to witness he can see as well as you can ... And if he be twenty years old, they'll swear he comes but seven next grass, if they find the buyer has not judgement enough to discover the contrary.[54]

Clearly, buying horses in the seventeenth century is somewhat like buying second-hand cars in the twenty-first.

What do you have to pay for a quality mount? The high cost of horses for noblemen's coaches has already been mentioned. Occasionally Lord Bedford will pay as much as £50 for a riding mount, such as the bay gelding he buys in 1671; he pays £38 for a strawberry stallion the same year.[55] Ordinary people do not go to this level of expenditure. All of the twenty-two horses owned by a Buckinghamshire esquire are worth less than £9.[56] A gentleman living in Lincoln has three horses and a colt worth a total of £30 – significantly more valuable than the six working horses on a farm he owns, which are worth a total of £18.[57] A yeoman might spend £5 on a horse, a tradesman £3 or so. The bottom of the scale is represented by the poor beasts that hauliers and carriers use for pulling their caravans. One Bristol haulier in 1686 has ten 'ordinary' horses, valued at an average of £2 3s each. Those owned by the widow of another Bristol haulier in 1689 are all past their prime: one 'old flea-bitten nag' is worth £1 10s; 'an old clubfooted bay gelding', £1 15s; 'an old brown hollow-backed nag', £1 15s; and 'a lame one-eyed brown mare', £1.[58] Blind horses are not suitable for riding, only for adding power as part of a team.

An alternative to all this expense is to hire a horse. This is a booming trade at this time, and has been since about 1630.[59] Rates vary from place to place: some people hire horses from inns, others from private individuals. In a number of places in Berkshire the rate is set at 1d per mile. However, in other localities you can get a standard day-rate of 12d.[60] Another form of horse hire is to ride with the post, stopping every 10–15 miles for a fresh mount. Although this is fast, it is much more expensive: 3d per mile, plus 4d per mile to the post boy (who will return the horse to its station). Schellinks rides with the post from Southwark to Rye in April 1663: he does the first 20 miles in three and a half hours (5¾mph), despite having to dismount and lead his horse down a steep hill near Farnborough.[61] Pepys also rides with the post one day in January 1661: he leaves London after 2 p.m. and reaches Rochester by 6 p.m., covering the 29 miles in less than four hours (7¼mph). Six months later, riding again with the post, he manages 55 miles in nine hours (6mph).[62] A young Ralph Thoresby travels the 204 miles from London to Leeds in just four days in February 1678 – even though the days are short and the roads muddy.[63]

Inland Waterways

Seventeenth-century people think of rivers as the arteries by which heavy loads can be conveyed over long distances efficiently and cheaply. They are also a quick and relatively safe way for individuals to travel. The trouble is that not everyone lives near a major river, and so a journey often has to integrate road and river transport. There is also the problem that many rivers are tidal, which leaves little flexibility as to the departure time of a ship or ferry. If there are insufficient passengers when the time comes to set sail, the boat master may decide to hang on for the next tide. You may well be in your stage-coach, willing it on to catch your ferry, despite the pouring rain and rutted roads, only to find that when you get to your point of embark-ation there won't be a sailing today after all.

The 57-mile journey from Canterbury to London neatly illustrates why you should not think of roads and rivers as alternatives but as complementary forms of transport. If you are travelling in early November 1661, for example, you'll need to get up before daybreak to make sure you catch the stagecoach at 7 a.m. By 1 p.m. you'll be in Sittingbourne, where the coachman will stop for an hour for you to have a meal. Then he'll take you via Rochester to Gravesend, arriving by 6.30 p.m. Here you will have just enough time for supper at the King's Head and to book yourself a place on the Long Ferry up the Thames to London. Your conveyance will be a tilt-boat – a large covered barge (a 'tilt' being an awning) – that is either rowed by men in the boat itself or pulled by a separate rowing boat of four oarsmen. If you're lucky, and the wind and tide are favourable, the journey should take about four hours, so you might reach Billingsgate by midnight.[64] Why take the trouble of changing to the boat, you might ask, rather than taking the stagecoach all the way? The answer lies in the fact that the stagecoach will not set out until the next day, and then it will take five hours to complete the journey to London, so you'll need to pay 12–18d for a bed in Rochester or Gravesend, plus the extra 5s for the coach. Travelling all the way by coach will thus cost you an extra 6s 6d and delay you by twelve hours or so.

When you get to London and look at the Thames you will see just how important river transport is to seventeenth-century people. There are tilt-boats and tide-boats, barges and wherries, hoys and ketches scattered all across the wide surface of the lapping water or, at low tide, heeling over awkwardly on a mud bank. Naval frigates are mixed in with coasters and merchantmen from all over the world. At Queenhithe there are boats arriving on a regular basis from Reading, Windsor, Maidenhead and all the other towns upstream. So many ships are waiting to unload at the twenty legal wharves on the north bank of the river that some of them have to be unloaded into small ships called lighters, which then ferry the goods ashore.

Among all these practical vessels you might see some unusual ones – the gilt royal barge, for example, or the similarly splendid craft used by the lord mayor and aldermen of the city. Noblemen also have their own barges, with twenty or thirty liveried oarsmen and a dining room with glass windows for the owner and his guests.[65] The word 'yacht' enters the English language in August 1660 when the city of Amsterdam sends a present of the 66ft *Mary* to Charles II. Pepys admires it greatly on arrival but, the following year, he sees a yacht built by the Kentish shipbuilder Peter Pett and decides that it is even better.[66] The king agrees and commissions a total of twenty-five yachts over the course of his reign. Several of them – the *Cleveland*, the *Portsmouth* and the *Fubbs* – are named after those other pleasure-vessels of his: his mistresses.[67]

Wherries are by far the most common boats on the Thames – there are more than 2,000 of them. They are sharp-bowed 22ft rowing boats that serve as river taxis, with room for five passengers. Those operated by a single waterman are called 'scullers'; those with two oarsmen are known as 'oars'.[68] Oars are faster than scullers (unsurprisingly) and therefore cost twice as much. Fares are 1d for a straight river crossing (2d for oars), and from 2d (or 4d) for a short journey up or down the river. Oars will charge you 8d for a one-way trip to Greenwich (12d if against the tide). Carrying people straight across the river is one of the mainstays of their business as there is still only one bridge; if you are at Temple or the Tower it is a long way to walk to cross on foot. There is only one ferry at this time too – the Horseferry – which runs between Lambeth and Westminster. Fares for this start at 2d for a man and a horse and increase to 1s 6d for a coach and two horses, 2s for a coach and four, and 2s 6d for a coach and six. Although the lord mayor petitions the king in 1663 for permission to establish another ferry, he is turned down. His attempt the following year to persuade the king to replace the Horseferry with a stone bridge is likewise ignored. Thus the wherries continue to ply their trade back and forth across the river, protected by royal benign neglect.

In the past, transport on the river after dark was forbidden. Nowadays it is permissible when the passengers are personally known to the watermen and are 'of honest conversation'. Nevertheless Willem Schellinks believes that it is unsafe to travel by night on the river because of the river pirates, who attack the boats and 'beat up the passengers, demanding their money'.[69] Pepys, however, has no such worries; he often uses wherries to get home after a late night in

Greenwich or attending to business in Whitehall. One moonlit night
he takes a wherry from Westminster and the waterman tells him some
bawdy stories about what has gone on in his boat. Once, he says, he
carried a lady from Putney on just such a moonlit night as this. As
he was rowing her along in the darkness, she bade him lie down in
the boat and make love to her, which he did.[70] Given what we know
about Samuel Pepys, it's a surprise he wasn't tempted to become a
night-time waterman himself.

Travelling by water is not without its challenges. It is easy to slip
on the wet wooden stairs when heading down to the river at low tide,
or to lose your footing as you step into a wherry or fall out of it when
it is hit by a big wave. The last of these misfortunes puts an end to
Major George Ansely in April 1660: a non-swimmer, with heavy boots
and coat pockets full of silver, he doesn't stand a chance when his
wherry goes down.[71] After a terrible gale in January 1666 Pepys looks
across the river and cannot see a single boat afloat except those that
have broken loose of their moorings. In February 1698 the Long Ferry
from Gravesend overturns in a storm with sixty people on board, only
seven of whom survive.[72]

Then of course there is the small matter of seasickness. Willem
Schellinks describes setting out from Gravesend one morning in
December 1661 with seventeen companions in a lighthorseman (a
large rowing boat which also has a sail):

> We headed straight into the wind, which was blowing up strongly and
> it stormed so badly that our foremast snapped while we were under
> sail, and in the end we had to strike our main sail and take it in because
> our gunwale was continuously dipping under water, and the ladies
> groaned loudly and the gentlemen swore and threatened the waterman
> mightily ... They could not use the oars properly, as the tide was
> running against the raging wind and the river ran so hollow, and the
> boat kept shipping water, so that in the end several guzzlers of our
> company presented the morning offering to the river god. Indeed they
> were so generous as to throw freely to the fish all kinds of English
> fancy sustenance, such as sack, Spanish wine, buttered eels, spirits,
> brandy, small and strong beer, cakes, pudding and other delicacies.[73]

If the wind is against you coming up the Thames, the tide may
turn before you reach your destination, which will severely delay you.

Then there is the cold – the sort that bites into you when your coat is wet with spray. When the London fog sinks down on the city, the watermen are plunged into an opaque blindness. If the fog mingles with the city's smoke, it forms smog; then men have to beat drums to let the watermen know the way to the north bank.[74] And don't forget the dangers of London Bridge, which, as the old saying goes, was built 'for wise men to go over and fools to go under'. The narrowness of the gaps between the starlings or platforms on which the piers of the bridge stand means that, at certain times of the tidal ebb and flow, the rushing of water between them is very dangerous. Only four of the nineteen arches are navigable, and one of them has a large lump of masonry in it, which fell from the bridge in 1437. 'Shooting the bridge' here is most unwise. Doing so when the tide is at its greatest ebb, after dark, is near suicidal.

The rivers elsewhere in Britain tend not to be as heavily used by passengers as the Thames. Your most frequent experience will be the innumerable short ferry journeys across them for a penny or two. However, crossing the estuary of a large river can be quite challenging, as Celia Fiennes finds out when she takes the Cremyll Ferry from Plymouth across the Hamoaze (the estuarine stretch of the Tamar) in 1698:

[This] is a very hazardous passage by reason of three tides meeting; had I known the danger before I should not have been very willing to have gone it, not but this is the constant way all people go, and saved several miles riding. I was at least an hour going over; it was about a mile but indeed in some places, notwithstanding there was five men rowing, and I set my own men to row also, I do believe we made not a step of way for almost a quarter of an hour; but blessed be God I came safely over. But those ferry boats are so wet, and then the sea and wind is always cold to be upon that I never fail to catch cold in a ferry boat as I did this day.[75]

Rivers are the arteries of trade: some navigable river networks penetrate inland for upwards of 70 miles. Of the twenty-six English towns mentioned in chapter 2 as having more than 5,000 inhabitants in 1670, only Leeds, Salisbury, Manchester, Coventry and Birmingham are not on a navigable river. Some of these waterways are not very substantial – such as the Stour at Canterbury, the Lark at Bury

St Edmunds, and the Cam at Cambridge – but even these small rivers permit the shipment of bulky items. Substantial barges regularly float down the Severn from Worcester to Bristol carrying wheat, malt, textiles, ironware and linen; a few days later they make the return trip upstream from Bristol with wine, tobacco, grocery wares, coal, lead and wool. Light goods might be transported even further up the river. The lightweight cargo boats on the Severn and Wye, called trows, have masts that can be taken down to go under bridges; they carry fruit and other foodstuffs all the way upstream to Shrewsbury.[76]

England's network of rivers is a tremendous asset to the nation but clearly it could be improved if all the rivers were navigable and they all joined up. Two recent initiatives – William Sandy's clearing and deepening of the River Avon to Stratford upon Avon (completed in 1640) and Sir Richard Weston's pioneering canal from Guildford to Weybridge (completed in 1653) – demonstrate what is possible in terms of engineering and commercial advantage. Gradually the idea spreads. In 1674 Carew Reynel declares that 'this nation might be greatly advantaged by cutting of rivers and making them navigable from one town to another and so breed a good commerce where [there] was none before'. He suggests building a canal from London to Bristol and cutting one right across the country in the north of England, so that ships can pass from the Irish Sea to the North Sea.[77]

River improvement, people start to realise, is a real possibility. Several River Navigation Acts are passed to allow barges of 24–70 tons to gain access to previously inaccessible new wharves. The River Stour is deepened in the 1660s to move coal from Staffordshire; the River Salwarpe is similarly cleared to transport salt from Droitwich. The River Avon is gradually improved to allow barges to reach Salisbury by 1684. The Great Ouse is made navigable as far as Bedford in 1689; the upper reaches of the River Trent likewise, first to Wilden Ferry and then, in 1699, to Burton on Trent.[78] The businessman Thomas Patten clears the obstructions in the Mersey, thereby connecting Warrington with Liverpool, and suggests improving the rivers Mersey and Irwell so that Manchester might have a wharf. In 1699 permission is granted to improve the rivers Aire and Calder so that barges can reach Leeds and Wakefield. Long before the canal-building craze of the next century, many improvements to the natural waterways of England are undertaken, facilitating the early stages of what will one day come to be known as the Industrial Revolution.

Seafaring

In Great Britain we often think of the defensive advantages of being an island but just think how much of an advantage the sea is for the industrial integration of the country. It is here that all the rivers *do* meet up – you can sail from one to another without having to cross any international borders. That is not the case for most other countries, whose waterways run through neighbouring states or, in the case of France and Spain, empty into seas thousands of nautical miles apart. As a result, Britain has an unrivalled commercial transport network – and that means there are thousands of ships and mariners available to help you sail around the coast or further abroad.

English shipping is growing rapidly in this period, both in respect of the number and size of ships. Back in the 1580s its total volume was 67,000 tons. By the start of our period, 1660, it has grown to three times that, being 200,000 tons.[79] Then it grows even more rapidly, driven by wars with the Dutch, Caribbean commerce, the trade with North America, the demand for coal in London, the expansion of the East India Company and the importation of grain from Eastern Europe. At the same time, the cost of shipbuilding comes down, from £8 to £5 per ton.[80] In 1686 the total volume of English shipping stands at 340,000 tons – more than five times its size at the time of the Spanish Armada.[81]

Rates of fighting ships in the Royal Navy, 1676[83]

Rate	Burden (tons)	Crew (men)	Cannon	Number in fleet
First Rate	1,300–1,500	750–850	90–100	6
Second Rate	730–1,230	410–640	56–80	8
Third Rate	629–1,055	340–400	53–70	20
Fourth Rate	305–646	170–280	34–60	33
Fifth Rate	158–337	110–170	22–32	16
Sixth Rate	28–287	25–80	4–18	18

Integral to this maritime strength is the Royal Navy. In 1672, it has a total of 238 ships in service, manned by 29,154 sailors, some from as far afield as Scotland and Ireland.[82] On top of these crews there are the shipwrights, timbermen, sail makers, rope makers, anchor makers, gun founders, administrators and suppliers of provisions who keep the whole fleet active. It is no exaggeration to say that the Royal Navy is a nationwide industry, and its warships are icons of British pride.

As the schedule of fighting ships above makes clear, the Royal Navy of Pepys's day is highly organised – due in no small part to Pepys himself. Whereas the navy of Elizabeth's reign had captains who were not permanent salaried officials, men who did not wear uniforms and an approach to discipline that can be called capricious at best, Pepys's navy is a well-integrated fighting machine. The rating of ships, for example, relates to the salaries paid to the officers on board. The professionalism that is sweeping across the rest of society also has a profound effect on the Royal Navy.

When you step on to the deck of a ship of the line, you are treading on a piece of technology that costs considerably more than a stately home. A First Rate requires on average £22,000 to build and an extra £12,000 to fit out. The most expensive English ship of all, the *Royal Sovereign*, has a price tag of over £65,000. Running costs are eye-watering too: the navy will spend almost £13,000 keeping a First Rate at sea for six months – in supplies, wages, maintenance, and so forth. And it can only operate for half the year, being lower in the water and thus too vulnerable in rough winter weather. The same applies to Second Rates. Hence Third Rates and Fourth Rates, which can be used all year around, are the workhorses of the Royal Navy. Operating costs of a Third Rate add up to £7,300 for six months.[84]

It would be unwise to travel in a warship during wartime – that is, during the years 1665–7, 1672–4 and 1689–97. Ten ships are sunk in just one battle in June 1666. The following year the Dutch sail up the Thames and sink a dozen English ships in their own harbour, capturing the British flagship, the *Royal Charles*, at the same time. Having said that, if you do take to the seas, sooner or later you will end up in a warship. This is because the Royal Navy is more closely integrated with ordinary life than you might imagine. Warships sometimes act as guards for valuable cargoes carried in merchantmen. If you are in a foreign port and seek a passage back to England, you may pay for passage on a warship. The mariners serving aboard contract only to serve for the single expedition, so a man might do one expedition aboard a Royal Navy ship and the next aboard a merchantman, or vice versa. Civilian ships, such as packet ships and merchantmen, are regularly attacked by foreign vessels and have to arm themselves; therefore their captains are keen to employ crew with experience in the Royal Navy. Aristocrats and important gentlemen often use naval vessels for their private ferrying about. And then there is the matter of pressing men for service. You may simply have no choice in whether or not you wish to serve on a warship – if the press gang comes looking to fill a quota and its captain decides that your physique and experience meet the requirements, then it's a naval life for you.

Most of the ships you will come across in a British port are small compared to the great ships of the line. The largest are the merchantmen belonging to the East India Company, which are 400–600 tons burden. Almost all other trading vessels are below 300 tons, with the most common, coasters, being in the range of 60–100 tons. Approximately a quarter of all mercantile shipping is used to transport coal around the coasts and to Europe.[85] The entire English fishing fleet amounts to 23,000 tons, one-third of the size of the coal trade. Smaller vessels are a mixture of sloops, ketches, galliots, hoys, pinks, smacks, flyboats and doggers. Sir William Petty even builds a prototype catamaran in 1663. I wouldn't sail in it if I were you, though: it sinks almost as soon as it is launched.[86]

NAVIGATION

Just as in the modern world, if you want to sail to a particular destination, you need to travel from the appropriate port. This principle also applies to the legal quays of London. To cross the Channel to France you will need to go to the Custom House Quay. For Scotland, you'll need the Hermitage, which is a wharf near St Katharine Docks. Boats for Colchester leave from Smarts Quay; those for Ipswich and King's Lynn from Dice Quay. Sandwich and Dover are served from Sabb's Dock. Plymouth, Dartmouth, Poole, Weymouth and ports in Ireland are served from Chester's Quay, and so on.[87]

Once out at sea, you'll need to place your trust in the ship's pilot. These days, he will be a trained navigator who is licensed to operate in certain stretches of water by Trinity House, the London-based authority founded in 1514 that oversees British maritime affairs. This is just as well, for navigation can prove difficult even in well-known seas. Grand Duke Cosimo III sails to England in 1669 in an English ship – and you would have thought that an English navigator could find his way up the English Channel. Yet although he constantly checks the time, his speed, his direction, the depth of the water and the quality of the seabed, the ship somehow manages to land on the coast of Ireland. The mistake is put down to the uncertainty of the soundings, the bad time-keeping of the ship's clock, the inexperience of the steersman in the night and the captain's tendency to interfere with the pilot's navigation.[88]

The underlying problem is the inability to calculate longitude at sea. People understand that the secret lies in accurate time-keeping, but spring-driven watches are unreliable and pendulum clocks are unusable at sea. Another difficulty comprises the poor maps and charts. Most seafarers are still using 'waggoner' charts (so called because they were drawn up by Lucas Janszoon Waghenaer). First published in 1588, these are strewn with errors, as many English captains know. They show the Isles of Scilly in the wrong place, for example, and the Dogger Bank is depicted 24 miles from its actual location.[89] Cometh the hour, cometh the man: in 1681 Captain Greenvile Collins is given command of the yacht *Merlin* and told to survey the coasts of Britain (including Scotland) in greater detail than ever before. This he does over the next eight years: his nautical charts are published in 1693 as *Great Britain's Coasting Pilot*. Such is the accuracy of Collins's work that it will continue to be republished for the next hundred years.[90]

Trinity House also has oversight of all the lighthouses up and down the country. You will be pleased to hear that from the 1660s there is a positive programme of improvement. The old lighthouses at Harwich, Dungeness, Lowestoft and North Foreland, which previously used candles in their lights, are all rebuilt as high towers carrying coal-fired braziers. New lighthouses are constructed at Old Hunstanton in 1665; St Agnes on the Isles of Scilly in 1680; and Winterton on the Norfolk coast in 1687. Work begins on the Eddystone, 9 miles off the coast of Devon, in 1696 – the first lighthouse in the world to be constructed on an isolated rock far out at sea. This is a remarkable piece of engineering: it is 80ft high, on a rock that is submerged at high tide, with a base of granite bound by iron and copper, and topped by a glass lantern room lit by candles. At the time of its construction the Nine Years' War is still in progress, so its designer and builder, Henry Winstanley, is guarded each day by a ship from Plymouth. Unfortunately one day the protection fails to show up and a French privateer captures him, destroys his work and takes him to Paris. When he hears of the deed, Louis XIV immediately orders Winstanley's release, famously commenting that 'France is at war with England, not with humanity'.

LIFE AT SEA

There is no doubt that life at sea is tough, and the further you sail, the tougher it is likely to be. Even if you have a perfect outward journey, there is a nagging worry that things will not be so wonderful on the way back. Ralph Thoresby's voyage from Hull to Rotterdam in 1678 is fast, taking just 48 hours to sail the 250 miles, with no greater problem than a bout of seasickness. On his return, however, his vessel is struck by a tremendous storm and blown on to its side on a sandbank in the North Sea. Poor Thoresby has to lie there, with waves crashing over him, for sixteen hours before the storm abates.[91] Ship-borne diseases are hardly any more merciful. When the *Britannia* arrives in Philadelphia in 1699, half of the 100 passengers aboard are dead.[92] One of the reasons why Edward Barlow starts writing his journal is so that people 'may understand in part what dangers and troubles poor seamen pass through'.[93]

If you are considering a voyage, here are a few things you can expect. Sleeping arrangements are basic and uncomfortable. As an ordinary sailor, Barlow has a cabin that is 'like a gentleman's dog kennel', as he has to crawl into it on all fours. This is not unusual; another description of such cabins is 'nasty holes, which breed sickness and in a fight are very dangerous'.[94] In later years you won't get a cabin; instead you'll be given a hammock in which to sleep, and allocated a space just 14 inches wide in which to hang it. You'll have to provide your own mattress, pillow and blankets. In contrast, the captain's cabin is spacious and luxurious. Even on a Fourth Rate ship, it is the full width of the stern and 24ft long. On a larger vessel it is furnished with oil paintings and gilt carvings. Schellinks describes the captain's cabin aboard the Third Rate *Henrietta* as 'a splendid, large and expensively furnished room'. As for the lieutenant's cabin, Schellinks and his companions are entertained there with 'claret, ale and delicious beer', which suggests it is easily capable of entertaining a party. So is the mate's cabin, to which Schellinks and companions repair for the next round of drinks.[95] In later years these lesser officers' cabins are reduced in size, to a mere 6ft by 5ft and they are divided by canvas partitions rather than wooden walls.[96] The captain's cabin, however, remains spacious and opulent.

Women are only to be found aboard ship in certain circumstances. Obviously there are those who are bound for a new life in North America or the Plantations. Some travel as indentured servants. The East India Company, however, does not permit men to bring out their womenfolk to India and the Far East, even if they are going to be stationed out there (although a handful of wives do slip through the net). The Royal Navy has a policy of allowing wives and girlfriends to stay with their men on the first leg of a long voyage, but no further. This, combined with the cramped hammock arrangements, leads to some lewd displays just after setting sail: in the gloom below deck you may well see 'a man and woman creep into a hammock, the woman's legs to the hams hanging over the sides'.[97] Not even officers are allowed to take their womenfolk outside British waters. Captain Sir William Jennens is dismissed and imprisoned for taking his wife on convoy duty in the Mediterranean in 1670.[98] It is well within British waters that the adventurous twenty-year-year-old Anne Chamberlyne takes part in a sea battle – the Battle of Beachy Head in 1690 – serving in the ship commanded by her brother. She survives the battle, but dies in childbirth the following year.

When it comes to food, the difference between the lot of the ordinary seamen and the officers is as great as the inequality of their sleeping quarters. Standard fare for a sailor in the Royal Navy is a gallon of beer (served by ladle from a barrel) and 1lb of biscuit every day, as well as a weekly ration of 4lbs salted beef, 2lbs pork, three-eighths of a fish, a quart of peas, 6oz of butter and 12oz of cheese.[99] On paper, it looks a good calorie count for a working man. However, measures are sometimes cut short by the ship's purser. The beer tends to go off or is watered down. Butter goes rancid, biscuits are attacked by beetles. The corks in barrels and liquor bottles are gnawed by rats. In the Mediterranean, rice might be substituted for fish, olive oil for butter, and raisins for beef. These alternatives do not go down well with the men. You will also find that the cooking facilities restrict the preparation of the food. Having a large fire on board a wooden ship is clearly hazardous: the heat has to be contained within a hearth of

600–2,500 bricks, depending on the size of the ship. That additional weight restricts the positioning of the galley; normally it is located in the hold or on the middle gundeck in a large ship. In either location it is both smoky and dark, making it very difficult to cook, especially if you are catering for hundreds of men. Most food for the ordinary sailor is therefore simply boiled in large cauldrons. Officers, in contrast, may dine on roasted meat and rich puddings. On 10 July 1675, having just sailed passed Lisbon, the naval chaplain Henry Teonge is invited to the captain's cabin to dine with all the officers of the squadron; they feast on

> Four dishes of meat, viz. four excellent hens and a piece of pork boiled in a dish; a leg of mutton and turnips; a piece of beef of eight ribs, well-seasoned and roasted; and a couple of very fat geese; last of all, a very great Cheshire cheese – a rare feast [even when on] shore. His liquors were answerable: canary, sherry, Rhenish, claret, white wine, cider, ale – all of the best sort – and punch [as plentiful as] ditch water.[100]

Ultimately it will be the smell, the 'pestilential funk', that will be your lasting memory of travelling on a Restoration ship, not the size of the cabin or the food. The only way of airing the lower decks of a ship is to leave open the gun ports, but this cannot be done in rough seas and, even when the water is calm, it is inadequate. The stink tends to rise from the very bottom of the vessel. Algae, fungi and bacteria cover the surfaces of whatever solids are in the dark salt-water soup down there. Every so often all the rocks and old pieces of iron used as ballast have to be taken out and left on the shore to be rinsed by the waves, while the bilge is washed down with vinegar.[101] Needless to say, 'every so often' is not often enough. The smell is not helped by the rotting food in the hold, the steam and smoke of the galley, the cooking smells, the vomit, and the excrement either dropped directly into a dark corner by its producer or thrown into the bilge by a servant who can't be bothered to go up on deck to empty an officer's chamber pot.

On the question of sanitation, the captain has his own outdoor seat of easement – a wooden seat with a hole in it, emptying directly into the sea – on the quarter gallery, a narrow private balcony at the back of the ship, just outside his cabin. For the ordinary sailor, relief from the call of nature is to be had at one of the pissdales on deck – a urinal attached to a lead pipe – or the 'heads', at the bow of the ship.[102] These days not only is the bow blessed with timber grating, but there are a couple of seats of easement there for you to use, one facing the other, each with their back to the timber wall of the bow. On the plus side, the rising and falling of the ship mean that this area is regularly washed with water from the spray and waves. The downside is that you are unlikely to spend any length of time here reading a book.

As you lie in your hammock in the dark below deck, swaying with the heaving of the ship and the stink of the bilge ever in your nostrils, you might reflect that you've come a long way since lying on that feather bed in London. There was almost complete silence in your room in the capital, except for the slow tick of the longcase clock and the chambermaid making her way up the stairs, and you wondered what tomorrow would bring. Now you are listening to the creaking of the ship's timbers, the distant waves and the nearby squeaking of rats scampering across the boards beneath you. And you may still be wondering what tomorrow will hold. Somewhere out there on this dark sea are the pirates you have heard so much about – Sir Henry Morgan, the conqueror of Panama; and Henry Every, the man who captures the richest prize ever taken by a pirate (and is never caught). More worrying still are the numerous Barbary corsairs, who sail the Mediterranean and Atlantic waters and even enter the English Channel, looking for boys like Joseph Pitts to sell in the slave markets of North Africa. Who knows, they may have already sighted your ship on the horizon and be waiting to attack at dawn.

As the vessel rides another wave and sinks down into yet another trough, and the hammocks all sway and creak on their ropes in the dark fug, you might think of your fellow seafarers. The dream of travelling the world has become a reality for many men – from Edward Barlow spending his life at sea, seeing strange animals in the most exotic locations, to William Dampier navigating his way around the world three times, to describe the flora and fauna of faraway places. You could say that, by 1700, we have come to terms with the world. So as you lie there and reflect, it might strike you as ironic to realise that the next revolution in travel will take place back onshore, in England.

If you sail to the River Tyne, put ashore near Newcastle and take a barge upstream, you will see some wooden rails near the riverbank.

Every so often you will see a horse arrive, pulling a train of wagons along those rails. Those wagons are full of coal – each train contains four or five chaldrons (about 10½–13 tons). You will not believe a single horse could draw so much weight. Coal merchants here can clearly see how easy it is to convey huge loads on wheels set on rails.

It is a wonderful moment in time. People are only just becoming aware of their ability to change the world.

8

Where to Stay

The practicalities of finding accommodation vary from age to age. One of the problems of the Restoration period is the sheer number of people on the road. You might be planning to stay at a favourite inn, only to find on arrival that you have just been beaten to it by a stagecoach from London, so the best rooms have all gone. Another issue arises from the practice of tipping. In the modern world, we think of a tip as a small reward in return for a particular service; in the seventeenth century, it has much more to do with the status of the giver than the service rendered. If you want to be treated as a gentleman, you will pass a sixpence or a shilling to almost every deserving person of lower status that you meet. You will tip the servants in your host's house as readily as those at an inn. You will give money to the poor and to beggars on the highways, to people who help you with directions and to the washerwoman who comes to clean your clothes. The readiness with which you distribute silver is an important indicator of your largesse, and in many places that will have a bearing on where you may stay overnight.

Inns

There are ways to secure the best room in an inn, even if it doesn't have a vacancy. If you turn up late one night and give the impression that you are a wealthy gentleman, then the landlord will find room for you, even if it means waking up someone who is already asleep and asking him to vacate the bed. In June 1668, Mr and Mrs Pepys and their two servants are travelling in rural Wiltshire (having just been to see Stonehenge) when they come to a small inn at 10 p.m. There is a pedlar asleep in the best bedroom. Not for long, though. Soon Samuel and his wife are enjoying the warm space he has vacated, with their servants Will and Betty in a truckle bed in the same room. You can see why the landlord has been so helpful when you look at the bill: Pepys pays 9s 6d for his accommodation, including stabling and fodder for their horses. The pedlar would have paid only a quarter of that.[1]

You will recognise an inn by its sign: all inns and taverns are required by law to have an identifying emblem clearly displayed.[2] For the most part, these are exactly what you would expect: painted wooden boards swinging on an iron bracket above the front of the building, just as in the modern day. They creak in the wind, in true 'Highwayman' style. Look carefully, however, and you'll see the signs are undergoing a revolution. A hundred years ago they all had simple images, such as the King's Head, the Red Lion, the White Hart, the Crown, the Mitre, the Grosvenor Arms, and so on. The only compound names you'd ever come across would be religious or heraldic symbols, such as the Eagle and Child, the Bear and Ragged Staff and the Rose and Crown. Nowadays it seems every new inn is called by a juxtaposition of two nouns, such as the Crown and Anchor or the Fox and Hounds. There is a trend for bizarre combinations: the Razor and Hen, the Magpie and Crown, the Leg and Seven Stars, the Whale and Crow, and the Shovel and Boat.[3] Marketing is the reason for the change. Innkeepers want a distinctive name that stagecoach users and operators will remember. The proprietors who name their premises like this are also giving a signal to prospective customers that their premises are up to date and equipped with all the latest conveniences (such as chamber pots).

Another new way of drawing in guests is the construction of a strikingly elaborate inn sign. The White Hart at Scole, Norfolk, is the benchmark here: its sign is probably the most elaborate ever constructed in England. Built in 1655 by James Peck, a Norwich merchant, it crosses the whole highway and is covered with dozens of the most ornate carvings. It shows biblical scenes, such as Jonah coming out of the whale's mouth; angels, shepherds and figures from classical mythology, including Bacchus and Cerberus; Prudence, Fortitude, Old Father Time and the coats of arms of many hoped-for patrons. The inn itself isn't bad, either. It looks handsome from the outside – new red brick, with fashionable Dutch gables – and the rooms are very comfortable. Thomas Baskerville visits in 1681 and speaks well of its ale and beer.[4] As a result, this becomes one of the most famous hostelries in the country. Other methods of attracting high-status customers' attention include providing entertainments such as a cockpit and a bowling green, and advertising the fact that royal visitors have stayed there. If you take a coach to Guildford, no doubt you will want to book in at the Red Lion and pay extra to stay in the room once occupied by Charles II. At the Swan in Market Harborough you can sleep in the same bed in which Charles I once spent the night.[5]

Some town inns are substantial premises. The Red Lion in Guildford, for example, has more than fifty rooms. A few in London are even larger, especially the coaching inns outside the gates and those in the centre that were rebuilt after the Great Fire. The largest inn in Lincoln, the Angel, has twenty letting chambers. These are not numbered, but are named after heraldic symbols: 'the Hart', 'the Angel', 'the Crown', 'the Bell', and so forth – thereby allowing illiterate travellers to identify their room. Furnishings in the Angel's chambers range hugely. The most sparsely furnished is the Green Room, which has just a four-poster bedstead with curtains and valance around it, and a feather bed (i.e. a feather-filled mattress) within the bedstead and a bolster. The most lavish is the Little Cross Room, which has a better-quality four-poster bed with hangings and all the usual accessories, plus a set of cane chairs, a table and a looking glass. In both rooms, a basin and ewer of water will be provided when you turn up so that you can wash your face and hands. Note that not all rooms are for sleeping in: the Great Cross chamber is arranged for meetings with twenty-two chairs of Turkey work (chairs upholstered with embroidered cloth) arranged around four tables.[6]

The majority of rooms in an inn have several beds in them. A fine one in a large Bristol inn has seven: two bedsteads with feather beds, a flock-filled bed and bedstead, two more nondescript beds and two truckle beds for servants. This isn't a dormitory – it's a high-status room, as you can see from the fact it also contains six Turkey-work chairs, seven 'plush chairs' (upholstered with a soft rich fabric, such as silk or cotton with a long, soft nap), two looking glasses, a cypress-wood cupboard and side cupboard and a table with a carpet across it.[7] Obviously the room is often shared by various users, not all of whom are necessarily acquainted. This is something you'll need to get used to. You may even have members of the opposite sex staying in the same room. In 1660 Pepys goes to lie down at his inn and finds the next bed occupied by an attractive woman. Being Pepys, he naturally thinks of making love to her and goes so far as to kiss her hand, but does not actually try his luck.[8] It is not unknown for foreign gentlemen travelling in England to go to their bedchambers only to find a woman disrobing.[9] Not everyone is happy with this state of affairs: Celia Fiennes, for one, is concerned that in some places ladies have to share a room with strangers. *Have* to share, you might ask: surely you can refuse? In some inns, the beds are nominally free and the costs are included in the prices of food and stabling. But that means you cannot complain that someone else is lodged in your room, if you have not paid for it. This way the landlord can cram even more people into his inn, night after night, and make more profit than if he were to charge for the room.[10]

You will also be expected to share beds. If you stay at the English Champion in Ware, Hertfordshire, you can sleep in the famous Great Bed of that town, which is 10ft 9 inches square and 7ft 6 inches high and sleeps twelve people. (Chances are that it's the person in the middle who has to get up in the middle of the night.) Samuel Pepys and Dr Clerke think nothing of sharing a bed when they stay at an inn together in April 1662.[11] Sometimes servants share a bed with their master or mistress. Pepys has been known to sleep in a truckle bed at an inn and let his maidservant share the main bed with his wife (although, unsurprisingly, his wife never allows him to share the bed with their maid).

Foreign travellers praise English inns highly for their accommodation and victuals; however, these tend to be better-off travellers staying at the best establishments. As they travel in groups and with servants, they rarely have to share a room. They also avoid some of the other problems that ordinary travellers face at an inn. Being woken by your roommates getting up at dawn can be tiresome – especially if you are sharing a bed with them. Then there's the snoring, and having to listen to other people use the chamber pot in the night. You may find the prospect of being the second person in the night to use the said article a trifle unpleasant, especially if the first one's aim was not so good. There's only one thing worse – waking up in the middle of the night and putting your foot in the said chamber pot and tipping it over. I suspect such inconveniences will outweigh even the discomfort of the fleas. These are everywhere, and so common that people tend to find their biting amusing, especially when they bite other people. When Pepys shares a bed with Dr Clerke, he is delighted to learn in the morning that the fleas attacked Dr Clerke in the night and not him.[12]

Stately Homes and Country Houses

The wealthy people of Britain live in a wide range of dwellings, from medieval castles to Tudor mansions and up-to-date stately homes. Even at the end of the century, older structures outnumber those built since 1660, and owners show great imagination in adapting and updating their ancestral piles. Having said that, I imagine it is the new architecture you most want to see. And well you might, for the Restoration period sees some of the finest country houses ever built in Britain.

The chances are that you will not have heard of the architects of the places where you might stay. *The* most famous architect, Sir Christopher Wren, only designs one or two private residences: his time is rather taken up with churches, monuments and St Paul's Cathedral; public buildings in London, Oxford and Cambridge; and palatial wings for the royal family's residences at Kensington Palace and Hampton Court. Wren's assistant, the ubiquitous Robert Hooke, is probably the second most famous name – but his fame rests largely on his scientific work for the Royal Society. His architecture, like Wren's, is predominantly of a public nature, although he does design some fine houses, including Ragley Hall in Warwickshire, Ramsbury Manor in Wiltshire and Montagu House in London. The two most famous English baroque architects, John Vanbrugh and Nicholas Hawksmoor, only start designing stately homes at the very end of our period. However, if you have never heard of Hugh May, Roger Pratt and William Talman, then you are in for a treat.

Hugh May is the architect of Eltham Lodge, built in 1663–4. This is a 'double-pile' house – an arrangement developed by Inigo Jones earlier in the century. It consists of a simple two-storey rectangular block with a central corridor running the length of the building on both floors, with rooms on either side – thus a 'double-pile' because it has a 'pile' of rooms at the front and another at the back. Like Inigo Jones's houses on the Covent Garden piazza, Eltham Hall makes use of brick and pilasters. It is quite modest, with only seven windows on each floor at the front. However, its appearance is so pleasing that it attracts many others who want something similar on a grander scale. Lord Clarendon commissions May to design him a house at Cornbury, Oxfordshire, but with a front elevation eleven windows wide. After that, May designs

Berkeley House, the most westerly of the stately structures on the north side of Piccadilly. This has colonnades connecting the main building to service wings on the street, thereby creating an impressive quadrangle. By 1666 May's star has risen sufficiently for him to be appointed one of three Commissioners for rebuilding the city after the Great Fire of London (the others being Roger Pratt and Christopher Wren). Important private commissions follow in the 1670s – at Cassiobury Park, Hertfordshire, and Windsor Castle.

May's fellow Commissioner in 1666, Roger Pratt, begins his architectural career almost accidentally when his cousin, Sir George Pratt, asks him to design a new stately home for him at Coleshill. Undeterred by his lack of training and experience, he sets about the task with care and enthusiasm – and a conversation with Inigo Jones. Like May, his starting point is the 'double-pile' house. At Coleshill you enter directly into a splendid double-height hallway with a grand pair of staircases. This provides a centre around which the rest of the living space is laid out; all the servants' quarters are in the attic or in the basement. But that description does not do justice to the elegance of the structure. It is astonishing – both grand and beautiful – and everyone says so. Flushed with this success, Pratt goes on to design three more great houses: the graceful Kingston Lacy in Dorset; the slightly more imposing Horseheath Hall in Cambridgeshire; and the astonishing Clarendon House on Piccadilly (next door to Berkeley House). This last building is described by John Evelyn as 'without hyperbole, the best contrived, the most useful, graceful and magnificent house in England'.[13] Unfortunately, it is also one of the shortest-lived: it is bought by the duke of Albemarle and demolished for its materials in 1683. But it inspires other fine houses of all shapes and sizes – everything from the magnificent Belton House in Lincolnshire to the more modest Groombridge Place in Kent and the exquisite little jewel of the Old House in Kibworth Harcourt, in Leicestershire.

If you visit in the last two decades of the century you will find many houses showing traces of May's and Pratt's ideas. People living in villages near these mansions quickly become used to seeing the architectural novelties of brick walls and Palladian architraves and pilasters, which might look quintessentially British to you but are utterly foreign in their eyes. The new aesthetic reaches Scotland too, when Sir William Bruce designs Kinross House in the Palladian style in 1686, drawing much inspiration from Clarendon House. But arguably the most important private building of the whole period is a piece of work that looks beyond the achievements of May and Pratt and their contemporaries and anticipates the English baroque of the next century. It is designed by the irascible, curmudgeonly and supremely arrogant William Talman, who falls out with all his patrons, tries to steal Sir Christopher Wren's job and is capable of producing work that barely passes as mediocre. Yet Talman also produces the sublime design that captivates the imagination of the whole country, creating Britain's most-loved stately home: Chatsworth, in Derbyshire. Here, in 1686, the earl of Devonshire asks him to remodel the south front of the Elizabethan house. Talman builds in stone, positions his pilasters not in the centre of the front but at the corners, and raises the balustrade in such a way that he conceals the roof entirely, creating a house that is at once majestic, beautifully proportioned and welcoming. The earl is so impressed that he asks him to do the same to the east front. This is completed by 1696. Celia Fiennes drops by a year later, while work is in progress on the west front; she devotes more space to describing this property than to any other house she visits. She is especially struck by the large panes of glass employed, as window glass can normally be made only in small sections; someone tells her the panes at Chatsworth cost 10s each.[14]

The effort that goes into these buildings extends to the grounds as well. The underlying philosophy is to combine house and estate in one design. Look at the careful way the windows are positioned in relation to the whole front: everything is symmetrical, laid out in carefully calculated ratios. You will find the same attention to order in the gardens. These are all formal squares – squares within larger squares, in many cases – and the lakes are often rectangular, with cupids spouting an arc of water. Lawns are set in squares and, while on the subject, just think how much effort it is to maintain a lawn when all the tools you have are scythes, shears and rollers. There is a real determination to design and control everything. Even parkland is laid out in straight lines. Long, straight avenues of trees lead from the house as far as the eye can see, often ending in an obelisk on the horizon. At Coleshill, Celia Fiennes remarks that

> all the avenues to the house are fine walks of rows of trees. The garden
> lies in a great descent below the house, of many steps and terraces
> and gravel walks with all sorts of dwarf trees, fruit trees with standing

apricots and flower trees, abundance of garden room and filled with all sorts of things improved for pleasure and use.[15]

She finds a similarly satisfying layout at Wilton, which has 'many gravel walks with grass squares'. But she is even more impressed by the water features there. As the success of Sir Samuel Morland makes clear, there is a fashion for all things to do with pumps and water displays. At Chatsworth, Celia goes into ecstasies when she sees the fountains:

> There is a large park and several fine gardens one without another with gravel walks and squares of grass with stone statues in them and in the middle of each garden is a large fountain full of images – sea gods and dolphins and seahorses – which are full of pipes which spout out water in the basin, and spouts all about the gardens ... there is one basin in the middle of one garden that's very large and, by sluices beside the images, several pipes play out the water, about thirty large and small pipes altogether. Some flush it up that it froths like snow ... there is another green walk and about the middle of it by the grove stands a fine willow tree: the leaves, bark and all look very natural ... and all on a sudden by turning a sluice it rains from each leaf and from the branches like a shower, it being made of brass and pipes to each leaf but in appearance is exactly like any willow.[16]

Elsewhere she praises the introduction of greenhouses, orange trees and lemon trees, aviaries, sculptures and grottoes. Most great houses have at least one deer park, and many have two (one for red deer, one for fallow). When John Evelyn visits Swallowfield in Berkshire (another house designed by William Talman), he is most impressed by the number of the trees: 'there is one orchard of 1000 golden and other cider pippins; walks and groves of elms, limes, oaks, and other trees ... [and] two very noble orangeries ...'[17] The reason he can count so many trees is, of course, because they are laid out in straight lines.

Gradually you start to realise there is more going on here than just a lot of extravagant gardening, with a preference for regularity and extravagant water features. There is a deliberate attempt to control nature – just as merchants are attempting to improve rivers so that barges can reach large towns, and scientists are trying to determine how the world really works mechanically. Look in the libraries of these gentlemen and you will find books on how to fertilise land, how to prune fruit bushes, how to maintain orange trees in a cold climate, and so on. Many of them are Fellows of the Royal Society and look at the manipulation of nature as part of the scientific progress of mankind. You can see the same desire in the range of flowers they employ in their formal gardens: roses, daffodils, tulips, violets, lilies, sunflowers, hollyhocks, lupins, pinks, marigolds, peonies, poppies, anemones, hyacinths, carnations and primroses.[18] Any botanical intruders are identified as weeds and swiftly removed. A great house is thus a design set in an ordered environment, where everything is established according to a perception of divine harmony: nothing is left to chance. The father of English landscape design, William Kent, is only born in 1685, and several decades have yet to pass before he proposes a more 'natural' landscaping. In the meantime, the task of laying out a formal garden is dominated by the Brompton Park Nursery, run by George London and Henry Wise. It is they who design the gardens at Chatsworth and Hampton Court. And it is they who construct the maze at Hampton Court. Other places (such as Patshull Park) are beginning to experiment with topiary. As you can see, the gardens of a rich man's country house are a work of art in every sense.

Let us turn now to the interiors of these houses. Some of them include some of the most lavish decoration that any age has ever seen.

You might not be familiar with the name of Antonio Verrio but, as far as dramatic painting goes, he is without rival as 'the best hand in England', to quote Celia Fiennes.[19] She is not alone in thinking so. At Windsor, John Evelyn goes to see St George's Hall, lately built to the design of Hugh May, and it is not the architecture that blows him away so much as 'the stupendous painting of the hall'.[20] The scale and skill of his ceilings will astound you. So too will their sensuality – not even Charles II has seen so much naked female flesh. Verrio works in his native Italy and in France before coming to England in 1672, at the invitation of Lord Montagu, to paint the staircase and great chamber of Montagu House. That leads to his work at Arlington House, Ham House and, from 1674, Windsor Castle, where he spends twelve years painting twenty ceilings and three staircases, in addition to St George's Hall and the king's chapel. In James II's reign he paints the chapel at Whitehall and lays out the gardens there. After the Glorious Revolution of 1688 he leaves the court to decorate Burghley and Chatsworth. His finest work is undoubtedly the Heaven Room at Burghley, probably the most astounding chamber in any private house in Great Britain. Stand in the middle of the room, look around and be amazed: gods and goddesses cavort amidst garlanded classical columns; caped warriors charge down on you from the heavens on horses; naked nymphs float effortlessly above the gazes of their bewitched menfolk ... The whole effect is like standing inside a temple of love watching a divine orgy in mid-air, discovering that you too can fly – and casually being invited by all the gods and goddesses to join in.

The great castles and stately homes of Britain also display a large number of pictures with which we are familiar – true Old Masters. In this matter too, things are changing, but in ways that might not immediately be noticeable. Our eyes are used to seeing paintings from the Renaissance through to our own time, so we forget that decorating houses with pictures in frames is a comparatively recent thing. In Elizabethan times it was not unusual for an aristocrat to have a long gallery where he displayed portraits of royal and historical figures as discussion points, and family portraits for reasons of pride. However, even the very wealthy had very few pictures in any other rooms. This changes in the seventeenth century: Sir John Brownlow has 153 pictures of various sorts at Belton in 1686; Sir John Lenthall has 145 paintings at Besselsleigh Manor in 1682; and Lord Bedford has 103 portraits at Woburn Abbey in 1700. And although most gentry families don't have quite so many, most still have forty or more by the 1680s. Sir Thomas Spencer of Yarnton Manor, Oxfordshire, has fifty paintings: his family portraits hang in his two parlours and an adjacent withdrawing room; his long gallery is stuffed with portraits of kings, queens and renowned ministers in the traditional fashion; and the grand staircase is where he hangs fifteen paintings whose subjects include Covent Garden, a parrot, a Dutchman, a Dutchwoman, two magpies, an ass, a horse and a mare, James II, a woman milking a goat, and a landscape. The sudden demand for Old Masters of course pushes up the price: some collectors, especially the royal family, pay huge amounts for great works of art. Sir James Oxenden of Dene, Kent, has a collection worth more than £2,000, including a battle scene for which he pays £310 and a painting of 'Christ arguing with the lawyers', which costs him £250.[21] But this only inspires the aristocracy to acquire further paintings. The more expensive an artwork is, the more it is admired and desired.

When it comes to decorative art, one name calls out to be mentioned above all others: Grinling Gibbons. He is the most renowned and sought-after woodwork sculptor of the age – or of any age, for that matter. Born in Rotterdam to English parents, he trains in the Low Countries and comes to England in 1667. Three years later John Evelyn is out for a walk in the wintry countryside around Deptford when he notices a poor solitary thatched cottage. Being of a curious disposition, he looks in the window. Inside is young Grinling, now twenty-two years of age, carving a copy of Tintoretto's *Crucifixion*. No mere symbol, this work has more than one hundred figures gathered around the cross. Evelyn is astonished. Soon it becomes clear that Gibbons's real talent lies not in religious scenes, but in decorative and high-relief ornamental work: fruit and acanthus leaves are sculpted to stand out in an extraordinarily lifelike way. In 1672, while living in an inn in London, he carves a pot of flowers in wood 'so thin and fine that the coaches passing by made them shake surprisingly'.[22] Hugh May employs him along with Verrio to create decorative panels and overmantels for Cassiobury Park and Windsor Castle. Later Gibbons moves on to produce incredibly lifelike figures of gamebirds and fruit tumbling down the walls of dozens of great houses, including Belton and Chatsworth. He surpasses himself in the Carved Room at Petworth House in Sussex, sculpting musical instruments, vases, royal regalia and even sheets of Purcell's music, out of limewood.

As you may have gathered, much of this incredible richness in design and decoration is due to foreign influence. You've already come across foreign styles changing the direction of fashionable clothing; almost everything in the foregoing passages about the magnificence of great houses also depends on foreign innovations. The introduction of Palladian architecture may owe much to Inigo Jones but it needs to be remembered that its origins lie with Palladio in sixteenth-century Italy. Verrio too is an Italian, and Gibbons trained in the Low Countries. The sense of order in garden design is very much a French style. This openness to foreign influences is to be noted in other decorative arts too. The leading ironwork master of the day is a Frenchman, Jean Tijou. Arguably the most important architectural sculptor is Caius Gabriel Cibber, from Schleswig-Holstein. Charles II's and James II's long exile in France has left them with a taste for all things French, not just Catholicism; William III's origins similarly open the door to many Dutch influences. The new styles gradually seep through the layers of gentility so that all gentlemen adopt them. This international character of the design, layout and decoration of the English country house is unprecedented.

All this rebuilding is not cheap. Evelyn hears a rumour that the total cost of Berkeley House in London is £30,000.[23] Ramsbury Manor costs Sir William Jones and his executors £17,257.[24] Belton costs £10,000 to build and £5,000 to decorate. Charles II pays Verrio more than £7,000 for his ceilings and staircases at Windsor Castle.[25] A normal gentleman's seat will cost much less – in the region of £3,000–4,000 – but, even so, it is a huge outlay, underlining yet again the difference between the rich and the rest.

So, if you are lucky enough to stay at one of these places, what will it be like? Are you going to find yourself in a cold architectural museum? Or will it be warm and comfortable? What facilities might you expect? What furnishings, conveniences and delights?

If you are being put up in a top-notch state bedroom, you won't be shown to your 'room' so much as your apartment, consisting of a reception room, an antechamber, a bedroom, a garderobe and a closet – a style of living first modelled in France and brought to England after 1660.[26] On a smaller scale, your apartment might consist of just a bedroom, garderobe and closet (the closet being a small chamber to which you might retire to read in private, rest on a daybed or write letters). As your servant opens each of the doors for you, you will notice that he turns a handle of brass and does not lift an iron latch, as in the past. Inside, the walls are covered in brightly coloured wool-and-silk tapestries: these exclude draughts and are warmer than painted plaster. More often than not, the hangings in question are from Flanders or France but you may have a set from the English tapestry works at Mortlake. Below the tapestry there is normally a low section of exposed panelling, which acts as a sort of lavish skirting board. Floor coverings are fitted rush mats at the start of the period but increasingly these go out of fashion as people start to employ rugs and even carpets on the floor (previously carpets were only used to cover chests and tables). Heating in each room is provided by a marble fireplace, artificial lighting by gilt candlesticks. If you want a continuous night-light, stone mortars are available. Once your servant has departed, you will be able to gaze at yourself in a large mirror hung on the wall and sit on one of the silk-covered upholstered chairs with low seats and high backs. As for the bed, this will be a good feather bed with a very-high-canopied four-poster frame, silk damask curtains, silk quilts and a matching valance. A new fashion at the end of the century is for the bed not to be a four-poster one with curtains all round, but a half-tester, with a canopy only above the head end and the curtains swept back. Sheets are made of holland. The fabric of the bed hangings may be 'chintz': brightly coloured hand-painted and -dyed cotton, often from India rather than China, which comes to England at the end of the century. You might have window curtains made of a similar material or dyed muslin. There may be a cupboard or chest of drawers in the room for important personal possessions. Towards the end of the century, tables are placed in front of mirrors to serve as dressing tables. Washing facilities include a jug of water and a basin in which to rinse your face and hands. In the garderobe you will find your close stool: a large wooden box with a top that, when lifted, reveals a velvet-covered seat with a hole in the middle and a removable pan underneath. Toilet paper is available for wiping; alternatively you might be provided with disposable pieces of woollen cloth.

As you sit in your bedchamber you will inevitably start to think that this is not so different from the modern world. True, the artificial lighting here is still entirely done by candles, and the tapestries particularly date the room, but in terms of the general level of comfort – the softness to be found in the textiles, for example, and not just the bed – you will feel at home. Much the same applies to the rest of the house. There is a balance between comfort and splendour in a fashionable Restoration home. Walk into a dining room and look around: in all probability it will have a symmetrical, moulded plaster ceiling and finely carved panelling. The marble fireplace will be furnished with firedogs and a cast-iron fireback, or perhaps a fire basket. The classic seventeenth-century floor is made of large squares of black-and-white marble. Portraits in gilt frames hang on the walls. A longcase clock ticks away in the corner. The table, covered with a white linen cloth, may well be set for dinner, with candelabra, plate warmer, plates of silver, pewter or china, wine glasses, white linen napkins, silver salt cellar, spoons and even knives and forks. You might see musical instruments hung on the walls: Pepys plays his violin and his lute in his dining room, which is decorated with green cloth hangings and gilt leather.[27] As you wander through to the parlour, you may well come across a set of upholstered armchairs and a couch or sofa – the ultimate benchmark of comfort. You might also find cane chairs and japanned (black lacquer) furniture, chests of drawers and screens, escritoires or desks (these being slopes placed on a table) and ornamental ceramics from the Far East.

In a few houses you will find specialist rooms set aside for the use of the owners and their guests. These include chapels, libraries, 'cabinets of curiosities', muniment rooms, billiard rooms, music rooms and, just occasionally, bathrooms and smoking rooms.[28] You might even come across a house with a room equipped with a flushing loo, such as at Beddington in Surrey, although these are so rare I would not recommend hanging on until you find such a facility.[29] On the other hand, some of the older houses have not been altered for the last 200 years. Many still retain their old medieval halls. Arrive at Oakley Park, Shropshire, in the 1660s and you will find that Sir Matthew Herbert's hall is equipped with a long table with two benches along either side, a chair at the head, two side tables, one picture and a single candlestick, all of which are described as 'old and worn out'.[30] Similarly there are many gentleman's residences where you might walk through the old hall and see muskets, halberds, swords, pikes, shields, helmets and all other sorts of armour left over from the days when gentlemen would use their manor houses for keeping the armour of the local militia. In Elizabethan houses with long galleries, the spaces are increasingly used to house the picture collections that gentlemen are busy forming. Thus a great country house can be everything from a place to sleep and eat, to a museum, an armoury, a venue for musical performances and indoor games, a library and a place of religious worship. Some are even venues for stage plays.[31] In fact, choose the right stately home and you might well find that you never actually need to leave.

Town Houses

Some aristocratic town houses are practically stately homes in an urban setting. They are built on a similar scale and have their lavish reception rooms, stately apartments, formal gardens and even their own stables. However, for the most part, town houses differ significantly from the gentleman's country seat. They don't have the space to provide the same range of facilities. Nor do they need to do so.

The provision of fresh food and drink is never far away; carriage and horse hire are similarly close at hand; and gardens, theatres and recreational spaces are within a short ride or walking distance. At the same time, there is more noise and less space. Your experience of staying in a town house is thus likely to be very different from your visit to an up-to-date country house.

Let us say you are going to pay a call on the physician Henry Corbet (whose coach was mentioned in the previous chapter). He lives in an old-fashioned hall house in Lincoln. Once the hall would have been the most important room in the house; now it is hardly used, with just a table, bench and six leather-covered chairs there. These days the principal rooms are the parlours, which are panelled. In the best one Dr Corbet has two tables and fourteen chairs, a comfortable couch, curtains in the windows and a stove. Wander through into his second parlour and there you will find a round table with four chairs and a cupboard. The cellar is stacked with casks and glass bottles; the dairy is similarly full of small beer vessels; and there is a brew house too. The dining room has a leather 'carpet' draped across the table and gilt leather hangings around the room, with pictures suspended over the top. In Dr Corbet's best bedchamber there are chests of drawers, dressing boxes, chairs, pictures and other furnishings, which, with the bed and its hangings, add up to the princely sum of £62 – considerably more than the value of the contents of the most lavish room in the best inn you can find in town. Add the furnishings of five more chambers – one of which includes his library – and his kitchen, and the total value of his moveable possessions in this house adds up to more than £300.[32]

Even though Dr Corbet's house is old, you can see indications of Restoration luxury that you would not have found regularly before the Civil Wars. The stove, couch, pictures and window curtains are perhaps the most obvious. But a newly built house suitable for a 'man of ability' shows its modernity in its fixtures and fittings, as well as its furnishings. Sash windows start to appear in the 1670s: Robert Hooke installs them at Ragley Hall, Ramsbury Manor and Montagu House; Christopher Wren does likewise at Hampton Court; and William Winde copies them at Belton. By the end of the century London is leading the way in the production of sash windows for ordinary town houses.[33] As for the windows themselves, they are glazed with blocks of rectangular panes of glass up to 5 inches wide – very different from the small diamond quarrels in a lattice of leadwork that were previously used. Beams are not left exposed as they were in earlier houses; rather they are covered with plaster ceilings, which are often elaborately moulded. In some places painted hangings are used in place of tapestries, to add to the warmth and contain the draughts. Staircases are given banisters with turned balusters and, where space allows, are built around an open stairwell. The panelling in reception rooms is far more sophisticated and elegant than it used to be, and doorframes are carved with pediments above the internal doorways. The doors themselves are no longer simply vertical planks nailed together, but panelled by a joiner and provided with handles. The front door may even have a bright new door knocker on it.[34]

One of the most notable and welcome features of all this modernisation is the development of new methods of heating. There has been a shortage of firewood in England since the sixteenth century: now people are increasingly turning to coal. Iron fire baskets, 'grates' or 'cradles' have been introduced, so coal and charcoal can be burnt for domestic heat in town houses.[35] Enclosed iron stoves are employed to produce continual heat all day; some can be used for cooking too. Once Tudor stone chimneystacks rose through the house, allowing large logs to be burnt inefficiently, and draughts to descend when the fire was not raging; now town dwellers are rebuilding their chimneys in brick, with smaller apertures and a more efficient draw, so there is less risk of the sulphurous smoke from a coal fire or stove entering the room.[36] The fireplaces have surrounds of carved marble with fine architectural features, which stand proud of the wall, creating a useful display ledge. Although the royal family still burns only wood in its apartments, and the aristocracy tends only to buy coal for specific purposes, such as airing rooms when they are not in residence, it is most probable that coal will keep you warm on your visit to a town, especially London. By 1700, the capital's citizens are importing 335,000 chaldrons (444,000 tons) per year to warm their toes.[37] In Scotland, the faster-burning Scottish coal is used along with peat, which is still burnt even in such a prosperous town as Aberdeen.[38]

Another indicator of modernity in Dr Corbet's house is the number of pictures he owns. The 'middle sort' are filling up the walls of their houses with artworks, especially concentrating on the staircases, dining rooms and other areas that visitors might see. One wealthy Lincoln citizen, Elizabeth Manby, has fifteen pictures on the walls of her staircase, three in her dining room, and a framed landscape in one of her lavishly decorated spare bedchambers. At this level you don't have to pay Old Master prices: a portrait in oils in 1660 might cost you £3 10s, which includes a suitable frame.[39] In 1675 the Bristol painter John Roseworme has a stock of eighteen paintings at £1 each in his studio; he also has an oil of 'three Roman ladies giving their father suck' at £3; eight landscapes at 7s 6d each; two battle scenes at 5s each; various ordinary and higher quality 'faces' of the day at 6–8s each.[40] Alternatively you can go into a dealer's shop and select artwork off the wall. Even a relatively poor man might have a small art collection. In 1668 the organist of Bristol Cathedral, Thomas Adeane, owns six paintings, each worth just a shilling.[41] Prints of famous paintings and views are cheap too, obtainable from stationers' shops. The choir-master of Lincoln Cathedral, William Norris, has twenty-three prints of various sizes in his hall, worth £1 in total.[42] Views of Italy and France are popular subjects, as are prints of churches and antiquities. By 1700, images are essential to the rich decoration of a town house.

Not everyone is sufficiently prosperous to bedeck their house with artwork or even decent furniture. Richard Hazeltine, a labourer in Lincoln, has a small house with a hall and two chambers in which he has furniture worth £2; clothes, 10s; a brass pot, 5s; a broken pewter flagon, 5s; and hearth furniture, 3s. Outside he also has a cow worth £1; a sow, 10s; and a colony of bees, 16s.[43] He can't provide for guests to stay with him. Nor can Richard and Charity Griffin of Exeter: the best they can do is offer you their truckle bed. Their combined posses-sions include this and their own bed, cooking utensils, basic furniture such as a chest and a bench, bed linen and a few bits of brassware. All their moveable possessions come to £3 17s 6d – and they are by no means the poorest people in town.[44] There are many others whose possessions simply aren't worth valuing.

When it comes to sanitation, everyone – rich and poor – faces the same problem. It is well illustrated by Pepys's experience of the morning of 20 October 1660. As he goes down to his basement to see where a new window can be put in, he steps into 'a great heap of turds'. Thus he discovers that his next-door neighbour's cesspit is full and is overflowing into his house.[45] It doesn't matter how many chamber pots you have, or how plush the seats on your close stools: they all have to be emptied somewhere. In May 1663, Mrs Pepys and her maid between them manage to spill 'the pot of piss and turd' upstairs.[46] Fortunately everyone can laugh about it. You won't laugh, however, if you witness someone defecating in the dark corners of Whitehall Palace. According to Anthony Wood, courtiers have a habit of 'leaving their excrements in every corner, in chimneys, studies, coal houses, cellars'.[47] Rich and not-so-rich alike have to arrange the periodic emptying of their cesspits and the transportation of the contents to one of the laystalls on the outskirts of the city. This process has to be undertaken at night. In July 1663 workmen labour all night, until six o'clock in the morning, to clean Pepys's 'house of office' (as it is called). It is just as well that they take their time, for the sake of cleanliness, when everything has to be carried through the house.[48]

Rural Houses and Cottages

As we have seen, three-quarters of the population live in a rural area. Thus you are far more likely to find yourself staying with the country people 'who fare indifferently' and the poor 'who fare hard' than with the nobility or gentry. I recommend that you avoid staying with Defoe's lowest sort, the miserable, 'who really pinch and suffer want', as they can't afford to feed themselves, let alone another mouth.

Ordinary country folk have a different set of priorities when it comes to housing. Whereas the wealthy demonstrate their cultural sophistication by rebuilding their country houses, and urban professionals can spend all their spare cash on pictures, carpets and similar luxuries, the less fortunate are more concerned with protecting themselves against the next bad harvest. They do not rebuild their houses simply on account of fashion. In fact they don't rebuild them at all, if they can help it. They do not build new houses, either, except where the old one proves unsafe or a farmer has managed to consolidate his land through enclosure and wants a new farmhouse situated in the middle of his farm. When this happens, his old house in the village is immediately freed up, to be used as cottages, thereby adding further to the housing stock.

This is not to say that rural housing doesn't change. Since the mid-sixteenth century people have been modernising their homes, adding fireplaces and chimneys, porches, glass windows, staircases and extensions. Most of those improvements are complete by the early seventeenth century; you won't come across a hearth still set in the middle of the hall floor, with smoke billowing around the room, except in Scotland and the remotest parts of England and Wales.[49] Similarly, few cottages south of the Scottish border are completely unglazed. But what you will find in both countries are old houses that still have halls open to the rafters, or with little private space, or with a newly built parlour wing tacked on to an old hall. This is the most common reason for late-seventeenth-century construction work: farmers and tradesmen who have prospered require more living accommodation for their families and servants, who are no longer content to sleep beside the hall fire every night.

Look at Nether Fletchamstead Hall, near Coventry, the house of a yeoman, William Meigh, from the 1660s. With its mullion windows on both floors and high chimneys, it is obviously a high-status building from earlier in the seventeenth century – but one that has been modernised by a farmer with cash to spare. Indeed, at the time of his death in 1685 William's goods and chattels are worth over £520.[50] However, his hall is sparsely furnished at the time of his demise: just the traditional long table and bench, another small table and the furniture for the fireplace – shovel, tongs, andirons and a newly bought grate for burning coal. The hall is no longer the grand centre of the house that it once was; in fact, an extra bedchamber has been built above it. The focus has shifted to the next room, the parlour, where William has a drawing table, a round table, a cupboard, a chest, an armchair, six chairs upholstered with Russia leather and another coal-burning grate with tongs and fire shovel. In a second hall there is nothing but an old iron turret clock and a fire grate. The rest of the rooms on the ground floor include the buttery, the kitchen, a mill house (where there is a malt mill installed) and a dairy or cheese chamber. All of these are utilitarian. Walking through the bedchambers on the first floor, you will see that they are all quite comfortable as far as sleeping goes: the best ones have feather beds with curtains, valance, counterpane, rugs and blankets; and there are besides many chairs and stools. What you will not see are pictures, carpets, screens, japanned furniture, mirrors and cushions. There isn't a single book in the house, or a chamber pot. Apart from the Russia-leather chairs, the nearest thing to a modern luxury item in the whole house is a practical tool: a smoothing iron, in the bedchamber over the buttery. William Meigh is a man with a barn full of rye, wheat, oats, barley, vetches and peas; 40 acres of corn in the fields; ninety-two sheep; nine horses; six pigs;

fifty-eight cows, bulls, heifers and calves; and several hundredweight of cheese – you'd have thought he'd have spent a little bit on luxuries, but no. Nor is he the exception. The improvements of the late seventeenth century lie in the quality of everyday items, such as the furniture. Separate chairs and stools have replaced benches; some of the chairs are upholstered. Cupboards have come to replace shelves. Much of the furniture is now made by a specialist joiner. Otherwise, the wealth of a prosperous farmer is largely in his fields and barns; there are very few non-necessities.

It will not surprise you to hear that the houses of poorer people also have few luxuries. When Thomas Jeffery of Dunsford, Devon, dies in 1691, the lease of his cottage is worth £10 – more than half the value of everything he owns. In the bedchambers there are just three old beds besides two coffers – nothing of decoration at all. Similarly there is nothing in the hall except a storage cupboard, a table and form, a settle and his cooking pots. Apart from the glass windows, nothing much has changed domestically from the time of his great-grandfather. Those at the bottom of the social ladder have every reason to feel that the changes of the age have passed them by.[51]

You will of course be making a mental note not to stay with people like Thomas Jeffery. They have little to offer you in terms of comfort. But it cannot be repeated often enough that the majority of people (62 per cent) fall into this category: labourers, cottagers and paupers – the poor 'who fare hard'. They don't have a choice between burning coal or wood; they cannot afford either. Peat is the standard fuel of the poor right across Great Britain – from Cornwall to Scotland – but it is not available everywhere. Celia Fiennes notes that, around Penzance, there is no fuel except 'gorse, furze and fern'; and that people living near Swanage in Dorset 'take up stones by the shores that are so oily as the poor burn it for fire, and it's so light a fire it serves for candle too, but it has a strong offensive smell'. Near Peterborough she sees 'upon the walls of the ordinary people's houses the cow dung plastered up to dry in cakes which they use [for] firing – it's a very offensive fuel but the country people use little else in these parts'.[52] In Wiltshire, Thomas Baskerville notes the poor of Highworth doing the same thing: daubing the walls of their cottages in cow dung to dry it over summer, for use in winter.[53] In Scotland, seaweed is dried and used, along with cow and horse dung.[54] And don't forget that these fuels are not only used for heating, but for cooking and lighting too. Candles are unaffordable if you have barely enough food to eat. Therefore, if you think that visiting a city is a multi-sensory experience, with all the smells of the ordure and the smog, then rest assured that visiting the homes of the rural poor can be just as much an assault on the senses. One of the few things you don't have to worry about, though, is the next-door neighbour's cesspit overflowing. The advantage of living in the country is that there is plenty of space for you to dig a hole.

9

What to Eat, Drink and Smoke

If you think that by visiting Restoration Britain you are returning to a healthier way of life, with a diet that is natural and more wholesome, you are in for a shock. Putting aside for the moment the heavy smoking and drinking, you will be surprised by what people consider a healthy diet. In the modern world, we balance the tastiness of a few types of meat with our nutritional needs. In the Restoration, people simply see lots of animals and think God put them all on Earth for their benefit. It is almost as if Noah's Ark were a menu. This is Edward Chamberlayne's list of abundant English foods:

> What plenty everywhere of sheep, oxen, swine, fallow deer, conies and hares ... red deer, goats [and] roe [deer]. What abundance of hens, ducks, geese, turkeys, pigeons and larks; of partridge, pheasants, plovers, teals, thrushes, merles, fieldfares, ouzels or blackbirds; wild ducks, wild geese, swans, peacocks, buntings, snipe, quails, woodcocks and lapwings. [England] wants not sandlings, knot, curlew, bayning, dotterel, roe, char, chough, maychit, stint, sea plover, pewits, redshanks, rails, wheatears, herons, cranes, bitterns, bustards, puffins, godwits, heath-cocks, moor-pouts or grouse thrushes and throstles. What plenty of salmon, trout, lamperns, gudgeons, carp, tench, lampreys, pikes, perches, eels, breams, rock, dace, crayfish, flounders, plaice, shads, mullets. What great abundance of herrings, whitings, mackerel, soles, smelts, pilchards, sprats, oysters, lobsters, crabs, shrimps, thornback ... prawns, ruffs, mussels, cockles, conger, turbots, cod, skate, [mades?], scallops, etcetera. What great plenty of apples, pears, plums, and cherries. How doth England abound with wheat, barley, rye, pulses, beans and oats; with excellent butter and cheese; with most sorts of edible roots and herbs.[1]

This does not point to a balanced diet, in any sense of the word. For a start, it is very heavy on the meat side. Chamberlayne lists several sorts of fruit but no vegetables beyond 'edible roots and herbs'. Indeed, vegetarians will have a tough time because it is widely assumed that everyone wants to eat flesh. Another imbalance is the unsustainability of the animals in question: people consume so many wild birds that some of them soon find themselves on the well-plucked path to extinction. A third imbalance is the level of fat on their plates. Monsieur Misson observes that when the English eat beef in a dish, 'they will besiege it with five or six heaps of cabbage, carrots, turnips or some other herbs or roots, well-peppered and salted and swimming in butter'.[2] People do not hesitate to use cream and eggs in abundance too. One recipe for a tansy (a flavoured egg pudding) reads:

> take fifteen egg yolks and six whites, beat them very well, then put in some sugar and a little sack [dry Spanish wine], and about a pint of cream, then put in tansy, spinach and primrose leaves, or the like, chopped as small as possible, and beat them all well together, then put it in a skillet and set it over the fire, stirring it continually till it be pretty stiff, then put it into a pan and fry it with sweet butter, and make sauce for it with rosewater, butter and sugar.[3]

Such a diet of plentiful meat and lashings of butter and cream will certainly make you put on weight, but you need to be wealthy to afford it. If you are poor, you can rule out almost everything on Chamberlayne's list. A chicken will set you back at least 1s, which is one-eighth of the weekly wages of a master carpenter. If the value of that chicken were to rise in line with the wages of carpenters, then at the time of writing (2016) you'd have to pay £66.49 for a similar one.[4] And that is a minimum. As for fruit, a single pear costs 1d, or $^1/_{96}$ of a skilled craftsman's weekly wages: the equivalent of approximately £5.54 in modern money.

This shows you just how precious food is in Restoration England. But don't forget that these prices are averages: there is far greater fluctuation from year to year than in the modern world. The principal reason is the Little Ice Age – the global cooling of the seventeenth century. Old people in England still remember the famine of 1623 in Cumberland and Westmorland. You don't have to be that old to recall the food shortages of the 1640s and the sieges of the Civil Wars, when many people were reduced to eating cats, dogs, rats and mice.[5] Famine remains a real fear in all ranks of society, for it sends prices skywards and triggers outbreaks of crime and disorder, which in turn affect the urban and wealthy. This is one of the reasons why gentlemen like Pepys and Evelyn are particularly attentive to the weather. The month of June 1661 is so wet that Londoners fear the crops will be destroyed and famine will ensue.[6] Across England that year prices do hit near-record heights. If you don't want to feel hungry, do not visit England in 1660, 1661, 1673, 1674, 1696 or 1697, when the cost of wheat goes well over 125 per cent of the long-term average. Low prices (25 per cent below the average) are recorded in 1685, 1687, 1688, 1689, 1690 and 1694.[7]

Without doubt, the worst place and time in which to find yourself in Restoration Britain is Scotland between 1693 and 1700, otherwise known as the 'ill years'. The population of the northern kingdom declines by about 10 per cent overall. In the worst-affected area, the Highlands, one-fifth of the population dies.[8] How can this happen? Why does Scotland fare so much worse than England? These are pertinent questions to ask, when the famine of 1696–7 is a Europe-wide phenomenon. There are several reasons. Perhaps the most important is the predominance of subsistence farming in Scotland: people consume what they grow themselves and store or barter any excess. When there are harvest failures, anyone retaining a surplus hoards it; others are forced to eat their seed corn, meaning they have nothing to plant the following year. Successive harvest failures amplify the dangers. Three consecutive years of poor harvests are enough to bring even a well-developed market economy to its knees – as shown by the famine of 1594–7 in England – but the Highlands are not a market economy, food does not change hands in times of dearth, and Scotland suffers *seven* bad harvests in the 1690s. Obviously the poorest people are left dependent on the relief administered by their parishes; but where there is no relief system in operation, or where the people live too remotely, or where there is no local market at which to buy corn, relief is ineffective. Poorly fed women find it difficult to conceive. New mothers cannot produce milk and their babies die. Men emigrate in search of work – and thereby deprive the land of half its workforce. The reasons why England and Wales get off relatively lightly are that the weather there is better, there are fewer poor harvests and, when they fail, the losses are not as severe as they are in Scotland. Most important of all, the 680 market towns in England and Wales distribute any surpluses so that the poor-relief system can do its work more efficiently.

As you travel around the island you'll discover further constraints on what you might eat. Seasonality is obviously a factor, and this can include seafood as well as lamb and fresh fruit. People already repeat the mantra that they should only eat oysters when there is an 'r' in the month.[9] Prices vary considerably as the year goes by: fresh eggs in winter are scarcer and more expensive than in summer (as chickens respond to the amount of light they enjoy). Cooking processes can also create problems, even in a well-appointed town house. John Evelyn dines one evening at the Portuguese ambassador's residence and is served fowls 'roasted to coal'.[10] And if this can happen when roasting on a spit – a form of cooking open to inspection – then just imagine how much harder it is to bake things. If you don't know your oven, how long do you leave things in there? There is no window, no temperature control, and if you open the door you risk losing all the heat. Thus in November 1660 Elizabeth Pepys manages to burn all her tarts and cakes when she and Samuel move into their new house, with its oven built into the side of the kitchen fireplace.[11] Two months later she and her husband go to dinner with Mr and Mrs Pierce, where they are presented with 'a calf's head carbonadoed [grilled], but it was [so] raw we could not eat it'. Pepys adds that Mrs Pierce 'is such a slut that I do not love her victuals', referring of course to her lack of tidiness in the kitchen rather than her morality.[12]

In case you are wondering, few people actually die of food poisoning, despite the health risks of eating poorly cooked meat. The statistician John Graunt studies the Bills of Mortality for the London area and concludes that your risk of a fatal case of poisoning is just 14 in 229,250, or 1:16,375.[13] If it's any reassurance, you are more likely to cut yourself and bleed to death than be poisoned.

Local and Regional Foods

The 'ill years' in Scotland are a reminder that you cannot generalise about food across the whole of Great Britain. Location determines what you can eat more than anything else. If you do travel north of the border, it would help if you are partial to oats, which are served up at almost every meal in every Scottish household. In fact, they make up three-quarters of the entire calorific intake of every man, woman and child there.[14] They might be baked into clapp bread or dished up in pottage (or porridge), or served as oatcakes. Even if you are a hardened Scottish patriot, it is likely that the diet of oats will prove a little monotonous.

A local abundance can work in two ways: it can lead to a very boring and imbalanced diet, if there is no alternative, or it can become a regional speciality. Pilchards might be plentiful in Cornwall – a little too plentiful for some – but the plenitude underpins the local economy and, if you do like pilchards, then that is the place to seek out the best. You can say the same for mullet in Sussex and herring on the East Anglian coast. As Celia Fiennes makes her way around the country she frequently finds it difficult to obtain good food, but she praises the crab and lobster of Brownsea Island and the Isle of Purbeck, and the salmon of the River Severn, and she expounds at length on the char from Lake Windermere. In Somerset she enjoys the apples and pears and extols the virtues of the local cider, while in Devon she has clotted cream on an apple tart.[15]

One writer who definitely appreciates regional food is Thomas Baskerville. In Gloucestershire he notes a huge amount of sage cheese being sold at a fair. In Gloucester itself he comes across 'yelver cakes' made of eels. He notices extensive liquorice supplies in Pontefract. He sees herring caught, cured and smoked by the boatload at Yarmouth.[16] These local specialities cause him to consider how many foods are named after their place of production. He can think of Cheddar cheese, Warfleet oysters, Herefordshire cider, Banbury cakes, Tewkesbury mustard, Scotch collops (see below), Studley carrots (from Studley in Wiltshire), Thames sprats, Besselsleigh turnips, Bartholomew Fair roast pig, Southwark Fair roast pork, and saffron from Saffron Walden. He notes down a few foods that have become the subjects of rhymes: 'Hampshire honey is current goods for every man's money'; 'Dorset ewes for the early lambs / and Warwickshire breeds most excellent rams'; 'Canary sack and Bristol sherry / will make a sad man's heart be merry'. He also mentions some foreign foods and drinks that have already gained an international reputation: Westphalia hams, Nantes brandy, Caribbean rum, Turkish coffee, Persian sherbet, East Indian rice, West Indian maize, Brazil sugar, Bermuda oranges, French claret, Russian sturgeon and Jamaican spice.[17] Already there is a sense in which the whole world is a larder.

Fasting

In the Middle Ages good Catholics were not allowed to eat meat on Fridays, Saturdays and Wednesdays or on any day in Lent and Advent. In England this tradition outlasted the Reformation and only started to decline in the 1590s. Now few people except Catholics forgo meat on any day of the week. This goes for eating meat in public as well as in private: you can enjoy a shoulder of mutton in a London tavern on a Friday and no one will bat an eyelid.

The idea of fasting has not quite gone away, however. There is a general feeling that Lent is still a time when you should prioritise spiritual matters and not eat meat or eggs. In 1661 the king emphasises this by ordering that everyone should keep the Lenten fast. Men like Lord Bedford dutifully observe this royal request and eschew all flesh. Others ignore it. Pepys doesn't think it realistic because the alternative is to eat fish, which the poor generally cannot afford. But Pepys himself illustrates a more significant problem: lack of self-control. On 27 February 1661 he conscientiously resolves to observe the forty days' fast. He manages just one day before giving in and eating meat. On 10 March he dines on 'a poor Lenten dinner of coleworts and bacon'. Which bit of bacon does he think doesn't count as meat? A week after the bacon, he and his wife tuck into a joint of beef, and on 26 March he is delighted to declare at dinner to Mrs Turner and everyone else at the table that *they* might have eaten no meat that Lent, but that he has 'had a good deal of good flesh'. In 1663 he forgoes meat on just one day in the whole of Lent.[18] Having said these things, even much later in the century many people continue to believe in the virtues of fasting. In 1682 Hannah Woolley lists a selection of dishes that you might consume during Lent and on other fasting days, including a very novel thing for the English table: baked potatoes.[19]

There are other reasons why people fast. Charles II orders that 30 January be kept as a fast day in memory of his father, as that was the day of his execution. Pepys finds a one-day fast much easier to observe than the full forty days of Lent. Then there's the belief that a religious fast can alleviate poor weather. It is ordered that Wednesday, 12 June 1661 be kept as a fast day due to the recent rain, to avert the sickness and diseases that might be expected to follow. The following year, 15 January is similarly decreed to be a fast day, so that people might pray for more seasonable weather, to avert the danger of plague.[20] Bearing in mind the extraordinarily high prices of corn in 1660 and 1661, and the approaching onslaught of the plague of 1665, we can perhaps understand this precaution. At the height of the plague, several days are set aside as 'solemn fast days'. As the century nears its conclusion, after the religious crises of the 1680s, the links between fasting and fruition become most unfashionable, in the eyes of good Anglicans. Natural philosophy also helps break the superstitions surrounding fasting, so fewer people entertain the idea of forgoing food as a sacrifice during the reign of William III.

Mealtimes and Manners

The three-meal ritual of breakfast, lunch and supper has not always been with us. Few people in Britain ate breakfast before the mid-sixteenth century. Travellers and harvest workers did, and so did those with long working days ahead of them. But most people ate two meals a day: a late-morning dinner (the main meal of the day) and a late-afternoon supper. However, as more and more individuals work for others rather than themselves, and are accordingly obliged to observe what we might call 'office hours', they cannot get away with a late-morning mealtime as well as an afternoon one. In most places it has become usual to have one break for lunch, rather than a late-morning dinner, and to leave supper until after the day's work is done. This has now become normal even among country people. Thus you will find people eating their main meal at noon and their supper at various times in the evening. But breakfast retains its ambivalent character: is it a meal or not?

The most common foodstuff for breakfast is beer. The old tradition of travellers beginning the day with a pint or two before they set out is still observed by some gentlemen – Thomas Baskerville, for example. Townsmen too might begin the day with a 'morning draught' of beer. Bread and butter is seen as a good countryman's breakfast, and Baskerville himself doesn't always insist on a pint but will opt for bread, cheese and cold tongue if they are available.[21] The range of foods that Pepys has for breakfast is quite extraordinary. Sometimes he has a morning draught of cakes and ale; on other occasions he heads to a tavern and has 'turkey pie and goose' or 'good wine, anchovies and pickled oysters'. One of his breakfasts consists of 'mince pie, brawn and wine'.[22] Then again, frequently he goes without breakfast altogether.

Dinner – the main meal of the day – varies with the degree of formality attached to it. A quick lunchtime meal at a tavern may amount to nothing more than a single course consisting of one dish. At the other extreme, a properly laid-out meal in a nobleman's dining room will consist of three courses: two meat courses and a sweet course, each one consisting of up to a dozen different dishes. Note that, at such a dinner, you are not expected to consume *everything* in front of you: you should pick what you want from each dish, as you would from a modern buffet. At least, that is what you are supposed to do. Some people do try to consume everything in sight. Monsieur Misson remarks that 'the English eat a great deal at dinner; they rest a while, and [go] to it again until they have quite stuffed their paunch. Their supper is moderate: gluttons at noon and abstinence at night.'[23] Supper is a single course in a nobleman's house but, despite Misson's comment about abstinence, this too might include several dishes. On top of that, you might be offered a late-evening meal of cold meat or a 'sack posset'. Sack is a dry wine, typically from Spain; in a 'sack posset' it is mixed with cinnamon, nutmeg, sugar, egg yolks and cream, and served warm. The purpose is either to fortify you for your journey home or to knock you out so that you don't notice the chill of your bedchamber.[24]

When it comes to the mechanics of eating, you need to be prepared for all eventualities. In the 1660s, when you sit down at a dinner table, you will probably not see a knife or a fork in front of you. You will be expected to provide your own eating knife, which you will wipe on your napkin at the end of the meal and take home with you. As for forks, these are an Italian innovation and rarely encountered in Britain, except when eating fruit in syrup in a gentleman's house. If places are formally laid at a table, the arrangement is a knife and napkin, not a knife and fork. This includes some quite prestigious events: if you dine with the lord mayor of London at the Guildhall, you will see napkins and knives are laid out, but not forks.[25] The reason napkins are essential is that you need to hold a piece of meat in order to cut it, and you will lift it to your mouth using your fingers, thus covering yourself in juices and sauce at both stages of the operation. Lorenzo Magalotti is somewhat perturbed to find that English people don't generally use forks in 1669; one of the few times he encounters them is at a dinner in the king's presence.[26] By the 1690s, however, you can sit down in a country-house dining room with a knife, fork and spoon ready at your place setting.[27] The transition to modern eating practices is practically complete – at least amongst the well-to-do.

To understand why this transition comes about, it is necessary to look at the implements more closely. At the start of the period, the eating knife that you carry around with you will have a pointed end as well as a sharp blade. This end is for spearing the meat and lifting it from the dish on to your plate. When forks are introduced, people use them to do the spearing, so the knives no longer need to have sharp points. Forks also serve the purpose of steadying the meat on your plate while you cut it, so initially they have just two tines. But soon it becomes apparent that, if you can use a fork to put meat on your plate, you may as well use it to lift the food to your mouth, keeping your fingers clean. Very soon people start using forks with three or four tines, to help with that process. Four-tined forks are also more popular as they hurt less if you accidentally jab your lip with one. People start to carry around their own knife and fork in a case, in the way they used to carry their own knife on a belt, but soon genteel hosts provide sets of cutlery for their guests, and the practice falls out of fashion.

The transition from fingers to forks is also reflected in the plates in use in gentlemen's houses. You have to be very rich to afford to eat off silver: in 1670 it costs about 5s 8d an ounce, so a single 18oz silver plate is likely to cost £5 or more, and a full dinner service will set you back more than £300. Pewter is employed much more frequently because, being predominantly made of tin, it is much cheaper (about 1d per ounce) and can be polished to look like silver.[28] But cutting your food with a knife will score a pewter plate and so, as people increasingly use a fork to steady their meat and cut more decisively, the surface gets damaged. China thus starts to take the place of pewter, as it resists knife cuts. Plates made by Staffordshire potters soon become the fashionable thing to have, many of which are slip-ware decorated with royal portraits or emblems of Restoration loyalty.

Ordinary people do not experience these same changes. You need to have a substantial income to care about *how* you eat, rather than what you eat. Most craftsmen and country workers still do not use forks in 1700. They might obtain pewter plates, in order to show off to their neighbours, but not china. Most of them eat off wooden platters: these tend to be round and with a depression in the middle, and not square like old-fashioned trenchers. Similarly the common people drink their ale and beer out of earthenware pots rather than glasses, which are habitually used for wine. The eating and drinking habits of the rich and poor have probably never varied as much as they do in the 1690s.

Food in a Wealthy Household

The real cost of food – roughly fourteen times greater than in the modern world – indicates that the meals enjoyed by the wealthy are bound to be different from those consumed by the poor. But the comparison by which we established this involved chickens and pears: two ordinary types of food. When it comes to delicacies, there are some things that even well-off townsmen never get to taste. A single carp, for example, can cost as much as 20s – two and a half times a skilled workman's weekly wages.[29] Just consider how much you earn in a week: would you spend more than twice that much money on a single fish?

For this reason, even noblemen economise on food. Lords with extensive lands usually maintain a home farm, which provides meat, poultry, vegetables, herbs, dairy, corn and fruit for their daily use. They also draw their game from their own parks: deer fend for themselves through the winter months and, unlike cattle, do not require the investment of large amounts of fodder and shelter. Landowners similarly draw on their own ponds and rivers to provide them with fish. Yet despite such economies, feeding a household of dozens of people is still expensive. The earl of Bedford does not operate a home farm at Woburn – only the deer park, gardens and ponds contribute to his table – so his kitchen clerk has to obtain a considerable proportion of his lordship's food from grocers, private suppliers and the marketplace.

One week's grocery bill at Woburn Abbey

Meat

27 stone 2lbs of beef at 1s 8d per stone	£2 5s 5d
A breast of veal	1s 10d
A side, a neck and a breast of mutton	10s 4d
12 stone of pork	18s 6d
16¾lbs bacon	16s 9d
Tripe	1s 8d
Sheep's feet	6d
A neat's (cow's) tongue	10d
subtotal	£4 15s 10d

Poultry

5 domestic pigeons	4s 7d
18 wild pigeons: 6 at 6d, 6 at 5d and 6 at 4d	7s 6d
3 pullets	4s 8d
7 chickens: 5 at 1s 2d; 2 at 1s	7s 10d
4 hens	4s 6d
2 capons	4s 2d
A cock for broth	1s 2d
subtotal	£1 14s 5d

Dairy

24lbs of butter: 1lb at 9d, 5lbs at 8d and 18lbs at 6d	13s 1d
1lb of butter for oatcakes	5d
Milk	2s 7d
Eggs	3s 1d
Newly laid eggs	7d
subtotal	19s 9d

Fish

3 lobsters	2s
4 salt fish and a side	4s 10d
6 flounders	1s 8d
subtotal	8s 6d

Fruit and vegetables

6 oranges and 3 lemons	6d
Asparagus	4s
Onions	2s
Herbs	1s 8d
subtotal	6s 4d

Bread and flour

3 bushels of coarse flour	8s
Bread for the pantry	2s 4d
Bread for the kitchen	1s
subtotal	11s 4d
Total	£8 16s 2d

The above sums do not reflect the true level of consumption at the Abbey. The week in question is in late March, which is Lent, a lean time of year even if you are not fasting. There are only a few references to the fish caught and the fruit consumed. In the 1690s, the earl regularly pays 10–15s each for large pike, one of his favourite foods. Looking ahead to his kitchen clerk's bill for one week in late July, and bearing in mind that apples, pears, quinces and many other fruit are supplied by his own orchards, you can see that even things that grow on trees are pricey.

One week's fruit bill at Woburn Abbey	
5 baskets of red raspberries	5s 10d
3 baskets of strawberries	4s 6d
8½ dozen pears	8s 6d
10 dozen white plums	10s
6 dozen red plums	6s
4 dozen Morocco plums	8s
10 dozen Newington peaches	£1
4 dozen great apricots	£1 4s
4lbs carnation cherries	8s
Lemons and oranges	5s 6d
6lbs cherries	1s 9d
Pears	1s 3d
Currants	10d
Codlins and gooseberries	1s 10d
Plums	2s 3d
	Total £5 8s 3d

These bills don't include the spices used, which are bought in bulk from grocers in town and kept in store until consumed. These too can be expensive: 8s for 1lb of cloves; 1s 9d for 1lb of ginger; and 4d for 1lb of rice. Sugar costs between 6d and 8¼d per pound for ordinary, 1s 4d per pound for smooth and anything from 1s 3d to 2s per pound for double-refined.[30] Overall, if you think in terms of a gentleman's table costing him £10–15 per week, or between thirty and forty-five times the weekly wages of a skilled worker, you will begin to understand the scale of expense. In 1663 and 1664 the earl's kitchen clerk's total expenditure amounts to £735 and £758.[31]

What does the food look like when it arrives on the dinner table? Much depends on the ways in which it is stored. Keeping fish and meat fresh, in the absence of refrigerators, is quite a struggle and the various methods devised by kitchen staff over the centuries tend to curtail its suitability for certain forms of cooking. One popular method is to pickle it. Valuable fish such as salmon, sturgeon and pike are regularly pickled, as are anchovies. Newcastle salmon, which is boiled in strong beer and salt before being pickled, can keep for a whole year.[32] Cooked beef can also be pickled in vinegar or boiled in brine and hung to dry by the fire. The head and foreparts of a pig are made into brawn, which, being soused in its own liquid, lasts a long time. Hares are often minced, beaten with marrow or suet and encased in pastry, sealed with butter, sometimes with the ears protruding from the pastry. Lobsters are boiled and buried in brine-soaked bags in sea-sand, so they last up to three months. Eels and lampreys are regularly 'potted' – baked in butter, drained and then sealed under more butter (to a depth of three fingers) – in which condition they can last many months. Salmon, smelts, mackerel, lobsters and shrimps are also preserved in this way. Potted fish soon becomes fashionable, displacing cold fish pies from the tables of the wealthy. Meat too is potted, especially beef, ham, hare and tongue, being minced and beaten with butter, then pressed to remove the air, and covered with more butter.[33]

Fresh meat is normally roasted on a spit in front of the fire, which is turned by hand, by a small dog trained to walk within a wheel, or by gravity (which requires a driving weight to be wound up, turning the spit as it slowly descends). Frequently the meat is stuffed before it is roasted. Fresh fish too might be roasted: oysters are cooked on wooden spikes attached to the spit; pieces of sturgeon are spitted, pike roasted whole and eels skewered on a spit in an S shape. Meat and smaller fish might also be 'broiled' (grilled) on a gridiron; steaks cooked in this way are called 'carbonadoes'. Most meats can be fried or baked in pastry – although the skill required to do either of these things should not be underestimated. The cautious cook might therefore prefer to follow recipes that call for the meat to be stewed or boiled in broth.

Just as the British in this period become international in their fashion sense, so they do in their cuisine. Many forms of French cooking are adopted, such as casseroles, fricassees (meat chopped small and fried in butter with white wine, salt and ginger) and hashes (sliced meat stewed in a strong broth of herbs, spices and wine, served on sops of bread or toast).[34] Spanish recipes also influence the diet of the wealthy in the form of 'olios': cooked pieces of meat, fowl, poultry and sweet-breads piled high on a bowl, with the juices in which they have been cooked poured over them. Italian pasta appears regularly on the English dinner table, in the form of macaroni and vermicelli. Even Scotland has a dish to offer, in Scotch collops: pieces of lamb or beef cut into medallions and fried with claret, vinegar, onions, nutmeg, lemon peel, anchovies, horseradish and oysters.[35] Not all these recipes appeal to everyone: John Evelyn declares that Portuguese olios are 'not at all fit for an English stomach, which is for solid meat'.[36] And it is true to say that the real joy for an Englishman is to eat whole joints of meat, or roasted birds and fish. A whole fish is either served on sops of bread or toast with butter melted over it or in a sauce made from berries: gooseberry sauce for mackerel, barberry sauce for boiled pike. White fish is often served in a parsley sauce (melted butter strewn with chopped parsley and thickened with flour). You will also come across fish baked in breadcrumbs and served with the traditional melted butter on top.[37]

So, sitting down with Samuel Pepys one lunchtime in January 1663, at his new dining table (which cost the princely sum of £2 10s) in his handsome dining room, you might not yet have a place setting with a fork, but you may expect a first course of three dishes – 'oysters, a hash of rabbit and lamb and a chine of beef' – and then a second course of 'a great dish of roasted fowl, which cost 30s, and a tart', followed by a third course of fruit and cheese. All this fills him, his wife and his six guests, but not so much that they cannot manage a supper a few hours later. Both meals add up to the princely sum of £5.[38] Pepys's finest feasts are those he provides to friends on 4 April each year – the anniversary of his operation for the bladder stone. In 1663 he has eight guests to celebrate with him and his wife, and together they consume 'a fricassee of rabbits and chicken, a leg of boiled mutton, three carp, a side of lamb, a dish of roasted pigeons, four lobsters, three tarts, a lamprey pie, a dish of anchovies and good wine of several sorts'.[39] Note that, in 1663, 4 April falls in Lent. This is not a great year for abstinence in the Pepys household.

It has to be said that the wealthy do not always eat in a lavish fashion. Indeed, some of their dishes are most unappetising. Calf's head is unlikely to appeal to the majority of modern British diners. Snail porridge is to be found on Restoration dining tables, having been imported from France along with stewed, fried and hashed snails and snail pie. Pepys invites his wife's tailor – a Mr Unthank – to dine with them one evening and their repast consists of 'nothing but a dish of sheep's trotters'.[40] Pepys is similarly known to share 'a good udder' with a friend and to serve up his favourite offal to his guests, such as 'a most excellent dish of tripe of my own directing, covered with mustard'.[41] With such things on the menu at his house, you might think twice before accepting an invitation to dinner.

Inns, Cookshops and Taverns

When the coach in which Ned Ward is travelling stops late one evening at an inn called the English Champion, in Ware, Hertfordshire, he and his companions ask the landlord what they might have for dinner. 'Eels,' the man replies. It soon transpires that eel is the only thing available. On the positive side, Ned and his companions all like eels. Moreover, they can have them boiled, fried, baked, stewed, roasted, toasted, coddled, parboiled, soused or doused, as they desire. Everything is fine – until they receive the bill: 2s 6d per head is a lot to pay for eels, however they are cooked.[42]

When you turn up at an inn you won't be able to peruse a menu. Often you will have no choice as to what to eat. However, it is not unheard of for clients to buy something in the market and take it to an inn and ask for it to be cooked for them. Willem Schellinks fancies goose one day, so buys a fat bird for 16d and has the cook at his inn roast it for him.[43] This bring-your-own-ingredients service can also apply to non-residents. Pepys is rather fond of lobster, so he takes one to a local alehouse for lunch, where it is cooked for him.[44] So, while in some respects the fare in an inn is extremely restricted, in others it is remarkably flexible. In certain roadside establishments the landlord will bring wine, beer or food out to serve to people in a hurry as they wait in their coaches. In some town taverns, private rooms are available for men to drop by and conduct business; they are free to send the potboy out for food from a cookshop.

The quality of the meal you will enjoy varies considerably, according to where you choose to dine. The cheapest fare is obtained from hawkers selling hot pies in the street and marketplace, if you don't mind the gristle inside the pastry and the flies on the outside. A step up from these are the cookshops in large towns and cities. Normally they will have several joints of meat roasting over a spit: the best have four spits working at once, cooking several pieces of meat simultaneously: beef, mutton, veal, pork or lamb. You can have whatever meat you want, and you can direct it to be sliced with fat on, or lean, well done or rare. You'll be given a bread roll with your meat and you can add salt and mustard at the counter. Some cookshops also serve pies and will cook portions of poultry for you.[45] Don't expect the highest standards of hygiene, however. At a cookshop in Bartholomew Fair, Ned Ward watches as

A swinging fat fellow, the overseer of the roast to keep the pigs from blistering, who was standing by the spit in his shirt, rubbed his ears, breast, neck and armpits with the same wet cloth which he applied to his pigs ... so scouring out again through an army of flies encamped at the door in order to attack the pig-sauce, we deferred our eating till a cleaner opportunity.[46]

A notch up from cookshops are the 'ordinaries' – modest eating houses where you can have a set two-course meal for 1s, each course consisting of a single dish (one of which will be beef).[47] Higher up the food chain again is a city tavern: a typical dish of the day is a meat chop (of lamb or veal) with bread, cheese and beer, at a total cost of 1s.[48] Note that this is a minimum; a fashionable location may well charge you twice as much: the King's Head in Charing Cross costs 2s 6d a head. The top-quality French eating houses in London (the word 'restaurant' is not yet in use) can cost much more. A meal at Chatelin's in Covent Garden will set you back 8s 6d per head in the 1660s, and Pontac's Head in Abchurch Lane in the city of London in the 1690s might cost more than a guinea (£1 1s).[49] But the most expensive places of all to eat are the inns that cater to the aristocracy. The English Champion in Ware might not be able to offer anything other than eel but the Red Lion in Cambridge can serve almost anything you want – as long as you can afford it. This is the earl of Bedford's bill for *one meal* at the inn, in 1689.

The earl of Bedford's dinner at the Red Lion, Cambridge,
16 October 1689[50]

First course

A brace of carp stewed with some perches arranged around them	£1 9s
A chine of mutton and a large chine of veal	£1
For making a pastry	13s
A dish of tongues, udders and marrowbones, with cauliflowers and spinach	11s 6d
A couple of geese	8s
A hash of calf's head with sweetbread	11s 6d
A dish of turkeys	12s
A dish of collared pig	[on the house]
A dish of stewed oysters	6s
A couple of pullets with oysters	6s
A grand salad	1s
subtotal	£5 18s

Second course

A dish of wild fowl	£1 4s
A jowl of sturgeon	[on the house]
A dish of fat chickens and rabbits	8s
A stand of pickles with oysters, anchovies and tongue	4s
A dish of snipes and larks	6s 6d
A large Westphalia ham with tongues	£1 5s
For recruiting [sending out for] a dish of tarts	3s
A dish of partridges	4s 6d
A dish of whipped syllabubs	7s 6d
A dish of artichokes	3s 6d
A salmagundi	2s
A dish of fruit	3s 6d
For lemons and double refined sugar	3s 6d
For oil and vinegar	2s 6d
For butter for my lord's table	4d
For cheese for the servants	1s
For bread and beer	£6 19s 8d
subtotal	£11 18s 6d
Total	£17 16s 6d

This meal is not a special occasion – it is only marginally more expensive than the one the earl and his family consume the previous day (£15 3s 6d). But the thing to note is the range of foodstuffs that can be provided at such a hostelry. If you are travelling in Restoration Britain and have money, and stay at the right place, then you will want for nothing.

Food in Ordinary Households

If there is one economic law that is historically true in all times and places, it is that the less wealthy a household is, the greater the proportion of its income is spent on food. The earl of Bedford's kitchen expenditure amounts to less than 10 per cent of his total income. A gentleman with one-twentieth as much will spend a much larger proportion on feeding his household, and a prosperous yeoman with an annual income of £50 will spend a greater proportion still. But as the figures in chapter 3 make clear, about two-thirds of the households in England have an income below the average of £32 per year, and in Scotland the average is even lower. Working people spend far more than half their income on food and drink. Even if you rule out spending 1s a day on a dinner at an inn or alehouse, and stick to an allowance of 6d per day for all three meals, that still adds up to more than £9 per year. This is what Edward Barlow's father has, in order to feed his whole family, consisting of his wife and six children – and that's without any deduction for rent, firewood, clothing or parish dues. If your income amounts to less than a penny a head per day for each member of your household, almost all of it has to be spent on food.

Lack of money to buy ingredients is one obvious reason why eating with Restoration husbandmen and cottagers is so different from dining with their social superiors. Another is a limited range of cooking utensils: they cannot afford a range of skillets and trivets, frying pans and saucepans. A third is the lack of fuel. In Cornwall, Celia Fiennes discovers to her horror that firewood is in such short supply that her hosts cannot roast meat for her: they have to boil it in a cauldron over a fire of furze.[51] A fourth limiting factor is the law. You can't just take fish from a river: they are the property of the landowner. In addition, Parliament passes an Act in 1671 prohibiting ordinary people from hunting or trapping game, even when it is on their own land. Things aren't quite as extreme as in the next century, when the law allows gamekeepers to shoot poachers on sight, but nevertheless the legislation adds to the poor man's misery.

How do people manage? The answer, in a nutshell, is thrift. Everything that can possibly be consumed from an animal is saved: bones, intestines, fat, brains, tongue, heart, kidneys, liver and hooves. No child in a hungry family is likely to turn down food on the grounds that he or she 'doesn't like it', so every part of any animal is used. Obviously, if you are lucky enough to own a few hens, you don't eat them but rather keep them for their eggs, and you only eat the bird when she has ceased to lay. But thrift has its creative side too, in making the most of the few assets available. You don't grow flowers or grass in your garden (if you have one) but a variety of herbs, onions, peas, beans, cabbages, kale, parsnips, turnips, beetroot, and so forth, which may well be the difference between life and death in a year of high prices. Apples, if stored carefully in the right conditions, can be kept for a year, and other fruit can be dried or made into preserves. If you own a cow, you don't kill it for its beef, but aim to benefit from the blood as well as the milk and the calves, by drawing off limited amounts of blood from cuts in its legs and mixing it with herbs and oats to produce blood puddings. You can cautiously try out new crops too. It is at this point that workers in the north-west of England start to plant potatoes as a staple crop: they find that not only are potatoes good for breaking up the soil and excellent insurance against a harvest failure, but they are also more nutritious per acre than wheat.[52]

Creative thrift extends to cooking methods, to compensate for the lack of utensils and fuel. Celia Fiennes might be shocked at the lack of firewood, but ordinary people up and down the country have been dealing with the problem for decades. Perhaps the most important efficiency in this respect is cauldron cookery. In a large cauldron of brass or iron, several things can be cooked at once. Meat can be inserted in an earthenware jug with herbs and salt (hence 'jugged hare') and cooked alongside vegetables in a net within the boiling water, with the juices adding to the cauldron water to make a pottage broth. Puddings too can be cooked in this way, and they can be made with almost any form of ingredients. Cauldron cookery is especially useful where charcoal or coal is the only available fuel: the acrid coal smoke prevents broiling or roasting but does not harm the food in a simmering cauldron. Iron fire-baskets are developed to facilitate the use of alternative fuels. Baking also reduces the need for firewood, as the oven is heated through burning dried undergrowth. Thus, rather than roasting a piece of meat, it can be encased in pastry and baked in a pie, cutting the cost.

For the poor and the ordinary household living near the sea, fish are a staple part of the diet. Oysters are eaten by everyone, rich and poor alike, although for the poor they may constitute a meal in themselves. A little further inland, pickled sprats and herrings and salt cod remain affordable but, as you travel further from the sea, the costs of carriage put them beyond reach. In Scotland, haddock and whiting are dried and smoked over seaweed fires on the shore by fishermen's wives. But for the majority throughout Britain, for whom meat is a rare or unaffordable luxury, the most important staple foods are bread (or oatcakes) and cheese. With respect to the latter, soft cheeses made with full-fat milk tend to be expensive but hard cheeses, made with skimmed milk, are cheaper and last a long time. As for bread, wheaten loaves from a baker are costly, but if you can bake your own with barley, rye, oats or maslin (a mixture of wheat and rye), you can cut costs significantly. Make it with a mixture of peas, beans and oats or barley, and you can reduce costs still further. For this reason it is important to have your own oven. This is one of the reasons why so many cottages have their fireplaces rebuilt at this time, with the addition of a bread oven. Take your fuel, such as dried gorse or bracken, and keep shovelling it in till the fire is roaring, heating the bricks or stones, and, when the oven is hot enough, sweep out the fire and ashes and insert your loaves in their troughs on a long-handled peel. Close up the oven with its oak door or slab of stone, and seal it with clay or mud. And if there is sufficient heat left afterwards, use it to bake pies or pastries, which require lower temperatures.[53]

What to Drink

In listing all the drinks available in England in 1676, Chamberlayne mentions 'wines from Spain, France, Italy, Germany and Greece ... brandy, coffee, chocolate, tea, aromatic, mum, cider, perry, beer and many sorts of ale'.[54] He could have mentioned many other things too, such as mead, which is enjoying something of a revival among the gentry (as an alternative to wine in the mornings); and metheglin, a herbal variation on mead, which remains popular in Wales. One drink Chamberlayne does not mention is water. This is not because it is so common that it goes without saying; rather, because it is rarely drunk. Its 'coldness' in medicinal terms means that physicians warn against drinking it, even if it is purified by boiling. Although many cities in the Restoration period – including London, Norwich, Exeter, Edinburgh, Leicester and Shrewsbury – have water piped from their rivers to the yards of wealthy people's houses, it is not for drinking purposes but for cleaning and cooking. London's pumping wheel, installed in 1656, can raise the water 93 feet, and an artificial channel or 'new river' supplies water to a reservoir in Islington and from there to houses in the north of the city; but these services are expensive and the people who can afford them are not the sort who drink water.[55]

ALE, BEER, MUM AND CIDER

Ale, brewed from malted barley and water, has been the traditional drink everywhere in Britain except the Highlands of Scotland for centuries. It continues to be drunk in great quantities, and in various forms. The problem is that it only lasts a few days after brewing. Beer, which includes hops, keeps for much longer, so this is the most common drink in England. Mum, a heavy ale brewed from wheat, flavoured with aromatic herbs and left to ferment for a couple of years, is another variation. But this general classification conceals a great number of regional differences. Herbal ales are popular in the north of England. In Cheshire, Lancashire, Derbyshire, Devon and Cornwall, ale is made with malted oats as well as barley, and in parts of Kent it is made with a mixture of the two.[56] Welsh ale or cwrw is made from kilned barley, which imparts a smoky flavour. Suffice to say, wherever you go, the local beer will be distinctive.

Then there are the specialist ales and beers. Cock ale is famous on account of it supposedly being a cure for consumption (tuberculosis). The basic drink is brewed from ordinary malted barley: the distinct ingredient is the cock, which is parboiled, steeped in sack and then left to soak in the ale with raisins, dates and spices. Alehouses that sell it are often named after the drink – for instance, 'Cock-ale Tavern'.

Old Pharaoh is another distinctive ale that gives its name to the alehouse where it is sold in Barley, Hertfordshire; Ned Ward describes it as 'a stout, elevating malt liquor'.[57] Margate ale, otherwise known as Northdown, is a strong drink favoured by Pepys for getting unsuspecting people tipsy. Coloquintida is small beer flavoured with colocynth, the bitter cucumber.[58] On top of these specific brands you have generic ale recipes. Buttered ale is boiled with butter, sugar and nutmeg and thickened with beaten eggs. Aleberry is similar, but thickened with oats and drunk in Scotland; and caudled ale is mixed with honey or sugar and egg yolk, which is recognised as a restorative for ill people. Lambswool – ale mulled with eggs, spices, sugar and the pulp of roasted apples – is a popular drink on Halloween, Christmas Eve and Twelfth Night.

Beer is not generally drunk out of glasses. Unless you are in an upmarket establishment, where pewter vessels might be used, you'll drink from a wooden tankard. The range of beers and ales available, and their sensitivity to their storage conditions, means that travellers remark on the quality of the beer and ale rather as modern British people talk about the weather. Schellinks remarks on the 'very good beer' kept in the caves below Dover Castle and the 'excellent beer' at the Dolphin Inn in Sandwich.[59] In Nottingham, ale and beer are stored well in cool cellars cut into the rock beneath the town.[60] Beer generally retails at 2d or 3d a quart (two pints). Ale is slightly cheaper. Small beer, which is weak and meant for children, is cheaper still. Yorkshire ale is very strong and thus more expensive – 'it will always cost you a groat [4d],' says Celia Fiennes.[61] Bottled beer has improved greatly since its introduction in the reign of Elizabeth (when the bottles would often explode) and may be found in small towns as well as cities. Most brewing is still done in people's homes, however; the difficulties of transporting beer any great distance mean that large breweries are a thing of the future.

Cider is most famously produced in Herefordshire, Somerset and Devon, although it is by no means confined to these regions. French cider too is imported and available in London. Varieties are generally named after the types of apples that produce them. In Herefordshire, a premium is set on cider made from Scudamore apples. Redstreak cider is also highly prized, being very strong. Prices tend to be higher than those for ale: Thomas Baskerville pays 6d a quart for cider in Herefordshire in 1673; bottled cider retails at 6d per bottle in 1693.[62]

WINE

If you are a wine connoisseur, you have come to perhaps the most exciting time ever in the history of wine production. And the English play a major part in the story. This is not because of any developments in the production of English wine. Although there *are* a few domestic vineyards (on Lady Batten's estate at Walthamstow, Essex, for example), English wines are almost never offered for sale.[63] Rather it is due to the fact that the emerging London bourgeoisie treat wine as a status symbol and thus create a considerable demand for it, leading to the development of fine wines in Bordeaux and new methods of making wine in Burgundy.

To understand all the excitement, you need to know something about how wine is bought and stored. First, it is illegal to sell it in bottles, due to an Act of Parliament of 1636. Yet bottling wine is the most convenient way to keep it and take it from your cellar to the dining table or banqueting house.[64] Gentlemen thus buy wine by the barrel and bottle it themselves. You place an order with a bottle-maker for dark-glass vessels with attached glass discs that include your initials, crest or coat of arms and the date. Note that these are expensive – a dozen can cost as much as 4s 5d – so you do not bottle up any cheap rubbish.[65] At the same time as this move to bottled wine is taking place, consumers are starting to use corks to close the bottle, instead of plugs of oiled hemp or glass stoppers.[66] They have not yet realised that by binning wine (laying it on its side so that the cork remains damp) they can improve it while it is in the bottle, so the majority of wines are still drunk while 'green' or young. When you go to a wine tavern, however, you will probably not see any sign of this oenological revolution. The cellars are full of casks and barrels, each one marked with the wine's place of origin. And when it is served, it will normally be brought to your table in a flask or jug and poured into wine glasses. The bottling and recording of the vintages of wine are entirely a private obsession of the rich.

Let us begin with champagne. You have no doubt heard the story of Dom Pérignon, the legendary wine grower at the abbey of Hautvillers, who is said to have invented the sparkling drink. It isn't true, sadly. In fact, the exact opposite is the case. Pierre Pérignon is indeed the treasurer at Hautvillers (from 1668) but his self-appointed mission is to eradicate the bubbles, not add them.[67] In the Champagne region, located in the cooler north of France, cold spells regularly halt the fermentation process in the barrel, so a second fermentation starts when the temperature rises. This creates an unwelcome effervescence in the red and white wines of the region. Thus, if you go to Hautvillers, you'll find Dom Pérignon devising methods of pruning and spacing out his vines and storing the wine in appropriate conditions, in order to increase the chances of the wine maturing normally, without any fizz. Meanwhile a local landowner, the marquis de Saint-Évremond, is in London, living it up in the city following his exile from France. Of course he has his own wines sent to him, and he and gentlemen of his acquaintance have it put into bottles. As it happens, English bottles are stronger than French ones, and when the second fermentation takes place inside, many of them are able to withstand the pressure. Champagne as we know it then quietly develops, in the darkness of English cellars. The well-to-do soon start talking about this special new drink: in 1676 the playwright Sir George Etherege declares his taste for *sparkling* champagne in his comedy *The Man of Mode*.[68] Demand quickly exceeds supply. Champagne growers rub their hands with glee. Dom Pérignon may be aghast but the rest, as they say, is history.

The other hugely significant development in this period is the move to import fine wines from Bordeaux. In the mid-1650s managers of vineyards start to think more scientifically about wine production: how many vines should be planted per acre, how hard the pruning should be, and so forth. One of them is Arnaud de Pontac, whose Haut-Brion estate yields some exceptionally good red wine. No doubt Charles II is already familiar with it as a result of his years in France for, very soon after his accession, he sets about acquiring it in considerable quantities.[69] The king's example is followed by many Londoners: Pepys cannot resist finding out what all the fuss is about and heads to the Royal Oak Tavern in Lombard Street on 10 April 1663 to try it for himself. His verdict is that Haut-Brion has 'a good and most particular taste that I never met with'.[70] Arnaud de Pontac notes that his order book is filling with London clients and sees a great opportunity. In 1666 he sends his son François-Auguste to open a wine tavern in London to push the wine. Known as 'Pontac's Head' or simply 'Pontac's', it sells Haut-Brion to the rich dining set and quickly becomes the most prestigious place to eat in the capital. John Dryden, John Evelyn, Daniel Defoe and Jonathan Swift all dine there. The philosopher John Locke is so impressed that he visits the vineyard in 1677. Of course as soon as you have won over the literati, your publicity takes on a life of its own. So successful are the Pontac family in this respect that in England their name becomes synonymous with fine claret, even after the other great 'new clarets' – Margaux, Lafite and Latour – have started producing comparable wines.[71]

Dozens of other wines are available in London and, to a lesser extent, in the other major wine-importing centre of Bristol, and from these places they are exported all over the country. The range covers the full A to Z – from 'A' for Alicante, a Spanish wine, to 'Z' for Zante, a Greek one. The most common red wine is ordinary claret, imported from Bordeaux. If you want white, the easiest to obtain is Rhenish, from the Rhine. Malmsey is imported from Greece, Canary from the Canary Islands, Candy from Crete, Vernage from Tuscany and La Ribera from Spain. Italian Chianti makes its first appearance in the English market, in both its white and red forms.[72] Rumney is a sort of sweet wine made in the Greek style but imported from Spain. The delightfully named Brown Bastard is a sweet blend from Portugal. Sack we have already encountered: it takes its name from *seco*, the Spanish word for 'dry'. This is one of the few wines you might be able to taste in an aged state: Pepys tries a thirty-year-old Malaga sack in 1663 and considers it 'excellent but more like a spirit'.[73] Another significant development at this time is the introduction of Iberian wines to the British market. Sherry starts to be imported in quantity from Jerez but as yet it is still not fortified. Port, too, is beginning to make its way to England in an unfortified state: in 1692 Job Bearsley starts a port business, taking strong red wines from the Douro valley to the port of Oporto and then to London (the company is still going in the twenty-first century, under the name Taylor's).

Now for the bill – and you can see why wine is a status symbol. An Act of 1660 lays down a maximum retail price for wine: Spanish and sweet wines must sell at 1s 6d or less per quart; French wines at no more than 8d; and Rhenish wines at not above 12d per quart. The penalty for breaking this law is £5 but you can guess how effective it is likely to be, especially after Pontac's opens its doors to a wealthy clientele. There you will have to spend about 7s for a bottle of Haut-Brion and 2s for lesser wines. Elsewhere, a quart of your standard claret is normally about 1s, sherry about 1s 8d a quart and Canary 2s in the 1670s.[74] In London, at a good wine tavern, expect to pay about

2s 6d for a quart of sack.[75] Most wealthy gentlemen buy wine by the cask, hogshead or tun: for example, the earl of Bedford pays the famous London wine merchant James Houblon £10 for two hogsheads of port in 1664.[76] In 1678 the importation of French goods, including wine, is forbidden, forcing merchants to turn to Spain and Portugal to make up the shortfall. The balance swings back to French wines in 1685, when the ban on imports is relaxed, and although wine tariffs on French wines are increased by £8 a tun, the duty on other wines increases by £12, making French wines more affordable again. In 1689 there is another embargo on French wine, which is lifted in 1696, but then the duty placed on it is increased by a massive £25 per tun, making it ridiculously expensive – and worth smuggling into the country illicitly.[77] Even drinkers of Haut-Brion blink at the prices charged by London wine merchants after 1696. But oenophiles tend not to compromise on quality, even when prices are so high, and the new clarets all remain in demand.

SPIRITS

Distilling is an ancient art but unknown in Britain until the late Middle Ages. Even then it was not employed for recreational drinking but for medicinal purposes. Apothecaries distilled concoctions in which plants had been dissolved in order to obtain their *essence*. Sometimes they produced 'strong water' or aquavitae, which is close to pure alcohol. It was the Dutch who gave us our first recreational spirit. In the late sixteenth century people (including English soldiers in the Low Countries) took a liking to drinking *genever* (gin) distilled from the juice of juniper berries. Now the popularity of spirits is spreading – not least because you are able to distil as much hard liquor as you want without having to pay punitive taxation rates. People accordingly experiment with distilling anything and everything they can lay their hands on: malt, molasses, fruit, snails and chickens. Yes, you may be offered 'cock water' as well as cock ale: this is not a synonym for urine (but you may wish it was). The thinking goes like this: if cock ale is so good for you, surely the distilled *essence* of cock should be even better. Likewise snail-water, which is snails distilled with sack and herbs. If you have any taste, you will eschew these for good old brandy. Sir Edward Dering declares in 1670 that brandy drinking in Kent has

'grown of a sudden to a very great mischief, it being now sold generally in every village, and the sellers despising the authority of the
justice of the peace, as thinking themselves not within the statutes
for selling ale and beer'.[78] Obviously those with money are not content
with home-distilled drinks but seek out the best French brandies.
These cost 3s 8d per gallon if you are buying in bulk, or 1s per bottle.[79]

At the same time as brandy is sweeping England, the practice of
distilling corn-based drinks is spreading in Scotland, so that men and
women there give up drinking water, milk, buttermilk and whey
and start drinking whisky every day. Making whisky remains a family
affair, however, so little of it makes its way south of the border. As a
result, it is Irish whiskey that first comes to the attention of the English.
Another imported strong drink is rum – short for 'rumbullion'. It is
also known as 'kill-water', which gives you an inkling of its potency.
Other strong drinks that you may be offered include punch – which
is served in a bowl with a piece of toast floating on top (hence 'to
drink a toast') – and arrack, which is a mixture of brandy, cider, fruit
juices, water, spices and sugar.[80]

COFFEE, CHOCOLATE AND TEA

The first coffee house in England opens in Oxford in 1650. It is soon
followed by one in London in 1652. By 1660 coffee is so popular that
the government decides to tax it, but this does not stop the craze; the
number of coffee houses continues to grow – despite a fear that
drinking coffee makes you infertile. By May 1663 there are no fewer
than eighty-two in the capital, and by 1700 there are perhaps a thousand.[81] You'll also find them in Bristol, York, Exeter, Bath, Norwich,
Yarmouth, Chester, Preston, Warwick, Edinburgh, Glasgow and probably many other large towns. They are male-only establishments; apart
from serving maids, no women are allowed in (which perhaps explains
the origin of the theory that men who drink a lot of coffee do not
have children). Apart from that, they are non-exclusive, as long as you
pay. In London, Lloyd's and Garraway's primarily cater for serious
businessmen. St James's Coffee House and the Cocoa Tree are for
politicians – if you are a Whig, make sure you go to the latter and
not the former, which is for Tories. Most coffee houses do not permit
discussion of religious matters but those that do are to be found near

St Paul's. If you are keen on literature, then Will's Coffee House in Covent Garden is the one for you, as that is where John Dryden holds court, informing everyone what he thinks of the latest book or play.[82]

Generally speaking, coffee houses consist of just the one room with a few tables and chairs for the drinkers. Some premises are larger. Enter the Great Lower Coffee Room run by John Kimber in Bristol and you'll see three tables with chairs, benches and stools, a clock, coffee dishes and glasses on the counter and a fireplace. There are bare boards on the floor, and a smell of coffee and stale tobacco in the air. A second coffee room upstairs is similarly equipped, but this one also has such luxuries as a couch, a mirror and window curtains.[83] As with taverns, some proprietors use historical relics to attract customers. A few of these are hilarious: one London coffee house purports to have 'Pontius Pilate's wife's chambermaid's sister's hat'.[84] Pay 1d as an entry fee and you can stay as long as you want to, drinking dishes of hot black coffee from the great urns in which it is made, and smoking clay pipes of black tobacco, which are also available.[85] There you might read the selection of weekly newspapers and news-letters, or debate important matters in your club – a 'club' at this time being an informal sharing of costs equally amongst a regular group of friends.

If you want to buy coffee to drink in your own home, it costs about 3s per pound until 1689, when excise duties increase; thereafter it steadily rises to 6s per pound in the 1690s. You'll need to buy a coffee pot and porcelain cups: the pot will cost you just 6d, but the cups are 1s 6d each, as they are imported from China.[86] However, coffee remains predominantly a social drink, enjoyed in public establishments. There is something odd about someone in the seventeenth century who wants to drink coffee by himself. Wine, yes, but not coffee. And wherever you drink it, it still incurs the wrath of some. According to the author of *A Satyr against Coffee*, the drink is made with 'the scent of old crusts and shreds of leather burnt and beaten to powder. It [is] the essence of old shoes ... horse-pond liquor, witches tipple out of dead men's skulls ... a foreign fart.'[87]

In the late 1650s, coffee houses near the Royal Exchange start to offer Chinese tea for sale. It is immediately popular, despite the enormous expense: the first dealers charge up to £10 per pound. In 1660 Thomas Garway, a coffee-house owner who wishes to expand his tea business, reduces his prices to as little as 16s per pound and advertises widely. That does the trick. Pepys takes his first sip on 25 September 1660.[88] By the end of the year, tea has joined coffee in being taxed. Prices stabilise at about £3 per pound for the highest quality and less than £1 for the lowest, after the East India Company starts to import it in 1664.[89] Thus if your visit to Restoration Britain leaves you gasping, a restorative cuppa is not out of the question – although you won't find any familiar varieties. There are three main types, all from China (Indian tea won't reach Britain until the nineteenth century). Boehea is a black leaf tea that leaves the boiling water looking brownish-red. Singlo is a leaf of a bluish-green colour that is strong enough to stand being reused three or four times. The third sort, Bing or Imperial, is a green tea, and the most costly of the three. All of them are drunk very weak by our standards and without milk, although many people add sugar and egg yolks.

Tea is just as much a social drink as coffee but, in marked contrast, it is usually consumed by groups of people in private homes. It follows that you need the appropriate apparatus for serving such a luxury to other people of high status: tea dishes, teapot and sugar bowl, and a silver salver on which to place everything. The tea dishes and teapot should, of course, be genuine Chinese porcelain items, which the East India Company will be only too happy to supply – at a price of 4s per tea dish and 10s for the teapot. The alternative is an English silver teapot; London silversmiths start to make these from 1670. With such status attached to it, wealthy households want to have their own tea sets, and thus they domesticate the drink. Moreover, in the privacy of their own homes, ladies can partake in the ceremony of serving tea, in defiance of being excluded from male-only coffee shops. The bills at Woburn Abbey show that the earl of Bedford and his countess start to drink tea at home from 1685 and consume much more of it than they do coffee, investing in several tea sets and even tea tables.[90]

The third new hot drink, chocolate, is even more outlandish and mysterious, being a product of the cocoa bean, to be found in the forests of Latin America. The Spanish and Portuguese have occasion-ally imported chocolate cakes to their own countries in past decades but their recipes have long been a closely guarded secret. This changes in 1655 when the English capture the island of Jamaica, where the Spanish have planted a number of cacao trees. Two years later a London entrepreneur starts advertising 'an excellent West India drink called chocolate'. It catches on immediately and, like coffee and tea, is subject to taxation from 1660. Part of the allure is that it makes for an excellent breakfast drink, not least because it is believed that it settles the stomach: Pepys occasionally has chocolate for his morning draught, on one occasion choosing it specifically because he has been drinking heavily the night before.[91] To make a chocolate cake, take 1lb of cocoa powder and add 6oz of white sugar, ½oz of cinnamon, one grated nutmeg and a vanilla pod. Blend these ingredients together with a roller over a gentle heat and press it into moulds while warm. To turn this into the drink, you will crumble some of the cake into red wine boiled with egg yolks and sweetened with sugar. Alternatives are made with milk, water and brandy, or purely with choice port or sherry.[92] The last option makes for quite some breakfast.

Smoking

The final consumable commodity that we come to is tobacco. As you are probably aware, the Elizabethans introduced it to these shores in the 1560s and it has been popular ever since, despite King James I publishing a diatribe against it, in which he declared it to be 'a custom loathsome to the eye ... and hateful to the nose'. Every foreign visitor to England comments on how much the common people smoke. In the words of Lorenzo Magalotti:

> It is a common custom with the lower order of people, however, rather than with the nobility, who are less given to it, after dinner or at public houses, when they are transacting business of any kind, to take tobacco and smoke, so there does not pass a day in which the artisans do not indulge themselves in going to the public houses, which are exceedingly numerous, neglecting their work, however urgent it may be.[93]

Willem Schellinks notes that one morning in Cornwall 'a lot of country people were at the market – everyone, men and women, young and old, puffing tobacco, which is here so common that the young children get it in the morning instead of breakfast, and almost prefer it to bread'.[94] Monsieur Misson and Celia Fiennes also remark on the very heavy consumption of tobacco by women and children in the western counties. Thomas Baskerville, riding through the Gloucestershire town of Winchcombe at 4 a.m. one morning, sees all the old women of the town seated in their doorways and smoking their pipes, doing their knitting.[95]

You have got to wonder, in an age of so much hardship, why people smoke so much – especially the poor. One reason is that the government encourages smoking as it increases the revenue raised by taxation on tobacco imported from Virginia. Monsieur Misson volunteers another: smoking makes people philosophical. He suggests that no one smokes so well as an English clergyman, and that as English theology is so profound, then tobacco must encourage profound thinking.[96] But the principal reason is, no doubt, sheer enjoyment – and it needs to be said that it is a pleasure unconfined by health warnings. In fact, most people believe that smoking is *good* for your health. It is widely seen as a prophylactic against the plague – hence boys at Eton College are liable to be beaten for *not* smoking. It is believed to give the smoker a clear voice, a sweet breath, clear sight, good hearing and a better sense of smell, and to be a cure for melancholy.[97] With all these things going for it, you can see why people give it to their children and smoke it themselves in large quantities. Boys in some parts of Devon and Cornwall take a pipe to school with them and smoke it at designated hours in the company of their tutors, learning how to hold the pipe and draw in all that nourishing smoke.[98]

So, how much is smoking 'in large quantities'? The answer is a heck of a lot. The earl of Bedford personally consumes about 30lbs of tobacco per year; this amounts to well over an ounce and a quarter per day. Yet no one remarks on him being a heavy smoker. Moreover, none of that tobacco is smoked with any filters – why would you, when it is thought to be good for your health? Rather, the smoke is inhaled through disposable clay pipes (cigarettes are a nineteenth-century invention). These pipes can be used three or four times at most, but they are not expensive: ordinary ones are nine for a penny. Tobacco costs 3s 4d per pound for Virginia, 10s per pound for Spanish.[99]

In case you are wondering, Lord Bedford lives to the age of eighty-seven.

10

Health and Hygiene

'What should you do when you get ill?' is one of the most important questions that confronts and defines a culture – and, indeed, civilisation in general. It does not matter whether the answer is based on medical observation, reason, superstition, religion or a combination of all of these things; what is important is that there is an answer of some sort and that it is convincing. For everyone lives with the knowledge that, at any moment in time, something could happen that will bring them to the point of suffering and death. No one wants to be told that there is no hope of alleviating their pain. No one wants to hear that their child's sickness is incurable. Even if you are plainly going to die and the physicians' attempts to help you have failed, you still need professional advice – even if it is just to know how long you have got to live, so that you can write a will and make your peace with God. For this reason, when we look at a society and take note solely of the healthy people, as if only healthiness is normal, we are missing a major part of what is going on. Indeed, when you consider the sense of shame associated with some infections, and the fear of death and the economics of medicine, as well as the impact of the sicknesses themselves, you can see that society would not function the way it does without illness.

As you travel through Restoration Britain you are going to be left in no doubt that this applies to the rich every bit as much as the poor. In marked contrast to the last chapter, in which we compared the food and drink of the wealthy with the fare of their less fortunate contemporaries, illness strikes everyone equally, without regard for high status. When Charles II rides in procession through London on his birthday in 1660 he has *two* brothers, James, duke of York, and Henry, duke of Gloucester. A few months later, on 13 September, Henry dies of smallpox. Three months after that, the king's sister, Mary Henrietta, dies of the same disease. Heartbreakingly, John Evelyn loses two of his daughters to smallpox within six months in 1685. In 1694 it claims the life of Queen Mary, wife of William III. The rich might be able to afford better food and better-qualified physicians but their life expectancy is no greater than that of ordinary people. In this period, a life of privilege also hangs by a thread.

Nowhere is this more in evidence than with regard to the loss of children. Just look at the royal family. The average lifespan of Charles I's nine children is just twenty-four; only Charles II and James II make it past thirty. Just two of James II's eight children by his first wife live to adulthood, and only one of his ten by his second wife (not counting two miscarriages). Princess Anne is arguably the most unfortunate member of the whole family: apart from her seven miscarriages, five of her ten children are stillborn. Two die within hours of being born, two more die of smallpox at the ages of two and one, and the last dies at the age of eleven. Despite seventeen pregnancies, she dies childless. Adding this up, it appears that of the thirty-five legitimate royal pregnancies in the period 1660–1700, only three children live to see adulthood.

Medical Thinking

In order to find your way around the medical landscape, you need to know how contemporaries understand illness. They have no idea about bacteria or viruses; the microscopes of the day are not powerful enough to see anything so small. But this does not mean they don't know – or *think* they know – what causes a disease. For more than a millennium there has been a basic understanding that the health of the body depends on a balance of four humours – blood, choler, yellow bile and black bile – just as the Earth is composed of four Aristotelian 'elements' (earth, air, fire and water). Too much choler makes you choleric, too much blood makes you sanguine, and so forth; combinations of these imbalances result in disease. The humours can be upset by any number of things. Eating rotten meat or breathing noxious vapours arising from stagnant water may be the cause, or an unfortunate alignment of the planets. Once the humours are out of kilter and the sickness has taken hold, then it can spread from you to other people and disrupt the balance of their humours too, and so on. Moreover, as the humours fluctuate in relation to one another, people think that one disease can morph into another, so food poisoning can lead to a fever, which can turn into measles.[1]

Given the volume of experimental work being undertaken by the Royal Society and its Fellows, you won't be surprised to hear that things are changing. Other philosophies are emerging: for instance, that the world is not made up of four elements but of many tiny particles or atoms. William Harvey's discovery of the circulation of the blood, published in 1628, has dispelled the ancient belief that there are two types of blood: venous, made in the liver, and arterial, made in the heart, both of which ebb and flow about the body. The awareness that classical writers were mistaken on this subject also permits physicians to be bold and question other aspects of ancient teaching. Practitioners working in the wake of Paracelsus propose 'iatrochemical' explanations of the health of the body – *iatro* being Greek for 'medical' – concentrating on salt-, sulphur- and mercury-based medicines to cure illnesses. 'Corpuscular' natural philosophers, such as Thomas Willis and Robert Boyle, who subscribe to the theories of Jan Baptista van Helmont, stress the importance of alkalis and acids on physiological processes. Those who favour 'iatrophysical' theories use the laws of physics to describe the process of breathing and similar bodily functions and, by implication, to explain why the body's organs fail.

The other strand of medical thinking that might confuse you is the degree to which it involves religion. We have already seen in chapter 4 how people judge each other according to their faith, so that people do not trust physicians of a different creed. The reason underlying this is that the physician has to act as a conduit of God's healing power and, if he displeases God, then the cure will not work, no matter how skilled he is. This is why, when physicians apply for licences to practise from a bishop, they are examined not only on their medical knowledge but also on their personal life. However, that is just the start of the crossover between religion and medicine. Prayer is essential to a full cure, in many people's eyes; medicine by itself is not enough. Then there is the problem of why a benign God makes us unwell. One answer to this conundrum is that sickness serves a purpose. Most good Christians still see diseases as being sent by God to give lesser sinners a chance to redeem themselves on Earth, partly or wholly, through physical suffering, so that they might still go to

Heaven. This is why dying 'a good death' is so important: you must be grateful for your chance to feel pain. Even children suffering excruciating illnesses are expected to be stoic. On the other hand, many people believe that ailments are sent by God as punishments. Plague especially falls into this category. The fact that rich and poor alike can be wiped out gives it an egalitarian edge that people associate with divine judgement. As you can see, the all-encompassing religious outlook of the time means that people are in continuous dialogue with their faith about why they fall ill, why they are made to suffer and what they might do to relieve themselves of that suffering.

Another spiritual angle on seventeenth-century illness is the belief that God did not just make all the diseases at the time of Creation, but created the cures too: the antidotes are to be found somewhere in the world, if you just look hard enough. All the medicinal herbs seem to confirm this. The fact that so many plants can ease pain also points to a merciful Creator: among these you will come across cloves for alleviating toothache, *colchicum* (a crocus) for easing gout, and *guaiacum* (a resin) for treating syphilis and many other ailments. Jesuit's bark, or cinchona, in particular seems to be the clinching proof of this philosophy. The bark contains quinine and is a genuine natural remedy for the symptoms of malaria. The English physician Robert Talbor becomes internationally famous in the 1670s for his apparently miraculous cures, which employ Jesuit's bark. This faith in the medical properties of Creation in turn encourages people to explore more of the world and discover more medicinal plants, giving further vitality to the 'scientific crusade' that we discussed in chapter 4.

Not all ailments can be blamed on the humours or divine judgement; people know that what they eat and drink can also affect their health. Indeed, you may find that they 'know' it with even more certainty than you do. Aristotle suggested that six 'non-naturals' govern day-to-day well-being: diet, evacuations, exercise, air, sleep and the passions; these lead people to conclude that, if they are unwell, it is probably because they have neglected to care properly for themselves. On top of these six non-naturals, you can add a seventh – exposure to cold – as a reason why people believe they become unwell. Pepys associates his pain in urinating in November 1662 with his 'having taken cold this morning in staying too long barelegged to pare my corns'. In September 1665, while staying away from home, he has particular reason to rue exposing himself to cold:

And so I to bed, and in the night was mightily troubled with a looseness (I suppose from some fresh damp linen that I put on this night);
and feeling for a chamber pot, there was none ... so I was forced in
this strange house to rise and shit in the chimney twice.[2]

There are good reasons why, if you are staying in someone else's
house, they will offer to send the maid up with a bed pan to warm
your bed before you get in it.

Taking the Waters

The awareness that what goes into the body affects its health does
not apply just to those things you eat and drink; it also includes
anything that enters the body accidentally through skin pores and
orifices. But if dangerous substances can enter the body in this way,
then so can beneficial ones. Therefore bathing in mineral-rich water
can be good for your health. Moreover, if the idea is to get a dose of
the minerals into you as quickly as possible, why bother bathing
in the water? Just drink it. For these reasons, the spa towns become
hugely popular at this time. Most members of the great, the rich and
the middle sort go to 'take the waters' at least once a year. Even the
less well off embrace the trend: the sailor Edward Barlow bathes in
'a brave well which is counted very good to bathe in against many
diseases' at Buxton in Cheshire.[3] One place no one goes to bathe,
however, is the sea. If you go to the beach you'll have all the sand to
yourself, even on the hottest day of the year. The idea that sea water
might be imbued with some of the properties of spa water is one for
the next century.

The principal spa town in Britain is, of course, Bath, where the
hot sulphurous springs have risen for centuries. These are directed
into three principal baths (the King's Bath, the Hot Bath and the
Cross Bath) and two subsidiary ones (the Queen's Bath and the Leper's
Bath). The largest of these, the King's Bath, consists of a big rectangular pool with a canopied cross in the middle. This cross has stone
seats in porticoes all around it, where you can sit up to your neck in
the hot water. According to Edward Jorden, author of *A discourse of
Naturall Bathes and Mineral Waters*, the benefits of doing so are that
the hot waters

warm the whole habit of the body, attenuate humours, open the pores, procure sweat, move urine, cleanse the matrix, provoke women's evacuations, dry up unnatural humours, strengthen parts weakened, comfort the nerves and all nervous parts, cleanse the skin and suck out all salt humours from thence, open obstructions if they be not too much impacted, ease pains of the joints, and nerves and muscles, mollify and discuss hard tumours, etc.[4]

These properties are good for treating 'palsies, contractions, rheums, cold tumours, effects of the skin, aches, etcetera . . .' Jorden even claims that the waters can help with 'stupidity'.[5]

The best time to bathe is in the morning, an hour or two after the sun is up. Ladies enter the water in voluminous stiff yellow canvas bathing gowns; these billow out when filled by the water, concealing their figures and thereby preserving their modesty. Gentlemen wear drawers and waistcoats of the same sort of yellow canvas. Poorer men and women have to go into the baths in their own linen shifts (women) or shirts and drawers (men), which cling to the body.[6] Jorden recommends that you should also cover your head to protect it from cold airs. He further suggests that you should spend as long in the water as you can stand, at least an hour or two, and to do this every day for as long as you can afford – ideally twenty or thirty consecutive days. If you have a particular ailment and your physician so advises, you should tell one of the attendants and he will arrange for hot water to be pumped directly over the affected area. Schellinks, who visits Bath in 1662, notes that some men and women have more than a thousand blasts of hot water delivered on to their heads and backs. There are attendants waiting in the water with knives to cut off your corns, warts and nails, for a small fee. It is a good thing that the baths are drained after each morning session and allowed to refill for the next day.[7]

The bathing ritual is very different at another popular spa, Harrogate in Yorkshire. For a start, there are no baths in the town itself, only wells. These produce two sorts of mineral water: 'sulphurous' and 'chalybeate' (that is, rich in iron). When Celia Fiennes visits, she reports that the chalybeate well is 'the sweet spa'. As for the other:

the sulphur or stinking spa [is] not improperly termed for the smell being so very strong and offensive that I could not force my horse near the well. There are two wells together with basins in them that

(*Left*) The process of executing traitors differs between men and women. Men are drawn to the gallows, hanged, cut down while still alive, disembowelled and then beheaded and their bodies cut into quarters, as shown here. Women are simply burnt at the stake.

(*Below*) Titus Oates is responsible for spreading fear stories about a Catholic plot in 1678–81. Thirty-five innocent men are executed as a result. When he himself is tried, his penalty is to be fined, imprisoned for life, unmercifully flogged and annually exhibited in the pillory. Here the crowds are turning out to witness the 1687 pillorying outside Westminster Hall.

An elegant new country house in Belsize, Middlesex, and an equally elegant coach, painted by Jan Siberechts in 1696.

Dating from 1655, the sign of the White Hart Inn in Scole, Norfolk, is adorned with coats of arms, biblical scenes, angels, shepherds and figures from classical mythology. The marketing of inns takes off with the development of coach travel.

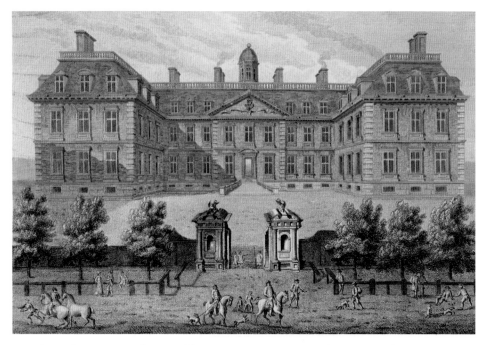

Clarendon House, designed by Sir Roger Pratt, stands on Piccadilly in West London. Despite being hailed by John Evelyn as 'the best contrived, the most useful, graceful and magnificent house in England', it is demolished in 1683, just sixteen years after its completion.

The remodelling of Chatsworth in Derbyshire is begun by the duke of Devonshire in 1686. Not only is the house an architectural triumph, the gardens and fountains astound all those who see them.

(*Left*) Grinling Gibbons's ability to carve the most exquisite forms in wood is unprecedented and unparalleled. This typical example of his work is to be seen in Petworth House, in Sussex

(*Below*) Chintz – elaborated multi-coloured painted or stained calico from India – starts to arrive in England in the seventeenth century, and proves very popular with the wealthy for upholstery, bed curtains and similar draperies.

(*Below*) This table clock looks 'timeless', if you'll pardon the pun: a design that hardly betrays its origins in Thomas Tompion's workshop. But nothing like it existed before the 1660s, and even then the early clocks had only one hand. This example also chimes the hour and quarter-hour

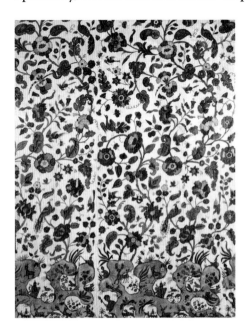

Antonio Verrio is considered by many to be 'the finest hand in England'. His work at Burghley, especially the Heaven Room, shown here, is incredible. It does not just dominate the room, it causes everyone who enters to fall silent in admiration.

Even the wealthy consume many animal parts that we regard as unpalatable. The wine is more likely to be to your taste: in the 1660s the French start to produce fine clarets, which are imported by the English at enormous expense.

(*Left*) Edward Barlow comes from a background of grinding poverty but heads to sea at the age of thirteen and, most remarkably, teaches himself to read, write and draw. His life is recorded in his journal: this is his ship, the *Sampson*, caught in a hurricane in 1694.

(*Below left*) William Dampier is the third Englishman to circumnavigate the globe – he goes on to repeat the feat twice more. Immensely curious, his career is that of an explorer, writer, collector, merchant and part-time pirate.

(*Below right*) The Chinese scholar Shen Fuzong, who visits England in 1687, painted by Godfrey Kneller. With Shen's help, the Frenchman Philippe Couplet introduces the works of Confucius to the West the same year.

Mary Beale (*above left*) has a good claim to call herself the first professional female artist in Britain … and Aphra Behn (*above right*) can call herself the first professional female writer. Here Behn appears painted – fittingly – by Beale.

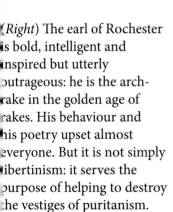

(*Right*) The earl of Rochester is bold, intelligent and inspired but utterly outrageous: he is the arch-rake in the golden age of rakes. His behaviour and his poetry upset almost everyone. But it is not simply libertinism: it serves the purpose of helping to destroy the vestiges of puritanism.

JOANNES EVELYN ARMIG.
REG. SOCIETATIS SOC.

Two great diarists: Samuel Pepys (*above left*) and John Evelyn (*above right*) both painted by Godfrey Kneller. Of all the literary genres, it is the art of self-awareness that reaches its apogee in this period, and these two men are its greatest exponents.

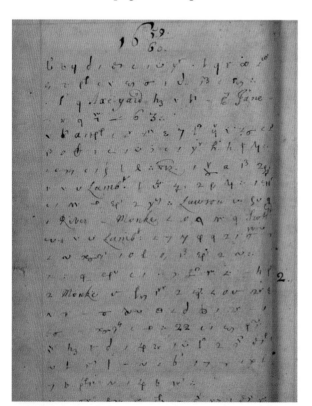

And here is a page from the greatest literary artefact of the age, the diary of Samuel Pepys showing his shorthand – by which means he conceals the astonishing honesty from his wife and servants.

the spring rises up in, which is furred with a white scum which rises out of the water: if you keep it in a cup but a few hours, it will have such a white scum over it ... The taste and smell is much like sulphur, although it has an additional offensiveness like carrion or a jakes [earth toilet].[8]

This is what you are supposed to drink. The water imparts its mineral qualities and at the same time opens your bowels to remove all impurities from your body. In Celia's case, 'I drank a quart [two pints] a morning for two days and hold them to be a good sort of purge if you can hold your breath so as to drink them down.'

After you have emptied your bowels in this fashion, you should make your way over the hills to St Mungo's Well, seven miles away. There you may immerse yourself in the mineral spring. But unlike Bath, you won't be spending a couple of hours sitting in a warm soup: the water is freezing. This suits our Celia, who declares, 'I always choose to be just where the springs rise [because] that is much the coldest.'[9] By her day Thomas Sydenham's advocacy of cold-water bathing and taking fresh air, especially for those suffering from a fever, has started to become popular.

Ralph Thoresby regularly goes to Harrogate. Normally his first morning draught after arrival upsets his constitution so much that he can do very little the following day. In 1680 this means he has to miss church – hence taking the waters upsets his conscience as well as his bowels. Thereafter, however, he delights in spending days drinking the sulphurous water, walking for exercise in the company of new friends and riding with them to St Mungo's Well, shivering alongside them in the chill water, and finally dining with them after the day's ordeals are over.[10] But not everyone is so enamoured of taking the waters. Thomas Baskerville states that

At your first coming hither you shall meet with a troublesome delight, an importunity among the women here almost as eager as that of the watermen of London, who shall be your servant to fill water to you when you go to the wells, or bring it to your lodging when you do not. And this clamour we were fain to endure because we were not resolved to drink the water, this evening and next morning – for they got into our chambers before we got out of our beds – with pots of water one cries out 'I am pretty Betty, let me serve you.' Another cries

'Kate and Coz Dol, do let we tend you,' but to tell you the truth, they fell short of that, for their faces did shine like bacon rind, and for beauty may vie with an old Bath guide's ass, the sulphur water had so fouled their pristine complexions.[11]

Your physicians and friends will no doubt suggest that you try various other spas. Tunbridge Wells is popular with the wealthy: coaches come down from London, and there are coffee houses and trinket shops around the walk that leads to the spring.[12] If you can't actually get there in person, you can have the water bottled and sealed with a cork and despatched to you wherever you are in the kingdom. Epsom waters are similarly conveyed in corked stoneware jars. But wherever you drink them, these waters will have much the same effect. In 1662 Schellinks observes men and women in Epsom taking different routes away from the well after they have drunk several pints and putting down 'sentinels in the shrubs', as he delicately puts it.[13]

If you think that the theory of the humours is a little odd, the fashion of paying a small fortune to 'take the waters', freeze yourself in a cold spring, swim in other people's cut toenails, warts and corns and violently empty your bowels in public every morning will surely strike you as utterly bizarre.

Hygiene

You might have gathered by now that your ideas about personal cleanliness do not exactly accord with those of the seventeenth century. This is not because people don't care about hygiene. Pepys takes the matter very seriously. When he visits Bath in June 1668 he cannot help but think, as we do, that so many unhealthy bodies entering the same water are more likely to spread their diseases further than cure them.[14] The difference between seventeenth-century cleanliness and our own is broadly one of necessity. In the modern world, we don't all wash our hands before every meal, let alone afterwards. This slackness would strike a seventeenth-century man as disgusting: washing your hands is that much more important when you eat with your fingers. As for bathing in the same water as other people, it is not that they don't care about the risks of infection but that the medicinal properties of the water outweigh the risks. You can see the same thinking applied in folk remedies. In Orkney and Shetland, if you get a bleeding nose you block it with pig dung. You use cow dung on a bruise, human urine for jaundice, and sheep droppings boiled in milk for smallpox.[15] People don't normally stick pig dung up their nose or sweeten their milk with sheep's excrement but the circumstances of the ailments require them to suspend normal behaviour. This general point explains many of the supposedly dirty aspects of life in the past: it is not a matter of negligence, but one of priorities.

Ideas about what constitutes normal 'cleanliness' are constantly changing. Most ordinary people will wash their hands, wrists, faces and neck – the parts that show – with cold water every morning. They rarely have a bath for the sake of cleanliness: the risks of infection from the impure water are too great. Instead, when necessary, they rub themselves and their hair vigorously with linen 'rubbers' or towels. This exfoliates the skin and removes any extraneous dirt. Wearing clean linen shifts, shirts and drawers then soaks up any sweat on the body: these garments can easily be washed, so that effectively the body is kept clean by linen, which in turn is cleaned in soap and water. Washing the whole body, bit by bit, in a basin of water is another way of cleaning oneself. For safety's sake, the water is boiled and then allowed to cool.

Apart from one visit to Bath, Pepys does not immerse himself in water for the whole ten-year period of his diary. In this he is not unusual. However, some people do take baths. One reason is medical treatment. Your physician may recommend that you bathe by yourself in hot water infused with certain unguents or herbs in order to cure a malady. Or he may advocate regular cold baths. As early as 1693, fashionable people are following Thomas Sydenham's advice that cold baths are good for your health.[16] This view is given powerful support in 1697 when Sir John Floyer publishes his seminal work *An Enquiry into the Right Use and Abuse of Hot, Cold and Temperate Baths in England*, in which he encourages cold-water bathing on the basis that it stops up the pores and invigorates the bather. Another reason for the growing popularity of bathing is that the practice is recommended by a few wealthy practitioners: Sir John St Barbe has a bathing house at Broadlands, in Hampshire, and Thomas Povey, a London merchant, has a bathroom at the top of his town house.[17]

The rise in bathing for the sake of cleanliness is mainly due to the influence of the Middle East. British diplomats who travel to Morocco or Turkey note that Muslims bathe regularly and expect others to keep themselves fastidiously clean. They return to Britain with their notions of purity altered, if not turned upside down. British slaves who have escaped or been liberated from their North African bondage similarly come back telling people about Muslim washing habits. Joseph Pitts's description is particularly interesting:

> They have a great many hammams or wash-houses to bathe themselves in, which they go into almost naked ... they leave their clothes in an outer room, put on a pair of clogs or pattens, and so walk with their guides into the hot places where, after they have been a little while, they grow into a great sweat, and having continued in it for some time, they have their armpits shaved by their guide, and then retire into a private room where they have their pudenda also shaved, accounting it very beastly to have it otherwise; after which they lie down on the smooth pavement and one of the guides or tenders, being ready with a glove made of coarse stuff or camlet, without fingers, and stuffed with something for that purpose, rubs their body all over, and cleanses it from filth. This they are very dexterous at, for as they are rubbing most parts of the body they will bring the rolls of filth like a worm (it may be two inches in length) under the glove upon the person's arm that he may see what need he stood in of cleansing ... Having washed all over and at last with soap, the guide for a while leaves every person to himself to throw water on his body, and this they may have from two cocks, one hot, the other cold, which run into an earthen pan or else a great basin of marble so that they may make the water of whatever temper of heat, or cold, they please.[18]

'Turkish baths' like this now exist in London. Elizabeth Pepys goes to one in 1660, on the eve of her visiting the queen.[19] She probably doesn't get the full shave down below – Samuel would surely mention it if she does – but otherwise it seems the Middle East is teaching Londoners how to be properly clean. Her very attendance at a hot bath on the eve of an auspicious occasion tells you that people have a positive attitude towards cleanliness, even if it does not affect their everyday behaviour.

Another development mentioned by Pitts is that now people are using soap to clean their hands and bodies. Most liquid soaps, which are used to clean clothes, are smelly and irritate the skin, but now cakes of Castile soap are cheap enough (3d per pound) that you might use it simply to wash your hands. Edward Jorden notes that washing your hands in the Cross Bath at Bath will make your 'finger ends shrink and shrivel as if [you] had washed in soap water'.[20] If you would prefer not to be bothered by body lice (as even a fastidious gentleman like Pepys is, from time to time), then you will make sure that you have a regular change of clean clothes and wash your hands and body with soap every day. Then your only physical irritants will be the fleas in the beds in the inns in which you stay. And toothache.[21]

Diseases and Their Remedies

The landscape of illness is an extraordinary terrain, some parts of it as fast-shifting as a chalk cliff being eroded by spring tides, other parts as constant as the peaks of a mountain range. It is difficult to know at any given time which diseases fall into which category. Seventeenth-century people have even less idea than you. For example, they have no way of knowing that the plague of 1665–6 will be the last major outbreak in Britain; they remain in fear of it for decades. Moreover, some illnesses they suffer from are simply unknown to modern medicine. You will find it even harder to determine which ailments affect us but not them. In short, all diseases are like stories, in that they come amongst us, linger for an indefinite period, are passed between cultures, change in their telling over decades, centuries or millennia, and then disappear. And after they have been forgotten, there is nothing left to say how they started, continued and ended.

One of the clearest illustrations of the differences you can expect to encounter is a comparison of the major causes of death. In the modern world, the eight biggest killers in Britain are heart disease, lung cancer, emphysema/bronchitis, stroke, dementia, pneumonia/influenza, bowel cancer and either prostate cancer (for men) or breast cancer (for women). Compare these to the biggest killers of adults, as reported in the London Bills of Mortality.

Principal causes of death in London (by %)

Disease	1663–4	1673–4	1683–4	1693–4	Average
Consumption (tuberculosis)	20.58	18.41	16.19	16.15	17.83
Convulsions	6.52	10.35	15.99	20.50	13.34
Ague and fever	13.03	10.26	11.58	18.12	13.24
Griping in the guts	5.95	11.69	12.35	7.46	9.36
Smallpox and measles	4.85	10.27	8.56	6.27	7.49
Teeth	6.01	6.21	5.19	6.26	5.92
Old age	6.97	4.91	5.77	5.60	5.81
Dropsy (oedema)	5.99	4.72	3.17	3.07	4.24

Although some of these terms probably fold into their modern equivalents – someone dying of old age in the seventeenth century would perhaps be diagnosed with heart disease or dementia in the twenty-first century – there is hardly any common ground between the two. No one suffers from smallpox in the modern world, and very few from tuberculosis in modern Britain. Measles and oedema are not major killers. 'Convulsions' are fits predominantly suffered by children, which are rare occurrences in the twenty-first century. On the other hand, cancer is not a worry for most Restoration people: they are more concerned with their teeth. *What? Deadly* toothache? We all know that to visit the past is to run the risk of dental caries and fearsome surgical instruments but the pain of primitive dentistry is as far as our imagination goes. We never think of there being a significant risk of death from dental problems. But there you go – the landscape of illness is, indeed, constantly changing.

PLAGUE

Plague is an intermittent disease, hence it does not appear in the above list of major causes of death. In the five years of 1660–64, just sixty-one people die of it, out of 85,096 people buried in the London area

(0.07 per cent). On this basis it hardly warrants a mention. Even if all the Bills of Mortality for the period 1660–1700 are taken into account, plague only ranks as the fifth-biggest killer.[22] However, in terms of perception, it ranks as the most feared disease by a long way. In 1665, 68,596 people in the London area are reported to have died from plague. But that figure is an under-recording: people bribe the searchers to say they don't have the plague – that their loved one has died of spotted fever or an ague instead – so that their house won't be boarded up with them inside. The average annual number of deaths in London from all causes in the five years before the plague of 1665 is 17,019; therefore the actual number dying of the plague that year is more likely to be around 80,000 – one-fifth of the population of the city.

As you are probably aware, the plague is caused by a bacterium, *Yersinia pestis*, which lives in the guts of fleas, which in turn live on the black rats that infest households in every town and village in Britain. When the fleas bite a human, they pass on the infection. If the infected person himself has fleas, these too can become infected when they bite him. They may then carry the plague to the next person to wear his clothes. People at the time do not know that rats and fleas are the agents of their doom; they suspect dogs of conveying the disease.

If you catch the plague, your temperature will rise to about 40°C. You will vomit, suffer headaches and become feverish and perhaps delirious. A blackish-green carbuncle will develop on the skin where the flea bit you, and the lymph nodes in your groin, neck and/or armpit will swell into black buboes. After a while you will develop the 'tokens' of the plague: a mass of large subcutaneous spots that can be almost any colour from orange and purple to blue and black. Most diagnoses of plague are made by 'searchers' – two women in every parish who visit the house of a deceased person carrying white wands and, for the fee of one groat (4d), will examine the corpse to discover what he or she died of, and inform the authorities.

The Great Plague of 1665 is, of course, not the first epidemic to hit Britain. London has suffered many minor outbreaks over the previous hundred years or so, with major ones occurring in 1563, 1603 and 1625. All three of those killed more than one-fifth of the population. Each new onslaught is termed 'the Great Plague', as the immediate suffering is considered worse than anything that has ever happened before. The same is true of the plague of 1665, although, proportionally speaking, isn't quite as deadly as the three outbreaks mentioned above.[23] People have short memories. Indeed, it is precisely this shortness of memory that contributes to the spread of the plague in 1665. Past experience has led to the development of a series of Orders about what magistrates should do to control the disease when it is found in a locality. They are to meet every three weeks, consult the searchers, arrange for the killing of dogs and levy a local tax for the maintenance of the sick. If the searchers find an infected person, the house is to be closed up with all the occupants inside; a red cross is to be painted on the door and a watchman set to ensure that no one goes in or comes out. Dire punishment is threatened on those who leave: to escape is to commit a felony for which you can be hanged, whether or not you have the plague. Such orders are, of course, aimed squarely at preventing the spread of the disease, but in 1665 some people don't remember how deadly an outbreak can be. They see the incarceration of victims as cruel and uncharitable. In April, one of the first houses to be infected is in the parish of St Giles-in-the-Fields. The magistrates order it to be sealed up but the neighbours object to such unchristian behaviour: they obliterate the red cross on the door, force the padlock that has been placed on it and release all the inhabitants as if they were victims of an injustice.[24] You can understand their feelings but they are making a terrible mistake. The infected victims emerge and mingle with their rescuers – and the plague spreads rapidly through the parish. More than 3,000 people die in St Giles-in-the-Fields as a consequence.

If you visit London in the latter half of 1665, your memory of the experience will probably never leave you. The sight of the painted red crosses – sometimes whole streets of doors boarded up, one after the other, with watchmen standing by – is deeply disturbing. Seeing some of the noble town houses in Covent Garden piazza so marked is no less disquieting than the boarding-up of old wooden houses in the alleys. Nowhere is safe. The streets are empty, many of the shops are shut. Parish bells ring out constantly, especially at night as corpse after corpse is carried to burial. Bodies are left in coffins in the lanes. People are found dead in their houses or lying in the streets, on the steps of wharves or floating in the river. People in the street cover their faces, avoiding even the gaze of the searchers with their white wands as they go from house to house. Fires are lit in the streets to fumigate the air. Men of substance who can leave the city do so; those who cannot, for reasons of business, send their wives and families into the country. Each day they gather in coffee houses and eagerly reach for the Bills of Mortality to find out if there is any abatement in the disease, only to find it growing worse and worse. Some weeks in August they read that more than 6,000 have died. At the height of the epidemic, in September, more than 8,000 die every week. By then there is no longer any hope of shutting up all the victims, and fear takes hold as people realise that those whom they meet in the street might have the disease. On 7 September, John Evelyn travels through the city to St James and says it is 'dangerous to see so many coffins exposed in the streets, now thin of people; the shops shut up and all in mournful silence, not knowing whose turn it might be next'.[25] By this time there is grass growing in some of the roads. Boats and wherries lie unused at the riverbanks, their watermen dead, or fled for fear that those who would employ them are carrying the pestilence. The following month Pepys writes:

> But Lord, how empty the streets are, and melancholy, so many poor sick people in the streets, full of sores, and so many sad stories over-heard as I walk, everybody talking of this dead and that man sick, and so many in this place and so many in that. And they tell me that in Westminster there is never a physician and but one apothecary left, all being dead.[26]

Across the whole of England, 86,859 more people are buried in 1665 than on average in each of the previous five years. The mortality in and around the capital accounts for the great majority of these deaths. But the rest of the country is not unaffected. There is terror in the provincial towns as their inhabitants realise that those fleeing London may well be bringing the plague with them. Fairs and gatherings of people are banned. Inns are closed, the inn signs removed by order in towns such as Northampton, so that travellers will not linger.[27] Exeter forbids access to all men and merchants arriving from London.[28] Along the highways men and women expire and, in some cases, are left to rot by the country folk, who fear to touch the dead bodies. A man who walks all the way from London to Dorchester is denied entry to the town and dies in a small hovel on a farm. Rather than bury him, the local people dig a huge hole beside the hovel and tip it and its dead occupant into it, burying the building as well as the man. Outside the well-guarded gates of Southampton, a family of three dies on a hillside, the wife's last act being to scratch a hole in the ground with her bare fingers for her dead husband, leaving his body half-buried as she herself dies.[29]

Over the course of 1665 and 1666, the disease breaks the defences of many towns. In Ipswich more than 1,000 of its 8,000 inhabitants are swept away. In Colchester the pestilence kills 4,817 people, half the population.[30] But the place that will probably stick in your mind more than any other is the village of Eyam, in Derbyshire. A parcel of cloth from London is opened in September 1665 by a servant, George Viccars, who, on finding the contents damp, unpacks everything and hangs it before the fire. After three days, the tokens of the plague are clearly visible on him; on 6 September he dies. Before the month is out, five more have died of plague. Twenty-two die in October. The disease continues at a lower level through the cold months, killing a few people every week, but everyone knows that the death toll will rise sharply when May and June bring warmer weather. Some suggest fleeing to the towns but the rector, William Mompesson, warns them that they thereby risk infecting many thousands more people. Instead he persuades them to isolate their entire village. A line marked by boundary stones around the parish is not to be crossed by anyone coming to or leaving Eyam. Food is to be brought to a certain point and paid for by money left in a stone cistern, where it is washed by running water. And then the terrible wait begins. Nineteen die in June 1666, fifty-six in July. Helpless and alone, the people of Eyam perish in their self-imposed isolation, tended only by each other and their minister. One woman, Elizabeth Hancock, loses her husband and all six of her children in the space of one week in August 1666 – and buries them all with her own hands near her house. Later that month, William Mompesson loses his beloved wife, Catherine. He writes to his patron, Sir George Savile:

This is the saddest letter that ever my pen did write, the destroying angel having taken up his quarters within my habitation. My dearest dear is gone to her eternal rest, and is invested with the crown of righteousness, having made a most happy end. Had she loved herself as well as me, she had fled from the pit of destruction with her sweet infants, and might have prolonged her days. But she was resolved to die a martyr for my interest.

The final burial from the plague in Eyam takes place on 11 October 1666. As Mompesson writes in his closing words on the tragedy: 'Our town has become a Golgotha, the place of a skull. My ears have never heard such doleful lamentations – my nose never smelled such horrid smells, and my eyes never beheld such ghastly spectacles.' In total, 267 people in Eyam perish due to the plague – 38 per cent of the population, twice the proportion that dies in London.[31]

OTHER DISEASES AND AILMENTS

The disease most likely to kill you in the seventeenth century is consumption – or tuberculosis, as you know it – which is the cause of death for more than one in six people in London and probably most of the urban and suburban areas of Britain too. People do not know that it is infectious: when several members of the same household contract it, people think the family has an inherited weakness. John Evelyn is convinced that the 'thick, dirty, smoggy air' that hangs over London is at least partly responsible, he declares in *Fumifugium*. 'This makes them vulnerable to thousands of diseases, corrupting their lungs and disordering their bodies, so that catarrh, coughs and tuberculosis are more prevalent in this city than any other in the world.' However, the actual cause is a bacterium. This is spread through infected cow's milk and the sneezing and coughing of those who already have the disease – hence its concentration in densely populated areas. Parish churches also encourage the disease to spread. Evelyn writes, 'is there under Heaven such coughing and snuffing to be heard as in the London churches and assemblies of the people, where the ... spitting is incessant'.[32] Symptoms vary enormously – the swelling of the lymph nodes in the neck that typify the King's Evil are a form of tuberculosis – but the classic ones are coughing up blood, weakness of the limbs, weight loss, sweating at night and fever. According to Nicholas Culpeper's *Pharmacopoeia Londinensis*, remedies include eating green walnuts, a bezoar stone (a concretion formed in the stomach of a goat) or the flowers of mallow bruised and boiled with honey and taken with a liquorice stick.[33] However, the physician John Symcotts notes in his casebook:

> Those that have a long, dry cough, wax lean and thin, feel unequal heats, especially after meals, have a quick and small pulse, covet the fire much, yet are hot within, and being [away] from the fire grow cold in hands and face, look pale and are often or continually troubled with a hoarseness, I never saw recovered.[34]

So, if you catch tuberculosis, it looks as though you are doomed – even if you do swallow the hardened product of a goat's gastrointestinal system.

'Ague and fever' comprises the third most common cause of death in the Thames region, but in the coastal marshes of Essex, Kent and Sussex, the Fens of Lincolnshire and Norfolk, the Ribble district of Lancashire, the Somerset Levels and the Holderness of Yorkshire, it accounts for more suffering than any other type of disease. The reason is that 'ague and fever' includes malaria, the greatest killer in human history. As you will no doubt be aware, malaria is spread by mosquitoes carrying the *Plasmodium* parasite. People living in the areas mentioned above often describe the disease as 'marsh fever'; other descriptions are 'tertian ague' (because it recurs every third day, counting inclusively, so every 48 hours) or 'quartan ague' (every fourth day, or 72 hours). This reflects the regular bursting of red blood cells in the body after they have been infected. Symptoms are shaking, high temperature, profuse sweating, headache, vomiting and diarrhoea. The one efficacious remedy is quinine, which, as we have seen earlier, is contained in Jesuit's bark. There are many dozens of alternative recipes and pills prescribed by physicians and apothecaries, but none are likely to do you any good.

'Griping in the guts' is a disease with which you are probably not familiar. It is better known to you as a form of dysentery, like 'the bloody flux', which is separately recorded in the Bills of Mortality but is far less common in Restoration London. The infection is carried by a bacterium and is particularly associated with the faeces: eating with your fingers and not washing your hands thoroughly, or washing your hands with contaminated water, is thus potentially fatal. You will surely know if you have dysentery by the bloody diarrhoea that follows. Culpeper suggests a large number of remedies, from vine leaves to pomegranate flowers and sorrel seeds.[35] Richard Tomlinson, another apothecary, suggests just as many in his *Medicinal Dispensatory*, from comfrey to cinquefoil and wild mulberries, but the high death rate in London testifies to the shortage of effective remedies. The same applies to dropsy. This ailment, being a swelling of part of the body, is a consequence of other maladies and thus has a wide range of causes. Go to an apothecary complaining of dropsy and you may well be given a pill containing such things as 'spurge-olive macerated in vinegar', dwarf-elder seeds, milwort roots and agaric.[36] Agaric, in case you are wondering, is a white fungus that grows on the larch tree in Italy and opens your bowels as effectively as the spa waters of Harrogate and Epsom. Otherwise it has no medicinal value whatsoever.

The Bills of Mortality group smallpox and measles together for the years 1687–1700. The reason for this is perhaps because they are both associated with children and young people, and in both diseases the skin is marked with disfiguring spots. Both are viral infections – not that seventeenth-century people know that – and are easily confused in the early stages. However, there are significant differences between them, not the least of which is their deadliness. In the period prior to 1687, smallpox kills more than ten times as many Londoners as measles: an average of 1,199 per year, compared to 109. But there are epidemics of both diseases from time to time, which increase your likelihood of infection. In 1674 no fewer than 795 citizens die of measles (the following year just one person does). In 1681 smallpox claims 2,982 lives; in 1666 just 38 die of it. Robert Hooke's servant Tom Giles is diagnosed with measles by Dr Diodati in 1677 but, when the red spots turn into the telltale pustules, it is clear that in fact he has smallpox. When he starts pissing blood, Dr Diodati advises him to be let blood at the nose and mouth: two surgeons accordingly remove 7oz of blood from his arm and from under his tongue. He continues to cough up blood and, when the doctors next come, they break the news to him that he is going to die. He expires shortly afterwards.[37] Hooke's beloved niece and housekeeper, Grace Hooke, recovers from the measles that same year, only to catch smallpox in 1679. She is prescribed 'Gascoyne powder', a fashionable new remedy, which makes her sweat profusely, and eventually she recovers. Even if you survive, you may well be marked for life with the scars of hundreds of pustules across your face. The good news is that, if you recover from the disease, you are immune thereafter. Evelyn, who loses two daughters to smallpox in 1685, comments on a woman whom he sees that year encouraging other young children to play with an infected child, in the hope of them catching the disease while still very young.[38]

The last major fatal disease in the Bills of Mortality is 'teeth'. In order to try and avoid your teeth killing you, you can use a dentifrice (a tooth powder) like the one sold by Robert Turner of London, which is supposed to 'scour and clean the teeth, making them white as ivory ... it fastens the teeth, sweetens the breath, and preserves the gums and mouth from cankers and impostumes'.[39] An 'impostume' is an abscess, and this is why the teeth are such a big killer. Pus-filled abscesses form inside the tooth or near the root when there is poor dental hygiene (and it has to be said that the tooth cloths of the day aren't up to keeping people's mouths clean). If the infection turns to blood poisoning, or swells and blocks the airway, it can prove fatal. If you have unbearable toothache, you have a range of options. You can try to ignore the problem and risk an abscess. You can ask a blacksmith to yank out the offending tooth with a pair of pliers. Or you can go to a tooth-drawer, a surgeon or an 'operator for the teeth' such as Peter de la Roche (one of the two royal dentists) and ask him to use a specialist instrument to remove the problematic tooth.[40] One such instrument is a 'pelican' – a metal claw fixed to a metal arm that is hinged to a support: the claw is placed around the tooth, the support is jammed against the jaw, and the tooth is levered out as the surgeon holds the patient's head firmly between his knees. Another instrument is a 'key': a hook that protrudes sideways from the barrel of a key-like tool. Using a left-hand and a right-hand key in conjunction, the dextrous surgeon can remove a tooth with greater precision than someone using a pelican. To say all such extractions are painful is to state the obvious: the advantage of this form of dentistry is not that it stops the pain but that it might save your life. Pain relief is available in the form of opium compounds (if you can afford them) or substantial quantities of alcohol. Apothecaries also have a large number of medicines for fastening the teeth, for loosening a tooth prior to having it pulled out, and for making all your teeth fall out. According to Culpeper, tooth removal may be brought about through the application of powdered earthworms. When Ralph Josselin's wife, Jane, is plagued with toothache, rather than earthworms, she reaches for that other good old cure-all, tobacco.[41]

You might want to watch out for a few other diseases too. Rickets is a skeletal deformity in children: it appears out of nowhere about 1630 and thereafter increases in prevalence. You are no doubt aware that the cause is not being exposed to enough sunlight, resulting in a deficiency in vitamin D. The development of the disease is thus a consequence of increasing urbanisation in the city of London – a quite avoidable problem – yet between 300 and 500 children die from it every year. 'The French pox', otherwise known as syphilis, is a sexually transmitted disease that, unsurprisingly, is on the rise in the capital. In the 1650s only six people were reported to die from it each year.

But in the swinging 1660s, under the rule of the merry monarch, the average annual number of deaths reported in London is at least ten times this number.

When it comes to mental illness, it is not the deadliness of the disease that is so distressing: it is the unremitting difficulty of dealing with someone who outwardly has nothing wrong with them and yet cannot behave in an ordinary manner. Classical medicine dictates that there are four varieties of madness: frenzy, mania, melancholy and fatuity, all brought on by different imbalances in the humours. Laymen add lunacy – supposedly caused by the phases of the moon – and 'distraction'. Culpeper suggests black hellebore for those who are driven mad with melancholy, rosemary flowers as a means to strengthen the brain, and drinking whey to 'help' with melancholy and madness, but these are of little real effect.[42] Thus families tend to keep their mad relatives at home in a cellar or a barn, locked away from public view.[43] There are a few private mad hospitals advertised in the London press from the 1650s, but the costs are high. Most famously there is Bethlehem, popularly known as Bedlam, the London hospital for the mad in Bishopsgate. If you wish to, you can go and watch the patients: the building is open for the curious to enter, like a permanent freak show, in order to raise funds. When it is rebuilt on a magnificent scale, to a design by Robert Hooke in 1676 at Moorfields, just to the north of the city wall, it is given long galleries from which visitors can view the inmates. Sadly, the majority of them will unwittingly entertain the prurient crowds for the rest of their days and never leave these walls.

One final medical problem must be mentioned, namely childbirth. It is a sad fact that for every 1,000 children born in England, 17 mothers are buried. That equates to a 1.7 per cent chance of dying every time you fall pregnant – which means a one-in-twenty chance of death if you have three children and almost a one-in-ten chance if you have six. Overall, 4 per cent of all women die giving birth.[44] One of the advantages of living in London at this time is that the Chamberlen family is based in the city. Dr Peter Chamberlen, who heads the family at the beginning of our period, has inherited a secret that enables women who are experiencing a difficult labour to give birth safely. Normally, if a child cannot be born, a surgeon will be called in by the midwives, to pull out the child with hooks and ropes, which invariably kill the child. In extreme cases the child is cut into pieces while still in the womb, for easy extraction. Obviously the use of sharp blades is hugely dangerous to the mother too, and many deaths are actually caused not by the childbirth itself but by frantic attempts to save the mother. The Chamberlens' secret machine, which they transport in a misleadingly large, elaborately carved wooden case, is actually quite small: a pair of obstetric forceps. Over the years the family has refined these so that the steel blades are curved to fit the head of the infant. No one else in Europe can offer you this service. When the Chamberlens operate, they don't allow anyone else to be present but the woman in labour. The secret makes the family both rich and envied, so that the College of Physicians in London has an uneasy relationship with Dr Chamberlen, his sons Hugh, Paul and John, and his grandson Hugh, all of whom practise midwifery. Only when the last member of the family dies without an heir in 1728 will the secret be discovered – for the benefit thereafter of every surgeon, midwife and, of course, every anxious expectant mother.[45]

Medical Practitioners

In Restoration Britain you are your own first medical responder – much more so than in the modern world, where you can simply pop along to see your local GP. A consultation with a physician or a surgeon is expensive, even if he lives nearby, so you don't want to pay out for medical advice if all you're suffering from is a cold. In addition, as most people live in the country and most medical practitioners live in towns, you will need to factor in the cost of his travel. Your messenger, who will contact the physician on your behalf, will have to pay his travel expenses in advance if you want to be seen in person, and even a relatively lowly provincial practitioner will charge about 2s 6d per mile.[46] Ralph Josselin frequently describes his family's illnesses as well as his own in his diary, but he almost never consults a physician because he lives at Earls Colne and the nearest doctors are at Braintree (9 miles away) and Colchester (10 miles). Thus, if you can deal with the illness yourself, you will do so.

To help you in your self-diagnosis and self-medication there are a great number of medicinal tracts available, such as John Tanner's *The Hidden Treasures of the Art of Physick Fully Discovered*, and popular books aimed at women, such as the late countess of Kent's *A Choice Manual or Rare Secrets in Physick and Chirurgery*. There are also affordable pharmacopoeias in the stationers' shops, such as Culpeper's English translation of the *Pharmacopoeia Londinensis*, which concentrates on cheap ingredients that are to be found in the fields, woods and hedgerows (hence its later popular name, *Culpeper's Herbal*).[47] *The Ladies Cabinet Enlarged and Opened: Collected and Practised by the Late Right Honourable and Learned Chymist, the Lord Ruthven* contains 270 medicinal recipes covering such diverse subjects as how to make artificial spa water, how to cure toothache with oil of cloves and opium (which sounds promising) and how to cure poor hearing with 'oil of snakes and adders' (which does not). In case you are wondering, this last recipe begins 'Take snakes or adders when they are fat, which will be in June or July, cut off their heads and take off their skins and unbowel them and put them into a glass gourd ...' The recommendation for gout in your feet is even more bizarre: 'Take an ox's paunch new killed and warm out of the belly, about the latter end of May or beginning of June, make two holes therein and put in your feet ...'[48] Mind you, it could be worse. When the bishop of Worcester suffers from gout in 1698, the archdeacon of London writes to him with an infallible remedy: 'drinking fresh urine of a cow, then fasting, a pint every morning'.[49] As a gout sufferer myself, I will be sticking to the tried-and-tested old recipe of the *colchicum* crocus; I don't hold with these newfangled cow's paunch and urine-drinking recipes.

Most people will not self-diagnose and self-medicate without talking to someone else about their symptoms. Therefore, unless you happen to have a physician in the family, you would be well advised to seek the advice of the womenfolk in the immediate vicinity. Old women and nurses have a poor reputation as medical practitioners and are often lampooned as careless, drunken hags, but you would be wise to trust their experience, especially with regard to diagnosis. When someone is seriously ill, the poor and old women of the parish are paid to attend them. They have thus seen at first hand a large number of ailments in every stage and have considerable experience of which medicines and healthful broths are effective and which are useless. What's more, in the 1650s the role of the medical 'nurse', as we understand it, suddenly comes to the fore. Before that decade, 'nursing' meant just wetnursing; now it also applies to women looking after the sick on a semi-occupational basis, requiring them to have certain skills and experience. Payments for nurses attending infectious illnesses such as smallpox and plague can be relatively high – 8s per week is usual, and higher fees are known. Payments for nursing mentally ill patients can also reach these levels.[50] Nurses are not allowed actually to diagnose or prescribe – although you would be wise to pay heed to their wisdom on both accounts. If there are some efficacious pills available from the local apothecary, no one will mind if she sends out for some for you.

If your symptoms leave you in doubt about what is wrong with you, and your family and friends can't help you, and the old women of the village are shaking their heads, then you have no choice but to seek the advice of a doctor. But what is a 'doctor' at this time? And where do you find one?

Before 1660, the term 'doctor' was used only in respect of men who had doctoral degrees from a university: you would come across doctors of divinity more often than doctors of medicine. But now the term is used much more loosely in medical contexts. Physicians and surgeons who only have a licence might be called 'doctor' by their patients. Thomas Sydenham calls himself 'Dr Sydenham' long before he actually obtains a doctorate. Even some apothecaries might use the title. What you need to know is how all these professions work in theory, and what each one does in practice.

PHYSICIANS

Physicians deal with the inner workings of the body, diagnosing illnesses and prescribing treatments. The most highly qualified are those who have studied at a university and emerged with a medical degree, either an MB or an MD. The best connected and most respected are also Fellows of the Royal College of Physicians or its Scottish equivalent, which is founded in Edinburgh in 1681. These are the most expensive medical professionals you can employ. Expect to pay a medical bill in the region of £2 per visit – although treatment of a serious disease can easily be ten times as much.[51] They will travel long distances for their wealthy clients, which is a good thing, if you are one; on the downside, they will frequently be unable to come to your aid if they are preoccupied with helping someone who is richer than you. Also, such men tend to be based in London and Edinburgh; a 1693 list of physicians printed by John Houghton only notes provincial

Fellows in Shrewsbury, Bath, Exeter, Canterbury, Northampton, Gloucester and Bishop's Stortford.[52]

If you can't afford one of the top-flight medical degree-holders, your next best bet is to send for a licensed physician. There are many sorts of medical licences available: some granted by the royal colleges, some by the Lord Chancellor, some by the universities and some by the bishops of England. To qualify for one from the Royal College of Physicians, a candidate has to pass three examinations in anatomy and physiology, pathology and the use of medicine. Needless to say, these require a good deal of knowledge. An easier qualification – and by far the most common at this time – is to apply for a bishop's licence. The applicant will be examined by a suitably qualified physician, who will then make a recommendation to the bishop's official as to whether or not to grant a licence. In many cases a petition will be submitted on the applicant's behalf by former clients, attesting to the effectiveness of his treatments and the purity of his moral life. Expect to pay a licentiate a consultation fee of 2s 6d or more, not including travel. Medicines are extra, too. On this subject, note that wealthy people generally pay twice as much as the poor. The reason is not a discount for the less well off but that physicians will prescribe the best medicines the patient can afford.

The lowest ranks of physicians on the qualification spectrum are self-taught men and women who prescribe and diagnose without any qualifications. These include gentlewomen who feel an obligation to help their tenants and their families; clergymen and their wives who are likewise called to help those whom the Lord has smitten; and apothecaries who take it upon themselves to advise their clients about which medicines are useful against certain diseases (but without any diagnostic training). In addition you will come across many itinerant practitioners, mountebanks and quacks. Sorting out the good from the bad amongst this lot is quite a headache. None of these unqualified practitioners are supposed to charge for their advice, so if they levy a hefty fee, that is one reason to be suspicious. Having said that, a clergyman might not charge you a penny and be full of goodwill, but will yet kill you through sheer medical ignorance. Be particularly cautious of those who stand up in marketplaces shouting about how wonderful their elixir is, or their ointments – especially one 'Alexander Bendo' on Tower Hill (it's actually the rake Lord Rochester in disguise). Likewise, don't trust men who arrive at your door offering to sell you cure-all pills. As with most things in life, if it sounds too good to be true, it's neither good nor true.

Will any of these physicians be able to cure you? Obviously it depends on your ailment as well as their experience. Even the best-qualified Fellows of the College are helpless to save their richest clients from time to time. It is salutary to remember the story of Sir Edmund King, MD, FRCP, physician to Charles II. In February 1685 he saves the king's life by quickly drawing blood during an apoplectic fit. The king is deeply grateful and orders that Sir Edmund be paid a reward of £1,000 – and then promptly dies.

If there is one physician who should be singled out above everyone else as being the best equipped to help you, it is Thomas Sydenham. He studies at Oxford in the 1650s, obtains a Bachelor of Medicine degree and moves to London, where he passes his examinations to obtain a licence from the Royal College of Physicians in 1663 and sets himself up in practice. He is never invited to become a Fellow of the College, and only late in life does he obtain a doctoral degree. What makes him so influential and successful is that he is original and not frightened to follow his own path, and does not feel obliged to stick to medical rules set down in the third century. Rather than seeing humoral imbalance as constructing illnesses, so that one disease can mutate into another, he sees each ailment as specific, caused by particles of morbific matter. He thinks symptoms are indicators of nature's efforts to rid itself of these morbific particles, and therefore the physician should work with nature, not against it. He is firmly opposed to the process of letting blood, and equally firm in his belief that every patient is unique. As John Locke says of him, 'you cannot imagine how far a little observation carefully made by a man not tied up to the four humours, or salt, sulphur, and mercury, or to acid and alkali, which had of late prevailed, will carry a man in the curing of diseases'. If a man is wasting away, Sydenham might prescribe him a roast chicken. If a woman has smallpox, he will not wrap her up to make her sweating worse or draw blood and further weaken her, but will get her up and about, making her breathe fresh air. With regard to consumption, he is the first English physician to advocate the use of Jesuit's bark as a remedy. Richard Talbor's fame in prescribing this cure for the ague is largely learnt from Sydenham's book on the subject. Sydenham remarks to John Locke in 1678 (the year Talbor is knighted by Charles II), 'I never got £10 by it; he has got £5,000.'[53] In the end, time will give Sydenham his due reward. Talbor will largely be forgotten, but Sydenham's fame lives on, in the efficacy of his cures and the originality of his methods, from which he becomes known as 'the English Hippocrates'.

APOTHECARIES

Apothecaries make up and sell the medicines that are prescribed by physicians – thus their businesses lie at the very heart of the medicalisation of society. Consider this fact: back in 1600, if people were suffering from a sickness that would eventually kill them, only about 5 per cent would seek professional medical help, even in the relatively prosperous south-east of England. The vast majority would either accept their lot or consult amateurs, such as clergymen's wives. Now, in the period from 1660 to 1689, about one-third of all seriously ill people in the south-east seek professional medical help when facing death; from 1690 on, half do. Other parts of England are only a little way behind. And the single factor that has changed this attitude to medicine more than any other is the availability of new medicinal substances. The value of the medicinal drugs imported in 1700 is roughly fifty times greater than it was in 1600.[54]

The ever-increasing demand for drugs and medicaments is what underlies the changes in attitudes to medicine; it also explains why the medical profession is expanding and changing so rapidly. In Canterbury, the number of apothecaries who are freemen of the city doubles over the course of the century – from thirteen in 1610 to twenty-seven in 1700. In Exeter, the number quadruples, to twenty-five.[55] Moreover, the volume and variety of medicines that they purvey are greater than ever before. In 1685, about a ton of Jesuit's bark arrives in London, along with half a ton of bezoar stones, ten tons of senna and a ton of opium. Many of these go straight into pre-ordered pills and potions, made up by apothecaries and sold over the counter. And this is where the apothecaries come into conflict with the physicians. The physicians realise the apothecaries are giving advice to their customers and think they are trespassing on ground that is rightly theirs, thereby doing them out of money. But is it an apothecary's fault if a woman enters his shop asking for Gascoyne powder? Why should he not sell it to her? After all, it is the cure that matters. By 1700 towns and cities are awash with apothecaries giving you advice about their wares.

Entering an apothecary's shop is quite a striking experience. The walls are lined from ground to ceiling with shelves on which row above row of chemists' blue-and-white ceramic jars are stored. You can read the names of all the exotic substances on the jars: agaric, aloes, ambergris, aniseed, bezoar stone, dragon's blood, gum traganth, Jesuit's bark, lignum vitae, opium, rhubarb, sarsaparilla, sassafras, senna, sulphur and wormwood, to name just a few. Among these you will also find bottles of distillations such as aquavitae and jars of herbs and ground spices (cinnamon, cumin, cloves, pepper, and so forth). Apothecaries also sell luxury consumables like chocolate, tea and coffee. There is a long table running down the middle of the room where the apothecary grinds roots to powder in a pestle and mortar, weighs out his wares on a set of scales, and bottles them up for the customer. Note also the spatulas and sets of ladles hanging on the walls, and the order book on the work surface. Above your head you may well see exotic trophies suspended from the ceiling, such as the skull of a shark or a stuffed crocodile. Nearby are his moulds for making pills, which, once prepared, are kept in drawers ready to be offered to customers. Among the medicines you'll also come across less desirable things: processed millipedes ground up and dissolved in wine (to provoke urine), woodlice boiled in oil (to be dropped into the ears), snakes' flesh (for the eyes), powdered burnt crab (for the bites of rabid dogs), sparrows' brains (to provoke lust) and the ashes of the head of a coal-black cat (for better eyesight).[56] To be fair, only about 10 per cent of medical recipes involve the body parts of animals. But even this small percentage is significant, for there is something fundamentally different from modern medicine in their grinding up animals and dissolving them in wine or oil for health reasons. It is reminiscent of people's attitude to food: that every creature has been put on Earth by God for mankind's benefit.

Perhaps most unpleasant of all the things you can find in an apothecary's shop are the human body parts. Most apothecaries will stock *mummia* – powdered mummified corpses from Egypt. Pepys goes to see one that has not yet been ground up at a merchant's warehouse in May 1668, noting that the body is all black and hard. The vendor gives him an arm as a souvenir. What could be the medical uses of powdered mummy? Rub it into your skin, you'll be told, to improve the tone. Alternatively, dissolve *mummia* in alcohol and drink it to cure internal bleeding. In fact, why stop at Ancient Egyptian bodies? A good apothecary will be able to supply you with the fat of recently deceased men to rub into your aching joints. The same unguent is also supposed to cure the scars of smallpox pustules. Charles II consumes powdered skulls in alcohol. This isn't some quack cure: it is recommended to the king on good medical authority. The noted physician Dr Thomas Willis – the holder of *two* medical degrees, a Fellow of the Royal Society and a Fellow of the Royal College of Physicians – prescribes a mixture of powdered human skull, ambergris, musk and chocolate as a remedy for apoplexy. The great scientist Robert Boyle also recommends powdered human skull as a medicine in cases of convulsions.[57] And Thomas Brugis has this recipe for the 'falling sickness' (epilepsy):

> [Take] a man's skull that has been dead but one year, bury it in the ashes behind the fire, and let it burn until it be very white, and easy to be broken with your finger; then take off all the uppermost part of the head to the top of the crown, and beat it as small as is possible; then grate a nutmeg, and put to it, and the blood of a dog dried and powdered; mingle them all together, and give [it to] the sick to drink ... both when he is sick, and also when he is well, the quantity of half a dram at a time in white wine.[58]

It sounds like a witch's brew. Frankly, the idea that smoking tobacco is good for your health is looking increasingly attractive.

SURGEONS

Whereas physicians traditionally deal with the inward illnesses of the body, surgeons deal with the outward aspects – problems of the skin, wounds, tumours, the breaking of bones, and so forth. As a result, their tasks tend to be less theoretical than those of the physicians, involving less ancient nonsense about humours and more practical observation. Indeed, many surgeons are very effective – for the good reason that, in a violent age, they have plenty of opportunities to practise. People are constantly injuring themselves and getting into fights. Many surgeons serve with the army or navy and learn such things as how to cauterise a wound or amputate a limb in the heat of battle. Even a surgeon working at one of the two London hospitals – St Bartholomew's and St Thomas's – will see a regular stream of broken and fractured limbs from road-traffic accidents and building-site calamities; rapier wounds from duels; gunshot wounds from murder attempts; and knife wounds from drunken fights. Add to these the skin diseases, swellings, spots, tumours, ulcers, buboes, aneurisms, hernias, fistulas, polyps, wens and rashes that occur on a daily basis, and you can see that a hospital surgeon works hard for his salary of £30 per year.

Having said a surgeon's work involves less theoretical nonsense than a physician's, there are elements that will cause you to scratch your head in disbelief. One of these is phlebotomy. The idea of drawing blood from a patient persists for a remarkably long time – long after the humoral theory that gave rise to it has fallen by the wayside. We have come across people having their blood let – Robert Hooke's servant, Tom Giles, in 1677 (for smallpox) and Charles II in 1685 (for apoplexy) – but almost everyone experiences it at some time in their life. Pepys has 16oz of blood drawn from his arm in 1662 – purely as a prophylactic precaution – and his arm is so badly affected the next day that he has to stay at home.[59] The experience costs him the large sum of 5s, too.[60] It is not money well spent. Phlebotomy weakens the body and unnecessarily puts you at risk of blood poisoning. Joseph Binns, a surgeon at St Bartholomew's Hospital, has to deal with several cases of bloodletting that result in gangrene.[61]

The other aspect of a surgeon's practice that will astonish you is the degree to which he will depend on laxatives. The first thing Joseph Binns does when faced with a new case is to prescribe a suppository, clyster or enema – anything to empty the patient's bowels. Headache? You'll be needing a laxative, sir. Broken leg from a cart accident? Laxative. Gunshot wound? Laxative first, then I'll remove the bullet. An ale-drawer at the Castle Tavern in Paternoster Row goes to see Binns after he has been smashed in the head with a tankard. Binns prescribes a suppository. Then he lets blood. And only after these two things have been done does he remove the splintered bone, dress the wound using warm medications and bandage up the patient's head. Before the patient leaves, Binns writes him a prescription of a suppository every day. The man recovers – as do the majority of Binns's patients, to be fair – but you suspect that if they gathered at the Castle to discuss their experience, they would all remark on how keen their surgeon is to make them shit like crazy. He even prescribes a laxative in a case of diarrhoea.[62]

The nature of surgery means that surgeons have to see their patients in person – they cannot simply diagnose by letter or by messenger, as some physicians do. This means that they tend to spread themselves out around the country, basing themselves in even the smallest towns. They build up relationships with people in their neighbourhoods and so they often obtain a medical licence on the strength of a petition signed by present and former clients. And because they are often the only medical practitioner in the area, they increasingly take on the role of a physician as well, diagnosing internal ailments and prescribing medicines. Thus they too start to be called 'doctors', even if they do not have any sort of medical degree. Some obtain licences to practise both medicine and surgery. In their practices you can see the beginnings of the modern General Practitioner's role.

When all is said and done, however, these men are still surgeons, and anaesthetics are still more than a century away in the future. That means these men are probably going to cause you more pain than you have ever imagined. You only need to take one glance into a surgeon's tool case to realise that your nerves are going to be severed and shredded, your blood is about to be spilled as freely as ale in a drunken man's tankard, and your bones are going to be lucky if they manage to retain the strength and consistency of custard. The shiny metal specula are enough to make you shudder – both the wide, screw-threaded ones for keeping your mouth wide open during dental work, and the narrow ones with teeth, for extracting objects in difficult-to-reach cavities. When you then see the scalpels, the knives, the skull saws, the bone saws, the pliers, the 18-inch-long pincers, the razors, the specially curved amputating knives, the drills for trepanning, the *elevatorium biploidum* (for lifting a smashed part of the skull), the syringotome (for opening fistulas) and the oversized sharp fork (used for mastectomies), you are going to quail.

One of the most feared regular operations – perhaps second only to limb amputation – is the 'cutting for the stone'. If you have a case of calculus in your bladder, not only will you feel excruciating pain but you will also regularly be pissing blood, vomiting and experiencing severe chills. The condition is dangerous – between forty and sixty people die of it every year in London. But the treatment is not exactly a walk in the park, either. It involves you being tied down to an operating table and having a 3-inch (7.5cm) incision made by the surgeon between your scrotum and your anus. He will then pull your nether regions apart, exposing the bladder, and will slice into this; when there is a big enough hole in your bladder, he will insert his fingers to feel for the offending article. When Pepys undergoes this operation, the surgeon, Thomas Holier, pulls out a stone the size of a snooker ball.[63] In his case, the calculated risk pays off. Not only does Pepys celebrate with a massive slap-up meal on the anniversary of the operation every year thereafter, but he freely offers advice to other people who are suffering from bladder stones. In 1669 John Evelyn persuades Pepys to show his stone to his brother, Richard, who is very worried about the operation. Pepys succeeds in talking Richard into it, and the date is set but, at the last minute, Richard backs out. He dies in agony in May 1670, although the stone in his bladder is later found to be no larger than a nutmeg.[64]

From a surgical point of view, however, cutting for the stone is one of the definite surgical success stories of the age: twenty times as many people die from the condition as die from the treatment. If you ever find yourself thinking that seventeenth-century medical knowledge is no good, think again. It could well save your life.

II

Law and Disorder

Lady Alice Lisle isn't your typical revolutionary. For a start, she's a gentlewoman. She's in her seventies, somewhat deaf, deeply religious and doesn't travel far from her beautiful home, Moyles Court in Hampshire. She has had nothing to do with politics for the last twenty years – ever since her husband, John Lisle, an MP who signed King Charles I's death warrant, was assassinated by two Irish extremists while in exile in Switzerland. However, when the duke of Monmouth clashes with forces loyal to King James II at the Battle of Sedgemoor on 6 July 1685, his defeat sets in motion a train of unforeseeable events. On 25 July, a nonconformist clergyman, John Hickes, who is in hiding with a friend after the battle, sends a note to Lady Alice asking if he and his companion can stay at Moyles Court. She innocently says yes, and invites them to dine with her that evening. A local labourer informs the military commander in the region, Colonel Penruddock, that Lady Alice is harbouring fugitives from justice. Penruddock searches the house and grounds the next morning and discovers Hickes and his friend hiding in a malthouse. He arrests them and their hostess, and takes all three to Winchester to stand trial. After a month in prison awaiting the arrival of the Chief Justice of the King's Bench, Lady Alice enters the dock. She is accused of sheltering traitors. That would be bad news in any circumstances, but two things make her situation very grave indeed. One is that her trial is the first of about cases concerning the supporters of the duke of Monmouth, so it is going to set the tone for the rest. The other is that the Chief Justice who will hear her case is none other than George Jeffreys, better known to you as Judge Jeffreys, probably the most notorious judge in all English legal history. He ruthlessly tears apart the testimony of those bold enough to speak in Lady Alice's defence. After a trial lasting six hours – a very long time by the standards of the day – the jury find her guilty, and Judge Jeffreys sentences her to be burnt alive for high treason. Traumatised, Lady Alice appeals to the king for mercy. James II decides that ruthlessness is the best policy. He merely changes the sentence from burning to beheading. On 2 September 1685 Lady Alice is led out of the inn where she has spent her last night and makes a short speech from the scaffold. She forgives those who have acted against her but insists that her only crime was to shelter a minister of the Church, on the grounds that he was a man of the cloth. She then kneels down and her head is cut off with an axe.[1]

Lady Alice's fate could have been worse. A few weeks later, Elizabeth Gaunt is accused in London of arranging the accommodation of her friend James Burton, who is also in hiding after Sedgemoor. When Burton is caught, he turns king's evidence and betrays Elizabeth. She is tried at the Old Bailey for treason on 19 October 1685. Although there is no evidence of her actually acting against the king – only that she helped Burton – she is found guilty and sentenced to be burnt to death. Her pleas for clemency fall on deaf ears. King James even refuses her the mercy of being strangled prior to being engulfed in flames. On 23 October she is taken to Tyburn. On the scaffold she holds up a Bible and makes a speech in which she declares that she only arranged to shelter Burton out of care for his wife and children, 'in obedience to the contents of this book'. She then arranges the straw of her pyre around her and dies with great dignity despite the agony – 'in such a manner that all the spectators melt in tears'.[2] Burton, the real traitor to James II, receives a royal pardon in return for betraying her.

These two examples of justice are not everyday occurrences, but they are indicative of common attitudes to the law. If you are accused of a crime, *your* highest priority will be that you have a fair trial. But in the seventeenth century the justice system has higher priorities, such as the safety of the monarch, the stability of the realm and the supremacy of the Anglican religion. Many judges would rather see a miscarriage of justice than set a suspected traitor free. Another strikingly different priority is the determination of many judges to uphold the law by applying the most horrific punishments possible. This is why Elizabeth Gaunt is burnt alive for her charity. Ironically, it is also why she sets about facing death so stoically – to show that the punishment is not so terrible that it makes her regret her actions. In the modern world we don't need such ghastly punishments as beheading old ladies or burning women to death to keep the vast majority of people on the straight and narrow; the near certainty of being caught and spending a long time in gaol is normally a sufficient deterrent. But in an age when it is difficult to track down a criminal, all the emphasis has to be placed on the agony that the state can inflict; it has no other methods at its disposal.

Another priority of the judges who will sit in judgement on you is the maintenance of the social order. As a result, the protection of land and chattels is considered far more important than the protection of mere lives. You can be hanged for the theft of something worth a few shillings but merely branded for killing a man or beating a servant to death. Nor is this emphasis weakening: from the 1690s, crimes against property that merit the death penalty are added to the statute books at the rate of about one per year.[3] If you think this is wrong – that a life is more valuable than possessions – then brace yourself for worse. Certain crimes committed by women are dealt with more harshly than those by men, for in carrying them out, women upset the natural order of things. If a man kills his wife, the crime is murder and the worst punishment is hanging; but if a woman kills her husband, the crime is petty treason and the punishment is to be burnt alive. In some cases, women are judged with a presumption of guilt. The Infanticide Act of 1624 presumes that an unmarried mother whose baby dies is guilty of killing the infant. Unless she can show that she is married or that the child was suffering from an illness, it will be deemed 'undeniable' that she killed her baby by strangulation and she will hang for murder.

The moral climate of the time demands that certain crimes are dealt with especially severely. Consider bigamy: what do you think is an appropriate punishment for someone who has married a second husband or a second wife? You might say that, as divorce is impossible, it is likely to happen quite often, and thus is an unremarkable crime – if it is a crime at all – and so the most appropriate punishment would be a fine. Restoration judges often deliver a sentence of death. Sixty-one people are indicted for bigamy at the Old Bailey between 1674 and 1700; thirty are found guilty, and six of those are sentenced to hang. James Cary, for example, marries Ann Clear in 1681 and, having left her, marries Mary Sergeant in 1694. The case being proved upon him by production of the 1681 parish register, he is found guilty and hanged. Similarly in 1693 Mary Stokes is accused of having married four men. She is hanged because she is 'an idle kind of slut, for she would get what money she could of them and then run away'.[4] One university-educated man who is said to have married no fewer than seventeen rich old women up and down the country is brought to the Old Bailey in 1676. He pleads guilty to four offences, confident in the knowledge that he will be transported to the West Indies. He obviously fancies a life overseas, seducing plantation owners' widows. The judge shakes his head and sentences him to the gallows.[5]

Other crimes are punished severely on account of their being considered against nature. Foremost among these are unlawful sex acts, which include rape, sodomy and bestiality. Marital rape is not a crime, as a man may do what he wants with his wife, and the rape of a servant is likewise not considered contrary to the order of things. However, outside the household, sexual crimes are taken seriously. The law is especially severe on men who force themselves on girls under the age of ten, who are deemed too young to be able to give their consent. Sadly, law courts regularly have to try men like William Harding, who in 1680 entices the eight-year-old Sarah Southy into a cellar by offering her apples; there he rapes her, stopping her mouth to prevent her from crying out. The crime is only discovered because he infects her with venereal disease. As for sodomy, this is a capital offence even when consensual (as explained in chapter 4). When not consensual, juries find it particularly horrific. Mustapha Pochowachett is a Turk who shares his bed with his fourteen-year-old Dutch servant, Anthony Bassa; one night in 1694 he stops the boy's cries with a pillow and rapes him: the jury has no hesitation in sentencing Pochowachett to death for buggery.[6]

Such is the level of revulsion caused by some reported sexual acts that the normal standards of evidence and judgement are suspended. A case in 1677 illustrates this well, and is worth quoting at length:

A married woman lately living without Cripplegate, that appeared to be between 30 and 40 years of age, was arraigned for that she having not the fear of God before her eyes, nor regarding the order of nature, on the 23 of June last, to the disgrace of all womankind, did commit buggery with a certain mongrel dog, and wickedly, devilishly, and against nature had venereal and carnal copulation with him. It was proved that the prisoner was a person of a lewd conversation, and lodging in a room into which there were several holes to look in at from the next house, they had often seen her in the very acts of uncleanness with villains that followed her; but one day one of the witnesses (a young woman) happening to cast her eye in, saw her use such actions with a dog as are not fit here to be recited. At which being amazed, she called up another woman, and after that a man, who all saw her several times practising this beastliness, and fully evidenced the same in court, where the dog was likewise brought, and being set on the bar before the prisoner, owned her by wagging his tail and making motions as it were to kiss her, which it was sworn she did do when she made that horrid use of him. For herself she had nothing to say, but denying the fact, alleging it was malice in the witnesses, which her husband, who appeared in her behalf likewise suggested, but could not make out any quarrel or occasion of any such malice in the least; whereupon after full consideration of all circumstances she was brought in guilty.[7]

You may think this amounts to a fair trial. Three witnesses would be enough to secure a conviction in a modern court. But let's look at the circumstances a little more closely. The crime is seen only through holes in the wall, which, if they went unnoticed on the other side, must be very small and discreet. The witnesses are all known to each other. All three are present on the day of the deed, and thus probably live next door to the accused. They often spy on her, by their own confession. They have a negative view of the men she entertains in her bed, whom they call 'villains', and by implication they have a low opinion of the woman herself. Thus they are clearly prejudiced against her, even before 23 June. Then comes the day of the supposed act. Maybe they are all genuinely horrified by what they see. Maybe they just hate their 'lewd-tongued' neighbour and decide to get rid of her. Maybe they fear her dog will bring plague into their row of houses, as she lets it into her bedchamber. We don't know. But you might notice that, although there is time for all three of them to witness the offence over and over again, they do not send for a constable or a person of similar authority. They collude in reporting her, because they want her dead: we can say that categorically because there are no lesser punishments handed out for crimes of this sort. The judge does not pick apart their evidence for its flaws; nor does he interrogate the first woman as to why she spies on her neighbour. He does not ask how the holes came to be there in the first place – or even if there actually are any holes for that matter; instead, he accepts her dog's mere recognition of its owner as confirmation of her offence. That is what this case comes down to: three people who dislike their next-door neighbour and see that they can exploit her weaknesses. If a judge in such a case does not want to give a woman in such a position the benefit of the doubt, then that is the end of her.

If you find yourself accused in this way, you may well have to resort to bribery to clear your name. In 1694 Edward Barlow, by now a very experienced mariner, beats an insubordinate sailor with a cane for refusing to carry out orders. Ten days later that sailor is one of four men who die aboard the ship. Most people would assume that the cause of death is an illness (as four men die at once), but the beaten man, swearing to his last breath that the blows are the cause of his suffering, persuades his fellow sailors that Barlow is responsible for his death. These men then tell the sailor's widow back in England. She searches out Barlow on his next visit home and threatens to have him arrested for manslaughter. Barlow thinks he has nothing to worry about but his friends persuade him that he is better off paying the woman £50 in compensation rather than risk a trial.[8]

High status and wealth also underlie influence that modern observers would describe as 'improper'. You will have difficulty accepting the means by which most MPs are elected: they either bribe the voters in their constituency or secure the goodwill of the land-owner, who directs his tenants to vote one way or the other. John Evelyn's brother, George, has to pay out £2,000 on food and drink to secure his Parliamentary election – and he feels it is unjust only on account of the large sum required.[9] Perhaps more reprehensible still is the practice of siphoning money out of government budgets. The Writer of Tallies is an office that originally had a salary of £91 per annum in the reign of James I. By the end of the century various office-holders have managed to raise that to nearer £300 – but, far more importantly, the incumbent charges fees worth £6,000 annually and has secured a pension worth £1,500 per year – all funded by deductions from ordinary soldiers' pay.[10]

I've said it before, but it is worth repeating: justice is a relative concept in all ages. If it is fairness you want from your legal system, I suggest you visit a period of history that prioritises the person over property, reality over religion, science over superstition, equity over influence and fairness over the process of the law. In finding such a time, I wish you luck.

Policing

The word 'police' is not yet in use in England; it still has to make the jump across the Channel from France. Nevertheless, there are several officers and organisations that perform similar roles. Every county has a sheriff, a Lord Lieutenant and one or two deputy lieutenants; these men, along with the Justices of the Peace, are responsible for maintaining law and order in their localities. On the whole, the Lord Lieutenant is primarily responsible for guarding against foreign threats, and the sheriff against domestic ones, including crimes. Every town has its bailiffs or beadles. Each county has its militia, a local force of part-time, semi-trained men who can be called out to put down riots or break up unlawful assemblies. Parishes have at least one constable, appointed by a local Justice of the Peace or by the parishioners: his role is to arrest suspects and bind them over, and to make enquiry into the circumstances of a crime. Often he will continue his usual occupation alongside his legal responsibilities, so you might find yourself being arrested by a baker, a butcher or a candlestick maker. In London, each of the twenty-six wards has a constable who breaks up quarrels and, in more serious cases, arrests the culprits and marches them off to the stocks or prison. Bellmen keep a watch for open and broken windows at night.[11] Selected citizens are obliged to patrol the streets of their ward, armed with halberds. These men constitute the town watch, and their like is to be found in most towns up and down the country.

It is worth knowing a few things about the powers of the sheriff and constables, just in case you find yourself on the wrong side of the law. The sheriff is responsible for maintaining the king's peace; executing the king's writs and instructions; summoning juries to try accused people; hanging them or otherwise punishing them, as directed by the king's justices; collecting fines; and examining smaller pleas in the county court. He and his officers are legally empowered to arrest you without showing a warrant. They may detain you at any time of day or night, and even on a Sunday (although no action at law may proceed against you on a Sunday, nor can any document against you be dated that day). A sheriff may break open any house to arrest you or to apprehend your goods in the case of a felony. Constables have similar powers in that they may arrest you for breaking the peace but, if they do so, unless it is night-time, they are obliged to take you straight to the county gaol – they are not permitted to lock you up in a private house or in the parish stocks. A constable may not arrest you for a violent act after it is done except with a warrant. He may arrest people on suspicion of felonies, especially nightwalkers, and he can search suspected bawdy houses for loose women. He may also detain people who sleep during the day. It stands to reason that, if you are sleeping in the daylight hours, you must have been up part of the night and probably up to no good. But it seems a bit tough if you are arrested simply for having a nap.[12]

The Administration of Justice

So you've committed an offence, the constable has raised the hue and cry and all the neighbours have chased after you and caught you. Now you are in the county gaol. No doubt you're cold and damp, surrounded by several dozen men and women in the same dark cell, some eyeing you up to see what you might have that's worth stealing or whether they can take advantage of you in some other way. What now? Of course, it depends on what you are accused of. Is your offence merely a misdemeanour? Or is it a felony, such as murder, housebreaking, rape or theft of something worth more than 12d? Either way, you are likely to be lingering in this dank cell for weeks, awaiting your day in court.

The seventeenth-century justice system operates at many levels. The highest courts in the land are those of King's Bench, Exchequer and Common Pleas. It is highly unlikely that you will have anything to do with these. Although King's Bench has the power to call in cases from lesser courts, it doesn't interfere with felonies, and you will only end up here if you appeal a judgement from a lower court or have taken part in a riot.[13] However, lawyers from all three courts regularly travel around the country to sit as assize judges. In that capacity they try those arrested for felonies – crimes sufficiently serious that they normally require a death sentence. Lesser offences (misdemeanours) are dealt with at a local level, by magistrates. Although magistrates no longer hang miscreants, they still have a wide range of powers, from imposing fines and floggings to more general administrative matters, like licensing. They also deal with routine local business, like bastardy disputes and bridge repairs, in the petty sessions. At a yet lower level there are manorial courts that will fine you if you cause a legal 'nuisance', such as allowing your cesspit to overflow on to the highway or letting your cattle trample someone's crops.

Running alongside this secular justice system is a similar hierarchy of ecclesiastical courts. At the top are the archbishops' courts, which have authority over the provinces of Canterbury and York. At the next level down are the consistory courts, which preside over individual dioceses. And below that are the archdeaconry courts. All these ecclesiastical courts deal with routine matters like probate administration and ecclesiastical buildings, but they also hear cases concerning the moral law. If you are an adulterer, your case will be heard by an ecclesiastical court. If you are a drunkard, philanderer, blasphemer, slanderer, defamer or someone who does not attend church every Sunday, it is the archdeacon's apparitor who will send for you and threaten you with dire punishment, unless you can produce compurgators or compurgatrices in court to swear to your innocence. On the whole these courts, like the manorial courts, exist in order to maintain order amongst neighbours; nevertheless you should be aware of their existence, lest you fall foul of their high moral standards.

At your trial you will face a few legalistic difficulties. First, there will be no assumption that you are 'innocent until proven guilty'. Experts in jurisprudence on the Continent are just beginning to discuss this idea but it has not yet touched British shores.[14] The next big problem you will encounter is that you don't have the right to remain silent in court. If you are asked a question, you have to answer. Standing mute is not an option. Then there is the lack of lawyers. A legal case is basically a confrontation between you and the person who is accusing you, in front of a judge and jury. No lawyer can speak for you until 1696, and then only in cases of treason or a misdemeanour – those accused of a felony have to defend themselves.[15] The thinking here is that, if you are innocent, the judge will ascertain this and direct the jury accordingly, so lawyers are unnecessary. That might set alarm bells ringing with you, and quite rightly. From the 1690s, lawyers start to appear for the prosecution – especially in cases of treason, sedition and libel – so things are doubly stacked against you, if you don't have a lawyer. Moreover, cases proceed bewilderingly fast. You might be on trial for your life but do not expect to have a hearing that goes on much beyond half an hour. Some are over in less than ten minutes.

When your trial begins, the indictment will be read out, detailing your supposed crime. A grand jury will be asked to decide whether the accusation is sufficiently well founded to proceed to trial. The prosecution can testify at this stage but you may not say anything in your defence. If the grand jury decides there is insufficient evidence, the case is dismissed and you are free to go. Forget about the weeks you spent in that miserable cell awaiting this moment; there is no such thing as compensation for wrongful detention. If the grand jury decides you do have a case to answer, then the indictment is marked as a 'true bill' and the case proceeds before a petty jury. First, you will be formally charged. Then you will be required to hold up your hand to acknowledge that you are the person accused and will be asked to enter a plea. If you plead Guilty, then the judge will proceed to sentencing forthwith. If you plead Not Guilty, the trial begins. Do plead one way or the other; if you refuse, there is a particularly grue-some ordeal awaiting you (described below).

Presuming you plead Not Guilty, you will be summoned into court by a crier, to stand before the bar that separates you from the scarlet-robed judge and his assistants. The judge then calls for twenty-four men to serve as a jury, selects twelve and asks if you have any objection to any of them hearing your case. You may object to up to twenty potential jurors in an accusation of a felony, or thirty-five in a case of treason; each one rejected will be replaced. When a set of twelve jurymen has been agreed, the indictment will be read out, as will your deposition. Witnesses for the prosecution will be called to give evidence under oath. You may inter-rogate them – indeed you must, for the onus is on you to prove yourself innocent, and you won't have a lawyer to do it for you. When all is said and done, the judge gives a summing-up speech and sends out the jurymen to consider their verdict. They are not allowed food, water or heat while they deliberate your fate; the law requires them to come to a unanimous decision as quickly as possible. In the 1660s, they can be locked up for contempt of court if their verdict displeases the judge. In 1670 this changes: a jury refuses to find two Quakers guilty of unlawful assembly and the judge imprisons them without food until they change their verdict. When they refuse to do so, he fines them 40 marks (£26 13s 4d) each. The foreman, Edward Bushel, refuses to pay the fine and so goes back to prison. He obtains a writ of habeas corpus and not only gains his freedom, but makes legal history. In granting the writ, the judge, Sir John Vaughan, establishes that juries are henceforth free to reach verdicts contrary to those of the judge. Bushel's Case is another little step along the long road to civilisation.

Scottish and English law are both descended from feudal law, and thus have much in common, but there are a number of important differences. Scottish law has its own hierarchy of courts, with the local and burgh courts at the bottom, the sheriffs' courts above them, and the High Court of the Justiciary (established in 1672) and the Court of Session at the top. Serious crimes such as murder, rape, treason, heresy, witchcraft and counterfeiting are dealt with by the High Court of the Justiciary. Scottish law has borrowed much more heavily from Roman law, so the processes and procedures vary from their English equivalents. Juries can still be locked up by a judge throughout the period. Torture is permitted (whereas it is not in England), and women are not normally allowed to give evidence. Punishments also differ. Witchcraft in Scotland is a heretical crime punishable by burning – although the condemned person has to be strangled first. There is no writ of habeas corpus, therefore you cannot insist that you be charged or released. But what will strike you as the greatest difference is that the king's writ is largely ignored in the Highlands and Islands. This is, after all, the only place left in Britain where you can still encounter the blood feud and medieval-style robber barons. Although the government tries to force the heads of all the clans to come to Edinburgh once a year to give sureties for the good behaviour of their clansmen, many do not attend. Even if they do, they are a law unto themselves. In 1671 Macleod of Assynt levies a tax on ships entering the water of Loch Inver; he also captures a neighbour and holds him to ransom. When the sheriff takes action against him, he defends his house with 400 men. After the government has issued a commission of fire and sword against him in 1674, Lord Seaforth and Lord Lovat storm his house with 800 troops, using a battering ram. They arrest him and drag him to the Tolbooth for trial – but the case against him is found Not Proven by a jury who are terrified of his revenge. And so Macleod returns to Assynt to carry on as before.[16]

Punishments

As you may already have realised, most punishments are carried out in public, partly to shame the condemned person and partly to deter others. In some cases, public humiliation is a key element of the penalty. Several men are arrested in 1660 for having sat in judgement on Charles I, even though they did not sign his death warrant. They are sentenced to forfeit their lands, titles and honours and to be imprisoned for life; but their punishment also involves them being drawn on a hurdle to the gallows every year, with a rope around their necks, as if they were going to be hanged. Nor do you need to have sat in judgement on a king to suffer such ignominy. As anyone who has spent any length of time standing in the pillory will tell you, it is not the pillory itself that inflicts the damage but the behaviour of the public. Executions are carried out in front of large crowds, and accounts of hangings are widely circulated in broadsides and official publications. *The Ordinary of Newgate's Account of the Behaviour, Confession and Dying Words* is one example, produced every time someone is executed in London. Its message is simple: the wages of sin are death – and not just any form of death, but a particularly agonising one.

PUNISHMENTS FOR TREASON

Of all the public executions that you really want to avoid, being burnt at the stake is surely the worst. Fortunately for men, it is not a punishment that we have to face in this period. Although, technically speaking, men can be burnt to death for heresy, this law has not been enacted in England since 1612 and is repealed in 1671. Women, however, are required to be burnt for treason as well as heresy. So there are days when the air at Tyburn and Smithfield is rank with the smell of wood smoke and burning flesh. Dozens of women die in this way, some for high treason and others for petty treason.

High treason not only includes offences against the king's person but also clipping the coin of the realm. Many people try to supplement their income by shaving off a small amount of metal from the rim of a coin, normally by clipping it with a pair of pliers and then filing down the edge. These filings are then melted down and sold. When women are found guilty of this offence, they are normally burnt at the stake, in accordance with the medieval law of treason. Edward Conyers and his wife Jane are two such coin-clippers. One day in early 1683 Jane sends their daughter out to buy bread and other groceries with two recently clipped shillings. One of the tradesmen is suspicious of the coins and reports the girl to a constable, who questions her. The girl breaks down and confesses that her father clips coins and that they have files, shears and melting pots in their house. A warrant is issued, the tools are discovered and both Edward and his wife are arrested. Found guilty of high treason, they are both sentenced to death. They die on the same day: Edward is drawn and hanged; Jane is burnt to death.

There are four different forms of petty treason: when a servant kills his or her master; when a child slaughters his or her parent; when a clergyman murders his bishop; and when a wife kills her husband. The first and last are by far the most common. In the last case, let's consider the crime from a woman's point of view. On the whole you don't have a great deal of say in whom you marry; most fathers want to marry off their daughters as soon as they can, both those at the top end of society (to make family alliances) and those at the bottom (to alleviate the burden of having to support them). Therefore although in theory a bride can say 'no' at the altar, she is under enormous pressure to say 'yes', even if her intended spouse stinks, drinks, snores, spits, gambles, blasphemes and is unfaithful and abusive. Suppose she says 'yes' to a man whom she grows to despise. Suppose they have rows and he beats her. Imagine that, in the course of one of their fights, she grabs the nearest thing to hand in order to defend herself. Unfortunately for one young woman in this situation in London in 1662, she jabs her husband with a tobacco pipe and the stem breaks: a sharp fragment enters his body and he bleeds to death.[17] At the trial it is plain to see that she struck her husband in anger and killed him, whether she meant to or not. She is guilty of petty treason, and there is only one punishment considered suitable.

The woman is taken from the gaol where she is held to the place of execution in a cart. Thousands of people follow her along the way, shouting at her, if they feel the need to vent their feelings, especially if they are relatives of the deceased; others throw things, such as rotten eggs. At the place where the punishment is to be enacted, she is manhandled from the cart to the huge oak stake, set hard in the ground. There an empty tar barrel that has had the bottom knocked out of it is passed over her head. Chains are placed around her body, fastening her to the stake. A long thin rope is looped around her neck and threaded through a hole in the wood. A clergyman then speaks to her of the approaching moment of doom, to help her make peace with the Almighty and to ask her to address the crowd, repenting of her sin. He prays with her. When he withdraws, dry straw is pushed into the barrel and strewn on the ground around her. Faggots are piled on top of the straw and close to her body, inside the barrel. Beadles stand guard with long staffs, using them to push back the raucous crowd where necessary. All the while street vendors are shoving their way between the people, selling pies and bottles of beer, or printed broadsides carrying woodcuts of previous hangings and burnings. Many families have been waiting for hours to get a good view, their children scurrying around between the mass of people, bored with the delays. But now the waiting is over, and they stand open-mouthed as the executioner sets fire to the straw.

When the flames rise, the faggots are alight and smoke is billowing around, the executioner *may* pull on the rope and strangle the condemned woman, her arms outstretched as she bids adieu to her friends in the crowd. As we have seen, in Scotland strangulation is a legal requirement of the sentence; in England it is not. Unless the king has forbidden it (as in the case of Elizabeth Gaunt), it is an act of mercy entirely at the executioner's discretion. If she has committed a particularly heinous crime and the crowd wants to hear the woman scream as she burns, he may dispense with the rope altogether. This is what happens to the woman who kills her husband with a tobacco pipe. On other occasions the wind whips up the flames too quickly and the executioner has to back off and is unable to hold on to the rope, even if he intends to be merciful. On such occasions you will hear the terrified screams of the victim and the gasps of the crowd, and you will start to encounter sensations more primitive than any you have come across in any other walk of life – terrible smells and sounds, and the profound shock that the society that you are visiting will render down a human being to just so much meat and fat, and let her die in agony, until she is mere ashes and splintered bone.

Men who are found guilty of petty treason, such as killing their employer, are 'drawn and hanged'. The penalty for high treason is to be 'hanged, drawn and quartered'. The 'drawn' bit of these sentences is the process of 'drawing' or dragging the condemned man to the gallows on a hurdle, so that he is humiliated in front of the crowd. If you are found guilty of high treason, the judge in court will declare that you shall be

drawn upon a hurdle or sledge to the place of execution, where you shall be hanged by the neck and cut down immediately, that your privities and your entrails may be separated from your body and burnt before your face; your head shall be severed from your body and your body divided into four quarters, to be disposed of according to the king's good pleasure.[18]

When a traitor's head is cut off, it is held aloft immediately with a cry of 'God save the king!' Some traitors are allowed to have a linen cap placed over their face, so that when they are cut down from the scaffold, it is not their head but their heart that is first cut out and lifted for the public to applaud.[19] The quartering involves cutting the corpse in half down the middle with a special broad-bladed axe, and then separating the chest of each half from the abdomen. In the case of political traitors, the four quarters of the torso, each with a limb attached, are set up above the gates of a town where the deceased is well known. Heads are put on spikes on London Bridge, the city gates and occasionally Temple Bar. It might strike you as utterly incongruous but it is a fact that in an age in which you can drink champagne and chocolate, listen to lectures by Isaac Newton and hear Purcell's operas, bloody pieces of human corpse are still hooked up above the main roads into the cities.

PUNISHMENTS FOR FELONIES

Most people who are sentenced to death are simply hanged, just as they have been for hundreds of years. In some places the familiar one-armed gallows is the instrument; in London it is the three-sided timber structure, which enables a dozen or more people to be despatched simultaneously. Many condemned felons dress up especially for the occasion: you might consider putting on a hat, cuffs and nosegay to mark the day. Some men even dress as bridegrooms on the day of their death. However you choose to be attired, you will be taken on a cart from gaol with other condemned prisoners and a clergyman to the traditional place of execution. Expect a large crowd to have gathered to watch you die. Some spectators might also have dressed specially: if you are a handsome young criminal known for your dashing and romantic gestures – like Claude Duval, a highwayman who has been known to dance with the wives and daughters of the men he has robbed – you might depart this world watching girls wearing white dresses strewing flowers from baskets before you.[20]

Along the way you should be given a final quart of ale. When you arrive at the gallows you might be allowed to say a few words or read a speech, as long as you do not make a claim to innocence (if you do, you will be cut short). Then a blindfold will be placed over your eyes, a noose around your neck and, with a crack of the whip, the horse and cart will suddenly be driven away, leaving you suspended in mid-air, slowly strangling yourself with your body weight, bobbing against the bodies beside you. Friends might leap on to you, hoping with such a sudden tug to break your neck. If they fail, the instinct to breathe will soon make your body twitch, which is called 'dancing' at the end of the rope.

There are two principal variations on the above routine, reserved for special crimes. Pirates are hanged under the jurisdiction of the court of Admiralty. They are generally held in the Marshalsea Prison at Southwark and led across London Bridge and through the city to Wapping in a processional cart in front of huge crowds, like those heading to Tyburn. They too are given a quart of ale along the route and permitted to make a final speech. But they are hanged at the water's edge, at low tide. Crowds watch from boats on the river as well as on the bank. After their dance of death has come to an end, they are not taken down from the gallows but left there for the tide to come in and wash over their heads three times. The worst of them are denied burial: their bodies are covered in tar and placed into a gibbet (a metal frame) and displayed for years to come, as a warning to others. It's a grisly sight, when you look out from a boat heading upriver and see the sunken cheeks and black eye sockets of a man's skull and the shrivelled skin on his bones, to the accompaniment of gently lapping water and the call of the gulls.

The other variation is to hang felons near the scene of their crime – a penalty most commonly applied to highwaymen. Highway robbery strikes a particular nerve throughout the whole of society. The thought that it might befall you at any time while travelling about your regular business is horrifying. Consider the case of Mr Robert Leaver on 11 July 1699. You might think he has taken every precaution necessary to avoid being robbed. Although it is late – between 10 and 11 p.m. – he is travelling on horseback with a servant and is carrying a sword, as well as pistols. Nevertheless, he is accosted by a gang of highwaymen led by Edmond Tooll as he crosses Finchley Common. The highwaymen rob both men and take their horses. Tooll leads his victims away from the road and his men set about tying them up. But Mr Leaver refuses to lie face-down and they stamp on his face and stomach in the darkness. He pleads for his life but, as he does so, one of them shouts that his servant is undoing the rope that ties him. Tooll then shoots a pistol in the darkness and hits Mr Leaver in the back. He slowly bleeds to death over the course of the night and the following day. But he lives long enough to give evidence. When Tooll is apprehended some months later and brought to the Old Bailey for trial, he remarks that he should have stabbed Mr Leaver in the heart. Unsurprisingly, he is sentenced to be hanged in chains near the place of the crime.[21] His body too is covered in tar and exhibited in a gibbet on the common. Sometimes the blackened corpses of highwaymen can be seen at waysides two or three decades after the execution, 'shrunk to their bones', as Pepys observes.[22] Each one becomes a landmark in its own right, as everyone in the locality knows exactly where 'the highwayman' creaks in the wind, day and night, eerily watching the road for travellers in death as he watched it in life.

If you are judged guilty of manslaughter rather than murder, then you will not be hanged for your crime. Instead you will be branded on the thumb (unless you are a peer of the realm, in which case you will not need to undergo this humiliation). Branding is also still used to denote those who have claimed Benefit of the Clergy. This is a remnant of the medieval custom whereby someone who could read was presumed to be a clergyman and therefore was not liable to be executed as a felon but instead was handed over to his bishop for punishment. These days many people are literate and lots of criminals claim Benefit of the Clergy for a first offence. They are not handed over to a bishop, but released; the branding on the thumb is to make sure they don't claim the privilege twice. You'll get a 'T' if you are convicted of theft, 'M' for manslaughter and 'F' for any other felony. You do still need to be able to read: if you claim Benefit of the Clergy and cannot read, then you will hang. Women are able to claim a limited version of the privilege but only when the stolen goods are worth less than 10s. In 1691, however, the law is changed: women henceforth can claim Benefit of the Clergy on the same terms as men. Don't turn to crime too eagerly, though, whichever sex you are. From 1699 you will be branded on the left cheek for theft, close to the nose. On the plus side, it still saves your life. On the negative, it makes it very difficult to get a job – not to mention what it may do to your romantic prospects.

Another alternative to hanging is transportation to the Plantations. From the 1660s certain classes of criminal who are sentenced to death can apply for a royal pardon in return to agreeing to serve a period as an indentured servant in the West Indies or America (although Maryland and Virginia refuse to accept condemned felons from 1670). The king's motive in proposing this measure is, as we have seen, a labour shortage overseas. However, English judges see transportation as serving a useful legal purpose: it allows them to impose a sentence that is stricter than the mere branding of the thumb and yet more lenient than death. Consider the case of Philip Johnson, who is tried in April 1683 for killing an infant, John Hill, aged about six months:

> John Hill's mother kept a public house in St Martins Parish, where of a Sunday night, at the beginning of the last month, Johnson came in to drink brandy, and after one quartern would have another, and go drink it in a private room with one he called his wife, which the land-lady refusing him, he threatened revenge before Saturday following. And on the Wednesday after about eight at night, came in a very rude manner, and breaking her windows, with other abuses, saying he had not yet revenge enough, the woman running to strike him, or defend her goods with the child in her arms, he struck it on the head with his stick, of which blow it died about seven hours after. Yet the jury being of the opinion that he had no premeditated malice to the child, but as it was accidentally in the woman's arms whom he might strike at, they found it manslaughter.[23]

It is easy to see why the judge in this case wants Philip Johnson to face a more severe punishment than mere branding, and so off he goes to Jamaica for a minimum of seven years.

Transportation is also a useful sentence in cases where the law would normally require the death penalty but there are serious miti-gating circumstances. In February 1682 Elizabeth Brown is found guilty of stealing a diamond ring, which she sells to a goldsmith. It easily counts as felony, for the value of the stolen item is far above 12d; so according to the law, she should be taken to Tyburn and hanged. But Elizabeth is not yet twelve years of age. The sentence of transporta-tion is thus used as a means to give her a second chance at life, albeit with the next seven years working as an indentured servant overseas.[24]

OTHER PUNISHMENTS

If you do not enter a plea you will be sentenced to suffer *peine forte et dure* ('strong and hard pain'), commonly referred to as 'being pressed'. The full penalty is as follows:

> That the prisoner shall be sent to the prison from whence he came, and put into a mean house, stopped from light, and there shall be laid upon the bare ground without any litter, straw or other covering, and without any garment about him, saving something to cover his privy members and that he shall lie upon his back, and his head shall be covered, and his feet bare, and that one of his arms shall be drawn with a cord to one side of the house, and the other arm to the other side, and that his legs shall be used in the same manner, and that upon his body shall be laid so much iron and stone as he can bear, and more, and that the first day after he shall have three morsels of barley bread, without any drink, and the second day he shall drink so much as he can three times of the water which is next the prison door, saving running water, without any bread, and this shall be his diet until he die ...[25]

In 1673 David Pearce and William Stoaks refuse to hold up their hands at the Old Bailey; they feel they should be tried in their native counties, where their supposed crimes have been committed, with local juries. The judge gives them one day to decide whether they would prefer to be tried in London or pressed to death; on returning to court, they both raise their hands. James Parker similarly refuses to plead in 1676 and is pressed under several hundredweight of stone before he gives in to the pain and asks to be tried. He is eventually hanged. Henry James refuses to plead in 1672 because his crime is 'so odious both in the sight of God and man' that he believes he does not deserve a trial. It takes him two days to die under the weight of the stones.[26]

The need for criminals not just to suffer, but to be *seen* to suffer, explains why imprisonment is only rarely used as a punishment. If you lock people up, the public forgets about them, and that is no deterrent. Although there are lots of prisons up and down the country, they are mainly used for holding people while they await trial.

There are some exceptions to this. Judges do occasionally impose a custodial sentence on a criminal but normally only in conjunction with some other penalty. Titus Oates's penalty for falsifying a Catholic conspiracy, with fatal consequences, is to be heavily fined, imprisoned for life, unmercifully flogged and annually exhibited in the pillory. If you are sentenced to serve a term of imprisonment, bear in mind that this might amount to a death sentence in itself. Most prisons are crowded, unsanitary and disease-ridden. Typhus is not called 'gaol fever' for nothing. The Old Bailey is open to the elements precisely so that the diseases of Newgate Gaol do not enter the court with the prisoners. Gloucester Prison – within the walls of the old castle – is said to be the best in England, with plenty of air, a bowling green and a 'neat garden', according to Thomas Baskerville. He writes in 1683 that 'if I were forced to go to prison and make my choice I would come hither'.[27] Fair enough. But convicted criminals don't get to choose where they are locked up. In 1661 Schellinks rides into Colchester and sees a very old man who has stolen a pig 'chained to a post in the street, with heavy iron rings around his neck and feet, his feet locked together and with a chain fixed to his neck, asking passers by for alms to keep himself from starving, else he would die from hunger and thirst'.[28] It seems the magistrates in Colchester have found a form of imprisonment that *is* publicly visible and thus can act as a deterrent.

Debt is another reason why people are imprisoned. Debtors are locked up in the Fleet Prison in London until they pay off what they owe. It is not quite imprisonment as you might imagine it: they have to pay for their lodgings and are allowed to go out in the daytime, if accompanied by a warden. But some people spend years there, unable to pay off their debts, with their lodging bills mounting higher and higher. There is some relief from the oppression by a measure of 1670, which allows the poorer debtors to swear an oath that they have less than £10 in the world; then those who insist on them being locked up until they pay have to fund their maintenance in the gaol, but this does not help people like Moses Pitt, an enterprising publisher who attempts to produce a scholarly atlas of the world in twelve volumes. After volume four he is heavily in debt and is imprisoned in the Fleet Prison in 1689 as a result. The title of his next book tells you what he thinks of his first two years in prison. In full it reads: *The Cry of the Oppressed: Being a True and Tragical Account of the Unparallel'd Sufferings of Multitudes of Poor Imprisoned Debtors, in Most of the Gaols in England, Under the Tyranny of the Gaolers, and Other Oppressors, Lately*

Discovered Upon the Occasion of this Present Act of Grace, For the Release of Poor Prisoners for Debt, Or Damages; Some of Them Being Not Only Iron'd, and Lodg'd with Hogs, Felons, and Condemn'd Persons, But Have Had Their Bones Broke; Others Poisoned and Starved to Death; Others Denied the Common Blessings of Nature, as Water to Drink Or Straw to Lodg On; Others Their Wives and Daughters Attempted to be Ravish'd; with Other Barbarous Cruelties, Not to be Parallel'd in Any History, Or Nation: All which is Made Out by Undeniable Evidence. Together with the Case of the Publisher. In all he spends seven years in the Fleet for debt. (And publishers think they have it hard today ...)

Corporal punishment still ranks high on most judges' list of favourite sentences. In London it tends to fall into two categories: whipping and the pillory. A boy, Philip Clarke, who is found guilty in 1690 of shoplifting a pair of gloves, is sentenced to be whipped through the streets of London, from Newgate Gaol to Aldgate, his hands being bound to the back of a cart. This is no easy punishment: the purpose is to draw blood. Women and children are sent to Bridewell for 'the correction of the house', which amounts to being whipped at the post. Thomasine Burton is found guilty in 1689 of shoplifting 60 yards of black crêpe, worth £3, which was discovered on her. As she was caught red-handed, she should be hanged. The jury shows mercy and so does the judge: they declare the true value of the goods to be merely 10d and the judge sentences her to be whipped at Bridewell, the reformatory prison, rather than through the streets.

The pillory is perhaps the best-known means of humiliating a criminal. You put your head and hands between the locked boards that hold you fast, and you face the crowd. For an hour. So what? you might think; an hour is not that long. And besides, isn't it quite funny to see someone exhibited like that? Ah, no. You certainly won't be laughing. That hour is likely to change your life for ever. It might even be the end of you, as the pillory occasionally proves fatal. In its grip, you are exposed for people freely to inflict their feelings on you – or, to be more specific, to express their feelings about you and your crime. They have the rare chance to show what they really think about those who attempt sodomy or murder, who blaspheme or spread misleading rumours, or who commit fraud or perjury. People in the crowd feel *their* reputations are under scrutiny too. In the case of boys and young men, there may well be attempts to outdo each other in viciousness. So they throw rotten eggs and vegetables at you; they empty buckets of urine and excrement over your head; they hurl stones, broken bricks, pieces of wood and dead cats at you. Sometimes they accidentally kill the condemned person. Even if they do not, your reputation is completely shot. You will never again hold up your head in the same town.

As we've seen, the Church courts in both England and Scotland are still in business, and these deal out the official punishments for immorality, such as having to stand in the marketplace on market day dressed in a white sheet, confessing that you've been found guilty of fornication. Again, the emphasis is on humiliation. This is especially sharp when you have to admit to adultery with a married man in front of all your kin and friends, as well as your own husband and his family. Excommunication still exists as a penalty, and is used as a punishment for those who have failed to perform their lesser penances or who have transgressed in a particularly ungodly manner. In England, such punishments carry less stigma than they did in the past. The Scots are far more assertive, trying fornication in the secular courts, along with incest, sodomy, bestiality, buggery and rape. Adultery too is taken seriously north of the border: adulterers are heavily fined; notorious adulterers are banished and, very occasionally, hanged.[29]

The extremists who would prefer to see fornication and adultery punished severely start to take matters into their own hands, especially after 1688, when it seems that God has put an end to the flagrantly immoral dynasty of Charles II and James II. Zealous magistrates have prostitutes arrested and publicly flogged. Societies are established for the reformation of manners; by 1699 they exist in London, Coventry, Chester, Gloucester, Hull, Leicester, Liverpool, Newcastle, Nottingham and Shrewsbury; and twelve more are being considered in other British towns.[30] They raise money to employ lawyers to prosecute brothel keepers and their clients. The Tower Hamlets society in London produces an annual Black List of the hundreds of lewd and scandalous persons they identify. More than a thousand prosecutions for sexual indiscretions are tried by magistrates in the capital every year. Offenders are flogged through the city or are set to hard labour. Brothel keepers are heavily fined. As a result, the majority of sexual policing and punishment is being organised by these societies by 1700.[31]

Alongside this new prudery you have older 'rough justice' – otherwise known as the court of public opinion. You will probably be aware of the cuckold's horns or antlers that are set above the door of a house

where the housewife has been unfaithful. Sometimes there are processions to mark the fact, led by a man holding aloft the cuckold's horns
on a pole, as the news of the woman's infidelity is spread around the
village. Occasionally this turns into a full skimmington ride. This involves
the villagers all gathering with blazing torches before the immoral house,
banging drums and pots and pans and generally creating a hullaballoo
for three nights; after three nights' interlude, they return for three more
nights, and then a third period. At the end they solemnly burn effigies
of the unfaithful wife and her cuckolded husband before the house.
In some places a skimmington ride involves a procession led by a man in
a white cap on a horse, wearing cuckold's horns and a fake beard, with
pots clanking under the horse's belly. He is followed by several hundred
people chanting and beating drums. When they come to the door of
the offender, they all start to sweep the threshold, one by one. They
are not supposed to enter the house but sometimes things get out of
hand and the errant husband is seized and placed on a horse facing
backwards, or the unfaithful wife is thrown into a pond or placed on
the ducking stool – a contraption normally maintained by manor courts
for teaching scolding women to keep their silence – and she is dunked
in the pond or river. It is a cruel punishment: the shame stings far more
than the cold water.

Evading Justice

It might seem that crime is on the rise and punishments are being
more frequently handed down than ever. Indeed, many people will
tell you that the country is going to the dogs. But people always talk
like this. They do not remember what things were really like in the
past; they hear about dozens of recent crimes and contrast those with
the few instances they can remember from their youth, and so convince
themselves that law and order are breaking down. In actual fact, the
crime figures are improving in Restoration Britain. Levels of law-
breaking vary, of course, but the underlying trend is downwards.
Despite the new Acts against theft and damage to property, the death
penalty is being less frequently applied. In the Middle Ages one in
three of those arrested for a felony would hang. In Elizabethan
England, between one in four and one in five would. By 1700, that
figure is down to about one in ten.[32]

One reason for this decline is a greater tolerance in society. Whereas before the Restoration, men worked to uphold one Church and to resist nonconformism, now there is less rigour in the maintenance of a single strict code of observance. Toleration in religious matters is accompanied by a more general relaxedness in matters to do with petty crime. You could say that jurymen are seeing greater virtue in being reformers of manners than persecutors of sin. In addition, the greater individualism in society encourages jurors to be more considerate of other individuals and more forgiving: they judge them as they would want to be judged themselves. Women accused of stealing valuable goods might well find themselves pronounced guilty by a jury that insists that the goods are worth less than the 10s threshold for hanging. Similarly many men accused of murder are found guilty of manslaughter purely because the circumstances of the killing are such that they do not deserve to hang. The English demeanour is softening in this regard, just as we observed with regard to cruelty in chapter 4.

If you are a woman facing a charge of felony, there are two other ancient legal traditions that may save you from the gallows. The first is that a married woman can claim marital coercion in her defence. As a wife is meant to obey her husband in all respects, if he commands her to break the law, then it is hardly her fault if she does so. This can play hugely to a woman's advantage, as the case of a London woman accused of clipping coins in 1677 shows:

> It is supposed her husband was the person that did actually clip, and that her business was to get money in fit for the purpose. It being proved that she often changed milled money for other but always desired that which was large or otherwise would not take it, which occasioned suspicion and her apprehension: which alarming her husband, he fled, and cannot be heard of. There were taken in her lodging abundance of files, melting pots and other implements of that kind, produced in court. However, because under such circumstances, our merciful laws, in favour of marriage, are pleased to suppose the wife's act to be done by coercion of the husband, and that he by flight had acknowledged his own guilt, she was brought in not guilty of the treason.[33]

That judgement saves her from being burnt to death.

The other advantage in women's favour that is being more frequently employed in this period is that pregnant women are not hanged. If sentenced to death, you may claim you are 'quick with child'. At this, a 'jury of matrons' will be assembled from those women present in the courtroom and, if there is sign of movement in your womb, then the death sentence is respited. You will stay in prison until the child is born. In theory, the death penalty can be inflicted after the birth but in practice most women are allowed to live. In 1685 twenty-nine women are sentenced to death at the Old Bailey, of whom eight (27 per cent) are found to be pregnant. The following year, six out of fourteen condemned women (43 per cent) are deemed to be quick with child. These are very high proportions when you consider that only about 5 per cent of women in London are likely to be carrying an unborn child in the fifth month of gestation or later at any given time.[34] You have to conclude either that pregnant women have a disproportionate desire to rush out and commit serious crimes – or that the women who have watched the trial and who form the jury of matrons often reach verdicts in favour of the condemned woman, regardless of whether she is pregnant or not. Considering the many gross disadvantages that women suffer on account of the law, it seems fitting that some escape condemnation and the ultimate penalty – through the compassion of those who are prepared to tell a lie to save their lives.

12

Entertainment

It is often said that you can judge a society by the way it treats its poor and needy, but it could also be argued that the spirit of an age is just as well gauged by what the people choose to do for fun. Of course, 'fun' is likely to include a wide range of activities and engagements, reflecting all the various interests, tastes and local customs of the time, not to mention wealth. Many townsmen and women find no greater pleasure in life than in dining well with convivial company. But, as a true traveller, you will no doubt want to look beyond the dining room and try to experience everything the period has to offer, from the sport of kings to the literature of the gutter press.

The Fun of the Fair

In chapter 5 we saw how some of the larger fairs remain important places for buying and selling, even if they offer drinking, gambling and other diversions on the side. But some fairs have lost their original *raison d'être* altogether and have developed into places of pure entertainment – although much of the entertainment on offer is anything but 'pure'. Foremost among these is Bartholomew Fair, held in West Smithfield, London. For most of our period it lasts two weeks, starting on the eve of St Bartholomew's Day (24 August), although in 1691 the authorities restrict it to three days. It is a labyrinthine mass of several hundred booths of iniquity, entertainment, vice and curiosity, and few Londoners can resist visiting it every year.

What are the attractions? You need to see for yourself. Ask your coachman to set you down at St Bartholomew's Hospital, which is as near as you can get to the fair before the stalls, booths, tents, platforms and crowds block your way. Perhaps have a drink first – it is not a bad idea to fortify yourself with a quart of strong beer before venturing further, to where the smells of unwashed bodies, roasting pork and tobacco smoke will warm your nostrils, and the noise of the crowds, drummers, trumpeters and street performers will assault your ears. Watch the dandies of the streets as they stroll through the crush of people with their silver-topped canes; and women 'who are no better than they ought to be' as they take in with a glance the looks of their respective admirers. People-watching is a key attraction. In fact, this is what Bartholomew Fair is really all about, with its actors, tumblers, sword-swallowers, fire-eaters, conjurors, gamblers, wrestlers, bearded women, acrobats, dandies, pickpockets, cardsharps, inventors, pretty women and handsome men. Look up at the galleries erected in the streets around Smithfield: here you'll see a group of amateur players performing the beheading of Holofernes by Judith or re-enacting the fall of Troy. Listen to the criers in the alleys advertising freak shows. Every pleasure here is transitory, every commodity temporary. Even the tokens and presents that you might buy – such as the broadside ballads, or baubles made of glass with objects suspended inside – are ephemeral.[1]

One act you will not want to miss is the rope-dancing. Pay a sixpence for entry to the enclosure and you will see some extraordinary antics performed by acrobats – some of them on a high tight rope, some on a low slack rope and some even on a trapeze. In 1698 Ned Ward sees all sorts of people making their way along the high rope with a pole in their hands: 'plump-buttocked lasses' who wear breeches under their petticoats, and then remove those petticoats when they are up above the crowd; and a huge Irishwoman whose thighs are 'as fleshy as a baron of beef', who 'waddles along the rope like a goose over a barn threshold'; and 'Doctor Cozen-Bumpkin', an idle fat chap who lies down, as if to sleep on the slack rope. But the prize of the show is 'The German Maid'. Ned quite loses himself in admiration and lust, for she 'does wonderful pretty things up the rope, having such proportion in her limbs and so much modesty in her countenance that I vow it was as much as ever I could do to forbear wishing myself in bed with her'.[2]

Many of the most renowned performers on the ropes in the 1660s and 1670s are Italians but perhaps the finest of all is an Englishman, Jacob Hall. Pepys sees him perform several times and is mightily impressed. His act includes flip-flops and somersaults on the rope, as well as 'flying over thirty rapiers' and 'flying through hoops'. The ladies are very fond of him, deeming him to be part Hercules and part Adonis. Such is his allure that the king's ex-mistress, Lady Castlemaine, takes Hall as her lover in 1667 and provides him with a salary for services rendered.[3]

Animals also perform on the high ropes. John Evelyn describes going to see them at the other major London pleasure fair in September 1660:

> I saw in Southwark, at St Margaret's Fair, monkeys and apes dance and do other feats of activity on the high rope; they were gallantly clad à la mode, went upright, saluted the company, bowing and pulling off their hats; they saluted one another with as good a grace as if instructed by a dancing-master. They turned heels over head with a basket having eggs in it without breaking any; also with lighted candles in their hands and on their heads without extinguishing them, and with vessels of water without spilling a drop.[4]

In 1660 you might be lucky enough to see the derring-do of a rope-dancer called 'The Turk' who performs barefoot. His stunts include dancing blindfold on the high rope with a twelve-year-old boy tied to one of his feet, who dangles 20 feet below.[5] He also stands on his head on a very high mast, before diving off it and sliding down a rope on his chest, head-first, with his arms outstretched – ouch! Visit around 1700 and perhaps you will witness an Italian family who have an act which consists of the father pushing out across the high wire a wheelbarrow containing two of his children and the family dog – all the time balancing a duck on his head, which quacks to the audience and causes much laughter.[6]

Even more dangerous is the act of 'Richardson, the famous fire-eater', whom Evelyn witnesses at work in 1672:

> He devoured brimstone on glowing coals before us, chewing and swallowing them; he melted a beer glass and ate it right up; then, taking a live coal on his tongue, he put on it a raw oyster, the coal was blown on with bellows until it flamed and sparkled in his mouth, and so remained until the oyster gaped and was quite boiled. Then he melted pitch and wax with sulphur, which he drank down as it flamed; I saw it flaming in his mouth a good while.[7]

You can't help but feel there have to be easier ways of making a living.

While the rope-dancers, sword-swallowers and fire-eaters are amazing, another prime draw of the fairs will horrify you. The intense curiosity of the age has an unwelcome side-effect in making spectacles of the less fortunate. This is harmless when it is limited to displaying animal deformities – such as the horse with hooves like ram's horns, or the goose with four feet and the cock with three, which are on show at Bartholomew Fair in 1663 – but it is deeply disturbing when it comes to human beings. Here you will discover the dark side of people-watching. If you want to see an Irishman so tall he can reach a point 10ft 6 inches above the ground and whose hand spans 15 inches, then the fair is the place for you. Then there's the Hairy Woman, who is not just bearded but completely covered in hair, including hair coming out of her ears and in tufts on her nose.[8] Roll up, roll up, to watch a forty-six-year-old dwarf who stands just 1ft 9 inches high, but whose arm span is 6ft 5 inches: he walks upon his hands and can jump on one arm onto a 3ft-high table. In 1681 you can view 'The Eighth Wonder of the World': a man born with no arms, who combs his hair and shaves with his feet and takes off his hat with his toes to salute the visitors. He can also use a knife and fork, thread a needle, write a letter and fill a glass from a bottle with his feet, for the spectators' amusement. The most distressing sights of all are the pairs of conjoined twins – the 'two-headed child' exhibited in 1699, or in 1682 the girls joined by the crowns of their heads, with their bodies diametrically opposite to one another, so that neither can ever sit upright or move, but can merely roll from side to side until they die.[9]

It is in this setting that many people make their first acquaintance with figures from Italian *commedia dell'arte*. You may see them in the form of marionette puppets, but they also appear as half-masked actors and even as rope-dancers. You probably know most of its famous characters: the colourfully dressed servant, Harlequin; the boastful coward, Scaramouche; the sad clown, Pierrot; his love, Columbine; the old man, Pantaloon; and the devilish Punch, with his beaked nose, warty forehead, projecting chin, hunchback and pot belly. Yes, the short-tempered, stick-wielding, conniving selfish buffoon is with us by 1662, speaking to the audience through a tin whistle or swazzle and prompting laughter in all ranks of society. People don't come to the fair just to gape and point at other people's deformities; they also come to see the common imperfections and deviousness of humanity – and thus, in part at least, to laugh at the monstrosity of what we ourselves are.

Now imagine all this on ice.

The Thames freezes above London Bridge several times in our period – and in the Long Frost of 1683–4 a 'frost fair' is held on the river. On 2 January 1684 the ice seems to be solid enough for people to walk across it. On 5 January some wag has a bet with a gentleman that he dare not drive his coach and six across it – only for the gentleman to demonstrate that the ice is indeed strong enough to bear them all. Within three days there are booths, eating houses, cookshops, alehouses, puppet shows and rope-dancers on the river. Coach trips are taken up and down the Thames. People hire skates and try ice-skating. Bulls and bears are baited on the ice, and a whole ox is roasted on 2 February.[10] The event becomes one of the marvels of the age; many painters depict it, and all the London writers mention it. And those ladies and gentlemen who pay 6d to have their names printed upon the Thames at a specially erected printing press have a lasting memento of the event – a small compensation for living through the coldest winter ever recorded.

Baiting Games

As described in chapter 4, the baiting of animals was banned by the Puritans. Now it is back, big time. Bears are thin on the ground but bull baiting may be seen in almost every town and village where cattle are slaughtered. The bull is led into the bullring, which is nothing more than a wide-open space set aside for the purpose of the spectacle. A 15ft rope is tied firmly to his horns and the other end to a ring attached to a stake driven deep into the ground. The crowd gathers around. The butchers hold their yapping dogs by the ears, ready to release them on the bull. Let Monsieur Misson tell you what happens next:

> The dog runs at the bull; the bull, immoveable, looks down upon the dog with an eye of scorn, and only turns a horn to him to hinder him from coming near. The dog is not daunted at this; he runs round him and tries to get beneath his belly in order to seize him by the muzzle or the dewlap, or the pendant glans, which are so necessary in the great work of generation. The bull then puts himself in a posture of defence; he beats the ground with his feet, which he joins together as close as possible, and his chief aim is not to gore the dog with the point of his

horn but to slide one of them under the dog's belly (who creeps close
to the ground to hinder it) and to throw him so high in the air that he
may break his neck in the fall. This often happens. When the dog thinks
he is sure of fixing his teeth, a turn of the horn, which seems to be
done with all the negligence in the world, gives him a sprawl thirty feet
high and puts him in danger of a damnable squelch when he comes
down. This danger would be unavoidable if the dog's friends were not
ready beneath him, some to give him a soft reception with their backs,
and others with long poles, which they offer him slant-ways, to the
intent that, sliding down them, it may break the force of his fall ...
Sometimes a second frisk in the air disables him from ever playing his
old tricks but sometimes too he fastens upon his enemy and when once
he has seized him with his eye-teeth, he sticks to him like a leech, and
would sooner die than leave his hold. Then the bull bellows and bounds
and kicks about to shake off the dog. By his leaping, the dog seems to
be of no manner of weight to him, although to all appearance he puts
him to great pain. In the end either the dog tears out the piece he has
laid great hold on, and falls, or else remains fixed to him with an
obstinacy that would never end if they did not pull him off ... While
some hold the bull, others thrust staves into the dog's mouth and open
it by main force. This is the only way to part them.[11]

Cockfighting is another bloody spectacle that engages huge crowds.
The inveterate sportsman Charles Cotton declares in his 1674 work,
The Complete Gamester, that it is 'a sport so full of delight and pleasure
that I know not any game in that respect is to be preferred before
it'.[12] It is so popular that you may well come across people setting
their birds against each other in the street or in farmyards. However,
the most highly charged events are held in the town cockpits.

Cockpits have a round area in the centre, which will either be covered
with sawdust (if on the ground) or rush matting (if raised on a table,
as in a modern boxing ring). Tiers of benches surround the fighting
area, so that everyone has a good view of the action. The spectators
range across society – from civil servants and gentlemen, to apprentices,
bakers, draymen, butchers and the poor in general. What is more, they
all gamble on the outcome; many people bet far more than they can
afford, so there is a sense of anticipation in the air. When the fighting
birds are brought forward from the wooden cages where they have
been kept, you can see that they have had their crests and low-hanging

wattles cut off. They have been fed with pepper, cloves and the yolks of eggs prior to the occasion, to make them more vigorous in battle. They also have long, sharp spurs of silver or steel affixed to their legs prior to being taken into the ring. Enter during the course of a fight and you will be greeted by a fug of smell and noise – chicken droppings, sweat, tobacco smoke and beer – and a highly charged audience yelling with eye-popping enthusiasm for the blows inflicted by one bird on another. Lorenzo Magalotti describes one cockfight he attends:

> As soon as the cocks are put down they walk around the field of battle with great animation, each watching for an opportunity to attack his rival with advantage. The first who is attacked places himself in a posture of defence, now spreading himself out, now falling, in his turn, on the assailant, and in the progress of the contest they are inflamed to such a pitch of rage that it is almost incredible to such as have never witnessed it with what fury each annoys his adversary, striking one another on the head with their beaks and tearing one another with the spurs, till at length he that feels himself superior, and confident of victory, mounts on the back of his opponent and never quits him till he has left him dead, and then, by a natural instinct, crows in applause of his own victory.[13]

The dead birds are sold to a butcher or cookshop proprietor after the show. Any bird that tries to run away from the fight has his neck wrung on the spot, and similarly ends his career in the catering industry.

Sports and Games

In his *Anglia Notitia*, Edward Chamberlayne declares that

> For variety of divertissements, sports and recreations, no nation doth excel the English. The king hath abroad his forests, chases and parks, full of variety of game; for hunting red and fallow deer, foxes, otters; hawking; his paddock courses, horse races etcetera; and at home, tennis, pelmel, billiards, interludes, balls, ballets, masks, etcetera. The nobility and gentry have their parks, warrens, decoys, paddock-courses, horse races, hunting, coursing, fishing, fowling, hawking, setting dogs, tumblers, lurchers, duck-hunting, cockfighting, guns for birding,

low-bells, bat-fowling, angling, nets, tennis, bowling, billiards, tables, chess, draughts, cards, dice, catches, questions, purposes, stage plays, masques, balls, dancing, singing, all sorts of musical instruments, etcetera. The citizens and peasants have hand-ball, football, skittles or nine-pins, shovel-board, stow ball, golf, torl-madams, cudgels, bear-baiting, bull-baiting, bow-and-arrow, throwing at cocks, shuttlecock, bowling, quoits, leaping, wrestling, pitching the bar, and ringing of bells, a recreation used in no other country in the world.[14]

This list sounds exhaustive but it is by no means complete. He's forgotten to mention hurling – the West Country ball game, similar to an extra-violent game of rugby. As for 'bow-and-arrow', archery might no longer be what it was in the Middle Ages, but 350 archers still turn up regularly to shoot at the marks on Finsbury Fields to the north of London, and prizes of silver arrows are competed for annually in Yorkshire as well as Scotland.[15] Then there are the spontaneous pleasures that occasionally arise, such as ice skating on the canal in St James's Park or on the frozen Thames, or pleasure-boating on a lake. Think of all the children's games, such as 'shoeing the wild mare' and cross and pile (heads or tails). And what about all the adult games that the above list does not include, such as cricket and hockey? In short, if you are wealthy and can turn your back on all the social inequality, illnesses and suffering, your life is probably one big pleasure zone. In fact you have so much choice, you will probably not know quite which game to choose. Therefore, here are brief descriptions of some of the most popular games and sports enjoyed in Britain.

ANGLING

Those who love angling will doubly enjoy their visit to the seventeenth century, first on account of the fishing itself and, second, for the chance to meet all the heroes of modern angling. Thomas Barker's *Barker's Delight or the Art of Angling* is first published in 1651, and two years later Izaak Walton's famous work, *The Compleat Angler*, hits the stationers' shelves. It is interesting to compare the various editions of these works to trace the development of the sport. For example, neither author mentions using a reel in early editions but both do in those published in the 1660s. Modern hooks are available from the London shop of Charles Kirby (inventor of the Kirby Bend). Fishing lines also improve with the development of a varnished gut line in the 1660s; the use of a gaff, for raising large fish, is first noted by Thomas Barker in the 1667 edition of his work. As a result of these developments, fly-fishing develops, as described at length by Charles Cotton in a considerable addition to the fifth edition of *The Compleat Angler* (1676). Fly-fishing obviously catches on quickly (if you will pardon the pun), for Magalotti is quite astonished to see English fishermen about their business in 1669. He writes:

> Their mode of angling here is very different from the common one; for, where our fishermen hold the hook still for a long time in the same place, these keep it in continual motion, darting the line into the water like the lash of a whip; then, drawing it along a few paces, they throw it in afresh, repeating this operation till the fish is caught.[16]

BILLIARDS

Billiards is older than you perhaps imagine. Not as old as Shakespeare would have you believe when he puts the words 'let's to billiards' into Cleopatra's mouth – thus implying that the pharaohs might have been hustlers on their evenings off – but dating back to before 1600. In its early days, however, it resembled more a form of table golf than the modern game. It is traditionally played with a 'mace', defined by contemporaries as a 'short, thick truncheon, or cudgel'.[17] This is used to push the ball around the table in the early form of the game. In the 1660s players start to turn the mace around and strike the balls with the tail end of it, or the 'cue' (from *queue*, the French word for 'tail'). The reason for the reversal is that the edge of the table is marked by rails and it is difficult to push the ball away from the rails with the thick end of the mace. By 1674, when Charles Cotton publishes the first edition of his *The Complete Gamester*, the edges of the table are surrounded with cushions or 'banks' stuffed with flax or cotton, and they have six 'hazards' or holes, like modern tables. Some versions of billiards are like the game we know as pool; others have a hoop ('the port') and a skittle ('the king') on the table as well. Billiard tables can be expensive: it costs the earl of Bedford £25 3s 3d to have a full-size one covered in green cloth installed at Woburn Abbey in 1664.[18] This does not put people off. Most towns and country houses have a table by 1680. John Evelyn, Samuel Pepys, John Locke, Celia Fiennes and Monsieur Misson all play billiards when they have the chance.

BOWLING

'A bowling green or bowling alley', writes Charles Cotton, 'is a place where three things are thrown away besides the bowls, *viz*: time, money and curses.'[19] Nevertheless you will find greens and alleys everywhere – and I do mean in the most extraordinary places. A Scotsman even builds one on a Thames barge.[20] In short, the whole nation is obsessed by the game. Willem Schellinks notes that there is a bowling alley in the Fleet Prison, just as there is one in Gloucester Gaol.[21] Almost every nobleman's and gentleman's residence has a bowling green. As he travels around the country, Thomas Baskerville makes a special record of which inns have particularly good greens: the Swan in Bedford; the Bull in Bury St Edmunds; the George Inn in Watton; and the Bear at Speenhamland, to name just a few.[22]

What is the reason for this popularity? First, there is the gambling. As with so many other sports and games, people place large sums on bowling and thus it is enormously exciting. Another reason is that it is one of the very few games that men and women can play together. Thus couples can play against other couples, as Pepys does with his wife and another couple in 1661.[23] This adds a social aspect and perhaps a sexual *frisson* to the game. But in case you are planning to win your true love's heart in this manner, be warned: it is a high-risk strategy. According to Cotton, bowling 'is the best discovery of humours, especially in the losers, where you may observe fine variety of impatience, while some fret, rail, swear and cavil at everything, others rejoice and laugh'.[24]

CARD GAMES

People of all sorts play cards – although separately: rich and poor don't play each other. Cotton lists no fewer than two dozen games in his *Complete Gamester*, namely 'ombre; primero; basset; picquet; lanterloo; English ruff; honours; whist; French ruff; brag; cribbage;

high game; gleek; all-fours; five cards; costly colours; bone-ace; wit and reason; the art of memory; plain-dealing; queen nazareen; penneech; post and pair; bankasalet; and beast'. If you want the rules to any of these, his book is the best place to look.

Huge amounts of money are lost on cards. Cotton refers to landed estates generating £2,000 and £3,000 each year being lost in this way.[25] In view of such financial ruin, the government passes the Gaming Act of 1664, whereby all losses of more than £100 are unenforceable. But the reality is that all ladies and gentleman play, and £100 is still a lot of money; moreover, people can lose £100 on numerous occasions if they are determined to risk that sum repeatedly.

CHESS

You know all about chess, the 'royal game', as it is sometimes called in the seventeenth century. However, there are still a few little discrepancies. Watch out for when one of your pawns reaches the far side of the board and is liable to be promoted: you can only change him to a piece that has already been taken, so you cannot have a second queen. Do clarify a few rules before you start, not least because many people bet large amounts on chess. For instance, in addition to 'checkmate' and 'stalemate', there is 'blindmate': this is when your opponent puts you in an inescapable check but does not say 'checkmate', not realising what he has done. Some people might tell you the game is over nonetheless; others that the game and the bet are both forfeit, or that the game is won but the bet is forfeit.

CRICKET

Cricket, unlike chess, is very far from reaching its modern form. It is not mentioned at all in *The Complete Gamester*, and the first set of rules won't be written down until 1744. However, you will frequently come across village cricket matches as you travel around the country. From its obscure roots as a form of stool-ball in the south-east of England, it has grown immensely and is now spreading faster than ever. The prime reason is, of course, aristocratic gambling: lords and gentlemen wager large sums that their team will win. But one should not neglect local pride, either. After all, it is not the taking part that matters, so much as hammering the visiting village's best bowler so hard that he has to walk back home to retrieve the ball.

In order to join in with a game during the Restoration, you'll need to be aware of some basic differences. There is normally just the one wicket and one batsman. The bat is curved, like a long-toed hockey stick. The bowler bowls underarm and aims to get the leather-clad ball through the wicket, which has just two stumps and a crosspiece. The ball may be rolled along the ground or it may bounce but, as the wicket is quite low, so too will be the delivery. If you're in bat, you must run to the bowler's crease and back to your own wicket and tap the umpire's staff, in order to score a run. Any number of players may be on the field – it is not limited to eleven aside – and there are no pads, gloves, helmets or any set costume. There are no organised teams: you just turn up and play when the captain asks you to do so. Finally, women do not play high-stakes matches alongside men. They are expected to play the old game, stool-ball, from which cricket developed (see below). If they do insist on playing cricket, it is normally at the instigation of some indignant cricket captain's daughter.[26]

FENCING

Fencing is still one of the accomplishments that form part of a young gentleman's education. In these days of duelling, that is just as well. Men go to fencing schools to learn how to fight and they practise in open fields with sticks. Most public fencing displays, however, are not between gentlemen, but between working men competing for prizes. Fights are put on in theatres and inns so that gentlemen can place bets on the outcome. Schellinks goes to the Red Bull playhouse in May 1662 to see a fight between a butcher's man and a porter: they don't have the requisite weapons so they borrow swords from the gentlemen present: 'it was dreadful to watch,' comments the artist.[27] Turn up at the New Theatre near Lincoln's Inn Fields in 1663 and you too can see fencers lacerating each other for the entertainment of the cheering crowd. Pepys goes along to spectate on 1 June and comments:

> it was between one Mathews, who did beat at all weapons, and one
> Westwicke, who was soundly cut several times both in the head and

legs, that he was all over blood. And other deadly blows they did give and take in very good earnest, till Westwicke was in a most sad pickle. They fought at eight weapons, three bouts at each weapon. It was very well worth seeing, because I did till this day think that it has only been a cheat; but this being upon a private quarrel, they did it in good earnest; and I felt one of their swords, and found it to be very little, if at all blunter on the edge, than the common swords are. Strange to see what a deal of money is flung to them both upon the stage between every bout. But a woeful rude rabble there was, and such noises, made my head ache all this evening.[28]

FOOTBALL

David Wedderburn is a schoolmaster in Aberdeen who writes a book, *Vocabula*, in 1633 to teach his pupils Latin by way of everyday expressions. The basic idea is nothing new: schoolmasters have been doing this for centuries. Wedderburn's stroke of genius is to include a section on the terms that his pupils might use on the football field. At first, sales of the book are slow – unsurprisingly, as no one is allowed to play football during the Commonwealth period – but after the Restoration, both the game and the book gain in popularity. Perhaps more use could be made of this method by modern teachers – promoting not only Latin, but also international understanding on the football pitch? I look forward to the day when I walk past playing fields and hear shouts of *Praeripe illi pilam si possis agree* (Tackle that fellow, if you can) and *Nisi cavesiam occupabit metam* (If you don't look out, he will score).

Football has been around for a good many years by 1660 and it has now acquired some unwritten rules. Teams play in a closed field that has a gate at each end, and each gate is a goal. The teams must have equal numbers and when someone kicks the ball over the hedge, thus putting it out of play, it must be fetched and kicked (not thrown) back in from where it went out. You may not simply kick another player in the shins; you have to make some attempt to play the ball. If you catch the ball on the full, without it bouncing first, you may make a mark with your heel; from that spot you may kick the ball without fear of being tackled.[29]

You will come across places where football is still banned. Although Winchester permits its boys to play it, the universities of Oxford and

Cambridge most certainly do not. Elsewhere, after the fall of the Commonwealth, many villages start happily playing football again with their neighbours every Sunday. Some Puritans still call it breaking the Sabbath, but more forward-thinking people realise there is less evil in playing football than in seeing young men in the alehouse. Monsieur Misson notes that the London youths play football up and down the streets in winter and explains to his readers that it is 'a charming exercise'.[30] Other foreigners do not find it charming. One Swiss traveller, having seen the windows of London houses and carriages smashed by football-playing youths, is shocked when the players, hearing the complaints of householders and passengers, simply laugh at them.[31]

GOLF

Golf is an expensive game. The feather-stuffed leather balls are whacked so hard that they easily lose their shape or split apart. You normally require one new ball per hole per player, so at 4d per ball, a round of golf across eighteen holes will cost you 6s in balls alone. The clubs, too, tend to break: each club lasts about ten holes. Iron-headed clubs are likely to cost you 2s each.[32] Of course, you can pay much more than this. On his visit to Scotland in 1679, James, duke of York, plays a round of golf. John Douglas of Edinburgh accordingly supplies a gross of top-quality golf balls at 5d each, costing a total of £3; he also provides sufficient 'sticks' for four players for a further £3 9s 2d.[33]

As it happens, that round has a claim to be the first international match between England and Scotland. The duke has an argument with a couple of his English-born noble attendants about whether golf is an English game or a Scottish one. The Englishmen's claim is not without foundation: Chamberlayne's list of English games includes golf; moreover, the English have been playing a similar game, stowball, for centuries (see below). But the duke, being of Scottish descent, stoutly defends the Scots' claim. And being who he is, he doesn't try to settle a historical question by asking a historian but decides it should be settled by a match. Thus he seeks a suitable Scottish partner and is told about John Patterson, a cobbler, who is the local champion. Thus it is that a duke and a cobbler set about defending Scottish honour. They defeat the upstart English lords, and that is that. If only all historical questions were answered so easily.

HORSE RACING

Horse racing costs a fortune – from the purchase or breeding of the horses to their training and stabling, veterinary bills, saddles and bridles and the price of merely travelling to and entering a race. Charles II spends £10,000 a year just stabling his horses. But 'the sport of kings' is even more expensive if you really *are* the king, as you have to entertain your guests and visiting dignitaries during the races, and provide food and drink of the highest order. Moreover, in 1660 the royal palace at Newmarket is in ruins – destroyed by the Puritans, who also tried to wipe out the breeding of racehorses. Charles thus has to rebuild the sport from scratch.

It takes him six years to get Newmarket properly up and running again as a great social event. Races recommence in 1663, and three years later Charles lays out the Round Course, to be run every October. He draws up a set of twenty articles or rules specially for this race: jockeys have to weigh less than 12 stone; they may not pull each other off or hit each other; they may not be servants or grooms; the entry fees of the horse that comes second are to be paid by the horse that comes last, and so on. All this may not sound unusual, but producing a *written* set of rules is unprecedented. Almost every other sport or game has acquired its rules gradually over the years and has never written them down; no royal authority dictates how you must play chess, for instance, or football, golf or cricket. Most sports will not have a set of written rules until the next century.

The king's initiative immediately finds favour with the aristocracy. The pattern of twice-yearly meetings established by the king at Newmarket is quickly followed at Epsom. Londoners also make the journey out to Banstead Downs in Surrey to watch the racing there. Studs develop specialist breeds of racehorses and by the time Monsieur Misson visits England in 1697, many are able to complete a traditional 4-mile course in sixteen minutes (in case you are wondering, the modern world record is half that). He watches one horse run 20 miles in fifty-five minutes. John Aubrey claims to know of a horse by the name of Peacock that can cover the 4 miles of the Salisbury Race in a little over five minutes.[34] Even though this time is not reliable it is evident that truly fast horses are to be found, despite the best attempts of the Puritans to wipe them out. Aristocrats accordingly reserve their largest and most ambitious bets for this sport, laying down stakes of up to £2,000 on a single race.[35]

HUNTING AND HAWKING

For many people the heyday of hunting is past. Wild boar have long since been hunted to extinction, and deer hunting is on the wane as more and more land is enclosed for agriculture. Most of all, the art of hunting with hawks is rapidly dying out. The earl of Bedford still keeps birds of prey: in 1671 he spends a total of £51 14s on birds, including £15 for a lanner and £8 for a goshawk.[36] The king too hunts with birds of prey from time to time. But, generally speaking, the art of falconry is fading fast.

One reason for this is the rise of fox hunting. Only a few rich men can come together to hunt with their birds of prey, but many people can ride in pursuit of a fox and enjoy the thrill of the chase. Being a large group of people, there is a strong social side to this form of hunting too: the Bilsdale Hunt in Yorkshire, established in 1668, is just one of several organised hunts that are set up in this period. Another reason for the decline in hunting with birds of prey is the growing popularity of guns among the rich. As a result of the Game Act of 1671, you must have an income of £100 per year to hunt with a gun, so the use of one becomes a status symbol. Guns are also easier to keep than birds, and a marksman can take a more personal interest in the kill than he can by merely letting loose a well-trained bird of prey.

PELL-MELL

Pell-Mell, or Pall-Mall, is a game like croquet. It comes to England in the reign of Charles I and finds favour with the aristocracy, who head to the Pall-Mall court on the south side of St James's Square, in London. Discontinued during the Commonwealth period, the game is restored to its former glory in 1660. It is played on a long, narrow enclosure with an arched hoop at either end. The players take turns striking the boxwood ball until they hit it through both hoops, with the one who does so first being declared the winner. Like most

Restoration games, it would be tedious if it weren't for the danger-ously high bets placed on each match.

RUNNING

Although competitive running must be one of the oldest sports of all, and is frequently mentioned in texts from the ancient world (just think of fleet-footed Odysseus in the *Iliad* or the original Olympic games), people don't think of it as a sport. But that changes in this period – and you can guess the reason why: gambling. Often two gentlemen will bet on their champion runners, just as they would on their horses. Pepys watches a 'foot race' in Hyde Park in August 1660 between an Irishman and an Englishman called Crow, who was once Lord Claypole's footman (a servant who runs alongside his master's coach). They run three times around the park (a total distance of about 12 miles) and Crow wins by more than two miles. Obviously being a footman is great training. Three years later, the king is present to watch a famous race on Banstead Downs in Surrey, between a man called Lee, who is the duke of Richmond's footman, and Tyler, a famous runner. The bets are all on Tyler winning but, again, the footman comes home first.[37]

It would be wrong to suggest that *all* the competitive running in the country is the result of gambling. We've already come across 'smock races' in which women undress to their smocks and run races for the prize of a new garment or a silver spoon. There are also old team games still being played in some parts of the country. Schellinks comes across a 'run' in Kent in the summer of 1661: teams of twenty men each gather in two corners of a level field and play what amounts to a complicated form of tag in front of several hundred spectators.[38] But none of these local traditions and games develop sets of rules or encourage the pursuit of excellence. Ironically, then, it is the vice of gambling that gives rise to the virtuous sport of athletics.

STOOL-BALL

Stool-ball – not be confused with stow-ball (see below) – is a traditional game not unlike cricket. The stool is the wicket. The teams are normally all-female but in some places the competition takes place between teams of young men and women, with the reward being a tansy – the flavoured egg pudding we encountered in chapter 9. However, as people do not wager large sums on the game, it does not come to much wider attention. It remains a ball game played among milkmaids and the boys who fancy them – or at least fancy their tansies.

STOW-BALL

Also known as stop-ball, this is very much like golf in that it is played with clubs or 'sticks' and hard, feather-filled balls. John Aubrey is of the opinion that it is only played in North Wiltshire, North Gloucestershire and part of Somerset, but in fact it is much more widely known: John Locke refers to it being played in Tothill Fields, in Westminster.[39] The difference between golf and stow-ball is that in golf the players try to sink a ball down a series of holes, whereas in stow-ball they hit out from a mark and set out for a distant pole, taking it in turns to hit the ball around it and back to the starting point. It can completely kill a conversation; a good striker of the ball will be hundreds of yards ahead of his opponent in a short while. Golf, on the other hand, requires some finesse to be displayed every few hundred yards, not just pure striking power. Thus players remain in proximity to one another and conversation can be maintained. And, most importantly in the Restoration period, golf gives gentlemen eighteen opportunities to bet, not just one.

TABLES

This is not actually a game in itself; rather, the word 'tables' denotes the board we use for playing backgammon, in conjunction with a set of dice. At this time people do play backgammon but they also play many other games besides, using the same tables. Charles Cotton mentions eight in his *Complete Gamester*: verquere, grand trick-track, Irish, backgammon, tick-tack, doublets, sice-ace and ketch-dolt. However, his explanations of the rules will leave you a little confused. Here is his instruction for ketch-dolt:

> The first throws and lays down from the heap of men without the tables, what is thrown at it might be sice-deuce. If the other throw

either sice or deuce, and draw them not from his adversary's tables to the same point in his own, but takes them from the heap and lays the ace down, he is dolted and loses the game, or if he but touch a man of the heap and then recall himself, the loss is the same.

Got that? No, nor have I. Stick to backgammon.

TENNIS

Forget about lawns and cucumber sandwiches: tennis in this period is exclusively of the indoor sort that we know today as *real tennis* or *royal tennis*. The ball is served on to the roof of the penthouse that runs along the left-hand side of the court and it can be played off the walls as well as the penthouse roofs. There are winning boxes called galleries that allow a point to be won instantly. It is a remarkably complicated game – especially when you consider that a ball bouncing twice on the server's side does not necessarily lose him the point but sets up a series of chases, which he can win later in the game by having the ball bounce twice closer to the back of the court than the second bounce of the ball he missed to set up the chase. Are you with me? It makes Charles Cotton's description of tables look straightforward. But the game is popular with the rich and that is what counts.

WRESTLING

Wrestling needs little explanation. You'll find it going on at fairs and in all sorts of open-air locations around the country. In London, if you just step beyond the wall out into Moorfields or go to the old Bear Garden on Bankside, you'll be bound to see a bout in progress. The umpire, or 'vinegar', throws two leather belts into the ring: the two contestants strip down to their breeches or drawers, take up the belts and put them on above the waist. No striking below the belt is permitted, but kicking your opponent's legs away is allowed.[40] And that's just about all you need to know.

There are two reasons to get excited about the wrestling matches, besides the action itself. First, there are the long-standing rivalries, such as that between the men of Devon and Cornwall, or those of the west and the north. The other reason is the betting – wrestling is one of the few sports in which the bets and prize money rival the money placed on horse races. Visit London on 19 February 1667 and make your way to St James's Park: a team of West Countrymen are set to take on a team of Northerners for the colossal prize of £1,000. The king is presiding and the umpires are the northern peer Lord Gerard and Sir William Morice, MP for Plymouth. Many large bets are placed. There is a lot of shouting from a crowd of working men and women, many of whom look as if they've been through a good few bouts themselves. Gentlemen like Evelyn stand in small groups, watching the straining muscles, the grasping and the crashing, as first one man brings his opponent down on the cold, hard ground, and then the next. The enormous prize means that everyone is spellbound by the spectacle being played out before them.[41]

I am glad to say that the West Countrymen win.

Sightseeing

The idea of travelling for pleasure is a relatively recent phenomenon. Even in the mid-sixteenth century, during 'the age of exploration', it was rare. People did travel long distances but only when they had to; most people found it safer and cheaper to stay at home. Now, however, driven by the immense curiosity that is the hallmark of the Restoration period, people are on the road for no other reason than they want to see the sights. You could say that, as far as tourism goes, the Rubicon has been crossed.

Most foreign travellers coming to Britain have a desire to see four towns in particular: Windsor (because of the castle), Oxford and Cambridge (because of the universities) and London (of course). Among the most popular destinations in and around the capital are Whitehall Palace (especially Inigo Jones's Banqueting House); the Royal Exchange; the royal tombs in Westminster Abbey; Nonsuch Palace (until 1682, when Lady Castlemaine has it demolished and sells the materials); St Paul's Cathedral (before it is destroyed by the Great Fire); Hampton Court; the royal tapestry works at Mortlake; and the Tower of London. Entry fees apply at some places: 3d to see the royal tombs and 12d for entry to the Tower. The latter may seem expensive but it's worth it. Here you will find not only Domesday Book and the archives of the English government since the reign of William I but also the royal menagerie, the royal armoury (including the armour of Henry VIII) and the Crown Jewels, which Colonel Blood unsuccessfully attempts to steal in an armed raid in 1671.

Foreign visitors and domestic travellers alike all want to see Stonehenge. It is counted one of the wonders of Britain by almost everyone who mentions it. Celia Fiennes, John Aubrey and Samuel Pepys all visit. Evelyn sees it and describes it as 'a stupendous monument'.[42] Monsieur Misson declares that the stones are 'a rarity worth a man's while to go a great journey to see' and adds that

> it is impossible to conceive either that they grew there or that they were brought thither or what use they could be designed for. This has given occasion to abundance of enquiries and to very long dissertations, and after all we are just as wise as we were before.[43]

He is quite right in that last assertion. Some people think that giants built it in ancient times, others think it is Saxon; some consider it the work of the Danes or Vikings, and Inigo Jones reckons it is Roman. Schellinks visits and outlines some of the theories he has heard, such as that it was brought by Merlin from Ireland, and that it was erected as a memorial by the Roman general who fought the Saxons, Ambrosius Aurelianus. Even Grand Duke Cosimo III alights from his carriage with Lorenzo Magalotti to view the stones in 1669 and, like everyone else, they are impressed by the dimensions and the engineering feat required to raise the upper stones into place. When Evelyn takes a chisel and tries to chop a bit off, he finds the stones harder than he thought. As the potential for archaeology to reveal our distant past is just beginning to dawn on learned men such as John Aubrey and John Conyers, Stonehenge stands as an icon of the combined sophistication and mystery of the unrecorded past.[44]

Apart from Stonehenge, it is the cathedrals and stately homes that attract the discerning traveller. Most of these will be open to you as long as you are of high enough social standing – you won't find the servants at Chatsworth showing labourers around the palatial rooms or the gardens. In case the idea of knocking on a duke's front door and asking to have a look around still worries you, rest assured: it is rare that an important man forbids travelling gentlemen and ladies a view of his house and gardens. If he has orange trees and Celia

Fiennes comes by and asks to see them, of course he will want to show them off to her. If his home is a fine Tudor residence with splendid furniture newly imported from France, of course he will welcome visitors who might regale other people with tales of the history of his family and the fineness of his furnishings, and thereby increase his social standing.

Museums

The gentleman's residence is the place where you will find the most interesting collections. Not only do gentlemen have the wherewithal to buy the best artefacts, they also have the necessary contacts to acquire them, the education to appreciate them, the space to keep them and – most of all – the desire to show them off. Thus learned men from the late sixteenth century on take great pride in their 'cabinet of curiosities': a room in their house devoted to interesting objects, normally of an ancient or exotic nature, which cause people to marvel, reflect or think differently about the world.

The grandfather of all these museums is Tradescant's Ark, a collection put together by John Tradescant the elder and his son, John Tradescant the younger. The elder John travels far and wide collecting rare specimens of plants and other interesting items, including trips to Russia and North Africa. His son travels three times to America searching for new flowers, plants, minerals and shells. Both men also have a wide array of contacts who send back exotic specimens from abroad, and they have useful connections with the nobility, who urge their own agents to send intriguing items to the Tradescants. In this way, by 1638 the Tradescants' collection has acquired a pre-eminent status amongst museums in England. Among many other things, they have the following items on show in that year:

> two ribs of a whale ... a salamander; a chameleon; a pelican; a remora; a lanhado from Africa; a white partridge ... a flying squirrel; another squirrel like a fish; all kinds of bright-coloured birds from India; a number of things changed into stone, among them a piece of human flesh on a bone ... all kinds of shells; the hand of a mermaid; the hand of a mummy ... all kinds of precious stones; coins; a picture wrought in feathers; a small piece of wood from the cross of Christ ... two

cups of rhinoceros horn ... Indian arrows such as are used by the executioners in the West Indies – when a man is condemned to death, they lay open his back with them and he dies of it ... the robe of the King of Virginia; a few goblets of agate; a girdle such as the Turks wear in Jerusalem; the passion of Christ carved very daintily on a plum stone; a large magnet stone ... a scourge with which Charles V is said to have scourged himself; a hat band of snake bones ...[45]

In case you're wondering, 'the robe of the king of Virginia' is a huge deerskin cloak stitched with thousands of white shells that once belonged to Powhatan, chief of the Virginian Native Americans and father of Pocahontas. But all this hardly gives you any idea how rich and diverse the museum is. In 1656 a 183-page description of the collection is published: *Musæum Tradescantianum, or a Collection of Rarities preserved at South Lambeth, near London*, the first museum catalogue to appear in Britain. When the younger John Tradescant dies six years later, he leaves the collection to Elias Ashmole. Ashmole combines the Tradescants' museum with his own and donates everything to the University of Oxford in 1683, where it is exhibited in a new purpose-built building, the Ashmolean Museum.

The Ashmolean is unusual in that it opens its doors to the public. Anyone can visit, on payment of a small entry fee. Many gentlemen are dismayed by this: they do not wish to share their visitor experience with the ranks of 'ordinary folk'. Tough, I say, if that's your view. The museum in Chetham's Hospital in Manchester is similarly aimed at the public. You will need to have the right contacts if you wish to see the East India Company's collections, including their birds of paradise, on show at India House. Sir Thomas Browne's London residence does not so much *have* a cabinet of curiosities, but *is* one: there you may see his famous egg collection as well as his assorted medals, books, plants, and so on. Ralph Thoresby not only visits all the museums in the country, but manages his family's own museum in Leeds, which is especially strong in its coin collections. By the end of our period the most sought-after tickets in London are to the immense cabinet of curiosities belonging to William Charlton (reputedly worth £50,000), the Royal Society's own collections in Gresham College, and the collection being formed now by Sir Hans Sloane, a wealthy physician. Sir Hans is only forty years old when the century ends – he still has more than fifty years of life left in him – but when he finally dies, he will possess an unrivalled collection. It not only includes Charlton's collection (which will be bequeathed to him) but many of the other major collections now being formed in England, including those of explorers like William Dampier. And, inspired by Ashmole, Sloane does a very good thing: he hands his museum over to the nation, thereby making it available for everyone to see. It will one day become the foundation collection of a new British Museum.[46]

Fine Art

Country houses and royal palaces double up as the nation's art galleries. If you consider that there are more than 16,000 gentlemen and people of similar high status in England in the 1690s, and if they have an average of just 15 paintings each (and some have ten times that number), then they possess about 240,000 artworks between them. If the greater clergy, men in administrative offices, greater merchants and lawyers – a total of 24,000 men – have an average of just 5 paintings a head, then they possess a total of 120,000 artworks. Add the thousands of artworks distributed amongst the royal palaces, urban guildhalls, livery companies, captains' cabins in ships of the line, and the art gallery that forms part of the Bodleian Library, and you can see there are probably in excess of 400,000 paintings in England – to say nothing of those in Scotland and Wales. Of course, there are hundreds of thousands of prints too. There is now an 'art world' in Britain that simply didn't exist a hundred years ago. If you are an aficionado of fine art in the Restoration period, you can have months of fun travelling around the country viewing the collections of your fellow gentlemen.

John Evelyn is a good example. He has been to Italy and seen the paintings of Leonardo and many other old masters in situ. Nowadays, based very close to London, he does not need to travel far to continue his interest. Every time he goes to Whitehall he can pop into the Banqueting House, look up and see the ceiling painted by Rubens. Elsewhere in the palace – which the artist Schellinks describes as 'full of outstanding paintings by old and new Italian, Dutch and other masters' – he can seek out paintings by Raphael, Holbein and Titian. In 1676, when dining with the Lord Chamberlain, he views a Raphael, a Leonardo and two paintings by van Dyck. Three years later, when dining at Buckingham House, he is able to inspect Titian's *Venus and Adonis* as well as other paintings by Titian, Bassano and van Dyck. Such is his knowledge of fine art that he is sought out by friends to accompany them to auctions. When Lord Melford falls on hard times and has to sell his collection in 1693, Evelyn goes along with friends and sees the hammer come down on a Murillo composition for £84 (which he deems 'dear enough') and a portrait by Rubens for £20. (Yes, I know what you're thinking: a Rubens for just twenty quid is a *very* good reason to visit Restoration Britain.) The following year he sees Corregio's *Venus* – acquired by Lord Mulgrave for £250 – which he declares 'one of the best paintings that I ever saw'. Clearly, if Old Masters are your thing, then the lack of a public 'national gallery' need not prevent you from indulging in your passion.[47]

In assessing artworks at this time, you will hear people talking in terms of the 'hierarchy of genres'. This is first promulgated by the French writer André Félibien in 1667 and very quickly adopted across Europe. According to this philosophy, the most important artworks are those of a historical and religious nature, of which the supreme examples are allegorical. Next in the hierarchy are portraits, followed by paintings of everyday life, such as a housemaid washing a doorstep or a housewife gutting fish. Fourth are landscapes; fifth, paintings of living animals; and at the bottom of the pile, pictures of dead animals and still-life paintings. This gradation has nothing to do with the skill required and everything to do with a painting's message: it is much easier to impart a moral lesson through depicting people and events than it is by merely showing animals and objects. A historical picture of the fall of Rome thus has meaning in the way that a goose on a pond or a flower in a pot frankly doesn't. It is important to realise that seventeenth-century people think like this: on the one hand, you have art; and on the other, you have mere pictures.

Everywhere you look, in the galleries of the great and the grand, you will see the lasting influence of Sir Anthony van Dyck. He was born in Antwerp in 1599, studied with Rubens, travelled extensively in Italy and lived intermittently in London until his death in 1641. His legacy was nothing short of a new style of portraiture in England. One glimpse at an English painting and you can see from the naturalism, pose and expression of character whether it is a pre- or post-van Dyck work. He also assisted in the purchase by Charles I of many Continental art collections, including that of the Gonzaga dukes of Mantua. Thus, even though he has been dead for nearly twenty years, you will still hear his name mentioned everywhere that fine art is appreciated. He is to British art at this time what Inigo Jones is to British architecture – the late-lamented father of all that is deemed excellent.

There are many good artists working in Britain in the wake of van Dyck. Indeed, the Restoration heralds a veritable invasion of artistic talent from the Continent. First and foremost is Sir Peter Lely, who steps into the role that van Dyck occupied prior to the Civil Wars. Born in Westphalia in 1618, Lely arrives in London soon after van Dyck's death and paints for a string of aristocratic clients. When Charles II returns to Britain in 1660, Lely is well qualified to slip into the role he always wanted: that of the king's principal painter. He portrays the king, the queen, the king's mistresses, the duke and duchess of York and many members of the aristocracy, as well as producing a few religious paintings. He also paints sets of portraits, including *The Windsor Beauties* (three-quarter-length portraits of a dozen of the most beautiful women at court), a similar set of 'beauties' for Lord Spencer's house at Althorp, and *The Flaggmen*, the duke of York's grizzled naval officers in the Second Dutch War (who are about as far from 'beautiful' as it is possible to get). If you want your own portrait painted, you will need to book an hour-long sitting at his house on the north side of Covent Garden piazza, where he will sketch your pose and paint your face and hands, and then pass over the work to one of his many assistants for finishing, while charging you the top rates. From 1670 these are £20 for a head study, £30 for a half-length and £60 for a whole-length picture. To put this fee in perspective, the Bristol painter John Roseworme, mentioned in chapter 8, charges just 7s for an ordinary-size portrait and 15s for a large one. Unsurprisingly, Lely grows rich but, rather than investing in a country estate, he spends his money on more art. By the time of his death in 1680 he has amassed one of the greatest art collections in Europe, numbering 575 paintings – including works by Rubens, Tintoretto and Bassano, and no fewer than twenty-four works by van Dyck – and more than 10,000 prints.[48]

Lely's position as the leading society portrait painter is quickly assumed by two other foreign-born artists, Willem Wissing (from Holland) and Sir Godfrey Kneller (from Lübeck), underlining how international the British art scene is in these years. Evelyn goes to have his picture drawn in October 1685 by 'the famous Kneller'. He sits again for him in 1689, with a copy of his famous book *Sylva* in his hand, for a portrait to be given to his friend Samuel Pepys. 'Kneller never painted in more masterly a manner,' writes Evelyn of that work.[49] Evelyn and Pepys are both much less complimentary about the other society portrait painter of the time, John Michael Wright. Pepys notes that there is a world of difference between Lely's work and Wright's, when he visits their studios on the same day in June 1662. Evelyn surveys Wright's portraits of the judges in the Guildhall in 1673, for which the artist has been paid no less than £1,000, and declares, 'I never took Wright to be any considerable artist.'[50] However, it is Wright who paints arguably the most iconic image of the whole Restoration: the full-length crowned figure of Charles II enthroned, holding his orb and sceptre and looking straight at you, as if you are being judged on a charge of high treason. Subtle it isn't; powerful it most certainly is. And if it is the mark of a good artist to leave a feeling as well as an image imprinted on your mind long after you have moved away from the canvas, then Wright is a good artist, whatever Evelyn says.

As you tour the country houses of Britain surveying the works of so many painters, you will no doubt find your own favourites. However, since so few of them are remembered in later centuries, it is worth naming a few more. Again, what will strike you is how many are foreign-born and foreign-trained. For example, there are leading portrait painters in John Closterman (born in Osnabrück), Jacob Huysmans (born in Antwerp), Gerard Soest (born in Westphalia) and John Baptist Medina (Spanish, but born in Brussels). For landscapes, you could apply at the studios of Adam de Colonia (born in Rotterdam), Adriaen van Diest (born at The Hague) and Jan Siberechts (born in Antwerp). For history paintings, there is Michael Dahl (from Stockholm); for historical murals on the scale of Verrio, there is Louis Laguerre (from Versailles); and for the finest marine painter of the age, look no further than Willem van de Welde (from Leiden). It is surely not a coincidence that as Britain reaches out and embraces the world – from trading in the Far East to controlling the plantations in the West Indies and the settlements in North America – the rest of Europe embraces Britain and enriches it culturally.

All this might give you the impression that there are no home-grown artists of note. Far from it. There is an explosion of interest in art amongst the natives too, both at an amateur level and at a professional one. Both Evelyn's and Pepys's wives take up painting as a hobby. Ralph Thoresby buys a set of sixty crayons for 2s 6d in 1677 so that he can copy the portraits of the founding fathers of the Protestant Church.[51] Amongst the professionals there are some striking characters, such as John Greenhill, a pupil of Lely whom some say is as good as his master. Although married, he is the heart-throb of the dramatist Aphra Behn, but he lives in an extremely dissolute manner in Covent Garden and eventually dies in a drunken stupor at the age of thirty-five. Then there is Isaac Fuller, another heavy-drinking artist, who paints naked nymphs by the dozen on the ceilings of Oxford college chapels, and similar themes on the walls of London taverns. He also produces portraits of writers and a vibrant, if somewhat bizarre; series of history paintings recounting Charles II's escape from the Battle of Worcester. Fuller's pupil, John Riley, who is far more mannered than his master in his painting as well as his lifestyle, becomes a court painter after the accession of William and Mary; he too displays a streak of unorthodoxy in that he paints grand, full-length portraits of royal servants, including Bridget Holmes, the woman in charge of emptying the king's chamber pot. Alongside these mavericks you have the perfectionists: the best miniaturists of the age are Samuel Cooper at the start of our period and Thomas Flatman at the end, both of whom have the uncanny ability to make you feel that *you* are the one being observed through the tiny frame, and that the sitter is in the real world, gazing at *you*. John Scougal emerges as the pre-eminent portrait painter in Scotland. Robert Robinson tries single-handedly to eclipse the hierarchy of the genres by producing accomplished work in every form, from history and allegory down to landscape, still-life and genre works. The even more versatile Robert Streater produces pioneering landscapes that are the equal of most Dutch specialists. Not only that, but he paints the ceiling of the Sheldonian Theatre in Oxford, which Pepys, Wren and their friends go to see in 1669, whereupon some of the company declare his work to be comparable with that of Rubens.[52] Despite the generally low opinion of animal painting and still life, Francis Barlow devotes his career to producing exquisite paintings of birds and animals and compensates for the 'lowness' of his art by becoming the first professional etcher in Britain.[53] Nor should we forget Marmaduke Craddock, who produces paintings of birds of such liveliness and colour that you cannot help but smile. True, most of them are ducks, so no one will ever compare a Craddock with a Rubens, but he has his place. You will know what I mean when you see one of his ducks.

Finally, we must welcome the first professional female painters to grace these shores. Four women are named by William Sanderson in his survey of the art scene in England at the start of our period, namely Mrs Joan Carlile, Mrs Mary Beale, Mrs Sarah Brooman and Mrs Weimes.[54] The last two women keep a very low profile, but the first two are boldly breaking new ground. Pride of place is given by Sanderson to Carlile. She tends to portray her sitters standing in their very best white satin dresses in Elysian woodland scenes. After Carlile's death in 1679, and perhaps even some years beforehand, Mary Beale becomes the unrivalled queen of British painting. Her husband, Charles Beale, is a deputy clerk in the patents office. When his job looks as if it is in jeopardy, Mary takes the upper hand and sets herself up as a professional artist, with her husband and sons as her assistants. Charging just £10 for a full-length portrait and £5 for a half-length, she quickly attracts a wealthy clientele. Sir Peter Lely comes to her studio, is impressed and invites her to see his manner of working. In 1671 her income from painting is £118; by 1677 it has reached £429. After earning such sums and always setting aside 10 per cent of her income for the poor, she begins to paint more freely and in a more original way for the rest of her days. Her younger son, Charles Beale, carries on her tradition and becomes a successful portrait painter in his own right after her death in 1699.

Libraries and Literature

Although over half the male population is literate, this does not mean that every other man owns a book. Most of those who can read do not even own a copy of the Bible – perhaps one in ten countrymen has one – and the majority of those who *do* have a Bible have no other book.[55] For this reason, ecclesiastical libraries and country houses are important local resources. Many town churches have libraries of about fifty to one hundred books, mainly of a theological nature, and all the cathedrals have larger libraries than this. As for private collections, most gentlemen will happily allow access to respectable people wishing to consult their books, in the same way that they are happy to show off their houses. Ralph Josselin uses Lord Mandeville's library at Kimbolton Castle, for example, and the poet Andrew Marvell uses the earl of Anglesey's in London.[56] Thus, if you live near Northfleet in Kent, your nearest significant library will be that of the physician and traveller Edward Browne, which contains 2,500 volumes. The library of Ashwellthorpe Hall, Norfolk, contains more than 1,400 volumes; that of the historian Sir Peter Leycester at Tabley Hall, Cheshire, has 1,332; and there are 340 volumes at Ashe House, Devon.[57]

The greatest private library in Britain at this time is that owned by Arthur Annesley, earl of Anglesey, which extends to 30,000 volumes, many of which are kept at his mansion on Drury Lane. This collection is, sadly, broken up and auctioned off after his death in 1686. The next largest in the London area known to John Evelyn in 1689 is that of Edward Stillingfleet, bishop of Worcester, who has 6,000 books at his house in Twickenham. Evelyn's own library contains an impressive 5,000 printed volumes and 500 manuscripts. But it concerns him greatly that, after the loss of Lord Anglesey's collection, there are no great private libraries in the London area. What's more, most of the important manuscript collections are closed to scholars. Sir Robert Cotton's library of about 800 medieval manuscripts is inaccessible. A similar library of 762 manuscripts collected by Dr Isaac Vossius, canon of Windsor, which Anthony Wood describes as 'the best private library in the world', is also tucked away, awaiting sale, after its collector's death in 1689. The 'Old Royal Library' of 2,000 manuscripts collected from the time of Edward IV is locked up at St James's Palace.[58] It is indeed a lamentable situation, and one that will be properly reversed only in the next century.

The nearest thing to a public library at this time is Chetham's Library in Manchester. Set up under the terms of the will of Humphrey Chetham, a wealthy merchant of the town, it is open 'for the use of scholars and others well affected' from 1655. It is small but growing steadily: in 1685 it holds 2,455 volumes, all chained to their shelves to prevent theft.[59] A much larger research library is the Bodleian in Oxford. Back in 1610 its founder, Thomas Bodley, did a deal with the Stationers' Company whereby a copy of every title published in England would be lodged there. The library's annual growth rate is enhanced further by major donations, such as the bequest of 8,000 books by the lawyer, John Selden, in 1654. Several Oxford colleges also have good libraries: Evelyn especially mentions Magdalen College, Christ Church, University College and Balliol College.[60] For this reason, if you have to undertake any serious research, Oxford should be your destination. If you are in Cambridge, Trinity College Library is your best bet.

What if you choose instead to build your own collection of books? If you buy new, prices are closely related to production costs, so the larger the book, the more expensive it is. A folio Bible (the largest size, with the best layout and largest print) may well cost you 10s; one in quarto, 7s; one in octavo (modern hardback size), 4s; and one in duodecimo (roughly modern paperback size, with the smallest print), 3s 6d.[61] According to *A Catalogue of all the Books Printed in England since the Dreadful Fire of London, 1666* (1673), a new, two-volume, illustrated folio-sized *Aesop's Fables*, printed by John Ogilby, costs £3; a first-edition quarto of John Milton's *Paradise Lost* (1667) is 3s; and a first-edition octavo of Milton's *Paradise Regained* (1671) will set you back 2s 6d.[62] Rare books can go for far higher prices than these. In February 1688, at an auction held in London, you'll have to bid more than £9 15s for John Gerard's *The Herball or Generall Historie of Plants* (third edition, 1633) and more than £40 for a set of Jean Blaeu's *Le Grand Atlas, ou Cosmographie blaviane* (twelve volumes, Amsterdam, 1663).[63] Pricey though these are, they are a fraction of their relative cost today, so wealthy gentlemen can still build up valuable libraries of choice printed books. Two copies of the recent fourth folio edition of Shakespeare's works (1685) sell at that same auction for 15s each.

In selecting what to read, obviously you will maximise you choice if you visit right at the end of our period. The number of new books (including pamphlets) published in England every decade increases by 300 per cent over the course of the century. In Scotland that figure is an even more impressive 800 per cent, as shown in the table below.

Number of books published in Britain, 1610–99[64]									
	1610s	1620s	1630s	1640s	1650s	1660s	1670s	1680s	1690s
England	4,290	5,029	5,578	18,455	12,658	11,344	11,975	18,538	17,116
Scotland	134	147	214	403	285	356	393	895	1,289

As a result, a total of more than 120,000 titles have been printed in England and more than 4,400 in Scotland from medieval times to the start of the year 1700: as many books are published in the British

Isles during the forty years of the Restoration period as were printed in the previous two centuries. And these figures do not include books in English published in foreign countries. You can add titles from such regions as the Low Countries (where 746 English books and pamphlets appear between 1610 and 1699), France (702), Germany (25), Switzerland (8), Italy (8) and America (925).

PROSE WORKS

When it comes to what to read, most seventeenth-century people opt for divinity. The afore mentioned *Catalogue of all the Books Printed in England*, which covers the period from October 1666 to December 1672, extends to seventy-nine pages, twenty-two of which are devoted to religious titles. The next-largest categories are history, ten pages; and law and public Acts, nine and a half pages; followed by medicine, six pages; and poetry and plays, six pages. Architecture, music, gardening, science and recipe books – each of these barely fills up a page of titles. As for fiction, there is no such category. So many aspects of modern life are recognisable in Restoration times, yet in our reading habits we are almost opposites. The seventeenth-century predilection for divinity accounts for more than a quarter of all new books published. In the modern world, fiction similarly accounts for more than a quarter of all new titles published. But they don't read much fiction, and we don't read much divinity.[65]

Having said this, fiction is beginning to rear its head in the seventeenth century. In 1678 John Bunyan's *The Pilgrim's Progress from this world to that which is to come, delivered under the similitude of a Dream ...* is published. Ten years later, Aphra Behn brings out *Oroonoko*, the story of a fictional prince protesting against slavery in Spanish America. Both of these are definitely novels and both have a strong moral current; if you want to begin to read through the corpus of English fiction from its earliest days, they are a good place to begin. However, you need to remember that Bunyan and Behn would be quite upset if you were to refer to their books as 'novels', for at this time the word denotes a short romance. And in that sense there are other contenders for the title of the earliest English novel. For example, *Tudor, a Prince of Wales: an historical novel* and *Capello and Bianca: a novel* both appear in 1677. Earlier still are the 'cast adrift' stories of exploration, which read like modern science-fiction works. One is *The Isle of Pines* (1668) by Henry Neville: a survival story of a single man marooned on a deserted tropical island with an abundance of food and four young, attractive women, by whom he sires four separate tribes. An even earlier piece of imaginative fiction is *The Blazing World* (1666) by Margaret Cavendish: a very strange story of a girl who, having been shipwrecked on the way to the North Pole, enters a 'Blazing World', marries its emperor and discovers his subjects are all men in the form of bears, foxes, geese, worms, fish, flies, magpies and ants, and helps him conquer the rest of the real world when she returns. If you then add novels translated from the French, there are even more from which to choose. In December 1660, when Pepys sits up reading in bed with his wife, he ploughs through Thomas Fuller's *Church History of Britain* while she reads *Artamène, or the Grand Cyrus*, a novel published in the 1650s by the Frenchwoman Madeleine de Scudéry. You might presume that her choice is a light, quick romp, compared to her husband's worthy tome. In fact, *Artamène* extends to two million words in ten volumes and is the longest 'novel' ever published, however you define the word.[66]

Pepys's choice of reading in December 1660 draws attention to the fact that people read a great deal of history at this time. Indeed, if you know anything about the great historical works of the past, you will be impressed by the roll call of famous titles. The first two volumes of Gilbert Burnet's *History of the Reformation in England* appear in 1679 and 1681. Lord Clarendon writes *The History of the Rebellion and Civil Wars in England* in these years (although it will not actually be published until 1702–4). Perhaps most important of all, Sir William Dugdale's massive achievements, *Monasticon Anglicanum* (three volumes, 1655–73) and *The Baronage of England* (three volumes, 1675–6), are produced: these break new ground in terms of attention to detail and providing access to the source materials, as well as building a national picture of the history of monasteries and the major families. Other historians use Dugdale's great reference books as frameworks and produce national- and local-history works of a similarly high level of research. Personally, I am most inspired by Joshua Barnes's magisterial *History of that Most Victorious Monarch Edward III* (1688), a huge undertaking of more than 900 folio pages, which will not be superseded as the best work on that monarch until the twenty-first century. As for Thomas Fuller, whose *Church History* is Pepys's choice of bedtime reading, he also writes *The History of the Worthies of England* (1662), a biographical account of the most eminent gentlemen of each county and thus an early biographical dictionary, which sets the pattern for many other reference works. While the Restoration is well known as the period of the Scientific Revolution, it is sometimes forgotten that it also sees huge advances in history writing.

When it comes to philosophy, the fuse is lit when Thomas Hobbes publishes his *Leviathan* in 1651. In 1666 Parliament blames the book for being the cause of atheism and blasphemy, which, it argues, have led to the recent twin disasters of plague and the Great Fire. Several bishops in the House of Lords propose that the seventy-eight-year-old Hobbes himself be burnt alive as a heretic. In 1683, four years after his death, the book and his other works are indeed publicly consigned to the flames.

Why does *Leviathan* cause such an extreme reaction? It introduces the intelligentsia to the idea of the social contract – the agreement between individual members of a society that underpins all political life. Hobbes returns to first principles, asking why does society exist. He imagines mankind to have originally been in 'a state of nature' when 'the life of man [is] solitary, poor, nasty, brutish, and short'. He argues that in this state, men have rights – including the right to kill each other – but that they might give up these rights to live together in peace. For example, men in a certain community might agree to protect each other so that they may defend their communities against potential attackers. This is the basis of the social contract, and it provides the foundation for government. Hobbes recognises only three possible forms of rule – monarchy, aristocracy and democracy – and declares that monarchy is the most desirable of them all. But he insists that the basis of the monarch's power lies in the social contract and not in divine power. Therefore religion has no place in government. He thus undermines the ancient concept of the divine authority of kings – and that is why he lands himself in hot water (and his books on hot coals). That is also why it is the most important book published in England between the King James Bible in 1611 and Newton's *Principia Mathematica* in 1687.

Hobbes's original thinking is taken up by other philosophers, most notably John Locke and Algernon Sidney. Building on Hobbes's idea that the rule of the monarch is dependent on the social contract, Locke argues in his *Two Treatises of Government* (1689) that the king cannot have absolute power over his subjects because his authority rests on his undertaking to protect the life and liberty of his people. Thus, if the king does not serve his people in a way commensurate with their collective interests, they should remove him from power. It goes without saying that this is political dynamite but, curiously, people at the time don't quite appreciate how significant it is. Perhaps that is just as well. Algernon Sidney produces some similar arguments against absolute monarchy and the divine right of kings in his book *Discourses Concerning Government* (1683). Like Hobbes before him, he argues that the right to govern is vested in a government by the people and that, without their consent, a king has no mandate to rule. The book is unambiguous on such issues – and it is too much for the king. Charles II has the man arrested and tried for treason. Judge Jeffreys steps well beyond the limit of his authority in order to bring in a guilty verdict. Sidney is beheaded on 7 December 1683. In his speech from the scaffold he declares that 'we live in an age that makes truth pass for treason' and asserts that he stands by what he has written. He thus becomes a true martyr for liberty.

POETRY

For the most part, 'literature' at this period means poetry. As Monsieur Misson puts it:

> The English have a mighty value for their poetry. If they believe that their language is the finest in the whole world, though spoken nowhere but in their own island, they have proportionably a much higher idea of their verses: they never read or repeat them but with the most singular tone in the world. When they happen in reading to go out of prose into verse, you would swear you no longer heard the same person: his tone of voice becomes soft and tender; he is charmed, he dies away with rapture.[67]

Well put, I say, and true. But who are the writers who can charm and soften the heart of an Englishman?

It seems that, in all ages, three-quarters of the poetry sold is by dead poets, three-quarters of what is sold by living writers is by the leading two or three poets of the day, and three-quarters of the rest is bought by the poets' family and friends. In listing the leading English writers for an Italian audience, Magalotti mentions Chaucer, Spenser, Drayton and Shakespeare – all of whom are deceased.[68] The *Catalogue of all the Books Printed* reinforces this dominance of the dead: it includes volumes of poetry published in 1666–72 by Aesop, Virgil, Horace and Ovid and by ten dead English poets. Laying aside those whose books are published anonymously, just nine living poets have new books out in the six years in question – Abraham Cowley, Sir John Denham, Henry King, Margaret Cavendish, John Milton, John Dryden, Edward Howard, Edmond Waller and Robert Wild. And Margaret Cavendish is generally thought by contemporaries to be one of the worst poets of all time. Mrs Evelyn thinks she should not be allowed out of the house, let alone published.

In deciding what to read, your choice may be influenced by the fact that in 1668 Charles II takes the bold step of appointing a poet laureate – the first time such a role has officially been conferred in Britain. The first incumbent of the post, John Dryden, is an accomplished writer of both poetry and plays. But he rather unwisely follows his royal master towards the Church of Rome and, having converted to Catholicism, has to forgo the poet laureateship on the accession of William and Mary in 1689. His successor in the role is his Protestant rival, Thomas Shadwell, whose work Dryden has repeatedly attacked for its inanity. Shadwell dies in 1692, whereupon Nahum Tate is appointed to the laureateship. Again, Tate is unlikely to trouble anyone writing a list of 'Restoration books you should read before you die'. I don't mean the man any disrespect – you have to take your hat off to anyone who attempts a 1,400-line verse translation of Girolamo Fracastoro's Latin poem on the subject of syphilis, in heroic couplets – but the poet laureateship is hardly a good pointer to the best literature of the 1690s.

So whom should you read?

Endless anthologising over the years means that you probably already have the top ten names lodged in your mind: John Milton, John Dryden, Samuel Butler, Andrew Marvell, Abraham Cowley, Henry Vaughan, Thomas Traherne, John Wilmot earl of Rochester, Edmund Waller and John Oldham. Several of these – Traherne, Vaughan and Marvell – are considered 'metaphysical poets' in modern times but they themselves would not recognise any such classification; there is no metaphysical 'school' as such. Nor is Marvell accorded the sort of fame he enjoys in the modern world for poems such as 'To his coy mistress' and 'The Definition of Love'. Most of his lyrical poems do not appear in print until his widow publishes his *Miscellaneous Poems* in 1681, three years after his death. Samuel Butler's fame rests almost entirely on his *Hudibras*. Although he does publish other works in the same vein, nothing comes close to that initial success. Lord Rochester never publishes any of his poems in his own lifetime; they circulate in manuscript and scandalise or delight those who read them, but his life is more like a sparkler than a flame, throwing instants of light in all directions and extinguished all too soon. Cowley's poetry is published before 1660, and the same is largely true of Vaughan and Waller – although Waller's most famous lines, from 'Of the last verses in the book', appear in the fifth edition of his *Poems*, published a year before his death in 1687. In case you don't know them, here they are:

> The seas are quiet, when the winds give o'er,
> So calm are we, when passions are no more:
> For then we know how vain it was to boast
> Of fleeting things, so certain to be lost.
> Clouds of affection from our younger eyes
> Conceal that emptiness, which age descries.

> The soul's dark cottage, battered and decayed,
> Lets in new light through chinks that time has made;
> Stronger by weakness, wiser men become
> As they draw near to their eternal home:
> Leaving the old, both worlds at once they view,
> That stand upon the threshold of the new.

Let me return to John Dryden, the most popular poet of the age. On 23 November 1658 he takes part in the funeral procession of Oliver Cromwell alongside John Milton and Andrew Marvell: all three poets are fervent supporters of the Commonwealth and write panegyrics to the Protector in life and death. You would have thought that meant all three are on very dangerous ground when Charles II takes power. But Dryden, the youngest of the three, assimilates himself to the restored monarchy almost overnight. He writes *Astræa Redux* ('Justice brought back') to welcome the return of the Stuart dynasty, dismissing the Commonwealth as a time of anarchy. And as soon as the king reopens the playhouses that were forbidden by the Puritans, Dryden starts writing plays. He clearly knows which side his bread is buttered: we will return to him as a playwright in due course. But although the stage gives him wealth and fame, he never turns his back on poetry and continues to produce original verse and translations as well as plays until he dies in 1700. At its worst, Dryden's verse is overblown and tedious. At its best, however, it is witty and light. This is a song from the comedy *Marriage à la Mode* (1673):

> Why should a foolish marriage vow,
> Which long ago was made,
> Oblige us to each other now,
> When passion is decayed?
> We loved, and we loved, as long as we could,
> Till our love was loved out in us both;
> But our marriage is dead, when the pleasure is fled:
> 'Twas pleasure first made it an oath.
>
> If I have pleasures for a friend,
> And further love in store,
> What wrong has he, whose joys did end,
> And who could give no more?
> 'Tis a madness that he should be jealous of me,
> Or that I should bar him of another:
> For all we can gain is to give ourselves pain,
> When neither can hinder the other.

Most of Dryden's published works are longer poems, however. In these he ranges from satire to religion and back, with a surprising integrity in both departments. If you dip into his work, including the poems he wrote to be incorporated in his many plays, you will come across a mass of trinkets of wit, and quite a few jewels. 'Plots, true or false, are necessary things / to raise up commonwealths and ruin kings' ... 'Love's the noblest frailty of the mind' ... 'Here lies my wife: here let her lie! / Now she's at rest, and so am I'. And these striking lines from his play *Aureng-Zebe*:

> When I consider life, 'tis all a cheat;
> Yet, fooled with hope, men favour the deceit;
> Trust on, and think tomorrow will repay:

Tomorrow's falser than the former day;
Lies worse; and while it says, we shall be blest
With some new joys, cuts off what we possessed.
Strange cozenage! None would live past years again,
Yet all hope pleasure in what yet remain;
And, from the dregs of life, think to receive
What the first sprightly running could not give.
I'm tired with waiting for this chymic gold,
Which fools us young, and beggars us when old.

Without doubt the most gifted writer to appear in print during these years is John Milton. Blind since 1652 and a committed republican, he begins *Paradise Lost*, his epic account of the fall of mankind from Heaven, in 1658, the year of Cromwell's death and the deaths of his second wife, Katherine, and their infant daughter. As a polemicist on behalf of Cromwell's government, justifying Cromwell's actions in a number of prose works, Milton both objects to the Restoration on principle and knows it is a time of great danger for him. When the king returns he goes into hiding. His books and tracts are collected and burnt in London by the public hangman. While he himself is not listed amongst those excluded from the general pardon issued in August 1660, when he emerges from hiding he is arrested and locked in the Tower. He loses most of his money. Living in reduced circumstances and dependent on amanuenses to write down his poetry, which he dictates to them, Milton struggles to bring up his teenage daughters. In fact they turn against him bitterly. At the age of fifty-four he marries his third wife, Elizabeth Minshull, who is thirty years younger than him. When his daughter Mary is told of her father's marriage, she replies, 'it is no news, to hear of his wedding, but, if I could hear of his death, *that* would be something'.[69]

Fear, prison, impoverishment, grief, family strife and blindness – *Paradise Lost* is not composed in the easiest of circumstances. Nonetheless, after nine years it is complete and ready for the press. Milton signs a book contract in April 1667 and receives £5 payment in return for the first edition of 1,300 copies. Ten thousand lines by which he hopes to 'justify the ways of God to men' do not perhaps strike the modern traveller as the most compelling subject, but the poem is nothing short of sensational. Reading it is like being on a literary rollercoaster, shooting through valleys of darkness and heavenly light in turn. With Satan as a lead character, and Adam and Eve being cast out of Paradise as the story's pivotal moment, the speeches are as powerful as the Devil whispering in your ear. This is Satan, taking his first view of Hell, into which he has just been cast:

'Is this the region, this the soil, the clime,'
Said then the lost archangel, 'this the seat
That we must change for Heaven, this mournful gloom
For that celestial light? Be it so, since he
Who now is sovereign can dispose and bid
What shall be right: farthest from him is best
Whom reason hath equalled, force hath made supreme
Above his equals. Farewell, happy fields
Where joy forever dwells. Hail horrors, hail
Infernal world, and thou profoundest Hell
Receive thy new possessor: one who brings
A mind not to be changed by place or time.
The mind is its own place, and in itself
Can make a Heaven of Hell, a Hell of Heaven.
What matter where, if I be still the same,
And what I should be, all but less than he
Whom thunder hath made greater? Here at least
We shall be free; the Almighty hath not built
Here for his envy, will not drive us hence:
Here we may reign secure, and in my choice
To reign is worth ambition though in Hell:
Better to reign in Hell, than serve in Heaven.

Yet amid the fire and brimstone, the smoke and Stygian gloom (which reflects Milton's own permanent darkness), beautiful descriptions emerge, such as that of evening in Eden:

Now still came evening on, and twilight grey
Had in her sober livery all things clad;
Silence accompanied, for beast and bird,
They to their grassy couch, thee to their nests
Were slunk, all but the wakeful nightingale;
She all night long her amorous descant sung;
Silence was pleased: now glowed the firmament

With living sapphires: Hesperus that led
The starry host, rode brightest, till the Moon
Rising in clouded majesty, at length
Apparent queen, unveiled her peerless light,
And o'er the dark her silver mantle threw.

Some of Milton's contemporaries understand the greatness of the poem from the moment they read it. At the end of October 1667 the poet and architect Sir John Denham rushes into the House of Commons carrying a newly printed sheet of *Paradise Lost*, wet off the press, declaring it to be 'part of the noblest poem that ever was wrote in any language or any age'.[70] The public as a whole is slower to catch on. Only when the fourth edition appears in 1688 does the work take off. After that it becomes *the* national epic in English: the equivalent of the works of Homer, Virgil and Dante in their respective languages. By then, of course, Milton is dead – but thus he conforms to my rule about three-quarters of the verse sold being by dead poets.

Music

As you walk along a London street in one of the better neighbourhoods at dusk on a summer's evening, all sorts of sounds will greet your ears. Horseshoes clacking on the cobbles, and iron-tyred wheels grinding against the stones. Masters calling to their servants, children being reproved by their mothers or governesses, window shutters being pulled closed with a slam. And high above it all, the plucked sounds of a lute and the low whistle of a recorder as a lady and a gentleman while away their evening playing a dance tune. A few doors down, there is singing, as a private recital is given in a gentleman's house. From another building you can hear the strains of a quartet of lute, harpsichord, viol and violin on the first floor. In a yard behind a house in the next street there's a girl singing a tune to herself, as she gathers in the washing from a line. A few blocks away, in a tavern, there is some raucous tune-wrestling as the drinkers join in with a soloist on the choruses of a well-known bawdy jig. From the open window of a smart house comes the delicate sound of an accomplished young lady playing the virginals in front of her proud parents and their dinner guests. Passing the parish church, you might hear the organ, cornets and choirboys practising a motet for the following morning. And if you walk along Seething Lane, maybe you will hear Samuel Pepys playing his lute and singing to himself in his chamber after an argument with his wife. There is music everywhere in the Restoration city – in every house, among men and women, rich and poor, young and old.

Listening to all this playing and singing, it is easy to forget that before the Restoration you would have heard few tunes. The Puritans forbade church music. Cathedral choirs were disbanded. Church organs were broken up. Groups of musicians who regularly played during services were rendered unemployed. The theatres, which had used music for interludes and amusements before, during and after the plays, were all closed down. The musicians and choir of the Chapel Royal were disbanded. Masques and lavish balls were no longer held, as they had been at Charles I's court. In taverns and inns, censorious magistrates took action to prevent the playing of songs that did not conform to their own high standards of propriety. Music did not disappear entirely but people were not allowed to sing and dance freely, and very little music was performed in public. When the Restoration sees the theatres open again, the churches allowed to restore their old organs and the cathedrals permitted to have choirs, it is as if all the windows in Britain have suddenly been opened at once and music is heard ushering in a million trills and bright cadences into the sunlit morning of a new age.

Royal music cannot simply resume where it left off in the 1640s. Too many skills have been lost; too many traditions have dwindled into obscurity. But Charles II rises to the challenge of re-energising it. He appoints twenty-four violinists, following the example of *Les vingt-quatre violons du Roi* who serve Louis XIV of France.[71] The old Master of the King's Music, Nicholas Lanier, is reappointed to his position, and the king recruits new musicians from the Continent to serve under Lanier. As a result, there are as many foreigners playing music in England in the 1660s and 1670s as there are painters from the Low Countries working here. Unsurprisingly, the king reaches out first to the French, and establishes a permanent band called the King's French Music. That group is disbanded in 1666 when Charles grows bored of them and decides he would like an Italian troupe instead. So Vicenzo Albrici and his brother Bartolomeo are brought over to run the King's Italian Music that same year, supported by two female

Italian singers, two Italian castrati, a tenor and a bass.[72] When Nicholas Lanier dies in 1666, his successor as Master of the King's Music is a Catalan-born, French-trained musician, Louis Grabu. All the foreign musicians who come to court also perform in private houses all around London. At one performance that Evelyn attends in 1679, all four musicians are from the Continent.[73] The rejuvenation of royal music means the breaking down of national barriers, and England resuming its long-lost place in the wider musical world.

The most important facet of this development lies in the developing orchestra. In 1673 four French wind players arrive at court and before long they start playing alongside the king's violinists. In the 1680s English trumpets are added to the mix. Nicholas Staggins, Master of the King's Music in 1685, writes music for the coronation of James II that involves violins, violas, basses, trumpets and oboes. The modern orchestra grows out of just such ensembles. The patronage of the royal family means that England is part of this international develop-ment in the last two decades of the century – alongside courts in Italy, Germany and France.[74]

Don't imagine for a moment that all these Continental influences damage English traditions. Now that the restrictions of the Commonwealth are lifted, the old songs and dances have a new lease of life too, both at the palace and in the country. Key to this is a guide to the dances, *The Dancing Master, or Directions for Dancing Country Dances*, by John Playford. First produced under Cromwell's government, the book soars in popularity after the Restoration, going through many editions by 1700. By the time the tenth edition appears in 1698, many famous English tunes are represented, including 'Cuckolds all a-row', 'Jamaica' and 'Lillibullero', all with instructions as to how to dance to them. New songs are published too – some written by 'serious' composers and circulated in their song books; others by anonymous writers and plastered up on tavern walls (with directions that they should be sung to this or that tune); and still others sold as broadsides by street sellers who sing the very songs as they walk along. Then there are the professional songwriters like Thomas d'Urfey. Hundreds of his songs are published in this period, many of which will one day be collected in the six volumes of his *Wit and Mirth: Pills to Purge Melancholy*.

Another musical development in this period is the public concert. Musical performances are essentially private affairs in the 1660s. You may see a gentleman gather a few musicians together, and some of them may be paid professionals, but they will play only for an invited audience. Hence it is enormously significant that on 30 December 1672 the violinist John Banister holds the first proper public concert in rooms adjacent to the George Tavern near the Temple, London. Admission is 1s per head. The scene is theatrical. Curtains are drawn back to reveal the performers on the stage. All the musicians are first-rate, playing music composed or selected by Banister and able to extemporise as necessary, to the delight of the audience. Banister continues to hold such events regularly until his death in 1679. By then a second series of public concerts is under way in Clerkenwell, managed by Thomas Britton: these are held weekly for the next thirty-six years. London musicians start to hold a public performance of a new composition in honour of St Cecilia, the patron saint of music, every year on the saint's feast day (22 November). In the late 1690s this becomes a competition, with large prizes for the winning composer. By 1700 the public concert is a regular fixture on the London entertainment programme.[75]

After a while of listening to everything from milkmaids' songs to harpsichord recitals and anthems, you will no doubt start to wonder who composes the best music? All that baroque sound that we associate with the period – where does that come from? One famous name obviously leaps out but, before we come to him, it is worth listening to his contemporaries. Matthew Locke and Henry Lawes are the most significant composers in England in the 1660s: Locke is the Composer in Ordinary of the King's Violins, and Lawes the author of three books of airs and a gentleman of the Chapel Royal. In the 1670s a younger generation of composers emerges, represented by Pelham Humfrey, William Turner and John Blow. Humfrey dies young, aged twenty-seven, but not before his education at the French court has influenced all his fellow composers in England. Turner contributes anthems for the royal household, sings in the Chapel Royal and dashes across London to perform his music in the theatres. Blow is the organist of Westminster Abbey: he composes dozens of anthems for the court and one of the first English operas, *Venus and Adonis*, in 1683. This is the pattern for all the leading composers: producing sacred music for the Chapel Royal, anthems for state occasions and dramatic music for the theatres.

Then we come to Henry Purcell.

Born in 1659, Purcell experiences the death of his father when he is five, and so his mother is forced to move with her six children into cheaper accommodation. But Purcell is musically gifted and obtains a place in the Chapel Royal, studying under the direction of Henry Cooke and then Pelham Humfrey. In 1682 he is given the prestigious position of organist in the Chapel Royal, and from that year until his early death at the age of thirty-six, he is incredibly prolific, producing more than sixty anthems, forty-eight hymns and a dozen services for the Chapel Royal, besides more than fifty 'catches' (songs by several voices sung in sequence); twenty-four odes; about two hundred popular songs; incidental music for more than forty plays; five dramatic operas (*Dioclesian, King Arthur, The Fairy Queen, Timon of Athens* and *The Indian Queen*); a full-scale opera, *Dido and Aeneas* (1689); and more than a hundred instrumental works, including sonatas, minuets, jigs, preludes, airs, hornpipes, pavanes, suites, voluntaries, sonatas, overtures and marches. Works such as his overture to *The Indian Queen* and the trumpet tune from the same piece; 'Dido's Lament' from *Dido and Aeneas*; the rondeau from the incidental music to *Abdelazer*; the 'symphony' from Act Four of *The Fairy Queen*; and his haunting 'Music on the Death of Queen Mary' all escape the confines of their own time and are still cherished in the modern world. Not only does Purcell's fame not fade down the centuries but his music does not, either.

The Theatre

If music was quietened by the Commonwealth, drama was silenced. The playhouses were closed on 2 September 1642 and converted to other purposes. The only performances were in private houses, behind closed doors. Every time the brave proprietors of the Red Lion Theatre in Clerkenwell attempted to put on a public performance, the authorities came knocking. The Globe Theatre was demolished and tenements built on the site. By 1660, despite the growing fame of Shakespeare, the space where he and his fellow actors had held the people of London in thrall was home to washing lines and screaming infants, whining schoolboys and lean old men.

The one little bit of light that shines out of the darkness of the eighteen years of Puritan suppression is a dramatic opera entitled *The*

Siege of Rhodes. In 1656 Sir William Davenant had a brilliant idea. If he were to have his play about the Ottoman siege of Rhodes in 1522 set to music, he could advertise it as a recital and thus get around the law. Moreover, he could use scenery, which previously had not been seen in the English theatre. He thus commissioned five leading composers to write the music (including Matthew Locke, Henry Lawes and Henry Cooke), and persuaded John Webb to design the sets. In September 1656 the curtain rose on *The Siege of Rhodes*. It is often said that necessity is the mother of invention: in this case, censorship was the father. Davenant's idea of a play punctuated by songs, dancing and pieces of instrumental music with lavish scenery introduced dramatic opera to the London stage. Consequently the development of Restoration drama owes much to his vision – especially his use of stage sets and music.

As with so many other cultural aspects of the Restoration, the royal family plays an important role. On 6 June 1660 the king's brothers go to see a play, Ben Jonson's *Epicene*, at the Red Lion in Clerkenwell.[76] A month later the king grants Thomas Killgrew and Sir William Davenant the exclusive right to stage plays in London. Killigrew's troupe receives the king's patronage and is thus permitted to call itself the King's Company, and Davenant's the duke's patronage, making his company the Duke's Company. Thus two main acting companies are formed, which will remain the pattern for theatre in London for the next 150 years.

The King's Company under Killigrew first makes its home at Gibbon's Tennis Court in Vere Street. It enjoys a big advantage over its rival: it has the rights to all the plays that had once belonged to the old company of the King's Men – and that includes the works of Shakespeare and his contemporaries. Killigrew soon draws up plans for a new Theatre Royal in Bridges Street. This opens in 1663, having cost Killigrew and his partners no less than £2,500, and is admired by many, not least because it allows the most lavish stage sets to be displayed. In 1669 Killigrew pays the artist Isaac Fuller the stupendous sum of £335 for painting the scenery for Dryden's *Tyrannic Love*: the play runs for fourteen consecutive days and takes an amazing £100 per day. All goes well until the evening of 25 January 1672, when a fire starts under the stairs at the back of the theatre. By the morning, the building is a smoking ruin and all the stock of scenery and costumes built up over the years is reduced to ashes. Although the theatre is rebuilt, at a cost of £4,000, the King's Company never fully recovers from the disaster. Audiences dwindle and box-office takings shrink. Retaining an in-house prostitute is indicative of the management's wayward priorities. On 16 November 1682, the King's Company ceases to be an independent outfit and merges with the Duke's Company, under the management of the latter, henceforth calling themselves the United Company.[77]

Sir William Davenant is a better businessman than Killigrew. He takes the Duke's Company first of all to the Salisbury Court Theatre while he waits for Lisle's Tennis Court in Lincoln's Inn Fields to be converted for him. His problem is that he has almost no plays: Killigrew has virtually the whole repertoire. Only in December 1660 does Davenant acquire the right to stage eleven classics, including nine plays by Shakespeare. But he gains a great advantage over Killigrew in that he secures the services of Thomas Betterton, the leading actor of the day. In 1661 Davenant's troupe moves into the new Duke's Theatre in Lincoln's Inn Fields and opens with a revival of his own dramatic opera, *The Siege of Rhodes*. It is a smash hit, running for twelve consecutive days (when most plays only last for three). Two months later he puts on *Hamlet*, with Betterton in the role of the prince. The leading man and the dramatic scenery do the trick. Thereafter the company goes from strength to strength until Davenant's sudden death in 1668 – and even then it remains in good hands, as Betterton and Henry Harris take over the running.[78] In November 1671 the company moves to new premises, the Dorset Garden Theatre. Richly decorated, with carvings by Grinling Gibbons, it costs a whopping £9,000. There, with even better capacity for employing scenery and music, the company puts on dramatic operas and increasingly elaborate shows. In April 1682, after taking over the King's Company, the new United Company stages its musical spectaculars at the Dorset Garden Theatre and its ordinary plays at the Theatre Royal. Everything goes smoothly until 1695, when a divisive manager of the United Company, Christopher Rich, upsets Thomas Betterton and his leading ladies, and almost all of the actors walk out on him. They set up independently, back at the old Duke's Theatre in Lincoln's Inn Fields – and London once again has two theatre companies.

Here are some things to bear in mind if you are planning to see a play. First, the theatres are closed during Lent. They are also shut during the plague of 1665. Some people still want them to be shut permanently: even in 1680 Ralph Thoresby is still too fearful of the moral judgement of others to step foot inside a theatre.[79] Others, however, go to the theatre more than once per day – although doing so might soon empty your purse. The cheapest seats are generally the benches at the front of the pit and the seats in the upper gallery, costing 12d. The best seats in the pit are 2s 6d. The most expensive seats are the boxes in the circle, which, depending on where you are, can cost up to 4s a seat. As a result, where you are seen to sit is all-important: if your work colleagues in a 2s 6d box see you slumming it in the 1s 6d seats, you might not hear the last of it, come Monday morning.[80] As a result, there is a whole range of people in the audience. The upper gallery is full of servants; the middle gallery is crowded with citizens' wives and daughters, serving men, journeymen and apprentices; the pit is where the professional men sit, plus a few 'beaus, bullies and whores'; and the boxes accommodate the gentlemen and their womenfolk.[81]

But what should you go and see?

You will soon find that theatregoers don't discriminate that much: the hardcore go to see almost everything that is performed. Whether a play is a success or not depends on how many times they see it, and how many of their friends they persuade to go along too. In 1660 Pepys goes several times to see both *The Bondman* by Philip Massinger and *Epicene* by Ben Jonson. He attends the first three performances of Davenant's *Love and Honour* in October 1661 and watches Dryden's *Sir Martin Mar-all* no fewer than seven times in total. In the first eight months of 1668 he goes to the theatre seventy-three times, and over the whole ten-year period of his diary he sees at least 140 different plays.

Another thing that will perhaps surprise you in this period is how many *old* plays are performed. It is somewhat peculiar that all of fashionable London is engaged in hearing speeches that are generally more than fifty years old. The reasons are clear enough, and you can hardly blame Killigrew and Davenant. After all, if *you* had the rights to Shakespeare's works, would you put on a play by a novice writer in their place? As a result, you can go to the theatre in the 1660s and watch most of the great dramatic works from 1590 to 1620, including Shakespeare's *Hamlet, Othello, Twelfth Night, A Midsummer Night's Dream, Romeo and Juliet, The Merry Wives of Windsor* and *Henry IV, Part One.* You can see Ben Jonson's *Epicene* and his *The Alchemist*; Christopher Marlowe's

Dr Faustus; John Webster's *The Duchess of Malfi* and *The White Devil*; Francis Beaumont's *The Knight of the Burning Pestle*; and almost everything that John Fletcher ever wrote or co-wrote. Mind you, the opportunity to see all these classics of the stage does not mean that your fellow theatregoers will appreciate them. Pepys declares of Webster's *White Devil* that he has 'never had so little pleasure in a play in my life'. He thinks *Twelfth Night* a 'silly play' and says *A Midsummer Night's Dream* is 'the most insipid, ridiculous play that ever I saw in my life'.[82]

What about new plays? Obviously at the start of our period, there aren't many. Why would you write a play if you knew you could not have it performed publicly? But after 1660, new writers very quickly fill the vacuum. In fact, if it had not been for Shakespeare and Marlowe, we would probably think of the Restoration period as the golden age of the English stage. With this in mind, here are a few of the many playwrights that emerge out of the dramatic void:

• **John Dryden** is the most successful writer of the age and also the most senior of the new playwrights listed here. Although not yet thirty at the time of the Restoration, he finds success with his second solo play, *The Indian Emperor*, performed by the King's Company at the Theatre Royal in 1665. Even greater acclaim follows in 1667 when he accepts Davenant's invitation to collaborate on a version of Shakespeare's *The Tempest* for the Duke's Company; he writes *Sir Martin Mar-all* for the same company that same year. In 1670 he writes the first 'heroic drama' in his *The Conquest of Granada*, performed by the King's Company. In total he writes fifteen plays, three for the Duke's Company and the rest for the King's. Several of his works are revived in the early 1690s, when they are given music by Henry Purcell. Dryden has a good claim to be the first prominent writer to live entirely from the earnings of his pen, and it is the stage that delivers him most of that income, even though the publication of his translation of Virgil's works in 1697 earns him a cool £1,400.

• **George Etherege** is a few years younger than Dryden but a completely different character. He is a friend of Lord Buckhurst, Sir Charles Sedley and the earl of Rochester. Or, to put it more directly, he is a self-indulgent profligate rake and a part-time genius who could achieve full-time success if he were not so lazy. His first play, *The Comical Revenge or Love in a Tub*, written in 1664, is very well received, but he does not produce another for four years. His third and last play, *The Man of Mode or Sir Fopling Flutter* (1676), is his greatest hit. It is about a rake, Dorimant, and his intentions to seduce a beautiful heiress who has recently arrived in town. In its frivolous, lascivious wit, you can see why the idea of being seen entering a theatre still fills Ralph Thoresby with dread in 1680.

• **Sir Charles Sedley**'s first play, *The Mulberry Garden* (1668), is nothing special; it displeases Samuel Pepys in both its words and its incidental music. His *Antony and Cleopatra* (1677) is also unlikely to entice Pepys to see it a second time. However, his third, *Bellamira* (1687), performed by the United Company in 1687, is a success. The dissolute rake has grown up and yet still he has as sharp a wit and as cold an eye as ever. Where there is beauty, there is now also disease; where there is money, there is avarice; where there is unbridled lust, it leads to rape. Such is the logical end of libertinism, you may feel. Sedley, having lived it, breathed it and been exhausted by it, now writes its epitaph.

• **Aphra Behn** starts writing for the theatre in 1670. Over the next seventeen years she produces fifteen plays, in addition to her novels, short stories and poetry. As a result she may be said to be the first woman in Britain to make a living from her pen. Her most successful play is *The Rover*, which takes as its subject a band of English émigré libertines in Naples and Madrid, with the rake Willmore as a lead character. Willmore might be based on John Wilmot, Lord Rochester, a friend of hers. A woman of striking originality, who treads a delicate line between conformity (so as not to threaten the establishment too much) and revolutionary ideals (for example, in showing compassion for a black slave in her novel *Oroonoko*), Aphra is a close friend of many other playwrights and becomes an inspiration for the next generation of women writers. Her plays too are revived in the 1690s and performed with Purcell's incidental music: the rondeau composed by Purcell in 1695 to accompany her *Abdelazer, or the Moor's Revenge* (1675) is one of his best-known pieces.

• **William Wycherley** is educated in France and is set for a career in law when he is seduced by the stage. In turn his success with his first play, *Love in a Wood*, leads to him being seduced by the king's ex-mistress, Lady Castlemaine, in 1671. Known as a great wit, Wycherley becomes famous when the King's Company perform his third play, *The Country Wife*, in 1675. The key character is a rake called Mr Horner who comes to town and pretends to be impotent so that men of quality trust him with their wives. He seduces several of them, including a young naïve 'country wife' whose husband, Mr Pinchwife, has married her for her inexperience – thinking her so innocent she will not know how to cuckold him. Horner teaches her thoroughly, and soon she discovers she has a vocation. At the end of the play the society ladies all realise they have been sharing Horner's favours but agree to keep the secret. Mr Pinchwife, who rightly suspects Mr Horner of cuckolding him, is eventually persuaded that it is in his interests to pretend that his wife has not been unfaithful. It causes a scandal: a scene in which two ladies have sex with Horner offstage while claiming to inspect china becomes notorious, being widely seen as offensive to female dignity, but it is successful, and that is what counts. Wycherley's friends (including the duke of Buckingham, the earl of Rochester and Lord Buckhurst) acclaim its brilliance. Its success allows Wycherley to go even further in his next play, *The Plain Dealer* (1676), which stuns audiences with its sharp exposé of contemporary morality. Two years later in a bookshop in Tunbridge Wells he hears a beautiful young lady, who turns out to be the wife of the earl of Drogheda, ask for a copy of *The Plain Dealer*. When he himself is pointed out to her, and he compliments her on being a woman who can stand 'plain dealing', she replies, 'I love plain dealing, especially when it tells me of my faults.' A romance follows and, when Lord Drogheda dies, she marries Wycherley.[83]

• **Thomas Shadwell** is Dryden's rival and successor as poet laureate. He is the author of eighteen plays, of which the most successful are the comedies he writes in his late forties, including *The Squire of Alsatia* (1688) and *Bury Fair* (1689). His lasting claim to fame, however, is *The Virtuoso*, performed at the Duke's Theatre in 1676. This is the play in which he lampoons Robert Hooke as 'Sir Nicholas Gimcrack', a natural philosopher who attempts a number of pointless scientific experiments. Often described as a satire on the Royal Society, it is actually much more sophisticated than that, being a criticism of some intelligent men's great folly in pursuing pointless and meaningless knowledge rather than that which will actually benefit mankind. When Sir Nicholas claims to be able to swim as well as any fish, his nieces' suitors, Bruce and Longvil, tease him on the matter:

> *Longvil*: Have you ever tried [to swim] in the water, Sir?
> *Gimcrack*: No, Sir, but I swim most exquisitely on land.
> *Bruce*: Do you intend to practise in the water, Sir?

Gimcrack: Never, Sir; I hate the water, I never come upon the water, Sir.

Longvil: Then there will be no use of swimming.

Gimcrack: I content myself with the speculative part of swimming, I care not for the practical. I seldom bring anything to use, 'tis not my way. Knowledge is my ultimate end.

Bruce: You have reason, Sir; knowledge is like virtue, its own reward.

In the end, Sir Nicholas has his estates seized in order to pay off the debts he has incurred in the pursuit of his scientific investigations. He is ruined. Shadwell isn't, though; he does rather well out of it. Unfortunately, he suffers from gout and takes opium to control the pain: he dies of an overdose in 1692.

• **Thomas Otway** is a writer of tragedies. True to his art, he dies in 1685 at the tender of age of thirty-three. The epitome of the struggling poetic genius, he begs for bread on Tower Hill and, when someone gives him the wherewithal to buy some, eats it so fast that he chokes on it and dies. By then he has written many tragedies, including two great ones, *The Orphan or the Unhappy Marriage* (1680) and *Venice Preserv'd* (1682).

• **John Vanbrugh** is a name that you probably associate more with architecture than drama, as he sets out the plans for Castle Howard in 1699 and designs some of England's greatest baroque masterpieces in the next century, including Blenheim Palace. However, the same hand is responsible for two sophisticated, yet popular, comedies of marriage and sex, *The Relapse* (1696) and *The Provoked Wife* (1697).

• **William Congreve** is the youngest, and arguably the greatest, playwright of those named in this selection. His first play, *The Old Bachelor*, is helped along by Dryden, has the best possible cast and is performed with incidental music by Purcell. Unsurprisingly, it is a great success when the United Company produces it in 1693. His second work, *The Double Dealer* (1694), makes less of a mark, but his third, *Love for Love*, is handed over to the star actors who break away from the United Company in 1695 and they do it more than justice. It runs for thirteen days and is so popular it lands Congreve a share in the ownership of the new company. It is followed by an even bigger hit, a tragedy called *The Mourning Bride* (1697). The first line will be familiar to you – 'Music has charms to sooth a savage breast' – as will the closing lines of Act Three: 'Heaven has no rage like love to hatred turned, / nor Hell a fury like a woman scorned.' Finally, in 1700, you can see his fifth and last play, *The Way of the World*. And after that closes, that's it, even though Congreve is not yet thirty. All you have left are his lines ringing in your memory – maybe you use some of them yourself:

'You have such a winning way with you' (*Old Bachelor*)

'Courtship to marriage, as a very witty prologue to a very dull play' (*Old Bachelor*)

'She lays it on with a trowel' (*Double Dealer*)

'See how love and murder will out' (*Double Dealer*)

'No mask like open truth to cover lies, / as to go naked is the best disguise' (*Double Dealer*)

'Women are like tricks by sleight of hand, / which to admire, we should not understand' (*Love for Love*)

'Say what you will, 'tis better to be left than never to have been loved' (*Way of the World*)

Of course it is not all about the theatres and the scripts. Many people go to see a play simply because a particular fine actor is starring in it, or because the leading lady excites their passion. In this respect one name dominates and leaves all others trailing in its wake: that of Thomas Betterton. When the theatres reopen, Pepys initially thinks that Michael Mohun is 'the best actor in the world', but he revises this in 1661 when he sees Betterton play in *The Bondman*.[84] When Betterton plays Hamlet in 1663, his performance gives Pepys 'fresh reason never to think enough of Betterton'.[85] Moreover, Betterton is still giving incredible performances thirty years later. One of the reasons for the acclaim of William Congreve's first play in 1693 is that Betterton is playing the leading role, alongside the two leading ladies of the day. While there are other great male actors – Michael Mohun, William Wintershall, Charles Hart and Edward Kynaston – they all play second fiddle to Thomas Betterton.

And the ladies?

Actresses are a new phenomenon in Restoration Britain. In 1660, female roles still have to be played by men or boys. Edward Kynaston starts his career as a pretty boy-actress whom Pepys describes as 'the loveliest lady that ever I saw in my life – only her voice not very good'.[86] Then, on 3 January 1661, Pepys sees a real woman on stage for the first time, in a performance of *The Beggar's Bush*. He appreciates the change. Later that year he records that 'a woman came afterward on the stage in man's clothes, and had the best legs that ever I saw; and I was very well pleased with it'.[87] He has seen his first 'breeches role'. The theatre managers realise they can tantalise the audience by revealing the shapely figures of actresses in male clothing, consisting of stockings and tight breeches, instead of the voluminous long skirts or dresses they would normally be expected to wear. Dressed as men, they can behave in sexually confident and promiscuous ways, even making speeches of love to another woman. Such is the sexual tension created by actresses in these roles that men become obsessed with them, including rich and powerful lords, who make them their mistresses. Evelyn notes in 1666 that he sees 'foul and undecent women now (and never till now) permitted to appear and act, who inflaming several young noblemen and gallants, became their misses, and to some, their wives'.[88] If he hopes to remove women from the stage, he is fighting a losing battle; 'breeches roles' remain popular for the rest of the century.

Of all the leading ladies you could watch, Elizabeth Barry takes the starring role. At the age of fifteen she enters the Duke's Company and plays minor roles. She is hopeless. But she is also full of character, has a good voice and an expressive face, and the earl of Rochester has his eye on her. He wagers he can make her a leading actress within six months, and accordingly takes her off to the country where he forces her to play roles from Aphra Behn's plays over and over again. When she comes back to London in March 1676, she takes a leading role in Etherege's *The Man of Mode* – and scores her first big hit. The following year she gives birth to Lord Rochester's daughter, but continues to deliver acclaimed performances while pregnant. In 1678 Lord Rochester casts her aside, blaming her for sharing her favours with others. (Talk about the pot calling the kettle black!) She goes on to have dalliances with Lord Buckhurst, George Etherege and Sir Henry St John. Delivering lines that allude to her uncorrupted virgin innocence, when everyone knows she has been repeatedly seduced, must be tough – the audiences laugh openly – and she is still only eighteen. But she manages to fight her way through the shame and wins hearts by the hundred. One of those hearts belongs to the impoverished playwright Thomas Otway, who swears undying love for her. She does not reciprocate but she does play the lead roles in his tragedies *The Orphan* and *Venice Preserv'd*. So adept is she at expressing emotion in these two plays that audiences are spellbound. She becomes the *Famous* Mrs Barry there and then. Thus she is the one for whose performances you should queue longest.

In the 1690s Mrs Barry acquires a rival, Anne Bracegirdle. Anne has the good luck to grow up in the household of Thomas Betterton, and begins her stage career at about the age of six, playing a pageboy in Thomas Otway's *The Orphan*. After a few minor parts, she plays her first 'breeches role' in 1689, at the age of eighteen. She has the figure for it. Moreover, she has the spirit. The actor-manager Colley Cibber later recalls that

> she had no greater claim to beauty than what the most desirable brunette might pretend to. But her youth and lively aspect threw out such a glow of health and cheerfulness, that on the stage few specta-tors that were not past it could behold her without desire.

On top of that, she can sing beautifully too. The temptation grows too much for Captain Richard Hill, who, together with his young friend Lord Mohun, attempts to abduct her in 1692. He is prevented from doing so by one of her fellow actors, William Mountfort. In the ensuing fight outside her house, Hill runs Mountfort through with his sword and kills him. That would put most ladies off acting in breeches for life, but not Anne. She carries on winning more hearts, developing her tragic roles and becoming an even finer comic actress. When in 1695 the United Company divides, it is largely because Anne, Mrs Barry and Thomas Betterton agree together that they do not want to be pushed around by Mr Rich any longer, and they know their audience will follow them wherever they go. Thus, when the three of them perform the premiere of William Congreve's *Love for Love*, at the Lincoln's Inn Theatre on 30 April 1695, you have the best actor and finest actresses of the age in one of the best plays of the period. They all take a leading role also in Congreve's next two plays. Of all the nights to be at the theatre since the days of Burbage playing Shakespeare, these are surely the best.[89]

There is one other actress you will make an effort to see while you are in Restoration London. She is, after all, the most famous by a long way. Nell Gwynn trades on her feminine charms from the outset, becoming the lover of the actor Charles Hart not long after she has been released from Newgate Gaol, where she has been imprisoned for theft. By the age of fifteen she has made it on to the stage and proves she can play comedy well. After Charles Hart throws her aside for Lady Castlemaine, she begins an affair with Lord Buckhurst. In 1668 she becomes the king's mistress and gives up the stage: her first child by the king is born in May 1670. Later that year she returns to perform in Dryden's *The Conquest of Granada*, but when it is over, so too is her acting career. Off she goes to play the more demanding role of the lowest-born of the king's mistresses, without any script or prompt, in front a different critical audience each day, whose members are disposed to dislike her on the grounds of her wildness, indiscretion, religion, morality and low birth – and their envy. And yet Nell wins them over. What is more, she secures the king's affections for longer than any of her rivals. When Charles lies dying, Bishop Burnett hears his last words: 'Let not poor Nelly starve.' To his credit, James II, to whom the message is passed, makes sure she is well looked after for the last two years of her life. She dies in her house in Pall Mall, in November 1687. Touchingly, in her will she leaves a bequest for the prisoners in Newgate Gaol.[90]

So now the play is over. The applause has died down. People around you are rising from their seats and making their way to the exits along the galleries and at the back of the pit, shuffling along in the shadows of the candlelight. Boys and ushers wait to extinguish the lights as the audience leaves, smiling to the clientele. Outside there is a chill in the night air. The candle lanterns are bright, the mirror-backed lamps on the hackney carriages even brighter. The carriages queue for some distance back into the darkness, waiting to take people home, light after light after light. Boys scamper here and there, pestering the exiting theatregoers for a commission. Very well, it has been a long day. Let us pay one of them a sixpence to light our way. And let us reflect on how far we have come, how much this city of London has grown; how it has been riddled with plague, burnt down, rebuilt and seen all manner of men and women come and go. Let us think how much we have learnt. That play we saw this evening: it may have been bawdy, rude even, but in tearing away the veneer of respectability, the writer has spoken to us about real life. In Cromwell's day, when there was no theatre, everything was about ideals and how good things should be in a godly world, yet many of us only paid lip service to such virtuous dreams. Some of the biggest idealists were rotten to the core, it turned out. Now we see the true morals of society laid bare. We talk about things. We laugh at ourselves. Look up at the stars: more of them are known to us than ever before. Do we know ourselves any better than we did before?

At home, you close the door and take off your overcoat. The fire has dwindled to embers in the fireplace, the maidservant has already retired for the night. Only a lamp burning on a shelf lights the stairway. Perhaps you'd like to pour yourself a glass of wine from a bottle, before heading up to bed. Take the lamp with you and count the chimes as the longcase clock rings out in the parlour. A few seconds later the bell in the parish church tower a block away rings the hour. Then, up in your chamber, you sit. There is silence. Put the lamp down now and watch it glow against the wooden panelling. You undress and wash your face and hands in a bowl on a linen-covered table. Beside it stands the looking glass you'll gaze into in the morning, and the combs your maidservant will use to dress your hair in preparation for the day ahead. But therein lies a question: what does the day ahead hold?

So many things, so many.

Envoi

Oh eternity! Eternity! Eternity!
What shallow conceptions we have of it!

Mr Sharp, quoted by Ralph Thoresby, Diary, p. 238

At the start of the Restoration period, approximately 1,560 of my direct ancestors were alive – not including any distant uncles, aunts or cousins.[1] The same applies to you, to a greater or lesser extent, depending on your age. In marked contrast, I have only thirty-four blood relatives within five degrees of consanguinity alive today – and that includes uncles, aunts, nephews, nieces, cousins, first cousins once removed and second cousins. In other words, my ancestors represented 500 times as great a proportion of the population in 1660 as my whole extended family does at the time of writing. I don't know who all those ancestors were, and I don't imagine that you know all of your late-seventeenth-century predecessors either, but that doesn't matter. The point is this: as you look further and further back in time, your nation's history increasingly becomes your family history. Go back to the eleventh century and every person then living in your country who has a descendant alive now is your ancestor.[2] You could say that the more remote a period is, the more personal it is to each of us. At times, that can be alarming – especially when you consider that the common ancestors of the English include men like King John. But if you want to know what you and your countrymen are *really* like, take a good long look in the mirror of a thousand years.

Seeing our ancestors up close, however, raises some very interesting questions – about us as well as them. Could you cope with spending months at sea in all weathers, soaked and cold for much of the time, as Edward Barlow did? I don't think many of us could face that with equanimity, even if we were not called upon to fight naval battles on a regular basis. In fact, it would be a hard task adapting to the seventeenth century even if you were to live your whole life safely on land, in the comfort of a smart London house. Could you become inured to the constant cruelty to animals and the beating of children? Could you cope with the hardship and prejudices thrust upon Restoration women? What would you think if, as a judge, you had to pass a sentence of hanging, drawing and quartering on a fellow human being? Or if, as an executioner, you had to carry out the sentence of burning a young woman alive for stabbing her abusive husband? Could we, as members of the public, condone such things? Could we justify the extreme social inequality? Some of these questions might make you shift uncomfortably because, as you surely realise by now, the answer to them all is: yes, we *could* condone and justify such things, for our ancestors did so. We may regard them as inhumane atrocities now but, as outlined at the start of this Envoi, our character is more fully exposed in the mirror of a thousand years than it is in the sensitive politeness of the present day. If we were in the same position as our ancestors, under the same pressures, with the same traditions behind us and the same levels of ignorance and knowledge, then we would see ourselves behave in much the same ways as they did.

Now factor into this reflection the environmental context in which these people lived. Consider the extreme cold, the famine of the ill years in Scotland, the unpredictability of the harvests, the brutality of the naval wars with the Dutch Republic, the French and the Jacobites, and the suffering caused by so many terrible diseases. How would you manage in a boarded-up house with the plague or smallpox, watching your children suffering in terror? How could you face the day ahead? Would you not simply sling a rope over a beam and do away with yourself?

It is obvious that our ancestors suffered many hardships that do not affect us in the modern world. It is equally obvious that the vast majority of them enjoyed very few comforts and freedoms that we do not. Yet although life was so much harsher, only half as many people killed themselves as do today. To be precise, the suicide rate in England in 1700 was just 56 per million. It reached a peak of 303 per million in 1905 (in the middle of the supposedly halcyon days of the Edwardian period) and fell back to roughly 100–120 per million during the Second World War, at which level it has fluctuated over the last fifty years.[3]

Herein lies a fascinating question: if the way of life we have observed in this book was so much worse than it is in the modern world, why did so few opt out of it?

You might think that the make-up of the population provides an explanation: children under fifteen represented a greater proportion of the population in the seventeenth century than they do now, and children are less likely than adults to kill themselves. But that isn't the answer. The proportion of the population aged under fifteen was even greater in the highly self-destructive Edwardian decade than it was during the Restoration period (about 34 per cent compared to 30 per cent). Also, it had only declined to about 25 per cent by the mid-1960s, when suicide rates stabilised at just over 100 per million. Some historical questions cannot be answered by historical research alone, and no doubt some people will argue that therefore they should not be asked in the first place. Yet the question of why people carry on living while suffering incredible hardship – and its corollary, why do more people kill themselves today, despite enjoying a far higher standard of living – is a profound issue indeed. It is the sort of problem for which historical evidence is of little use; instead you must get up from your desk and go for a very long walk.

At the start of this book I posed another important question: is it true that 'the changes in English society ... between the reign of Elizabeth and the reign of Anne were not revolutionary'? The quotation comes from Peter Laslett's highly popular and influential book, *The World We Have Lost* (1966). Laslett was a historical demographer, and many of the research questions he asked were thus of a quantitative nature: how many people were there in a household, what proportion of the population was illegitimate, at what age did men and women marry, how many children did they have, and so on. However, he failed to give sufficient weight to some profound aspects of life that could not be so easily measured. For example, seventeenth-century people experienced a great shift in understanding how the world works – from a belief system rooted in superstition, religion and magic to one underpinned by scientific experimentation and rationalism – but that does not show up in a table of household sizes or population growth. The decline in hanging people for witchcraft in England is just one example of how this shift in understanding had a practical effect on everyone, not just the intellectuals. Another example is the end of hanging heretics and nonconformists and allowing the latter to worship in their own churches. Another is the fact that educated people became increasingly humanitarian in outlook, abhorring 'cruel and unnatural punishments'. People started to believe that the plague had ceased to kill with its old regularity. They became much less ideological and more frequently chose paths that led to earthly pleasures rather than Heavenly rewards – such as wandering in the New Spring Gardens or going to Newmarket, drinking champagne or travelling across the country to see Stonehenge or the Lake District. Most of all, they increasingly saw themselves as individuals, and not mere elements of larger religious and social entities – hence the increase in the number of diaries written in this period.

Over the fifty years since Laslett's book came out, social historians have been able to measure a far wider range of social phenomena. The resulting data show that society did indeed undergo a series of profound revolutions in the seventeenth century. In chapter 10 we saw how no more than 5 per cent of dying men sent for a doctor in 1603; in 1702 the majority did so. The implication of those figures is that people no longer simply looked to divine powers for their physical well-being, they looked to educated and professional men. If that shift in life-preserving power, from Christ to the professional, is not revolutionary, then nothing is. Similarly, people understood by 1700 that mathematics was essential to a huge number of social functions, from calculating life tables to answering specific scientific and economic questions, such as the weight of air or the balance of trade with other nations, or the size and wealth of the population. They no longer had to rely purely on vague philosophical theories. These developments illustrate the profound effect that the intellectual changes of the seventeenth century had on people's daily lives. You cannot calculate fire-insurance premiums on the strength of a theological argument about God's destruction of evil-doers' property. You can if you employ mathematicians to establish the risk.

Enough of the past, it is time to return to our own world. But that involves saying goodbye not just to the changes and chances of the Restoration period but also to its people. In writing this book I have grown familiar with many characters, and I hope you have come to appreciate the finer points of some of them too. I am sad to say goodbye to the intrepid Celia Fiennes and the heavy-smoking earl of

Bedford; the straight-talking Edward Barlow; the maverick Lord Rochester; and even the dry Ralph Thoresby. I will also miss the sesquipedalian Ned Ward and the sociable Willem Schellinks; the refined Italian Lorenzo Magalotti and the Anglophile Monsieur Misson. But I will miss even more listening to our two great diarists: Samuel Pepys, the foremost exponent of the medium, and his friend John Evelyn, the most erudite and sympathetic gentleman to have left a personal record of the period. Saying goodbye to them all is hard. In finally closing the door that leads to their world, I know that their opinions, jokes, insights and reminiscences are all going to be replaced with an unending silence. So, as I do close it, I find myself straining to hear a final word from one of them. And a voice does reach me. To my surprise, it does not belong to one of these characters. Nor is it that of King Charles II whispering sweet nothings to one of his mistresses, nor Milton calling out in his blindness, nor the London theatregoers shouting for an encore from Mrs Barry. Instead it is that of humble Joseph Pitts of Exeter, the fourteen-year-old boy who was captured in the English Channel by Barbary pirates in 1678 and sold in the slave markets of Algiers. If you remember, after fifteen years of slavery, he made the pilgrimage to Mecca and, after another year or so, managed to return to England. He was thus thirty when he returned, the same age as the king at his Restoration. What you don't know is that, when he finally came home, Joseph learnt that his mother had died and his friends had given up all hope of ever seeing him again. But his much-loved father was still alive. Joseph himself tells the story best:

I thought it would not be prudent to make myself known to my father at once, lest it should quite overcome him; and therefore went to a public house not far from where he lived and inquired for some who were playmates before I went to sea. They told me there was one Benjamin Chapel lived near there with whom I had been very intimate while a lad. I sent for him and acquainted him who I was, desiring that he would go to my father and bring it out to him by degrees. This he readily undertook, well knowing he should be a most welcome messenger, and in a little time brought my father to me. The house was soon filled with the neighbourhood, who came to see me. What joy there was at such a meeting I leave the reader to conceive of, for it is not easily expressed. The first words my father said to me were

'Art thou my son Joseph?' with tears. 'Yes, father, I am,' said I. He immediately led me home to his house, many people following us, but he shut the door against them and would admit no one until, falling on his knees, he had returned hearty thanks to God for my signal deliverance.

If you listen carefully at the door to the past, what you hear most – above all the distant sounds of daily life and death – is the beating of the most unstoppable heart.

Abbreviations used in the Notes

All places of publication are London unless otherwise stated.

AHEW	Joan Thirsk (ed.), *The Agricultural History of England and Wales, vol. v: 1640–1750* (Cambridge, 2 vols, 1984–5)
Anglia Notitia	Edward Chamberlayne, *Anglia Notitia* (9th edn, 2 vols, 1676)
AR	Mark Overton, *The Agricultural Revolution* (1996)
Barlow's Journal	Basic Lubbock (ed.), *Barlow's Journal of his Life at Sea in King's Ships, East & West Indiamen & other Merchantmen from 1659 to 1703* (2 vols, 1934)
Baskerville	'Thomas Baskerville's Travels in England, temp. Car. II', in *The Manuscripts of his Grace the Duke of Portland preserved at Welbeck Abbey*, Historical Manuscripts Commission 13th report, part 2 (1893), pp. 263–314
BEG	Stephen Broadberry, Bruce M. S. Campbell, Alexander Klein, Mark Overton and Bas van Leeuwen, *British Economic Growth 1270–1870* (2015)
Bristol	Edwin and Stella George (eds), *Bristol Probate Inventories 1657–1689*, Bristol Record Society, vol. 57 (2005)
Buckinghamshire	Michael Reed (ed.), *Buckinghamshire Probate Inventories 1661–1714*, Buckinghamshire Record Society, no. 24 (1988)
Cosmo	Lorenzo Magalotti, *Travels of Cosmo the Third* (1821)
Crisis	Peter Clark and Paul Slack (eds), *Crisis and Order in English Towns 1500–1700* (1972)
CUHB	Peter Clark, *The Cambridge Urban History of Britain, vol. 2 (1540–1840)* (Cambridge, 2000)
D&D	Ian Mortimer, *The Dying and the Doctors: The Medical Revolution in Seventeenth-Century England* (2009)
DEEH	H. E. S. Fisher and A. R. J. Juřica (eds), *Documents in English Economic History: England from 1000 to 1760* (paperback edn, 1984)
Enclosure	J. R. Wordie, 'The chronology of English enclosure, 1500–1914', *The Economic History Review*, 36, 4 (1983), pp. 483–505

EoaW	A. F. Scott, *Everyone a Witness: the Stuart Age* (1974)
Essex	Francis Steer (ed.), *Farm and Cottage Inventories of Mid-Essex 1635–1749* (Colchester, 1950)
Evelyn	William Bray (ed.), *The Diary of John Evelyn* (Everyman's Library edn, 2 vols, 1966)
Fashion	Avril Hart and Susan North, *Seventeenth- and Eighteenth-Century Fashion in Detail* (2009)
FDB	C. Anne Wilson, *Food and Drink in Britain* (paperback edn, 1991)
Fiennes	Christopher Morris (ed.), *The Illustrated Journeys of Celia Fiennes* (1982)
Gamester	Charles Cotton, *The Complete Gamester* (5th edn, 1725)
GFS	Hannah Woolley, *Guide to the Female Sex* (3rd edn, 1682)
Global Crisis	Geoffrey Parker, *The Global Crisis: War, Climate Change and Catastrophe in the Seventeenth Century* (2013)
HECSC	C. Willett Cunnington and Phillis Cunnington, *Handbook of English Costume in the Seventeenth Century* (3rd edn, 1972)
HELS	Elizabeth Foyster and Christopher A. Whatley, *A History of Everyday Life in Scotland, 1600 to 1800* (Edinburgh, 2010)
Hooke	Richard Nichols, *The Diaries of Robert Hooke, the Leonardo of London, 1635–1703* (Lewes, 1994)
Josselin	E. Hockliffe, *The Diary of Ralph Josselin*, Camden Third Series, 15 (1908)
King's Highway	Sidney Webb and Beatrice Webb, *English Local Government: the Story of the King's Highway* (1913)
Later Stuarts	Sir George Clark, *The Later Stuarts 1660–1714* (2nd edn, Oxford, 1955)
Lincoln	J. A. Johnston, *Probate Inventories of Lincoln Citizens 1661–1714*, Lincoln Record Society (1991)
London Spy	Kenneth Fenwick (ed.), *The London Spy by Ned Ward* (Folio Society edn, 1955)
LSCCS	David Brandon, *Life in a Seventeenth-Century Coffee Shop* (Stroud, 2007)
Magna Britannia	Daniel Lysons and Samuel Lysons, *Magna Britannia being a concise topographical account of the several counties of Great Britain* (6 vols, 1806–22)
Markets	Colin Stephen Smith, 'The Market Place and the Market's Place in London, c. 1660–1840' (UCL PhD thesis, 1999)
Misson	*M. Misson's memoirs and observations in his travels over England. With some account of Scotland and Ireland* (1719)
Noble	Gladys Scott Thomson, *Life in a Noble Household, 1641–1700* (1937)

OCSH	Michael Lynch, *The Oxford Companion to Scottish History* (Oxford, 2001)
OCW	Jancis Robinson, *The Oxford Companion to Wine* (3rd edn, Oxford, 2006)
ODNB	*Oxford Dictionary of National Biography*: http://www.odnb.com/
OED	*The Oxford English Dictionary*: http://www.oed.com/
Ogg, *Charles II*	David Ogg, *England in the Reign of Charles II* (2 vols, Oxford, 1934; 2nd edn, 1956)
Ogg, *J. & W.*	David Ogg, *England in the Reigns of James II and William III* (Oxford, 1963)
Old Bailey	Old Bailey Online: https://www.oldbaileyonline.org/
Pepys	Robert Latham and William Matthews, *The Diary of Samuel Pepys: a New and Complete Transcription* (11 vols, 1970–83)
Pepys Companion	Robert Latham and William Matthews, *The Diary of Samuel Pepys: a New and Complete Transcription: Companion* (1983) [vol. x in the above series]
PFR	Margarette Lincoln (ed.), *Samuel Pepys: Plague, Fire, Revolution* (2015)
Pharmacopoeia	Nicholas Culpeper, *Pharmacopoeia Londinensis or the London Dispensatory* (4th edn, 1654)
PHE	E. A. Wrigley and R. S. Schofield, *The Population History of England 1541–1871: A Reconstruction* (1980)
PL	Stephen Porter, *Pepys's London* (2011)
PN	J. D. Davies, *Pepys's Navy: Ships, Men & Warfare 1649–1689* (2008)
Rugg	William L. Sachse (ed.), *The Diurnal of Thomas Rugg, 1659–1661*, Camden Third Series, 91 (1961)
Schellinks	Maurice Exwood and H. L. Lehmann (eds), *The Journal of William Schellinks' Travels in England 1661–1663*, Camden Fifth Series, 1 (1993)
SED	Joan Thirsk and J. P. Cooper (eds), *Seventeenth-century Economic Documents* (Oxford, 1972)
SSW	The Survey of Scottish Witchcraft: http://www.shca.ed.ac.uk/Research/witches/
Sufferers	Lucinda McCray Beier, *Sufferers and Healers* (1987)
Thoresby	Joseph Hunter (ed.), *The Diary of Ralph Thoresby* (2 vols, 1830)
ToH	Peter Brears, 'Seventeenth-century Britain', in Peter Brears, Maggie Black et al. (eds), *A Taste of History* (1993)
Travel in England	Joan Parkes, *Travel in England in the Seventeenth Century* (Oxford, 1925)
TTGEE	Ian Mortimer, *The Time Traveller's Guide to Elizabethan England* (2012)

TTGME   Ian Mortimer, *The Time Traveller's Guide to Medieval England* (2008)

Urban growth   E. A. Wrigley, 'Urban growth and agricultural change: England and the Continent in the Early Modern Period', *The Journal of Interdisciplinary History*, 15, 4 (1985), pp. 683–728

WCH   J. T. Cliffe, *The World of the Country House in Seventeenth-century England* (1999)

WWHL   Peter Laslett, *The World We Have Lost* (2nd edn, 1971)

Notes

Introduction

1. Devon Archives and Local Studies Service: QS 1/9 fol. 51r (4 April 1654), 55r (11 July 1654). The baby was ordered to be passed from place to place until it reached her husband (who refused to look after it). • **2**. *Global Crisis*, p. 22. • **3**. *The London Gazette*, 24–8 Jan. 1684. • **4**. *WWHL*, p. 167.

1. London

1. *Schellinks*, p. 48. • **2**. John E. N. Hearsey, *London and the Great Fire* (1965), p. 97. See also Claude de Jongh's views of the bridge, dated 1630 (at Kenwood), 1632 (Yale Center for British Art) and 1650 (V&A). • **3**. Jonathan Swift, 'A description of a city shower' (1710). • **4**. Sir John Hobart, quoted in *PL*, p. 20. • **5**. The figures here are from vol. 36 of the Survey of London, http://www.british-history.ac.uk/survey-london/vol36/pp25-34, downloaded 6 Nov. 2015. • **6**. *Schellinks*, p. 58. • **7**. *Cosmo*, p. 200. • **8**. In 'A Ramble in St James's Park'. • **9**. https://www.royalparks.org.uk/parks/hyde-park/about-hyde-park/history-and-architecture, downloaded 19 Oct. 2016. • **10**. This is a paraphrase. Brydall's line was half in Latin. He actually wrote: 'It [London] is stiled the epitome or breviary of all England, the seat of the British Empire, the king of England's chamber, *camera regis, reipublicæ cor, & totius regni epitome*' (p. 15). • **11**. Misson was writing much later, in 1697, but the comment is about some old houses that pre-dated the Fire. See *Misson*, pp. 134–5. Note: the book is sometimes attributed to its editor, François Maximilien Misson (e.g. *ODNB*). However, the original French edition (1698) has a dedication signed by 'H. M. de V.', referring to his brother Henri Misson. It is not clear who was the actual author. • **12**. Defoe, *Journal of the Plague Year*, quoted in Hearsey, *London and the Great Fire*, p. 19. • **13**. Rosemary Weinstein, 'New urban demands in Early Modern London', *Medical History*, Supplement no. 11 (1991), pp. 29–40 at p. 31, n. 11. The words 'if no'

have been deleted from the last line (after 'increase') to aid readability. •
14. Pepys, vii, p. 268. • **15**. Thomas Vincent, *God's Terrible Voice in the City*
(1667), quoted in *PL*, p. 136. • **16**. Pepys, vii, pp. 271–2. • **17**. Evelyn, ii, p. 12.
• **18**. As shown by melted pottery discovered by archaeological investigation
and now in the Museum of London. http://collections.museumoflondon.
org.uk/Online/object.aspx?objectID=object-750122, downloaded 9 Nov.
2015. • **19**. Pepys, viii, pp. 87, 114. • **20**. Hearsey, *London and the Great Fire*, p.
158. • **21**. Evelyn, ii, pp. 14–15. • **22**. Pepys, viii, p. 60. • **23**. Owen Ruffhead
(ed.), *Statutes at Large*, vol. 3 (1786), p. 289. • **24**. M. J. Power, 'East London
housing in the seventeenth century', in *Crisis*, pp. 237–62 at p. 244. • **25**. This
was later renamed the Hand-in-Hand Fire and Life Insurance Society. Note:
fire insurance had been invented at a slightly earlier date in Germany, in
1664, by the guilds of Hamburg. See *Global Crisis*, p. 635. • **26**. Edgar Sheppard,
The Old Royal Palace of Whitehall (1902), pp. 383–8. • **27**. Power, 'East London
housing', in *Crisis*, pp. 237–62 at p. 237. • **28**. PL, p. 208. • **29**. *Urban growth*,
p. 688; Ogg, *J. & W.*, p. 132. For Dublin, S. J. Connolly (ed.), *The Oxford
Companion to Irish History* (1998), p. 161, gives 50,000–60,000. • **30**. This is based
on a comparison of the population of London compared to the combined
total of the next-largest ten cities or towns in England in the years 1377, 1600,
1670, 1700, 1750 and 1800. For 1377, see *TTGME*, p. 10 (London's population
was just 59% of the combined total of the next-largest ten cities); for 1600,
see *TTGEE*, p. 16 (London was 225% the size of the next ten). For the other
dates, see *Urban growth*, p. 700. In 1750, London was 282% the size of the next
ten cities; in 1800 it was 172%; in 1861, 136%; in 1900, 160%; in 1951, 159%.

2. Beyond London

1. Thoresby, i, pp. 267–8. • **2**. Fiennes, p. 168. • **3**. Fiennes, pp. 166, 183. Blackstone
Edge was in Lancashire in the 17th century; it has been in West Yorkshire
since 1974. • **4**. Schellinks, p. 34. • **5**. Schellinks, p. 64. • **6**. Lincoln, p. 111.
• **7**. Schellinks, p. 130 (Dorchester); *BEG*, p. 106. • **8**. Most late-17th-century
writers regard Monmouthshire as part of England, not Wales, following its
adoption within the framework of English legal circuits in the reign of
Charles II. By this reckoning, its area of 507 square miles should be deducted
from the Welsh total and added to the English one. However, not all commentators saw it as English; Charles Davenant, for whom Gregory King drew
up his tables, did not. See *SED*, p. 802. • **9**. *Urban growth*, at p. 700, shows
rural employment in agriculture declining from 70% to 66% in this period.
However, Wrigley's definition of a town is a place with 5,000 or more people,
and thus includes many small towns in his 'rural' sample. If he had excluded

all small towns from this calculation, the level of agricultural employment would have been far higher. • **10**. The total population is from *Urban growth*, p. 700. Note: *PHE*, p. 528, gives a figure of 4.962 million. This was obtained by back-projection. In E. A. Wrigley, R. S. Davies, J. E. Oeppen and R. S. Schofield, *English Population History from Family Reconstitution 1580–1837* (Cambridge, 1997), p. 614, the authors use a different method (generalised inverse projection) to arrive at a figure for the midpoint in the five-year period 1696–1700 of 5.118 million. The authors did not regard Monmouthshire as part of England in this study. Gregory King put the population in 1695 at 5.5 million; *SED*, p. 772. To determine the rural population for England I have taken 75% of 5.06 million. The figure for urban density in 1695, adopting King's proportion of 25%, is 562 per square mile. • **11**. *Enclosure*, p. 502. • **12**. Ian Mortimer, *Berkshire Glebe Terriers 1634*, Berkshire Record Society (1995), xx. Parliamentary enclosures after 1738 account for a further 160,000 acres of the old county, or roughly one-third (using its pre-1974 boundaries). Relatively little enclosure took place in England in the early 18th century, as private agreements petered out and Enclosure Acts had yet to become popular as a means whereby landlords could secure control of the land. See *Enclosure*, p. 498. • **13**. These are Oxfordshire, Cambridgeshire, Northamptonshire, Huntingdonshire, Bedfordshire, Leicestershire, East Riding of Yorkshire, Rutland, Lincolnshire and Nottinghamshire. See *Enclosure*, pp. 500–1. County Durham should also be added to these counties; see *AR*, p. 149. • **14**. Figures adapted from *Enclosure*, p. 502. J. R. Wordie's statistics – about 47% enclosed by 1600, and about 71% enclosed by 1700 – have been adjusted to exclude the remaining commons in 1914: this is in order to focus on the decline of champaign country, not unenclosed spaces in general. • **15**. Robert C. Allen, 'Community and Market in England: Open Fields and Enclosures Revisited', in M. Aoki and Y. Hayami (eds), *Communities and Markets in Economic Development* (Oxford, 2001), pp. 42–69 at p. 62. • **16**. *BEG*, p. 54. This is a logarithmic scale and seems to show a rise in horses from about 0.32 million to 0.64 million. See also Nat Alcock, *People at Home: Living in a Warwickshire Village 1500–1800* (Chichester, 1993), p. 190; John Langdon, 'The Economics of Horses and Oxen in Medieval England', *Agricultural History Review*, 30, 1 (1982), pp. 31–40. As Langdon explains, oxen were cheaper than horses in the Middle Ages because, being held in common, many of their costs fell to the manor, not to the tenants. • **17**. *BEG*, p. 106. For comparison, there were about 23 million sheep in the UK in 2015, one-third of a sheep per person; about 10.9 million of these were in England, one-fifth of a sheep per person. • **18**. *AR*, pp. 100, 106. • **19**. *Pepys*, iv, p. 356 (29–30 Oct. 1663). • **20**. John McCann, *Clay and Cob Buildings* (3rd edn, Princes Risborough, 2004), p. 35. • **21**. *Fiennes*, p. 168. • **22**. *AHEW*, ii, pp. 409–11.

The total functioning in 1690 was put at 874 (including 73 in Wales) by John Adams. However, he must have included some desperately small places to reach that total; the 1693 figure is more useful when considered in conjunction with those for the earlier and later periods. The English cities were Durham, York, Carlisle and Chester in the province of York; and Canterbury, Rochester, Chichester, Winchester, Salisbury, Exeter, Wells, Worcester, Hereford, London, Lincoln, Ely, Norwich, Lichfield, Bristol, Gloucester, Peterborough and Oxford in the province of Canterbury. The Welsh cities – Bangor, St Asaph, St David's and Llandaff – were also part of the province of Canterbury. The diocese of Sodor and Man, in the Isle of Man, was also in the province of Canterbury. • **23.** There is a full survey in the History of Parliament volumes for 1690–1715 (available online at http://www. historyofParliamentonline.org/volume/1690–1715/survey/constituencies-and-elections, downloaded 20 Dec. 2015). The total I have given for England includes the eight Cinque Ports (Dover, Hastings, Hythe, New Romney, Rye, Sandwich, Seaford and Winchelsea) as well as Durham and Newark, which were enfranchised by an Act of Parliament in 1673. It does not include Monmouth, which included the out-boroughs of Newport and Usk, and which is included in the Welsh total. • **24.** John Toland, *The Art of Governing by Partys* ... (1701), p. 75. • **25.** http://www.clickonwales.org/wp-content/uploads/4_Factfile_Settlements.pdf, downloaded 24 Nov. 2015. Christopher Chalkin, *The Rise of the English Town, 1650–1850* (Cambridge, 2001), p. 8, suggests the population of Wrexham was just 2,500 in 1650. • **26.** Data from *Urban growth*, p. 700. • **27.** For Exeter houses at this time, see Michael Laithwaite, *Exeter Houses 1450–1700* (Exeter, 1966), p. 58. • **28.** Fiennes, p. 198. • **29.** *Cosmo*, p. 133. He describes the cathedral as 'a very considerable edifice; the architecture is gothic but it deserves praise for its size and for having its exterior ... ornamented with different figures in stone, both in high and low relief, representing saints both of the Old and New Testament. Many of these have been injured and broken in the time of Cromwell.' • **30.** *Cosmo*, p. 137. • **31.** *Cosmo*, p. 137. The awkward 19th-century translation has been smoothed a little here. • **32.** For this reference I am indebted to the excellent blog 'Demolition Exeter', http://demolition-exeter.blogspot.co.uk/, downloaded 25 Nov. 2015. For the ballast in the next sentence, see Michael Laithwaite, *Exeter Houses 1450–1700* (Exeter, 1966), p. 60. • **33.** Fiennes, p. 197. • **34.** *Fiennes*, p. 197. • **35.** *Baskerville*, p. 308. • **36.** *Cosmo*, pp. 124–5. • **37.** Philip Jenkins, *A History of Modern Wales 1536–1990* (2nd edn, 2014), pp. 34–5; Paul Slack, 'Great and good towns 1540–1700', in *CUHB*, pp. 347–76, at p. 350. • **38.** *Lincoln*, pp. 143–4. • **39.** *Fiennes*, p. 172. • **40.** Michael Faraday, *Ludlow 1085–1660* (Chichester, 1991), pp. 160, 168. The figure for 1700 is an estimate based on the 66 baptisms in that year, reported in *Abstract of answers and returns made* *pursuant to an Act passed in the forty-first year of King George III* ... (1802), p. 251, extrapolated using an approximate annual crude birth rate of 31 births per thousand people. • **41**. *Magna Britannia*, iii, pp. 99–101. • **42**. *Magna Britannia*, iv, pp. 22–6; *AHEW*, i, p. 7. • **43**. The 810 is Gregory King's urban 25% of the total population of England and Wales in 1700 (5.5 million), less the population of the large towns (850,000), divided between the 648 market towns and cities in England and Wales in 1693 with fewer than 5,000 inhabitants. • **44**. *Schellinks*, p. 81. • **45**. *Cosmo*, p. 140; *Fiennes*, p. 181. • **46**. For the population of Moretonhampstead: the parish registers indicate a total parish population of about 1,600, rising to 1,700 in the late 17th century, to which should be added a few Presbyterians after 1672. The borough had as many houses as the manor of Moreton in the 1639 survey of the manor and borough, and about another third of the population lay in other manors in the parish (Doccombe, Wray and South Teign). It is probable that the town supported about 40% of the parish population. Other details are from the 1639 survey (in the archives of the Rural History Centre, University of Reading) and the several 18th-century surveys in the Courtenay collection (Devon Heritage Centre, Exeter). See also Ian Mortimer, 'Index of Medical Licentiates, Applicants, Referees and Examiners in the Diocese of Exeter, 1568–1783', *Transactions of the Devonshire Association*, 136 (2004), pp. 99–134; Bill Hardiman and Ian Mortimer, *A Guide to the History and Fabric of St Andrew's Church Moretonhampstead* (Friends of St Andrew's, paperback, 2012); and *Magna Britannia*, vi, 2, p. 357. • **47**. *Baskerville*, pp. 289–90. • **48**. *OCSH*, p. 488. • **49**. Various dates are given for this landmark killing; I have gone with the one in *Later Stuarts*, p. 409. • **50**. Pepys to W. Hewer, Rawlinson MSS A 194, ff. 276–7, quoted in Arthur Bryant, *Samuel Pepys* (3 vols, 1954–8), ii, p. 379. • **51**. *A Trip to Barbarous Scotland* (c. 1708), quoted in *EoaW*, p. 49. • **52**. *Fiennes*, pp. 182–4. • **53**. The other 11 dioceses were Argyll, Brechin, Caithness, Dunblane, Dunkeld, Moray, Ross, Galloway, the Isles, Orkney and St Andrews. • **54**. For the average size of touns, see *HELS*, p. 31. • **55**. *HELS*, p. 37. • **56**. *CUHB*, p. 419. • **57**. Ogg, *Charles II*, i, pp. 400–2. • **58**. *HELS*, p. 5, states that 5.3% of the Scottish population lived in towns of 10,000 or more, i.e. Glasgow and Edinburgh. Robert Allen Houston, *Population History of Britain 1500–1750* (Cambridge, 1992), p. 20 (quoting Ian D. Whyte, 'Urbanisation in early modern Scotland: a preliminary analysis', *Scottish Economic History Society*, 9, 1 (1989), pp. 21–37 at p. 22), gives the same figure, based on a population of 53,000 in towns of 10,000 or more, and thus presuming a total national population of 1 million. However, the hearth tax of 1691 suggests a population nearer to 1.2 million, and a figure close to that of 1.265 million in Webster's census of 1755 is supported by *OCSH*, pp. 487–8. In addition, there seems to be some debate on the populations of the towns in 1700.

Older works tend to say 50,000 for Edinburgh and 12,000 for Glasgow. Paul Slack diplomatically puts the figure at '40,000 or more' in *CUHB*, p. 350, and states that Glasgow's population in 1700 was 18,000. David Harris Sacks and Michael Lynch in the same volume (p. 419) put Edinburgh, Canongate and South Leith at a total of 40,000; Glasgow at 15,000, Dundee at 9,000, Aberdeen at 10,000 and Ayr at 5,000 in 1691: thus they give a total large-town population of 79,000. Presuming the figure of 1.2 million is correct for the whole country in 1691, this suggests that 6.6% lived in large towns. If Slack's figure for Glasgow is correct, this would add 3,000 to the large-town urban population, meaning the proportion would be 6.8%. • **59**. *OCSH*, p. 220. • **60**. Sir Alexander Grant, *The Story of the University of Edinburgh During its First Three Hundred Years* (2 vols, 1884), i, pp. 224–5. • **61**. *HELS*, p. 220. • **62**. Robert Chamber, *Notices of the Most Remarkable Fires in Edinburgh from 1385 to 1824 . . .* (Edinburgh, 1824), pp. 13–15. • **63**. Alexander Reid, 'Aye Ready': *The History of Edinburgh Fire Brigade, the Oldest Municipal Brigade in Britain* (1974). This reproduces the Act Appointing a Company for Quenching of Fire (1703), which company consisted of 12 firefighters. It is sometimes said that the brigades set up by the London fire-insurance companies were the earliest fire services in the world, and they may have been (see chapter 1). However, these were private services, not municipal ones. According to Arthur E. Cote, P.E., and Percy Bugbee, *Principles of Fire Protection* (1988), p. 4, the world's first paid town fire service was set up in Boston after a fire in 1679, employing a fire chief and 12 firefighters and using an engine imported from England. Reid gives the credit for Britain's first municipal fire brigade to the Edinburgh force set up in 1824, because its staff were paid and not voluntary (as they were in 1703). Brian Allaway does likewise in his preface to the second edition (Edinburgh, 2004) of James Braidwood's *On the Construction of Fire Engines and Apparatus* (1st edn, Edinburgh, 1830). No mention is made of the earlier force, which, I presume, either fell into abeyance in the 18th century or failed to meet the test of a municipal fire brigade by the standards of 1824.

3. The People

1. *SED*, p. 775. • **2**. *PHE*, pp. 528–9. • **3**. *OCSH*, p. 488. For the emigration to Poland, see *Global Crisis*, p. 100. • **4**. This figure is based on the statistics for the early 1680s. Wrigley et al., *English Population History from Family Reconstitution*, p. 267. See also *WWHL*, pp. 132–3. • **5**. *Global Crisis*, p. 93. • **6**. The 1695 figures, which relate only to England and Wales, are from Gregory King, quoted in *WWHL*, p. 108; these have been adapted to provide a breakdown for the ages 60+. The figures for 2011 are for the whole of the UK, from the 2011 Census (http://www.ons.gov.uk/ons/dcp171778_270487. pdf, downloaded 4 Jan. 2016). • **7**. *Evelyn*, ii, p. 140 (Grafton); *Pepys*, iii, p. 297n.; iv, p. 107. • **8**. *WWHL*, p. 116. • **9**. *WCH*, p. 66. • **10**. *Josselin*, p. 169. • **11**. *Evelyn*, ii, p. 153. • **12**. *Evelyn*, ii, pp. 159, 174. • **13**. *Josselin*, p. 160. • **14**. *Fiennes*, p. 146. • **15**. *WWHL*, pp. 115–16. Alice is generally described as Mother George, née Guise. Mrs Reginald Lane Poole's catalogue of the paintings of Wadham College (R. Lane, *Catalogue of Portraits in the Possession of the University, Colleges, City and County of Oxford*, vol. iii, part 2 (1925), p. 218) suggests she was born in 1582, as Mother George was careful to relate that she was born in 'Saltwyche', Worcestershire (i.e. Droitwich) on Thursday, 1 November – and 1 November fell on a Thursday in 1571, 1575, 1582 and 1593; Mrs Lane Poole opts for the second-to-last, but with no explanation as to why. She adds that Mother George's father was Hugh Guise and her mother Bridgit Watkins. One Hugh Gise did live at the time in Hadzor, a mile from Droitwich, but he was married to a woman called Alice. Hugh and Alice Gise had the following children: Francis (baptised in July 1565), Johane (Dec. 1568) and Christopher Gise (Jan. 1575). There is therefore a gap in the recorded births of children around the time that Alice Guise is supposed to have been born (*c.* 1571) and it could be that Mother George was the child of Hugh and Alice, but baptised elsewhere; there is also the circumstantial evidence of the same name being borne by her possible mother. However, it should be noted that there was another Hugh Gise in the area, whose son John was baptised in St Andrew's, Droitwich, in February 1598. Also, children were born in the 1570s and 1580s to John Gise of Hadzor; William Guyse of St Andrew's, Droitwich; Richard Guyse of St Peter's, Droitwich; and Thomas Guyse of the same parish. None of these were called Alice or Mary (the other name associated with the portrait of Mother George in 1691). As for her children, her son John George was noted by Locke as being 77 in March 1681. While his baptism has not been found, three children surnamed George were baptised in the parish of St Giles in the years 1610–16, including one called Bridget George, so there is every likelihood that Alice married Richard George before 1610. In conclusion, the appearance of a Hugh Guise in Droitwich having children between 1565 and 1575 may be considered as supporting Alice's claim to have been born in the early 1570s, and the three Oxford baptisms also support her claim to have been married before 1610, but her exact age cannot be verified. She cannot have been 108 on 1 March 1681, when Locke met her, if she was born on a Thursday, 1 November, but she could have been 105 or 109. Nor can we be certain about the number of children she had. Given that she lived for another 10 years, there is a case to be made for hers being a rare case of genuine extreme longevity.

• **16**. *Schellinks*, p. 72. • **17**. *SED*, pp. 780–1. King did not group his status ranks according to class – these associations are my own – but given that he used terms such as 'greater sort', 'middle sort' and 'lesser sort', he clearly understood that such groupings could apply in the 1690s. • **18**. Thomas Blount, *Glossographia, or a Dictionary interpreting all such Hard Words of Whatsoever Language now used in our refined English Tongue* (2nd edn, 1661), under 'classe'. On the evolution of the terminology of class in the early modern period, see Keith Wrightson, 'Estates, Degrees and Sorts in Tudor and Stuart England', *History Today*, 37, 1 (1987). • **19**. Daniel Defoe, *The Review* (25 June 1709). • **20**. *Anglia Notitia*, i, p. 263–7. Note that this number was a relatively recent development; in 1603 there were no dukes, just one marquess, 19 earls, 3 viscounts and 40 lords: a total of 63 secular lords. • **21**. For wealth earlier in his career, see *Noble*, p. 366. For his wealth at death, see *ODNB*, under Bedford, quoting Thomson, *Russells in Bloomsbury*, p. 101. • **22**. *Noble*, pp. 23–5, 124, 203. • **23**. *Pepys*, iv, p. 22. • **24**. *Evelyn*, ii, p. 111; D. C. Coleman, 'Banks, Sir John, baronet (*bap.* 1627, *d.* 1699)', *ODNB*. • **25**. *Evelyn*, ii, pp. 152, 177; Michael J. Braddick, 'Fox, Sir Stephen (1627–1716)', *ODNB*; Richard Grassby, 'Child, Sir Josiah, first baronet (*bap.* 1631, *d.* 1699)', *ODNB*. • **26**. Sir Henry Craik, *The Life of Edward, Earl of Clarendon, Lord High Chancellor of England* (1911), p. 222. • **27**. B. R. Mitchell, *British Historical Statistics* (1988, paperback edn, 2011), pp. 166–9, analysed for the years 1670–1700 in my *Centuries of Change* (2014), p. 312. See also *BEG*, p. 60. • **28**. *DEEH*, pp. 207 (Trowbridge), 523 (carpenters' wages). • **29**. Devon Heritage Centre: Z1/21/2/1 10 March 1693. Counterpart of lease, for 99 years or 3 lives. • **30**. *Essex*, pp. 170–1. • **31**. *Barlow's Journal*, i, p. 251. • **32**. These examples are from *Pepys*, i, p. 307; ii, p. 207; iii, pp. 37–8, 105; iv, p. 109. • **33**. *SED*, p. 769. • **34**. *WCH*, p. 101; *DEEH*, p. 524. • **35**. *Hooke*, pp. 23–4. • **36**. *Josselin*, p. 136. • **37**. *Pepys*, iii, p. 53; iv, p. 86. • **38**. *Pepys*, iv, p. 95. • **39**. *Evelyn*, ii, p. 116. • **40**. *DEEH*, p. 526, quoting Daniel Defoe, *Giving alms no charity and employing the poor a grievance to the Nation* (1704), pp. 25–8. • **41**. Paul Slack, *The English Poor Law 1531–1782* (1990), pp. 26–7, 30 (table). • **42**. For example, those measures adopted by Huntingdonshire in 1676. See *DEEH*, pp. 448–51. • **43**. Ian Mortimer, 'Baskerville, Hannibal (1597–1668), antiquarian dilettante', *ODNB*. • **44**. This comes from the preamble to the 1697 Act of Parliament allowing for the establishment of a new workhouse in Exeter. • **45**. Ogg, *Charles II*, i, p. 124. • **46**. As several people have pointed out, the story does not correspond with the historical dates. However, that is not the point here. People believed it in the 1660s – indeed, Pepys himself believed it. See *Pepys*, ii, pp. 114–15. • **47**. *Pepys*, i, p. 269. • **48**. *Evelyn*, ii, p. 104. • **49**. *Evelyn*, ii, p. 253. • **50**. *Pepys*, iii, pp. 232–3. • **51**. *Misson*, p. 32. • **52**. John Miller, *James II* (3rd edn, 2000), p. 38. • **53**. *Pepys*, iv, p. 132 (dissection); p. 156 (horse's dung).

• **54**. The marquess of Halifax, *Advice to a daughter*, quoted in Ogg, *J. & W.*, pp. 78–9. • **55**. David Norbrook, 'Hutchinson, Lucy (1620–1681)', *ODNB*. • **56**. *Anglia Notitia*, i, pp. 291–6. • **57**. William Gouge, *Of Domesticall Duties* (1622), p. 337, quoted in Elspeth Graham, Hilary Hinds, Elaine Hobby and Helen Wilcox (eds), *Her Own Life: Autobiographical Writings by Seventeenth-Century Englishwomen* (1989), p. 8. • **58**. *Pepys*, iv, pp. 9–10. • **59**. *Anglia Notitia*, i, pp. 293, 299. • **60**. *Cosmo*, pp. 399–400. See also pp. 314–15 for the liberty of London women, even at night. • **61**. For example, 4 April 1661: Pepys left his wife at a gathering and returned home alone. See *Pepys*, ii, p. 66. For the potential seduction of a maidservant, see *Pepys*, iii, p. 152. He knew it was shameful, as he said so later, on p. 157. • **62**. *Pepys*, ix, p. 337. • **63**. This and the following instances of the law being favourable to women are from *Anglia Notitia*, i, p. 293. • **64**. Defoe, *Giving alms no charity*, quoted in *DEEH*, p. 526. • **65**. Divorce was very rare and was only possible for the very wealthy. Two forms were recognised in Restoration Britain: *a vincula matrimonii* (that the marriage should never have been contracted in the first place) and *a mensa et thoro* (that adultery had taken place). The latter precluded the divorced partners from remarrying after the divorce was complete. Only in 1700 did the duke of Norfolk's divorce *a mensa et thoro* result in an Act of Parliament specifically allowing him to remarry. Ogg, *J. & W.*, p. 78. For alimony, see *WCH*, p. 77. • **66**. *Misson*, p. 129. • **67**. *WCH*, p. 71. • **68**. Edward Albert Parry, *Letters from Dorothy Osborne to Sir William Temple (1652–54)* (1888), letter 19.

4. Character

1. *Barlow's Journal*, i, p. 261. • **2**. *Misson*, pp. 358 (hairs), 130 (coins). • **3**. Alan Macfarlane, *The Family Life of Ralph Josselin: An Essay in Historical Anthropology* (Cambridge, 1970), pp. 190–1. • **4**. *HELS*, p. 220. • **5**. John Aubrey, *Miscellanies* (1696). • **6**. *EoaW*, pp. 224–5, quoting Rev'd John Glanville's *Saducismus Triumphatus*. • **7**. *Evelyn*, ii, p. 282. • **8**. For examples of an almanac, see *Pepys*, i, p. 289; for a horoscope, *Evelyn*, ii, p. 92; for palmistry and gypsies, *Pepys*, iv, pp. 234, 284, 296. • **9**. *Pepys*, iv, p. 339 and n. • **10**. *Pepys*, i, p. 281. • **11**. *Evelyn*, ii, p. 199. • **12**. Harold J. Cook, 'Sydenham, Thomas (*bap.* 1624, d. 1689)', *ODNB*; Michael Hunter, 'Boyle, Robert (1627–1691)', *ODNB*. • **13**. As noted in James Sharpe, *Instruments of Darkness: Witchcraft in Early Modern England* (Philadelphia, 1997), p. 23, the decades around 1600 saw a marked increase in the number of witch trials. • **14**. Paula Hughes, 'Witch-hunting in Scotland 1649–50', in Julian Goodare (ed.), *Scottish Witches and Witch-hunters* (2013), p. 86. • **15**. Owen Davies, 'Witches in the dock: 10 of Britain's most infamous witch trials', *BBC History Magazine* (Dec. 2012).

• **16**. *SSW*, downloaded 25 Jan. 2016. • **17**. Robert Pitcairn, *Ancient Criminal Trials in Scotland* (3 vols, 1833), vol. 3, part 2, pp. 602–16. • **18**. *SSW*, downloaded 25 Jan. 2016. • **19**. *Misson*, pp. 129–30. • **20**. For example, see Moses Pitt's book, *An account of one Ann Jeffries now living in the county of Cornwall, who was fed for six months by a small sort of airy people called Fairies* (1696). • **21**. *Schellinks*, p. 123. • **22**. *Baskerville*, p. 268. • **23**. *Anglia Notitia*, i, p. 34. • **24**. *Cosmo*, pp. 426–62. • **25**. *Later Stuarts*, p. 27, gives 150,000–250,000. Ogg, *J. & W.*, p. 93, gives the proportions of faith amongst freeholders in 1676 as 2,477,154 conformists, 108,676 nonconformists and 13,856 Roman Catholics, but makes the point that Catholicism and dissent were more common in the northern province than these figures (based on the province of Canterbury) suggest. As the population of England in 1676 was about 5,003,488 (according to *PHE*, p. 528), this proportion would suggest considerably more than 200,000 people were living in nonconformist households. • **26**. This was especially the case in the aftermath of the Popish Plot of 1679. See John Cordy Jeaffreson (ed.), 'Middlesex Sessions Rolls: 1679', in *Middlesex County Records, volume 4, 1667–88* (1892), pp. 113–42. • **27**. *Pepys*, iii, pp. 266–7. • **28**. R. H., *The Clownish Hypocrite Anatomized* (1671). • **29**. *Later Stuarts*, p. 27 (30,000); *Schellinks*, p. 40 (Quakers in prison); *Pepys*, iv, p. 271 (100 arrests); *PL*, p. 144 (fine). • **30**. *Cosmo*, p. 428. • **31**. Robert Beddard, 'Anti-popery and the London Mob, 1688', *History Today*, 38, 7 (1988). • **32**. *PL*, p. 16. In 1697 Misson reckoned there were 60 or 70 Jewish families in London. See *Misson*, p. 144. • **33**. Famarez Dabhoiwala, *The Origins of Sex* (2012), p. 53. • **34**. Brian P. Levack, 'The Prosecution of Sexual Crimes in Early Eighteenth-century Scotland', *Scottish Historical Review*, 89, 288 (2010), pp. 172–93 at p. 175, n. 11. • **35**. *Barlow's Journal*, i, p. 286. • **36**. *Misson*, p. 311; *Thoresby*, i, p. 18. • **37**. *Pepys*, iii, p. 26 (music on a Sunday); i, pp. 220, 239. • **38**. *Misson*, p. 60. • **39**. *Pepys*, viii, 29 July 1667. • **40**. *Pepys*, iv, pp. 1, 30. • **41**. *Pepys*, ii, p. 209. • **42**. *Misson*, p. 287. • **43**. *Cosmo*, p. 397. The word order has been altered, with regard to the French, to make the meaning clearer. • **44**. *Pepys*, iii, p. 268. • **45**. *Evelyn*, ii, p. 351n. To be fair to that servant, the house was never the same again. • **46**. *Evelyn*, i, p. 378. • **47**. *EoaW*, p. 49, quoting *A Trip to Barbarous Scotland by an English Gentleman* (1709). • **48**. *Schellinks*, p. 75. • **49**. This was certainly the case in Devon. For some early-18th-century examples, see the militia assessments for Bere Ferrers and Egg Buckland (transcripts available at http://www.foda.org.uk/militia/documentindex.htm, downloaded 1 Nov. 2016). • **50**. Ogg, *Charles II*, ii, p. 492. • **51**. *Misson*, pp. 81–2. • **52**. *Misson*, pp. 81–2, 232–3; *Schellinks*, pp. 61–2; *PL*, p. 208. • **53**. Susan Dwyer Amussen, *Caribbean Exchanges: Slavery and the Transformation of English Society 1640–1700* (2007), p. 221. • **54**. *Anglia Notitia*, i, p. 299. • **55**. According to Miranda Kaufmann, he expressed this opinion in the trials of Chamberlain vs Harvey (1696), Smith vs Brown & Cooper (1701) and Smith vs Gould (1706). See http://www.mirandakaufmann.com/common-law.html, downloaded 14 March 2016. • **56**. Amussen, *Caribbean Exchanges*, pp. 219–20. • **57**. Devon Heritage Centre: Bishopsteignton parish register, 3/4/1708. • **58**. W. J. Hardy (ed.), *Middlesex County Records: Calendar of Sessions Books 1689–1709* (1905), p. 41. • **59**. Pepys, iii, p. 95. • **60**. Pepys, vi, p. 215. • **61**. Manuel Eisner, 'Long-Term Historical Trends in Violent Crime', *Crime and Justice*, 30 (2003), pp. 83–142 at pp. 85, 99. • **62**. Eisner, 'Long-Term Historical Trends', p. 99. Strangely, the Belgian propensity to violence continues to this day: at the time of writing, the murder rate in Belgium is 1.8 per 100,000, twice the UK figure. • **63**. Misson, pp. 305–6. • **64**. Keith M. Brown, 'Gentlemen & Thugs in 17th-Century Britain', *History Today*, 40 (Oct. 1990). • **65**. Much of what follows about duelling comes from Markku Peltonen, *The Duel in Early Modern England: Civility, Politeness and Honour* (Cambridge, 2003). For this point about it being the golden age of the duel, see p. 202. • **66**. Pepys, i, p. 20 (Chesterfield); *ODNB* (Tankerville); *Evelyn*, ii, p. 230 (Talbot); *Pepys*, ii, pp. 32–3 (Buckingham); *Evelyn*, ii, p. 355 (Seymour); J. Kent Clark, *Whig's Progress: Tom Wharton Between Revolutions* (2004), p. 218 (Wharton); *Pepys*, viii, p. 363. • **67**. Peltonen, *The Duel in Early Modern England*, pp. 206–8. • **68**. Sword duels were three times as lethal as pistol duels. They killed more than 20% of combatants, whereas pistol duels killed 6.5%. The reason was that honour could be satisfied by firing a shot (regardless of whether it hit or not) whereas, with a sword, blood had to be drawn. See Robert B. Shoemaker, 'The Taming of the Duel', *The Historical Journal*, 45, 3 (2002), pp. 525–45 at p. 528. • **69**. Misson, p. 216. • **70**. Schellinks, p. 62. This practice had begun slightly earlier, under Cromwell. • **71**. John Cordy Jeaffreson (ed.), 'Middlesex Sessions Rolls, 1670', in *Middlesex County Records, volume 4, 1667–88* (1892), pp. 17–24. • **72**. John Cordy Jeaffreson (ed.), 'Middlesex Sessions Rolls, 1657' in *Middlesex County Records, volume 3, 1625–1667* (1888), pp. 256–68. • **73**. Pepys, iv, p. 150 (devil); iii, p. 116 (whey). • **74**. Pepys, iii, p. 66 (cellar); iv, p. 8 (Barbados). • **75**. Schellinks, p. 73. • **76**. Pepys, ii, p. 214. • **77**. E. S. de Beer (ed.), *The Diary of John Evelyn* (Oxford, 1959), p. 540, quoted in *PL*, p. 59. • **78**. Anglia Notitia, i, pp. 52–3. • **79**. Pepys, ii, p. 17 (monkey); ii, p. 23 (canaries); iv, pp. 150–2 (blackbird). • **80**. Fiennes, p. 32. • **81**. D. B. Horn, *British Diplomatic Representatives 1689–1789*, Camden Third Series, xlvi (1932), *passim*. • **82**. Anglia Notitia, ii, pp. 284–5. • **83**. You can buy globes, by this period. Pepys does so in Sept. 1663 for £3 10s. See *Pepys*, iv, p. 302. • **84**. Pepys, ii, pp. 33–4 (Algerian slaves); *Evelyn*, ii, pp. 149, 195 (China and Japan); *Pepys*, iv, 11 Dec. 1663 (Königsberg). • **85**. Pepys, iii, pp. 172, 298; iv, pp. 189, 315, 350. Pepys owned books in Chinese and Russian. See *PFR*, p. 34. • **86**. News of Ameixial reported by Pepys on 25 June 1663 and published in *The Kingdom's Intelligencer*, 29 June –

Pepys, iv, pp. 198, 202–3. For Lima, see *Evelyn*, ii, p. 278. • **87**. Michael Hunter, 'Boyle, Robert (1627–1691)', *ODNB*, quoting Hunter, *Boyle by Himself* (1994), xlii. • **88**. Most of the details in this section are derived from Jeremy Lancelotte Evans, 'Tompion, Thomas (*bap.* 1639, *d.* 1713)', *ODNB*. • **89**. *Pepys*, i, p. 264. • **90**. *Fiennes*, p. 205; *Baskerville*, p. 291; *Evelyn*, ii, pp. 28, 180; Alan Marshall, 'Morland, Sir Samuel, first baronet (1625–1695)', *ODNB*. • **91**. *Hooke*, p. 65. The density of air is generally taken to be about 1.29kg per cubic metre. • **92**. Paul Pettitt and Mark White, *The British Palaeolithic: Hominin Societies at the Edge of the Pleistocene World* (2012), p. 145; J. S. Cockburn, H. P. F. King and K. G. T. Mcdonnell (eds), *A History of the County of Middlesex: volume one* (London, 1969), pp. 11–21. *British History Online*, http://www.british-history.ac.uk/vch/middx/vol1/pp11–21, accessed 13 Oct. 2016. • **93**. William Petty, *Political Arithmetick*, quoted in *DEEH*, p. 61. • **94**. *Evelyn*, pp. 134–5. • **95**. *Noble*, pp. 93–4. • **96**. R. A. Houston, 'The Development of Literacy: Northern England, 1640–1750', *The Economic History Review*, New Series, 35, 2 (1982), pp. 199–216 at pp. 206, 208; Houston, 'The Literacy Myth? Illiteracy in Scotland 1630–1760', *Past & Present*, 96 (1982), pp. 81–102 at pp. 92, 95, 97. • **97**. *GFS*, pp. 2–3. • **98**. Houston, 'The Development of Literacy', pp. 199–216 at p. 204; Houston, 'The Literacy Myth?', pp. 81–102 at p. 90. • **99**. *Evelyn*, ii, p. 267. • **100**. *Anglia Notitia*, i, pp. 320–1. • **101**. Dewey D. Wallace, jun., 'Morton, Charles (*bap.* 1627, *d.* 1698)', *ODNB*. • **102**. Macfarlane, *Family Life of Ralph Josselin*, pp. 165–6. • **103**. *Evelyn*, ii, pp. 217–21, esp. p. 219. • **104**. *Pepys*, i, p. 167; ii, pp. 43, 71, 73, 164, 169. • **105**. Ward, *London Spy*, p. 33. • **106**. George de Forest Lord (ed.), *Poems on Affairs of State: Augustan Satirical Verse, 1660–1714* (7 vols, 1963–75), i, p. 146. • **107**. de Forest Lord (ed.), *Poems on Affairs of State*, i, p. 424. • **108**. *Pepys*, vii, p. 371. • **109**. Quoted in Keith Brown, 'Gentlemen and Thugs in 17th century Britain', *History Today*, 40 (1990). • **110**. Quoted on the website of the National Portrait Gallery, http://www.npg.org.uk/collections/search/portrait/mw01903/Catherine-Sedley-Countess-of-Dorchester. • **111**. *Evelyn*, ii, p. 251. • **112**. *Evelyn*, ii, p. 100.

5. Basic Essentials

1. *Thoresby*, i, p. 10. • **2**. *Pepys*, iii, pp. 32, 35. • **3**. *Evelyn*, ii, p. 304. • **4**. Gordon Manley, 'Central England temperatures: monthly means 1659 to 1973', *Quarterly Journal of the Royal Meteorological Society*, 100 (1974), pp. 389–405, at p. 393. March 1674 averaged 1.2°C (in the modern world, the long-term average is 5.4°C); September 1694 averaged 10.5°C (12.7°C in the modern world); July 1695 averaged 13.4°C (15.1°C in the modern world); and May 1698 averaged 8.6°C (10.4°C in the modern world). The only periods of sustained high daytime temperatures (averaging 17°C or more for the month) were July and August 1666, July 1667, July 1669, July 1677, August 1679 and July 1699. • **5**. Baskerville, p. 299 (Cirencester); Pepys, ii, p. 239 (wassail bowl). • **6**. Ronald Hutton, The Rise and Fall of Merry England: The Ritual Year 1400–1700 (Oxford, 1994), p. 242. • **7**. Misson, pp. 34–5. • **8**. Chris Durston, 'The Puritan War on Christmas', History Today, 35, 12 (1985). • **9**. Durston, 'Puritan War', quoting Edward Fisher, A Christian Caveat to the Old and New Sabbatarians (1649). • **10**. Pepys, ii, pp. 44, 192; Pepys Companion, pp. 377–8; Schellinks, p. 73; Misson, pp. 330–1. • **11**. Pepys Companion, p. 164. • **12**. Bristol, p. 66. • **13**. Misson, pp. 36–7. • **14**. Pepys, i, p. 19. • **15**. Pepys states on 3 Sept. 1662: 'now the days begin to shorten and so whereas I used to rise by 4 a-clock it is not broad daylight now till after 5 a-clock, so that it is 5 before I do rise'. Pepys, iii, p. 185. And on 7 Jan. 1663 he says: 'up pretty early: that is by 7 a-clock, it being not yet light before or then'. Pepys, iv, p. 7. • **16**. Cosmo, p. 210. For 3 a.m. starts, see Pepys, i, p. 125; ii, pp. 135, 149. The latter two instances were prior to setting out on a trip. • **17**. Thoresby, i, p. 72. • **18**. John Aubrey, Brief Lives: A Modern English Version Edited by Richard Barber (Woodbridge, 1982), p. 204. • **19**. Pepys, i, p. 186. • **20**. The computerised comparison of the language reveals that 84% of the New Testament and 76% of the Old Testament of the King James Version were taken verbatim from Tyndale. See Jon Nielson and Royal Skousen, 'How much of the King James Bible is William Tyndale's? An Estimation based on Sampling', Reformation, 3 (1998), pp. 49–74. Also, when David Crystal read the King James Bible and counted therein a total of 257 idioms in daily use, he discovered only 18 were original to the team that put that work together: almost all the rest were the work of Tyndale. See David Crystal, 'King James Bible: How are the Mighty Fallen?', History Today, 61, 1 (January 2011). • **21**. Mark Stoyle, West Britons: Cornish Identities and the Early Modern British State (Exeter, 2002), p. 15; Later Stuarts, pp. 409–10. • **22**. Fiennes, p. 186. • **23**. Later Stuarts, p. 410; HELS, p. 165. • **24**. Pepys, i, pp. 260–1. • **25**. Evelyn, i, p. 357; Cosmo, pp. 222, 224. • **26**. The paper prices are from a 1674 inventory in Bristol, pp. 60–1. • **27**. Pepys, iv, pp. 263–4. • **28**. Anglia Notitia, ii, pp. 218–19; SED, pp. 367–9. • **29**. Anglia Notitia, ii, p. 219. • **30**. Misson, p. 222; Anglia Notitia, ii, pp. 218–19; Joan Day, 'Dockwra, William (bap. 1635?, d. 1716)', ODNB; Sir William Petty, Several Essays in Political Arithmetick (first published 1690; 4th edn, 1755), p. 171. • **31**. Josselin, p. 136. • **32**. Evelyn, ii, p. 311. • **33**. Evelyn, ii, pp. 278 (Sicily); Pepys, iv, p. 240 (Tangiers). • **34**. Pepys, ii, p. 56; iii, pp. 35–6. • **35**. D. J. H. Clifford (ed.), The Diaries of Lady Anne Clifford (Stroud, 1990), p. 232; Evelyn, ii, pp. 198 (flood of news), 349n. ('lecture nights'). • **36**. Asa

Briggs and Peter Burke, *A Social History of the Media: From Gutenberg to the Internet* (Cambridge, 2002), p. 76. • **37**. Briggs and Burke, *Media*, p. 76. • **38**. *Misson*, p. 283. • **39**. *Pepys*, i, pp. 281–2; iii, pp. 163, 221; *Evelyn*, ii, pp. 2, 90. • **40**. *Evelyn*, i, p. 366. Pepys notes the earl of Oxford's 'miss' too, and states that she is 'owned' by the earl. *Pepys*, iii, pp. 32, 58 and 86. In 1666 Evelyn has another swipe at lords' mistresses being onstage and refers to them as 'misses'. *Evelyn*, ii, pp. 19, 67 ('a miss as they call these unhappy creatures'). • **41**. *Pepys*, ii, pp. 199, 215; iii, p. 207. • **42**. *Pepys Companion*, pp. 100, 103. • **43**. *Cosmo*, p. 193. • **44**. *London Spy*, p. 31. • **45**. *Pepys*, i, p. 287. • **46**. *Fiennes*, pp. 64–5, 175. • **47**. J. P. B. Karslake, 'Further notes on the Old English Mile', *The Geographical Journal*, 77, 4 (1931), pp. 358–60. • **48**. *AHEW*, i, p. 8. • **49**. Thomas Keith, *The Complete Practical Arithmetician* (1824), p. 23. • **50**. The Scottish inch was 1.0016 of the imperial inch. See the data on the Scottish Archive Network page, http://www.scan.org.uk/measures/distance.asp, downloaded 14 March 2016. • **51**. *Pepys*, iii, p. 266n. • **52**. *PL*, pp. 165–6. • **53**. *Evelyn*, ii, p. 345. • **54**. *SED*, p. 707. • **55**. Richard S. Westfall, 'Newton, Sir Isaac (1642–1727)', *ODNB*. • **56**. *Pepys Companion*, p. 132. • **57**. This example is held by Royal Bank of Scotland Heritage Archives. See Object 91 on their website: http://heritagearchives.rbs.com/rbs-history-in-100-objects/going-the-extra-mile/cheque-1659–60.html, downloaded 16 March 2016. • **58**. For example, *Noble*, p. 104. • **59**. *PL*, p. 170. • **60**. Formally known as 'An account of tallies struck on particular funds, the payments made thereon, and the principal remaining due'. Ogg, *J. & W.*, p. 412. • **61**. I think it is fair to say this was a common expression in the early 18th century, if not the 17th. Although often associated with Benjamin Franklin, it was first recorded in Christopher Bullock's *The Cobbler of Preston* (1716) as 'Tis impossible to be sure of any thing but Death and Taxes'. It also appeared in several other pre-Franklin texts, including Edward Ward's *Dancing Devils* (1724), p. 43, and Daniel Defoe's *The History of the Devil* (1728), p. 302. There was also a variation, 'who would not appear against death and taxes?', in *The Gentleman's Magazine* (1733), p. 152. • **62**. 12 Charles II, cap. 4, cap. 23; Owen Ruffhead (ed.), *Statutes at Large*, vol. 3 (1786), pp. 147–62, 172. • **63**. Ogg, *Charles II*, ii, p. 435. • **64**. Details of the Free and Voluntary Present are from the National Archives website, http://www.nationalarchives.gov.uk/e179/notes.asp?slctgrantid=188&action=3, downloaded 13 March 2016. • **65**. Anne L. Murphy, 'Lotteries in the 1690s: Investment or Gamble?', *Financial History Review*, 12, 2 (2005), pp. 227–46; 10 & 11 William III, c. 17. • **66**. Ogg, *J. & W.*, p. 414. • **67**. *Baskerville*, p. 310. • **68**. 'Guilds, markets and fairs', in P. M. Tillott (ed.), *A History of the County of York: The City of York* (1961), pp. 481–91, http://www.british-history.ac.uk/vch/yorks/city-of-york/pp481-491, accessed 9 March 2016. • **69**. Mitchell (ed.), *British Historical Statistics*, pp. 719, 754. • **70**. Daniel

Defoe, *A Tour thro' the Whole Island of Great Britain* (3 vols, 1724–7), vol. 1, letter 1, part 3 (http://www.visionofbritain.org.uk/travellers/Defoe/4, downloaded 15 March 2016). • **71**. Edward Ward, *Step to Stir-Bitch-Fair with remarks upon the University of Cambridge* (1700), pp. 3, 14. • **72**. *Baskerville*, pp. 272–3. • **73**. These details are mostly from Defoe, *Tour.* The detail about Newton is from http://www.cam.ac.uk/research/features/stirbitch-mapping-the-unmappable, downloaded 15 March 2016. • **74**. Ward, *Step to Stir-Bitch-Fair*, p. 15. • **75**. *Pepys*, iv, p. 84 (haggling); i, p. 284 (inch of candle). • **76**. *London Spy*, p. 57. • **77**. The six that were discontinued are Bishopsgate, Eastcheap, Fish Street Hill, Old Fish Street, St Nicholas Shambles and St Paul's Churchyard. • **78**. By 1700 there were general food markets at Shadwell and Wapping (to the east of the city), Spitalfields (to the north-east) and Southwark (to the south). To the west of the city you had Bloomsbury, Brooke's Market (near Gray's Inn Road), Clare Market, Covent Garden Piazza, Hungerford Market (near Charing Cross), Newport Market, St James's Market and Westminster. In addition there were hay markets in Haymarket, Whitechapel, Southwark and Chapel Street (Westminster), and a Rag Fair on Tower Hill for second-hand clothes. See *Markets*, p. 216. • **79**. *Markets*, p. 27. • **80**. *Markets*, pp. 28, 102.

6. What to Wear

1. Christopher Dyer, *Standards of Living in the Later Middle Ages* (revised edn, Cambridge, 1998), pp. 316–17. Similar heights are noted for Scotsmen and women: 5′ 5″ to 5′ 7″ (165–170cm) for the men and 5′ 1″ to 5′ 3″ (155–160cm) for the women. See *OCSH*, p. 285. • **2**. Tim Allen, 'The Forgotten Chemical Revolution', *British Archaeology*, 66 (2002), http://www.archaeologyuk.org/ba/ba66/feat2.shtml, downloaded 22 May 2016. • **3**. *Lincoln*, p. 8. • **4**. For an example, see *Fashion*, p. 194. • **5**. C. Willett Cunnington and Phillis Cunnington, *The History of Underclothes* (1951), pp. 56–60. • **6**. Thirteen new pairs were valued at £1 2s 6d in 1680; a single second-hand pair at 1s 6d in 1685. See *Bristol*, pp. 112, 139. • **7**. *HECSC*, pp. 133–4. • **8**. *Fashion*, pp. 80, 96. • **9**. *Noble*, p. 339 (muslin); *HECSC*, p. 147 (Venetian lace). • **10**. *Pepys*, iv, p. 80. • **11**. E.g. '3 dozen of wooleing hose for men £2 2s 0d' in *Bristol*, p. 102. • **12**. *Pepys*, iii, pp. 204, 217, 224. For boots costing 9s, see *Bristol*, p. 67. • **13**. *HECSC*, p. 154 (red heels). • **14**. *Pepys*, i, p. 26; *HECSC*, p. 156. • **15**. *Pepys*, viii, p. 249. • **16**. *Buckinghamshire*, pp. 258–9. • **17**. *Pepys Companion*, p. 101. • **18**. *Pepys*, iv, pp. 343, 350, 357–8, 380. • **19**. *Pepys*, ix, p. 217. • **20**. *Noble*, pp. 341–2. • **21**. *PFR*, p. 125. For dog-skin gloves, see *Lincoln*, p. 110. • **22**. *Noble*, p. 341. • **23**. *Noble*, pp. 343–4. • **24**. *Lincoln*, p. 110. • **25**. *Lincoln*, p. xlviii. • **26**. In March 1785 *The Edinburgh Magazine* carried a letter written 20 years earlier, stating that the kilt had been invented by an English engineer, Thomas Rawlinson, in the 1730s. The author of the letter had known Rawlinson. There are other stories about the origins of the kilt, including variations on this one, but this is the prime first-hand account. • **27**. *HELS*, pp. 141, 156. • **28**. *EoaW*, p. 48, quoting *A Trip to Barbarous Scotland by an English Gentleman* (1709). • **29**. William Cleland, *A Collection of Several Poems and Verses* (1697), pp. 12–13. • **30**. *Fashion*, p. 190. • **31**. Julia Allen, *Swimming with Dr Johnson and Mrs Thrale: Sport and Exercise in Eighteenth-century England* (2012), pp. 163–4. • **32**. I have not found a case of a smock marriage for the years in question, but there are instances recorded earlier and later. At Much Wenlock in 1547 Thomas Munslow, smith, married Alice Nycols in her smock and bare-headed (Cunnington and Cunnington, *Underclothes*, p. 47). At Chiltern All Saints in 1714 John Bridmore married Anne Selwood in her smock 'without any clothes or headgear on' (William Andrews, *Old Church Lore* (1891), p. 186). The latter work has further references for smock marriages in 1723, 1738, 1776, 1771, 1797, 1808 and between 1838 and 1844. Amy Louise Erickson, *Women and Property in Early Modern England* (2002), p. 146, states that 'the idea of smock marriage was at least symbolic of the husband not getting any money with his bride from the early 17th century. Sir John Villiers protested he would take the heiress Frances Coke, daughter of Sir Edward Coke, "in her smock", implying (speciously) that he loved her for her person, not her money.' • **33**. *Pepys Companion*, p. 102, is quite wrong to suggest otherwise. The reference to 'plenty of literary evidence' is a single reference to a ballad in John Ashton (ed.), *A Century of Ballads illustrative of the life, manners and habits of the English nation during the Seventeenth Century* (1887), in which women ran in men's underwear for the sake of titillation. • **34**. *Pepys*, iv, p. 172. This seems to be the meaning here, given the 'naughty' context of women wearing drawers elsewhere. It is possible that he wondered whether she was wearing long drawers – i.e. stirrup drawers – to preserve her modesty. He discovered in May 1668 that the recently married Mrs Lowther wore long drawers at her father's house in London, for when he changed her shoes and tried to touch her thigh, he found them interrupting the progress of his hand. See *Pepys*, ix, p. 194. • **35**. Ashton (ed.), *Ballads*, pp. 277–9; Allen, *Swimming with Dr Johnson and Mrs Thrale*, p. 164. • **36**. Thomas Mace, *Musick's Monument* (1676), p. 232. • **37**. *Pepys*, iii, p.77; *Pepys Companion*, p. 101. • **38**. *Rugg*, p. 105. • **39**. John Bulwer, *Artificial Changeling* (1653), quoted in *HECSC*, p. 170. • **40**. *Fashion*, pp. 212–13 (braid, perfumed shoe), 214–15 (embroidered velvet pantofles). • **41**. *Misson*, p. 214. • **42**. *Fiennes*, p. 207. • **43**. *Bristol*, p. 54. • **44**. *Pepys Companion*, p. 102. • **45**. *Pepys*, i, p. 299. • **46**. *HECSC*, pp. 181–3. • **47**. *Pepys*, v, p. 78. • **48**. *Pharmacopoeia*, p. 146. • **49**. Quoted in *HECSC*, p. 187. • **50**. *Pepys*, iii, p. 239. • **51**. *Misson*, p. 214; *HECSC*, p. 187. • **52**. *Schellinks*,

p. 43; Iris Brooke, *English Costume of the Seventeenth Century* (2nd edn, 1950), p. 68. • **53**. *Essex*, p. 125. • **54**. *Fiennes*, p. 173. • **55**. *EoaW*, p. 49, quoting *A Trip to Barbarous Scotland by an English Gentleman* (1709). • **56**. *HELS*, p. 158. • **57**. Hannah Woolley, *The Gentlewoman's Companion* (3rd edn, 1682), pp. 294, 303. • **58**. *Pepys*, i, p. 19. • **59**. *Pepys*, i, p. 296. • **60**. *Noble*, p. 214. • **61**. For instance, 'two smoothing irons' were appraised at 2s in Bristol in 1689. See *Bristol*, p. 179. • **62**. *OED*, under 'iron' and 'ironing'.

7. Travelling

1. *Schellinks*, pp. 46, 48. • **2**. *Fiennes*, p. 22. • **3**. *Fiennes*, pp. 40–1. • **4**. *Fiennes*, p. 203. • **5**. *Thoresby*, i, p. 295. • **6**. *Fiennes*, p. 214. • **7**. *Baskerville*, pp. 271–2. • **8**. *Pepys*, iv, p. 139. • **9**. *Travel in England*, p. 14. • **10**. *Travel in England*, pp. 8–11; *HELS*, p. 253. • **11**. *Travel in England*, p. 27; *King's Highway*, pp. 22–3. • **12**. *King's Highway*, p. 147. • **13**. For a reference to an Elizabethan signpost in Kent, see *King's Highway*, p. 156. • **14**. *King's Highway*, p. 157. • **15**. *Fiennes*, p. 164. • **16**. *Travel in England*, p. 27. • **17**. *DEEH*, p. 65; *Fiennes*, p. 135. • **18**. *Baskerville*, p. 296. • **19**. *Cosmo*, p. 402; *Misson*, p. 172; Lettie S. Multhauf, 'The Light of Lamp-Lanterns: Street Lighting in 17th-Century Amsterdam', *Technology and Culture*, 26, 2 (1985), pp. 236–52 at pp. 251–2. See also E. S. de Beer, 'The early history of London street-lighting', *History*, new series, 25, 100 (March 1941), pp. 311–24. • **20**. £1 15s to light the space in front of twenty houses. See Ogg, *J. & W*, p. 133. • **21**. *Pepys*, viii, p. 174. • **22**. In 1636 there were 6,000 coaches in London; Sir William Petty estimated in 1676 that there had been a considerable increase in the number. See J. H. Markland, 'Some remarks on the early use of carriages in England', *Archaeologia*, xx (1824), pp. 443–76 at p. 468. If the population increase over the years 1636–70 – from about 300,000 to 475,000 – had resulted in a commensurate increase in the number of coaches, we should expect there to have been about 9,500 in 1670. • **23**. On 15 Dec. 1662 Pepys knocked off two pieces of beef from the side of the shambles in Newgate Market with his coach. The butchers stopped the horses and he was forced to pay them a shilling in reparations. *Pepys*, iii, p. 283. On 27 Nov. 1660 he came to a great 'stop of coaches' in King Street, caused by a falling-out between a drayman and a footman. *Pepys*, i, p. 303. • **24**. *Travel in England*, p. 79; *SED*, p. 381. • **25**. *Travel in England*, p. 80; *Pepys Companion*, p. 451. • **26**. *Travel in England*, pp. 71–2. • **27**. The chaise is first mentioned in *OED* in an entry dated 1701. • **28**. *Pepys*, ii, p. 110 for the chariot-vs-coach race. • **29**. *Pepys*, i, p. 286; *Pepys Companion*, p. 453; *Misson*, p. 306. • **30**. *Lincoln*, lxxiii, p. 75. • **31**. Markland, 'Some remarks on the early use of carriages in England', p. 463. • **32**. *Noble*, p. 208. This is actually described as a 'charet' but seems more to resemble a coach, with its glass windows and the high price. The total includes £53 10s for the basic frame and cab; £24 for velvet to line the cab; £10 14s to the glassmaker for windows; £14 10s to the fringemaker for adornments; and £25 for a painter to finish the decoration. • **33**. The earl of Bedford paid £25 for a horse in 1641 (*Noble*, p. 54). In 1680 the countess of Sunderland paid £100 for a pair of coach horses: see *Travel in England*, p. 76. • **34**. *Lincoln*, p. 75. Gregory King estimated the rental value of pasture and meadow at 9s per acre in 1688. • **35**. *Noble*, pp. 203, 206–7. • **36**. *Pepys Companion*, p. 453. • **37**. *Evelyn*, ii, p. 280. • **38**. *Pepys*, iv, p. 430. • **39**. *Evelyn*, ii, p. 221. • **40**. *Misson*, p. 39. • **41**. *Anglia Notitia*, ii, p. 219. • **42**. Coaches from the George Inn also made the journey to Wakefield, Leeds and Halifax (£2 per person, leave on Fridays); to Durham and Newcastle (£3, every Monday); and Bath or Bristol (£1, every Monday and Thursday). The Edinburgh trip took place every three weeks and cost £4 10s. See *EoaW*, p. 202, quoting *Mercurius Politicus* (1658); Markland, 'Some remarks on the early use of carriages in England', p. 474; *SED*, pp. 384–5. • **43**. *Schellinks*, p. 65. • **44**. *SED*, pp. 383–5. • **45**. *Travel in England*, p. 86. • **46**. *PL*, p. 164; see also *Pepys Companion*, p. 451. • **47**. Ward, *Step to Stir-Bitch-Fair*, pp. 3–4. • **48**. This is how Mrs Pepys lost a waistcoat in January 1663. *Pepys*, iv, p. 28. • **49**. *SED*, pp. 388–9. • **50**. *Evelyn*, ii, p. 20. • **51**. *Pepys*, ix, p. 474; *Josselin*, p. 159. • **52**. *Travel in England*, p. 70; *Evelyn*, ii, pp. 41, 274. • **53**. *Schellinks*, p. 93. • **54**. *London Spy*, p. 87: • **55**. *Noble*, p. 206. • **56**. *Buckinghamshire*, p. 181. • **57**. *Lincoln*, p. 88. • **58**. *Bristol*, pp. 151, 175. • **59**. A number of different sources attest to this, not least the Berkshire probate accounts: see Ian Mortimer (ed.), *Berkshire Probate Accounts 1573–1712*, Berks Record Society (Reading, 1999). Of the 162 accounts in this book, 84 relate to the period up to 1630; yet only one of those accounts mentions horse hire and, in that 1608 case, the accountant lived in London and probably hired his horse there. There are 16 references to horse hire in the remaining 78 accounts, which relate to the years 1631–51 and 1663–1712. The rates of appearance of references to horse hire are about the same in the period 1631–51 as they are after the Restoration. Early years see a predominance of hire by accountants in large towns. It is perhaps significant that hackney carriages started in London in the 1620s too. • **60**. The 1d per mile rate is evidenced in Mortimer (ed.), *Berkshire Probate Accounts*, pp. 159, 199, 215. Horse hire from Pangbourne to Woolhampton (9 miles each way) costs 1s 6d (1681); from Tilehurst to London (84 miles), 7s; and from Tilehurst to Oxford (25 miles), 4s. The first of these also gives a 3s price for three trips from Pangbourne to Woolhampton, which rather suggests a 1s rate. In 1680 there is a direct reference to 'one day's horse hire' at a rate of 1s for a Frilford accountant (*Berkshire Probate Accounts*, p. 214). • **61**. *Schellinks*, p. 178. • **62**. *Pepys*, ii, pp. 15, 133.

• **63**. *Thoresby*, i, pp. 12–13. His route was to Royston (41 miles) on day one; to Stamford (58 miles) on day two; to Tuxford (48 miles) on day three; and to Leeds (57 miles) on day four. In July 1680 he rode the route in the same time, going via Cambridge (54 miles) on day one; Casterton, Rutland (48 miles) on day two; Barnby Moor (58 miles) on day three; and reaching Leeds (43 miles) on day four (*Thoresby*, i, p. 49). • **64**. *Schellinks*, p. 65; *Baskerville*, p. 276. • **65**. *Misson*, pp. 11–12. • **66**. *Schellinks*, p. 58; *Pepys*, i, p. 287; ii, p. 12. For the yacht's dimensions, see the National Maritime Museum model of the *Mary*, http://collections.rmg.co.uk/collections/objects/66330.html, downloaded 9 June 2016. • **67**. *PN*, p. 63. • **68**. *Misson*, p. 21. • **69**. *Schellinks*, p. 70. • **70**. *Pepys*, i, p. 311. • **71**. *Rugg*, p. 72. • **72**. *Travel in England*, pp. 102–3. • **73**. *Schellinks*, p. 69. • **74**. This was in November 1699. *Evelyn*, ii, p. 357. • **75**. *Fiennes*, p. 203. • **76**. *SED*, pp. 370 (trows), 420. • **77**. Carew Reynel, *The True English Interest* (1674), pp. 42–3, quoted in *SED*, pp. 386–7. • **78**. T. S. Willan, 'The River Navigation and Trade of the Severn Valley, 1600–1750', *Economic History Review*, 8 (1937), pp. 68–79; idem, 'Yorkshire River Navigation 1600–1750', *Geography*, 22 (1937), pp. 189–99; *PN*, p. 116 (Bedford). • **79**. Mitchell (ed.), *British Historical Statistics*, p. 534; *PN*, p. 114. • **80**. Ogg, *J. & W.*, pp. 294–5. • **81**. *PN*, p. 114. • **82**. *PN*, p. 33. • **83**. *Anglia Notitia*, ii, pp. 155–7. • **84**. *PN*, p. 38. • **85**. *PN*, p. 115. • **86**. *Pepys*, iv, pp. 256–7. • **87**. *SED*, p. 352. • **88**. *Cosmo*, pp. 95–7. • **89**. *PN*, p. 146. • **90**. Elizabeth Baigent, 'Collins, Greenvile (d. 1694)', *ODNB*. • **91**. *Thoresby*, i, pp. 17, 25–7. • **92**. *SED*, p. 582. • **93**. *Barlow's Journal*, i, p. 228. • **94**. *PN*, p. 154. • **95**. *Schellinks*, p. 41. • **96**. *PN*, p. 76. • **97**. *PN*, p. 156. • **98**. *PN*, p. 156. • **99**. *PN*, p. 152. • **100**. Henry Teonge, *Diary* (1825), pp. 27–8. • **101**. Joe J. Simmons, *Those Vulgar Tubes* (2nd edn, 1997), p. 7. • **102**. Simmons, *Tubes*, pp. 43, 52.

8. Where to Stay

1. *Pepys*, ix, p. 231. • **2**. This has been the case since 1393. Jacob Larwood and John Camden Hotten, *English Inn Signs* (1951), p. 8. • **3**. Larwood and Hotten, *English Inn Signs*, p. 11. • **4**. *Baskerville*, p. 265 • **5**. *Pepys Companion*, p. 452; *Baskerville*, p. 307. • **6**. *Lincoln*, p. 105. • **7**. *Bristol*, p. 82. • **8**. *Pepys*, i, p. 150. • **9**. Lawrence Wright, *Warm and Snug* (1962), p. 125. • **10**. Wright, *Warm and Snug*, p. 128. • **11**. *Pepys*, iii, p. 70. • **12**. *Pepys*, iii, p. 70. • **13**. John Summerson, *Architecture in Britain 1530–1830* (9th edn, 1993), p. 141. • **14**. *Fiennes*, p. 106. • **15**. *Fiennes*, p. 47. • **16**. *Fiennes*, p. 105. • **17**. *Evelyn*, ii, p. 243. • **18**. *WCH*, p. 59. • **19**. *Fiennes*, p. 171. • **20**. *Evelyn*, ii, p. 235. • **21**. *Noble*, pp. 280–301 (Woburn); *WCH*, pp. 43, 45. • **22**. Katherine Gibson,

'Gibbons, Grinling', *ODNB*, quoting Vertue, *Notebooks*, 4.11. • **23**. *Evelyn*, ii, p. 82. • **24**. *WCH*, p. 19. • **25**. Kathryn Barron, 'Verrio, Antonio', *ODNB*. • **26**. Peter Thornton, *Seventeenth-Century Interior Decoration in England, France and Holland* (1978), p. 56. • **27**. *Pepys*, i, pp. 269 (decoration), 298. • **28**. *WCH*, pp. 30, 39; *Buckinghamshire*, p. 269 (smoking room at Shardeloes); *Evelyn*, ii, p. 117. • **29**. *WCH*, p. 38. • **30**. *WCH*, p. 24. • **31**. *WCH*, p. 161. • **32**. *Lincoln*, pp. 73–5. Note: I have presumed this is an old-fashioned house, on account of it having a hall and no room named as being the chamber over the hall (implying it was still probably full-height, and thus old). I have also presumed that the lack of reference to paintings or tapestries in the parlours indicates they were wainscoted. • **33**. Hentie Louw and Robert Crayford, 'A constructional history of the sash-window c. 1670–1725', *Architectural History*, 41 (1998), pp. 82–130. • **34**. Pepys bought a new-fashioned door knocker in Nov. 1662. *Pepys*, iii, p. 263. • **35**. For example, 'Abroad to look out a cradle to burn charcoal in at my office, and I found one to my mind in Newgate Market.' *Pepys*, iv, p. 409. • **36**. See *Misson*, pp. 37–8, for an account of how to light a coal fire and the need for a good chimney. • **37**. Mitchell, *British Historical Statistics*, p. 244. • **38**. *HELS*, p. 11. • **39**. *Pepys*, i, p. 302. • **40**. *Bristol*, p. 78. • **41**. *Bristol*, p. 35. • **42**. *Lincoln*, p. 120. • **43**. *Lincoln*, pp. 32–3. • **44**. Margaret Cash (ed.), *Devon Inventories*, Devon & Cornwall Record Society, NS 11 (Torquay, 1966), pp. 174–5. • **45**. *Pepys*, i, p. 269. • **46**. *Pepys*, iv, p. 155. • **47**. Quoted in Liza Picard, *Restoration London* (1997), p. 14. • **48**. *Pepys*, iv, pp. 252–3. • **49**. James Ayres, *The Shell Book of the Home in Britain* (1981), p. 34. • **50**. As the earliest inventory for this house dates from 1634 and it does not appear in the 1597 survey, I have presumed it was built between those two dates and thus had mullion windows. See N. W. Alcock, *Living in a Warwickshire Village 1500–1800* (Chichester, 1993), pp. 85 (wealth, inventory), 215 (date). • **51**. Cash (ed.), *Devon Inventories*, p. 162. • **52**. *Fiennes*, pp. 40, 144; Ayres, *The Home in Britain*, p. 31. • **53**. *Baskerville*, p. 298. • **54**. *HELS*, p. 11; Ayres, *The Home in Britain*, p. 34.

9. What to Eat, Drink and Smoke

1. *Anglia Notitia*, i, p. 6. • **2**. *Misson*, p. 314. • **3**. Quoted in *Pepys Companion*, p. 148. • **4**. This is based on the master carpenter having a gross salary of £25,000, including five weeks' paid holiday (£532 per week). Both the chicken and the pear cost – as proportions of a carpenter's weekly wage – fourteen times more in real terms than they do in the modern world. • **5**. *Schellinks*, p. 33. • **6**. *Pepys*, ii, pp. 112–13. • **7**. These dates are for prices in the Exeter corn market. See Mitchell, *British Historical Statistics*, p. 754. • **8**. *OCSH*,

p. 286; Stana Nenadic, 'Necessities: food and clothing in the long 18th century', in *HELS*, pp. 137–63, at p. 137. • **9**. Henry Buttes, *Dyet's Dry Dinner consisting of eight seuerall courses* (1599), section 4, under 'oyster'. • **10**. Evelyn, ii, p. 143. • **11**. Pepys, i, p. 291. • **12**. Pepys, ii, p. 3. • **13**. Charles R. Geisst, *Beggar Thy Neighbour: A History of Usury and Debt* (2013), p. 102. This would appear to be about 6–7 times the likelihood of dying from food poisoning in England and Wales in the 21st century. • **14**. HELS, p. 138. • **15**. Fiennes, pp. 39–40 (crab, lobster), 61 (cider), 64 (salmon), 166 (char), 204 (cream). • **16**. Baskerville, pp. 268 (herring), 294 (eels), 299 (sage cheese), 310 (liquorice). • **17**. Baskerville, pp. 274–6. • **18**. Noble, p. 141 (Lord Bedford); Pepys, ii, pp. 44–5, 52, 55, 60. • **19**. GFS, pp. 218–19. • **20**. Pepys, ii, p. 119; iii, p. 10. • **21**. Baskerville, pp. 263 (beer), 297. • **22**. Pepys, i, p. 9; ii, pp. 208, 228. • **23**. Misson, p. 313. • **24**. ToH, p. 201. • **25**. Pepys, iv, p. 354. • **26**. Cosmo, pp. 377–8. • **27**. As Celia Fiennes did when she dined at Bretby. See Fiennes, p. 155. • **28**. ToH, p. 196. • **29**. EoaW, p. 43. • **30**. Noble, pp. 165–6. • **31**. Noble, p. 144. • **32**. FDB, p. 58. • **33**. FDB, pp. 105, 111. • **34**. FDB, p. 101; ToH, p. 184. • **35**. ToH, p. 204. • **36**. Evelyn, ii, p. 143. • **37**. FDB, p. 56. • **38**. Pepys, iv, p. 14. • **39**. Pepys, iv, p. 95. • **40**. Pepys, i, p. 223. • **41**. Pepys, i, p. 263; iii, p. 234. • **42**. Ward, Stir-Bitch-Fair, p. 7. • **43**. Schellinks, p. 91. • **44**. Pepys, iv, p. 192. • **45**. Misson, pp. 146–7. • **46**. London Spy, p. 187. • **47**. Pepys Companion, pp. 417–18. • **48**. Pepys, iv, p. 301. • **49**. Pepys Companion, p. 417; Misson, p. 147. • **50**. Noble, pp. 218–20. • **51**. Fiennes, p. 207. • **52**. Although potato farming certainly helped, it did not cover more than 2% of the agricultural land in 1801. See AR, p. 102. • **53**. ToH, p. 193. • **54**. Anglia Notitia, i, p. 51. • **55**. PL, p. 13; Fiennes, pp. 136 (Norwich), 146 (Leicester), 186 (Shrewsbury), 198 (Exeter). • **56**. FDB, p. 385. • **57**. Ward, Stir-Bitch Fair, p. 8. • **58**. Pepys, i, p. 283 (Northdown); London Spy, p. 179 (Coloquintida). • **59**. Schellinks, pp. 38, 40. • **60**. Baskerville, p. 308. • **61**. Fiennes, p. 182; Pepys Companion, p. 105. • **62**. Baskerville, pp. 292 (Scudamore apples), 293 (Redstreak), 295 (prices); Fiennes, p. 41; Pepys, iv, p. 254; Noble, p. 181 (bottled cider). • **63**. Pepys, i, p. 317. • **64**. On 23 Oct. 1663 Pepys bought half a dozen bottles with his crest upon them, for the storage of wine. See Pepys, iv, p. 346. • **65**. Noble, p. 189. • **66**. OCW, p. 97. • **67**. OCW, p. 511. • **68**. Noble, pp. 192–3; OCW, p. 151. The same year (1676), Thomas Shadwell referred in his Virtuoso (Act 1, Scene 2) to Sparkes entering the playhouse 'ful of champagn, venting very much noise, and very little wit'. • **69**. Charles Ludington, 'The Politics of Wine in 18th-century England', History Today, 63, 7 (July 2013), http://www.historytoday.com/charles-ludington/politics-wine-18th-century-england, downloaded 1 Sept. 2016. • **70**. Pepys, iv, p. 100. • **71**. In his poem 'The Search after Claret' (1691) Richard Ames called Haut-Brion 'sprightly Pontac'. • **72**. FDB, p. 391. • **73**. Pepys, iv, p. 235. • **74**. Baskerville, p. 295. Note: these

were the prices in Worcester. • **75**. *Baskerville*, p. 308. • **76**. *Noble*, p. 197.
• **77**. Tim Unwin, *Wine and the Vine* (1991), p. 243. • **78**. *SED*, p. 86.
• **79**. *Noble*, p. 200. • **80**. *FDB*, pp. 400, 403. • **81**. *LSCCS*, p. 19 (infertility);
Clarke, *Later Stuarts*, p. 358. • **82**. *LSCCS*, pp. 50–1. • **83**. *Bristol*, pp. 118–19.
• **84**. *LSCCS*, p. 23. • **85**. *Misson*, pp. 39–40. • **86**. *Noble*, p. 168. • **87**. *LSCCS*,
p. 24. • **88**. *Pepys*, i, p. 253. • **89**. *FDB*, pp. 411–12. • **90**. *Noble*, p. 170.
• **91**. *Pepys*, ii, p. 88 (the morning after the coronation); iii, p. 227; iv, p. 5.
• **92**. *FDB*, pp. 408–10. • **93**. *Cosmo*, p. 398. • **94**. *Schellinks*, p. 121. • **95**. *Misson*,
pp. 311–13; *Fiennes*, p. 204; *Baskerville*, p. 303. • **96**. *Misson*, p. 313. • **97**. *HELS*,
p. 224. • **98**. Jorevin de Rocheford, quoted in *Fiennes*, p. 204 n. 13. • **99**. *Noble*,
pp. 345–6.

10. Health and Hygiene

1. See Alice Thornton's autobiography, quoted in *Sufferers*, p. 227. • **2**. *Sufferers*,
p. 164. • **3**. *Barlow's Journal*, i, p. 178. • **4**. Edward Jorden, *A discourse of Naturall
Bathes and Mineral Waters* (3rd edn, 1683), pp. 132, 134. • **5**. Jorden, *Naturall
Bathes*, p. 138. • **6**. *Fiennes*, p. 45. • **7**. *Schellinks*, p. 106; *Fiennes*, p. 46.
• **8**. *Fiennes*, p. 93. • **9**. *Fiennes*, p. 94. • **10**. *Thoresby*, i, pp. 54, 86, 234.
• **11**. *Baskerville*, p. 314. • **12**. *Fiennes*, pp. 125–7. • **13**. *Schellinks*, pp. 87–8.
• **14**. *Pepys*, ix, p. 233. • **15**. *HELS*, p. 224, quoting E. W. Marwick, *The Folklore
of Orkney and Shetland* (1975), p. 92. • **16**. Virginia Smith, *Clean: A History of
Personal Hygiene and Purity* (Oxford, 2007), p. 220. • **17**. *WCH*, p. 39; *Pepys
Companion*, p. 103. • **18**. Joseph Pitts, *Faithful Account of the Religion and Manners
of the Mahometans* (4th edn, 1738), pp. 69–70. • **19**. *Pepys*, i, p. 298. • **20**. Jorden,
Naturall Bathes, p. 134. Note that Jorden was addressing an educated and
wealthy readership in his book, not a bunch of washerwomen, which
rather indicates that he reckoned most gentlemen and educated women
would know what washing with soap might do to their fingers.
• **21**. For Pepys and lice, see *Pepys*, iv, p. 38. • **22**. The total number of people
recorded in the Bills of Mortality in the years 1660–1700 is 890,361. The total
number of plague deaths recorded is 70,735 (7.94%), 68,596 of them in 1665.
If the average number of deaths in 1660–64 (17,019) is subtracted from the
total number buried in 1665 (97,306) to take into account the maximum
levels of under-recording of the plague in 1665, the total is 80,287 (9.02%).
Adding the non-1665 plague deaths gives a total maximum of 82,426 (9.26%).
Over the whole period, 141,982 (15.9%) are recorded as dying of consumption (not including the King's Evil), 119,496 (13.4%) of convulsions, 111,499
(12.5%) of agues and fever and 85,984 (9.66%) of 'griping in the guts'.
• **23**. Paul Slack, *The Impact of Plague in Tudor and Stuart England* (1985),

p. 151. The Great Plague of 1665 killed more people, but they represented a smaller proportion of the population. • **24**. Walter George Bell, *The Great Plague of London* (1924), pp. 23–4. • **25**. *Evelyn*, i, p. 404. • **26**. *Pepys*, vi, p. 268. • **27**. Bell, *Great Plague*, p. 143. • **28**. Slack, *Impact of Plague*, p. 317. • **29**. Bell, *Great Plague*, p. 140. • **30**. A. G. E. Jones, 'The Great Plague in Ipswich', *Proceedings of the Suffolk Institute for Archaeology and History*, xxviii, 1 (1958), pp. 78–89 at p. 88; Charles Creighton, *History of Epidemics in Britain* (1894), ii, pp. 687–90; Slack, *Impact of Plague*, pp. 16 (Colchester), 138 (Norwich). • **31**. Bell, *Great Plague*, p. 296. It is frequently stated that the population of Eyam was 360 at the time. A detailed piece of analysis available at the Eyam Museum website indicates that the population was exactly 700, of whom 433 are known to have survived. See http://www.eyam-museum.org.uk/assets/files/eyam-population-1664–1667.pdf, downloaded 4 Sept. 2016. • **32**. Evelyn, quoted in Vanessa Harding, 'Housing and Health in Early Modern London', in V. Berridge and M. Gorsky (eds), *Environment, Health and History* (2012), pp. 23–44 at p. 38. • **33**. *Pharmacopoeia*, pp. 24, 70, 92. • **34**. F. N. L. Poynter, *A Seventeenth-Century Doctor and his Patients: John Symcotts, 1592?–1662*, Bedfordshire Historical Record Society, xxxi (1951), p. 49. • **35**. *Pharmacopoeia*, pp. 56, 58, 61. • **36**. Richard Tomlinson, *A Medicinal Dispensatory* (1657), p. 589. • **37**. *Hooke*, pp. 26–7. • **38**. *Evelyn*, ii, p. 236. • **39**. *Mercurius Politicus* (20 Dec. 1660), quoted in *EoaW*, p. 140. • **40**. *Pepys*, ii, p. 53. • **41**. *Pharmacopoeia*, p. 64; *Sufferers*, p. 141. • **42**. *Pharmacopoeia*, pp. 10, 30, 67. • **43**. Roy Porter, 'Madness and its institutions', in Andrew Wear (ed.), *Medicine in Society: Historical Essays* (Cambridge, 1992), pp. 279, 285. • **44**. *PHE*, p. 256 (1.7%); *Global Crisis*, p. 93 (4%). • **45**. For the design of the forceps owned by Dr Chamberlen and found in 1813 at Woodham Mortimer Hall, see Peter M. Dunn, 'The Chamberlen family (1560–1728) and obstetric forceps', *Archives of Disease in Childhood Fetal & Neonatal Edition*, 81 (1999), F232–5. • **46**. Eric Jameson, *A Natural History of Quackery* (1961), p. 29. • **47**. Andrew Wear, 'Making sense of health and the environment in early modern England', in Wear (ed.), *Medicine in Society*, p. 127. • **48**. Lord Ruthven, *The Ladies Cabinet Enlarged and Opened* (4th edn, 1667), pp. 63–5 (spa water), 70–1 (toothache), 86 (snakes), 127 (gout). • **49**. Barry Till, 'Stillingfleet, Edward (1635–1699)', *ODNB*. • **50**. *D&D*, pp. 154–5. • **51**. *D&D*, pp. 78, 112–15; Noble, p. 40 (£20 for a course of treatment for smallpox). • **52**. Jonathan Barry, 'John Houghton and Medical Practice in William Rose's London: The Medical World of Early Modern England, Wales and Ireland, 1500–1715: Working Paper Two' (April 2015), http://practitioners.exeter.ac.uk/wp-content/uploads/2014/11/EMP_WP2_Barry_Houghton.pdf, downloaded 6 Sept. 2016. • **53**. Harold J. Cook, 'Sydenham, Thomas (*bap.* 1624, *d.* 1689)', *ODNB*. • **54**. *PFR*, p. 39; Patrick Wallis, 'Exotic Drugs and English Medicine: England's

Drug Trade *c.* 1550–1800', LSE Working Papers 143/10 (2010), Table 1 and Figure 2. • **55**. *D&D*, pp. 58–9 (Canterbury). For the Exeter figures, 8 apothecaries were admitted freemen in the 45 years of Elizabeth's reign: at an average career length of 26 years, this suggests there were 4.6 apothecaries at any one time. In the period 1660–1700 the number admitted was 39, suggesting 24.7 apothecaries at any one time. It is assumed that Exeter apothecaries worked a comparable length of time to their Canterbury colleagues. • **56**. *Pharmacopoeia*, pp. 64–5. • **57**. Richard Sugg, *Mummies, Cannibals and Vampires: The History of Corpse Medicine from the Renaissance to the Victorians* (2011), pp. 58–9. • **58**. Thomas Brugis, *The Marrow of Physick* (1669), p. 65. Quoted in P. Kenneth Himmelman, 'The medicinal body: an analysis of medical cannibalism in Europe, 1300–1700', *Dialectical Anthropology*, 22, 2 (1997), pp. 183–203 at p. 197. On the subject in general, see Sugg, *Mummies, Cannibals and Vampires*). • **59**. *Pepys*, iii, p. 77. • **60**. *D&D*, p. 86. In Kent, some payments were as low as 6d; 2s 6d was not an unusual sum. Payments of 3s 6d and 4s are noted too in Berkshire and Sussex. • **61**. *Sufferers*, p. 63. • **62**. *Sufferers*, pp. 61, 74. • **63**. *PFR*, p. 38. • **64**. *Evelyn*, ii, pp. 42, 48, 98.

11. Law and Disorder

1. Michael J. Galgano, 'Lisle, Lady Alice (*c.* 1614–1685)', *ODNB*. • **2**. Melinda Zook, 'Gaunt, Elizabeth (*d.* 1685)', *ODNB*. • **3**. J. M. Beattie, 'The Pattern of Crime in England 1660–1800', *Past and Present*, 62 (1974), pp. 47–95 at p. 48. • **4**. *Old Bailey*, ref: t16931206-14. • **5**. *Old Bailey*, ref: t16760510-1. • **6**. *Old Bailey*, ref: t16940524-20. • **7**. *Old Bailey*, ref: t16770711-1. • **8**. *Barlow's Journal*, ii, pp. 451–3. • **9**. *Evelyn*, ii, p. 133; http://www.historyofParliamentonline. org/volume/1660–1690/member/evelyn-george-i-1617–99, downloaded 13 Sept. 2016. • **10**. Ogg, *J. & W.*, p. 64. • **11**. Luttrell Collection of Broadsides, 1683–4, quoted in *EoaW*, pp. 24–5. • **12**. John Brydall, *Camera Regis* (1676), pp. 43–58, 73–5. • **13**. J. A. Sharpe, *Crime in Early Modern England* (1984), p. 22. • **14**. Kenneth Pennington, 'Innocent until proven guilty: the origins of a legal maxim', *The Jurist*, 63 (2003), pp. 106–24. • **15**. Pennington, 'Innocent', p. 119. • **16**. Ogg, *Charles II*, i, p. 408. • **17**. *Schellinks*, p. 86. • **18**. *Misson*, pp. 324–5; *Old Bailey*, ref: s16901015-1. • **19**. *Schellinks*, pp. 82–3. • **20**. *Misson*, p. 124. • **21**. *Old Bailey*, refs: t17000115-19; s17000115-1. • **22**. *Pepys*, ii, p. 71. • **23**. *Old Bailey*, refs: t16830418-7, s16830418-1. • **24**. *Old Bailey*, ref: t16820224-15. • **25**. Andrea McKenzie, '"This Death Some Strong and Stout Hearted Man Doth Choose": The Practice of Peine Forte et Dure in Seventeenth- and Eighteenth-Century England', *Law and History Review*, 23, 2 (Summer, 2005), pp. 279–313, at p. 280. • **26**. McKenzie, 'Peine Forte et Dure', p. 302. • **27**. *Baskerville*, p. 295; N. M. Herbert (ed.), *A History of the County of Gloucester: Volume 4, the City of Gloucester* (1988), pp. 245–7. • **28**. *Schellinks*, p. 34. • **29**. Levack, 'Sexual Crimes in Early Eighteenth-century Scotland', pp. 174–6. • **30**. Faramerz Dabhoiwala, *The Origins of Sex* (2012), pp. 55–6. • **31**. Dabhoiwala, *Origins of Sex*, pp. 58–60. • **32**. Timothy Curtis and J. A. Sharpe, 'Crime in Tudor and Stuart England', *History Today*, 38, 2 (Feb. 1988). • **33**. *Old Bailey*, ref: t16771010-6. • **34**. This statement is based on the fact that there were about 14,730 christenings in 1685 and 14,694 in 1686. If just 5% were stillborn, there were at least 15,500 pregnancies per year between all the women of child-bearing age. Taking the population as about 520,000 at the time, and estimating that roughly half that number were aged 15–45 and assuming that half of those were women, just under 12% of women of child-bearing age became pregnant every year. However, a child is not felt to kick within the womb until about 4 months; thus the pregnancies should only have been discoverable for 5 months in the year, so the expectation that any woman of child-bearing age in court could have been found to be 'quick with child' in the manner used should be ($^5/_{12}$ x 15,500)/130,000, which is just under 5%.

12. Entertainment

1. *London Spy*, p. 181; *Pepys*, ii, p. 166. • **2**. *London Spy*, p. 182. • **3**. Philip H. Highfill, Kalman A. Burnim and Edward A. Langhans, *A Biographical Dictionary of Actors, Actresses, Musicians, Dancers, Managers and Other Stage Personnel in London, 1660–1800* (Carbondale and Edwardsville, 1982), vol. 7, pp. 23–5. • **4**. *Evelyn*, i, p. 345. • **5**. *Evelyn*, i, p. 325. • **6**. *EoaW*, p. 134. • **7**. *Evelyn*, ii, p. 83. • **8**. *Evelyn*, i, p. 325 (hairy woman). • **9**. Henry Morley, *Bartholomew Fair* (1859), pp. 315–32. • **10**. *Evelyn*, ii, pp. 196–7; *Travel in England*, p. 105; *PL*, p. 27; *Misson*, pp. 318–19. • **11**. *Misson*, pp. 25–7. • **12**. *Gamester*, p. 196. • **13**. *Cosmo*, p. 313. • **14**. *Anglia Notitia*, i, pp. 52–3. • **15**. This figure of 350 archers in Finsbury Fields relates to 1675 (http://www.bowyers.com/bowyery_finsburyMarks.php, downloaded 19 Oct. 2016). In Scotland, the group that would one day become the Royal Society of Archers was formed by 1676. The Musselburgh Silver Arrow, the world's oldest sporting trophy, has been offered every year since 1603. In England, the Scorton Silver Arrow has been competed for annually in Yorkshire from 1673. • **16**. *Cosmo*, pp. 145–6. • **17**. Randle Cotgrave, *A Dictionarie of the French and English Tongues* (1611), under 'billiard'. • **18**. *Noble*, p. 238. • **19**. *Gamester*, p. 223. • **20**. *Schellinks*, p. 60. • **21**. *Schellinks*, p. 71. • **22**. *Baskerville*, pp. 263, 265, 271, 285. • **23**. *Pepys*, ii, p. 90. • **24**. *Gamester*, p. 224. • **25**. *Gamester*, p. 17. • **26**. Many of these points are to be seen in the earliest painting of cricket, by Francis Haydon, which dates from 1743. In particular the ball casts a shadow in the painting, so it is off the ground, even though the bat is curved. Thus the statement one often reads about the ball being rolled along the ground in the days of the curved bat is unlikely to be wholly correct. As for women playing cricket, the *Reading Mercury* in 1745 recorded a game between 11 maids of Bramley and 11 of Hambleton (note: this was after the 1744 London rules were drawn up). No earlier references to women's cricket are known. • **27**. *Schellinks*, p. 83. • **28**. *Pepys*, iv, p. 167. • **29**. Christopher Rowley, *The Shared Origins of Football, Rugby and Soccer* (2015), p. 86. • **30**. *Misson*, p. 307. • **31**. Morris Marples, *A History of Football* (1954), p. 83. • **32**. Prices for apparatus come from National Library of Scotland MS.1400, f.253: http://digital.nls.uk/golf-in-scotland/assets/images/content/st-andrews/morice-accounts.jpg, downloaded 20 Oct. 2016. • **33**. National Library of Scotland Acc.13144: http://digital.nls.uk/golf-in-scotland/international/werden-pocket-book.html, downloaded 20 Oct. 2016. • **34**. John Aubrey, *Natural History of Wiltshire* (1847), p. 117. • **35**. *Misson*, p. 231. • **36**. *Noble*, p. 229. • **37**. *Pepys*, i, p. 218; iv, p. 255. • **38**. *Schellinks*, pp. 36–7. • **39**. Aubrey, *Natural History of Wiltshire*, p. 117; Locke in Lord King's *The Life and Letters of John Locke* (1830), i, p. 248. • **40**. *Schellinks*, p. 51. • **41**. *Evelyn*, ii, p. 23. • **42**. *Evelyn*, ii, p. 297. • **43**. *Misson*, p. 282. • **44**. *Schellinks*, p. 134; *Cosmo*, p. 149. • **45**. http://www.ashmolean. org/ash/amulets/tradescant/tradescant03.html, downloaded 21 Oct. 2016. • **46**. *Cosmo*, p. 326; *Evelyn*, ii, p. 69; *Fiennes*, p. 184; *Thoresby*, i, pp. 245, 298; *Misson*, pp. 27, 280–1; Marjorie Swann, *Curiosities and Texts: The Culture of Collecting in Early Modern England* (Philadelphia, 2001), p. 196. • **47**. *Evelyn*, ii, pp. 113, 132, 152, 327–8; *Schellinks*, pp. 60–1. • **48**. Diana Dethloff, 'Lely, Sir Peter (1618–1680)', *ODNB*; Ellis Waterhouse, *The Dictionary of 16th and 17th Century British Painters* (1988), p. 171. The earl of Bedford paid £31 for a three-quarter length picture of himself by Lely in 1675 and an extra £3 for the frame; a full-length portrait the following year cost the standard £60, plus £9 for the frame and £1 5s for a case in which to send it to Woburn Abbey. *Noble*, pp. 294–5. • **49**. *Evelyn*, ii, pp. 243, 301. • **50**. *Pepys*, iii, p. 113; *Evelyn*, ii, p. 89. • **51**. *Thoresby*, i, p. 9. • **52**. *Pepys*, ix, p. 434. • **53**. Waterhouse, *Dictionary*, p. 18. • **54**. William Sanderson, *Graphice* (1658), p. 20. • **55**. This is a very rough estimate, simply based on the number of Bibles mentioned in *Essex*. • **56**. Josselin, p. 7; M. Perceval-Maxwell, 'Annesley, Arthur, first earl of Anglesey (1614–1686)', *ODNB*. • **57**. Kees van Strien, 'Browne, Edward (1644–1708)', *ODNB*; *WCH*, pp. 163–4. For comparison, the earl of Bedford had 152 books at Woburn Abbey and 247 at his London house. *Noble*, p. 262. • **58**. William Bray (ed.), *Memoirs of John Evelyn ... comprising his diary, from 1641–1705/6, and a selection of his familiar letters* (5 vols, 1827), iv, p. 316. • **59**. A. C. Snape, 'Seventeenth-century book purchasing in Chetham's Library, Manchester', *Bulletin of the John Rylands University Library of Manchester*, 67 (1985), pp. 783–96 at p. 790. • **60**. Bray (ed.), *Memoirs*, iv, p. 315. • **61**. *Lincoln*, p. 36; *Essex*, p. 99 ('large Bible 10s'). • **62**. Robert Clavel, *A Catalogue of all the Books Printed in England since the Dreadful Fire of London, 1666. To the end of Michaelmas Term 1672* (1673). • **63**. Richard Landon, 'The Antiquarian Book Trade in Britain 1695–1830: The Use of Auction and Booksellers' Catalogues', *The Papers of the Bibliographical Society of America*, 89, 4 (1995), pp. 409–17 at p. 410. • **64**. These data are drawn from the English Short Title Catalogue maintained by the British Library: http://estc.bl.uk/ (searches downloaded 17 Oct. 2016). The statistics are for all languages published in the two respective countries. • **65**. According to the Publishers Association's *UK Book Industry in 2015*, the British National Bibliography contains 139,394 titles for that year, of which 35,918 are 'literature'. Sales of fiction titles in that same year accounted for 27% of the UK market, according to Nielsen. • **66**. *Pepys*, i, p. 312 and note. • **67**. *Misson*, pp. 210–11. • **68**. Agostino Lombardo, 'Shakespeare in Italy', *Proceedings of the American Philosophical Society*, 141, 4 (1997), pp. 454–62 at p. 454. • **69**. Gordon Campbell, 'Milton, John (1608–1674)', *ODNB*. • **70**. Campbell, 'Milton, John', *ODNB*. • **71**. John Spitzer and Neal Zaslaw, *The Birth of the Orchestra: History of an Institution 1650–1815* (2004), p. 268. • **72**. *Pepys Companion*, pp. 266–7. • **73**. *Evelyn*, ii, p. 141. • **74**. Spitzer and Zaslaw, *Birth of the Orchestra*, p. 274. • **75**. Peter Walls, 'Banister, John (1624/5–1679)', *ODNB*; Richard Crewdson, *Apollo's Swan and Lyre: Five Hundred Years of the Musicians' Company* (Woodbridge, 2000), pp. 117–20. • **76**. *Pepys*, i, p. 171. • **77**. *Pepys Companion*, pp. 434–8. • **78**. *Pepys Companion*, pp. 438–41. • **79**. *Thoresby*, i, p. 48. • **80**. *Pepys*, ii, p. 18 (prices); iv, p. 8 (cheapest seats). Pepys went to the theatre twice in one day on his 30th birthday; *Pepys*, iv, pp. 55–7. • **81**. *Pepys Companion*, p. 444. • **82**. *Pepys*, ii, pp. 190–1; iii, p. 208; iv, p. 6. • **83**. Kate Bennett, 'Wycherley, William (*bap.* 1641, *d.* 1716)', *ODNB*. • **84**. *Pepys*, i, p. 297; ii, p. 47. • **85**. *Pepys*, iv, p. 162. • **86**. *Pepys*, i, p. 224. • **87**. *Pepys*, ii, pp. 5, 35, 203. • **88**. *Evelyn*, i, 366; ii, p. 19. • **89**. J. Milling, 'Bracegirdle, Anne (*bap.* 1671, *d.* 1748)', *ODNB*. • **90**. S. M. Wynne, 'Gwyn, Eleanor (1651?–1687)', *ODNB*.

Envoi

1. One hundred years ago I had 12 ancestors alive. 150 years ago I had 20 alive on my father's side, so I assume 40 in all. 200 years ago I had 36 ancestors alive on my father's side, so double that makes 72. Beyond this, I do not know all the names and dates, but I estimate that on my father's side the total was 130, so 260 in all alive in 1766. If each of them had at least six ancestors alive 100 years earlier (as six is the difference between 100 years ago (12) and 200 years ago (72), and comparable to the difference between 150 years ago (40) and 250 years ago (260)), then I had in the region of 1,560 ancestors alive in 1666. • 2. See Ian Mortimer, *The Perfect King* (2006), appendix eight; see also 'Physics News Update', no. 428 (American Institute of Physics, 1999). The only group I can imagine for whom this would possibly be incorrect is the particularly rarefied bloodline of the royal families of Europe: in the case of the current UK monarch and her children, their English ancestry is a relatively small part of their genetic make-up and is comparatively limited, compared to the rest of us. The same caveat will not apply in the next generation, to the princes William and Harry. • 3. The figures for 2013 and 2014 are 120 and 108 per million respectively. See Ogg, *J. & W.*, p. 35; Kyla Thomas and David Gunnell, 'Suicide in England and Wales 1861–2007: a time-trends analysis', *International Journal of Epidemiology*, 39 (2010), pp. 1464–75 at p. 1465; http://www.ons.gov.uk/peoplepopulationandcommunity/birthsdeathsandmarriages/deaths/bulletins/suicidesintheunited kingdom/2014registrations, downloaded 29 Oct. 2016.

Illustrations

Portrait of Charles II by John Michael Wright (Royal Collection Trust; © Her Majesty Queen Elizabeth II, 2016/Bridgeman Images).

Portrait of James II by Peter Lely (© Boston Museum and Art Gallery, Lancashire/Bridgeman Images).

Portrait of Queen Mary II by William Wissing (Kenwood House, London; photo © Historic England/Bridgeman Images).

Portrait of William III, prince of Orange, by Godfrey Kneller (Bank of England, London; photo © Heini Schneebel/Bridgeman Images).

Portrait of Queen Catherine of Braganza, studio of Peter Lely (private collection; photo © Philip Mould Ltd, London/Bridgeman Images).

Portrait of Barbara Villiers, after Peter Lely (Geffrye Museum of the Home, London/Bridgeman Images).

Portrait of Louise de Kéroualle, duchess of Portsmouth, by Godfrey Kneller (Sudbury Hall, Derbyshire; National Trust Photographic Library/Bridgeman Images).

Portrait of Nell Gwynn, after Peter Lely (Army and Navy Club, London/Bridgeman Images).

View of London from Southwark, Anglo-Dutch school (Chatsworth House, Derbyshire, © Derbyshire Collection, Chatsworth, reproduced by permission of the Chatsworth Settlement Trustees/Bridgeman Images).

The Great Fire of London in 1666, by Lieve Verschuier (Museum of Fine Arts, Szepmuveszeti, Budapest/Bridgeman Images).

The piazza in Covent Garden, hand-coloured etching (© Victoria and Albert Museum, London).

Golden Square, engraving by John Bowles (private collection/Bridgeman Images).

Portrait of Sir George Rooke by Michael Dahl (private collection; photo © Philip Mould Ltd, London/Bridgeman Images).

Portrait of Lord Mungo Murray by John Michael Wright (private collection; photo © Christie's Images/Bridgeman Images).

Portrait of Bridget Holmes by John Riley (Royal Collection Trust; © Her Majesty Queen Elizabeth II, 2016/Bridgeman Images).

Portrait of Lady Anne de Vere Capel by Michael Dahl (Petworth House, West Sussex; National Trust Photography Library/Bridgeman Images).

Image of a flea, from Robert Hooke's *Micrographia*, 1665 (Bridgeman Images).

Dentist examining the tooth of an old man, painting by Gerrit Dou (private collection; photo © Bonhams London/Bridgeman Images).

Cheque of the Earl of Arran. Reproduced by kind permission of The Royal Bank of Scotland Group plc © 2017.

Frost fair on the Thames, winter of 1683–4, English school (Yale Center for British Art, Paul Mellon Collection/Bridgeman Images).

The King's Bath and the Queen's Bath, drawing by Thomas Johnson (private collection/Bridgeman Images).

Sir Thomas Armstrong's execution, engraving, 1684.

Titus Oates in the pillory, 1687, English school (Museum of London/Bridgeman Images).

View of a house and its estate in Belsize, Middlesex, 1696, Jan Siberechts (1627–c.1700) (© Tate London 2016)

The White Hart Inn in Scole, Norfolk, English school (private collection/Ken Welsh/Bridgeman Images).

Clarendon House, engraving (private collection/Stapleton Collection/Bridgeman Images).

View of Chatsworth from the south-west, painting by Thomas Smith of Derby (Chatsworth House, Derbyshire, © Derbyshire Collection, Chatsworth, reproduced by permission of the Chatsworth Settlement Trustees/Bridgeman Images).

Carving of musical instruments by Grinling Gibbons (Petworth House, West Sussex; National Trust Photographic Library/Andreas von Einsiedel/Bridgeman Images).

Indian hanging, dyed and painted cotton, c.1680 (© Victoria & Albert Museum, London).

William and Mary striking table clock by Thomas Tompion (private collection; photo © Christie's Images/Bridgeman Images).

Pigs' knuckles on a pewter plate, Flemish school (private collection; © Lawrence Steigrad Fine Arts, New York/Bridgeman Images).

The Heaven Room at Burghley House, by Antonio Verrio (reproduced courtesy of Burghley House).

Edward Barlow's ship, the *Sampson*, caught in a hurricane in 1694 (reproduced from Edward Barlow, *Barlow's Journal of his life at sea in King's ships, East & West Indiamen & other merchantmen from 1659 to 1703*, ed. Basil Lubbock, 2 vols, London, 1934).

Portrait of Michael Alphonsus Shen Fuzong by Godfrey Kneller (Royal Collection Trust; © Her Majesty Queen Elizabeth II, 2016/Bridgeman Images).

Portrait of William Dampier by Thomas Murray (National Portrait Gallery, London/De Agostini Picture Library/Bridgeman Images).

Portrait of John Wilmot, 2nd earl of Rochester, by Jacob Huysmans (Warwick Castle, Warwickshire/Bridgeman Images).

Mary Beale, self-portrait (National Gallery, London; photo © Stefano Baldini/Bridgeman Images).

Portrait of Aphra Behn by Mary Beale (St Hilda's College, Oxford/Bridgeman Images).

Portrait of Samuel Pepys by Godfrey Kneller (Royal Society of Arts, London/Bridgeman Images).

Portrait of John Evelyn by Godfrey Kneller (© The Royal Society).

Opening page of Pepys' diary. Reproduced by permission of the Pepys Library, Magdalene College, Cambridge.

Jacket details

Portrait of Charles II by John Michael Wright (Royal Collection Trust; © Her Majesty Queen Elizabeth II, 2016/Bridgeman Images).

Habits of Quakers (Stapleton Collection/Bridgeman Images).

Whitehall, from *Prospects of London* (O'Shea Gallery, London/Bridgeman Images).

Portrait of Nell Gwynne after Samuel Cooper (Valerie Jackson Harris Collection/Bridgeman Images).

Richmond Palace engraved by Michiel van der Gucht (Bridgeman Images).

Frontispiece from *The Theory of the Earth* by Thomas Burnet (Warden and Scholars of New College, Oxford/Bridgeman Images).

Raised embroidery of flower (private collection/Bridgeman Images).

Letters patent issued by Sir Edward Walker, 1664 (Christie's Images/Bridgeman Images).

Broadside of the Great Fire of London, 1666 (Bridgeman Images).

Image of a flea, from Robert Hooke's *Micrographia*, 1665 (Bridgeman Images).

The 'Definitive Design' for St Paul's Cathedral by Sir Christopher Wren (St Paul's Cathedral Library, London/Bridgeman Images).

Ironwork design for Hampton Court Palace by Jean Tijou (Bridgeman Images).

Index